Writers of Multicultural Fiction for Young Adults

WRITERS OF MULTICULTURAL FICTION FOR YOUNG ADULTS

A Bio-Critical Sourcebook

Edited by M. Daphne Kutzer

Emmanuel S. Nelson, Advisory Editor

GREENWOOD PRESS
Westport, Connecticut • London

Library of Congress Cataloging-in-Publication Data

Writers of multicultural fiction for young adults : a bio-critical
  sourcebook / edited by M. Daphne Kutzer.
      p.   cm.
    Includes bibliographical references and index.
    ISBN 0–313–29331–7 (alk. paper)
    1. Young adult fiction, American—Minority authors—Bio-
bibliography. 2. Young adult fiction, American—Minority authors—
Dictionaries. 3. Authors, American—20th century—Biography—
Dictionaries. 4. Pluralism (Social sciences) in literature—
Dictionaries. 5. American fiction—20th century—Bio-bibliography.
6. Ethnic groups in literature—Dictionaries. 7. Minorities in
literature—Dictionaries.   I. Kutzer, M. Daphne.
PS374.Y57W75   1996
813.009′9283—dc20   95–502

British Library Cataloguing in Publication Data is available.

Library of Congress Catalog Card Number: 95–502
ISBN: 0–313–29331–7

First published in 1996

Greenwood Press, 88 Post Road West, Westport, CT 06881
An imprint of Greenwood Publishing Group, Inc.

Printed in the United States of America

The paper used in this book complies with the
Permanent Paper Standard issued by the National
Information Standards Organization (Z39.48–1984).

10 9 8 7 6 5 4 3 2

CONTENTS

Introduction: What is Multicultural Literature?

M. Daphne Kutzer

This reference book includes fifty-one alphabetically arranged entries about writers of multicultural fiction for young adults. Each entry consists of a biographical introduction to the author, an overview of major young adult works, a section on the critical reception of the author's writings, a bibliography of works by the author, and a selected bibliography of criticism. While the individual bibliographies strive to be current, not all of the writers have been discussed in books or major articles during the last few years. The volume closes with a selected bibliography of works related to multicultural literature. The first part lists general studies, while other sections cite works on African-American, Hispanic-American, Native American, Asian-American, and Jewish literature.

The breadth of authors covered ensures a historical context for the issues raised by multiculturalism, and the sections on the critical reception of each author address such important issues as the authority and authenticity of the writer to comment on a different culture. Authors included range from the nearly forgotten, such as Laura Adams Armer, to the newly discovered, such as Graham Salisbury, Winner of the 1994 Scott O'Dell Award for Historical Fiction. Contributors to the volume are of many different ethnicities and include important scholars of children's literature, lending authenticity and authority to the book.

The term "multiculturalism" has become more than a buzzword; it has become a part of the American vocabulary, despite the fact that "multiculturalism" means different things to different people. Before we invented this particular term, one heard of "ethnic" studies, "minority literatures," "cross-culturalism," "world studies," and so on, but now we seem to have settled upon "multiculturalism" to mean all of these things, and perhaps more.

In a 1993 *Language Arts* interview with three experts in multiculturalism and children's literature, the term "multicultural" was defined respectively as "literature by and about people of color"; literature that "emphasizes respect for the different historical perspectives and cultures in human society"; and "literature of inclusion" (Madigan 169–70). But if multicultural literature is an inclusive literature, who, if anyone, is excluded, and why? We do not generally include the poor when we speak of multicultural literature, nor do we include the Deaf, or gays and lesbians, although persuasive arguments have been made for the culture of poverty, for the existence of a Deaf culture, and for "queer" culture. And, of course, some people of white European background have loudly argued that their culture is being excluded from this multicultural debate.

What is a poor editor to do? Obviously, some working definitions of multicultural literature had to be made before the table of contents for this book could be shaped. Early on I decided that for the purposes of this reference text, a definition that was fairly inclusive yet also workably narrow would be necessary if the manuscript were to be of manageable weight and size. Thus, "multicultural," in the context of *Writers of Multicultural Fiction for Young Adults*, refers to literature written in English about North American and Caribbean cultural groups that by virtue of race, ethnicity, or religious background differ from the culturally dominant white Europeans. This definition of multicultural excludes some superb writing from British Commonwealth countries, as well as from Africa and parts of Asia. But since the primary purpose of this text is to help teachers and scholars of young adult literature in North America, I made a decision to exclude writers who write about what might more accurately be called the global culture, rather than multicultural America.

So part of my editorial task was complete: a definition of "multicultural" that might not satisfy everyone, but that would give my text workable and useful shape. But what of the rest of the definition? What is "young adult" literature, anyway?

As with "multicultural," there are many ways to define "young adult literature." The loosest definition is one that includes all works read by teenage readers, whether meant for them or not: J. D. Salinger, Stephen King, Emily Brönte. This particular definition, like the more global definition of "multicultural," did not strike me as very useful. It might work, perhaps, for compilers of bibliographies of suitable reading for teenagers, or for lists of recommended texts for secondary school classrooms, but it was too broad for my purposes. Another definition of "young adult" literature might be books that are concerned with the postpubescent, rather than the prepubescent experience—in other words, books where concerns about romance, sexuality, and growing away from the family might be at the fore. Yet another might tie the label "young adult" to a specific reading level, concentrating on the level of diction and syntactic complexity of the text.

The definition of "young adult" used in this text is rather broad, but I hope not unmanageably so. I define "young adults" as those persons aged about twelve or above, although occasionally they might be as young as ten. Some of the authors discussed within this text write for the middle school audience as well as for the slightly older high school audience. I have included discussion of some of these books for younger readers because a number of older readers read below grade level, and might find these "simpler" books appropriate reading for themselves. Other children who have better reading skills might also, at times, be attracted to somewhat shorter and less complicated texts: those of us who have worked with young adults know that at one instant they seem very grown-up, and at the next they revert to a much more childlike self.

I have not included any authors who write primarily for the adult audience, even though their works may be suitable for young adults. The two writers who come closest to this definition are Raymond Andrews and Beatrice Culleton, but the former seems to have slanted at least some of his writing toward the young adult audience, and the latter consciously rewrote her adult novel for a younger audience—leaving out the graphic sexual language of the adult version. There are certainly any number of writers whose adult works might work very well for young adults: Amy Tan, Toni Morrison, Ann Petry (who wrote juvenile biographies, but no juvenile fiction), Leslie Silko. They are excluded, not because they are not important writers, but because they are best served by a text that focuses on adult works suited for teen readers.

Another limitation of this reference volume is that it is restricted, by and large, to writers who publish within the mainstream press, for the practical reason that these are the books most easily obtained by interested teachers, parents, and librarians. There are smaller, minority-owned, sometimes bilingual presses—among them Oyate and Piñata—that are publishing some wonderful literature, although they are more likely to be publishing books for younger children than for the young adult audience. The difficulty with books that come from mainstream houses is that they may, or may not, have been shepherded through by someone who, even if not a minority, is sensitive to and educated about minority issues. Authentic minority voices do issue forth from mainstream publishing houses, but I suspect that if these publishing houses had more minority editorial staff, the voices might be larger in number and louder in volume.

It is my hope that *Writers of Multicultural Fiction for Young Adults* will serve a number of different purposes. Since there has been increasing pressure on public schools to provide multicultural experiences for their students, teachers (many of whom were not exposed to any multicultural materials during their own schooling) need some guidance in choosing appropriate materials for the classroom. Unfortunately, many teachers assume that because a novel has, say, African-American characters and has won some awards that it is appropriate material for the classroom. This is the case with *Sounder,* although any number of African-American teachers, writers, and scholars have condemned this particular novel for reinforcing racist stereotypes of blacks in society. As the essay on *Sounder* within this volume suggests, the novel is still a powerful one, but ought to be approached cautiously. There are also some older and now lesser-known writers whose novels about ethnic minorities may pose some difficulties for contemporary readers, but which provide both accurate cultural information and a historical perspective on racial and racist attitudes in this country—Laura Adams Armer, Florence Crannell Means, and Jesse Jackson fall into this category. And then there are authors who may have gained a name for themselves in some circles as being authentic voices of their own cultural experience, but whose authority has been challenged. Jamake Highwater has dropped public mention of his supposed Native American ancestry, after intense and sometimes angry scrutiny by the Native American literary community. Highwater's work, as pointed out in Linda C. Jolivet's essay, raises some more troubling issues about authenticity, but much of his work does accurately reflect Native experience, whether he himself is Native American or not. Danny Santiago turned out to be not a Hispanic youth, but an elderly Yale-educated Anglo man. Nonetheless, Santiago's *Famous All Over Town* grew out of the author's experiences living in a predominantly Hispanic neighborhood, and it strikes many Hispanic readers as telling the truth about their lives.

The cases of Highwater and Santiago raise some other problematic issues concerning multicultural literature, the most important being what I will call the insider/outsider controversy. Can someone who is not a member of a minority culture write about it both accurately and sensitively? The case of Joseph Quincy Krumgold, among others, suggests that the answer is yes: his . . . *And Now Miguel,* a coming-of-age novel about a Hispanic child written by a middle-aged Jewish man, has consistently been praised for its sensitive and accurate portrayal of a culture not the author's own. Ginny Moore-Kruse, a noted expert on multicultural literature, has noted that "it is not a requirement that someone who writes about a culture be of that culture's same background. However, the farther one is removed from the experience or heritage about which one is writing, the more barriers there are to success, the harder writers have to work to attain cultural authenticity, and the more sensitive they need to be in order not to use hurtful images and erroneous cultural information" (Madigan 172). Krumgold had spent months with New Mexican sheep herders, working on a documentary film: an experience that obviously gave him ample time to observe and absorb the culture around him. The same can be said for someone like Laura Adams Armer, who spent years living in close proximity to the cultures about which she wrote. Their works may at times promote, without questioning, white ideas of progress and cultural validity, but the cultural information they convey to the reader is accurate, and just as important, their stories are powerfully written.

Another issue that is never far from my mind, although it has no overt presence in this volume, is that childhood is, in itself, its own culture. Marina Warner's recent *Six Myths of Our Time* suggests that children, no matter how defined by adult culture, are always defined as "the Other"— despite the fact that unlike other "Other" groups, children, at least white children, grow up to be the Self or the Subject in society; the child outsider grows into the adult insider. Yet, children are even more voiceless than adult members of "Other" communities—voiceless by virtue of their (relative) lack of literacy, and their absolute lack of economic, social, and legal power. Children do not get much opportunity to write (or film, or dance, or sing) their own culture for "outsiders," i.e., adults, and the culture they invent for themselves—in games, oral stories, schoolyard rhymes, and so on—is ephemeral.

Part of the purpose of children's literature, whether we acknowledge it or not, is to indoctrinate children into the culture of adulthood. In earlier times, this purpose was quite overt: one has only to think back to Puritan children's books of manners and prayers; or to nineteenth-century didactic tomes or classics like *Little Women* (whose title, perhaps, says it all); or in our own time to countless "problem novels" of the sixties and seventies that promised sex or other excitement to the reader, but were really thinly disguised jeremiads. Many multicultural books want to indoctrinate children into more tolerant attitudes toward those who differ from themselves or, conversely, to provide accurate mirror images of themselves to minority children. Whatever the agenda, it is still an adult agenda. This is not necessarily a good or a bad thing: but it is an aspect of the study of children's literature that is too often overlooked by teachers and scholars.

My own interest in what is now known as "multiculturalism" is long-standing and is rooted in my own childhood experiences of difference and intolerance. My earliest memory of intolerance dates to third grade, in 1960, during Kennedy's campaign for the presidency. I was standing by the pencil sharpener in the company of a crew-cut, plaid-shirted boy straight from Beaver Cleaver's neighborhood. We must have been having a civics lesson, because he turned to me and said, "I'd never vote for that guy! He's Catholic!" I thought this was very strange, since I was Catholic at the time, and this boy counted me as a friend, someone he did not complain about sharing a project or a game with. I could not fathom why someone's religion should matter so much to another person, and why it should be the sole criterion by which we should choose a president—or a playmate. I did not challenge the boy, however: at seven I was more interested in being accepted by my peers than in making what we might now call a "politically correct" point.

Seven or eight years later, my family was vacationing in Bermuda, and I was fascinated by the fellow who ran the sailboat rental franchise. He had what I thought of as an English accent, but was dark of skin, kinky of hair, and had beautiful green eyes. He let me fool around with the boats and treated me like a human being, something my fifteen-year-old self desperately desired. My parents, catching wind of this, told me I should not spend time with him because he was the "help" and I was a guest. I reacted with adolescent fury, rightly perceiving that my parents (who considered themselves Adlai Stevenson liberals) were actually more concerned about the young man's race than they were with his employment status; and also asserting that even if they were concerned about his servant status, that was hardly any better. As I grew older, I recognized my own racism in this incident: much of the young man's attraction for me was his "exotic" nature—something about which Edward Said, among others, has had much to say.

In editing this volume I hope I have achieved and maintained a sensitivity toward the complexities and difficulties—and pleasures and opportunities—of living in a multicultural society, whether one is part of the "Other" community or not. My own bicultural experience of living as a lesbian in a heterosexual world has made me keenly aware of how even well-meaning people not of my cultural group can get us "wrong," how lives that are "different" can be distorted by mainstream literature and media, and how varied the lives of individuals within a single cultural group can be.

Of course, *Writers of Multicultural Fiction for Young Adults* is not a complete volume by any means. I am especially sorry not to have been able to include an essay on Marie G. Lee, a Korean-American writer whose *Finding My Voice* and its sequel, *Saying Goodbye*, raise some compelling questions both about adolescence and about cultural identity and assimilation. I would also have liked to include an essay on Mitali Perkins' *The Sunita Experiment*, the story of an Indian girl living in San Francisco with her parents and trying to cope with assimilation issues. While there are novels for young adults about the adolescent experience in India itself, or the adolescent Indian and Pakistani experience in Great Britain, there is little about this particular North American population written for young adults. I expect this to change, just as I expect that by the time *Writers of Multicultural Fiction for Young Adults* actually sees print there will be another half dozen or more new multicultural writers on the scene.

My hope for this reference volume is that it will help teachers, librarians, students, and scholars to understand better some of the racial, ethnic, and cultural issues within our society, and that it will aid in presenting literature about these issues in the classroom. Multicultural literature *is* American literature, not merely a category of American literature. This will become even more evident in the next century, when, increasingly, the "average" U.S. resident will trace his or her ancestry to Africa, Asia, the Pacific Islands, Arabia, the Hispanic world—almost anyplace except Europe. *Writers of Multicultural Fiction for Young Adults* will, I hope, aid us in educating ourselves about our multicultural America.

ACKNOWLEDGMENTS

There are several people I would like to thank, without whose help this book would not have been possible. First, thanks to Rae Anne Barry and Charles O. Warren, Rae Anne for helping me find the road and Charlie for giving me a year to travel it. Second, thanks to Emmanuel S. Nelson, who was the impetus behind this volume. Many, many thanks to the reference staff at Feinberg Library at Plattsburgh State University, especially Gordon Muir, Tim Hartnett, and Mike Miranda. I would also like to thank Bernie Grabczewski of the Computing Support Center at Plattsburgh State, who unfailingly, unflinchingly, and even cheerfully has bailed me out of more computer difficulties than I care to count. Of course, none of these people are to blame for any of the book's shortcomings, but they are largely responsible for making editing an enjoyable, not an onerous, task.

WORKS CITED

Lee, Marie. *Finding My Voice*. New York: Laurel Leaf, 1992.
———. *Saying Goodbye*. Boston: Houghton Mifflin, 1994.
Madigan, Dan. "The Politics of Multicultural Literature for Children and Adolescents: Combining Perspectives and Conversations." *Language Arts* 70.3 (1993): 168–76.
Perkins, Mitali. *The Sunita Experiment*. New York: Little Brown, 1993.
Warner, Marina. *Six Myths of Our Time: Little Angels, Little Monsters, Beautiful Beasts, and More*. New York: Vintage, 1995.

RAYMOND ANDREWS
(1934–1991)

Mitchell Kachun

BIOGRAPHY

Raymond Andrews was born June 6, 1934, the fourth of ten children in a family of sharecroppers, in rural Morgan County, Georgia. If there could be such a thing as racial harmony in a segregated town, Andrews has written, it existed in his town of Madison. Nonetheless, race remained a central organizing principle in southern life. Morgan County's African-Americans fostered among themselves a strong sense of family and community which protected children from the worst aspects of white racism while preparing them to deal with that reality as adults.

Andrews grew up immersed in a black oral tradition, and nothing pleased young Raymond more than a good story, well told. Though his family was poor, and illiteracy was prevalent among the county's black population, Raymond's appreciation for storytelling evolved into a passion for reading. Even as a child, in a racial and economic environment hardly nurturing of literary aspirations, he wanted most of all to write. When the adult Andrews wrote, he wrote largely about the pervasive presence of race in southern life, and relied heavily on the oral tradition in developing his voice.

Andrews also grew up in the fields—planting, tending, and picking cotton until the age of fifteen. As mechanical cotton pickers began to replace manual labor in the fields, agricultural work for blacks became scarce. Andrews responded, as did many others across the South, by moving to the city. He went to Atlanta, where he worked at a variety of odd jobs while earning his diploma at night high school.

After serving four years in the air force and briefly attending Michigan State University, Andrews moved to New York City where he worked as an airline reservations agent from 1958 to 1966. On his thirty-second birthday Andrews quit his job and finally acted on his lifelong ambition to write. Later that year he married Adelheid Wenger, a Swiss national and former co-worker.

Writing full time, however, failed to provide financial support, and Andrews continued to work at various outside jobs between 1967 and 1984. He divorced in 1980, and, in 1984, returned to his roots in the South. He spent most of his remaining years living alone in an Athens, Georgia, studio. In November 1991, his health failing, Raymond Andrews took his own life in his Athens home.

MAJOR WORKS AND THEMES

Andrews finished his first novel in 1969, but it took another nine years before *Appalachee Red* was published by Dial Press. Two more novels, *Rosiebelle Lee Wildcat Tennessee* (1980) and *Baby Sweet's* (1983), set in the same fictional Georgia county of Muskhogean, completed a thematically coherent trilogy. Although Andrews' trilogy was well-received by reviewers, the books went out of print after Dial's demise in 1984, and remained so until reissued by the University of Georgia Press in the late 1980s. In 1990 he published *The Last Radio Baby*, an exuberant reminiscence of his first fifteen years. A fourth novel (actually, two novellas), *Jessie and Jesus; and, Cousin Claire,* was published in 1991.

All of Andrews' published works emanate directly from his experiences in the South. Many of the presumably authentic incidents and personages appearing in *The Last Radio Baby* can be found in Andrews' novels, adapted with minor alterations to fit the circumstances. Throughout his corpus, Andrews tells stories about African-American life in the rural South from the turn-of-the-century to the 1980s.

Andrews' style is colloquial—one can easily imagine these tales being told from a rocker by the fireside. The full range of life in his fictional Muskhogean County and its main town of Appalachee is explored with the respect and humor one expects from a long-time resident. The illustrations in all of Andrews' works, provided by his brother Benny, pleasantly enhance the narratives. The language of the third-person narrator is graphic and naturalistic; he deals as frankly and easily with sex, racial violence, and death as he does with family dinners and boyish pranks.

The novels provide an intimate, often hilarious, and at times brutal portrait of Muskhogean County's African-American community and of the whites with whom blacks' lives were inextricably linked. The reader learns about the violence, the sexual exploitation, and the undercurrents of fear and hatred that dominated race relations in the Jim Crow South. But Andrews ultimately emphasizes the uneasy understanding between whites and blacks that allowed them to coexist and under which African-Americans pursued their lives, their loves, and their aspirations.

Andrews reveals the complexity of life among the blacks—and whites—he knew while growing up. He recounts that some men loved their mules and their farms and their families; some loved fast cars and the lure of the city; some loved liquor and women. Some women loved listening to blues records and entertaining gentlemen callers; some lost themselves in church and family; some built a reputation by ministering to the sick and attending funerals.

Muskhogean County is peopled with strict religious moralists and unrepentant whorehouse operators; the evangelical Baptists of "Dark Town" and the "dicty" Methodists of "Light Town"; "town niggers" and "hole niggers"; razor-toters, barbecue purveyors, frustrated and underemployed black college graduates; Uncle Toms, lunatics, po' white trash, redneck cops, effeminate planters' sons, and every other stereotype imaginable. But personalities are never reduced to stereotypes. Andrews constructs his characters as complete and complex individuals, at times fantastic, but withal believable.

Andrews' unrelenting historical realism translates the thoughts and lives of everyday people into a sociohistorical survey of twentieth-century southern culture. His decision to set all of his works in the same locale allows the reader to experience with some intimacy the sociocultural milieu of several generations of white and black families, their acquaintances and interrelationships. The convoluted intricacies of race relations and racial identity pervade all of Andrews' works, as the personal lives and family histories of Muskhogean County's residents take shape.

Many of those lives and histories are patterned after the author's own family. Andrews' paternal grandmother was a light-complexioned woman of African, European, and Native American ancestry who maintained a long-term relationship with a prominent white planter. Though they neither married nor cohabited, their union produced numerous offspring whose racial identity was ambiguous and problematic. Composites of these individuals and their progeny are prominent inhabitants of Raymond Andrews' novels.

The racial ambiguity of the title character of *Appalachee Red* is a case in point. The son of a wealthy white man and his black maid, "Red" suffered years of rejection from both whites and blacks after being sent north from Appalachee as an infant. Serving his country in World War II only intensified Red's hatred for America's racial dissimulation. The novel pivots on his return to Appalachee after the war. There Red hopes to forge an identity and to extract vengeance from his father's family and from the racist sheriff who kicked his mother into a state of insanity years earlier. Red appears as a racial mystery in a time and place whose hypocritical official ideology admits of no gray area between black and white.

As "the reddish nigger"—his true identity remains unknown to Appalachee's inhabitants—exerts increasing control over the town, he disrupts the sense of order within the white and black power structures. Red liberates the sheriff's unwilling black concubine and takes her for his own. He establishes himself as the community's kingpin of vice. Challenging the racial order of the late Jim Crow South, Andrews ends the novel with Red's half-sister succumbing to her irresistible attraction for Red and driving off with him in his long black Cadillac. In the epilogue we find that Red has also slain the sheriff before disappearing forever.

Rosiebelle Lee Wildcat Tennessee and *Baby Sweet's* respectively establish the historical and genealogical background for the events depicted in *Appalachee Red* and carry the story into the mid–1960s. Red himself does not figure in the other novels, but many of the secondary characters, along with their extended families, ancestors, and descendants, are developed in considerable detail. *Rosiebelle Lee* outlines the interracial entanglements that provide the context for *Appalachee Red* as the community attends the deathbed of the matriarch named in the title (and patterned after Andrews' grandmother). *Baby Sweet's* describes the events surrounding the opening of Appalachee's first official whorehouse on Independence Day, 1966. Both novels make effective use of broad set pieces that allow Andrews to move among the company, shifting the reader's perspective and adding depth to the characters as their stories unfold. *Jessie and Jesus; and, Cousin Claire*, really an extension of the original trilogy, brings the story of life in Muskhogean County into the 1980s by recounting the bizarre exploits of a pair of beautiful and resourceful *femmes fatales*.

CRITICAL RECEPTION

Virtually all reviewers laud Andrews' melodic language, gift for storytelling, and boisterous humor. Warren J. Carson cites *Appalachee Red* as "one of the most comic novels of the twentieth century," largely based on Andrews' "knack . . . for turning tragedy, violence, and heartbreak in on themselves and rendering them comic without compromising their more serious aspects" (11). Frederick Busch, however, claims that Andrews is "somewhat prone to use of clichéd speech" (22). David Guy, in his review of *Baby Sweet's*, finds that the novel's voice "never varies" and "does not sound quite right in the mouth of a white woman" (6).

Andrews has been generally praised for his profound knowledge of life in the small southern town, and for his reconstruction of the intricate familial and social relationships that give the community coherence. Carson, in his detailed analysis of *Appalachee Red*, contends that Andrews' historical revisionism in "retell[ing] the history of the American South from the black perspective" (10) is one of the author's great achievements.

David Guy has expressed admiration for Andrews' ability to create "characters [who] are larger than life and often seem to represent phenomena as much as they do flesh and blood human beings" (6). Others, however, have interpreted this trait in a more negative light. Busch, in his generally positive review of *Baby Sweet's*, faults Andrews' tendency to refract America's multicultural experience through the language of blacks at the expense of "evoking an emotional response to that experience" (10). Characters who strike Guy as representing "larger than life" phenomena prove unsatisfying to Busch, who feels that "the novel's style and tone distance its characters" (22). Guy also feels that *Baby Sweet's* has a "haphazard" construction and needs "a more dramatic center" (6).

Appalachee Red, recipient of the Dial Press James Baldwin Prize for Fiction in 1978, is generally considered Andrews' best novel. The less enthusiastic reception of his subsequent books, combined with their unavailability for several years, left Andrews underappreciated until the early 1990s. The 1991 publication of *The Last Radio Baby* brought Andrews more prominently into public view. The College Language Association, an organization of African-American literary and linguistic scholars, held a symposium on his works at its 1991 annual conference.

Andrews' writing works as well for mature readers as for younger ones. He is only infrequently cited as an author of books for young adults. *Children's Books in Print* first began to list him in 1990/91, and then only for *Radio Baby*. Helen E. Williams, however, does include *Appalachee Red* in her volume, *Books by African-American Authors and Illustrators for Children and Young Adults* (Chicago: American Library Association, 1991).

BIBLIOGRAPHY

Young Adult Fiction by Raymond Andrews

Appalachee Red. Illus. Benny Andrews. New York: Dial, 1978.
Rosiebelle Lee Wildcat Tennessee: A Novel. Illus. Benny Andrews. New York: Dial, 1980.
Baby Sweet's: A Novel. Illus. Benny Andrews. New York: Dial, 1983.
The Last Radio Baby: A Memoir. Atlanta: Peachtree, 1990.
Jessie and Jesus; and, Cousin Claire. Atlanta: Peachtree, 1991.

Selected Studies of Raymond Andrews

"Andrews, Raymond." *Contemporary Authors, New Revision Series*. Ed. Susan M. Trosky. Vol. 42. Detroit: Gale, 1994. 10–11.
Busch, Frederick. Rev. of *Baby Sweet's*. *New York Times Book Review* 24 July 1983: 10, 22.
Carson, Warren J. *"Appalachee Red." Masterpieces of African-American Literature*. Ed. Frank N. Magill. New York: HarperCollins, 1992. 9–12.
Guy, David. Rev. of *Baby Sweet's*. *Washington Post Book World* 31 July 1983: 6.
O'Briant, Don. "The Literary Harvest of a Sharecropper's Son." *Atlanta Journal and Constitution* 28 Feb. 1988: J1, 3.

LAURA ADAMS ARMER
(1874–1963)

Linnea Hendrickson

BIOGRAPHY

Laura May Adams was born in Sacramento, California, on January 12, 1874, the third child of California pioneers Charles and Maria Adams. She attended public school in San Francisco, and was also educated at home. She studied painting and photography at the California Institute of Design, where she met her future husband, fellow artist Sidney Armer, who was to illustrate several of her books. From 1899 to 1902 she operated a successful photographic studio in downtown San Francisco. After her marriage in 1902, she continued to operate a studio and darkroom at home.

She photographed many of California's rich and famous. According to historian of photography Laverne Mau Dicker, Armer had the ability "to cut through surface artifice and lay bare the sitter's character" (135), an ability that would also be evident in her writing.

During the winter of 1905–1906, Laura, with her two-year-old son Austin, her husband Sidney, and a friend to care for Austin, traveled to Tahiti where Laura was commissioned to take photographs for the Oceanic Steamship Company (A. Armer 14). Armer continued to photograph and paint while managing her household and caring for her family, but it was not until after Austin was grown that Armer found her deepest inspiration among the Navajos.

In the summer of 1923, Laura, Sidney, and Austin traveled to the Navajo Reservation in a Buick touring car. The story of this colorful trip, and vivid accounts of Laura's subsequent adventures among the Navajos are related in *In Navajo Land*. For many years following this trip, Laura returned to the reservation, often alone, to paint and write. She saw herself as always seeking the beautiful.

Befriended by trader Lorenzo Hubbell, who also figured in some of her books, she encountered other writers in this remote land, including the young Oliver LaFarge and an already famous D. H. Lawrence, whom she observed at a Hopi snake dance and mistook for a Mormon missionary.

Armer won the confidence of Navajo medicine men and was allowed to make hundreds of copies of sacred sand paintings and gained admittance to ceremonies no woman had ever been allowed to see. In 1928 she made a film of the nine-day Mountain Chant, the first Native American motion picture directed in the Indian tongue, a valuable documentary that was shown at the American Museum of Natural History in New York in the fall of 1928.

In 1931, her first novel, the story of a young Navajo boy destined to be a medicine man, was published to great acclaim. *Waterless Mountain* was awarded the Longman's Juvenile Fiction Prize, and in 1932 the Newbery Medal.

She continued to write and to paint, completing, in addition to five more books for children, a cactus identification guide (*Cactus*, 1934), a book of essays (*Southwest*, 1935), and *In Navajo Land* (1962).

MAJOR WORKS AND THEMES

Waterless Mountain accurately captures much of the Navajo way of life, its beliefs, its ceremonies, and even the patterns of its language. The book begins slowly as the reader is introduced to the life, thoughts, and dreams of Younger Brother, a sensitive child, who, like Armer herself, seeks to understand what lies below the surface of things.

Midway through the book Younger Brother, now twelve years old, sets out alone on his pony, heading for the Western Ocean in search of the mythological Turquoise Woman. Along the way he strikes up an acquaintance with a white boy in a car, encounters unsavory Navajos who try to steal his pony, and stays with a widowed kinswoman who, before he leaves, loses her handsome new husband and everything she owns in a disastrous flood.

Upon returning home, Younger Brother goes back to his peaceful pattern of life, moves closer to his goal of becoming a medicine man, and thinks about seeking a mate with whom to share his life. At the end of the book, while dancing all night with a girl, Younger Brother feels at one with his people and with the earth, and realizes that there is a new song in his heart: "A song of his people who had lived in the land when the Ancients dwelt in the cliffs. . . . It was the song of his people, who carried on, who persisted, who danced to the throbbing music of their hearts" (211).

Like Younger Brother, Armer was a dreamer and a seeker of beauty and of "the deep heart of things." The patterns of her narrative follow the patterns of the Navajo legends that Armer knew so well. Younger Brother's quest was also her own.

Dark Circle of Branches (1933), Armer's second Navajo story, also portrays the life of a medicine man, this one based on the life of the real Na Nai, known as "the Crawler" because he was born with no feet. The book begins before The Long Walk of 1864, when the Navajos were rounded up from their homes and hiding places, and taken to the far side of New Mexico, to Bosque Redondo at Fort Sumner, where many of them perished. Na Nai, his medicine man uncle, and his sister survive the Long Walk and the years of imprisonment, but Na Nai's mother does not.

Within this story is the story of two Mexican children, Juan and Pedro, who have been kidnapped by the Navajos, just as Navajo children were kidnapped by the Mexicans. They were slaves to Red Singer's son, who treated them unfeelingly. Na Nai's medicine man uncle, however, welcomed them into the tribe as though they were his own children. The children are rescued by their father during the Long Walk, but long afterward, when the Navajos have returned to their homeland, Pedro returns to his Navajo family to start a trading post.

The stories of the Mountain Chant are interwoven with the story of Na Nai, as is the symbolism of the dark circle of branches, representing the head of Klishto the great horned serpent, within which the ceremony is held, and the fire burning in the darkness, representing the pole star.

Like *Waterless Mountain* the story is beautifully written, its prose echoing the poetry of the chants: "The rainbow arched across the eastern sky. The red of its outer rim glowed like fire against shell pink clouds and the blue on its inner side shone with such color as Na Nai had never seen. Under the rainbow the moistened earth lay peacefully with growing corn in the valleys, and with the cliffs of Tsegi trimmed in brilliant quills of the sunrays" (12).

Armer's third Navajo book for children, *The Trader's Children* (1937), illustrated with her own photographs, was less successful. The book looks at life among the Navajos from the perspective of the children of a trader, rather than from within the Navajo culture. The photographs make it seem less like a story than a documentary. Two of the characters in the book, the children's aunt and uncle, sound very much like Laura and Sidney Armer.

Her fourth book for children, a boldly colored picture book entitled *The Forest Pool* (1938), was a Caldecott honor book. The illustrations, unusual for the time, consist of eight brilliantly colored plates in a style reminiscent of Diego Rivera. The story is a simple one of a young Mexican boy, his parrot who says only, "I have been here before," and the iguana who lives at the forest pool.

Little Diego and his friend Popo walk through the forest to the pool where, in addition to the iguana, they find mysteriously hidden pearls, pearls about which the parrot had brought a puzzling message long ago. The family keeps the pearls, but the iguana, who looks wise, "as if he knew all of the past," returns to his home in the dark woods by the forest pool where he will be happy.

Armer's last children's book, *Farthest West* (1939), was greeted with mixed reviews. It is the story of a group of school children, including one half Native American child, who attempt to save California's coastal redwoods from lumber interests.

CRITICAL RECEPTION

Little has been written about Armer. Only the Newbery Award–winning *Waterless Mountain* remains in print. Unfortunately, its latest edition, published by Knopf, lacks the wonderful aquatint illustrations of earlier editions.

From the first, *Waterless Mountain* was greeted with acclaim, and it continues to be held in high regard. J. W. Maury wrote in the *Boston Transcript*, December 2, 1931: "From first to last there is not a jarring note in *Waterless Mountain*. It is a book beautifully conceived and excellently wrought" (6).

Anne T. Eaton in the *New York Times*, October 18, 1931, praises Armer's sympathy for and knowledge Indian ways and says that "nothing in this book is finer than the author's presentation of the poet of a primitive [*sic*] people and his response to the beauty and mystery" around him (19).

An anonymous reviewer in *New Mexico* magazine, November 1931, writes that it is hard to imagine a white author capturing certain qualities in the book, but that Armer's time spent in the desert helped her "capture the true mythology of the Navajos." The book, we are told, "will both thrill and inform the youthful reader" and is lively, rather than "dry-as-dust" (33).

This same reviewer also points out that the Navajos in the story are free of the "romanticism and tomfoolery" that can be "wrapped like a blanket" around fictional Indians (33).

Dark Circle of Branches was also praised for its sensitive portrayal of Navajos. Withers Woolford, in *New Mexico* in April 1934, wrote that there is not much action in the book because "there can be [none] in [any] book that aspires to picture Indian life, unless it is of years of war. But there is a great understanding of Indian life and a deep meaning for those who live through the pages of the book" (37).

The reviewer in Mary Jo Lass Woodfin's *Books on American Indians and Eskimos* noted that "the author's reverence for her subjects emerges constantly" (22).

Mary Lystad, writing in *Twentieth Century Children's Writers*, suggests that "Armer's place in American literature derives from her authentic and humanistic portrayal of Navaho [*sic*] life, within its own context and within a larger American context. . . . Her novels were fore runners of later books on the American Indian and their problems of reconciling native traditional, rural values with an American secular, urban world" (31).

Armer captured Navajo life at a particular moment in history, and for that alone her work is valuable, but she also captured it in a way that few other writers have. The interweaving of myth and story is closer to the work of Native American writer N. Scott Momaday than to that of other Anglo writers, and has closer affinity with the magical realism of Gabriel García Márquez or Virginia Hamilton than with earlier stories of Native American life.

BIBLIOGRAPHY

Young Adult Fiction by Laura Adams Armer

Waterless Mountain. Illus. Laura Adams Armer and Sidney Armer. 1931; 1959. New York: Knopf, 1993.

Dark Circle of Branches. Illus. Sidney Armer. New York: Longman, 1933.

The Trader's Children. Illus. with photographs by Laura Adams Armer. New York: Longman, 1937.

The Forest Pool. Illus. Laura Adams Armer. New York: Longman, 1938.

Farthest West. Illus. Sidney Armer. New York: Longman, 1939.

Books Illustrated by Laura Adams Armer

Jones, T. E. [Theodore Elden]. *Leaves from an Argonaut's Note Book: A Collection of Holiday and Other Stories Illustrative of the Brighter Side of Mining Life in Pioneer Days*. Illus. Laura Adams Armer. San Francisco: Whitaker & Ray, 1905.

Other Works by Laura Adams Armer

Cactus. Illus. Sidney Armer. New York: Stokes, 1934.
Southwest. Illus. Laura Adams Armer. New York: Longman, 1935.
In Navajo Land. Photographs by Laura Adams Armer, Sidney Armer, and Austin Armer. New York: McKay, 1962.

Selected Studies of Laura Adams Armer

Armer, Alberta. *Working Hands*. 1981. [Family history. Privately printed by Alberta Armer. Copy at University of California, Davis.]

"Armer, Laura Adams." *Contemporary Authors*. Ed. Jane A. Bowden. Vols. 65–68. Detroit: Gale, 1977. 31–32.

"Berkeley Sees Copies of 'Sand Paintings.' *Art Digest* 1 Oct. 1929: 8.

Britton, Jasmine. "*Waterless Mountain* Wins Newbery Medal." *Publishers Weekly* 30 Apr. 1932: 1878–79.

Dawdy, Doris O. *Artists of the American West: A Biographical Dictionary*. Chicago: Sage Books, 1974.

Dicker, Laverne Mau. "Laura Adams Armer: California Photographer." *California Historical Quarterly* 56. 2 (1977): 128–39.

Eaton, Anne T. Rev. of *Waterless Mountain*. *New York Times* 18 Oct. 1931: 19.

Helbig, Alethea, and Agnes Perkins, eds. *Dictionary of American Children's Fiction, 1859–1959: Books of Recognized Merit*. Westport, CT: Greenwood, 1985.

"The John Newbery Prize Book." *Journal of the National Education Association* 21 (1932): 265.

"Laura Adams Armer." *Something about the Author*. Ed. Anne Commire. Vol. 13. Detroit: Gale, 1971. 2–6.

"Laura Adams Armer." *Wilson Library Bulletin* 6 (1932): 666, 670.

Lystad, Mary. "Laura Adams Armer." *Twentieth Century Children's Writers*. Ed. D. L. Kirkpatrick. 2nd ed. New York: St. Martin's, 1989. 30–31.

Maury, J. W. Rev. of *Waterless Mountain*. *Boston Transcript*, 2 Dec. 1931: 6.

"Newbery Medal Award." *American Library Association Bulletin* 26 (1932): 644–45.

"Newbery Medal Award." *Library Journal* 57 1 May 1932: 430.

Peterson, Linda K., and Marilyn L. Solt. *Newbery and Caldecott Medal and Honor Books: An Annotated Bibliography*. Boston: G. K. Hall, 1982.

Woodfin, Mary Jo Lass. *Books on American Indians and Eskimos*. Chicago: American Library Association, 1978.

Woodfin, Mary Jo Lass. Rev. of *Waterless Mountain*. *New Means*. April 1934: 37.

WILLIAM HOWARD ARMSTRONG
(1914-)

Thomas J. Morrissey

BIOGRAPHY

Born in Lexington, Virginia, September 14, 1914, William H. Armstrong attended Augusta Military Academy, from which he graduated in 1932. He earned a B.A. (*cum laude*) and Phi Beta Kappa key at Virginia's Hampden-Sydney College in 1936, and attended the University of Virginia at Charlottesville (1937–1938). Armstrong married Martha Stonestreet Williams in 1943. Three children, two sons and a daughter, were born to them before Martha's death in 1953. Armstrong taught history for thirty-six years, first at Virginia Episcopal School from 1939–1944, and then at Kent School in Connecticut, from 1945 until his retirement in 1976. His historical interests ranged from ancient to contemporary, with a special emphasis on the theme of social justice.

Having spent his first thirty years in segregated Virginia, he developed a keen interest in the effects of racial discrimination, from which sprang *Sounder*, the novel for which he is famous; its sequel, *Sour Land*; and a biography of Lincoln. A dedicated teacher, Armstrong shared his pedagogical expertise in a number of works aimed at improving student learning (1956–1976). He was awarded the National Association of School Administrators School Bell Award in 1963. In 1970, *Sounder* won Armstrong both the American Library Association's John Newbery Medal and the Lewis

Carroll Shelf Award. Hampden-Sydney College granted him an honorary Litt.D. in 1986.

MAJOR WORKS AND THEMES

Armstrong's fame rests on the success of the novel *Sounder* (1969) and the 20th Century Fox film based on the book (1972). This novel and its sequel, *Sour Land* (1971), constitute his contribution to multiculturalism. According to Nancy Huse, Armstrong originally intended *Sounder* to include the events of *Sour Land* as well, but Harper & Row persuaded him to write two novels. Neither book is truly multicultural in the sense that it portrays with accuracy the lives of a racial or cultural minority. It would be difficult to get a full picture of African-American life in the pre–Civil Rights Movement South from either of these novels; in fact, reading *Sour Land* could give one the impression that there is no such thing as African-American culture.

Published within five years of the Civil Rights and Voting Rights acts and just a year after the assassination of Martin Luther King, Jr., *Sounder* was an instant success. The book is the story of a poor black sharecropper family in the rural South suffering but persevering under a racist economic and legal system. That none of the human characters has a name suggests that they represent universal types. The black boy who desperately wants to learn to read is every black child who is denied a good education in the South and every child of any race who wonders at the mysteries of nature and questions the conventions of adult society. The scenario of an absent father, a searching son, and a loyal dog echoes *The Odyssey*. The hunting dog Sounder is both a symbol of the symbiotic kinship between humans and nature and the living bond between father and son. The elderly black schoolteacher who introduces the boy to Montaigne represents what poor Southern African-Americans can become with educational opportunity.

Lyrical language and precise description expose for readers the maturation of a young mind in a corrupt world. In the first chapter, the boy dreams of the biblical flood. In his version, floating cabins can come together to form a community and put an end to loneliness. In the next chapter, he learns how racism undermines community and perverts language. When the sheriff who has come to arrest the father for stealing pork from a smokehouse calls the man "boy," the boy in the story thinks the sheriff means him. Likewise, when the sheriff says, "Chain him up" (24), the boy thinks he means Sounder until the lawmen chain his father. This is the first of many bitter lessons. Ultimately, the boy will learn to conquer the despair that such cruelty can engender by learning to read, thus opening up for him the liberating life of the mind. Armstrong's use of lyrical language and literary allusion in the service of an admirable theme results in a story that can be read and appreciated by both young adult and adult audiences.

The novel's principal weakness—and it is a serious one—is that the book's universal context is more believable than its local context. Armstrong's fiction distorts the reality of Southern black life. The mother and father are passive victims of oppression. The family lives in a lonely cabin and seems to have no support system. There is no image of traditional or powerful social institutions—community, extended family, or church. That the young hero has never heard a black man called "boy" is a little hard to believe. That the black schoolteacher appears to be an elderly bachelor who has no familiarity with black writers suggests that the novel's vision of what an African-American can attain through education is sterile and anything but multicultural. Still, *Sounder* is an evocative novel that has moved many readers.

In contrast, *Sour Land* is painfully slow, culturally inaccurate, and thoroughly depressing. Its hero is Moses Waters, the boy of *Sounder* grown to old age. An itinerant schoolteacher, he comes to Virginia where he works to improve the lot of the weak and apparently dwindling black population. He also serves as a day laborer and nighttime tutor on the farm of a liberal white man, Anson Stone. Unlike his biblical namesake, Moses does not lead his brethren to freedom, nor does he bring the waters of life to their sour land (save for the garden around his quaint cottage). After agreeing to testify against whites who raped a black teenager (she later dies from the assault), Moses is himself murdered. Moses teaches the Stone children the classics and much else, but he never breathes a word about the work of any African-American thinker, leader, or artist. The book's over-written romantic ending tries to suggest that Moses' death is a hopeful event, but since his life and the cultural life of blacks in general seems to be a dead end, it seems today to be a convenient way to dispatch a character who has no future.

CRITICAL RECEPTION

Sounder could not have won the Newbery Medal had it not received a strongly positive critical reception. Zena Sutherland's response to the novel is fairly typical. She writes in *Saturday Review* that "somber as the book is, it is moving and tender, and inexorable. The human characters have no names; they are a symbol of all the poor, black and white, who face indignity with courage" (30). *Commonweal* calls it a "biting indictment of the treatment of Negro farmers in the South" (257). Writing in the *New York Times*, June Jordan recommended the book to young and old but raised a series of questions about the origin of the story and the accuracy of the character portrayals, which have continued to bother black critics. Rae Alexander, who compiled a list of acceptable biracial books for young people on behalf of the NAACP, considers *Sounder* a racist book because it perpetuates the image of impotent black characters who cannot serve as adequate role models for African-American youth. He writes that "when you study the Black actors in *Sounder*, you wonder how black people could have survived social genocide since 1619" (62). Applying criteria established by Julius Lester, Albert V. Schwartz also dismisses *Sounder* for its lack of authenticity. He questions Armstrong's ability to retell a tale told to him by a black man. He asks why the book has no black speech, no real black spirituals, no characters who fight back, no mention of the white landowner for whom the blacks toil, and no references to black writers. In her article in *Children's Literature Association Quarterly*, Nancy Huse reviews much of the *Sounder* criticism as she reconsiders the novel after encountering resistance to it from students born after its publication. She claims that participant readers, those who share Armstrong's cultural origins and perspectives, love the novel for its craft and message while observer readers, mainly blacks, reject the craft because of the book's falsification of their reality. She writes: "For participant readers the literary imagery of *Sounder* extends their knowledge of racism . . . for observer readers, the extension of such knowledge is like waving the perennial red flag before the bull" (69).

The 1972 film of *Sounder* differs in significant ways from the novel. In his article on the transition from print to film, Leonard J. Deutsch notes among the major revisions the fleshing out of characters, the strength of the family and community, the change in sex of the schoolteacher from male to female, and, above all, the change to an "upbeat ending" (222). Although some critics think that the changes are an improvement, Deutsch thinks that "each of the works makes rich and effective use of the properties inherent in its own art form" (224).

Sour Land met with mixed reviews. The *Horn Book* reviewer describes it as "a sincerely idealistic and elegiac presentation of one of America's tragic dilemmas" (285). To Diane G. Stavn in *Library Journal* the book celebrates "the ultimate inviolability of the human soul," but she finds Moses "too noble to be interesting" (1121). However, Alice Walker, a decade away from *The Color Purple*, calls the book a "crushing disappointment" to those who loved *Sounder* (8). As it turns out, that is just about the most positive comment she makes. Walker dismisses Moses as "Uncle Remus' grandson," who serves whites and knows nothing of his culture. She concludes with this stinging indictment: "Your death, like your life, is perfect. But absolute perfection is inhuman, which means, Moses Waters, that to your re-creator, the man who dragged you from childhood, you were never even real" (10). Lois Kuznets compares and contrasts the two novels. She sees *Sounder* as a novel for children and *Sour Land* as a novel with adult concerns and conventions. For her, "*Sounder* depicts a quest for self-transformation clearly and sweetly fulfilled in the best tradition of the children's classic," but in its sequel "adult pessimism for life on this earth prevails" (29). She argues that Moses Waters is a Christ figure whose figurative resurrection is his influence on "the good Whites" (24).

BIBLIOGRAPHY

Young Adult Fiction by William Howard Armstrong

Animal Tales. Illus. Mirko Hanak. New York: Doubleday, 1970.
Barefoot in the Grass: The Story of Grandma Moses. New York: Doubleday, 1970.
Sounder. Illus. James Barkely. New York: Harper, 1969. London: Golancz, 1971.
Sour Land. Illus. David Armstrong. New York: Harper, 1971.
Hadassah: Ester, The Orphan Queen. Illus. Barbara Byfield. New York: Doubleday, 1972.
The McCleod Place. Illus. Eros Keith. New York: Coward McCann, 1972.
The Mills of God. Illus. David Armstrong. New York: Doubleday, 1973.
The Education of Abraham Lincoln. Illus. William Plummer. New York: Coward McCann, 1974.
My Animals. Illus. Mirko Hanak. New York: Doubleday, 1974.
Joanna's Miracle. Nashville: Boardman, 1977.
The Tale of Tawny and Dingo. Illus. Charles Mikolaycak. New York: Harper, 1979.

Selected Studies of William Howard Armstrong

Alexander, Rae. "What Is a Racist Book?" *The Black American in Books for Children: Readings in Racism*. Ed. Donnarae MacCann and Gloria Woodard. Metuchen, NJ: Scarecrow, 1972. 57–62.
Deutsch, Leonard J. "The Named and the Unnamed." *Children's Novels and the Movies*. Ed. Douglas Street. New York: Ungar, 1983. 215–26.
Huse, Nancy. "*Sounder* and Its Readers: Learning to Observe." *Children's Literature Association Quarterly* 12.2 (1987): 66–69.

Jordan, June. Rev. of *Sounder*. *New York Times Book Review* 26 Oct. 1969: 42.

Kuznets, Lois. "Sweet and Sour Land: A Critical Comparison of the *Sounder* Novels." *Illinois English Bulletin* (Spring 1978): 23–29.

Rev. of *Sounder*. *Commonweal* 21 Nov. 1969: 257.

Rev. of *Sour Land*. *Horn Book* 47 (June 1971): 285.

Schwartz, Albert V. "Sounder: A Black or White Tale?" *The Black American in Books for Children: Readings in Racism*. Ed. Donnarae MacCann and Gloria Woodard. Metuchen, NJ: Scarecrow, 1972. 89–93.

Stavn, Diane G. Rev. of *Sour Land*. *Library Journal* 96 15 Mar. 1971: 1121.

Sutherland, Zena. Rev. of *Sounder*. *Saturday Review* 20 Dec. 1969: 30.

Walker, Alice. Rev. of *Sour Land*. *New York Times Book Review* 9 May 1971: 8+.

BETTY LOU BAKER
(1928–1987)

Thomas J. Morrissey

BIOGRAPHY

Although Betty Lou Baker is best known for her novels set in the Southwest, she was an easterner by birth, having been born in Bloomsburg, Pennsylvania, and having attended school in New Jersey. She was an avid reader as a child and enjoyed making up acrostic puzzles. Baker was married in 1948 and divorced in 1965. She had one son, for whom she wrote *Little Runner of the Longhouse* (1962), a tale about the New Year's celebrations of the Iroquois. She held a number of jobs, including dental assistant and shop owner, and served as editor of *Roundup* magazine. Baker had a passion for western lore. Her novel *Do Not Annoy the Indians* (1968) resulted from the discovery of a century-old timetable of the Butterfield Overland Mail Company, a stagecoach service that later became Wells Fargo, and from conversations with Gordon C. Baldwin, the anthropologist to whom the book is dedicated. A two-time winner of the Western Heritage Award (1964, 1971), she also won the Western Writers of America Spur Award in 1968. Her western home was Tucson, Arizona.

MAJOR WORKS AND THEMES

Most of Baker's multicultural fiction consists of historical novels based on southwestern history from the Spanish conquest on. Although her work is uneven in quality, the best of her books display a remarkable sensitivity to and appreciation of Native peoples and cultures.

Among her best novels is *Killer-of-Death*, which earned the author a well-deserved Western Heritage Award in 1964. Set in nineteenth-century Arizona, it is the fictional autobiography of an Apache warrior who comes to manhood as his people make their last great stand against U.S. aggression. The history in the novel is real, and the first-person narration adds to the novel's sense of authenticity. Killer-of-Death, the teenage title character, is at once familiar and alien to readers his age. He has a family and a community. His mother is quiet and kind, his father wise and patient. He and his brother are close, and they have a playful little sister. However, there are some big differences, too. Killer-of-Death is one of the People; their foes call them "Apache" from the Pueblo for "enemy." They hunt, gather, grow a little corn, and steal whatever else they need in raids against other tribes or Mexicans. In fact, Killer-of-Death's younger brother is of Mexican birth, having been captured as a child and raised as one of the People.

The narrator gives us what seems to be a first-hand glimpse of Apache society. He tells of their religion, ethical code, and rites of passage. We see southern Arizona through his eyes—the Mexicans and "white eyes" (Yankees) are clearly interlopers who give civilization a bad name. We share Killer-of-Death's adventures, including his saving the life of the great war chief Mangas Colorado, as well as his fear that he has a sickness because killing enemies is repugnant to him. In the end, however, we understand and sympathize with the young warrior's accommodation to killing enemies. The Mexicans treacherously murder hundreds of Apaches at a feast, and the American cavalry, using heavy artillery, blasts the Apache off their ancestral lands. After he and his people are sent to a reservation some distance from their former home, the desperate Killer-of-Death sends his only son to the infamous Carlisle Indian School where, he hopes, the boy will learn the white man's ways and return to help the Apaches survive the twentieth century.

The Shaman's Last Raid (1963) is a light-weight comedy lacking seriousness of purpose and multicultural vision. An elderly Apache shaman who knew Geronimo and who has spent his entire adult life longing to go on a cattle raid teaches his off-reservation grandchildren much about the old ways. However, the shaman's descendants are moving further away from their cultural roots with each generation, and accommodating to the ways and expectations of whites seems to be the only viable answer for the characters. The novel's uncritical tone reinforces the impression that accommodation is inevitable and even desirable.

Baker reaches back to the early days of the Spanish conquest in *Walk the World's Rim* (1965). Chakoh, an Avavare of East Texas, joins conquistadors on a trip to Mexico City and a quest for Cibola. The geographical journey is also a cultural one: the young Indian traverses technological and social barriers. Chakoh, whose people are preagricultural, is exposed to buffalo hunters, settled agriculturists, and the splendor and squalor of Mexico City. There, Chakoh mimics the ways of the monks who take charge of his education. After the death of his friend Esteban, a black slave who is killed by Pueblos at Cibola, Chakoh decides to retrace his steps and bring agriculture and Catholicism to his people. Baker exposes Spanish cruelty at every opportunity: their lust for gold and bright stones undermines their humanity, overcomes their Christianity, and leads to the scenes of poverty and abuse that Chakoh witnesses in Mexico City. The "world's rim" is a descriptor of the long journey in uncharted regions, but it is also a metaphor for life on the margin. When Chakoh decides to return to his own people, he is escaping from the center of the world, but he is carrying with him from the hub of New Spain the seeds of colonial expansion and cultural assimilation.

The Blood of the Brave (1966) is a slow-moving novel that traces the plotting and intrigues surrounding Cortez's conquest of Mexico. The book shows the daring of the conquistadors as well as their avarice and bigotry. The Spaniards marvel at the wonders of Mexico, but they do not hesitate to topple the pyramids so that the stones can be used for a church.

Do Not Annoy the Indians (1968) reads like a TV sitcom set in Arizona in the 1850s. The Barnes children set out from Philadelphia with their mother to join their father in Arizona, where he works as a stagecoach station master. Their adventures with local Yumas help to erase anti-Native prejudices. In Yuma mythology, a spirit created Yumas, Mexicans, and whites, but expelled the non-Yumas from Arizona because they were greedy. The clash of white and Native values is evident. The Native point of view gets a fair airing, but there is little overt condemnation of white imperialism.

And One Was a Wooden Indian (1970) is an engrossing and often funny book about cultural difference. It has a happy ending, but lurking just outside the boundaries of comedy is the reality of American aggression and racism. An Apache with poor eyesight, Hatilshay, and his superstitious friend Turtlehead accidentally get mixed up with the U.S. cavalry. Their translator is a Christian Papago who believes until late in the book that if he acts like a white man he will be treated as one. The two Apaches get a fleeting glimpse of a wooden statue that they believe to be a spirit carving designed to turn Turtlehead into wood through magic. Hatilshay, Turtle-head, and the tribe's shaman spend the rest of the novel trying to capture and destroy the figure.

Cultural and linguistic confusion creates the comedy and hints at the potential disaster. The Native Americans come to realize that the whites do not recognize tribal or individual differences among Native peoples. Since they are from different tribes, they communicate with each other using the old lingua franca, Spanish, but the Papago and Yuma, whose tribal ways are more eroded, also speak the new lingua franca, English. In their amusing efforts to communicate, they scoff at Yankee ways. Hatilshay laughs at the concepts that anyone can own land and that coined money can have value.

Sight is an important metaphor in the book. Hatilshay sees poorly, for which he is often ridiculed, but the shaman sees in him the gift of predictive foresight. When Hatilshay has the opportunity to keep a Yankee spyglass, he returns the beloved instrument, fearful that by gaining the ability to see distant objects, he will lose the ability to see distant events. He will not allow modern technology to eclipse ancient values.

The Natives in this remarkable novel are individuals. One cannot read it and come away with the notion that all Native Americans look, act, or think alike, or that the very term "Indian" is anything but a convenient catchall invented by ethnocentric invaders.

A Stranger and Afraid (1972) repeats the theme of a young Native American returning home after seeing the Spanish. Sopete joins Coronado, hoping to find the Plains tribe from which he was captured by Pueblos as a child. Young readers are shown life at Cicuye Pueblo—the farming, the ceremonies, the societies, and kivas—as well as Spanish brutality toward the people. Sopete finally leaves the Spaniards and settles among the Wichitas. In Baker's last novel about Native Americans, the message is unequivocal: Coronado's last act is to plant a giant cross; Sopete's is to knock the cross over and burn it.

In 1977 Baker wrote a history for young adults entitled *Settlers and Strangers: Native Americans of the Desert Southwest and History as They Saw It*. Although she was not a Native American, her history is brutally honest. From Coronado's attack on Hawikuh in 1540 to the hanging of Pueblo holy men in 1847 and the subsequent seizure of Pueblo, Navajo, and Apache lands, the story is the same: Euro-American racism, religious bigotry, and greed carry the day. It seems fitting that this book comes at the end of her career as a writer of historical fiction about Native Americans; it is as though once she succinctly told the history that inspired her earlier novels, there was nothing left to say—she had paid her tribute to the Native people of her region.

CRITICAL RECEPTION

Reviews are usually, but not always, favorable. *Killer-of-Death* is described as a "moving first person narrative" (Libby) and a "haunting tale" (Hood). M.S. Libby calls *The Shaman's Last Raid* "a splendidly funny story." Evelyn R. Downum describes *Walk the World's Rim* as "an engrossing account," but Thomas Fall says that it "does not effectively come alive." According to Marjorie Stephenson, *The Blood of the Brave* is "exciting fiction"; however, W. J. Jacobs finds it "undistinguished in characterization," although he does like the "realistic descriptions of human sacrifices on blood-stained Aztec idols." Zena Sutherland accurately attributes to *And One Was a Wooden Indian* "a perceptive and emphatic understanding of cultural conflict."

The reviews sometimes reveal the cultural biases of the reviewers and misinterpret the author's major themes. Baker does not subscribe to the myth of the "vanishing Indian," that convenient distortion of reality that allowed Americans to put Natives on coins and products while stealing their land and attempting to eradicate their cultures. Failing to understand that Baker is not weeping over a lost culture but praising a living one, Robert Hood says in a review of *Killer-of-Death* that "through her the Apache rides again, powerful, courageous, fiercely proud—and doomed." Again writing for the *New York Times*, this same reviewer calls the shaman of *The Shaman's Last Raid* an "old buck" whose "Geronimo-like raid" gives his great-grandchildren "a quiverful of trouble." Baker's condemnation of Spanish colonial policy is evident in book after book, yet Jacobs writes of *The Blood of the Brave* that its "underlying theme is the bravery of the Conquistadors in the struggle they waged in the New World for the sake of 'gospel, glory, and gold.' "

BIBLIOGRAPHY

Young Adult and Children's Works by Betty Lou Baker

Little Runner of the Longhouse. Illus. Arnold Lobel. New York: Harper, 1962.
The Sun's Promise. Illus. Juliette Palmer. New York: Abelard Schuman, 1962.

The Shaman's Last Raid. Illus. Leonard Shortall. New York: Harper, 1963. Reissued as *The Medicine Man's Last Stand.* New York: Scholastic Books, 1965.

Killer-of-Death. Illus. John Kaufmann. New York: Harper, 1964.

The Treasure of the Padres. Illus. Leonard Shortall. New York: Harper, 1964.

Walk the World's Rim. New York: Harper, 1965.

The Blood of the Brave. New York: Harper, 1966.

The Dunderhead War. New York: Harper, 1967.

Do Not Annoy the Indians. Illus. Harold Goodwin. New York: Macmillan; London: Collier Macmillan, 1968.

The Pig War. Illus. Robert Lopshire. New York: Harper, 1969. Kingswood, Surrey: World's Work, 1971.

And One Was a Wooden Indian. New York: Macmillan, 1970.

The Big Push. Illus. Bonnie Johnson. New York: Coward McCann, 1972.

The Spirit Is Willing. New York: Macmillan, 1972.

A Stranger and Afraid. New York: Macmillan; London: Collier Macmillan, 1972.

Dupper. Illus. Chuck Eckart. New York: Greenwillow, 1976.

Partners. Illus. Emily McCully. New York: Greenwillow, 1978.

Save Sirrushany! (Also Agotha, Princess Gwyn, and All the Fearsome Beasts). Illus. Erick Ingraham. New York: Macmillan, 1978.

All-by-Herself. Illus. Catherine Stock. New York: Greenwillow, 1980.

The Great Desert Race. New York: Macmillan, 1980.

Santa Rat. Illus. Tom Huffman. New York: Greenwillow, 1980.

Danby and George. Illus. Adrianne Lobel. New York: Greenwillow, 1981.

Worthington Botts and the Steam Machine. Illus. Sal Murdocca. New York: Macmillan, 1981.

Seven Spells to Farewell. New York: Macmillan, 1982.

The Turkey Girl. Illus. Harold Berson. New York: Macmillan, 1983.

My Sister Says. Illus. Tricia Taggart. New York: Macmillan, 1984.

The Night Spider Case. New York: Macmillan, 1984.

Other Works by Betty Lou Baker

Great Ghost Stories of the Old West. Ed. Betty Lou Baker. New York: Four Winds, 1968.

Arizona. New York: Coward McCann, 1969.

At the Center of the World: Based on Papago and Pima Myths. Illus. Murray Tinkelman. New York: Macmillan, 1973.

Three Fools and a Horse. (Apache Folk Tale). Illus. Glen Rounds. New York: Macmillan, 1975. Kingswood, Surrey: World's Work, 1977.

Settlers and Strangers: Native Americans of the Desert Southwest and History as They Saw It. New York: Macmillan, 1977.

Latki and the Lightning Lizard. (Indian Folk Tale). Illus. Donald Carrick. New York: Macmillan, 1978.

No Help at All. (Maya Legend). Illus. Emily McCully. New York: Greenwillow, 1978.

Rat Is Dead and Ant Is Sad. (Pueblo Folk Tale). Illus. Mamoru Fumai. New York: Harper, 1981.

And Me, Coyote! (Native-American Folk Tales). Illus. Maria Horvath. New York: Macmillan, 1982.

Selected Studies of Betty Lou Baker

Buckmaster, Henrietta. Rev. of *The Blood of the Brave. Christian Science Monitor* 3 Nov. 1966: B12.

Coleman, Jean. Rev. of *And One Was a Wooden Indian. Library Journal* 96 (15 May 1971): 1809.

Cosgrave, M. S. Rev. of *Walk the World's Rim. Book Week, Spring Children's Issue* 9 May 1965: 32.

Downum, Evelyn R. Rev. of *Walk the World's Rim. Library Journal* 90 16 Mar. 1965: 1546.

Fall, Thomas. Rev. of *Walk the World's Rim. New York Times Book Review* 11 July 1965: 34.

Gurko, Miriam. Rev. of *And One Was a Wooden Indian. New York Times Book Review* 14 Feb. 1971: 20.

Hood, Robert. Rev. of *Killer-of-Death. New York Times Book Review* 27 Oct. 1963: 39.

Hood, Robert. Rev. of *The Shaman's Last Raid. New York Times Book Review* 12 May 1963: pt 2, 26.

Jacobs, W. J. Rev. of *The Blood of the Brave. New York Times Book Review* 11 Sept. 1966: 34.

Libby, M. S. Rev. of *Killer-of-Death. Book Week* 16 Feb. 1964: 14.

Libby, M. S. Rev. of *The Shaman's Last Raid. New York Herald Tribune Books* 12 May 1963: sec. 12:14.

Maples, H. L. Rev. of *The Blood of the Brave. Book Week* 14 Aug. 1966: 13.

Rev. of *And One Was a Wooden Indian. Horn Book* 47 (Apr. 1971): 171.

Rev. of *The Blood of the Brave. Horn Book* 42 (Aug. 1966): 437.

Rev. of *Killer-of-Death. Horn Book* 40 (Feb. 1964): 63.

Rev. of *Killer-of-Death. Library Journal* 88 (15 Oct. 1963): 4078.

Rev. of *The Shaman's Last Raid. Horn Book* 39 (Apr. 1963): 75.

Rev. of *Walk the World's Rim. Horn Book* 41 (Apr. 1965): 174.

Sheehan, Ethna. Rev. of *The Blood of the Brave. America* 115 (2 July 1966): 14.

Sorenson, Marian. Rev. of *The Shaman's Last Raid. Christian Science Monitor* 9 May 1963: 4B.

Stephenson, Marjorie. Rev. of *The Blood of the Brave. Library Journal* 91 (15 June 1966): 3262.

Sullivan, Peggy. Rev. of *The Shaman's Last Raid. Library Journal* 88 (15 May 1963): 2140.

Sutherland, Zena. Rev. of *And One Was a Wooden Indian. Saturday Review* 53 (14 Nov. 1970): 31.

White, Fidelis. Rev. of *Walk the World's Rim. Best Sellers* 25 (15 May 1965): 96.

NATHANIEL GODDARD BENCHLEY
(1915–1981)

Karen Fauls-Traynor

BIOGRAPHY

Second in the Benchley trio of authors, Nathaniel Goddard Benchley was born November 13, 1915, in Newton, Massachusetts. His father, Robert Benchley, was a well-known humorist and actor. Nathaniel Benchley's son, Peter, would later become a novelist, most famous for the 1974 best-seller *Jaws*. While literary talent seems to be a legacy in the Benchley family, each of the three exhibited his own unique style and choices for subject matter.

Nathaniel Benchley attended the Phillips Exeter Academy in New Hampshire from 1931–1934 and graduated from Harvard University in 1938 with a degree in English. He claims he began his career as a writer because it seemed to be the only thing he could do, but it is likely that he was influenced by the eventful career of his father. Believing that a writer's career should start with experience as a reporter, his first literary positions included being a feature writer for a weekly paper called *The Connecticut Nutmeg*, city reporter for the *New York Herald Tribune*, public relations writer with the U.S. Navy, and assistant editor for *Newsweek* magazine. After leaving *Newsweek*, he began freelancing, first with magazine articles and eventually with short stories and adult and juvenile fiction.

From 1941–1945, Benchley was called to active duty in the U.S. Naval Reserve, first in the position of reporter for the Public Relations Office, and later, at his own request, in active sea duty on destroyers and submarines in the Pacific. His wartime experiences are reflected in several of his works.

Nathaniel Benchley married Marjorie Bradford on May 19, 1939. They had two sons: Peter Bradford, born in 1940, and Nathaniel Robert, in 1946. The Benchley family moved from New York City, where Nathaniel had spent most of his adult life, to Nantucket Island in Massachusetts in 1969. Nantucket provided the perfect setting for Benchley's other interests of fishing, boating, and painting. He professed to be an amateur painter, but in actuality often sold his works. Benchley loved living and working on Nantucket, but often found many distractions during the summer months when the tourist season was at its peak. He established a disciplined schedule of writing, calling for a minimum of one thousand words per day, and refrained from social activities to reinforce the idea that he was working, not vacationing. When not working, he spent his time on the ocean with his sons, boating and fishing and, occasionally, hunting sharks. It was from these childhood experiences that his son Peter is said to have developed his fascination with sharks that led to the novel *Jaws*.

In 1960 Benchley began writing books for children, and in 1970 wrote the first of five novels directed at young adults. He continued to write books for adults as well.

Nathaniel Benchley died on December 14, 1981, of a liver infection, in Boston, Massachusetts.

MAJOR WORKS AND THEMES

Nathaniel Benchley was a prolific and versatile writer. In total, he published eighteen adult novels, two biographies (including a well-received tribute to his father), two screenplays, twenty children's books, and five young adult historical novels. He also contributed numerous articles and short stories to periodicals such as the *New Yorker*, *Esquire*, *Vogue*, *McCalls*, and *Ladies Home Journal*.

In examining Nathaniel Benchley's life, there are many apparent influences on his works. His low-key, satirical humor was no doubt an inheritance from his father. His years on Nantucket are reflected in the settings of many of his works, and his interest in nature shows in the animal protagonists in many of his children's books. Naval experiences are related in some of his adult novels, most notably in his 1961 book *The Off-Islanders*, the basis for the movie *The Russians Are Coming! The Russians Are Coming! A Necessary End*, published in 1976, was also drawn from his military experience.

Benchley began writing children's books in part because of a belief that children should be motivated to read books instead of watching television. In his view, the components of a good juvenile book included humor, suspense, and language that did not talk down to children. He once gave the example of E. B. White's *Charlotte's Web* as the ideal children's novel because it could be enjoyed by children as well as adults. Of the twenty children's books written by Benchley, his most successful was *Red Fox and His Canoe* (1964), about the mishaps of a young Native American boy who is anxious to assume adult responsibilities. *Small Wolf* (1972) and *Running Owl, the Hunter* (1979) also featured Native American characters.

Benchley believed in the need for young adult works to bridge the gap between child and adult fiction, especially for teenagers with limited reading abilities. His goal was to tell a story as "cleanly and neatly as possible" and he spent considerable time on meticulous research, including travel to the sites of his stories. In 1970 he began to write historical novels for teens, first with *Gone and Back,* a story of the Oklahoma land rush as told through a young man's experiences. In 1972 he produced *Only Earth and Sky Last Forever*, a story from the Native American perspective of the events leading up to the Battle of Little Big Horn. Benchley had read an article that detailed an interview with a Native American survivor of the famous battle. He was charmed by the individual's personal motive, to win the affections of a girl, that led to his role in the events. Although essentially a tragic story, it is lightened by Benchley's humor and characterization of the boy.

Benchley's next young adult novel was *Bright Candles: A Novel of the Danish Resistance*, published in 1974, followed by *Beyond the Mists* (1975), a Viking tale that includes a description of the Vikings' encounters with Native Americans when they arrived in the New World. His final novel written for young adults was published in 1976, *A Necessary End,* a description of a young man's experience with submarine combat in the Pacific during World War II.

CRITICAL RECEPTION

Nathaniel Benchley brought a new level of excellence to the books he wrote for his younger audiences. His children's novels were imaginative, lively, humorous, and written with language that challenged rather than bored. Many of his books for young children were part of the Harper I Can Read Series and were engaging and informative while meeting the standards for the reading level.

His historical novels for young adults were thoughtful, substantial, and well researched. In 1973 he was the recipient of the Western Writers of America Spur Award, for *Only Earth and Sky Last Forever*. The *New York Times* selected *Gone and Back* as an Outstanding Book of the Year for Young adults in 1971 and the American Library Association voted *Bright Candles: A Novel of the Danish Resistance* as Best Book for Young Adults of 1974.

Benchley's style of writing has historical events come to life in a way that makes his work more than required reading. His well-developed characters draw the reader into the story so that the outcome is eagerly anticipated. *Center for Children's Books Bulletin* calls *Only Earth and Sky Last Foreve*r (*CBB-B*) "poignant" and "powerful," noting that its "bleak" ending is "balanced by the tender love story, its note of dismay by the stirring hopefulness of the battle" (119). Of *Bright Candles, CBB-B* says "Benchley shows a segment of the Danish people seldom included in stories of World War II. . . . Style, dialogue, characterization and setting are treated with consummate skill" (171).

Robert Benchley was not of Native American descent, but chose to write *Only Earth and Sky* from the perspective of a young Sioux boy. Although Benchley was writing at a time when attention and sensitivity to ethnic issues was not always common practice, this raises a question for the young adult reading his work today. Often writers are criticized for choosing subjects outside the realm of their personal experience, especially as relating to racial and cultural issues. It is obvious that Benchley considered this, as demonstrated by his note in the preface of *Only Earth and Sky Last Forever*: "The main events in this work of fiction are true, and as historically accurate as the conflicting records allow. . . . As for the language, I have not tried to make too close an approximation of the way Indians spoke, or how their language would sound if translated literally; the Tonto or 'heap big paleface' type of dialogue is also not suited to this story . . . I have made the people speak what sounds most natural to the modern ear."

Although Benchley's attempt to remain neutral is admirable in face of other works of that time period that use language that demeans Native Americans, the reader is left to wonder how the story could have been different if told with a genuine voice. As written, it is an engaging story, but the impartial language leaves the reader with the question, "Is this really how they would have said this?"

Benchley was careful to research his topics thoroughly, as evidenced by his bibliography at the end of *Only Earth and Sky Last Forever*. *Catholic Library World* commented of this book that information on Indian beliefs and customs was "well integrated" and that the details "make this book a source of authentic knowledge of the Indian way of life" (506). Benchley often traveled to the site of his stories and spent time in Denmark when doing research for *Bright Candles*.

Benchley found being the son of an already famous writer to be both a help and a hindrance. His work received more attention because of his connections, but was also compared to that of his father. He made it a point to write in a completely different style to avoid comparisons, and was largely successful in finding his own voice and his own audience.

BIBLIOGRAPHY

Young Adult Fiction by Nathaniel Goddard Benchley

Gone and Back. New York: Harper, 1970.

Only Earth and Sky Last Forever. New York: Harper, 1972.

Bright Candles: A Novel of the Danish Resistance. New York: Harper, 1974. London: Deutsch, 1976.

Beyond the Mists. New York: Harper, 1975.

A Necessary End. New York: Harper, 1976. London: Deutsch, 1978.

Children's Works by Nathaniel Goddard Benchley

Red Fox and His Canoe. Illus. Arnold Lobel. New York: Harper, 1964. Kingswood, Surrey: World's Work, 1969.

Oscar Otter. Illus. Arnold Lobel. New York: Harper, 1966. Kingswood, Surrey: World's Work, 1967.

The Strange Disappearance of Arthur Cluck. Illus. Arnold Lobel. New York: Harper, 1967. Kingswood, Surrey: World's Work, 1968.

A Ghost Named Fred. Illus. Ben Shecter. New York: Harper; Kingswood, Surrey: World's Work, 1969.

Sam the Minuteman. Illus. Arnold Lobel. New York: Harper, 1969. Kingswood, Surrey: World's Work, 1976.

The Flying Lesson of Gerald Pelican. Illus. Mamoru Funai. New York: Harper, 1970.

The Several Tricks of Edgar Dolphin. Illus. Mamoru Funai. New York: Harper; Kingswood, Surrey: World's Work, 1970.

Demo and the Dolphin. Ilus. Stephen Gammell. New York: Harper, 1971.

Feldman Fieldmouse. Illus. Hilary Knight. New York: Harper, 1971. London: Abelard Schuman, 1975.

The Magic Sled. Illus. Mel Furukawa. NY: Harper, 1972. Rpt. as *The Magic Sledge*. London: Deutsch, 1974.

Small Wolf. Illus. Joan Sandin. New York: Harper, 1972. Kingswood, Surrey: World's Work, 1973.

The Deep Dives of Stanley Whale. Illus. Mischa Richter. New York: Harper, 1973. Kingswood, Surrey: World's Work, 1976.

Snorri and the Strangers. Illus. Don Bolognese. New York: Harper, 1976. Kingswood, Surrey: World's Work, 1978.

George the Drummer Boy. Illus. Don Bolognese. New York: Harper, 1977. Kingswood, Surrey: World's Work, 1978.

Kilroy and the Gull. Illus. John Schoenherr. New York: Harper, 1977. London: Abelard Schuman, 1979.

Running Owl, the Hunter. Illus. Mamoru Funai. New York: Harper, 1979.

Snip. Illus. Irene Trivas. New York: Doubleday, 1981.

Walter the Homing Pigeon. Illus. Whitney Darrow, Jr. New York: Harper, 1981.

Selected Studies of Nathaniel Goddard Benchley

"Benchley, Nathaniel." *Contemporary Authors: New Revision Series.* Ed. Linda Metzger. Vol. 12. Detroit: Gale, 1984. 55–57.

"Benchley, Nathaniel." *Twentieth Century Children's Writers.* 2nd ed. Ed. D. L. Kirkpatrick. New York: St. Martin's, 1983. 77–79.

"Benchley, Nathaniel." *Twentieth Century Children's Writers.* 3rd ed. Ed. Tracy Chevalier. Chicago: St. James, 1989. 80–81.

De Montreville, Doris, and Elizabeth D. Crawford, eds. *Fourth Book of Junior Authors and Illustrators.* Crawford, NY: Wilson, 1978. 36–37.

"Nathaniel Benchley." *Something about the Author.* Ed. Anne Commire. Vol. 25. Detroit: Gale, 1981. 39–45.

"Nathaniel Benchley." *Something about the Author.* Ed. Anne Commire. Vol 28. Detroit: Gale, 1982. 43.

Rev. of *Bright Candles. Center for Children's Books Bulletin* 27 (July 1974): 170–71.

Rev. of *Only Earth and Sky Last Forever. Catholic Library World.* 44 (Mar. 1973): 506.

Rev. of *Only Earth and Sky Last Forever. Center for Children's Books Bulletin* 26 (Apr. 1973): 119.

JAMES BERRY
(1924-)

Kwame S. N. Dawes

BIOGRAPHY

James Berry was born in rural Jamaica in 1924. The fourth of six children,
Berry left Jamaica at the age of seventeen for the United States as part of a
wartime contract labor scheme. His stay in the United States lasted four
years after which he returned to Jamaica deeply bothered by the treatment
of blacks in America. He continued to live in his coastal village until 1948
when he tired of the limited possibilities in the island and traveled to Britain.
In London, Berry worked during the day and studied at night to gain a
marketable skill. He trained to be a telegraphist and worked in that occupa-
tion for several years. Eventually, he was made redundant. According to
Berry the event was fortuitous because it allowed him an opportunity to
devote himself to writing full time. About that time he began to publish
short stories and to write plays for the stage.

Berry has said that his preoccupation with questions of race and identity
began as early as his preteen days in Jamaica where he lived in a village
that had whites and blacks. Even at that stage, he was bothered by the
established belief systems that sought to demean the character and person
of blacks, even as they privileged the status and ascendancy of whites. He
was also acutely aware of the intensely painful slave history that marked
his people's past. Alarmed by the implication of inferiority that such a
background suggested, Berry has committed his work to trying to retrieve

the humanity and dignity of blacks all over the world. He rarely compounded the tension between the races by dwelling on vengeance and what he has described as the process of "being burdened with an imbalance of injustice." Instead, he has sought in his work to create dialogue through a two-way process of culture sharing and respect.

This commitment to celebrating the identity and dignity of blacks has led Berry into social activism and the advocacy of black writing in Britain. He was, for years, one of the few voices of the Black British experience that sounded throughout the British literary community. In 1976 he edited the book *Bluefoot Traveller*, a book of Black British poetry which contained some of the early works of many of the currently popular and successful Black British poets. He continues to guide and support the work of black writers in Britain and the Caribbean.

His writing has earned him a great deal of attention in Britain and the United States, and his numerous awards include The Greater London Arts Association Fellowship in 1977, the National Poetry Competition Award in 1981 for his poem "Fantasy of an African Boy," the Grand Prix Smarties Prize for his book *A Thief in the Village* in 1987, the Signal Poetry Award for his collection of juvenile poetry, *When I Dance*, the Order of the British Empire for Service in poetry in 1990, and the Society of Authors Chomondeley Award for Poetry in 1991.

Berry has published three volumes of adult poetry and one volume of verse for children. He has also published several books for children—mainly fiction. His reputation was established in the area of adult poetry, and his *Lucy's Letters and Loving* secured his position as a clever chronicler of black existence in Britain. His editing credits are impressive and include at least four anthologies of West Indian-British and black British verse.

Berry lives in England although he is a regular visitor to Jamaica. He lives in Brighton where he writes steadily and continues to work with younger writers. He is an avid cricket fan and music lover and has a strong affinity for jazz, reggae, and classical music. He remains as committed as ever to his task of speaking to the experience of blacks or people of the African diaspora in as eloquent and heartfelt a manner as possible. He writes from experience but also with a deep passion for conveying the realities of history and people's experiences.

MAJOR WORKS AND THEMES

Berry's juvenile literature was prompted by what he regarded as a vacuum in that area of writing for West Indian children in Britain. The peculiar circumstances of the Black British experience may help to explain this reality better. Much of the black population in Britain originated in African or Caribbean countries. The two communities remained fairly distinct from each other, largely because of the circumstances and the timing of their arrivals in the United Kingdom. Many Caribbean people arrived in England just about the time Berry landed there. They settled into occupations in London, Birmingham, and Manchester and started the process of making families. Many of the blacks in Britain are second-and third-generation Caribbean people who have a lasting tie to the tenacious culture of the Caribbean, while evolving a new and distinct subculture called the Black British. With the advent of reggae and the unique culture that it generated, along with the presence of fairly prominent Caribbean writers in Britain during the fifties and sixties, there is a clear cultural context for much of what is now termed Black British culture. However, despite this, the education system in Britain for years failed to recognize the presence and needs of children with different cultural backgrounds than the traditional white British children. At the same time, many Caribbean parents wanted to ensure that their children developed a sense of pride in their origins. The absence of children's books to meet this need prompted writers like Berry, John Agard, and Neville V. Nichols to start to seriously create narratives that would meet the need.

Berry's first children's novel was published in 1987 when his book *A Thief in the Village* was published by Hamish Hamilton. This collection of children's stories is set in rural Jamaica. It is clear from the stories that Berry uses his memories of a Jamaican childhood to explore the complex world of growing up and trying to gain a sense of place in society. His works are all set in Jamaica, and, with the possible exception of one story, they are all set in the rustic rural landscape of Jamaica. There is a quality of nostalgia that permeates these works even if they do not become quagmired in overt sentimentality. There is a constant theme that runs throughout these stories. They explore, more often than not, the underdog, invariably a child in his or her early teens. The antagonists in many of the narratives are other strikingly but believably cruel children who either torment the protagonists with teasing or some systematized process of alienation. Ultimately, in these narratives about peer dynamics, the struggle is for acceptance. This theme is prevalent in the majority of the works, and the object of belonging is usually something physical—a bicycle ("Becky and the Wheels and Brake Boys"), a mouth organ ("The Mouth-Organ Boys"), a mongoose ("Elias and the Mongoose"). In some instances, the peer pressure is exerted through an intense process of teasing and related alienation. We see this in the story

"Tukku-Tukku and Samson" in which the triumph of the distanced boy is expressed with his being accepted by friends at the end of the story. In "Elias and the Mongoose," Berry opts for a less optimistic ending. In fact, there is a growing sense that Elias will continue to be harassed by his peers for keeping a mongoose and for being different. The comment on childhood cruelty is poignant and allows Berry to avoid easy sentimentality.

If there is a positive trend in the first stories in the book, those in the latter part of the book possess a certain seriousness of theme that is sophisticated and complex. The title story, "A Thief in the Village," characterizes the humor and pleasant reconciliatory quality that we see in the first half of the collection. After false accusations and arrests, it is discovered that the Rastafarian man accused of praedial larceny is really innocent, and a more respected individual is guilty. The whole community has shamefully allowed itself to respond to its prejudices and misguided biases. The revelation of truth at the end is underscored by the narrator's (a young girl) acceptance of the Rastafarian man, evidenced in her visiting his place. Here is a dilemma that has been averted, and a clear lesson of absolute truth is given to the reader. Such clarity of message is intentionally blurred in the latter part of the book. No longer do underdogs, like the young protagonist in "The Mouth-Organ Boys," come to be accepted by their erstwhile cruel and unfair companions. Another example is Tukku-Tukku, the short, stumpy boy who beats Samson up after suffering many defeats at the hands of Samson in the past. He further manages to win the respect, friendship, and admiration of friends who once spent all their time laughing at him and insulting him. These emotionally satisfying endings are replaced by the more complex "Elias and the Mongoose" in which the propensity to tease and harass a boy who is physically handicapped is not altered at the end of the work, even after the intervention of an adult. What is more disturbing about the way the narrative ends is the recognition that the cruelty of the boys has been nurtured by the indifference (and some would argue collusion) of adults in the mistreatment of the boy Elias. This is the beginning of a series of darker narratives that suggest to young readers that everything cannot end happily, nor can everything be understood in life.

The pathos of the story "Fanso and Granny-flo" bears this out profoundly. In this story, Berry deals with the difficult theme of absentee fathers and the legacy of rootlessness and confusion that they leave behind when they depart. Fanso, who lives with his grandmother and whose mother lives and works in the city, does not know his father, who it turns out, abandoned his mother before the birth of Fanso. The story begins as Fanso tries to understand this fatherlessness in a world in which his friends all have some knowledge of, if not a relationship with, their fathers. He has to contend with certain painfully sociological theses which argue that a fatherless child is invariably poor. This process of questioning and seeking to retrieve his father introduces a series of complex emotional challenges for his grandmother, who is clearly certain that it is in the boy's best interest to forget his father. The tension between these two ways of looking at the fatherhood issue rests at the center of the narrative. Berry manages, then, to convey the complicated feelings of both adults and children and never, in any way, softens the tension that is contained in this situation. Berry does not trivialize the experiences of the characters. When Fanso's father does appear, the reader shares Fanso's joy in finally finding his father, but also recognizes the audacity of the father in trying to bribe his way into acceptability. Unquestionably presented as the wayward and irresponsible male—at least in the eyes of the grandmother—his return creates turmoil in the household because the son, Fanso, is elated to finally see his father, and the grandmother is appalled at his return. It is his willingness to confront these sometimes unattractive emotions in his characters that makes Berry such a successful writer.

In keeping with his commitment to construct narratives that speak to the black children of Britain, who have very little literature to refer to that speaks of their experience, Berry wrote the collection of children's poems, *When I Dance* (1988). The collection, however, is distinct in its commitment not to "speak down to" children with doggerel or simplistic verse. In fact, much of the poetry is directed at black children only in that the poems offer a way of viewing the world that is distinctly black—they offer images and narrative experiences that black children can associate with. Also, a number of the personae in many of the poems are children, and so the poems tend to view the world from that perspective. Berry, however, experiments with various poetic structures, including the call-response "Diggin Sing" and "Me Go a Granny Yard," the poetic drama "Sunny Market Song," the song "Let Me Rap My Orbital Map" and "Listn Big Brodda Dread, Na!," and the lyrical "Seeing Granny," "My Hard Repair Job," and "Coming Home on My Own." He writes about children's dreams for success in life, presents admonitions about education and its value, and tries to enter the mind of hurt and alienated children in a language that he thinks they will identify with. His use of dialect is extensive in many of these poems, creating a British-flavored Jamaica-speak that only rarely rings some false notes. There is a mission in this collection, as Berry states in his revealing introduction to the book, and the mission is to create songs and poems for black children in the schools of Britain. In this sense, the collection is very successful.

Having demonstrated his ability in the use of verse for children and in the shorter narrative format, Berry attempted a longer, novel-length narrative in his next effort. His book *Ajeemah and His Son* (1991) is his most ambitious children's book to date. It is telling evidence that Berry is a writer of children's literature to be contended with.

James Berry's *Ajeemah and His Son* falls perfectly into the category of retrieved stories of slave narratives written by Caribbean writers. The narrative is a very simple one. Ajeemah and his son Atu are walking home one afternoon a few weeks before Atu is to be married to his sweetheart and village heartthrob, Sisi, who will figure greatly in the narrative as a symbolic representation of the nostalgic African past. The duo is captured by African slave traders and taken to the coast to be shipped to the New World. Soon, the father and son find themselves at sea, heading away from Africa. The trauma of this leaving is vividly captured in the sounds of moaning and wailing coming from the hull and in the personal, emotional pain felt by Ajeemah and his son. It is important for Berry to establish the act of slave captivity as the wrenching of a people from their home and people.

In Jamaica, they are separated when sold to white planters. Ajeemah is christened Justin by his planter. Atu becomes a field hand and eventually assumes the role of troublemaker and dangerous slave. Both men are allowed to express their intense hatred and bitterness toward white men and what they have done to them. Both express their sense of insult and degradation at the hands of white men through lengthy and involved monologues and dreams. Both speak of a need for revenge, and a need to assuage their anger by plotting their escape, and thereby attaining vengeance. Ajeemah plots a revolt that has to be aborted because of betrayal by a slave called Kaleb. Atu steals a gun and begins to plot his vengeance by trying to steal some shells for the gun. Eventually, he buys a foal and feeds the animal until it becomes a full-grown creature. But his planter covets his horse and simply takes it away. It belongs to the plantation, he is told. Atu breaks the legs of the horse and admits to the act after the horse is destroyed. He is brutally whipped and the next evening he is found in the roadway of the plantation with a knife in his chest. The reader assumes suicide, but this is not made clear. Ajeemah senses the death of his son and goes mad. This insanity leads to his meeting Bella, who nurses him and gives him guidance about how to survive in the world of slavery. Ajeemah has a change of heart. He accepts his fate, acknowledging that he will never return to Africa, and he starts a new life in Jamaica with Bella. They have a child whom they call Sisi, and the story ends with the marriage of Sisi.

Berry's story has a certain popular currency, especially in the United States where there is a revival of the need to celebrate the Africanness of those of African heritage. It plays into the easy, but attractive, stereotype of idyllic Africa, filled with family men, leaders, and warriors, and of the raping of that land by white-inspired bandits. Berry does not portray them as stock villains—he allows them a certain cold logic that is far more disturbing and daunting than an easy stereotype would be.

As a narrative for young adults, it is a challenging work that allows for the exploration of adventure and the excitement of danger and action, but at the same time it seeks to be an educational piece that celebrates African-ness and the African identity with some dignity. If Berry offers a means of coping with the anger blacks may feel about their past, it lies in the idea of getting along with the business of making a life that is filled with dignity. Africa, in this context, is a memory, and the families left behind, while they may not have been forgotten, remain an unknowable and unretrievable fact of memory. Indeed, Berry does not take us back to Africa. His revisit of Africa is merely a way of contextualizing the origins of the modern blacks of the New World. It is not an attempt to retrieve that past and apply it fully to the present.

His most recent collection of stories, *The Future-Telling Lady* (1991), retains much of the style and themes of his earlier collection, *A Thief in the Village*. The language reflects Berry's growing capacity to find the right combination of complexity and profound simplicity in the rendering of tales in this selection. Some of the stories are longer and more involved, but they all remain located in the Jamaican landscape of Berry's memory. Pieces like the title story, "The Future-Telling Lady," examine the childhood fascination with magic and the supernatural, while another, "Banana-Day Trip," looks at the engaging life of a young boy who enjoys chanting lyrics in "rap" fashion. The introduction of rap in a piece that is so clearly located in a period that predates rap tells us something of Berry's own connection with Jamaica and the Jamaican landscape. While most of his stories do not offer a journalistic view of modern Jamaican life, they remain effective narratives about the magic and adventure of childhood experience. Berry ends the collection with a clue to his passion for the story as a way of communicating, and in this way he links himself with the great Jamaican storyteller/novel-ist/poet Andrew Salkey. The final story is a folk tale about Mr. Mongoose (the subject of much bawdy wit in Jamaican life) which Berry manages to retrieve from memory. Typically it recalls the Anancy trickster tales and the pattern of come-uppance that characterizes many black folk tales that derive from West African life. Berry retells the story with energy and wit.

CRITICAL RECEPTION

Berry has received limited attention by critics in Britain and the United States for his fiction writing. He is recognized for the task that he has undertaken—to give voice to the black people in Britain—but he is also seen as possessing a wonderful use of language and imagination in his clear and lucid narratives. His use of the Jamaican dialect has received very strong praise from some critics in Britain, but this praise has not been uniform. Unfortunately, Berry, like many Black British writers, has been ignored by scholars in Britain, and his long period away from the Caribbean has led to a dearth in critical attention from Caribbean scholars as well. Significantly, Berry was excluded from the critical biographical volume *Fifty Caribbean Writers*, edited by Daryl Dance and published by Greenwood Press in 1986, despite having published several critically successful volumes of poetry at the time. There still remains a tremendous amount of work to be done on his poetry and on his children's writing.

BIBLIOGRAPHY

Young Adult Fiction by James Berry

The Girls and Yanga Marshall: Four Stories. London: Longman, 1987.
A Thief in the Village. New York: Orchard; London: Hamish Hamilton, 1987.
When I Dance. New York: Harcourt Brace Jovanovich; London: Hamish Hamilton, 1988.
Ajeemah and His Son. New York: HarperCollins, 1991.
The Future-Telling Lady. New York: Wila Pearlman, 1991.

Poetry by James Berry

Fractured Circles. London: New Beacon, 1979.
Lucy's Letters and Loving. London: New Beacon, 1982.
Chain of Days. London: Oxford UP, 1985.

Anthologies Edited by James Berry

Bluefoot Traveller: Poetry by West Indians in Britain. Rev. ed. London: Nelson; London: Limestone, 1976.

Dance to a Different Drum: Poetry Anthology. Brixton: Brixton Festival Community, 1983.

News for Babylon: The Chatto Book of West Indian British Poetry. London: Chatto and Windus, 1984.

Other Works by James Berry

"Acceptance Speech." *Boston Globe/Horn Book* Award. *Horn Book* 70.1 (1994): 50–52.

Selected Studies of James Berry

There is no extended analysis of James Berry's work. What little there is is devoted almost exclusively to his poetry. In *Come Back to Me My Language*, by Canadian critic Ted Chamberlain, a few lines are given to Berry's contribution to the work of Caribbean writers in Britain, and a very brief analysis of one of his poems from the collection *Lucy's Letters and Loving* is included to illustrate the evolution of language in West Indian writing. Beyond this, Berry's work has had little extensive attention in significant publications. His work has been reviewed briefly in *The Observer, Poetry Review, Bananas, Stand, The Listener,* and *Times Literary Supplement.* Stewart Brown, renowned West Indian critic, has published a brief analysis of Berry's writing in a promotional pamphlet put out by the British Council in 1991 in their Contemporary Writers Series. In it, he celebrates Berry's position as "perhaps the first Black British poet," and Berry's significant capacity to write exuberantly of the black experience while being painfully realistic about the struggles that blacks (particularly in Britain) have to go through.

Brown, Stewart. "James Berry." *Contemporary Writers: James Berry.* Pamphlet London: British Council, 1991.

Chamberlain, Edward. *Come Back to Me My Language.* Urbana: U of Illinois, 1993.

FRANK BONHAM
(1914–1988)

John P. Madison

BIOGRAPHY

Frank Bonham, a third-generation Californian, was born in Los Angeles, and, except for service in the U.S. Army (1942–1943), was a self-employed writer all his life. He sold his first short story at the age of twenty to a detective magazine. His love of reading and interest in writing reportedly developed while recovering from periodic respiratory problems during childhood and early adulthood. Asthma forced him to drop out of Glendale Junior College, and he moved into his parents' cabin in the San Bernadino Mountains. During two years of relative isolation, he wrote more than one hundred short stories, of which ten were published. In 1938 he married Gloria Bailey, and they had three children.

Bonham worked as an apprentice to Ed Earl Repp, a western fiction writer, and eventually became a successful writer of westerns, publishing more than two dozen in twenty-five years. Additionally, more than five hundred of his pieces—novelettes, serialized novels, and short stories—have been published in *American, McCall's,* and the *Saturday Evening Post* as well as in various mystery and western periodicals. During the 1960s, he also wrote screenplays and scripts for several television series, including *Death Valley Days, Restless Gun, Shotgun Slade,* and *Wells Fargo.*

While investigating material for a mystery novel, he learned of the exploits of Merrill's Marauders, a group of Japanese-American servicemen recruited from the internment camps and sent to fight behind the Japanese army lines in Burma. This led to the publication, in 1960, of Bonham's first young adult novel, *Burma Rifles: A Story of Merrill's Marauders*. This fortuitous change in the genre and audience of his writing coincided with a reduced market for both westerns and mystery novels. Many of Bonham's subsequent twenty-five young adult novels reflect his concern with issues in the lives of African-American, Mexican-American (Chicano), Native American, and Japanese-American young people. His books for young people were nominated for and won several awards. In 1980, he was awarded the Southern California Council of Literature for Children and Young People prize for his contributions to the field of children's literature. Bonham died in Arizona in 1988.

MAJOR WORKS AND THEMES

The publication of *Durango Street* (1965) established Frank Bonham as a writer of contemporary realistic fiction for adolescents—a new direction after many years as a successful writer of mystery and western novels for adults. This candid and convincing (for its time) presentation of gang life in a depressed area of a West Coast city was a publishing breakthrough. Poverty, racism, school failure, and alienation had not formerly been considered appropriate topics for twelve-to-eighteen-year-old readers. Bonham's protagonists, almost all teenage minority males, are racially, sociologically, and attitudinally different from conventional main characters. Although Bonham consistently remained on the outside of his stories, he demonstrated an awareness that stemmed from his personal experience with minority children and youth in the poorer areas of Los Angeles during the 1960s and 1970s.

After publication of *Mystery in Little Tokyo* (1966) and *Mystery of the Fat Cat* (1968), Bonham became recognized as a writer of realistic mysteries with minority group characters and urban settings. Although his mysteries place less emphasis on "issues" and have contrived plots, the characters are realistic and successful, and the stories are humorous and readable.

The Nitty Gritty (1968) contains many of the same issues presented in *Durango Street*. Charlie Matthews is a poor African-American and lives in an urban ghetto in a California city. His school performance is marginal, and he is unsuccessful in his search for employment. His adult male role models are disappointing, and his attempt at escaping from his home environment leads to disaster. The climax contains a level of bloodshed and violence previously not found in contemporary realistic fiction for adolescents.

Bonham presents the experience of a Mexican-American teen in *Viva Chicano* (1970). Kenny Duran, recently released from reform school, tries to avoid gang membership and involvement with drugs. An idealized father image (a legacy from an absent male parent), combined with a deep desire to honor his Chicano heritage, creates relationship problems between Kenny and his overwhelmed mother. Bonham successfully presents intragroup cultural and racial tensions through skillful characterization and good storytelling.

In *Cool Cat* (1971), Bonham returns to the setting of *Mystery of the Fat Cat* and reintroduces Buddy, an ambitious motivated teen who is trying to earn money. Several aspects of the topic of drugs and drug sales are explored as the title character turns out to be an undercover narcotics agent. The contemporary life of Native Americans is presented in *Chief* (1971). Henry Crowfoot (Chief) is the hereditary chief of a small tribe. Although this novel contains some intentional stereotypical characters, it is exciting and allows readers to become involved in the clash of cultures when a legal attempt is made to get recognition of a long-forgotten and outdated treaty.

Cool Hankins, the main character in *Hey, Big Spender* (1972), is paid to interview down-on-their-luck applicants for a daily prize given by Breathing Man, a former vagrant who has inherited a large sum of money ($500,000). Social responsibility and a common sense approach suggested by Cool's foster mother persuade Breathing Man to use his money to establish foster homes for abandoned children. This is a much gentler presentation of the deprivation felt by poor people than is found in his other works.

In *The Golden Bees of Tulami* (1974), one of Bonham's several fantasies for adolescents, an African stranger (Kinsman) introduces a special soporific honey to the residents of Dogtown. The honey-laced candy induces feelings of peace, harmony, and brotherhood. The negative reaction of government officials stops the production and puts an end to the possibility of world peace.

Although Frank Bonham's books for young adults are written for a general audience, he shows a special sensitivity to those readers who are members of minority groups. Although the main messages are cautionary, they are based on reality as expressed by an interested and compassionate observer. Bonham creates real people who are facing real problems. He uses humor and compassion to soften what could be depressing stories of hopeless lives. The often insurmountable problems faced by his African-

American, Mexican-American, and Native American characters of the 1960s and 1970s, however, are tame when compared to news stories of drive-by shootings, crack cocaine, hightech weapons, and contemporary gang life of the 1990s.

CRITICAL RECEPTION

As one of the first writers to convincingly enter the world of teenage inner-city males and to tell their stories, Bonham was received positively at first by reviewers and critics. James McBride in the *New York Times Book Review* (1965) writes that *Durango Street* is "a forthright presentation of a social problem which teenagers want and deserve to know more about." Zena Sutherland writing in the *Bulletin of the Center for Children's Books* (1965) says that *Durango Street* is a "candid and powerful novel about teen-age gangs and the tortuous protocol of intramural gang fights." Jane Manhorne in a review of *The Nitty Gritty* in the *New York Times Book Review* (1969) writes that Bonham is "faithful to the argot and atmosphere of the city. . . . Parents drink their beer and send their truant kids off to make a few pennies at the shoeshine parlor."

Although Bonham's novels for young people were generally well-received, the publication of *Cool Cat* (1971) met with mixed reviews. In a review in the *Bulletin of the Center for Children's Books* (June 1971), Zena Sutherland writes that although this book "grimly mirrors the ghetto scene," it "lacks direction or focus." Bonham's skill in characterization is demonstrated, but the story line is difficult to follow.

John T. Gillespie in *More Juniorplots: A Guide for Teachers and Librarians* (1977) declares in his review of *Chief*, "The Indians' plight is realistically portrayed without sermonizing or condescending, although many of the characters express a natural bitterness and disillusionment with the values of present-day America" (52). Bonham's sincerity, storytelling skill, and choice of interesting main characters more than compensate for an occasional lack of focus or tendency to be obviously didactic. His "young adult novels are realistic depictions of the problems encountered by underprivileged black, Chicano, Indian, and Japanese-American youth. Based on Bonham's observations and experiences in volunteer social work in impoverished areas of the West Coast, his work is neither moralistic nor exploitive; rather it seeks to involve the young people he writes about by depicting a world they understand," says James G. Lesniak in *Contemporary Authors*.

BIBLIOGRAPHY

Young Adult Fiction by Frank Bonham

Burma Rifles: A Story of Merrill's Marauders. New York: Crowell, 1960.
War Beneath the Sea. New York: Crowell, 1962.
Deepwater Challenge. New York: Crowell, 1963.
Honor Bound. New York: Crowell, 1963.
The Loud, Resounding Sea. New York: Crowell, 1963.
Speedway Contender. New York: Crowell, 1964.
Durango Street. New York: Dutton, 1965.
Mystery in Little Tokyo. Illus. Kazue Mizumura. New York: Dutton, 1966.
The Mystery of the Red Tide. Illus. Brinton Turkle. New York: Dutton, 1966.
The Ghost Front. New York: Dutton, 1968.
Mystery of the Fat Cat. New York: Dutton, 1968.
The Nitty Gritty. New York: Dutton, 1968.
The Vagabundos. New York: Dutton, 1969.
Viva Chicano. New York: Dutton, 1970.
Chief. New York: Dutton, 1971.
Cool Cat. New York: Dutton, 1971.
The Friends of the Loony Lake Monster. New York: Dutton, 1972.
Hey, Big Spender. New York: Dutton, 1972.
A Dream of Ghosts. New York: Dutton, 1973.
The Golden Bees of Tulami. New York: Dutton, 1974.
The Missing Persons League. New York: Dutton, 1976.
The Rascals from Haskell's Gym. New York: Dutton, 1977.
Devilhorn. New York: Dutton, 1978.
The Forever Formula. New York: Dutton, 1979.
Gimme an H, Gimme an E, Gimme an L, Gimme a P. New York: Scribner, 1980.
Premonitions. New York: Holt, 1984.

Adult Fiction by Frank Bonham

Last Stage Valley. New York: Simon and Schuster, 1948. Kingswood, Surrey: World's Work, 1950.
Bold Passage. New York: Simon and Schuster, 1950. London: Hodder and Stoughton, 1951.
Snaketrack. New York: Simon and Schuster, 1952.
The Outcasts of Crooked River. London: Hodder and Stoughton, 1953.
The Feud at Spanish Ford. New York: Ballantine, 1954.
Night Raid. New York: Ballantine, 1954.
Rawhide Guns. New York: Popular Library, 1955.
The Wild Breed. New York: Lion, 1955.
Border Guns. London: Muller, 1956.

Defiance Mountain. New York: Popular Library, 1956. London: Consul, 1962.
Hardrock. New York: Ballantine, 1958. London: Muller, 1960.
Tough Country. New York: Dell; London: Muller, 1958.
Last Stage West. New York: Dell; London: Muller, 1959.
Sound of Gunfire. New York: Dell; London: Muller, 1959.
One for Sleep. New York: Fawcett, 1960. London: Muller, 1961.
The Skin Game. New York: Fawcett, 1960. London: Muller, 1963.
Trago. New York: Dell, 1962.
By Her Own Hand. Derby, CT: Monarch, 1963.
Cast a Long Shadow. New York: Simon and Schuster, 1964.
Logan's Choice. New York: Fawcett, 1964.
Break for the Border. New York: Berkley, 1980.
Fort Hogan. New York: Berkley, 1980.
The Eye of the Hunter. New York: Evans, 1989.

Selected Studies of Frank Bonham

"Bonham, Frank." *Contemporary Authors, New Revision Series.* Ed. James G. Lesniak. Vol. 36. Detroit: Gale, 1992. 45–48.

"Bonham, Frank." *Contemporary Literary Criticism.* Ed. Dedria Bryfonski. Vol. 12. Detroit: Gale, 1980. 49–56.

Carlson, Ruth Kearney. *Emerging Humanity: Multi-Ethnic Literature for Children and Adolescents.* New York: Wm. C. Brown, 1972.

De Montreville, Doris, and Donna Hill, eds. *Third Book of Junior Authors.* New York: Wilson, 1972. 42–43.

Gillespie, John T. *More Juniorplots: A Guide for Teachers and Librarians.* New York: Bowker, 1977.

Manhorne, Jane. Rev. of *The Nitty Gritty. New York Times Books Review*, 19 Jan. 1969: 28.

McBride, James. Rev. of *Durango Street. New York Times Book Review*, 5 Sept. 1965: 20.

Mercier, Jean F. "Frank Bonham." *Twentieth-Century Children's Writers.* Ed. Tracy Chevalier. 3rd ed. Chicago: St. James, 1989. 116–17.

Sutherland, Zena. Rev. of *Cool Cat. Bulletin of the Center for Children's Books* 25 (June 1971): 153.

Sutherland, Zena. Rev. of *Durango Street. Bulletin of the Center for Children's Books* 19 (Oct. 1965): 127.

Manuscript Collection: Kerlan Collection, University of Minnesota, Minneapolis.

BRUCE BROOKS
(1950-   )

Karen Herc

BIOGRAPHY

Bruce Brooks was born in Washington, D.C., in 1950. After his parents divorced when he was six, he split his time between Washington and North Carolina, where his mother's family lived. Both of these places became locales for his fiction.

Brooks experienced some feelings of isolation since he always felt somewhat of an outsider, shuttling from the North to the South. He learned to adapt in order to make friends; he became skilled at reading people and discovering how best to fit in with different groups.

His situation in Washington was very different from that in North Carolina because the schools he attended in Washington were integrated, while the ones in North Carolina were not. Brooks was able to observe the results of the 1954 *Brown v. Board of Education* case firsthand in the South, and the inequalities that he saw in relations between blacks and whites affected him profoundly.

In 1972 Brooks graduated from the University of North Carolina at Chapel Hill. He worked at different jobs, including printer, reporter, and teacher, then attended the Iowa Writers' Workshop. He graduated from the University of Iowa with an M.F.A. in 1982. He now writes full time.

Brooks lives in Silver Spring, Maryland, with his wife, Penelope, and their two sons, Alexander and Spencer.

MAJOR WORKS AND THEMES

All of Brooks' characters are intelligent, talented, and precocious. Jerome Foxworthy, the gifted narrator of *The Moves Make the Man* (1985), is no exception. *Moves*, Brooks' first book, is probably his most controversial, since Jerome, the thirteen-year-old protagonist, is an African-American, while Brooks himself is Caucasian.

The debate over whether authors of one race are capable of expressing the innermost thoughts and feelings of characters of another race, or whether they even have the right to try, has been raging for some time in all branches of literature, including children's literature. Brooks was not aware of the furor that some earlier books for children depicting the African-American experience as written by non-African-Americans had caused, largely because he was not very attuned to the children's literature field. He did not intend *The Moves Make the Man* to be a book specifically for young readers; he simply wrote the book that he felt a need to write at the time. Brooks says of the main character in this book:

I don't pretend to know what all thirteen-year-old black kids sound like, but I do know what Jerome sounds like. The verisimilitude that depends on duplicating a type never comes into it. The accuracy of the voice arises from identity; the character is not a type but an individual. It does not reflect an age group or a race. I can speak as this kid speaks. I know this guy and how he speaks. The voice arises entirely from who Jerome is (McDonnell 189).

Jerome is the first African-American student to integrate a school in North Carolina in the 1950s. Besides being an honors student, he is also a great basketball player. An early scene pits Jerome against the extremely racist basketball coach of his new high school. The coach sets up an unfair test for him when Jerome wants to prove he belongs on the team. A few of the players attempt to stand up to the coach so Jerome can join the team because they want a player with his ability on their side, but the scene ends with Jerome leaving the gym alone.

Basketball plays an important role in this story: the "moves" referred to in the title are moves made on the basketball court, and, by extension, in life. Jerome debates the honor of making a move on an opponent with his friend Bix, a disturbed white boy. Bix's obsession with honesty makes him incapable of hiding any animosity toward Jerome because of his race. He accepts Jerome as a person and thinks everyone else does too, so the next time Jerome encounters a racist Bix appears more hurt than Jerome. Jerome is used to it; Bix is not, and since Bix previously considered the racist man a friend, his faith in his own judgment is shattered.

Ultimately, *The Moves Make the Man* is more about Bix than Jerome, since Jerome writes the book to tell Bix's story. Jerome's stable, loving family contrasts sharply with Bix's dysfunctional one, and because of his family's support, Jerome proves more mature, more centered, and simply better able to cope than Bix.

As he did with Jerome, Brooks chooses an unlikely narrator for his second novel, *Midnight Hour Encores* (1986). This time he enters the mind of a sixteen-year-old girl. Like Jerome, Sibilance is talented and eloquent. Unlike Jerome, she can be a bit insufferable. Sib is one of the premier cellists in the world and her success in music makes her disdainful of anyone who does not share her skill, knowledge, and taste in composers, including her father. Brooks wrote this book after becoming a father, and he considers *Encores* to be primarily about the relationship between Sib and her father. The book includes a passage in which Sib's father compares being a parent to being a cello virtuoso, since both involve making sacrifices for what you love.

With *No Kidding* (1989), Brooks begins using third-person narration. *No Kidding* challenges its readers with its portrayal of twenty-first century Washington, D.C., where 69 percent of adults are alcoholics. The protagonist, fourteen-year-old Sam, supervises his younger brother and has responsibility for his alcoholic mother after his father leaves.

The agenda of his book is obvious, but Brooks manages to tell a story in the midst of the anti-alcohol message. He shows alcoholism as a disease that affects people of all races, since it affects both black and white people in the book. The acceptance of characters in the story is notable because it is so matter-of-fact. Sam meets an African-American man who talks with him about the various ways of treating alcoholism, and he later helps an African-American friend who becomes drunk again after six years of sobriety. Race relations are not the main theme of the book, but the fact that they are presented in such a low-key way shows Brooks' hope that by the twenty-first century acceptance will be so common that it is unnoticeable.

Everywhere (1990) returns from the future to the South in the 1950s and to first-person narration. The narrator, a ten-year-old boy, never identifies himself other than by saying his grandfather named a rose, "Peanut," after him. After his grandfather suffers a heart attack, the African-American town nurse comes to his grandparents' house and brings her eleven-year-old nephew, Dooley, to entertain the narrator. Dooley tells him they can save his grandfather by switching his soul with that of an animal's, and the short book consists of their attempt to do so, and the results.

Dooley educates the narrator in a number of ways, pointing out that his aunt is not an actual nurse since no nursing school will admit an African-American woman. This story is written for younger children than Brooks' others, and the narration is not as subtle, but it does seem like the reasoning of a sensitive child. The boy worries not only about his grandfather, but also about the way he treats Dooley. When he accidentally shrinks from Dooley's touch, he bursts into tears and cries on Dooley's shoulder in a combination of grief for his grandfather and guilt because he does not want Dooley to think he moved away because of Dooley's color. The intelligent boy struggles to form his own opinions and to carve out some kind of a relationship with an African-American child in segregated Virginia.

What Hearts (1992), Brooks' latest novel, also features an extremely bright child, Asa. The book consists of four short stories depicting Asa at different times in his life. Like Brooks, Asa moves from Washington, D.C., to North Carolina with his mother after his parents divorce when he is six. As he gets older, Asa, his mother, and his stepfather move a lot, and Asa learns to become a human chameleon by turning himself into whatever kind of person each child he meets can best relate to.

Asa uses baseball as a means of escape. The third part of the book features a Little League game in which Asa figures prominently. He is not the best player on the field, but he is the smartest and he loves and understands the game. Only at the end of that story does the reader learn that the baseball game described takes place entirely in Asa's head.

What Hearts is an unusually constructed coming-of-age story, but the four glimpses of Asa's life prove that he survives each hardship that befalls him, and will continue to do so as he grows into his intellect and develops emotions strong enough to compete with his intelligence.

In addition to his fiction, Brooks has written a number of nonfiction works. *On the Wing* (1989), *Predator!* (1991), *Nature by Design* (1991), and *Making Sense* (1993) all explore the animal world and illustrate the similarities and differences between humans and other animals.

His other nonfiction focuses on sports. *Boys Will Be* and *Those Who Love the Game* were both published in 1993. *Boys* glorifies being male. It points out things that Brooks says women will never understand, such as the merits of sweat. It includes sections about baseball, hockey, football, and tennis (in the form of a tribute to Arthur Ashe).

Those Who Love the Game is a biography of NBA basketball player Glenn "Doc" Rivers. The format consists of third-person reports of Rivers' words, with some first-person observations by Brooks added. Besides discussing various NBA players and family members, Rivers addresses the racism he has faced. He laments the fact that there are few African-American coaches in the NBA, and even fewer African-Americans in upper-level NBA management positions. Rivers says teamwork can overcome racism since "competition destroys all sense of color" (66). Rivers is an intelligent, sensitive man, and so fits in with all the other people Brooks writes about.

CRITICAL RECEPTION

Brooks' fiction has generally been very well received. However, some critics seem to think his greatest strength, the sophistication of his writing style, is also his greatest weakness. Brooks wants to challenge his readers, but reviewers are not always sure that very young adult readers are up to the challenge. For example, one reviewer "found some of the issues [in *No Kidding*] perplexing for young readers" although she still thinks "Brooks is a fine writer" (*Something about the Author* 25). Brooks is adamant about not writing down to young adults. He says, "We are capable as readers of a wild and intricate world of thought and response and feeling—things going on in different layers at the same time. I hope to write books that involve all those layers of thinking and feeling in my readers" (*Something about the Author* 23).

Brooks' fiction has won numerous awards. *The Moves Make the Man* won a Newbery Honor and a *Boston Globe-Horn Book* award. It was named a *School Library Journal* (*SLJ*) best book of the year and an American Library Association (ALA) notable children's book, and was called a notable book of the year by the *New York Times*. *Midnight Hour Encores* won such recognition as being named an SLJ best book of the year, an ALA notable book for young adults, and an International Reading Association's young adult choice. *No Kidding* also won honors from SLJ and ALA, being called one of the best books of the year for young adults by both of them. The ALA called *Everywhere* a best book of the year for children, and SLJ called it a notable children's book. *What Hearts*, in addition to its other awards, won a Newbery Honor medal.

Brooks has also won praise for his nonfiction nature series books; reviewers specifically credited him "for his grasp of his subjects and for injecting humor into the narratives" (*Something about the Author* 25). The striking photographs in these books give them a large appeal, and Brooks' conversational style makes it possible for the reader to ingest a great deal of information about the natural world painlessly.

BIBLIOGRAPHY

Young Adult Fiction by Bruce Brooks

The Moves Make the Man. New York: Harper, 1985.
Midnight Hour Encores. New York: Harper, 1986.
No Kidding. New York: HarperCollins, 1989.
Everywhere. New York: HarperCollins, 1990.
What Hearts. New York: HarperCollins, 1992.

Young Adult Nonfiction by Bruce Brooks

On the Wing: The Life of Birds: From Feathers to Flight. New York: Scribner, 1989.
Nature by Design. Knowing Nature Series. New York: Farrar Straus Giroux. In association with Thirteen/WNET, 1991.
Predator! Knowing Nature Series. New York: Farrar Straus Giroux. In association with Thirteen/WNET, 1991.
Boys Will Be. New York: Holt, 1993.
Making Sense: Animal Perception and Communication. Knowing Nature Series. New York: Farrar Straus Giroux. In association with Thirteen/WNET, 1993.
Rivers, Glenn, and Bruce Brooks. *Those Who Love the Game: Glenn "Doc" Rivers on Life in the NBA and Elsewhere.* New York: Holt, 1993.

Selected Studies of Bruce Brooks

"Bruce Brooks." *Artists and Authors for Young Adults.* Ed. Sonia Benson. Vol. 8. Detroit: Gale, 1992. 17–24.
"Bruce Brooks." *Something about the Author.* Ed. Anne Commire. Vol. 72. Detroit: Gale, 1993. 22–26.
"Bruce Brooks." *Speaking for Ourselves: Autobiographical Sketches by Notable Authors of Books for Young Adults.* Urbana: NCTE, 1990. 33–35.
McDonnell, Christine. "New Voices: New Visions: Bruce Brooks." *Horn Book* 63.2 (1987): 188–91.

ALICE CHILDRESS
(1920-)

Reinhard Isensee

BIOGRAPHY

Born to a poor and uneducated family on October 12, 1920, in Charleston, South Carolina, but raised in Harlem. Alice Childress' childhood did not seem to promise her a future career as an actress, playwright, and novelist. She was raised by her grandmother, Eliza Campbell, daughter of a former slave and a white sailor. Living in abject poverty Alice was unable to finish high school. Nevertheless, she profited from the encouragement of her teachers to continue writing, which she had discovered was something very enjoyable during her school years.

Her professional career started in 1940 when she gave her first performance as an actress in *On Strivers Row* in New York City. Here she worked as a drama coach, drama director, member of the board of directors, and personnel director with the American Negro Theater for twelve years. During this time she also earned a reputation as a respected actress, working with, among others, Ossie Davis, Ruby Dee, and Sidney Poitier. Her reputation was primarily based upon her performances in such productions as *Natural Man* (1941), *The Candy Story* (1953), *The World of Sholom Aleichem* (1953), and *The Cool World* (1960).

Although very successful in both acting and directing, Childress became more and more interested in play writing, thus following the fascination with writing she developed during her three years of high school. In the fifties Childress started her career as a playwright with pieces like *Just a Little Simple* (an adaptation of Langston Hughes' *Simple Speaks His Mind*) and *Gold through the Trees* (1952), the first play by a black woman to be professionally produced on the American stage. Her play *Florence* was also put on stage again at that time even though it had been produced by the American Negro Theater in a small loft in Harlem as early as 1949.

With *Trouble in Mind*, published during the year of the Montgomery bus boycott, Childress gained nationwide attention by receiving an Obie Award for the best Off-Broadway production of the 1956 season, making Childress the first woman ever to have won the award. It also brought her work into mainstream theater.

While remaining a prolific playwright, Childress also lectured at several colleges and universities in the 1960s. During this time she earned wide recognition by both the academy and theater audiences on several university campuses. Some of her plays, such as *The Wedding Band* (1966), were first produced at universities, and her activities as a scholar-writer at Harvard University from 1966–1968 helped to further establish her reputation as a politically committed writer.

Because the themes of her plays provoked mixed reviews, it was often difficult for her to get them produced, as, for instance, in the cases of *The Wedding Band*, *Wine in the Wilderness*, *The Young Martin Luther King*, and *The Freedom Drum*. In addition to her plays, she has also written columns for the *Baltimore Afro-American* newspaper and has devoted particular attention to young adult fiction—after writing two plays for young people during the 1970s (*When the Rattlesnake Sounds* and *Let's Hear It for the Queen*). In 1973 her first novel for young adults, *A Hero Ain't Nothin' but a Sandwich,* was published, followed by *Rainbow Jordan* in 1981. Both novels received prestigious national awards such as the *New York Times Book Review*'s Outstanding Books of the Year and the Coretta King Award.

Alice Childress has been married since 1957 to Nathan Woodard, a musician who composes music for her plays, and lives in New York City. She has one daughter, Jean, from her first marriage. Besides being active in the American Federation of Television and Radio Artists, the Dramatists Guild, the Actor's Equity Association, the Harlem Writers Guild, and the New Dramatists, Screen and Writers Guild, she frequently contributes to anthologies and journals such as *Masses and Mainstream, Black World*, and *Freedomways*. One of the essential motives of Alice Childress' career has been her dedication to social justice, which she has promoted not only in her writing but also by her activity in schools, community affairs, theater projects, and by her assistance to young black women playwrights.

MAJOR WORKS AND THEMES

Even at a first glance Childress' works clearly reflect her artistic concept of the function of writing. From a very early time she insisted on a notion of art that was based upon her experience as an African-American growing up among "the poor, genteel, and sensitive people who are seamstresses, coal-carriers, candy-makers, sharecroppers, bakers, baby care-takers, housewives, foot-soldiers, penny candy sellers, vegetable peelers" (A. Childress) in Harlem. Thus, her own background became the strongest force for her ambitions as a writer. At the same time it served as the major thematic inspiration for her works, dealing with the life of such people and their struggles to survive.

As she began to write, she resisted advice to focus on those blacks who were able to overcome their cruel living conditions and make the American Dream come true. Instead, she was interested in the life and fate of those who did not make it, those who were the losers in American society. From the beginning of her writing career Alice Childress thus directed her efforts to the interpretation of the "ordinary people" because in her view they were not ordinary but represented the masses of human beings. All of her texts articulate this self-imposed thematic focus on the nature and behavior of black people in everyday situations, on the complexity of the relationship in the black community, as well as on the inconsistent relationship between black and white people. Whereas she put special thematic emphasis on the role of black actresses and their experiences in the theater world in such plays as *Florence* and *Trouble in Mind*, she later broadened her themes to include more comprehensive problems of the racial struggle by blacks. In *Gold through the Trees* (1952) Childress depicts the similarities and differences in the situation of South Africans and African-Americans. With the civil rights movement gaining full momentum during the 1960s, she concentrated more and more on questions of race relations in America. *The Wedding Band* described the interracial love affair between a white man and a black woman in South Carolina at the time of World War I.

Enthusiastic about and inspired by the black liberation movement led by Martin Luther King, Childress took a more political approach in her plays written in that period, depicting either activities and activists of that movement—for instance in *The Young Martin Luther King* (1969) and *The Freedom Drum* (1970)—or investigating the role of ordinary African-Americans in bringing together black people of different social status—as in *Wine in the Wilderness* (1969). In this play it is a black woman in the ghetto who succeeds in uniting inner-city and middle-class blacks in the struggle for their common interests.

Even though suggested in her earlier works, it is here—as well as in the two novels focusing on female protagonists (*A Short Walk*, 1979; *Rainbow Jordan*, 1981)—that the author fully develops what may be called the central theme of her writings: the exploration of the experience of African-American women in America by questioning the life and aspirations of various groups and individuals in both historical and contemporary times. In dealing with race relationships, especially those of black and white, Childress attempts to portray the complex and unique life of human beings struggling to come to terms with life in a society that only recently began to recognize and respect "otherness" and "difference" related to ethnicity. At the same time, however, she makes us aware of her belief that American society, for the sake of a democratic and prosperous future, is not only fundamentally dependent on the contributions of its diverse ethnic groups but would also enormously profit from its multicultural composition. Based on her own painful childhood in Harlem, she concluded that many of the causes for the failure of individuals to function successfully in society could be traced back to their experiences as children and adolescents. As a result, Childress became more and more interested in the contemporary situation of young African-Americans living in inner-city environments.

Her first novel for young adults, *A Hero Ain't Nothin' but a Sandwich* (1973), which goes back to a suggestion by Ferdinand Manjo, an editor and author of children's books, and Childress' own long-standing interest in the impact of drugs on young people, tells the story of Benjie, a thirteen-year-old boy close to heroin addiction. Having spent all his childhood in the ghetto, the protagonist had had to adjust to the tough life in a hostile environment. Throughout the narrative the author lays special emphasis on Benjie's lack of communication and relationships with adults, including his mother. This situation, combined with his confusion and uncertainty, makes him vulnerable and receptive to drugs and criminal acts. Moreover, he also is neglected in school, which as an institution fails by and large in providing positive values. The theme presented in this novel points to the painful conditions of growing up as a black youngster in a ghetto district. What Childress suggests in the text as a hope for the Benjies in America is meaningful relationships with adults providing trust and friendship. By narrating the story through different perspectives (Benjie's, his teachers', the principal's, his mother's, etc.), the author is, as Elbert R. Hill maintains, "particularly effective in bringing out the uncertainty and ambiguity the various characters feel about their own identities."

Rainbow Jordan (1981), Childress' second young adult novel, is the story of three female characters living in an urban setting. Rainbow, a mature, fourteen-year-old black girl, is frequently left by her mother, who works as a go-go dancer, and therefore has to stay with Josephine, a fifty-seven-year-old social worker and dressmaker. The theme developed in this text is yet another example for the author's claim that meaningful communication between people can function as the key to overcome even severe problems in life. The particular achievement of this story is the literary strategy of building confidence and trust between the protagonist, who is at a very vulnerable stage of adolescence, and a woman going through a deep crisis in her marriage. In Childress' sensitive delineation, structurally established in the book through the narratives of three women, human strength derives from genuine respect of human beings. Rather than finding flawless adults, the reader is confronted with a relationship of two very different characters that is based on a gradually emerging commitment by adult and adolescent alike. Moreover, in contrast to Benjie in *A Hero Ain't Nothin' but a Sandwich*, who is solely dependent on the help of adults for solving his problems, it is the adult character of Josephine in *Rainbow Jordan* who finds a partner in Rainbow, the adolescent, for dealing with her own crises. What is revealed in the relationship between these two female characters is Childress' profound understanding of individuals and her humanistic view of the possibilities of mastering supposedly hopeless life situations.

In 1989 Childress published a novel for young adults that is again devoted to a "difficult" or controversial subject. The theme of this novel, however, does not solely center on ethnicity and the problems related to it. *Those Other People* is the story of young people whose "differences" most of all derive from sexual orientation and who find themselves in a severe conflict in trying to convey these differences to the social world that surrounds them. With seventeen-year-old Jonathan, protagonist of the novel, Childress portrays an adolescent who has been unable to come to terms with being homosexual in a homophobic culture. Setting her novel in a high school locale she competently creates a plot structure in which each of the characters is forced to confront exposure to social discrimination by taking sides for or against different sexual preferences. This happens in the text when the only two black students in a computer class are being harassed by a racist student and a girl is sexually assaulted by a teacher. Jonathan and the two black students overcome their fear and speak their minds. In this way the author provokes the reader to join the literary characters in reflecting on his or her own view on this issue.

CRITICAL RECEPTION

The critical reception of Childress' work has always separated her achievements into two major fields of accomplishment: her plays and activities in the American theater on the one hand and her novels, especially those for young adult readers, on the other. In contrast, Childress herself does not subscribe to such a view of her work but rather insists on the thematic and artistic interdependence of her plays and novels which in John T. Gillespie's assessment is particularly "revealed in the brilliant characterization and dialogue" of her novels. Attributing her writing style in fiction to her experience in theater, Childress admits: "When I'm writing a book, I visualize it all on stage. I'm very pleased when critics say my novels feel like plays. I've learned to lean on theater instead of breaking with it."

When assessing her reputation as a writer, such a separation, however, seems to be valid. Despite her consistent productivity in a wide variety of genres over the course of forty years, she has not received adequate critical attention. This is especially true for her contribution to the American theater where Childress was in the forefront of pioneering developments. Although academic and critical circles began to welcome her plays and novels from the 1970s on by inviting her as guest lecturer and writer-in-residence to several university campuses and by praising her artistic achievements as an outstanding playwright, it took the "official" critique much longer to recognize her work. In fact, her reputation as a writer has remained somewhat obscure up to the present time for several reasons. Some of the most relevant may be found particularly in the controversial themes of her texts, her uncomfortable honesty, and the uncompromising delineation of black experience in contemporary America. Producers and critics hesitated more than once to put her plays on stage because of disputes over theme and interpretation, as for instance in the case of *Trouble in Mind*, which Childress herself withdrew due to these disputes. The mixed reactions by critics to this play (and most of her other works), praising its compassion, humor, and pathos on the one hand and expressing their dislike of an uneven plot and propagandistic scenes on the other, nourished the belief that the production on larger stages would result in commercial losses. Other plays, even though they received favorable reviews at the time they were first produced, reached mainstream theater with great delay. This was especially true for her play *The Wedding Band*, which was produced at a commercial New York stage eight years after its initial publication. And when this play was run on an ABC network program, several local stations refused to broadcast it fearing the controversy it might cause among viewers.

However, this resistance to her work through the 1960s and 1970s could not diminish the lasting impact of her "exuberant celebration of black experience, her power as a great humorist, her love of life and people" (John Killens) on writers and audience/readers alike.

Despite the fact that Childress' young adult novels were enthusiastically praised as "one of the noblest creations in young adult fiction" (Alleen Pace Nilsen and Kenneth L. Donelson), as "beautiful books" (Anne Tyler), and for the "skillful use of expressive and often poetic idiomatic language" (Geraldine L. Wilson), as well as honored with multiple national awards, their themes still caused heated controversies over their "suitability" for adolescent readers. Some school libraries even banned *A Hero Ain't Nothin' but a Sandwich* (1973) from their shelves. In one Long Island, New York, library the book was reinstated only by order of the Supreme Court in 1983.

How does the author Childress come to terms with such a critical reaction to her work? What impact does it exert on her artistic principles? First of all, she deals with criticism in a rather self-confident manner, calling herself "one of the best known of unknown people" (according to Trudier Harris). In "A Candle in a Gale Wind," an essay published in 1984, Alice Childress more extensively articulates her position with respect to her critics by adhering firmly to her credo as an artist: "My stories and plays were usually labeled controversial and some were banned from a few school libraries and by several local television outlets when shown on national network. I do not consider my work controversial, as it is not at all contrary to humanism."

BIBLIOGRAPHY

Young Adult Fiction by Alice Childress

A Hero Ain't Nothin' but a Sandwich. New York: Coward, 1973.
A Short Walk. New York: Coward, 1979.
Rainbow Jordan. New York: Coward, 1981.
Many Closets. New York: Coward, 1987.
Those Other People. New York: Putnam, 1989.

Plays by Alice Childress

Florence. Produced in New York City at American Negro Theater, 1949.
Just a Little Simple. Produced in New York City at Club Baron Theater, 1950.
Gold through the Trees. Produced in New York City at Club Baron Theater, 1952.

Trouble in Mind. Produced Off-Broadway, 1955. Revised version published in *Black Theater: A Twentieth-Century Collection of the Work of Its Best Playwrights*. Ed. Lindsay Patterson. New York: Dodd, 1971.

String. Produced Off-Broadway, 1969.

Martin Luther King at Montgomery, Alabama. 1969.

A Man Bearing a Pitcher. 1969.

Vashti's Magic Mirror and The Freedom Drum. Produced as *Young Man Martin Luther King* by Performing Arts Repertory Theater (on tour), 1969–1971.

Majo: A Black Love Story. Produced in New York City at New Heritage Theater, 1970.

Majo and String. Dramatists Play Service, 1971.

The African Garden. 1971.

The Wedding Band: A Love/Hate Story in Black and White. New York: Samuel French, 1973. Produced in Ann Arbor, MI, 1966.

When the Rattlesnake Sounds. New York: Coward, 1975.

Let's Hear It for the Queen. New York: Coward, 1976.

Sea Island Song. Produced in Charleston, SC, 1977.

Gullah. With Nathan Woodard. Produced in Amherst, MA, 1984.

Moms: A Praise Play for a Black Comedienne. With Nathan Woodard. Produced Off-Broadway, 1987.

Screenplays by Alice Childress

Wine in the Wilderness: A Comedy-Drama. Dramatists Play Service, 1969.

Wedding Band. American Broadcasting Companies, 1973.

A Hero Ain't Nothin' but a Sandwich. New World Pictures, 1978.

String. Public Broadcasting Service, 1979.

Other Works by Alice Childress

Black Scenes. New York: Doubleday, 1971 (collection of scenes from plays).

Like One of the Family: Conversations from a Domestic's Life. New York: Independence Publishers, 1956. Reprinted with an introduction by Trudier Harris, New York: Beacon, 1986.

Selected Studies of Alice Childress

Abramson, Doris. *Negro Playwrights in the American Theater: 1925–1959*. New York: Columbia UP, 1969.

"Alice Childress." *Children's Literature Review*. Ed. Gerard J. Senick. Vol. 14. Detroit: Gale, 1988. 85–94.

"Alice Childress." *Something about the Author.* Ed. Anne Commire. Vol. 48. Detroit: Gale, 1981.

Benson, Sonia. "Alice Childress." *Artists and Authors for Young Adults.* Ed. Laurie Collier. Vol. 8. Detroit: Gale, 1992. 25–34.

Black Writers. A Selection of Sketches from Contemporary Authors. Ed. Sharon Malinowski. Detroit: Gale, 1989. 100–103.

Childress, Alice. "A Candle in a Gale Wind." *Black Woman Writers (1950–1980): A Critical Evaluation.* Ed. Mari Evans. New York: Doubleday 1984. 111–16.

"Childress, Alice." *Contemporary Authors, New Revision Series.* Ed. Hal May and James G. Lesniak. Vol. 27. Detroit: Gale, 1989. 100–103.

"Childress, Alice." *Dictionary of Literary Biography.* Vol. 7. *20th Century Dramatists Part One.* Ed. John MacNicholas. Detroit: Gale, 1981. 118–24.

Davis, Mariana. *Contributions of Black Women to America.* Columbia, SC: Kenday, 1982.

Gillespie, John T. *More Juniorplots: A Guide for Teachers and Librarians.* New York: Bowker, 1977. 51–74.

Hill, Elbert R. "A Hero for the Movies." *Children's Novels and the Movies.* Ed. Douglas Street. New York: Ungar, 1983. 236–43.

Hull, Gloria T., Patricia Bell Scott, and Barbara Smith, eds. *But Some of Us Are Brave.* Old Westbury, New York: Feminist Press, 1982.

Killens, John O. "The Literary Genius of Alice Childress." *Black Woman Writers (1950–1980): A Critical Evaluation.* Ed. Mari Evans. New York: Doubleday, 1984. 129–33.

Nilsen, Alleen Pace, and Kenneth L. Donelson. "Life Models: Of Heroes and Hopes." *Literature for Today's Young Adults.* 2nd ed. Glenview, IL: Scott, Foresman, 1985. 208–57.

Ortiz, Miguel A. "The Politics of Poverty in Young Adult Literature." *The Lion and the Unicorn* 2.2 (1978): 6–15.

Shockley, Ann. *Living Black American Authors.* New York: Bowker, 1973.

Smith, Jessie Carney, ed. *Notable Black American Women.* Detroit: Gale, 1992. 181–83.

Turner, Darwin. *Afro-American Writers.* New York: Appleton, Century, Crofts, 1970.

Tyler, Anne. "Looking for Mom." *New York Times Book Review* 26 Apr. 1981: 52–53, 69.

Wilson, Geraldine L. Rev. of *Rainbow Jordan. Interracial Books for Children Bulletin* 12.7 (1981): 24–25.

ANN NOLAN CLARK
(1896-)

Jeanne Whitehouse Peterson

BIOGRAPHY

The third child of five, Ann Nolan Clark, née Ann Marie Nolan, was born on December 5, 1896, in Las Vegas, New Mexico Territory. Her Irish Catholic parents, Patrick Francis and Mary (née Dunn) Nolan, with their sons Ben and Carol, moved from rural Illinois to this "mountain meadow" community in 1895, hoping the sunshine, altitude, and mineral springs would assist Patrick Nolan's recovery from tuberculosis.

Because her father, an independent merchant, built their home close to the railroad yards and the Gallinas River, Ann Nolan Clark grew up near the boundary between West and East Las Vegas, between Spanish-speaking Old Town and New Town's commercial blocks, where English was the language of choice. Her early cross-cultural experiences at home, school, and church, described in detail in her 1953 Newbery Award speech and in *Journey to the People* (1969) and "A Handful of Days" (1993), enabled Clark to develop the understanding she would need both as teacher and writer. She was Irish among Spanish, French, German, and Pueblo Indians, learning their ways, eating their foods, celebrating their feasts. In 1912, at the age of fifteen, Clark relished the feeling of becoming "something larger" as New Mexico officially joined the United States of America as its forty-seventh state.

In her introduction to *Journey to the People*, Annis Duff, long-time editor and friend, wrote how fortunate it was that "writer and teacher grew together in one person." In the beginning, however, Clark came to teaching out of necessity. Her early positions included teaching assistant in an English class at Highlands University, Las Vegas; teacher in the small German-speaking community of Optimo, New Mexico, during World War I; and, for two months in the spring of 1918, substitute teacher with the Bureau of Indian Affairs at Tesuque Pueblo, north of Santa Fe.

Anxious to leave home, young Ann followed her brother Carol to Ft. Lewis in Washington State where he was training for the military. Her parents brought her back to a teaching position in a mining camp near Gallup, where she met and married Thomas Patrick Clark, a baseball player working in the community. Several years after the birth of their son, Tommie, as the couple's differences became irreconcilable, Clark left her husband and returned to teaching. Fortunately, the principal at the school in Gallup was Mabel Parsons, a graduate from Columbia University and a self-avowed "Dewey Disciple." She became Clark's mentor and companion. As she would later state, Parsons "taught me everything I know about teaching," especially the value of home visits and the development of social or education programs which would affect entire families within the school community.

Four years later, Clark and Tommie followed Parsons to a school in a mining camp high in the mountains near Santa Fe. Within a few years they purchased a touring car, jackets, hats, and jodhpurs and advertised themselves as Tewa Tours, dedicated to guiding tourists through ancient Indian ruins and into modern pueblos. During these tours, or with her son and mother, Clark began exploring New Mexico's past. She delighted in the stories she learned of people, places, and events. Eventually, encouraged by George Fitzpatrick, editor of *New Mexico Magazine*, Clark began publishing articles based on her study of regional history.

In 1930, searching for financial security for herself and her son, Clark took the government test to become a teacher with the Bureau of Indian Affairs. While teaching in Black Rock School near Zuni Pueblo and then at the Indian School at Santa Fe, Clark began to recognize the problems in Indian education. Not only were children being asked to read stories about children who were unlike themselves, the stories they were given did not value Native children's "particular natures and needs."

In 1934, after elders of Tesuque Pueblo requested "the little teacher" who had once taught at their day school, Clark returned to this rural community. She knew she would miss the authors and artists she had met in Santa Fe, especially Mary Austin, whose book *The American Rhythm: Studies and Re-expressions of Amerindian Songs* had helped her notice differences in Native children's speech patterns. But she planned to make a home for herself and Tommie, and for her mother and Mabel Parsons, when either wanted to stay.

After 1937, during the New Deal for Indian Education, something memorable happened which affected Clark's life-journey. Realizing that nationally published textbooks were irrelevant to her Indian students, Clark decided to compose a geography book for her third graders, using the texture and cadence of the children's own speech as they described their homes, irrigation ditches, and fields. At the end of the year, five third graders took home copies of *Third Grade Home Geography*, which they had helped print on Clark's Kelsey Press, hand stitched and covered in bright calico. As she hoped, the books were read by the entire community.

When Willard Beatty, director of Indian education, saw the impact of Clark's work, he asked if she would consider writing a series of bilingual readers for children in other pueblos and on the Navajo and Sioux reservations. The work would be done on site and with anthropologists in Washington, D.C. By this time, Clark's son, Tommie, was on his own. She accepted and, in the next few years, completed twelve booklets (some of which have been reprinted and are still in use) before funds were diverted into projects for government defense, and Clark was given a heartbreaking assignment as part of a team in a Japanese Rehabilitation Center.

The early 1940s brought other turns in Clark's life. Her writing career developed as she and regional author Frances Carrey published *A Child's Story of New Mexico*, a textbook used to teach state history for more than thirty years. Viking Press accepted *Third Grade Home Geography* for publication in 1941 as *In My Mother's House*. Illustrated by award-winning Pueblo artist Velino Herrera, Clark's first nationally published book received several awards, including runner-up for the 1942 Randolph Caldecott Award given by the American Library Association. During these years changes occurred in Clark's family. Her father died, her son married, joined the Air Force, and, only one month after his own son's birth, died during combat in the South Pacific.

During the 1950s and 1960s, Clark won two major awards for her writing. In 1953, while on a lunch break in a cafe in Utah, Clark opened a letter from the American Library Association which informed her that *Secret of the Andes*, a mystical novel set in Peru, had won the coveted John Newbery Award—ahead of the now classic *Charlotte's Web*. Ten years later, in 1963, Clark received the Regina Medal from the Catholic Library Association for "continued distinguished contributions to literature for children." During these years Clark completed her assignment with the Bureau of Indian Affairs by assisting in the Adult Indian Education Project. She trained teachers and assisted in the writing of over one hundred books, including manuals for crafts and skills that were thought important to ensure productive work away from reservations. Following a serious accident in 1962, which kept her in the hospital for many months, Clark retired from the U.S. Department of the Interior to devote herself to her writing.

Throughout her lifetime as teacher and writer, Clark has become noted for her boundless compassion and fine sense of humor. As Annis Duff once wrote, she is seen as a "rare and shining human being" (*Journey* 15). In her later years she left the home she and Mabel Parsons built in Tesuque, New Mexico, for the warmth of the desert near Tucson, Arizona. For as long as her health allowed, Clark traveled and wrote books of the Basque in Idaho, the Irish, the Finnish-Americans and lastly, in 1975, of immigrants from war-torn Vietnam. She wrote the books she thought were needed.

"And what is a book from the writer's viewpoint? It is a part of the writer's life, his beliefs and his experiences, his values and his dreams, his development of craftsmanship and his endowment of talents. His writing is a part of his mind and his heart. It is a piece of the privacy of his inner being that he has pushed out into the openness of public acceptance, or public disapproval or public indifference" (*Journey* 66).

MAJOR WORKS AND THEMES

Ann Nolan Clark published her first novel for young people in 1943, two years after *In My Mother's House* brought her to national attention. *Little Navajo Bluebird* (1943), set on the Navajo Reservation during the late 1930s, is about the everyday life of Doli, or Bluebird as her family calls her. During the summer Doli decides to fly from her hogan to attend boarding school. Story events show Doli traveling with her parents to the trading post, learning to weave, staying with her sheep during a deluge, and participating in purification rituals following the death of a neighbor. Doli's simple, realistic response to her world accurately depicts the beliefs about nature a Native American child might hold, and is seen in this description of a rain storm:

Dusk was near before the rain stopped falling and only for a little while did Sun-Carrier show his face to give light to the rain-drenched land. Then he went to his western home and at once night came and filled the land (94).

In her picture stories, in *In My Mother's House*, first written for third graders in Tesuque Pueblo, and in the Little Herder Series, published bilingually for Navajo readers, Clark lovingly and accurately describes the young Indian's response to her material and spiritual worlds. Clark has broadened her audience to include non-Native children whom, she feels, must come to accept the lifestyles of others, as well as the teachers, librarians, and parents who select and share the books she has written.

Of her work, Clark once wrote, "I tell these things not to bewilder but to ask that white Americans recognize that other people have different values and different ways from those handed down to them and to ask that these values and ways be accepted with respectful minds and open hearts" (*Journey* 35).

In *Little Navajo Bluebird*, as in all her young adult novels, Clark shows her concern for young people who must grow up in a world not of their own making. Doli, secure in her life as a child of the People, can and will choose a path which embraces, yet extends, well beyond that of her parents.

In *Secret of the Andes* (1952), Clark enlarges upon this theme of growing beyond the security of one's heritage as she develops the character of Cusi, a child of the Inca, who must search for a place to belong, for a family, for home. As Cusi journeys away from the Andes toward Cuzco and back, he learns truths about his heritage, hears the legend of Inca gold, hidden from conquering Spaniards four hundred years before, and wonders about the role he must play in the preservation of his culture. Most importantly, Cusi learns to read the messages of his own heart. "Of course you knew," Cusi's guardian eventually tells him, "but you had to find out that you knew" (119).

While other American authors of young adult fiction began to explore the consequences of actions made by their youthful protagonists, one of Clark's major interests lay in the ways young people gained knowledge of their cultural heritage, their values and beliefs, and how they learned to listen to their own hearts as they chose future pathways. In each novel Clark's protagonist was instructed by an elder, or an Old One. In each, he or she was released from the patterns of the past, ready to select his or her "joyous journey."

During the 1950s, Clark's other novels for young people reflected her concern that Indians in Latin America be allowed to retain knowledge of their cultural heritage even after close contact with the dominant culture. *Santiago* (1955) is the seemingly tragic story of a twelve-year-old Indian who grows up as the foster child of a proud Guatemalan of Spanish descent. When Santiago is wrested away from his secure life by a clansman of his father, he must assume the clothes and posture of a burden-bearer for the first time in his life. He grieves when he leaves his Tia Alicia behind. But he, like Cusi in *Secret of the Andes*, learns he must understand the complexities of his heritage. This is his lot in life. Even now, forty years after publication, *Santiago* adequately reflects the pain young people feel when caught between two cultures. Clark wrote, "The old Indian's scorn cut through the boy's longing. Even she who loves you hates you because you are Indian—hates the race that bore you and wants you to pass, pass as a Spaniard, the murderers of your people" (36).

However, because Santiago was not trained from birth in the ways of his ancestors, his training fails. During the next five years the young man travels throughout Guatemala, learning the ways of those who gather coffee or chicle, until his path brings him back to his childhood home and the decision he must make about his future.

Just as Santiago learns from a wise old man what it means to be a burden-bearer, Paco, in *Paco's Miracle* (1962), learns to appreciate the beauties of nature and his kinship with all living things. In this mystical novel for young people, Clark merges the stories of Saint Francis' love of the animals with those of Christmas as celebrated by Hispanics in northern New Mexico. Paco, an orphaned child, repays the kindness of his adoptive parents and community by supplying decorations and wild honey after a severe winter snowstorm cuts the valley off from the necessary supplies. With the publication of this book, Clark begins to turn from Latin America and refocuses her attention on the southwestern cultural landscape. Now, however, she is interested in the role religious beliefs played within traditional French and Hispanic cultures.

Clark's concern for intergroup harmony, for the ways young people must acknowledge and value the past if they are to find their own pathways, is restated in each of her novels. Decisions, she lets her readers know, are never made easily, especially when they involve leaving home or accepting other ways of being or another faith.

With the publication of *Medicine Man's Daughter* (1963), Clark returns to the Navajo Reservation, to the landscape she brought to life twenty years earlier in *Little Navajo Bluebird*. In this story, however, the conflict between old ways and new ways is sharply drawn. Tall Girl, in training as a medicine woman, learns her nephew has been healed in a white man's hospital, not by a traditional sing. Her once-secure world crumbles. Tall Girl sees the healing as a message that sends her to boarding school—in the end, to study western medicine. As Tall Girl's aunt philosophically says, "Seasons change and we meet the changes. It then should follow that as the years change so do we meet those changes" (130).

But Tall Girl must meet the greatest challenge of all. She must forsake the Navajo abhorrence of death to embrace a Catholicism which centered itself on the crucifixion of Christ. During an interview Clark stated that she wrote *Medicine Man's Daughter* in part "to show the dreadful thing we were trying to do to the Indians—to make them Catholic, especially the Navajo" (Interview 1981). The reader who is outside the culture sees the many ways the beliefs of Native people have been ignored or changed by well-meaning but destructive outsiders.

During the late 1960s, responding to the restlessness she observed among America's youth, Clark wrote several novels of Europeans moving west-ward to America. She explored the ways young adults, well-steeped in the traditional values and beliefs of their cultures, could survive in new and dangerous settings. In *Year Walk* (1975), one of her strongest, most detailed books, Clark accurately depicts the culture of Kepu, a young Basque who comes from the Pyrenees to Idaho to herd sheep for his godfather. She explores the ways Kepu survives drought, fire, range wars, and being alone for most of the year. In the end, at the time when Kepu must decide to return to Spain or to stay, he knows the path he must choose. His decision is appropriate and believable, given the traditional values of loyalty and independence Kepu brought with him from his homeland.

Clark published *To Stand Against the Wind* in 1978, when she was eighty. In this painful story Em, a Vietnamese refugee, spends an evening honoring his dead and living family members left behind in Vietnam. In a series of flashbacks, Clark accurately depicts everyday events, such as cooking, cultivation of rice paddies, and traditional celebrations. But the backdrop of war is horrific: "friendly" troops kill Em's family members; his American friend, a reporter; even his all-important water buffalo. Clark makes us look at the ways war disrupts and destroys traditional patterns—forever. In the end, Em must accept his place as the remaining family member who must remember and cherish the past. Only then, Clark tells us, will Em and his relatives be able to move toward a future in this new land.

CRITICAL RECEPTION

During her years as an author, Ann Nolan Clark believed that books about people "should be made up of laughter and tears, joys and sorrows, and the peace of all the humdrum hours, because that is what life is made of" (*Journey* 95). In the beginning critics responded positively to the everyday quality of her stories. They were pleased with her realistic, unsentimental portrayal of Native American characters.

In 1953, in her article "Ann Nolan Clark: 1953 Newbery Award Winner," Evelyn Wenzel praised Clark's concern that teachers wait for youth to "read its own heart." She wrote: "Few teachers have given themselves so single-mindedly to understanding a people as Ann Nolan Clark in her long years of work among the Indians; and few writers have been able to effect communication between cultures so sensitively and artistically" (330–32). Ten years later, after Clark won the Regina Award for the continuing humanitarian quality of her writing, Claire Huchet Bishop praised Clark's dedication to the discovery of "the way Indians feel." Her work, Bishop maintained, "reveals a quiet and steady groping at an understanding from the heart" (282).

Of her early works, reviewers stated appreciation for the ways Clark portrayed unusual landscapes for her readers and how she developed believable characters whose lives, while bereft of material possessions, were "rich in feelings" (Bishop 285). They responded to the ways Clark showed the warmth of family relationships and yet how she might conclude her story—as in *Secret of the Andes*—with a "non-white happy ending" (Bishop 283).

Most importantly, Clark's reviewers commented on her poetic use of language. Bishop writes, "Her writing has the unhurried quality of the Indian song and its compelling rhythm" (285). May Hill Arbuthnot, commenting on Clark's writing in her *Children and Books*, notes that Clark's "cadenced prose is beautiful and unique" (453). Arnold A. Griese defines Clark's style as "her natural awareness of detail aimed at promoting imagery and a facility to communicate such images . . . through the use of appropriate concrete words [as well as] an effective use of simile, metaphor and personification" (655). Griese continues, stating that Clark's distinctive style is "akin to poetry" and for that reason young people may not readily select Clark's books for individual, private reading in the same way they might not choose poetry itself for private entertainment. But, he advises, considering "the strong themes contained in her writing, her effectiveness in building bridges of understanding between cultures, and the poetic quality of her style, it would seem important that every effort be made to properly introduce children to her stories" (657).

At times Clark is criticized for her "rhapsodic timbres," as in the *Kirkus Reviews* discussion of *Circle of Seasons*, but usually her use of language, the physicality of her rhythms, the expressive style "that is spiritual—even mystical at times" is highly praised, as in the review of *World Song* in the *Bulletin of the Center for Children's Books*. What is important to remember is that Clark heard the recurrence in Native American speech patterns and utilized these same rhythms or patterns when she wrote her young adult novels, especially *Secret of the Andes*. In this way Native American speech patterns integrated or moved into the dominant culture. Each time one of Clark's early novels was read aloud in home or school settings, young people were becoming accustomed to another way of speaking, thinking, and meaning.

Because Clark's stories involve everyday events, later reviewers at times seemed critical either of the ways Clark developed her characters or plot lines of her stories. However, Griese wrote in 1972, "If we define plot as the generation of a problem or conflict taken from within the everyday happenings of a child's life, and if the attempted solutions stem from the child's attitudes, actions, and inner resources, then her stories can be said to have rigorous plots" (656). Clark's characters are often caught up in the larger issues of cultural conflict that affect adults around them. As young adults they must learn all they can of their heritage, their cultural values and beliefs, before they are able to select an appropriate pathway to the future.

Seemingly, Ann Nolan Clark wrote as an outsider, as someone who was empathetic to, but not *of* the groups of which she wrote. "The challenge," she once wrote, "that urges and pushes, forces and compels me to write is *need*. It is the need I think exists for the kind of books I try to write" (*Journey* 88). And the need, as Clark perceived it, was to write about groups of people who were usually underrepresented in stories for young people.

The five qualities Clark asked of her books were those of *honesty* or a belief in what was written; *accuracy* or knowledge that the information for her story was factually correct; *reality* so that her story was filled with everyday happenings; *imagination* so that readers might make pictures with their hearts and minds from the words the author chose; and also *appreciation* of "all that life holds and all that life means" (*Journey* 90–98).

Throughout her writing career, Clark meant to bring the cultural beliefs of others to life so that youthful readers would feel empathetic to the choices and lives of others. She did this and she did this well, using, as she did, appropriate music—or rhythms and patterns—of language. What must be remembered is that Clark also wrote as an insider, as someone growing in the understanding of her own issues and problems, someone who wrote out of her own authentic truths. She, too, grieved the loss of her son, her family, and—like Cusi in *Secret of the Andes* or Em in *To Stand Against the Wind* —had to understand and cherish her past as she journeyed toward her future as teacher and writer.

BIBLIOGRAPHY

Young Adult Fiction by Ann Nolan Clark

Little Navajo Bluebird. Illus. Paul Lantz. New York: Viking, 1943.
Secret of the Andes. Illus. Jean Charlot. New York: Viking, 1952. New York: Puffin, 1976.
Blue Canyon Horse. Illus. Allan Houser. New York: Viking, 1954.
Santiago. Illus. Lynd Ward. New York: Viking, 1955.
World Song. Illus. Kurt Wiese. New York: Viking, 1960.
The Desert People. Illus. Allan Houser. New York: Viking, 1962.
Medicine Man's Daughter. Illus. Don Bolognese. New York: Farrar Straus, 1963.
Circle of the Seasons. Illus. W. T. Mars. New York: Farrar Straus, 1970.
Hoofprint on the Wind. Illus. Robert Andrew Parker. New York: Viking, 1972.
Year Walk. New York: Viking, 1975.
All This Wild Land. New York: Viking, 1976.
To Stand against the Wind. New York: Viking, 1978.

Works for Children by Ann Nolan Clark

Little Boy with Three Names: Stories of Taos Pueblo. Illus. Tonita Lujan. Washington, DC: U.S. Office of Indian Affairs, 1940. Ancient City Press, 1990.
Who Wants to Be a Prairie Dog? Illus. Van Tishnahjinnie. Washington, DC: U.S. Office of Indian Affairs, 1940.
A Child's Story of New Mexico. With Frances Carey. University Publishing 1941. 3rd ed. 1960.
In My Mother's House. Earlier version privately published as *Third Grade Home Geography.* Illus. Velino Herrera. New York: Viking, 1941. 1991.
The Pine Ridge Porcupine. Illus. Andrew Standing Soldier. Washington, DC: U.S. Office of Indian Affairs, 1941.
About the Grass Mountain Mouse. Illus. Andrew Standing Soldier. Washington, DC: U.S. Office of Indian Affairs, 1942.
About the Hen of Wahpeton. Illus. Andrew Standing Soldier. Washington, DC: U.S. Office of Indian Affairs, 1942.
About the Slim Butte Raccoon. Illus. Andrew Standing Soldier. Washington, DC: U.S. Office of Indian Affairs, 1942.
Buffalo Caller: The Story of a Young Sioux Boy of the Early 1700's, before the Coming of the Horse. Illus. Marian Hulsizer. Row, Peterson, 1942.
There Still Are Buffalo. Illus. Andrew Standing Soldier. Washington, DC: U.S. Office of Indian Affairs, 1942. New York: Haskell, 1958. Ancient City Press, 1992.
Bringer of the Mystery Dog. Illus. Oscar Howe. Washington, DC: U.S. Office of Indian Affairs, 1943.

Young Hunter of Picuris. Illus. V. Herrera. Washington, DC: U.S. Office of Indian Affairs, 1943.

Brave against the Enemy: A Story of Three Generations—of the Day before Yesterday, of Yesterday, and of Tomorrow. Illus. Helen Post. Washington, DC: U.S. Bureau of Indian Affairs, 1944.

Singing Sioux Cowboy Primer. Illus. Andrew Standing Soldier. Washington, DC: U.S. Indian Service, 1945.

Sun Journey: A Story of Zuni Pueblo. Illus. Percy T. Sandy. Washington, DC: U.S. Office of Indian Affairs, 1945. Ancient City Press, 1988.

Singing Sioux Cowboy Reader. Illus. Andrew Standing Soldier. Washington, DC: U.S. Indian Service, 1947.

Linda Rita. Washington, DC: GPO, 1948.

Magic Money. Illus. Leo Politi. New York: Viking, 1950.

Looking-for-Something. Illus. Leo Politi. New York: Viking, 1952.

The Little Indian Pottery Maker. Illus. Don Perceval. New York: Melmont, 1955.

Third Monkey. Illus. Don Freeman. New York: Viking, 1956.

The Little Indian Basket Maker. Illus. Harrison Begay. New York: Melmont, 1957.

A Santo for Pasqualita. Illus. Mary Villarejo. New York: Viking, 1959.

Paco's Miracle. Illus. Agnes Tait. New York: Farrar, Straus, 1962.

This for That. Illus. Don Freeman. San Francisco: Golden Gate, 1963.

Tia Maria's Garden. Illus. Ezra Jack Keats. New York: Viking, 1963.

Bear Cub. Illus. Charles Frace. New York: Viking, 1965.

Brother André of Montreal. Illus. Harold Lang. New York: Farrar, Straus, 1967.

Arizona Is for Young People. With Glenna Craw. Lincoln: Nebraska UP, 1968.

Along Sandy Trails. Illus. Alfred A. Cohn. New York: Viking, 1969.

In the Land of Small Dragon: A Vietnamese Folktale. With Dang Manh Kha. Illus. Tony Chen. New York: Viking, 1979.

Little Herder Series for Children by Ann Nolan Clark

Little Herder in Autumn. Illus. Hoke Denetsosie. Washington, DC: U.S. Office of Indian Affairs, 1940. Ancient City Press, 1988.

Little Herder in Spring. Illus. Hoke Denetsosie. Washington, DC: U.S. Office of Indian Affairs, 1940.

Little Herder in Summer. Illus. Hoke Denetsosie. Washington, DC: U.S. Office of Indian Affairs, 1942.

Little Herder in Winter. Illus. Hoke Denetsosie. Washington, DC: U.S. Office of Indian Affairs, 1942.

Works for Adults by Ann Nolan Clark

"Newbery Award Acceptance." *Horn Book* 29 (Aug. 1953): 249–57.

Journey to the People. Essays. New York: Viking, 1969.
"A Handful of Days." In *Something about the Author Autobiography Series.* Vol.
    16. Detroit: Gale. 33–109.

Selected Studies of Ann Nolan Clark

Arbuthnot, May Hill and Zena Sutherland. *Children and Books.* 7th ed. Glenview
    Ill.: Scott Foresman, 1986.
Bishop, Claire Huchet. "Ann Nolan Clark." *Catholic Library World* 34 (Feb.
    1963): 280–86, 333.
Griese, Arnold A. "Ann Nolan Clark—Building Bridges of Cultural Under-
    standing." *Elementary English* 49 (May 1972): 648–58.
Rev. of *Circle of Seasons. Kirkus Reviews* 38 (15 May 1970): 56.
Wenzel, Evelyn. "Ann Nolan Clark: 1953 Newbery Award Winner." *Elementary
    English* 30 (Oct. 1953): 327–32.
Whitehouse, Jeanne. "The Early Life of Ann Nolan Clark: A Contextual Biogra-
    phy." Diss. U of New Mexico, 1987.

BARBARA COHEN
(1932–1992)

Shirley A. Tastad

BIOGRAPHY

Born in Asbury Park, New Jersey, on March 15, 1932, Barbara Cohen was the daughter of innkeepers, Florence and Leo Kauder. She graduated from Barnard College in New York with a B.A. in English in 1954 and married Eugene Cohen, also an innkeeper. She earned her M.A. from Rutgers University in New Brunswick, New Jersey, in 1957. Throughout her high school and college years, Cohen was an avid writer, but in the years following graduation, she found little time for her passion. She occupied herself with teaching high school English and being a wife and mother of three daughters, Leah, Sara, and Rebecca. In 1972, she returned to the writing she loved and began her prolific career with the publication of her first children's book, *The Carp in the Bathtub*. Cohen struggled doing both teaching and writing; she reluctantly gave up her teaching career to become a full-time writer, the career she pursued for the remainder of her life.

Cohen was moved by the stories she heard as a child. She had spent her summers sitting on her grandparents' porch listening to tales told by and about family members. The events and stories from her own life were inextricably intertwined with the books she read and the books she wrote later in life. When she was eight years old, she moved into the Somerville Inn, the place her parents purchased the year before her father's death. The inn was a place of importance throughout her life and in her writing.

She earned numerous awards, including the American Library Association Best Books for Young Adults citations for *Unicorns in the Rain* (1980) and for *Seven Daughters and Seven Sons* (1982); Association of Jewish Libraries Best Picture Book award for *Yussel's Prayer;* the National Jewish Book Awards for *King of the Seventh Grade* and *Yussel's Prayer;* Kenneth Smilen Present Tense Award for *King of the Seventh Grade;* American Library Association Notable Children's Books citations for *Thank You, Jackie Robinson, I Am Joseph,* and *Seven Daughters and Seven Sons;* and the Sidney Taylor Award for lifetime work. The film adaptation of *Molly's Pilgrim,* her best known work, won an Academy Award for best live action short subject of 1985. In 1991, Cohen was inducted into the New Jersey Literary Hall of Fame. She died of cancer on November 29, 1992 in Bridgewater, New Jersey.

MAJOR WORKS AND THEMES

The bulk of Cohen's juvenile writings are for younger readers. She established her writing career with her first book, *The Carp in the Bathtub* (1972), the story of a Jewish guest who keeps a carp in the bathtub in order to have the freshest fish possible when making the Passover holiday delicacy, gefilte fish. The primary thread throughout Cohen's books, whether for younger or older readers, is the feeling of difference created by her Judaism. During her childhood and adolescence she experienced subtle anti-semitic prejudice and struggled to find her place as a Jew in a broader Christian society. She was able to share her sensitivity for the Jewish perspective with her readers. As the author of nearly forty books for children and young adults, she is perhaps most noted for her children's books, but the focus of this piece is her writing for the young adult audience.

Cohen's first young adult novel, *Bitter Herbs and Honey* (1976), is set in a small New Jersey town during 1916. It chronicles the subtle antisemitism that was a part of Cohen's life. Jewish life and customs are woven into a romance between a Jewish girl, Rebecca, and a Christian boy, Peter. Becky personifies Cohen's mother, who took a giant step into the twentieth century by wanting to go to college against her father's wishes. It reflects the feelings of guilt, elation, and understanding Cohen experienced when she dated a boy who was not Jewish. Becky discovers that her heritage is an integral part of her life, but she can balance it with her desire to become an educated woman.

R, My Name Is Rosie (1978), *The Innkeeper's Daughter* (1979), and *Thank You, Jackie Robinson* (1974) grew out of Cohen's childhood experiences while living at Somerville Inn. Of the three books, *The Innkeeper's Daughter* is the most autobiographical. She describes how sixteen-year-old Rachel, daughter of a widow, feels when she wears a sophisticated black dress to a party when the other girls are wearing skirts and blouses. She shares the struggles of being overweight and feeling isolated from her peers. Cohen subtly infuses Jewish lifestyle and the feelings of antisemitism with issues of intermarriage with non-Jews. *R, My Name is Rosie* was written with her sister Susan in mind. Rosie (Susan) desperately wants to have a pet, but her mother insists that an inn is not a place for a dog. Rosie shares a friendship with the bartender, Tex, and Cohen creates a story in which Rosie's life alternates with the fairy tales she elaborates with Tex.

The book *Fat Jack* (1980) grew out of a reminiscence Cohen had after an old high school acquaintance dropped by to visit. Cohen said that Jack was someone she could have loved, despite his great size. Jack and Judy's friendship grows through work on the play *Henry IV*, when Jack is asked to play the comic part of Falstaff and Judy plays a minor character. He fears ridicule because of his weight, but he agrees to play the part. Being valued as an individual even though overweight was an enduring theme in Cohen's work.

In *Unicorns in the Rain* (1980), Cohen constructed a re-telling of the biblical story of Noah and the Flood and set it in a future filled with fear and violence. Nikki, the main character in the story, has a special love for animals and frees a rare unicorn, only to cause its death in the flood that follows.

Set in Brooklyn in 1913, *Queen for a Day* (1981) is a Cinderella story of a girl, Gertie, who fills in for her Aunt Lilly as Queen Esther in the annual local Purimspiel. She loves the attention, but is disappointed when she must return to the drudgery of caring for her mentally ill mother. Although the book does not end on a happily-ever-after note, the reader realizes that Gertie has gained hope for a brighter future.

In the contemporary *King of the Seventh Grade* (1982), Cohen creates a character who discovers what it means to be a Jew. Vic, whose divorced parents have little time for him, resents being forced to go to Hebrew School to prepare for his Bar Mitzvah. He discovers that, since his mother is not Jewish, he is not a Jew. Realizing how much Judaism means to him, he converts and celebrates his Bar Mitzvah, including his non-Jewish friends in the events.

The heroine of *Seven Daughters and Seven Sons* (1982), Buran, travels with a trading caravan disguised as a boy in an attempt to help her family by selling goods. She becomes friends with Mahmud and later, when her identity is revealed, they become lovers. This re-telling of an Arabic folktale affirms Buran's value as a clever, intelligent female character in a society which held contempt for women.

Cohen's next two young adult novels, *Lovers' Games* (1983) and *Roses* (1984), deal with romance and are based on genres she enjoyed. *Lovers' Games,* modeled on a gothic romance, focuses on a heroine who undergoes a transformation after visiting a beauty shop and dress store. *Roses,* a contemporary *Beauty and the Beast*, presents the theme of accepting one's own sexuality and laying aside guilt and grief. Although Cohen expressed her pleasure in writing these books, neither was as well received as many of her other young adult novels. The characters are shallow and leave the reader wanting.

When writing *Coasting* (1985), Cohen chose to return to characters more reflective of people in her own life. She uses her children's experiences in college as a basis for the story. Maddy, a student at Barnard College, allows Metz to sleep on her floor while he looks for a job. Their friendship becomes strained when Metz takes advantage of Maddy's romantic affection for him. The two go their separate ways until Metz learns to reach out to others and Maddy decides that she is not as unattractive and overweight as she thought. Again, we see Cohen's sensitivity concerning weight and her desire for character (self) acceptance in spite of it.

In her next teen romance, *People Like Us* (1987), Cohen vicariously experiences the attention she never received in high school through her character, Dinah. Dinah, tall and thin, is noticed by the handsome football star, but must battle to get her family to accept him in this story of reverse prejudice. The book explores intergenerational misunderstandings coupled with Jewish family customs and concerns.

Tell Us Your Secret (1989) evolved during a two-week writers' conference for adolescents that Cohen taught. She used the book as a means of exploring the pain of the second-generation survivors of the Holocaust. The book focuses on interrelationships and personal growth through character dialogue and has received some criticism because the characters are unevenly drawn.

CRITICAL RECEPTION

Barbara Cohen, as an author of children's and young adult books, reflects an understanding of the feelings and emotions of her readers. Drawing on her childhood and adolescent experiences, Cohen created believable characters with real problems. Cyrisse Jaffee said of *The Innkeeper's Daughter,*

"A sensitive and satisfying semi-autobiographical novel. . . . This is one story about coming of age that is not laden with problems or crises, yet rings true" (86).

The predominant thread throughout Cohen's work is her focus on the feelings of those who feel unacceptable for one reason or another. Her vivid recollections center on how it feels to be an outsider, Jewish, overweight, and a member of a nontraditional family—growing up in an inn where her mother served guests alcohol. Cohen allows her readers to experience through her characters the insecurity and pain of being an outsider. In an attempt to maintain cultural and ethnic identity, outsiders have their own prejudices. Zena Sutherland says that *People Like Us* is a believable story concerning prejudice expressed by "people who decry bigotry in principle but feel their own bias is rational." Sutherland also notes that Cohen is "too good a storyteller to fabricate an unconvincing plot or unconvincing characters" (5).

Cohen's writing was her life and that life represented what it meant to be Jewish within the context of a Christian society. Her young adult novels capture the universal struggles of growing up and accepting oneself, acknowledging the part of one's life that represents the spiritual needs within us. Few mainstream authors have risked exploring the spiritual aspects of adolescence; yet Cohen unabashedly allows her characters to pursue their spiritual and cultural heritage amidst their broader Christian and secular worlds. In *King of the Seventh Grade,* Vic, a popular boy, wants to maintain his popularity with his non-Jewish friends, but he makes a spiritual decision to pursue his Jewish heritage. Adolescents need spiritual role models, whatever their faith, in literature to help them identify and accept themselves. "Well crafted, with sharply delineated characters, this probably has an extra dimension for Jewish readers, but Vic's perplexities and his eventual realizations will touch many" (*Booklist* 243).

BIBLIOGRAPHY

Young Adult Fiction by Barbara Cohen

Bitter Herbs and Honey. New York: Lothrop, 1976.
R, My Name Is Rosie. New York: Lothrop, 1978.
The Innkeeper's Daughter. New York: Lothrop, 1979.
Fat Jack. New York: Atheneum, 1980.
Unicorns in the Rain. New York: Atheneum, 1980.
Queen for a Day. New York: Lothrop, 1981.
King of the Seventh Grade. New York: Lothrop, 1982.

Seven Daughters and Seven Sons. With Bahija Lovejoy. New York: Atheneum, 1982.
Lovers' Games. New York: Atheneum, 1983.
Roses. Illus. John Steptoe. New York: Lothrop, 1984.
Coasting. New York: Lothrop, 1985.
People Like Us. New York: Bantam, 1987.
Tell Us Your Secret. New York: Bantam, 1989.

Works for Children by Barbara Cohen

The Carp in the Bathtub. Illus. Joan Halpern. New York: Lothrop, 1972.
Thank You, Jackie Robinson. Illus. Richard Coffouri. New York: Lothrop, 1974.
Where's Florrie? Illus. Joan Halpern. New York: Lothrop, 1976.
Benny. New York: Lothrop, 1977.
The Binding of Isaac. Illus. Charles Mikolaycak. New York: Lothrop, 1978.
I Am Joseph. Illus. Charles Mikolaycak. New York: Lothrop, 1980.
Lovely Vassilisa. Illus. Anatoly Ivanov. New York: Atheneum, 1980.
Yussel's Prayer. Illus. Michael Deraney. New York: Lothrop, 1981.
The Demon Who Would Not Die. Illus. Anatoly Ivanov. New York: Atheneum, 1982.
Gooseberries to Oranges. Illus. Beverly Brodsky. New York: Lothrop, 1982.
Molly's Pilgrim. Illus. Michael Deraney. New York: Lothrop, 1983.
Here Come the Purim Players! Illus. Beverly Brodsky. New York: Lothrop, 1984.
The Secret Grove. Illus. Michael Deraney. New York: Union of American Hebrew Congregations, 1985.
The Christmas Revolution. Illus. Diane de Groat. New York: Lothrop, 1987.
Even Higher. Illus. Anatoly Ivanov. New York: Lothrop, 1987.
First Fast. New York: Union of American Hebrew Congregations, 1987.
The Donkey's Story: A Bible Story. Illus. Susan Jeanne Cohen. New York: Lothrop, 1988.
Four Canterbury Tales. Illus. Trina Schart Hyman. New York: Lothrop, 1988.
The Orphan Game. Illus. Diane de Groat. New York: Lothrop, 1988.
The Long Way Home. New York: Lothrop, 1990.
Two Hundred Thirteen Valentines. Illus. Will Clay. New York: Holt, 1991.
Make a Wish Molly. Illus. Jan N. Jones. New York: Delacorte, l994.

Selected Studies of Barbara Cohen

Jaffee, Cyrisse. Rev. of *The Innkeeper's Daughter. School Library Journal* 25.8 (1979): 86.
Rev. of *King of the Seventh Grade. Booklist* 78.1 (1982): 243.
Sutherland, Zena. Rev. of *People Like Us. Bulletin of the Center for Children's Books* 39.1 (1987): 5.

BEATRICE CULLETON
(1949–   )

Julie A. Davies

BIOGRAPHY

The youngest of four children, Beatrice Culleton was born on August 27, 1949, in St. Boniface, Manitoba, to Louis and Mary Clara Mosionier. Growing up in foster homes in and around Winnipeg, she was a ward of the Children's Aid Society from the age of three. Although she was born into the Métis culture, her foster care placements were with white families. With the exception of several years with one sister, she was placed in foster homes separate from her siblings. At the age of seventeen, she moved to Toronto where she lived for seven years. She attended George Brown College and subsequently worked as a bookkeeper. Twice married, she lived on a farm in Oakbank, Manitoba, and then moved closer to Winnipeg, in Vita. At the time of this writing her two children, Billy and Debbie, are twenty-six and twenty-one respectively.

Both of her sisters, Vivian and Kathy, committed suicide. After the second suicide in October 1980, Beatrice decided to write. Her largely autobiographical novel, *In Search of April Raintree*, was published in 1983, followed the next year by a revised edition bearing the new title, *April Raintree.*

She became manager of Pemmican Press in 1983 and has worked with the Winnipeg Coalition on Native Child Welfare as well as the Manitoba

Métis Association. In 1985 she published a children's book, *Spirit of the White Bison*.

In 1990 she lived in Toronto where she was the playwright in residence at Native Earth Performing Arts. That same year she wrote an as yet unpublished play, *Night of the Trickster*. In addition, she completed a filmscript, *Walker*, for the National Film Board of Canada.

Culleton, the name under which her two books are published, is her name from her second marriage. She has since started using her birth surname, Mosionier, and any further work will be published under that name.

MAJOR WORKS AND THEMES

Just as Beatrice Culleton comes from a tradition that is neither entirely Native nor entirely white, she offers in *April Raintree* a work that is also not firmly grounded. This novel is neither autobiography nor fiction, nor is it a successful blending of both. Sometimes it seems as true as is imaginable, sometimes it seems to lie to us with impunity. This novel is also neither Native nor white. There are no recurring Native themes such as connection to the land, spirituality, communal cooperative living, or the wisdom of elders. Instead of mythic parallels drawn from centuries-old oral tradition, we have simply the story of two sisters, removed by a government agency from their neglectful, alcoholic parents and placed in the often bleak and horrific world of social workers and foster care homes. Likewise, a white tradition in Culleton's writing is equally absent. Nowhere in her text will the reader find the style, grace, and polished prose that critics of good literature praise. However, despite the often awkward, never artful writing, we find in *April Raintree* a story with the power to move, to teach, and to communicate.

Except for a brief time together, the sisters Cheryl and April Raintree grow up in a succession of separate foster homes. The description of the working of the foster care system and the clearly racist, sexist, and classist biases held by many of the social workers are presented in vivid detail. Although Cheryl is placed for a time with a family that cares for her and nurtures her, April's time is largely spent in an abusive setting where she is no more than an ill-treated servant. Cheryl is clearly Indian in appearance, and from an early age, with the support of her foster family, learns pride in her Métis heritage. April, conversely, looks more white and sees her only hope for a better life in assimilation in the white world. Cheryl enters university and becomes a regular worker at the Indian Friendship Center in Winnipeg. April rejects her Indian side and when presented with the opportunity, marries into white society. For both women, however, idealism meets with harsh reality. Unable to keep up with the demands of society, April's marriage collapses. Cheryl attempts to work with Native women but everywhere is faced with the "native girl syndrome" she was warned about by one of her childhood caseworkers. Eventually she, too, falls prey to alcoholism, prostitution, pregnancy, and a violent relationship. For her the disillusionment is too great and ends with a suicidal leap from the same bridge that claimed her mother years before. Through the loss of Cheryl, April comes to accept the reality of her own mixed heritage. Cheryl has left a son behind, however, and the reader is left to wonder if April will be able, through her nephew, to witness a new generation of Métis.

Initially conceived as a story about alcoholism, the novel *In Search of April Raintree* became a much more essentialist work, exploring the experience of living as a Métis, a person whose heritage is mixed Native and European.

The earliest settlement of Canada in the seventeenth century centered in large part around the enormously profitable fur trade with Europe. Both French and English settlers engaged in this rugged combination of business and adventure. As white men pursued the fur trade deeper into the wilderness of the Canadian interior, the trading posts they established became centers of economic activity for both the Native trappers and the white traders. Since the harsh winter and difficult terrain made winter travel impossible, many whites "wintered over" in these outposts. The economic, political, and personal alliances that formed between the Natives and the whites were often accomplished through the natural bridging skill of the Native women. The so-called country marriages between the white traders and the Native women produced generations of children known as Métis, or "mixed blood." In the nineteenth century, with the end of the reign of the major fur-trading companies, large groups of Métis people, especially in the area that became Manitoba, were left with one foot in each culture. Paul Wilson has suggested that while recognized as one of Canada's Native Peoples, the Métis are genetically "the epitome of Canadian history, a mingling of the blood and tradition of Europe with the aboriginal history of this continent" (30).

Just as the Métis evolved as a genetically and generationally layered people, the story *In Search of April Raintree*, revised a year later as *April Raintree*, offers to both reader and teacher a story containing many layers and versions. On the surface this supposedly true-to-life, "autobiographical fiction" proceeds often awkwardly. Writing in the journal *Ariel*, Helen Hoy finds, "The rhetorical conventions which her plain-speaking, expository narrative voice invokes are less those of fiction or even dramatized story-telling than of family history of the everyday recounting of personal experience, aligning her rhetorically with thousands of unofficial, daily chroniclers" (178). And like those unofficial chroniclers, Culleton's story within the text often shifts from the version of one protagonist to that of the next, or from first-person narrative to letter or journal entry to dialogue to prepared speeches to courtroom testimony. Outside the text there is further shifting. One year after the original publication, Culleton, at the urging of Manitoba Education, agreed to revisions of her text. In order to meet school requirements she removed sexually explicit language from the description of a rape and eliminated other scenes with overtly sexual content. Other parts of the narrative were tightened stylistically and in addition details in many scenes were either removed or added.

April's first foster mother, Mrs. Dion, explains to her that "telling the truth is always easier and better than telling lies" (*April Raintree* 22). But April and Cheryl find that advice confusing. They are often lied to, accused of lying, and forced to lie to protect themselves. In a sense, they learn to form their stories to suit their audiences. The true story of April Raintree and therefore the true story of Beatrice Culleton remain elusive. The text presents us with puzzles and challenges but ultimately offers a rich blending of reality and fiction and enormously valuable insights into poverty, racism, alcoholism, and an area rarely explored in fiction: the lives of children removed from their parents and placed in the foster care system.

In 1985, following the revision of *April Raintree*, Beatrice Culleton published a children's novella, *Spirit of the White Bison*. Although there are many Native legends and myths surrounding the white buffalo or bison, Culleton has chosen not to be influenced by them. She has instead crafted a native story that she hoped would be suitable for animation. *Spirit of the White Bison* is in the form of an autobiography of a female white bison called Little White Buffalo. The story is set in the nineteenth century, at the time of the nearly total extermination of the vast herds of buffalo on the North American plains. As Little White Buffalo learns about the world around her, she begins to understand the balance of nature. She experiences the dangers of the landscape and the weather. There is also the ever-present danger of predators, including Native and Métis hunters. The white bison calf learns to accept all of these as part of her world's natural order. She watches the Natives as they hunt buffalo to provide food, clothing, and shelter for their families. She is befriended by a Métis hunter named Lone Wolf who respects and values her as an exceptional creature. Neither of them, however, proves to be a match for the sweeping decimation that occurs when the white hunters with their organization and firearms arrive to clear the plains. *Spirit of the White Bison* aims to provide children with a glimpse into the past and hopefully constructs a lesson for the future.

CRITICAL RECEPTION

The reviews that followed the 1983 publication of *In Search of April Raintree* and its 1984 revision as *April Raintree* generally agreed that while stylistically awkward the first novel by a young Métis woman was a compellingly honest account of modern Native life.

Noted Canadian author Margaret Laurence provided the following for the publication of the revised edition: "One cannot read this moving account of two Métis sisters without feeling their terrible anguish, bewilderment and anger as they try in their different ways to live in a society that frequently rejects and abuses them, as it has rejected and abused their parents and ancestors. The story is a tragic one, yet its final outcome is one of affirmation and bitterly won resolve."

Others, however, writing for more objective publications, rarely reviewed this work in an entirely favorable manner. "What the book lacks in literary polish is more than made up for in compassion, understanding and beautifully controlled emotion" (Sigurdson 43). Reviewer Paul Wilson found it "an almost artlessly told story" and then compared it to Maria Campbell's *Halfbreed* as "a woman's search for identity and her struggle to overcome degradation and exist in harmony with two vastly different worlds, both potentially her own by birthright" (30).

In her opening paragraphs of "Contemporary Native Women's Voices in Literature," Agnes Grant begins a more careful critical evaluation. "Native literature," she asserts, "means native people telling their own stories, in their own ways, unfettered by criteria from another time and place" (125). She goes on to explain why *April Raintree* is at best called Native literature: "The style is admittedly very simple. Beatrice Culleton writes as she and many people like her speak. . . . Perhaps the style is painful for those immersed in skillful prose . . . but is it just to confuse simple style with a simplistic book? On the contrary . . . this book works to good effect, communicates, moves us . . . makes us see" (129).

In the most recent and most comprehensive critical work on Beatrice Culleton to date, Helen Hoy writes of teaching *In Search of April Raintree* to university students and then goes on to use postmodern theory to examine the text. In "Nothing But The Truth: Discursive Transparency in Beatrice Culleton," Hoy describes student reactions to the text as mixed. While some found the book "simplistic and poorly written" (157), others were deeply touched emotionally. Her own critical analysis follows and is both thorough and responsible. She finds that Culleton's writing "fuses pragmatic and artistic ends, and grows out of the consciousness of community. . . . Her book writes beyond the ending of the classic domestic novel or the romance quest, opening up beyond individual self-development into a vision of collective action. If novelty, authorial self-expression, and originality of execution give way in Culleton's aesthetic credo to instrumental and communal values, then her writing may require different methods of evaluation, recognizing their values also as artistic achievements" (171).

BIBLIOGRAPHY

Young Adult Fiction by Beatrice Culleton

April Raintree. Winnipeg: Pemmican Publications, 1984.
Spirit of the White Bison. Winnipeg: Pemmican Publications, 1985.

Other Works by Beatrice Culleton

"The Pain and Pleasure of that First Novel." *Pemmican Journal* (Winter 1981): 7–10.
In Search of April Raintree. Winnipeg: Pemmican Publications, 1983.
"Images of Native People and Their Effects." *School Libraries in Canada* (Spring 1987): 47–52.

Selected Studies of Beatrice Culleton

"Beatrice Culleton." *Contemporary Challenges: Conversations with Canadian-Native Authors*." Ed. Harmut Lutz. Saskatoon, SK: Fifth House, 1991. 97–105.
Bridgeman, J. M. "This Was Her Story: An Interview with Beatrice Culleton." *Prairie Fire* 4–5 (1983): 42–49.
Fee, Margery. "Upsetting Fake Ideas: Jeannette Armstrong's *Slash* and Beatrice Culleton's *April Raintree*." *Canadian Literature* (1990): 168–82.
Francis, Anne. Rev. of *In Search of April Raintree*. *Quill and Quire* (1983): 20.
Grant, Agnes. "Contemporary Native Women's Voices in Literature." *Canadian Literature* (1990): 124–32.
Hoy, Helen. "Nothing but the Truth: Discursive Transparency in Beatrice Culleton." *Ariel* 25.1 (1994): 154–84.
Moher, Frank. "April in the Métis Netherworld." *Alberta Report* 10 Oct. 1983: 50.
Russell, Judith. Rev. of *April Raintree*. *Queen's Quarterly* (1987):190–93.

Sigurdson, Norman. "Métis Novel Overwhelming." *Winnipeg Free Press*, 30 July 1983: 43.

Wilson, Paul. Rev. of *In Search of April Raintree*. *Books in Canada* (1984): 30.

Cliff (Chauncey Clifford Vernon) Faulknor (1913-)

Karen Sands

BIOGRAPHY

Chauncey Clifford Vernon Faulknor was born March 13, 1913, in Vancouver, British Columbia, the only son of George Henry Faulknor, a building contractor, and Rhoda Anne (née Baldry) Faulknor. He showed early promise as a writer, winning a short story contest before graduating from high school in 1929. However, the Depression years did not provide a conducive environment for a struggling young writer, and Faulknor spent the early thirties working at a variety of jobs, including clerking at a bank, harvesting in Alberta and Manitoba, working as a plumber, working in a mill, and acting as an assistant forest ranger in British Columbia.

The increasingly unstable world situation led Faulknor to join the Canadian army in 1937. He served first as an artillery gunner in the Royal Canadian Artillery, and then as a marine engineer sergeant for the Canadian Army Water Transport, beginning in 1939. In this capacity, Faulknor served out the rest of the war years. In 1945, at the age of thirty-two, Faulknor left the army and returned to British Columbia, where he began work on a degree in plant science at the University of British Columbia. He graduated in 1949 with first class honors and his B.S. in agriculture.

For the next several years, Faulknor served as a land inspector for the British Columbia Department of Lands and Forests. He enjoyed the opportunity to work outdoors, but he also longed to get back to writing. He began writing articles for newspapers in both Vancouver and Victoria, particularly the *Victoria Times*. However, he keenly felt his responsibility to his wife (since 1943), Elizabeth Sloan, and their two children, and it was not until 1954, when he was offered a regular position on the national farm magazine *Country Guide*, that Faulknor finally began writing full time.

His *Country Guide* work led him, after a year in Winnipeg, Manitoba, to Calgary, Alberta, where he became the magazine's western field editor, a position he held until 1975. Faulknor thrived in Calgary, and took a great interest in the people and events of western Canada, including the rodeo circuit which culminated every year in the events of the Calgary Stampede. He wrote nonfiction articles about western Canadian life for several magazines and newspapers in both Canada and England, including the cattle industry's *Cattlemen* magazine.

In 1957, his first short story appeared in *The Scout Annual*, a British magazine, and this began Faulknor's fiction career in earnest. After several years of publishing short stories in various magazines, Faulknor had his first novel published, *The White Calf* (1965). This book, an adventure story of a young Native American boy in the mid–nineteenth century, was extremely well received. Its reception led Faulknor to continue to write for young people.

Although Faulknor was successful as an author, both of fiction and nonfiction for children and adults, he always retained a tongue-in-cheek humility about his writing. Despite the many awards he received for his work, he continued to hold onto a recommendation from the plumbing firm he had worked with in the 1930s in case he ever needed to change careers. This need never materialized, of course. His early careers had taken him far away from the short story prize he had won in high school, but once Faulknor got the chance to write on a regular basis, he never stopped.

MAJOR WORKS AND THEMES

Faulknor wrote six novels for young people. Three of them, including his first novel, *The White Calf*, form a trilogy concerning the lives of a tribe of Native American Blackfeet in the mid–nineteenth century. Although Faulknor is not a Native American, he chose to tell the stories in this trilogy through the eyes of Eagle Child, a young member of the Piegan Blackfeet tribe.

The White Calf, the first story in the trilogy, tells the story of how twelve-year-old Eagle Child finds a white buffalo calf and, instead of shooting it, brings it back to the tribe as a symbol of good fortune sent from the gods to protect his tribe. As both boy and calf grow, Eagle Child learns that if he wants to be seen as a man, he must take the responsibilities of one, including eventually letting the white calf (who has become quite destructive) go back to the buffalo herd. As such, it is a pleasant *Bildungsroman* in the tradition of Marjorie Rawlings' *The Yearling*. Faulknor does a particularly good job with the relationships between the father, Night Rider, and his two sons, Eagle Child and War Bonnet. The story occasionally suffers from a change in point of view, from Eagle Child to War Bonnet, but by and large it is engaging and interesting.

As a work of fiction about Native Americans or First Peoples, *The White Calf* is still successful, but far from problem free. Faulknor does an excellent job with historical details, showing that his efforts at careful research are not entirely in vain. Faulknor consulted with both historians and Native Americans in writing his novel, striving for an accurate depiction of Native American life in the mid–nineteenth century. However, he did not entirely succeed. Much of the novel builds up to the annual Sun Dance, an important tribal ritual. Therefore, the fact that the Sun Dance is not ever described, and in fact is mentioned only before and after its occurrence, is a serious lapse in Faulknor's story. The reader is left to wonder why the Sun Dance seemed to hold such importance for the tribe if no time is given to it in the story. Faulknor's biggest failing, however, in *The White Calf* is its language. The Native Americans' speech is often stiff and somewhat overdone, sounding more like a bad Hollywood western than the natural dialogue of real people. Also, Faulknor lapses on occasion into a Eurocentric point of view—for example, Eagle Child describes the land surrounding the tribe's camp as empty, something no Native American who lived on the land would do. These problems detract from Faulknor's otherwise sensitive portrayal of the book's characters.

Unfortunately, the language and dialogue problems do not disappear in the remaining books in the series, though they become less frequent. For example, in the second book in the trilogy, *The White Peril* (1966), Faulknor introduces white Americans through Eagle Child's eyes. The whites are of great interest to Eagle Child, especially their weaponry and shipbuilding. However, although Eagle Child admires the whites, Faulknor depicts them as bigoted and stupid without exception. The only "good" white in this story is "the Tall One," who acts as a go-between for the Native Americans and the whites; however, he is only half-white, the other half being, of course, Native American. Any other white acting in the Native Americans' behalf does so only from fear of attack. This lack of balance in the portrayal of the whites may have been intended to make the young white reader think twice about how whites view themselves in history; unfortunately, it also makes Eagle Child seem naive and stupid for admiring such obvious villains. In the third book in the trilogy, *The Smoke Horse* (1968), the boys have grown up.

Faulknor's difficulty in attempting to sensitively portray the Native American also shows up in a novel that is not about Native Americans at all, *The In Betweener* (1967). In this story, Native Americans are referred to as "redskins" by an otherwise sympathetic character. Further, at one point in the story, the two white boys who serve as the story's main characters are interested in Indian lore. The tale of Indian lore that follows, however, is not about Native Americans at all but about white settlers "escaping." The author does not say from what the settlers are escaping, but the obvious answer is the "redskin." *The In Betweener*, while not as strong a story as *The White Calf*, does not have the dialogue and language problems apparent in Faulknor's Native American trilogy, and the more believable, less stilted, dialogue leads to the conviction that it is in *The In Betweener* that we get Faulknor's most authentic voice. If this is the case, then Faulknor's commitment to providing an accurate, sensitive portrayal of the Native American is left in serious doubt.

His novel, *Johnny Eagleclaw* (1982), tends to bear out this doubt. *Johnny Eagleclaw* is a story of Native Americans, but unlike the White Calf series it has a contemporary setting. The main character, Johnny, is a Native American young adult who leaves the school run by whites in order to become a rodeo star. The novel is an interesting examination of what it means to be a Native American in a white society—Johnny is accused of being an "apple," red on the outside and white on the inside, for example— but, like Faulknor's other novels, the story is marred by stiff dialogue and simplistic solutions to complex problems. The whites in the story are, as in *The White Calf* trilogy, mostly portrayed as obtuse and therefore unwittingly racist; Johnny's teacher at the white school and the daughter of the owner of the ranch where Johnny works are two examples of this characterization. A notable exception to this portrayal is the principal at the white school, who, though white, is the champion of the Native American students in his school. In this way, Faulknor has moved beyond the totally unbalanced picture of whites in *The White Peril*, but in all cases, white characters in Faulknor's Native American novels remain predictable and stereotyped.

It is unusual to find novels about Native Americans authored by whites that pay such close attention to historical detail as those written by Cliff Faulknor. Throughout his books, he confronts the stereotype that all Native Americans are the same, and he does not sentimentalize the life of the Native

American as many authors do. For his authentic portrayal of the tribal relationships and other details of Native American life, Faulknor certainly deserves a great deal of credit. Unfortunately, this effort is too often lost in Faulknor's uncomfortably stilted dialogue, and potential readers may be put off by this, thereby missing both the good adventure and interesting historical detail in Faulknor's novels.

CRITICAL RECEPTION

Despite winning several awards for his young adult fiction, including the Little, Brown Award for Fiction and the Vicky Metcalf Award, Faulknor has not received a great deal of critical attention. His first novel, *The White Calf*, which earned him the Little, Brown Award in 1964, was most heavily reviewed. This book won many recommendations from reviewers, and was subsequently published in Great Britain and the Soviet Union. *The White Calf* was also turned into a radio play and a Canadian Broadcasting Corporation television drama, which won the Alberta Television Drama Award in 1972.

None of Faulknor's remaining books received half that much attention. *The White Peril* was reviewed by many of the same publications which had examined *The White Calf*; however, reviewers were less enthusiastic. The *Library Journal*, for example, which had recommended Faulknor's first book, found *The White Peril* to be only "an average Indian adventure" (4330). Faulknor's third book in the trilogy, *The Smoke Horse* (1968), was not reviewed by the *Library Journal* at all. Perhaps one reason for this can be found in a comment made in *The Oxford Companion to Canadian History and Literature*. The reviewer, who enjoyed Faulknor's earlier books, claimed in regard to *The Smoke Horse* that "because the boys are grown up in this book they have lost their freshness and ebullience" (33).

In general, reviewers were impressed with Faulknor's ability to portray Native American life, both historically and in contemporary settings. *Books in Canada* called Faulknor's *Johnny Eagleclaw* "a sensitive portrayal of Johnny's fight against discrimination" (11) and *The Young Reader's Review* lauded *The White Peril* for "giving a sincere appreciation of the Indian's ways" (11). Most of the reviews, however, tended to focus less on Faulknor's stories as Native American novels and more on the books as adventure stories for boys. The *Times Literary Supplement* of London, for example, reviewed Faulknor's books with those of Jack London in an article titled "Wild and Tame." This focus on adventure is appropriate, for

Faulknor's books are more memorable for their exciting action than for their Native American characters.

BIBLIOGRAPHY

Young Adult Fiction by Cliff (Chauncey Clifford Vernon) Faulknor

The White Calf: The Story of Eagle Child, the Piegan Boy, Who Found a White Buffalo Calf Said to Have Been Sent by the Above Ones. Illus. Gerald Tailfeathers. Toronto: Little Brown, 1965. London: Dent, 1966.

The White Peril. Illus. Gerald Tailfeathers. Toronto and Boston: Little Brown; London: Dent, 1966.

The In Betweener. Illus. Leonard Shortall. Toronto: Little Brown, 1967.

The Smoke Horse. Illus. W. F. Phillipps. Toronto: McClelland and Stewart, 1968.

West to Cattle Country. Illus. Gordon McLean. Toronto: McClelland and Stewart, 1975.

Johnny Eagleclaw. Illus. Richard A. Conroy. Edmonton: John LeBel, 1982.

Other Works by Cliff (Chauncey Clifford Vernon) Faulknor

The Romance of Beef. Winnipeg: Public Press, 1966.

Pen and Plow. Winnipeg: Public Press, 1976.

Turn Him Loose. Saskatoon, SK: Western Producer, 1977.

Manuscript collection and archival material, The University of Calgary and The Kerlan Collection of the University of Minnesota.

Selected Studies of Cliff (Chauncey Clifford Vernon) Faulknor

Brenner, H. A. Rev. of *The White Peril*. *Library Journal* 91 (15 Oct. 1966): 4330.

Hamilton, K. A., ed. *Canada Writes! The Members' Book of the Writers' Union of Canada*. Toronto: The Writers' Union of Canada, 1977. 110–11.

MacDonald, Grace. "Cliff Faulknor." *Profiles*. Ed. Irma McDonough. Ottawa: Canadian Library Association, 1975.

Rev. of *Johnny Eagleclaw*. *Books in Canada* 11 (Dec. 1982): 11.

Rev. of *The White Peril*. *The Young Readers' Review* 3 (Nov. 1966): 11.

Sorfleet, John Robert. "Cliff Faulknor." *Twentieth Century Children's Writers*. Ed. Tracy Chevalier. 3rd ed. New York: St. James, 1989. 330–31.

Toye, William, ed. *The Oxford Companion to Canadian History and Literature (Supplement)*. Toronto: OUP, 1973. 32–33.

LOUISE FITZHUGH
(1928–1974)

Sherrie A. Inness

BIOGRAPHY

Author, artist, and illustrator Louise Fitzhugh was born in Memphis, Tennessee, on October 5, 1928, to Millsaps Fitzhugh and Louise Perkins. While Millsaps came from a wealthy Tennessee family and was a well-known attorney, Louise Perkins was his social inferior. Their marriage lasted for only a year; after a heated custody battle, Millsaps gained custody of his daughter. Young Louise was raised by her wealthy grandparents, but her childhood was often marred by unhappiness and insecurity.

Later on, growing up in Tennessee with her father and Sally Taylor, his new wife, Fitzhugh felt confined by the expectations of how a girl from a wealthy southern family should behave; she also abhorred the pervasive southern racism and disliked her social responsibilities. Her years at the Hutchinson School for young ladies only emphasized that her place was not in Memphis. In addition to disliking her role as a genteel southern debutante, Fitzhugh felt further alienated from her surroundings because she was a lesbian.

After a brief stay at Southwestern College in Memphis and at Florida Southern College in Lakeland, she left for the Northeast. New York City and Bard College offered Fitzhugh the intellectual and emotional freedom that she craved. Fitzhugh attended Bard, but left six months before graduation to pursue a painting career. Although still dependent upon family money for her weekly income, Fitzhugh managed to find her individual identity in New York City. She studied art and discovered the pleasures of bohemian Greenwich Village. She also met a wide range of artists and intellectuals, including Sandra Scoppettone, Maurice Sendak, Lorraine Hansberry, and Jane Wagner, who offered her the support that her family did not. They appreciated Fitzhugh for herself, and did not withhold their approval because she was a lesbian and an artist. Fitzhugh was not secretive about her sexual orientation, and found that New York was more conducive to being open about her sexuality than Memphis.

The early 1960s were an extremely productive time for Fitzhugh, a period in which she wrote the book *Harriet the Spy* (1964) that was to bring her lasting fame. Her art career also flourished. Her paintings—often satirical portrayals of people—reflected the same interest in satire and caricature that was evident in her children's fiction, which she had started writing in the 1950s.

The late 1960s and early 1970s were less productive for Fitzhugh, a possible reason being that her father died during that time, leaving her with many responsibilities connected with her inherited wealth. Only a few years later, time ran out for Louise Fitzhugh, too. On November 19, 1974, she met a tragically early death. At age forty-six, she died of an aneurysm in the brain, ten days before her third novel, *Nobody's Family Is Going to Change,* appeared. Rumors flew that she killed herself, but those have been largely discounted. Although her career was cut short prematurely, Fitzhugh made a notable impact on children's literature and will long be remembered for her sensitivity to what it means to be an outsider in our culture and for her astute portrayal of the adult world through the eyes of children.

MAJOR WORKS AND THEMES

Harriet the Spy (1964), Fitzhugh's second novel, is commonly regarded as her masterpiece, receiving far more attention than her first novel, the picture book *Suzuki Beane* (1961), which suffered from a thin plot and undeveloped characters. Challenging traditional notions of desirable deportment for girls, *Harriet the Spy* focuses on a nontraditional heroine, eleven-year-old Harriet M. Welsch, who delights in spying on people and in keeping a detailed notebook about others' shortcomings. The novel introduces many of the themes that Fitzhugh will continue to study throughout her writing career: loneliness, rejection, conformity, the place of the outsider in society, and the role of the artist. We also see the author's interest in revealing the hypocrisy of the adult world, seeing it through the eyes of a child.

The sequel to *Harriet the Spy*, *The Long Secret* (1965), is a less successful work. Harriet and Beth Ellen, the central characters, appear oddly washed out and colorless when compared to the vividly drawn characters of Fitzhugh's previous novel. *The Long Secret*, however, does have a few redeeming features. Like many of Fitzhugh's works, it perceptively explores the chasm that exists between parents and children. The novel also has a number of minor characters who are as fascinating as any of Fitzhugh's creations. The Preacher, an African-American man who quotes from the Bible, is one of the most sensitively portrayed characters in Fitzhugh's novel. Like many of Fitzhugh's outsiders, the Preacher provides a voice of reason about the world's foibles.

Bang, Bang, You're Dead! (1969), although not explicitly about racism, does focus on the issue of difference and our rejection of those who are in one way or another not like us. This picture book discusses how war is started simply because people see others as alien. The oversimplistic text, however, does not match the sophistication of Fitzhugh's drawings. Similarly, Fitzhugh's three *I Am* books (*I Am Three, I Am Four,* and *I Am Five,* which were published after the author's death) have simple story lines, geared toward very young children.

Fitzhugh's most important novel about racial issues is *Nobody's Family Is Going to Change* (1974), which was later made into a television movie and a Tony Award-winning play. This book tells the story of a well-off black family that can afford private schooling and a white maid, living in New York City. Emancipation Sheridan (Emma) is a fat black girl with dreams of being a lawyer. Her seven-year-old brother, Willie, imagines becoming a dancer, despite his father's desire that he become a lawyer. Emma and Willie's parents, William and Virginia Sheridan, cannot understand why their children wish to pursue such atypical careers.

The novel is particularly notable for its critique of stereotypical gender roles. Emma tells her mother, "Willie wants to do a girl's thing, and I want to do a boy's thing." That is unacceptable for Mr. and Mrs. Sheridan. Emma's mother assumes her daughter is looking forward to getting married and having children, and completely ignores Emma's ardent interest in the law. Mr. Sheridan believes his son should avoid being a dancer, since dancing is for "sissies." Even when Willie lands a role in a Broadway musical, his father is not thrilled, but, instead, appalled.

The novel is also about anger and people's needs to express their rage against injustice. Emma, for instance, joins a secret army of children who unite to defend children's rights. Willie resists his parents' attempts to take him away from the theater. Rather than being obedient children, Emma and Willie rebel against the society that pigeonholes them according to gender. Fitzhugh points out that anger can be a beneficial force, which can gradually change the world, but one must first change oneself and one's own attitudes.

Fitzhugh's novel lacks the usual happy ending in which parents and children resolve their differences; instead, the Sheridans retain the views they started with and still do not see eye to eye. The book's message, ultimately, is that some people will not change, that they are too set in their ways. Emma muses about her parents: "They are going to be the way they are the rest of their lives." However, by the end of the novel, Emma at least has recognized that she can still be a lawyer even though her father and mother disapprove. Fitzhugh's message for anyone who is an outsider is to believe in yourself, no matter what others might say. The novel also makes a plea for Emma, Willie, and other "misfits," those individuals who do not seem to fulfill society's expectations; individuals are unique, Fitzhugh points out, and they should not be forced to change in order to fit a single mold.

Fitzhugh's last novel, *Sport* (1979), which was first published five years after her death, touches on multicultural issues, but in a far less absorbing fashion than in *Nobody's Family Is Going to Change*. Sport, Harriet's friend and the book's hero, has a diverse group of friends, including a Chicano, a Jew, and a black, but these individuals appear stereotyped. This novel does have a few notable episodes, such as when Sport's mother reveals her anti-semitic feelings and when police officers want to arrest Sport and his friends because of their cultural backgrounds, but these few scenes do not stop the novel from being of less importance than Fitzhugh's other work. In *Sport*, Fitzhugh seems more interested in creating light-hearted farce than in tackling thorny social problems.

CRITICAL RECEPTION

Louise Fitzhugh's fiction has always met with both praise and condemnation. Adult readers are particularly uneasy with Fitzhugh's often scathing inspections of adult behavior and her emphasis on childhood cynicism. Early reviewers were particularly severe with *Harriet the Spy*, calling its heroine "egocentric and mean" (*Book Week*) or "disagreeable" (*Horn Book*). More recently, however, Fitzhugh's fiction has met with considerable praise. Some critics laud Fitzhugh's presentation of a non-saccharine view of children and their thoughts. Perry Nodelman writes that Fitzhugh's novels "cleverly express the differences between individuality and eccentricity, and between what one owes others and what one deserves oneself."

Fitzhugh's most important novel about multicultural issues, *Nobody's Family Is Going to Change,* has had a mixed critical reception. Kate Fincke remarks that the novel "is written with rare wit and intelligence. It is compelling and funny." Rosemary Stones calls it "undoubtedly" Fitzhugh's best, and identifies the work as "a landmark in writing for young people." Virginia Wolf, however, comments negatively about Fitzhugh's work: "This novel does not achieve the depth of psychological realism now recognized as a principal merit of *Harriet the Spy* and *The Long Secret.*" Wolf, as well as other critics, regards *Nobody's Family* as an inferior work in Fitzhugh's *oeuvre* because the book attempts to cover too many social problems, including racism, sexism, poverty, and bias against children and homosexuals. This does not prevent the novel from offering an insightful examination of how families function and the difficulties of having individual needs met within the family structure. The book also creates a memorable heroine, Emma, who recounts in an angry, rebellious voice her experiences as a young African-American woman both within a family and within the culture at large.

BIBLIOGRAPHY

Young Adult Fiction by Louise Fitzhugh

Harriet the Spy. New York: Harper, 1964.
The Long Secret. New York: Harper, 1965.
Nobody's Family Is Going to Change. New York: Farrar, Straus & Giroux, 1974.
Sport. New York: Delacorte, 1979.

Works for Children by Louise Fitzhugh

Suzuki Beane. With Sandra Scoppettone. New York: Doubleday, 1961.
Bang, Bang, You're Dead! With Sandra Scoppettone. New York: Harper, 1969.
I Am Five. New York: Delacorte, 1978.
I Am Four. Illus. Susan Bonner. New York: Delacorte, 1982.
I Am Three. Illus. Susanna Natti. New York: Delacorte, 1982.

Selected Studies of Louise Fitzhugh

Fincke, Kate. "The Breakdown of the Family: Fictional Case Studies in Contemporary Novels for Young People." *The Lion and the Unicorn* 3 (Winter 1979–1980): 86–95.

Nodelman, Perry. "Louise Fitzhugh." *Dictionary of Literary Biography*. Vol. 7. *American Writers for Children since 1960*. Ed. Glenn E. Estes. 133–42.

Rev. of *Harriet the Spy. Book Week*, 10 January 1965: 18.

Viguers, Ruth Hill. Rev. of Harriet the C Spy. *Horn Book* 41 (Feb. 1965): 74–76.

Wolf, Virginia L. *Louise Fitzhugh*. Ed. Ruth K. MacDonald. Twayne's United States Authors Series. New York: Twayne Publishers, 1991.

————. "A Novel of Children's Liberation." *Children's Literature* 5 (1976): 207–72.

PAULA FOX
(1923-)

Bruce Henderson

BIOGRAPHY

In John Rowe Townsend's *A Sense of Story*, Paula Fox says, "My career sounds like flap copy of the 1930s" (95). Indeed, not only has Fox held a wide variety of jobs throughout her life, but her childhood sounds like a plot out of one of her novels. Born in New York City in 1923 to Paul Hervey and Elsie de Sola Fox, she was sent to live with her maternal grandmother in Cuba at the age of eight; in 1934, upon Batista's rise to power, she returned to New York. In an interview with Augusta Baker, she recalls always feeling "transient," and notes that she did not see her parents very often. According to Baker, Fox always had the sense of "not knowing what was going to happen the next day." People beyond her family offered her what permanence she knew, a situation many of her child-protagonists would share.

She went to work at age seventeen, and among other jobs, worked as model, machinist (about which she writes poignantly in an essay in the *Horn Book*), teacher of English to Spanish-speaking children, reporter, script reader, and teacher of the developmentally disabled, as well as professor of English literature at the University of Pennsylvania. One sees in the range of occupations she has had the material upon which she will base both her sense of the difficulties of surviving in the economics of contemporary society, as well as the opportunities to develop the sensitivity to the inner lives of children and the disenfranchised which features so prominently in many of her novels. She attended Columbia University from 1955–1958, as well as the Juilliard School of Music.

She married Richard Sigerson in 1948; that marriage ended in divorce in 1954, but produced her two children, Adam and Gabriel. In 1962, she married Martin Greenberg. She currently lives in Brooklyn.

She has received numerous awards for her books for children and young adults, including a nomination for the National Book Award for children's literature for *Blowfish Live in the Sea* in 1971 and for *The Little Swineherd and Other Tales* in 1979; the Newbery Medal for *The Slave Dancer* in 1974; Newbery Honor Books for *One-Eyed Cat* in 1985 (which also won the Christopher Medal) and *The Village by the Sea* in 1989 (which also won the *Boston Globe/Horn Book* Award); and the Hans Christian Andersen Award in 1978. Her books have consistently been listed as "outstanding" and "notable" by such publications as the *New York Times*.

She has also written several novels for adults, perhaps most notably *Desperate Characters* (1970), which was subsequently filmed and won Shirley MacLaine an award at the Berlin Film Festival for her leading performance in it.

MAJOR WORKS AND THEMES

Paula Fox's works for young adults are so prolific that to identify one or two major themes is to do their complexity some manner of injustice; similarly, it would be impossible, in an essay of this length, to cover with depth all of her major books for young adults. Nonetheless, for the purposes of the reader interested in Fox's attention to multicultural issues, it is possible to see Fox consistently working through a few central concerns, as she writes both out of an interest in the adolescent's individual development and how that development is affected and contextualized by the difficult, often threatening, social world of contemporary society. First and foremost, her books are about *specific* characters—never as representatives of a particular culture or social class, nor even simply as products of their environment. The social and cultural milieu in which her young people (as well as her adults) find themselves is hardly unimportant to their development as characters, and in fact often is dramatically important to the changes they undergo, but Fox typically works with deftness and subtlety to suggest that people respond to their cultural environment in very different ways—and the mark of virtue for many characters in her books is their ability to thrive and learn from a situation that might diminish other characters.

In the broadest sense of the word, "culture" is any grouping of people who share beliefs, values, and practices; it is possible to argue that Fox's fiction is always concerned with conflicts between cultures and miscommunication between members of different, though sometimes intersecting, cultures. For example, in such books as *Blowfish Live in the Sea* (1970) and *The Moonlight Man* (1986)—and, to a lesser and more indirect extent in *The Village by the Sea*—while the characters all belong to a traditionally white American culture, the subculture of the alcoholic becomes an intrusion into the unity of family life. Similarly, *Lily and the Lost Boy* (1986) sets into most vivid contrast the differences (and similarities) between the American family on sabbatical and the Greek natives of the island where they are staying. Jim Hemmings' alcoholism becomes a kind of subcultural barrier that leads to different values from those of Lily and her family and to a carelessness on the part of Jack, Jim's son, that has tragic consequences for a young Greek child.

But in the narrower sense of the word "culture," Fox has also produced intriguing and challenging work for the young adult reader, work that has sometimes proven controversial to her adult critics. Her most important work on multicultural themes has centered on African and African-American cultures, and has been the focus of three novels, each, interestingly enough, from a different stage in her career: *How Many Miles to Babylon?* (1967), her Newbery Medal book *The Slave Dancer* (1973), and the more recent *Monkey Island* (1991).

How Many Miles to Babylon?, Fox's first major work for young readers, tells the story of James Douglas, a black child who lives in Brooklyn. His mother has been hospitalized—it is implied that she has suffered some kind of nervous breakdown—when his father abandons them. James lives with his three aunts, Grace, Althea, and Paul, and attends school, where his teacher is Miss Meadowsweet. All his mother has left him is a ring, which becomes a kind of magic talisman for him. A story of its African origins leads James to fantasize about his own family's African connections, to dream that his mother has been whisked away to Africa and to fantasize of himself as a lost African prince.

Fox establishes the cultural setting of the novel and James' blackness without sensationalizing it or drawing any particular attention to it: it is not a "problem" (in the sense of many of the young adult "problem novels" of race and ethnicity of the time), but it provides a specificity and authenticity against which James' experiences are better understood. In a wonderfully poetic passage early in the novel, James, woolgathering in class at school, ruminates on the varying degrees and shades of color among the people around him and in his life. This description not only gives us insight into James' own creative perceptions of the world, but also encourages the reader to think beyond simplistic divisions between black and white (and red and yellow, and so forth).

James is coerced by three tough boys of various ethnicities—Gino, Stick, and Blue—into participating in a dog-napping scam they have developed to make money. James ultimately escapes from the boys and returns the stolen dog to its owner, after a brief, but frightening encounter with a homeless man. When he returns home, he tells his aunts about his journey. There is a great surprise in store for him: his mother has returned from the hospital, smaller than he remembered, clearly having gone through a battle of her own. James emerges from his experience both changed and un-changed—still somehow questioning his identity: "He thought, who am I? I'm not a prince. How can I be a prince? Who am I?" Fox concludes this novel, "As though she had read his mind and heard his question, his mother held out her hand. 'Hello, Jimmy,' she said."

The conclusion is simple, but enormously effective. James has not undergone an unrealistic transformation, but is now more able to articulate his experiences to his aunts, perhaps because he has had to confront the life outside himself more directly. He also has a more realistic understanding of those around him: he comes to terms with the fact that his mother is as fragile and human a person as he is, not some queen out of an African magical tale. Similarly, her response to him helps him find his identity: throughout the novel, he has been referred to either as James (by the narrator) or as Prince (by the three boys). His mother calling him "Jimmy" is, in a sense, a reclaiming of the mother-child relationship, a re-estab-lishment of the primary bond that he has lacked.

Fox's next major work of multicultural fiction for young adults, *The Slave Dancer* (1973), won the Newbery Medal in 1974, and was controver-sial at the time of its publication. Some critics heralded it as a breakthrough book, both in terms of Fox's own career and in terms of the treatment of the history of slavery in juvenile literature; others reviled it for what they saw as its distortions of history (see Critical Reception for the arguments). While it continues Fox's theme of the development of individual character in the midst of cultural turmoil, it does so at what for Fox is an uncharacteristic remove from the contemporary scene and with a heightened drama, also uncharacteristic of her usually understated and implied commentary on racism and power imbalances between individuals and between cultures.

The Slave Dancer is set in 1840, and tells the story of Jesse Bollier, a thirteen-year-old boy of New Orleans, the titular "slave dancer" and narrator of the novel, who lives with his mother and sister in poverty, and who amuses himself by playing his flute and wandering through the slave market. One night, he is kidnapped and pressed into service aboard a slave ship, *The Moonlight,* bound for West Africa. He has been kidnapped because of his ability to play the flute and, therefore, his usefulness at "dancing" the slaves—getting them to perform the exercise necessary to keep them alive on the voyage back from Africa.

Over the course of the voyage, Jesse is treated with brutality by various members of the crew, and begins to sympathize with the black slaves, whom he sees treated with even greater violence and neglect than he; at the same time, Jesse is not without some of the prejudices and stereotypes of Africans he has been taught in America. One of the controversies of the novel is what the reader is to make of Jesse's statements, which to some extent hold the Africans responsible for their own enslavement, and for the enslavement of other Africans, and which, some critics argue, suggest Jesse's own dehumanization of the slaves.

The ship is destroyed in a storm, and Jesse is one of only two survivors, the other being Ras, a slave. The two are rescued by David, an older black man, who helps Ras escape to the North and Jesse find his way back to New Orleans and his family. We learn in a brief epilogue that Jesse is looking back from adulthood as he tells the story. In the last paragraph of the novel he admits that the experience of being "slave dancer" on *The Moonlight* has changed him forever: "I was unable to listen to music. . . . I would see once again as though they'd never ceased their dancing in my mind, black men and women and children lifting their tormented limbs in time to a reedy martial air, the dust rising from their joyless thumping, the sound of the fife finally drowned beneath the clanging of their chains."

In *The Slave Dancer*, Fox is ambitious in presenting intercultural relations and their impact on individual character. For one thing, she is working with highly contested historical materials in a time when not only were the "facts" of the history of slavery being questioned, but the identity position of those writing about slavery was also being scrutinized as never before. Thus, for a white woman, admittedly not a professional scholar or historian, to narrate the history of slavery and to tell it from the perspective of a white adolescent's experience (albeit filtered through his older self) was to thematize and complicate the act of fiction itself as a social and cultural performance—which was itself rife with intercultural tensions and conflicts.

In *The Slave Dancer*, the fact that Jesse narrates the entire novel makes it unclear for some readers where his historically positioned and constructed opinions about slaves and the relative culpability of blacks and whites in the process of enslavement ends and the author's (or the implied author's) endorsement or rejection of them begins. For example, even within the first-person point of view, we wonder, at some point, whether Jesse's statements about the Africans' own involvement in slavery are meant to reflect the adolescent's received teachings, which the older Jesse perhaps would no longer accept, or whether they continue what is, for some readers, a racist view of slavery. Even at this point, the question remains: to what degree is it reasonable for contemporary readers to assume that the author holds the same view of history as the characters she creates, who live in an imaginative world of a century and a half ago?

While this may seem as much a theoretical question as a textual one, it is an important one in considering *The Slave Dancer* as a novel for young adults about history and the degree to which cultural experience shapes individual character in the novel. One reading will dismiss the novel's use of history as distortive and simply inaccurate; another will see the potentially racist comments as a challenge to the young reader to question what constitutes "fact" and "history." Similarly, the reader's determination of whether Jesse's negative descriptions of the Africans is that of his adolescent, untransformed self or that of his older self will say a lot about the reader's evaluation of whether or not the experience has been truly transformative for Jesse—or whether there is some middle ground, some in-between psychology that accounts for seemingly contradictory positions. Again, to navigate the middle ground requires a sophisticated reader (which is not to say that the decision not to seek a middle ground, in which Jesse remains both racist and antiracist, even into adulthood, is necessarily a simplistic or immature reading) who is able to question the realism of relentless "consistency" in human character. It is clear, in the haunting conclusion of the novel, that Jesse accepts some degree of responsibility for his participation in the process of slavery, even though he himself was something of a "slave"—he clearly understands the degrees of slavery involved and his own relatively high position compared to those of the Africans. Is it possible to see his remarks that hold Africans responsible for some participation in the enslavement of other Africans (and the concomitant move to exonerate some of the whites to some degree) as a kind of defense mechanism, a rationalization to lessen his own sense of guilt? Or is it—as perhaps Fox is implying at least in part in her acknowledgment of Professor Wallace (in addition to performing an appropriate act of scholarly documentation and gratitude)—arguing for what was then and remains now an unpopular view of the history of slavery that she nonetheless holds to be true?

That *The Slave Dancer* raises these complex levels of interrogation suggests that, whether one praises or excoriates the novel, it possesses a power and magnitude worthy of consideration. On the one hand, it begins as a kind of "pirate" story (or "shanghai" story, to use Sheila Egoff's term), a "boys' book," not unlike *Treasure Island* or *Kidnapped*, but it ultimately emerges as something closer to Fox's own version of *Moby Dick*, in which the history of adventure also becomes a meditation on character, on comradeship, and on the individual's position in historical process and spiritual judgment.

The last of Fox's novels to be considered is *Monkey Island* (1991) in which she returns to New York City, but it is now a different and more harrowing landscape than what Anita Moss calls the "pastoral" in *How Many Miles to Babylon?* While it is true that, even in the earlier novel, Fox's protagonist James had to reckon with the dangers of city life, the dangers were surmountable and James was finally able to save himself and escape back to the comforts of home. In *Monkey Island*, there is a similar initial situation, in which the young hero's mother leaves home, but the different journeys of the protagonists of each novel are in stark contrast to each other: in *Monkey Island*, when the protagonist sets out on his journey, there is no guarantee that there is anyone to whom he can return—no loving aunts in the background, no secure, if poor, community that will welcome him back.

Clay Garrity and his parents live in a welfare hotel near the New York City/New Jersey border. When his parents, in despair and frustration, abandon him, Clay resorts to foraging in his neighbors' garbage for leftover food, and when Mrs. Larkin, a well-intentioned neighbor, discovers this and calls a social service agency, Clay, in terror of being separated permanently from his family, takes to the streets.

On the streets he quickly becomes part of one of America's most recently recognized subcultures: the homeless. Fox narrates his initiation into the world and practices of people without shelter. Clay is "adopted," so to speak, by two homeless men—Calvin, an older white alcoholic former teacher, and Buddy, a younger African-American man. The men help Clay find food and clothing, and protect him from some of the more violent attacks against the homeless. The title of the novel comes from a particularly frightening episode in which a group of rowdy young men (and a few young women) set upon the residents of the park, calling out "Monkey Island! Monkey Island! Where the monkeys live," thus effectively dehumanizing the homeless even more than circumstances have done. A note of racism is added when they call Buddy a "Nigger."

Clay ultimately is reunited with his mother (but not with his father), and the two struggle to re-establish their sense of family. Unlike *How Many Miles to Babylon?*, where the return to home was a full circle and the reintegration of James' mother seemed secure and optimistic, all that is secure at the end of *Monkey Island* is that Clay is off the streets: his mother acknowledges that she must still earn Clay's trust, and that he must find it in "a place beyond forgiveness."

Monkey Island, while not as graphically violent, for the most part, as *The Slave Dancer*, perhaps because of the immediacy of its subject, has a social and emotional power equal to it: the squeamish reader will be upset and the younger reader may find it traumatizing in its almost relentless vision of home as an absence rather than presence in the contemporary urban landscape. As with *How Many Miles to Babylon?*, it paints a multicultural world and suggests that homelessness and poverty are by no means unique to one racial or cultural group. At the same time, Buddy's blackness is acknowledged as one of many factors causing him to be especially targeted by the gang that attacks the homeless in the park. In the final chapter, when he and Clay are reunited, they talk about the incident in the park, and, when Clay, perhaps testing his own ability to forgive his parents for their abandonment of him, asks Buddy whether he can forgive those who attacked him and called him "Nigger," Buddy responds, "Forgive them! . . . Sorry is nice but short. *Nigger* is the longest word I know." There are some social transgressions, Buddy (and Fox) suggests, that can never warrant forgiveness—only a wary coexistence.

In all of Fox's novels, there is exploration of the problems of difference, and of the particularly difficult process for the adolescent of balancing tolerance and respect for other people with establishment and maintenance of personal values. In a sense, the protagonist's ability to understand what makes people different (whether that difference is value-free, as in race or ethnicity, or whether that difference clearly has negative effects, as in alcoholism) becomes the ethical quest, and it is only by gaining empathy for the experiences and lives of others that the protagonist gains a mature sense of self. In these three novels, the presence of multiple cultures becomes the particular backdrop for the rite of passage into selfhood: for James, it is the ability to integrate his fantasy of his culture (i.e., the African prince) into the reality of surviving a potentially dangerous and criminal adventure; for Jesse Bollier, the sometimes ambivalent and contradictory experience of historical processes becomes a backdrop for understanding people from cultures seemingly totally alien from his own and understanding his own growing awareness of being implicated within that process of slavery; finally, for Clay Garrity, it is his understanding of a kind of fluidity of cultural identity, on the one hand, when he can move from a position of security to membership in a stigmatized group (the homeless) within a very brief span of time, and, on the other hand, his recognition that even within the category of people called the "homeless," others outside that "culture" will maintain the traditional targeting of people according to race and other markers of group identity.

CRITICAL RECEPTION

With some notable exceptions, from the beginning of her career, Paula Fox's books for children and young adults have been reviewed with high praise; in recent years, her works have begun to receive scholarly attention, as well. Almost all of the reviews of her young adult books have identified her skill at characterization, her unflinching realism, and the sophistication of her representation of relationships between adults and younger people. In particular, her attention to the latter is often singled out as going beyond the stereotypical young adult "problem novel," in that the difficulties between younger people and adults never result in either a simplistic moralizing or in a flattening of the older character, in deference to the values of the primary intended reader (i.e., the young adult).

As one reads critical and scholarly surveys of children's and young adult literature in the late 1960s and early 1970s (such as John Rowe Townsend's and Eleanor Cameron's), one finds Fox's name mentioned as an heir to earlier writers who blended intellectual complexity and the subject of childhood and adolescence. It is only with 1973's *The Slave Dancer* that any sense of controversy arises. When *The Slave Dancer* was published and, with perhaps even more intensity when it was awarded the Newbery Medal, a number of African-American critics took both the author and the award committee to task for what they saw as a valorization of racist attitudes about slavery. Beryle Banfield, for example, evaluates the novel as "subtle racism. . . . Skillfully written, it repeats several racist historical myths" (*Black American* 35), such as the barbarianism of Africans, their intrinsic character defects, and their role in selling their own people into slavery. Similarly, Sharon Bell Mathis, in an essay whose title suggests its thesis, "*The Slave Dancer* Is an Insult to Black Children," makes many of the same arguments as Banfield, adding details that suggest what she sees as a dehumanizing effect of description, such as the narrator's analogy between the sounds of the slaves' feet and that of rats scuttling. Binnie Tate focuses on distortions of history, arguing in more detailed ways than Mathis about problematic elements in the novel's depiction of race, such as the use of the term "creole" to describe Jesse and its implications for determining his identity as black or white, given historical classifications and language use.

While most of the negative assessments of the novel emerge out of a concern for historical accuracy and for the implanting of destructive attitudes in young readers' minds, it is important to acknowledge that there has been some criticism of the novel for other reasons. Fred Inglis, for example, situating Fox's novel in a broader study of "value and meaning" in children's literature, sees *The Slave Dancer*, for all its stylistic power, as nonetheless simplistic in its addressing of the moral issues of slavery faced by its narrator-hero; Inglis compares the novel to *Huckleberry Finn*, for example, and finds Fox's treatment of similar ethical dilemmas of the positioning of the individual in the historical process of slavery too pat and reductive.

These opinions, while vocal and powerful and raising important concerns around issues of representation and historical accuracy, are one part of the critical response, but, clearly, given the novel's celebrity, many critics, teachers, librarians, and readers felt and feel otherwise about it. John Rowe Townsend, for example, felt so strongly positive about it that his revision of his essay on Fox for *A Sense of Story* focused almost exclusively on the merits of *The Slave Dancer*. Sheila Egoff, in *Thursday's Child*, suggests that, quite the opposite of being gratuitously graphic and reductive in its presentation of violence against the slaves (as well as against the sailors), the novel "restrained its [opportunity for sensationalism] in favor of emotionalism, all the stronger for its understatement" (170–71). Egoff sees the limits of description and the ambivalent moral perspective of Jesse as a function of a fourteen-year-old's language skills—that this is narratively appropriate. David Rees goes so far as to see in *The Slave Dancer* "a savage indictment of a whole society, intensely political in its overtones which ring down the ages to the present day" (122).

The place of *The Slave Dancer* in the contemporary canon of young adult novels seems fairly stable at the moment. While its historical accuracy may still remain in doubt for various readers and critics, its stylistic and narrative excellence is rarely disputed. Fox herself, acutely sensitive to the charges against the book, has remarked on the year of research she spent before writing *The Slave Dancer* (including living in New Orleans, near Rampart Street, the border between deeply segregated neighborhoods), and declared, in her Newbery Medal acceptance speech, "There are those who feel that slavery debased the enslaved. It is not so. . . . Slavery debased the enslavers, and self-imposed ignorance of slavery keeps the mind closed" (quoted in Nelson 1241).

In recent years, critics have begun to both look back retrospectively at Fox's career for patterns from book to book and to draw connections between Fox's works and those of other writers. The issues raised and perspectives brought to these analyses have ranged from the archetypal (as in Hazel Rochman's use of Fox's novels as examples of the stages of the heroic journey) to versions of New Historicism (as in Hamida Bosmajian's essay on "the outer limits" of children's literature, using *The Slave Dancer* as an example). Both Lois R. Kuznets and Anita Moss focus on *How Many Miles to Babylon?* in exploring different aspects of children's and young adult literature from rather sophisticated critical perspectives. Kuznets ties the novel (along with other recent novels by other writers) to pastoral literary traditions, identifying in James' adventure a continuation of the narrative pattern of escape to the "country" (Coney Island in this case) and ensuing return that goes back to centuries-old European and other texts. Moss' essay situates the novel in the metafictional tradition, seeing in James' fantasies about his mother's ring and in his retelling of his adventures to his aunts when he returns a commentary on the act of storytelling itself.

In the cases of both Kuznets and Moss, the critical perspectives acknowledge the placement of the novel as a children's or young adult work; at the same time, each essay employs critical perspectives and invokes literary traditions that extend beyond any simple system of division of texts between one kind of reader and another. Without ever losing the sense of the "childist" concerns (to use Peter Hunt's term) of the novel, both Kuznets and Moss also work to extend the value of the novel beyond one chronologically or developmentally defined readership and move criticism of Fox's writing beyond a consumerist approach to a consideration of what is appropriate for children and young adults to read. In this sense, they are themselves closely aligned to Fox herself as a writer, for whom the question of audience and limits is an open one and for whom the extension of intellectual, moral, cultural, and imaginative boundaries seems to be the bedrock of her art of fiction.

BIBLIOGRAPHY

Young Adult Fiction by Paula Fox

How Many Miles to Babylon? New York: David White; London: Macmillan, 1967.

Blowfish Live in the Sea. Scarsdale, New York: Bradbury, 1970.

The King's Falcon. Scarsdale, New York: Bradbury, 1969. London: Macmillan, 1970.

Portrait of Ivan. Scarsdale, New York: Bradbury, 1969. London: Macmillan, 1970.

The Slave Dancer. Scarsdale, New York: Bradbury, 1973. London: Macmillan, 1974.

A Place Apart. New York: Farrar, Straus, 1980. London: Dent, 1981.

One-Eyed Cat. Scarsdale, New York: Bradbury, 1984. London: Dent, 1985.

Lily and the Lost Boy. New York: Orchard, 1986. Rpt. as *The Lost Boy.* London: Dent, 1987.

The Moonlight Man. Scarsdale, New York: Bradbury. London: Dent, 1986.

The Village by the Sea. New York: Orchard, 1988.

In a Place of Danger. New York: Orchard, 1989.

Monkey Island. New York: Orchard, 1991.

Western Wind. New York: Orchard, 1993.

Works for Children by Paula Fox

Maurice's Room. Illus. Ingrid Fetz. New York: Macmillan, 1966.

A Likely Place. Illus. Edward Ardizzone. New York: Macmillan, 1967. London: Macmillan, 1968.

Dear Prosper. Illus. Steve McLachlin. New York: David White, 1968.

Hungry Fred. Illus. Rosemary Wells. Scarsdale, New York: Bradbury, 1969.

The Little Swineherd and Other Tales. Illus. Leonard Lubin. New York: Dutton, 1978. London: Dent, 1979.

Works for Adults by Paula Fox

Poor George. New York: Harcourt; London: Bodley Head, 1967.

Desperate Characters. New York: Harcourt; London: Macmillan, 1970.

The Western Coast. New York: Harcourt, 1972. London: Macmillan, 1973.

The Widow's Children. New York: Dutton, 1976.

A Servant's Tale. San Francisco: North Point Press, 1984. London: Virago, 1976.

The God of Nightmares. San Francisco: North Point Press, 1990.

Other Works by Paula Fox

"Newbery Acceptance Speech." *Horn Book* 50.4 (Aug. 1974): 347–50.

"One Human Heart: A Conversation between Paula Fox and Cathie Mercier." *Innocence and Experience: Essays and Conversations on Children's Literature.* Ed. Barbara Harrison and Gregory Maguire. New York: Lothrop, Lee and Shepard, 1987. 250–58.

"The Village by the Sea." *Horn Book* 56.1 (1990): 22–23.
"To Write Simply." *Horn Book* 57.5 (1991): 553–55.

Selected Studies of Paula Fox

Baker, Augusta. "Paula Fox." *Horn Book* 50.4 (1974): 351–53.
Banfield, Beryle. "Racism in Children's Books: An Afro-American Perspective." *The Black American in Books for Children: Readings in Racism.* Ed. Donnarae MacCann and Gloria Woodard. Metuchen, NJ: Scarecrow, 1985. 23–38.
Bosmajian, Hamida. "Nightmares of History: The Outer Limits of Children's Literature." *Children's Literature Association Quarterly* 8 (Winter 1983): 20–22.
Cameron, Eleanor. *The Green and Burning Tree: On the Writing and Enjoyment of Children's Books.* Boston: Little, Brown, 1985.
Egoff, Sheila. *Thursday's Child: Trends and Patterns in Contemporary Children's Literature.* Chicago: ALA, 1981.
Inglis, Fred. *The Promise of Happiness: Value and Meaning in Children's Fiction.* Cambridge: Cambridge UP, 1981.
Kaye, Marilyn. "Paula Fox." *Twentieth-Century Children's Writers.* Ed. Tracy Chevalier. 3rd ed. Chicago: St. James, 1989. 357–58.
Kuznets, Lois R. "The Fresh-Air Kids, or Some Contemporary Versions of Pastoral." *Children's Literature* 11 (1983): 156–68.
Mathis, Sharon Bell. "*The Slave Dancer* Is an Insult to Black Children." *Cultural Conformity in Books for Children: Further Readings in Racism.* Ed. Donnarae MacCann and Gloria Woodard. Metuchen, NJ: Scarecrow, 1977. 146–48.
Moss, Anita. "Varieties of Children's Metafiction." *Studies in the Literary Imagination* 19 (Fall 1985): 79–92.
Nelson, Harold. "*The Slave Dancer.*" *Beacham's Guide to Literature for Young Adults.* Vol. 3. Ed. Kirk H. Beetz and Suzanne Niemeyer. Washington, DC: Beacham, 1990. 1238–44.
Rees, David. "The Colour of Saying." *The Marble in the Water: Essays on Contemporary Writers of Fiction for Children and Young Adults.* Boston: Horn Book, 1980. 114–27.
Rochman, Hazel. *Against Borders: Promoting Books for a Multi-cultural World.* Chicago: ALA, 1993.
Sutherland, Zena, ed. *The Best in Children's Books: The University of Chicago Guide to Children's Literature, 1966–72; 1973–78.* Chicago: U Chicago P, 1973; 1980.
Tate, Binnie. "Racism and Distortions Pervade *The Slave Dancer.*" *Cultural Conformity in Books for Children: Further Readings in Racism.* Ed.

Donnarae MacCann and Gloria Woodard. Metuchen, NJ: Scarecrow, 1977. 149–53.

Townsend, John Rowe. *A Sense of Story: Essays on Contemporary Writers for Children*. Boston: Horn Book, 1971.

―――. *A Sounding of Story: New and Revised Essays on Contemporary Writers for Children*. New York: Lippincott, 1979.

In addition, Paula Fox's novels for children and young adults have regularly been reviewed in *Horn Book*; check index of year of publication (and subsequent year) for citations.

JEAN CRAIGHEAD GEORGE
(1919–)

Dona J. Helmer

BIOGRAPHY

Jean Craighead George, the daughter of entomologist Frank C. and Carolyn Craighead, was born July 2, 1919, in Washington, D.C. She is the sister of John and Frank Craighead, world experts on the grizzly bear. In 1944 she married ecologist and conservationist John L. George with whom she had three children: Twig, Craig, and Luke. The couple divorced in 1963.

She attended Pennsylvania State University where she earned her B.A. in 1941 and edited its literary magazine. She later studied painting and became a reporter for the International News Service (1941–1943) and the *Washington Post* and *Times-Herald* (1943–1946). She worked as a staff artist for *Pageant* magazine and the Newspaper Enterprise Association from 1946–1947. She worked as a staff writer for *Reader's Digest* from 1969–1974 and later as a roving editor for the magazine from 1974–1980.

During World War II, she met her future husband, who was a college roommate and friend of her twin brothers at the University of Michigan. The couple met in September of 1943 and married in January of the next year. Since John was still serving in the navy, Jean moved to New York to be near the Brooklyn Navy Yard. The couple acquired a fox pup, and Jean soon began working evenings on a book later titled *Vulpes, the Red Fox* (1948), which details the life cycle of a fox. According to Jean, John contributed "his observations of birds and animals and occasionally tapped out a paragraph" (*Journey Inward* 4). At the end of the war John decided to finish his Ph.D. at the University of Michigan with the help of the G.I. Bill of Rights.

After finishing his course work, John was offered a teaching position at Vassar. Jean took courses in painting and continued to write. The couple later acquired two minks and eventually collaborated on five more animal biographies. Two more children were born. It was a stressful time for the young couple. John failed to be renewed in his teaching position. Jean felt that the world was closing in. One day she sat down at her typewriter and started a story about a boy who ran away from his father and civilization. This story became the book *My Side of the Mountain* (1959). It was the first book that Jean signed alone (*Journey Inward 84*).

Although some critics felt that the boy's father would not encourage him to run away, the book was popular with young adults and was declared a Newbery honor book.

In her autobiography, *Journey Inward,* George notes her early interest in writing, sketching, and natural history. In fact, one of the major factors that influenced her work was her early orientation to the "outdoors," via her family and later her husband. George was interested in ecology and nature. Her family always had stray animals living with them. As she says, "The great advantage of raising the wild things I wrote about was that they behaved among us much as they would in the wild, so that by translating I would learn about them as in no other way—not even sitting out in the woods" (*Journey Inward* 90).

The Craighead family had a long tradition of caring for the land. William Penn's son had deeded a land grant to John Craighead in 1742. John was the youngest son of Rev. Thomas Craighead, a Scottish physician turned Presbyterian minister, who emigrated to New England in 1715. George's father was born in Yellow Breeches Creek at Craigheads, Pennsylvania. Her father studied forestry and entomology.

Every summer during her youth, while her father went west to supervise field research stations, she, her mother, and her twin brothers lived at the family house in Craigheads. During these summers "we too learned to follow the skunks, the snakes and the birds . . . we fished, swam, rode hay wagons and raised owls, falcons and guinea pigs. We really believed that if you were good, good would come back to you, and that work was salvation" (*Journey Inward* 33).

Her brothers were a big influence on her. While they were in high school, John and Frank wrote an article about falconry in the United States for the *Saturday Evening Post* and *National Geographic*. This article was responsible for introducing the sport of falconry to the American public. They would later become experts on river running and grizzly bears. Jean says that although she spent a great deal of time with the twins on their adventures, "I was always an outsider—almost as much so [as] an only child. So I dreamed up an imaginary companion for whom I began writing stories (*Journey Inward* 34).

Another important aspect of her life was her relationship with her husband. Although they were both deeply involved with the environment, they believed different things about child rearing and this tension eventually caused the disintegration of their relationship. They also disagreed about writing.

In the 1960s and 1970s George wrote over thirty books, mainly for children. She also published many articles for *Reader's Digest*. She originally felt that since she was not a scholar, she had no credentials, and therefore she put John's name on the first books. A *Reader's Digest* editor suggested they try a piece about "nature detectives," but John had received a letter from a colleague criticizing him for his popular writing and did not feel that he should be associated with such a venture. Jean described this as a perennial "battle between the scientist and the popular nature or science writer . . . scientists just do not trust those of their coterie who are popular writers. Science is pure, hard information, and needs no embellishments" (*Journey Inward* 94).

In 1963 the couple divorced, and John retained control of the royalties for the first six books. Jean was forced to write even more in order to support her children, but, in doing so, she became confident as both a writer and person.

During her early career George illustrated her own texts. Eventually she began to concentrate more on her writing. She became a full-time writer and gave up illustrating. One night her editor, Elizabeth Riley, ended her career as an illustrator by telling her that although she was a competent artist, she really needed good artists to illustrate her books. George said, "I felt a bit sad, for I loved to illustrate. But she was right; I had a style, but I could not hold a candle to the artists who were illustrating the children's books of the day" (*Journey Inward* 142).

Since that time George has continued to concentrate on her writing and storytelling. One of her books, *Julie of the Wolves* (1972), was awarded the Newbery Medal. Two of her works have been made into films.

MAJOR WORKS AND THEMES

Although the novels of Jean Craighead George have a wide variety of settings and plots, they share a common thread of nature facts and lore. Her characters are scientifically literate. They observe nature and use the scientific method to understand natural phenomena. Her major themes are the conflict between humans, particularly civilized humans, and nature; the conflict between civilization and humans, particularly Native peoples; and survival in the wilderness. Her best books deal with the place of humans in the ecological chain. George communicates the idea that humans are part of the ecology and have a responsibility for the earth and its creatures. Her novels tend to focus on young adults who learn to survive in alien situations in the wilderness through their observations of nature.

George has written four major works dealing with multicultural protagonists: *Julie of the Wolves* (1972), *Talking Earth* (1983), *Water Sky* (1987), and *Julie* (1994).

Julie of the Wolves is the story of a young Eskimo girl who runs away from her home after losing her mother and being married off at age thirteen. She becomes lost on the north slope of Alaska, but is saved from almost certain death by starvation and hypothermia by a wolf pack that teaches her the survival skills. Julie learns how to touch them so they bring up food from their food sack. During the course of the story, she matures and eventually goes back to civilization. The book is packed with accurate details of the Eskimo way of life and rituals, as well as information about wolves.

Julie of the Wolves evolved because George had read two interesting articles on wolves in *Scientific American.* Her editor at *Reader's Digest* sent her and her thirteen-year-old son to the Arctic Research Laboratory in Barrow, Alaska, for two weeks to do deep research for an article on wolves and the tundra. She later went to Denali, Alaska, in order to study a wolf pack there. The article was not published by *Reader's Digest,* but George was so intrigued by her study of the wolves that she used the information and combined it with speculation about a little girl her son had seen walking on the tundra. *Julie of the Wolves* deals with the ancient Eskimo ways and the conflict of that way of life in modern society. The American Library Association awarded it the 1973 Newbery Award.

The story of the young protagonist is continued in *Julie* (1994). Julie returns to her home and learns that her father has married a white schoolteacher who is now expecting a child. Julie teaches her stepmother the ways of the Eskimo, and they become friends. Her father has become a member of the tribal council and is an entrepreneur in charge of the penned tribal herd of musk ox. During a harsh winter, the wolf pack is hungry and threatens the livelihood of the people. Julie tries to lead her wolf pack away, but it is inevitable that the two species will clash. Julie's stepmother says that in Minnesota once an animal threatens the economic survival of the community, man has the right to kill the predator. Julie's father learns that the Minnesota way will not work in Alaska, and so he turns the musk ox free and lets nature run its course. The Natives will harvest the wool in the old ways from free-roaming musk ox and the wolves will take what they need for survival. Julie's stepbrother is born and is given the name of the wolf that helped her and was killed by her father.

Jean Craighead George shows a strong knowledge of anthropology in these two works. As Brian W. Alderson stated in his review of *Julie of the Wolves*, "the Eskimo says 'we live as no other people can, for we truly understand the earth" while noting that the entire Eskimo way of life is being threatened by civilization. Mary J. Lickteig, in her essay in *Twentieth-Century Children's Writers*, says the clash is symbolized by the use of the two names for the protagonist: Miyax (Ante or Eskimo) and Julie (Anglo or white). Julie/Miyax must decide for herself whether she will follow the old ways or the "new ways" of the white society.

Water Sky (1987) is also set in Alaska and reflects George's attention to detail and her search for authenticity. In preparation for this book, George spent six weeks on the ice off Barrow researching bowhead whales. Although this work is similar thematically to the Julie books, it also deals with a larger theme that is important to George. This book explores the place of humans in the world of nature. Since humans are part of ecology, what is their role? In *Water Sky*, the character has to learn how to use the elements of nature but not change them. He must learn to accept the world as it is. The character must also learn the difference between the Anglo and Alaskan Native philosophies of life.

The other work which deals with Native Americans is *The Talking Earth*. (1983). Although it also has a strong ecological theme it is not set in Alaska but in the Florida Everglades. The female protagonist, Billie Wind, does not trust the wisdom of the tribal myths and questions the tribal elders. She proposes going into the everglades on something like a vision quest but her two-day quest turns into a life-and-death struggle when her boat is destroyed in a fire. In the end, it is not the everglades that threaten her but the land developers who threaten the entire ecological system in the everglades. The character of Billie Wind is sensitively drawn by George, and by the end of the book Billie has an understanding and reverence for the old ways.

These novels by Jean Craighead George deal with a triangular clash of the whole ecological system, "natural people," and civilization and modern progress. At first the main protagonists in these novels do not realize or understand their place in either society or the ecological system. They do not understand the necessity of learning the old ways, of listening to tribal elders, and of learning how to "read" nature. The main characters eventually realize that their ability to survive is dependent upon their ability to utilize the traditional skills taught by elders. They must learn how to trap, to hunt, to observe and interact with nature, to read signs, and to protect themselves. As the characters mature, they learn that they must take this knowledge of nature and natural phenomena back to their people. George also feels that those individuals who have forgotten old ways must return to ways of living in harmony with nature. In these books, everything is made whole once the protagonist returns to the old ways and feels a rededication to harmony. George's female characters are strong and reliant. The books show a genuine respect for Native cultures. Each of these works has a ring of authenticity. George has carefully delineated young adult protagonists standing at the end of the twentieth century, yet representing much older cultures and traditions. She has accurately portrayed classic tribal dimensions in these works.

CRITICAL RECEPTION

Jean Craighead George's work has been acclaimed by critics and reviewers for her detailed descriptions of the habitat and life cycles of animals and her careful attention to factual details. The books are accurate from both an anthropological and an ecological viewpoint. Karen Nelson Hoyle in her article in the *Dictionary of Literary Biography* says that George tends to "meld accurate natural history with stories about adolescents."

Julie of the Wolves, perhaps George's best-known work, has consistently garnered positive critical attention. Lee Bennett Hopkins found *Julie of the Wolves* "a finely crafted novel evolving around a young Eskimo girl, who becomes lost on the north Slope of Alaska's tundra while on her way to visit her pen pal, Amy, in San Francisco . . . Her rich Eskimo heritage is an integral component of this novel that leaves the reader and the young heroine pondering the question—is contemporary life really civilized?" (1053). James Houston said that the novel was "packed with expert wolf lore, its narrative beautifully conveying the sweeping vastness of tundra as well as many other aspects of the Arctic, Ancient and modern, animal and human" (8), while Virginia Haviland compared it to Scott O'Dell's Newbery Award–winning *Island of the Blue Dolphins*. She said that the "superb narration includes authentic descriptions and details of the Eskimo way-of-life and of Eskimo rituals" (Haviland 54). Brian W. Alderson felt that *Julie of the Wolves* would appeal to readers because of the minority female protagonist who acts resourcefully and "because it sustains a powerful case not only for conservation but also for the preservation of man's material skills" (18).

In his analysis of the novel, Jon Stott offers some criticism of it:

In describing the thoughts and actions of Julie as she survives the tundra, Jean George discusses many of the old ways the heroine learns to understand and revere: the improvisation of songs during various activities, the paying of homage to spirits of slain animals, the drum dances, and the intuitive quality of carving. However, even though incorporated skillfully into the narrative, the material often has the quality of superimposed documentary. This is also the case in descriptions of Julie's actions: her gathering of food, mending of clothes, and building a home and sled. (224)

He goes on to say that George combined several stylistic elements to tell the story of a vision quest. It is at once a survival story, an accurate description of old traditions, and a keen observation of nature. He feels that Jean George often uses a "vision pastoral" and looks longingly to the past for a purer way of life. Overall, Stott's evaluation is a positive one: "*Julie of the Wolves* is, in my opinion, one of the best written American children's novels of the 1970s" (224).

The sequel to *Julie of the Wolves*, *Julie*, garnered respectful reviews, but ones more muted than those for its predecessor. Elizabeth Watson found that this story—as it looks at both traditional village life and village life as changed by technology—gives a view of these worlds "as they coexist, struggling with each other for a fragile balance. . . . While the text is neither as sparse nor as poetic as in the first book . . . the story is a strong and compelling adventure." (730).

George's other Alaskan novel, *Water Sky*, met with less critical success. Cheryl Penny in *Booklist* said that although there are exciting scenes and episodes and the evolving state of the Eskimo culture is handled well, the "romantic relationship . . . falls rather flat under the weight of a heavy load of symbolism about [the lovers'] separate cultures" (843). On the other hand, Ethel Heins praised the novel for its "fluency and conviction" and for the ways it dramatizes "the story in which the setting and the nature lore are as strong as the story but do not overwhelm it . . . The characters are strong, the plot is smoothly developed, and the setting vividly drawn in a novel imbued with understanding and respect for the rich traditions of Eskimo Life" (87).

Although Kay Webb O'Connell applauds the familiar themes in *The Talking Earth,* "conserving the earth from mindless development and destruction, ethnic integrity and the intricate beauty of a natural environment," she found the book less powerful and satisfying than *Julie of the Wolves* because it lacks the excitement generated by Julie's plight (74). However, novelist Betsy Byars, writing for *Book World* in the *Washington Post,* found that there was plenty of excitement and that Billie Wind is a protagonist with "just the right combination of guts, humor and curiosity to make the reader care about her" (17).

BIBLIOGRAPHY

Young Adult Fiction by Jean Craighead George

My Side of the Mountain. New York: Dutton, 1959.
The Summer of the Falcon. New York: Crowell, 1962.
Julie of the Wolves. New York: Harper, 1972.
The Talking Earth. New York: Harper, 1983.
Water Sky. New York: Harper, 1987.
On the Far Side of the Mountain. New York: Dutton, 1990.
Julie. New York: HarperCollins 1994.

Works for Children by Jean Craighead George

Vulpes, the Red Fox. New York: Dutton, 1948.
Vision, the Mink. New York: Dutton, 1949.
Masked Prowler: The Story of a Raccoon. New York: Dutton, 1950.
Meph, the Pet Skunk. New York: Dutton, 1952.
Bubo, the Great Horned Owl. New York: Dutton, 1954.
Dipper of Copper Creek. New York: Dutton, 1956.
The Hole in the Tree. New York: Dutton, 1957.
Snow Tracks. New York: Dutton, 1958.
Red Robin, Fly Up! Reader's Digest Books, 1963.
Gull Number 737. New York: Crowell, 1964.
Spring Comes to the Ocean. New York: Crowell, 1966.
The Moon of the Bears. New York: Crowell, 1967.
The Moon of the Owls. New York: Crowell, 1967.
The Moon of the Salamanders. New York: Crowell, 1967.
Coyote in Manhattan. New York: Crowell, 1968.
The Moon of the Fox Pups. New York: Crowell, 1968.
The Moon of the Monarch Butterflies. New York: Crowell, 1968.
The Moon of the Mountain Lions. New York: Crowell, 1968.

The Moon of the Wild Pigs. New York: Crowell, 1968.
The Moon of the Alligators. New York: Crowell, 1969.
The Moon of the Deer. New York: Crowell, 1969.
The Moon of the Gray Wolves. New York: Crowell, 1969.
The Moon of the Moles. New York: Crowell, 1969.
The Moon of the Winter Bird. New York: Crowell, 1969.
All Upon a Stone. New York: Crowell, 1971.
Who Really Killed Cock Robin? An Ecological Mystery. New York: Dutton, 1971.
All Upon a Sidewalk. New York: Dutton, 1974.
Hook a Fish, Catch a Mountain: An Ecological Spy Story. New York: Dutton, 1975.
Going to the Sun. New York: Harper, 1976.
The Wentletrap Trap. New York: Dutton, 1978.
The Wounded Wolf. New York: Harper, 1978.
River Rats, Inc. New York: Dutton, 1979.
The Cry of the Crow. New York: Harper, 1980.
The Grizzly Bear with the Golden Ears. New York: Harper, 1982.
The Wild, Wild Cookbook: A Guide for Young Foragers. New York: Crowell, 1982.
One Day in the Desert. New York: Harper, 1983.
One Day in the Alpine Tundra. New York: Harper, 1984.
One Day in the Prairie. New York: Harper, 1986.
One Day in the Woods. New York: Harper, 1988.
Shark beneath the Reef. New York: HarperCollins, 1989.
One Day in the Tropical Rain Forest. New York: Crowell, 1990.
Dear Rebecca, Winter Is Here. New York: HarperCollins, 1993.
The Fire Bug Connection: An Ecological Mystery. New York: HarperCollins, 1993.
First Thanksgiving. New York: Putnam, 1993.
The Missing 'Gator of Gumbo Limbo: An Ecological Mystery. New York: HarperCollins, 1993.
Animals Who Have Won Our Hearts. New York: HarperCollins, 1994.

Works for Adults by Jean Craighead George

Journey Inward. New York: Dutton, 1982.

Selected Studies of Jean Craighead George

Alderson, Brian W. "*Julie of the Wolves*." *Children's Book Review* 4.1 (1974): 18.
Byars, Betsy. "Growing Up Is Hard to Do." *Book World-The Washington Post* 6 Nov. 1983: 17.
Haviland, Virginia. "*Julie of the Wolves*." *Horn Book* 59.1 (1973): 54–55.

Heins, Ethel. "*Water Sky.*" *Horn Book* 53.4 (1987): 468–469.

Hopkins, Lee Bennett. "Jean Craighead George." *Elementary English* 50.7 (1973): 1049–53.

Houston, James. "A Magic Cabinet, Kissing Wolves and a Running Nose: *Julie of the Wolves.*" *New York Times Book Review* 21 Jan. 1973: 8.

Hoyle, Karen Nelson. "Jean Craighead George." *Dictionary of Literary Biography.* Ed. Glenn E. Estes. Vol. 52. Detroit: Gale, 168–74.

"Jean Craighead George." *Children's Literature Review.* Ed. Gerard J. Senick.Vol. 1. Detroit: Gale, 1976. 89–94.

"Jean Craighead George." *Contemporary Literary Criticism.* Vol. 35. Ed. Ann Block and Carol Riley. Detroit: Gale, 1985. 175–80.

Lickteig, Mary J. "Jean Craighead George." *Twentieth-Century Children's Writers.* Ed. Tracy Chevalier. 3rd ed. Chicago: St. James, 1989. 381–83.

O'Connell, Kay Webb. "*The Talking Earth.*" *School Library Journal* 30.4 (1983): 74.

Penny, Cheryl. "*Water Sky.*" *Booklist* 83.11 (1987): 843.

Shepherd, Kenneth. "Jean Craighead George." *Contemporary Authors.* Ed. Hal May. Vol. 25. Detroit: Gale, 1989. 156–58.

Stott, Jon. "Form, Content, and Cultural Values in Three Inuit (Eskimo) Survival Stories." *American Indian Quarterly* 10.3 (1968): 213–26.

Sutherland, Zena. "*Water Sky.*" *Bulletin of the Center for Children's Books* 40.5 (1987): 1987.

Watson, Elizabeth. "*Julie.*" *Horn Book* 60.6 (1994): 730–31.

Rosa Cuthbert Guy
(ca. 1925–   )

Ann M. Cameron

BIOGRAPHY

Much of Rosa Guy's work reflects the two locales that shaped her early life: Trinidad and Harlem. Although much about her early life in these two environments is sketchy, clearly both her island background and her subsequent life in the United States influenced her views and attitudes. Rosa Cuthbert Guy (rhymes with "me") was born in Trinidad, British West Indies, *circa* 1925. The exact date of her birth has been variously given as September 1, 1925, and September 1, 1928, and Guy has not cleared up the matter. The more likely of the two dates is 1925, given that she married in 1941. A birth date in 1928 would have made her thirteen at her marriage—possible, of course, but less likely than marriage at sixteen. Guy remained in Trinidad until the age of seven, staying there with relatives until she and her older sister Ameze could come to New York to join her parents, Henry and Audrey Cuthbert, who had come to the United States earlier. Assuming the earlier birth date, this would place her arrival date somewhere around 1932.

Guy did not leave the island influences behind in Trinidad. A sizable West Indian community was flourishing in Harlem at the time so a number of customs and attitudes originating in the Caribbean continued during her New York experience.

Shortly after the two sisters arrived to rejoin their parents, the family suffered a setback with the illness of Guy's mother, Audrey. Ameze and

Rosa went to live with cousins in the Bronx. Here they became acquainted with the ideas of Marcus Garvey, the influential and charismatic black nationalist leader who founded the Back to Africa Movement. Garvey favored the idea of creating a black central homeland in Africa and was influential in shaping the thinking of Malcolm X (to whom Guy dedicated her first novel). It was through this experience that Guy came to have a greater awareness of Africa and of the larger sense of the African diaspora. Guy's parents were not Garveyites so Garvey's ideas presented a new point of view to the young girls.

Guy's mother died around 1934, and the girls returned to Harlem to live with their father. Guy's mother, however, was to have a lasting impact on her daughters' lives even though the time they spent together was short. Guy acknowledges the debt she owes her mother. After her mother found out the girls were spending their Saturdays at the local movie theater watching characters like Tarzan and Stephen Fetchet, whom she regarded as denigrating to African-Americans, she insisted that they stay home on Saturdays. To fill the void, Rosa began to read, and she and her mother talked about those books. Her mother bemoaned the fact that no black writers were available, but she saw the books as a more positive alternative to the films. As a legacy from her mother, Guy explains that she became sensitized to "the plight of others" ("The Human Spirit" 129) and, further, developed "a deep and abiding love for myself and others which enabled me to overcome clichés imposed by generations" ("The Human Spirit" 132).

After Audrey Cuthbert's death, Guy's father briefly remarried. Guy's stepmother serves as the model for the exotic Dorine in both the novel *A Measure of Time* (1983) and the short story "She." Henry Cuthbert's second marriage ended, and he died sometime around 1937. Thus, in a period of five years, Guy had come to Harlem, faced the illness and death of her mother, suffered another dislocation in having to live with her cousins, and saw the remarriage and divorce of her father and his death. By this time she was approximately twelve years old.

Here begins a period which was to have a significant impact on Guy's life and on her writing. It is tempting to conclude that she faced a number of the same challenges as the character Edith Jackson, who is also an orphan, in her first Harlem trilogy for young adults. Rosa and Ameze were now orphans in Harlem, with the older Ameze taking care of Rosa for the first few years. When her sister became ill, however, Rosa was required to shoulder more responsibility and was forced to drop out of school. At fourteen she was employed in a brassiere factory where she continued to work, even after her marriage to Warner Guy in 1941 at the age of sixteen, staying at this job during his ensuing time in the service. Her son Warner was born in 1942.

While her husband was away during the war, Guy became involved in the American Negro Theatre (ANT), which was flourishing at the time. Other members of the theater who went on to greater fame included Sidney Poitier, Ruby Dee, Alice Childress, and Harry Belafonte. Guy's work with the ANT, however, was curtailed when, in 1945, she moved with her husband and son to Connecticut.

After the end of her marriage in 1950, Guy entered a new stage of her life, one in which she began searching for the appropriate avenue for her artistic talents and creativity. She returned to New York in 1950 and tried to reenter the theater world. The ANT was no longer viable, but it had been replaced by the Committee for the Negro in the Arts, which attempted to increase opportunities for blacks in the theater. It was at this time that Guy began to write for the theater, mounting the one-act play *Venetian Blinds*. Soon, however, she became discouraged with the theater. It was a dead end for black artists. As she explains, "I soon learned the limitations for advancement of the black artist on the American scene—limitations caused by the overwhelming prejudice in the society against the color of one's skin" (Gallo 85). Instead, she turned to writing fiction.

A significant product of her interest in writing and her collaboration with like-minded artists was the founding, with John Killens, of the Harlem Writers Guild, a workshop in which writers shared their work and perfected their craft.

Not until 1960 did Guy actually publish her first work, two short stories based in Trinidad, of which no texts survive. Her writing was increasingly being influenced by the Civil Rights Movement of the 1960s as well as by the independence efforts of various African countries. With Maya Angelou and Paule Marshall, Guy helped influence CAWAH (The Cultural Association for Women of African Heritage) to organize a protest at the United Nations in January 1961 on the occasion of the announcement of the death of Patrice Lumumba. Through this effort she was later to meet Malcolm X.

Guy's former husband Warner was murdered in 1962, and Malcolm X was assassinated in 1965. These traumatic events prompted Guy to publish her first novel, *Bird at My Window* (1966), dedicated to Malcolm, "the pure gold salvaged from the gutter of the ghettos in which we live." Shortly thereafter, in 1968, Martin Luther King, Jr., was assassinated. As a result of this violence, Guy decided to investigate the lives of young people in the South to record their attitudes toward the events occurring around them and to describe the circumstances of their lives. The result was *Children of*

Longing (1970), still one of Guy's most powerful books. It proved an inspiration and a sourcebook for Guy's later work. In its pages are the prototypes for a number of Guy's later fictional characters and first-hand stories that provide the impetus for later plots. Notably as well, the book contains an essay by the then-25-year-old Nikki Giovanni.

The 1970s witnessed some of the most significant of Guy's work. The Harlem trilogy of *The Friends* (1973), *Ruby* (1976), and *Edith Jackson* (1978) is probably still the most well known of Guy's writing, dealing as it so poignantly does with the tensions between West Indian immigrants and native-born African-Americans in Harlem. In each of the three major characters, the young women Phyllisia, Ruby, and Edith, Guy has developed sympathetic and detailed portraits of adolescents struggling against the obstacles that threaten to destroy their dreams. During this period (in 1981), Guy's sister Ameze died. *The Disappearance* (1979) begins the Imamu Jones trilogy about a sixteen-year-old African-American boy who also plays amateur detective. *New Guys around the Block* (1983) and *And I Heard A Bird Sing* (1987) complete the trilogy. These novels form the male counterpart to the earlier trilogy.

Much of Guy's reputation rests upon these six young adult novels, but her career has not remained static after the success of these early works. Her writing in the 1980s and 1990s has been marked by variety and experimentation. She has written two children's picture books, *Mother Crocodile* (1981), which is her translation of Birago Diop's retelling of an African tale, and *Billy the Great* (1992). Among other works, she has written an adult novel, *A Measure of Time* (1983); a literary fairy tale based on Hans Christian Andersen's *The Little Mermaid*, *My Love, My Love; or, the Peasant Girl* (1985); a novel featuring affluent white characters, *Mirror of Her Own* (1981); and another young adult novel *The Music of Summer* (1992). This last novel focuses on the intraracial bigotries of a group of African-American teenagers vacationing on Cape Cod. Guy enriches her work by introducing experiences gained from her past and from her travels to Europe, Africa, and the Caribbean. At various times she has lived in Haiti and in Geneva. Currently she resides in New York, writing, speaking, and spending time with her family, including her two grandchildren.

MAJOR WORKS AND THEMES

Rosa Guy's fiction presents a complex world where her characters, primarily teenagers and young adults, are poised at a significant point in their lives. They walk a tightrope between self-respect and self-destruction where the choices they make and the responsibilities they accept will affect the rest of their lives.

Most of Guy's central characters are African-American or African-Caribbean, characters whose lives are influenced by racial concerns. White racism is a prominent ingredient in the formation of Guy's fictional world. Always in the background is the implication of the white sense of superiority and the deprivation and economic hardship which the black characters must face. White racism, however, is felt more indirectly than directly. Very few white characters have much impact in the novels (except in *Mirror of Her Own*, which focuses on white characters). White racism manifests itself primarily in its effects on the circumstances in which the black characters exist and in the insidious attitudes it creates.

Poverty and lack of hope, for example, are a reality for characters like the orphaned Edith Jackson, who must try to keep her sisters together while being shuttled from foster home to foster home. She does not even dream of having nice clothes or an education because she sees these dreams as being completely out of reach. In the mean streets of Harlem, characters cope as best they can with the insurmountable obstacles that make their lives a dead end.

It is not only poverty, however, that results from racism. Even among Guy's middle-class African-American and African-Caribbean characters, racism results in what Guy has written of as the "American disease." It is a disease that infects all those black characters who "internalize [their] sense of inferiority and concretize the superiority of whites" ("The Human Spirit" 129). These characters create intraracial bigotry by devising their own caste system. Blacks with fair skin and straight hair reject their darker brothers and sisters because they remind them of those racial characteristics most despised by the white community.

This theme is most fully realized in *The Music of Summer*, in which a group of black teenagers goes to Cape Cod on vacation. Each of the characters is presented initially through physical descriptions of skin tone, hair, and eye color. Guy even introduces some ambiguity by describing the lighter-colored blacks as "fair." It is not even clear until later in the novel whether they are black or white. Sarah Richardson has been ostracized by her former friend Cathy Johnson, who has found a circle of friends richer and more fair skinned. These new friends clearly do not want to include Sarah. Their bigotry turns violent when, in a frenzy of hatred, they try to drown her. Racial bigotry turns inward as a result of white societal values.

Even African-Caribbean characters feel the brunt of this prejudice. Tensions arise from the clash between American-born African-Americans and the immigrant West Indians who are perceived as being elitist, of thinking of themselves as better than their Harlem neighbors. Some of the tensions in the friendship between the West Indian Phyllisia Cathy and the African American Edith Jackson result from the refusal of Phyllisia's father to allow her to be friends with a "ragamuffin." Melvin B. Rahming, in his book *The Evolution of the West Indian's Image in the Afro-American Novel,* argues that the West Indians have less a sense of being victims of racial injustice than do African-Americans in the United States. This results partly from the majority status of blacks in the West Indies and partly from what he describes as the greater success of the British in the West Indies in inculturating the people to think of themselves as being within rather than outside the British tradition. Guy refers to this concept herself when she explains how much of her early life was spent in absorbing British values: "[G]enerations of my family had spent and were still spending their lives learning things that had nothing to do with their lives on our little island in the sun and denigrating those who provided our sustenance" ("The Human Spirit" 128). The allegorical tale *My Love, My Love; or, the Peasant Girl* depicts the gulf that exists between the peasants on the "jewel of the Antilles" on which the novel is set and the upper-class blacks who live in their castles behind gates and guards.

Guy's novels, however, are not polemics about the evils of racism. Most of her work deals with the choices young people must make growing up in a world full of obstacles and pitfalls. These struggles are intensified by racial bias but also apply more universally to the situation of all young people. Ironically, sometimes the resources which allow young people to survive and succeed are the same as those by which they fail.

The family, for instance, can be a source of strength or of disorder. Often, in Guy's novels, it is through the sacrifice by one's family that the young person is given a chance of success. Sarah Richardson's mother, aunt, and uncle in *The Music of Summer* work and sacrifice in order to provide the money for her music lessons, her road to Juilliard and success. Families, however, can also be the source of pain. Wade Williams in *Bird at My Window* is diseased by his mother's lack of aspirations. The most serious threat to Guy's characters, however, often comes from lack of family altogether. Being an orphan had a significant impact on Guy's life, as it does for characters like Edith Jackson. Edith is robbed of her childhood because of the premature responsibilities of trying to keep her sisters together in various foster homes. It is only when she has lost the struggle to keep them together that she can even recognize the fact that improving her own life will make her a better person for everyone she loves.

Guy uses the metaphor of the orphan as an expression of the plight of all of the members of the African diaspora. Orphaned and set adrift from family and culture, they can only find success in the creation of a new culture and in acceptance of self. Destruction lies in material advancement at the expense of self-worth.

Guy's victims are those who are defeated by loss of self-worth in the vain hope of advancement within a society whose members despise them. Black women, for instance, only "advance" when they fulfill white ideals of beauty, have money, or reject the solidarity of all those of African descent. Ruby Cathy is a victim because she desperately wants to belong at any cost, looking for love in an almost desperate way.

Many of Guy's young characters are, in one way or another, looking for acceptance through love. They try all the permutations: family, friends, romantic heterosexual relationships, and, in *Ruby*, a homosexual relationship. It is only when characters learn to love themselves first, however, that other relationships take on meaning.

Guy's characters succeed in a variety of ways, one of which is through education or accomplishment. Imamu Jones succeeds by solving mysteries, Sarah Richardson succeeds by pursuing her education and her musical career, and Edith Jackson succeeds by agreeing to an abortion so that she can give herself a chance at a life off welfare. Often characters succeed through the help of an adult mentor like Mrs. Bates in *Edith Jackson* or Chere Mama in *The Music of Summer*.

What comes through clearly in all of Guy's work, however, is both the preciousness and precariousness of life. One decision, one event, one way or another can mean the difference between success or destruction. The world can be a harsh place, but even in the harshest environments of bigotry, poverty, and violence, love and family, self-respect and achievement can occur and triumph. The magical forest of Désirée Dieu-Donné in *My Love, My Love; or, the Peasant Girl* still holds its power to transform and cleanse, but also lurking there is the evil Papa Ge' with his top hat and cigar, playing capricious games with people's lives.

CRITICAL RECEPTION

From the very beginning, with the publication of her first adult novel, *Bird at My Window*, Rosa Guy was recognized as a novelist with promise. One reviewer, Thomas L. Vince, compared her work to that of James Baldwin, calling it "the most significant novel about the Harlem Negro since . . . *Go Tell It on the Mountain*." This early promise and concern with the setting of Harlem continues in the six young adult novels on which much of Guy's reputation rests, the trilogy beginning with *The Friends* in 1973—and featuring the three young female characters Phyllisia Cathy, Ruby Cathy, and Edith Jackson—and the trilogy featuring their male counterpart Imamu Jones, beginning with *The Disappearance* (1979). These novels, particularly *The Friends* and *Edith Jackson*, have consistently been named to best books lists for younger readers and for a time were a required part of the British high school curriculum.

It is in these novels that Guy displays some of her characteristic strengths, one of which is the development of character. Katherine Paterson, in a review of *The Disappearance*, cites Guy's ability to create unique characters who defy racial or gender stereotypes: "[A] great strength of Guy's work is her ability to peel back society's labels and reveal beneath them highly individual men and women" (21). Guy is especially successful at depicting the struggles that young men and women face growing up, particularly in the view of obstacles that not only discourage the attainment of dreams, but often discourage the desire to dream at all. Edith Jackson, for example, probably one of Guy's most successful and poignant characters, shoulders the responsibility of keeping her siblings together in foster homes at the expense of her own future. It is only late in the novel, in the face of her disintegrating family and an unanticipated pregnancy, that she decides with the help of her mentor Mrs. Bates to fulfill her own dreams and forge a life for herself. Hers is a courageous story of growing up in a hostile world.

Guy successfully depicts family relationships, particularly among the women in the family. The mothers and grandmothers often are strong matriarchs, but even here Guy does not rely on stereotypes. Mothers can hold families together, but they can also destroy them. Mumma, in *Bird at My Window*, stifles her son's dreams.

The setting of Harlem, so important in Guy's own life, forms a significant backdrop to her most highly praised novels. The place itself is vivid. Violet J. Harris, in *Black Women in America*, explains that "the reader smells the stench of Harlem tenements or the fresh, fragrant air of middle class enclaves" (508). Harlem can be both vital and energizing and also a deteriorating dead end, symbolic of confinement and disillusionment.

Guy is equally successful in depicting nature as a spiritual and shaping force. In both the quasi-fairy tale *My Love, My Love; or, the Peasant Girl* and in the young adult novel *The Music of Summer*, forest settings take on magical qualities as places of romance and transformation.

Guy has called herself primarily a storyteller, "a romancer," whose well-crafted tales are influenced by the oral traditions of the Caribbean. Critics often notice the care Guy takes in shaping her stories and in crafting the unmistakable dialect influenced both by her upbringing in the West Indies and by her life in Harlem.

Guy's work, however, has not been without its critics. At the same time that critics praise her vernacular language, others find it ponderous and pompous. Her female characters have generally been praised, even to the extent that a single characterization has saved a novel from universal criticism. The adult novel, *A Measure of Time*, achieved some qualified success only as a result of the strong portrait of Dorine, a character based on Guy's stepmother. Her male characters have not fared as well. One critic, Antar Sudan Katara Mberi, calls Guy to task for creating a "narrow, one-sided picture of men" while at the same time praising other aspects of her work. Furthermore, at times Guy lapses into stereotypes of the African know-it-all or of the Jew. It often seems as if the foreign characters are too good to be true and must save the Americans from their own weaknesses and delusions.

One criticism of Guy's work, however, that at times it is too dire, too hopeless, is perhaps more indicative of what is usually seen as one of her strengths, her willingness to take risks. In a recent retrospective attempting to place Guy's work in context with other Caribbean women writers, Selwyn R. Cudjoe looks back on *Bird at My Window* as "the impetus for a breakthrough of the second renaissance of African-American women's writing and [a novel which] signaled a new subject in the writing of West Indian women" (40). Cudjoe even goes so far as to call *Bird at My Window* a "magnificent achievement" that supersedes the narrative level and psychological depth of works like Richard Wright's *Native Son* and Ann Petry's *The Street* (40). Cudjoe is referring to Guy's willingness to deal not only with interracial bigotry, but also with the dynamics of intraracial hatred. At the same time that Guy exposes the cruelties toward all blacks perpetrated by the white majority, she also calls attention to the cruelties inflicted by native African-Americans on the immigrant Carribean population. A hallmark of her work is the simultaneous attempt to universalize the experience of all blacks in the Western Hemisphere and her depiction of the biases within that group.

Not only does Guy take risks in showing intraracial tensions, but she also stirred controversy in introducing the topic of lesbianism in her novel *Ruby*, arguably for the first time in a young adult novel. Guy's work can be stark and compelling, but it is also an emotionally demanding and uncompromising look at the lives of its characters.

Guy has also not hesitated to experiment with subject and genre. The line between her adult and young adult novels has always been indistinct. *Edith Jackson* and her other young adult novels, for instance, are equally compelling reading for adults. Probably the least successful in critical terms has been *Mirror of Her Own*, Guy's only novel that focuses primarily on white characters. Critics of the work, however, do not fault Guy's attempt to experiment with a new subject, but her failure to deliver her characteristically compelling and credible plot and multidimensional characters. Her experiment into literary fairy tale, *My Love, My Love; or, the Peasant Girl* and the young adult novel set on Cape Cod, *The Music of Summer*, both reach toward new territory and have generally been well received.

The promise that critics recognized in 1966 has flourished in a body of work that is varied and influential both in our understanding of the particularized settings of Harlem and the Caribbean and of individualized human responses to the struggles of becoming a distinctive and successful human being in those settings and in the face of daunting challenges.

BIBLIOGRAPHY

Young Adult Fiction by Rosa Cuthbert Guy

Bird at My Window. Philadelphia: Lippincott, 1966.
The Friends. New York: Holt, 1973. London: Gollancz, 1974.
Ruby. New York: Viking, 1976. London: Gollancz, 1981.
Edith Jackson. New York: Viking; London: Gollancz, 1978.
The Disappearance. New York: Delacorte, 1979. London: Gollancz, 1980.
Mirror of Her Own. New York: Delacorte, 1981.
New Guys around the Block. New York: Delacorte; London: Gollancz, 1983.
Paris, Pee Wee and Big Dog. New York: Delacorte; London: Gollancz, 1984.
And I Heard a Bird Sing. New York: Delacorte; London: Gollancz, 1987.
The Ups and Downs of Carl Davis III. New York: Delacorte, 1989.
Billy the Great. Illus. Caroline Binch. New York: Delacorte, 1992.
The Music of Summer. New York: Delacorte, 1992.

Adult Fiction by Rosa Cuthbert Guy

A Measure of Time. New York: Holt, Rinehart, 1983.
My Love, My Love; *or, The Peasant Girl*. New York: Holt, Rinehart, 1985.

Other Works by Rosa Cuthbert Guy

Venetian Blinds. Produced in New York, Topical Theatre, 1954.
Children of Longing. Editor. New York: Holt, Rinehart, 1970.
Diop, Birago. *Mother Crocodile*. Trans. Rosa Guy. New York: Delacorte, 1981.
"I Am a Storyteller." *Horn Book* 61.2 (1985): 220–21.
"Innocence, Betrayal, and History." *School Library Journal* (Nov. 1985): 33–34.
"The Human Spirit." *Caribbean Women Writers: Essays from the First International Conference*. Ed. Selwyn R. Cudjoe. Wellesley: Calaloux, 1990.

Selected Studies of Rosa Cuthbert Guy

Angelou, Maya. *Heart of a Woman*. New York: Random House, 1982.
Christian, Barbara. *Black Feminist Criticism: Perspective on Black Women Writers*. New York: Pergamon Press, 1985.
Cudjoe, Selwyn R., ed. *Caribbean Women Writers: Essays from the First International Conference*. Wellesley: Calaloux, 1990.
Gallo, Donald R., ed. *Speaking for Ourselves: Autobiographical Sketches by Notable Authors of Books for Young Adults*. Urbana, IL: NCTE, 1990.
Guinness, Gerald. *Here and Elsewhere: Essays on Caribbean Literature*. Rio Piedras, PR: Editorial de la universidad de Puerto Rico, 1993.
"Guy, Rosa." *Contemporary Authors*. 1st rev. Ed. Clare D. Kinsman. Vol. 17–20. Detroit: Gale, 1976.
Harris, Violet J. "Rosa Guy." *Black Women in America: An Historical Encyclopedia*. Ed. Darlene Clark Hine. Brooklyn: Carlson, 1993.
Holtze, Sally Holmes, ed. *Fifth Book of Junior Authors & Illustrators*. New York: Wilson, 1983.
Johnson, Dianne. "Perspectives on Unity and the African Diaspora: Examples from the Children's Literature of Lucille Clifton and Rosa Guy." *Work and Play in Children's Literature: Selected Papers from the 1990 International Conference of the Children's Literature Association*. Ed. Susan R. Gannon and Ruth Anne Thompson. Pleasantville, New York: Pace U, 1990.
———. *Telling Tales: The Pedagogy and Promise of African American Literature for Youth*. New York: Greenwood Press, 1990.
Kimmel, Eric A. "Guy, Rosa." *Twentieth Century Children's Writers*. Ed. Tracy Chevalier. 3rd ed. Chicago: St. James, 1989. 412–13.
LeSeur, Geta. "One Mother, Two Daughters: The Afro-American and the Afro-Caribbean Female Bildungsroman." *Black Scholar* 17.2 (1986): 26–33.
Mberi, Antar Sudan Katara. "Through a Teenager's Eyes." *Freedom Ways* 19 (1979): 47–50.
Norris, Jerrie. *Presenting Rosa Guy*. Boston: Twayne, 1988.

Paterson, Katherine. "A Family of Strangers." *Washington Post Book World* 11 Nov. 1979: 21.

"Rosa Guy." *Contemporary Literary Criticism.* Ed. Jean C. Stine. Vol. 26. Detroit: Gale, 1983. 140–46.

"Rosa Guy." *Something about the Author.* Ed. Anne Commire. Vol. 62. Detroit: Gale, 1990. 58–65.

Smith, Jessie Carney, ed. *Notable Black American Women.* Detroit: Gale, 1992.

Vince, Thomas L. Rev. of *Bird at My Window. Best Sellers* 25.20 (1966): 403.

VIRGINIA EDITH HAMILTON
(1936-   )

Janice E. Patten

BIOGRAPHY

Virginia Hamilton was born March 12, 1936, in Yellow Springs, Ohio, to her father, musician Kenneth James, and her mother, Etta Belle (née Perry) Hamilton. Today, she still lives on the same farm where she grew up in Yellow Springs, which was where her grandfather had settled after escaping slavery. Hamilton, one might say, seems rooted by her own birth to a sense of cultural history. Many of her own narratives reflect her upbringing, her heritage, and her family's fascination with storytelling.

Hamilton admits to being "a teller of tales" because of the way she heard tales told to her by her mother, by her maternal grandmother, and by other relatives who passed the time, embellishing their memories here and there with creativity and imagination as the stories warranted. Having escaped a life of slavery, her ancestors settled in this small rural community in Ohio. Her father owned a rare Gibson 1902 patent-pending mandolin and played in clubs all over the country, but never in the great concert halls from which he was banned because of his race. He was also an avid reader, devouring all kinds of literature from *The New Yorker* to DuBois' writings to the classics. Access to her father's library stimulated Hamilton's early love of literature. Her stories are created around the historical setting of this southern Ohio valley area, where fugitives from slavery fled and were helped to acquire land and begin a legacy of freedom. Her "Grandpa Perry" was brought north by his mother, who disappeared, perhaps because she was a "conductor in the Underground Railroad" (MacCann and Woodard 2:56). This tale was told by her grandfather to Hamilton's mother once a year, emphasizing the nature of slavery and the reasons for his escape, and why it should never happen to his grandchildren or to any others.

Even though she found these family narratives fascinating, she still felt "trapped" in this very small Ohio town. Unlike other young women her age, she found herself unwilling to settle for marriage at an early age. This escape route was therefore closed off, and because her family did not have much money, there were no economic means to enable her to move away. However, encouraged by her high school English teacher and a five-year scholarship procured by that teacher, Hamilton was able to attend the local college, Antioch, where she majored in writing. Attending college satisfied her for only a short time; she still yearned for experience away from her home. She left Antioch after three years for Ohio State University where after many writing and literature courses, she struck out for New York City. She began slowly, spending summers traveling between New York and Ohio until she finally left college to live permanently in the East Village section of New York. Mornings she worked as a cost accountant for an engineering firm, afternoons she wrote, and evenings she read voraciously. In between these busy times, she developed many friendships with other writers, artists, and musicians who mutually supported one another. She studied more, taking several writing courses. In one writing course under Hiram Hayden, she again found encouraging remarks regarding her talent for narration, particularly for her yet unpublished adult novel *Mayo*. His partners did not agree, and after a short while, she returned to a book she had started earlier while she had been at Antioch. This book later became her first published book, the award-winning *Zeely* (1967).

Hamilton met Arnold Adoff in 1957. She and her husband have both been writers-in-residence at Queens College of the City University of New York. She has lectured at the Library of Congress and has given numerous lectures at various colleges around the country and continues to appear in book talks for young adults. Describing herself as a "changing woman, working" (Hearne 59), she methodically devotes several hours each day to writing and the rest of the day is spent, as she says, "just living." She resides with her husband, poet and anthropologist Arnold Adoff; her daughter, Leigh Hamilton; her son, Jaime Levi; ten cats; and a dog in the small town of Yellow Springs.

MAJOR WORKS AND THEMES

In an effort to define a modern African-American identity, Virginia Hamilton has written down folk tales and myths in vibrant new ways in addition to writing new contemporary stories about young adults' struggles with self-assertion, validation, and insight. Her works of fiction demonstrate the transforming power of myth and cultural memory. While it is a commonly accepted fact that mythological tales help create a lasting bond between generations and establish a strong sense of cultural identity, it is also important to understand how this is accomplished. In her works, fictional heroes and heroines discover themselves as they slowly begin to differentiate between their individual perception of the world and that of a culturally imposed perception. Hamilton's protagonists eventually sort out modes of illusion, or false myths, from a reality based on newly recognized perception. *M. C. Higgins, the Great* (1974) illustrates Hamilton's facility with language, her profound understanding of the problematics of our modern world, her abiding trust in the human spirit, her belief in the power of heritage and the past to influence the present, and lastly, her integration of magical realism and illusion into the genre of young adult fiction. Hamilton's contribution to the canon of young adult literature is notable not only because she is a writer who captivates and entertains her audience, but also because she addresses the problems and cultural circumstances of African-Americans who need to know, just as we all need to know, that they "are not alone" ("Illusion and Reality" 15).

Hamilton's books are not about the African-American experience; they are written from within that experience, narrating stories without stereotypes and sociological didacticism. She prefers to be considered simply a writer, or a writer of a "parallel culture" (*Something about the Author* 56: 66). Hamilton possesses a sensitivity to the cultural conditions as they exist, and she presents her art as a means of preserving and passing on to young people a positive image and legacy. Following W.E.B. DuBois' logic, her books educate readers not in human hatred and centuries of prejudice, but familiarize them with the history and achievements of the black race, help them realize that being black is a normal, beautiful thing, and let them know that others like themselves have grown up to be beautiful, useful, and famous persons. Teaching children to be comfortable with their own physical realities inculcates in them an abiding faith that they are not isolated individuals, that they are indeed part of humanity. Hamilton's views on why we read good literature find a similar ground in C. S. Lewis' theory that we read "to know we are not alone" (*Horn Book* 1986). Reading a work by

Virginia Hamilton provides readers with not only good literature, but also a cultural consciousness, in an aesthetically enriching experience which is always historically authentic. The young adult experience adapts itself well to Hamilton's lingering descriptions, her focus on words, rather than actions, her characterizations, and her sense of journey—whether that be into one's own historical past, one's consciousness, or a cultural past.

And even though she speaks of taking "hold of a single theme of black experience," her books encompass many. In fact, Hamilton's prose should not be construed as offering a simple dichotomy, but rather a unique blending of music and text, of harmony and spirit, of words and visions. Indeed, there are themes in Hamilton's young adult literature which contain "strains through the whole of black history" (*Artists and Authors* 2:59–60). Throughout her works are themes of the wanderer; of the fleeing slave or the persecuted searching for a better place; of the black man hiding his true self, ever acting so that those who betray him will never touch him. But these themes are not simple; they are multifarious. Questions of a thematic nature presuppose an understandable, explainable text. However, some of Hamilton's themes remain buried under the textual palimpsest of her prose style, waiting to be uncovered. Nevertheless, motifs of alienation, of betrayal, of memory and its counterpart, amnesia, and of ancestry inform our reading of Hamilton's *oeuvre*. Because of her marvelous storytelling ability, her high intellectual achievements, and her obvious warmth and love of children, her work is often credited with raising the standard of American literature for younger readers.

Her prize-winning *M. C. Higgins, the Great* is just such a work. The book opens, as many of her works do, in an immediately captivating manner. We first encounter Mayo Cornelius (M. C.) sitting atop his 40-foot-high steel pole, a reward from Jones, his father, for swimming the Ohio River. His glistening pole, equipped with a bicycle seat, pedals, and a pair of wheels, creates a monumental illusion of flight, power, and perception, and links him to Icarus in Greek mythology in a highly suggestive way: to M. C.'s wrists are tied large heads of lettuce, leafy "wings." The pole glistens in the sunlight and reflects sharp beams of light across the dark valley forest of the Appalachians. These lettuce leaves and the bicycle parts synecdochically combine to give the illusion of flight and of omnipotence to M. C., as well as to the reader who perceives the scene. A blend of mythologies, the M. C./Icarus' illusion of flight gives an ominous foreshadowing of events—paralleling the misguided actions of Icarus in disobeying his father's warning and traveling too close to the sun to M. C.'s perilous underwater struggle and fashioning his own way against the modern forces of industrialization. Hamilton's protagonist presents a syncretistic image of a modern young adult fused with a seemingly timeless figure, as he blends with the harmonies of the natural world.

Hamilton narrates a poignant black folk tale, "The People Could Fly," in her book by the same name. The tale begins, "They say the people could fly. Say that long ago in Africa, some of the people knew magic. . . . And they flew like blackbirds over the fields. . . . Then, many of the people were captured for Slavery" (166). In what might be called a "code-language," one slave speaks to another, detailing a fantasy world of suffering, of magic power, retelling and retelling by those "who had only their imaginations to set them free" (173). In a similar manner *M. C. Higgins, the Great* is concerned with flight, escape and discovery. M.C.'s flight is solitary, and he acknowledges that "To be by himself in the perfect quiet was reason enough for him to wake up early" (2). His strange and magnificent pole is also a marker for the dead, marking the bones of ancestors actually buried around the pole. The gravestones themselves become at the end of the novel the cement that connects the living present to the past, aiding M. C. and his father to stem the tide of industrialization and impending doom from the sliding mass of Sarah's Mountain.

We witness yet another tension in the novel almost immediately as M. C. runs barefoot, "striding swiftly through the piney woods" trying to capture rabbits (3) and the Dude who captures voices in a "little box of a tape recorder" (3). M. C., with his friend Ben, beholds a harmony with nature, comprehending that freedom and communication do exist between dissimilar living things. Sarah's Mountain is itself a personality, a living, breathing being with a consciousness of its own significant history; it seems to breathe its own struggles from bondage, just as the escaped slave Sarah had fought for her freedom years earlier. This story is built on sorrow, yet out of this sorrow rises a sense of each man's unyielding human spirit and strength to fight. Hamilton's unique blending of mythology and realism creates a magical world which, she argues, shows how "our history as given in the myths shows our purpose . . . we must make the world a safe place for us to be ourselves" (*In the Beginning* xi).

M. C.'s friend Ben seems to be bred in this raw, unadulterated nature. His family remains isolated from the world, unspoiled, untouched by capitalism, by modernization. Ben's father, Mr. Killburn, recognizes that even though they are living in a vegetable-farming commune that is approached through a huge web of vines, he still holds "a half-forgotten dream awakened into life" (218) in which children can climb and play, where they are all part of a vast living universe—where the "soil is body." In a significant pause in the book, Killburn notes, "We don't own nothing of it. We just caretakers, here to be of service. . . . The truth is, we just a body wiggling and jiggling in and out of the light" (229). Feeling like an outsider himself in his connection with these six-fingered, red-haired blacks, the Killburns, M. C. shows us as well how, in some ways, we are all outsiders laboring to belong. This story also accentuates the theme of outsider/insider when the music-collecting Dude arrives to tape Banina's (M. C.'s mother) voice, and Lurhetta Outlaw and her car wander in to captivate M. C.'s heart. Banina's haunting melodic voice expresses the power of her individual secrets, of her own sorrow. Banina and other members of M. C.'s family communicate with each other by yodeling, a "magic belonging only to those of the hills" (169). Blending the echoes from the mountain in the form of yodeling, nature and man seem to be in harmony, communicating effort-lessly. Animated nature, mists, swimming in darkness, listening to beautiful soul music, living in a partial cave and among vines and natural vegetation all add to the novel's mystical, powerful, and dynamic realism. With each reading the themes and images in this book cohere in new and exciting ways.

Zeely (1967), Hamilton's first book, is similar in many ways to *M. C. Higgins*, but in some ways it does not have its richness of multiplicity. It demystifies African history from present circumstances and puts literary considerations before sociological/didactic ones. The protagonist Eliza-beth, who calls herself "Geeder," sees a strikingly beautiful, extremely tall Zeely first as a night-traveler, then as a Watutsi queen. In a moment of insight at the end of the novel, Geeder sees through this illusion and accepts Zeely for what she is. Yet, the story leaves the reader with the sense that illusion still remains—a unique blending in connection with Zeely's authen-tic nature. Is she not really a night-traveler after all?

As *Zeely* is a rural story, *The Planet of Junior Brown* (1971) is a city book, but one which also deals with the problems of realism and self-created illusion. Junior Brown is an enormously fat, precocious, and lonely boy, who lives with his overbearing, unhappy, lonely, chronically asthmatic mother, and finds an unlikely friendship with Buddy, who has no parents and lives in a fulfilling way on the street, and in the tenement buildings. The two boys find a peaceful haven in a concealed janitor's closet with another outsider, an ex-teacher now janitor. The janitor builds for these truant boys a large, rotating model of the solar system, where they all revolve around a new reality, a new illusion. The real world is also composed of planets of homeless boys located around the city, each with a "Tomorrow Billy" as leader, each also lost in the galaxy of the huge city. Buddy bonds with Junior Brown, finding him a place in his own dark, cold tenement building which is warmer in spirit than Junior's home. Hamilton works with an extended metaphor of playing and hearing music. Junior's piano playing is rendered silent by his mother's removal of the sounding strings, and by his piano teacher's refusal to allow his playing on her piano. Complexity of perception and multiple hauntings permeate this book as well, giving a powerful picture of inner-city life of the young and powerless. Buddy's spirit, his inventiveness, give an uplifting sense of hope in an otherwise bleak world.

The protagonist in *Sweet Whispers, Brother Rush* (1982) extends both M. C.'s and Junior Brown's situations to a commingling of a seemingly supernatural experience and a harsh reality involving a competent, bright teenager and absent parents, a retarded sibling, and a search for identity. Tree, short for Teresa, encounters events and sees herself experiencing them in a unique manner. Her brother suffers incomprehensible pain from a strange illness, and this leaves Teresa fearful and powerless. Hamilton employs a unique literary device: Brother Rush appears and through a small, "bright space," Tree penetrates her family's past, her own past, her mother's past, and perceives her own reality with a new understanding. Here we see a palimpsest approach tying myths and narrative ancestry to the present.

Ancestry also contributes to the mystery of the present in Hamilton's trilogy: *The House of Dies Drear* (1968), *The Mystery of Drear House: Book Two of Dies Drear* (1987), and *The Mystery of Drear House: The Conclusion of Dies Drear Chronicle* (1994). Thomas is a sensitive, self-sufficient, albeit lonely young man who embarks on a new adventure when his father, a Civil War historian, is transferred to a small Ohio town. Thirteen-year-old Thomas is both frightened and intrigued by the legends he hears, by a series of ghostly occurrences, and by the mysterious caretaker, old Pluto, in their new rented home which had been built by the abolitionist Dies Drear as a station in the Underground Railroad. In the midst of shadows, unexplained noises, and strange whisperings, Thomas discovers a labyrinth of tunnels, and he and his father unearth a cave which holds many treasures, and in so doing they also discover and uncover part of their own history, their own past. Thomas' appetite for mystery is whet as is ours, the readers. In addition to being a marvelous mystery, it is also a typical young adult story of maturation, of Thomas' growing awareness of and appreciation for the complexities of history, both collective and personal. A kind of serenity is achieved both for the characters as they enter this strange underground cave and for us readers as we come to know the simultaneity of the past and present, the collapsing of time and space in a fictive world.

Hamilton has written many other fascinating books for young adult readers, both fiction and nonfiction. Her interest in mythology and our quest for origins finds unique expression in her book *In the Beginning: Creation Stories from around the World* (1988). These twenty-five stories read like melodies, sung from the heart of diverse yet similar cultures around the world. In December 1994, the book was reissued with a reading cassette by James Earl Jones. "Myth stories present themselves as truth" writes Hamilton in her note from the author preface to the book (ix). At the end of each of these narratives is a comment by Hamilton about the myth itself. A young adult course might well begin with a study of this book, followed by reading one or more of her novels as applications and fictive worlds enhanced and informed by these mythical tales of origination.

Another recent nonfiction book that also collects a number of cultural narratives is *Many Thousand Gone: African Americans from Slavery to Freedom* (1993). Chapters in this, her latest collection, include "A Vanished Slave and His Return," "Elizabeth Freeman," "The Nat Turner Rebellion," "The Brave Conductor," and "The Tide of Freedom." Hamilton traces narratives from the beginnings of human slavery in Virginia in 1619. Trading in human beings began a year before the Pilgrims landed in Plymouth. In her afterword, Hamilton notes that in the ratification of the Thirteenth Amendment to the Constitution on December 18, 1865, slavery was formally abolished, and in the following year, the Civil Rights Acts were passed, "giving African Americans citizenship and protecting them from oppressive laws and codes" (145). Freedom brought with it responsibilities; African-Americans were now free to buy land, to educate themselves, to pursue their individual and collective desires, to write, to sing, to live together, and to read. This freedom, her book records, has always and will always be the goal of all people, but most poignantly for the African-Americans.

The People Could Fly: American Black Folktales (1985) brings together the special tales of the African-Americans in their confronting and living without freedom. This oral literature is divided into four sections in the book, representing the main body of black folk tales. She includes such familiar tales as Uncle Remus' "Bruh Rabbit," "The Beautiful Girl of the Moon Tower," and "John and the Devil's Daughter." Hamilton cautions her readers, though, as she intimates and articulates in many of her works, that these tales "belong to all of us" (xii). Created out of years of sorrow and suffering, these tales, nevertheless, offer readers a sense of hope and celebration. "Remember the voices from the past" she both warns and encourages her readers.

In all of her works, Hamilton's discourse articulates that a myth of a common and distinct origin in time and space gives an ethnic community a sense of cultural identity. It is precisely, however, this mythological quality which both simultaneously creates a semiotic visibility for that cultural identity and reinforces its own self-reflexive invisibility. We see this dynamically and synchronously limned in the characters of Tree, Thomas, and Junior Brown. Memory provides dreamlike sequences in narrative or gives an almost supernatural quality to the spatio-temporal frame. Ethnic traces give hermeneutic importance to several of Hamilton's narrative worlds. For example, Hamilton weaves ethnic traces through her books, providing readers with an unusual, often unsettling, sense of their own disorientation, misunderstanding, and misperception. Just as readers instantaneously experience a sense of otherness, they also observe a similar struggle in protagonists who put themselves in contact with the foundational world of their ancestors, reproduce themselves as members of an ethnic community, and subsequently identify themselves as different from the Eurocentric mainstream culture. This seeming fragmentation has a potential to cause inexperienced readers to feel themselves outsiders, as other. This reading experience is potentially positive because it replicates the feeling of otherness in the "parallel culture." As W. E. B. DuBois and others have pointed out, ethnic seeing cannot be separated from the seer, nor the seer from his act of seeing. The uncanny Junior Brown both finds himself and loses himself in a world created in a concealed closet, and in almost epic proportions he quests to hear his unheard music played; Elizabeth ultimately locates her identity when, in sorting out wild imaginings from unfamiliar mores, she loses her illusion of Zeely as an African princess; and Thomas re-covers and un-covers the mysterious history of the house of Dies Drear only after he reveals the identity of "invisible" intruders. As Ralph Ellison's fictional account of invisibility demonstrates, African-American individuality is predicated on the fact that one must both be simultaneously "other" and acculturated; one must see, be seen, and be not seen simultaneously.

Similarly, Hamilton's protagonists are both intersubjects, choosing to identify positively with their ethnic cultural history, and to acknowledge their difference from the dominant culture to which they also undeniably belong. Hamilton's texts are beautifully constructed intertexts, a profound narrative blend of past and present, of visibility and invisibility. For example, we can see *M. C. Higgins, the Great* as an intertext, specifically as M. C.'s struggles with the memory of his family's past, the mountain's memory of its own history of abuse, and his own search for individuation which provides a paradigm for this crisis. Here the crisis of memory and the crisis of identity become synchronous. "As he watched the shadowy figures in the kitchen, his thoughts seemed to float away from him. He fell into a kind of reverie as he heard, deep in his mind, a wild creature's roar. . . . Or was he the image, waiting for another part of himself to reach it?" (66). Each of the words in Hamilton's pattern of signification are polysemous. And indeed, this passage suggests an allegory of reading, the process of watching and gazing, seeing oneself, and waiting for another part of oneself to reach a new kind of comprehension.

Throughout Hamilton's career the oppositions generated by the semiotics of vision (imagining/seeing, blindness/sight, freedom/entrapment, memory/prophesy) provide crucial organizing principles for her narratives. Her characters perform variations of visionary seeing that often paradoxically preclude sensory apprehension. Young adults and teachers of young adult fiction and nonfiction alike are challenged by these imaginative, complex, and very literary works. Her fictive worlds and her characters' patterns of seeing suggest that there are no signifiers in the material world sufficient to mirror the African-American experience. Hamilton's words provide us with that metaphorical veil of which W. E. B. DuBois speaks. DuBois notes that before each segment of his writing stands a bar of Sorrow Songs—"some echo of haunting melody from the only American music which welled up from the black souls in the dark past. And finally, need I add that I who speak here am bone of the bone and flesh of the flesh of them that live within the Veil" (*Souls of the Black Folk* 2). Virginia Hamilton's works are much influenced by DuBois' thematics and his sense of double consciousness. Just as in literacy lay the true freedom for the black slave, so too Virginia Hamilton's literature of today generates a new awareness, a new freedom—intellectual as well as physical—a refusal to be enslaved by ideas, by cultural attitudes, by present circumstances. We put down a book of Hamilton's with W. E. B. DuBois' question silently hovering: "Would America have been America without her Negro people?" (*The Souls of Black Folks*).

CRITICAL RECEPTION

"Few writers of fiction for young people are as daring, inventive, and challenging to read—or to review—as Virginia Hamilton" writes Ethel L. Heins (*Horn Book* 505–06). David Guy remarks on Hamilton's plots, which at the outset often seem like any other young adult book, but adds that Tree in *Sweet Whispers, Brother Rush* longs for a larger world, for a real family, for some respect as a person, for a little romance "but finds them in an extraordinary manner. She is visited by a ghost—Brother Rush, her mother's brother." Guy continues to note that in reading this novel he felt the presence of a different kind of imagination, a poetic visionary. Katherine Paterson, a well-known young author, writes that Hamilton's style is always demanding, that she has taken ideas that "occur repeatedly . . . and bathed them in her unique black light" (56). One further note, in writing of *The Planet of Junior Brown*, Michael Cart says that the "book is like a perfectly executed piece of music; the author doesn't strike a single false note" (126).

Alleen Pace Nilsen and Kenneth L. Donelson note in *Literature for Today's Young Adults* that during the first forty-seven years of the Newbery Award only three winners portrayed protagonists of color (426). However, in 1974, Hamilton's *M. C. Higgins, the Great* earned several awards: the Newbery, ALA Best Young Adult Book, *Boston Globe/Horn Book* Award, Lewis Carroll Shelf Award, *New York Times* Outstanding Books of the Year, IBBY (International Board on Books for Young People) Honor List for Text, and National Book Award, breaking all previous records for the most awards given a young adult book. The characters in *M. C. Higgins*, as in Hamilton's other books, are all black, but as John Rowe Townsend notes, "there is no taint of racism in her books" (97) for she demonstrates that the experience of a people must come to mean the experience of humankind.

In terms of the critical reception of two of her books which are strictly biographical, but still aimed at the young adult audience, the response has been overwhelmingly positive. Marilyn Gardner writes, "The problem of the twentieth century is the problem of the color line . . . Hamilton's excellent biography, *W. E. B. DuBois*, is a tribute to the lifetime he spent trying to solve that problem." Hamilton's work, she notes, is "meticulously annotated, comprehensive and generally objective—too detailed for pre-teens, perhaps, but extremely good for slightly older readers" (B5). Zena Sutherland calls it a "sober record," "an affirmation of his life" (8). About her biography *Paul Robeson: The Life and Times of a Free Black Man* (1974), Elaine Landau remarks that the text remains unfictionalized and acquires chilling authenticity as each incident is fully documented by Senate testimony. One lone voice suggests that the complexity of Robeson's life eludes Hamilton.

Not all reviews have been positive. Jane Langton writes of *Arilla Sun Down* (1976) that "perhaps too many things are piled too precariously on too many edges. There is too much talking, too much explaining and forced Indian imagery" (39). Perhaps Alice Walker should have another look at Hamilton. Walker says that while her ideas in *The Planet of Junior Brown* are "interesting," the book "itself is surprisingly dull" (8).

Hamilton's own theory regarding the value inherent in young adult books often finds her at odds with publishers and other current trends which suggest that problem books are the new rage for young adults, that they only read to find answers to the complex issues in their own lives. She deliberately chooses a literary radicalism in the hope of removing traditional prose restrictions and creating new ways to approach literary forms from a perspective other than that of the majority. Just as Russian formalism sought to de-familiarize the familiar, so too do Hamilton's narratives seek to problematize and de-familiarize the standard, preconceived mythos, in her own words from the Greek sense of "word which means final authority" (*In the Beginning* x).

BIBLIOGRAPHY

Young Adult Fiction by Virginia Edith Hamilton

Zeely. Illus. Symeon Shimin. New York: Alladin, 1967.
The House of Dies Drear. Illus. Eros Keith. New York: Collier, 1968.
The Planet of Junior Brown. New York: Macmillan, 1971. London: Gollancz, 1987.
M. C. Higgins, the Great. New York: Collier, 1974.
Arilla Sun Down. New York: Greenwillow, 1976.
Justice and Her Brothers. New York: Greenwillow, 1978. London: Hamish Hamilton, 1979.
Dustland. New York: Greenwillow; London: MacRae, 1980.
The Gathering. New York: Greenwillow; London: MacRae, 1981.
Sweet Whispers, Brother Rush. New York: Avon, 1982.
The Magical Adventures of Pretty Pearl. New York: Harper, 1983.
A Little Love. New York: Philomel, 1984. London: Gollancz, 1985.
Junius over Far. New York: Harper, 1985.
The Mystery of Drear House: Book Two of Dies Drear. New York: Greenwillow, 1987.
A White Romance. New York: Philomel, 1987. London: Gollancz, 1988.
Cousins. New York: Scholastic, 1991.
The Mystery of Drear House: The Conclusion of Dies Drear Chronicle. New York: Macmillan, 1994.

Fiction for Children by Virginia Edith Hamilton

The Time-Ago Tales of Jahdu. Illus. Nonny Hogrogian. New York: Macmillan, 1969.
Time-Ago Lost: More Tales of Jahdu. Illus. Ray Prather. New York: Macmillan, 1973.
Jahdu. Illus. Jerry Pinkney. New York: Greenwillow, 1980.

Drylongo. Illus. Jerry Pinkney. San Diego: Harcourt, 1988.
The All Jahdu Storybook. Illus. Barry Moser. New York: Dial, 1991.
Plain City. New York: Blue Sky, 1993.

Other Works for Children by Virginia Edith Hamilton

W. E. B. DuBois: A Biography. New York: Crowell, 1972.
Paul Robeson: The Life and Times of a Free Black Man. New York: Harper, 1974.
Willie Bea and the Time the Martians Landed. New York: Greenwillow, 1983.
The People Could Fly: American Black Folk Tales. Illus. Leo Dillon and Diane Dillon. New York: Knopf, 1985. London: Walker, 1986.
Anthony Burns: The Defeat and Triumph of a Fugitive Slave. New York: Knopf, 1988.
In the Beginning: Creation Stories from around the World. Illus. Barry Moser. San Diego: Harcourt Brace, 1988.
The Dark Way: Stories from the Spirit World. Illus. Lambert Davis. New York: Harcourt, 1990.
Many Thousand Gone: African Americans from Slavery to Freedom. Illus. Leo Dillon and Diane Dillon. New York: Knopf, 1993.

Works for Adults by Virginia Edith Hamilton

"Illusion and Reality." Lecture. Washington, D.C.: Library of Congress, 1975.
The Writings of W. E. B. Du Bois. Editor. New York: Crowell, 1975.
"Changing Woman, Working." *Celebrating Children's Books: Essays on Children's Literature in Honor of Zena Sutherland.* Ed. Betsey Hearne and Marilyn Kaye. New York: Lothrop, Lee, and Shepard, 1981. 54–59.

Selected Studies of Virginia Edith Hamilton

Apseloff, Marilyn F. *Virginia Hamilton: Ohio Explorer in the World of Imagination.* Ohio: State Library of Ohio, 1979.
Cart, Michael. Rev. of *The Planet of Junior Brown. School Library Journal* 18.1 (1971): 126.
Gardner, Marilyn. "Rebels, Black and White." *Christian Science Monitor,* 4 May 1972: B5.
Guy, David. "Escaping from a World of Troubles." *Washington Post Book World,* 7 November 192: 14.
Haviland, Virginia, ed. *The Openhearted Audience: Ten Authors Talk about Writing for Children.* Washington, DC: Library of Congress, 1980.
Heins, Ethel L. Rev. of *Sweet Whispers, Brother Rush. Horn Book* 53.5 (1982): 505–506.

Johnson, Dianne. "Telling Tales: The Pedagogy and Promise of African-American Literature for Youth." *Contributions in Afro-American Studies 139.* New York: Greenwood, 1990. 61–71.

Landau, Elaine. "A Brave Man, Baby Gorilla, a Poisoned Planet." *New York Times Book Review*, 22 December 1974: 8.

Langton, Jane. Rev. *Arilla Sundown. New York Times Book Review*, 31 October 1976: 39.

MacCann, Donnarae, and Gloria Woodard, eds. *Authors of Books for Young People.* 2nd ed. New York: Scarecrow, 1971.

Moss, Anita. "Mythical Narrative: Virginia Hamilton's *The Magical Adventures of Pretty Pearl.*" *The Lion and the Unicorn* 9 (1985): 53–57.

Nilsen, Alleen Pace, and Kenneth L. Donelson. *Literature for Today's Young Adults.* 4th ed. New York: HarperCollins, 1993.

Paterson, Katherine. "Family Visions." *New York Times Book Review* 14 Nov. 1982: 41, 56.

Sutherland, Zena. Rev. of *W.E.B. DuBois: A Biography. Bulletin of the Center for Children's Books* 26.1 (1972): 8.

Townsend, John Rowe. "Virginia Hamilton." In *A Sounding of Storytellers: New and Revised Essays on Contemporary Writers for Children and Young Adults.* New York: Harper, 1974. 97–110.

"Virginia Hamilton." *Children's Literature Review.* Ed. Gerard J. Senick. Vol. 11. Detroit: Gale, 1986. 54–95.

Walker, Alice. Rev. of *The Planet of Junior Brown. New York Times Book Review*, 24 Oct. 1971: 8.

Works Cited

DuBois, W.E.B. *Essay and Sketches.* N.Y: Dodd, 1979. 198.

JAMAKE HIGHWATER
(1942?-)

Linda C. Jolivet

BIOGRAPHY

Controversy and mystery surround the background of Jamake Highwater. Publishers, biographers, and reviewers have sung his praises from the moment he made his first enigmatic entrance on the literary scene. But the fact that there is so little consistent information available regarding his origins, childhood, and family contribute to much controversy about his authenticity and his authority to write of Native experience.

Early reports place his childhood in Toledo, Ohio, in the late 1920s or early 1930s. Other accounts place his birth at about 1942, his birthplace as Glacier County, Montana, and his early years in Alberta, Canada (*Dictionary of American Children's Fiction* 102). Still other accounts quote the author as not knowing "where or when he was born." On occasion he has stated that he was born in Montana (*Children's Literature Review* 20). Perhaps these controversies are best discussed in *Awkwesasne Notes* (Summer 1984) and *Children's Literature Review* (vol. 17). His early promotional literature states he is of "Blackfeet/Cherokee heritage" (book jacket of *Anpao*, 1977). Ed Calf Robe, elder of the Blood Reserve of Blackfeet, gave Highwater the tribal name of Piitai Sahkomaapii (Eagle Son) in 1979. Yet recent publicity information fails to provide any information about his purported Indian heritage. The controversy surrounding his identity, the assertions from writers and researchers Duane Champagne, Elizabeth

Cook-Lynn, Jerry Reynolds, columnist Jack Anderson, and numerous others that Jamake Highwater is not Native American, was fueled not solely because he was writing as a "Native" writer, but some believed that he deliberately fabricated an Indian persona for literary and monetary gain. Highwater himself has consistently refuted allegations that he is not Native American, although he has done little to provide evidence of his heritage.

Critics have also called into question his claims of degrees in cultural anthropology and music, as well as his assertion that he speaks eleven languages and his self-promotion as a "tribal person." He is not registered with any particular tribe, but has talked about his childhood as if he were a member of a tribe. He has claimed himself a recipient of tribal wisdom and of the oral tradition. Statements such as "it's possible for everyone to find the Indian in himself" (*Children's Literature Review*) add to the scrutiny. Ward Churchill, in *Fantasies of the Master Race* (1992), has grouped Highwater with what he calls "plastic medicine men"—non-Native writers who appropriate and re-shape Native experience for their own profit. The Native American poet, critic, and anthropologist Wendy Rose agrees in her essay "The Great Pretenders: Further Reflections on White Shamanism." Here she states that although it is appropriate for non-Native peoples to write of Native subjects, they cannot pretend to be Native or to give a Native perspective. She uses the analogy of the Catholic Mass: a poet can use the iconography of the Mass, can even chant poetry as part of a Mass, but can never pass him or herself off as a priest. She believes that Highwater, among others, is doing exactly that (414).

Despite the almost universal condemnation of Highwater's Native credentials from within the Native American community, he is still being held up by any number of non-Native educators and critics as an authentic purveyor of Native culture and beliefs.

MAJOR WORKS AND THEMES

The recurring themes in Highwater's fiction focus on outcasts, tragic, abandoned loners, all of whom are shrouded in myth and fantasy. This is perhaps a reflection of his ambiguous, elusive, questionable identity and lack of a clear identification with the larger Native American community. Although a number of Highwater's earlier works focus on Indian art, music, and philosophy, as well as travel, his most celebrated works are based upon folklore which explores and celebrates the Native American oral tradition. *Anpao: An American Indian Odyssey* (1977) was his first well-received work of fiction. As Highwater notes in his afterword to the book, "I created

Anpao out of many stories of the boyhood of early Indians, and from my own experience as well, in order to make an Indian 'Ulysses' who could become the central dramatic character in the saga of Indian life in North America" (240). The tales relate the story of Anpao, who in order to marry the beautiful Ko-Ko-mik-e-is must travel to the house of the sun and have the scar from his face removed. In the beginning, Anpao is an outcast, living hand-to-mouth in a village not his own. After many obstacles, however, he finds the house of the sun, obtains the secret of the Medicine Lodge, and returns a hero. Based on the Blackfoot legend of Scarface as collected by John Bird Grinnell, the story combines the typical young adult theme of achieving self-understanding with parallels to Greek mythology, thus raising youth to heroic heights.

The Sun, He Dies: The End of the Aztec World (1980) shows that Highwater is interested in the heritage of all indigenous peoples in the Americas. The hero of the book is Nanautzen, or the Ugly One, an Aztec who becomes Montezuma's chief orator. It is through his eyes that we see the coming of Cortez and the destruction of high Aztec culture and civilization. Highwater bolsters his credentials to write this story by including maps, a glossary, an afterword, and a bibliography.

Legend Days (1984) is the first of the Ghost Horse trilogy, a fictional account of three generations of Northern Plains Indians, from the nineteenth century to the present. *Legend Days* is the story of Amana, a Native woman who survives (with the help of a spirit animal, a fox) the smallpox epidemic, yearns to help her tribe, and marries her invalid sister's husband. Its sequel, *The Ceremony of Innocence* (1985) picks up the story three years after the death of Amana's husband and after she has been driven out by her tribe for attempting to act as a warrior/hunter. She gives birth to a daughter, Jemina (whose father is French Canadian). Jemina grows up alienated from her Native ancestry, mimicking whites, and eventually marries a doomed Indian rodeo stunt rider, with whom she has two children. The novel does not spare the reader the bleakness of depression life and of Native difficulties with alcoholism and racism. Jemina has two children, one of whom, Sitko, is strongly attracted to his grandmother Amana and his tribal past.

I Wear the Morning Star (1986) is the last in the series, bringing us up to contemporary times. Sitko has been abandoned in an orphanage, where he resists attempts to break him and take away his Native heritage. Sitko constantly faces pressure to assimilate, but is aided in his resistance by his grandmother Amana. Sitko eventually finds redemption and identity in the role of the artist.

The books in the Ghost Horse trilogy were widely praised for "powerful, rhythmic prose" (Flanagan 336) and for the interweaving of symbol, supernaturalism, and realism. Yet Doris Seale in *Interracial Books for Children Bulletin* states that with the exception of *Anpao*, "none of [Highwater's] books *feels* very Indian and that by and large they lack some balance. Of *Legend Days* she says the "supernatural parts seem poorly integrated into the realistic whole of the narrative" (18–19).

Ceremony of Innocence also received some criticism for underdeveloped characters and an "overwrought style" (Rochman 6), but a more serious criticism of the novel has to do with the treatment of the individual. The willfulness and self-interest of the adolescent characters, common in mainstream young adult life and fiction, is not as common in a traditional setting, yet is taken as cause for celebration as the focal point of the novel. The title itself, a reference to the poet W. B. Yeats' poem "The Second Coming," is clue enough that there is a fairly Eurocentric focus in this "Native American" novel. Seale, again writing in *Interracial Books for Children Bulletin*, criticizes the lack of believable characters in the novel, and finds a problem in attempting to represent all of history through a few people. She writes that "one might also be tempted to cite the author for his helpless and ineffectual women, were it not for the fact that none of his characters seem competent to cope with life on any level." She also complains that any reader unfamiliar with Native history would come away from the novel unable to understand how Indians were able to survive at all.

Highwater's novel based on the life of Dr. Charles Alexander Eastman, *Eyes of Darkness* (1985), provides insight into typical criticism of his work by Native American writers. The book is the account of Yesa, later renamed Charles Alexander Eastman, a traditional and spiritual Sioux taken from his people at age seventeen to live the life of the white man. He grows up trying to use the white man's wisdom to keep Indian heritage alive. The sensationalizing of areas presented as matter-of-fact in Eastman's biography are exploited and touted as "exotic" in the Highwater novel. The theme of the individual going against traditional wisdom, or a young child questioning tradition in a Eurocentric manner, would be an anomaly in Native culture. Yet, since this is a common theme in the mainstream literary world, Highwater gives it a disproportionate degree of attention and celebration in his fictionalized biography.

Although reviews of *Eyes of Darkness* cite this work as "remarkable" and "a tale of desperation and hope, capturing the spirit of these tribes that perished without mercy" (*Kirkus Review* 990), the praise is couched in condescending and pitying language concerning the "disappeared" Indians.

There is an assumption that Native Americans mattered in the historical past, but are not part of the historical present.

CRITICAL RECEPTION

Highwater's books have been critically well received by the mainstream press. *Anpao* was named a Newbery Honor Book and a *Boston Globe/Horn Book* Honor Book in 1978. *Many Smokes, Many Moons* won the Jane Addams Children's Book Award in 1979.

Anpao received wide praise. James Norworthy wrote that "to say that Highwater did for American Indian culture what Homer did for the people of Ancient Greece may seem astonishing or perhaps overstated, but it is true" (235). Jane Yolen, on the other hand, questions whether it is a novel or an extended folk tale, and says, "It is nowhere as great a narrative as the *Odyssey*" (26). Yet, by and large critics agreed with Virginia Haviland, who praised Highwater's gift of a "poetic, dignified language" (64).

Praise for his other works has not been as unanimous, and even *Anpao* has come under reconsideration. Jon Stott, in a lengthy article in *Studies in the Literary Imagination*, recalls his earlier praise of the book, but goes on to be troubled by what he now perceives to be a heavier reliance on the theories of Joseph Campbell than on the truths of Native life and spirituality.

Mainstream critics are also troubled, in the Ghost Horse trilogy, by "strained and repetitive language" (Rochman 973) and "overwrought style" (Seale 6), as well as for lack of character development. From the Native point of view, however, Highwater's novels pose greater problems. Composite characters meshing Native traditions from different tribes cause discomfort among Native American critics more so than among non-Native critics. Although Highwater says in the afterword to *Anpao* that he believes "in the existence of some sort of transcendent Indian sensibility," not all Native Americans agree. Subtleties of individual cultures glossed over seem to take on a lesser importance among the mainstream reviewers and publishers, perhaps shedding light on the gap between those represented in the mainstream literary world and those calling for a high degree of cultural authenticity. Native American scholars suggest that Highwater's writings are for the "nonspecialist," while others cite his maladjusted characters, noting that they are symbolic, romanticized tragic figures, both titillating and melodramatic, one step away from the tragic and false figure of the "disappearing Indian" or the historical, as opposed to contemporary, Indian.

Another difficulty for Native readers of Highwater's work is the emphasis on characters who are often portrayed as being detached from the Indian communities from which they spring. The recurring figure of the individu-alistic, disconnected rebel is glamorized as a nonfunctioning outsider. While this may satisfy Highwater's predominantly Euro-American readership, it raises serious difficulties for the Native population, which is rooted in community and underplays the value of the individual.

When Highwater began publishing young adult fiction, there was little available fiction for this audience about the Native experience, and this perhaps accounts in part for the highly enthusiastic early reviews. Critical reception of his work has become increasingly lukewarm over the years, partly due to the controversy over his authenticity, but also because cultural and literary standards for Native American writers have risen substantially since the 1970s. Highwater has said that "a human being should be judged by his or her work" ("Indian Heritage Queried" 6), rather than by the authenticity of his background. While this may be true, and while no critic has seriously questioned the truth of the portrayals of Native hunting methods or of boarding school experiences, critics have expressed—and continue to express—an uneasiness that although the facts of Highwater's fiction may be true enough, he is not true to the spirit of the Native American worldview.

BIBLIOGRAPHY

Young Adult Fiction by Jamake Highwater

Anpao: An American Indian Odyssey. Illus. Fritz Scholder. Philadelphia: Lippin-cott, 1977.
The Sun, He Dies: The End of the Aztec World. New York: Lippincott, 1980.
Legend Days. New York: Harper, 1984.
The Ceremony of Innocence. New York: Harper, 1985.
Eyes of Darkness. New York: Lothrop, 1985.
I Wear the Morning Star. New York: Harper, 1986.

Verse for Children by Jamake Highwater

Moonsong Lullaby. Photographs by Marcia Keegan. New York: Lothrop, 1981.
Songs for the Seasons. Illus. Sandra Speidel. New York: Lothrop, 1994.

Works for Adults by Jamake Highwater

Journey to the Sky. New York: Crowell, 1978.

Many Smokes, Many Moons: A Chronology of American Indian History through Indian Art. NY: Lippincott, 1978.

Under the name "J. Marks," Highwater has also published a number of works on modern dance and culture, including a biography of Mick Jagger.

Selected Studies of Jamake Highwater

Adams, John. Rev. of *The Sun, He Dies. School Library Journal* 27.2 (1980): 167.

Anderson, Jack. "Lots of Smoke Rises around This 'Indian.'" *Washington Post District Weekly* 16 February 1984: D, C, H.

Churchill, Ward. *Fantasies of the Master Race.* Monroe, ME: Common Courage, 1992.

Dictionary of American Children's Fiction. Eds. Althea K. Helbig and Agnes Regan Perkins. Westport: Greenwood, 1993.

Flanagan, Kate M. Rev. of *Legend Days. Horn Book* 60.3 (1984): 336–37.

Hand, Dorcas. Rev. of *Legend Days. School Library Journal* 30.10 (1984): 84.

Haviland, Virginia. "Tales of the Tribes." *Washington Post Book World* 12 Feb. 1978: G4.

"Indian Heritage Queried: Highwater Refutes Charges." *School Library Journal* 30.8 (1984): 7.

"Jamake Highwater." *Children's Literature Review.* Ed. Gerard J. Senick. Vol. 17. Detroit: Gale, 1989. 19–32.

Momaday, N. Scott. "Indian Facts and Artifacts." *New York Times Book Review* 30 Apr. 1978: 42.

Norworthy, James. "Rev. of *Anpao.*" *Catholic Library World* 49.5 (1977): 235.

Rev. of *Eyes of Darkness. Kirkus Review,* 53.18 (Sept. 1985): 990.

Rev. of *The Sun, He Dies. Choice* 2 Oct. 1980: 248.

Rochman, Hazel. Rev. of *Ceremony of Innocence. Interracial Books for Children Bulletin* 17.1 (1986): 6.

———. Rev. of *I Wear the Morning Star. Booklist* 1 Mar. 1986: 973.

Rose, Wendy. "The Great Pretenders: Further Reflections on White Shamanism." *State of Native America.* Ed. M. Annette Jaimes. Boston: South End Press, 1992. 403–31.

Seale, Doris. Rev. of *Legend Days.* IBCB 16.8 (1985): 78–79.

Stott, Jon C. "Narrative Expectations and Textual Misreading: Jamake Highwater's *Anpao* Analyzed and Reanalyzed." *Studies in the Literary Imagination* 18.2 (1985): 93–105.

Yolen, Jane. Rev. of *Anpao. New York Times Book Review,* 5 Feb. 1978: 26.

BELINDA HURMENCE
(1921–   )

Miriam Bat-Ami

BIOGRAPHY

Belinda Hurmence, daughter of Eula and Warren Coleman, was born on August 20, 1921, in Oklahoma. She began her writing career at a very early age. In her interview with Scott Gillam, she speaks of early achievements and the encouragement she received at school: in first grade she won a competition prize of Potter's *Peter Rabbit*; later, in high school, Hurmence entered a national essay contest that won her an invitation to the White House for tea with Eleanor Roosevelt.

After college Hurmence worked for a brief time as a writer for *Mademoiselle*. Then, in 1951, she moved to New Jersey. Perhaps what influenced Hurmence greatly as a writer was her volunteer library work, begun in the 1960s in a neighborhood house in Morristown, New Jersey. Like so many other caring white adults, Hurmence was discouraged by the paucity of literature about African-American children, so she decided that she would try to write for the children who came to listen to her stories. She wanted them to see images of themselves in books.

Later, in 1968, when Hurmence moved to North Carolina, she continued reading to African-American children in a day center; and in 1980 her first contemporary middle-grade novel, *Tough Tiffany*, was published. This work centers on an eleven-year-old black girl who, in the circle of her poor yet closely knit family, stubbornly forges ahead.

Aside from *Tough Tiffany* and *The Nightwalker* (1988), two contemporary middle-grade novels, Hurmence has written primarily historical fiction and nonfiction. From 1980 through 1984 she completed three historical fiction works (two middle-grade novels and one adolescent text). Two of these books recreate the Civil War South and feature a black female protagonist (*A Girl Called Boy* and *Tancy*). For background research Hurmence carefully read thousands of typewritten pages of oral histories, assembled under the heading of *Slave Narratives*, which were amassed by writers working for the Federal Writers' Project in the 1930s. These ex-slave narratives also form the basis of three volumes of nonfiction which Hurmence has edited (*My Folks Don't Want Me to Talk about Slavery*, 1984; *Before Freedom, When I Just Can Remember*, 1989; and *We Lived in a Little Cabin in the Yard*, 1994). The first two of these nonfiction volumes, representing the voices of former North and South Carolina slaves, were ultimately combined into the single volume *Before Freedom* (1990).

Hurmence began writing because she wanted her African-American readers to see themselves and their past in literature, and, of the nine volumes Hurmence has thus far either written or edited, the majority are focused on black figures—people, both young and old, whose voices speak of the resiliency and courage of African-Americans. So Hurmence, in her introduction to *My Folks Don't Want Me to Talk about Slavery*, said "[These slaves] not only did the work [of homesteading], they endured through bondage to freedom. The idea for *My Folks Don't Want Me to Talk about Slavery* grew out of my admiration of those very real pioneers" (xii).

MAJOR WORKS AND THEMES

While its contemporary feel sets it aside from the majority of Hurmence's work, her first novel, *Tough Tiffany*, does provide a backdrop for what has consistently been Hurmence's brilliance as a children's writer: her dialogue and superb sense of place. While the narration of *Tough Tiffany* is in third-person standard English, dialogue is in what appears to be very real modern southern black dialect:

Mama said, "Tiff, how many times I tell you stop messing?" "I wasn't messing, Mama, it [sister's hair cream] was in my box. Can't I use something that's in my own box?" Dawn said, "How you think my stuff get in your box, the tooth fairy put it in there?" (18)

In referring to her use of dialect Hurmence is quoted as saying, "My own knowledge of black dialect I use in my stories comes, I think, because of my close connection with the black community" (*Something about the Author* 97).

Tiffany's ability to move beyond her circumstances and, in fact, to help those around her also makes her the first in a long line of Hurmence's positive female role models. As girls searching to find themselves and their place in the world, Hurmence's main characters are spunky, sensitive, intelligent, and resourceful. They also tend to be poor; yet, poverty seems to impel them to find strength within themselves: Hurmence's girls always figure out the best way to solve problems.

Tough Tiffany differs from Hurmence's later works, though, in that not only the voice it is written in but the issues it centers on are contemporary in nature: credit, budgeting, monthly payments, and unwanted pregnancies. Tiffany herself has to deal with a sister who becomes pregnant, a spendthrift mother, and a tough old grandmother. However, as in Hurmence's later works, family, although poor in money, is rich in warmth. A *Horn Book* reviewer refers to this kind of familial wealth that marks most of Hurmence's works: "While the circumstances of poverty are never diminished, the story offers an interpretation of family loyalty, love, and pride . . . showing that lack of wealth is not necessarily synonymous with lack of spirit, tradition, and hope" (Burns 297).

Hurmence began writing historical fiction when she wrote her second novel, *A Girl Called Boy* (1982). Most well known of all her novels, this book is unique among the many children's books written about slavery because it combines time travel fantasy with historical fiction. Boy, short for Blanche Overtha Yancey, a modern eleven-year-old child, is catapulted back in time when she shuns the power of her father's soapstone carving and sarcastically invokes a request to be transported across the water. "Take me over the water," she orders, and the tiny stone bird obeys (6).

A Girl Called Boy's theme is at once timeless and time-bound. Its timelessness has to do with the horrors of enslavement and the inalienable right all people have to be free. Its time-bound quality relates to the contemporary issue of modern identity. Boy, unlike Tiffany, dislikes hearing about her slave ancestors. When her father talks fondly about his African ancestry and the soapstone pocket piece handed down from generation to generation as a family good luck charm, Boy not only disparages the notion of magic, but she calls into question the whole idea of one's African roots. To her, one's feelings of linkage to Africa as a home country seem to negate one's identity as American. She says, "Oh, Daddy, you're not African— you're *American*" (3).

However, when Boy steps into the shoes of the woman after whom she is named, she learns to both respect her African heritage and value the experience of slaves. The child reader, traveling with Boy, gets to view slavery as an experience lived through by a modern American child.

In *A Girl Called Boy*, Boy has to solve the mystery of time and location. As she sorts out information and discovers that she has traveled back to the nineteenth century so, too, does the child reader answer puzzling questions of time and place. Boy also is on a quest to find the real Blanche Overtha Yancey. Tancy, in Hurmence's third novel, named after the central character, is a child of her own time, but she, too, is impelled to solve a mystery: she tries to discover who her mother is and if she is still alive. In this sense, quest after the mother seems to mark both these books and provides impetus for the plot.

Since *Tancy* spans the teen years of a slave girl during the last years of slavery and through the Reconstruction period, it is a young adult novel. Language and issues are age appropriate. Quite early on in the novel Tancy is raped by the son of her slave master, who, she finds out, is also her brother. The rape itself is not merely alluded to: it is an actual scene which is nearly repeated. When freedom comes, Tancy fights her way to independence by working at the Freedmen's Bureau, and one day, finally, she finds her mother.

As Hurmence so vividly described the life of slaves in *A Girl Called Boy*, in *Tancy* she vividly portrays life after slavery. Most compelling is the description of the Freedmen's Bureau itself where supposedly ex-slaves could go to get free land and find out the location of family members:

At the back of the building, a door with glass in its upper half admitted light to the hall. A forbidding flight of stairs ran up one side of the hall to some gloomy region above, posted against trespassers by a chain fastened across the stairs. . . . It was all very official looking and intimidating. (99)

The idea for *Tancy* (as in *A Girl Called Boy*) began to germinate in Hurmence's mind as she poured through the pages of slave narratives. So taken with these narratives was Hurmence that, while she worked with Clarion Books on her historical fiction, she worked with John Blair on editing the narratives themselves. Her feelings about the importance of documenting nonfiction seems to be voiced in her introduction to *We Lived in a Little Cabin in the Yard* (1994):

History books tend to focus on the politics of slavery, or its economics, and tactfully skirt the human mechanics of that unseemly institution. In the same vein, historical fiction mainly presents a romanticized or stereotypical version of slave life. The firsthand experience of a Susan Kelly, eyewitness of day-to-day life under the yoke, offers a better seminar to readers who would inform themselves about the realities of slavery. (xii)

While Hurmence's own historical fiction rings very true, it is also quite true that her nonfiction, written primarily for older children and adults, is both raw and compelling. It is also honestly contradictory from voice to voice, for some ex-slaves talk romantically about their masters—they speak out of the poverty of the thirties—and some vividly describe its horrors. Always, though, life is personalized, and always these people, culled from the many pages of narratives, give voice to a wretched time in American history. The reader, poring over these well-edited narratives, sees the slave quarters, the instruments of torture, the singing at corn-shucking time, the Yankees coming, and the long hill up from slavery.

Of Hurmence's nonfiction, *My Folks Don't Want Me to Talk about Slavery* (1984) contains twenty-one oral histories from ex-slaves of North Carolina, *Before Freedom, When I Just Can Remember* (1989) contains twenty-seven oral histories of former South Carolina slaves, and *We Lived in a Little Cabin in the Yard* (1994) contains narratives of twenty-one former Virginia slaves.

Hurmence's *Nightwalker* (1988), like her first and second works of historical fiction, depends upon mystery. Its main character is not black: she (Savannah) is, in a very small degree, part Native American. Savannah's father is part Coree. Slavery is not the issue: it is the environment. Hurmence's concern with the environment and the destruction of the natural land seems to continue in *Dixie in the Big Pasture* (1994), a book whose central character, as Hurmence herself states, is based on Hurmence's own aunt and the homesteading history of her family. But neither of these books is as powerfully written as Hurmence's books in which black characters are the central figures.

So, too, Hurmence's portrayal of Native peoples in both books is somewhat problematic, particularly in *Dixie in the Big Pasture*. While the child reader is supposed to feel sympathetic to the fact that Kiowa families kept yielding ground to pioneers, it seems more than likely that the reader will see the Kiowa way of life in a negative light. One is led to believe that ritual and ineptitude may have hastened the death of the Kiowa, Mrs. Sixteen. Dixie's mother, seeming somehow like the white protectoress, comes to the rescue with her eucalyptus rub, but it is too late. Hurmence also seems to emphasize the fact that Old Man Sixteen has, quite fortunately, become a Christian: Dixie's playmate is named after John 3:16. He is called John Three. One might say that Hurmence is striving for a realistic portrayal of a white pioneer family in 1907; and the fact that Dixie questions her own assumptions—she thinks of John Three as a "thieving Indian" at one point and then bows "her head in remorse"—is admirable (150). Still, there are problems, and, according to this reader, neither of these two recent works of fiction is as beautifully written nor as well constructed as *A Girl Called Boy* and *Tancy*.

CRITICAL RECEPTION

Hurmence's excellent use of dialogue in her portrayal of character and situation was noted by reviewers even with the publication of her first book. Of *Tough Tiffany*, Marilyn Kaye said "there's a spontaneity in dialogue and a natural warmth that shines through" (56–57). *Horn Book*, often not covering first books, also gave Hurmence a positive review. Accolades which followed were the American Library Association Notable Children's Book (1980) and the National Council of Social Studies (NCSS) Notable Children's Trade Book in the Field of Social Studies (1981), both for *Tough Tiffany*. The *Horn Book* was not quite as positive about *A Girl Called Boy*, complaining that the "time-slip device was thin" but praising Hurmence's excellent descriptions of slave times (Flowers 404). And Denise Wilm, in a *Booklist* review, applauded Hurmence "for breaking new ground here, for she's taken the well-used time-travel fantasy mode and freshened it with black characters and a vivid historical context" (1445). Reviews were also glowing in the *Bulletin of the Center for Children's Books* and in the *Children's Book Review Service*, and the educational scholars Evelyn Freeman and Linda Levstik cited Hurmence's book in their 1988 article "Recreating the Past: Historical Fiction in the Social Studies Curriculum." They told how "the fantasy frame allows the author to provide a double perspective on history" and explained ways in which the text can be used in a middle-grade classroom (332).

For *A Girl Called Boy*, Hurmence received the Parents' Choice Award and the National Council of Teachers of English (NCTE) Teacher's Choice Award (1984).

Of *Tancy*, Frances Bradburn, in the *Wilson Library Bulletin*, states, "Belinda Hurmence's young black slave, who at the end of the Civil War leaves her plantation home to seek her mother, is another shining image of women throughout our nation's history" (61). For this adolescent work, the

Society of Children's Book Writers and Illustrators awarded Hurmence the Golden Kite Award, and again Hurmence's book was a National Council of Social Studies award winner (1984). Aside from this the American Association of University Women presented Hurmence with an Award in Juvenile Fiction for *Tancy* in 1984 and for *The Nightwalker* in 1989. As for the nonfiction slave narratives, the *School Library Journal* gave Hurmence a Best Adult Book for Young Adults citation for *My Folks Don't Want Me to Talk about Slavery.* So, too, Robert Bealer, in his review says, "The voices of former slaves interviewed in the 1930's as part of the Federal Writers' Project ring instructively through this fine little book" (206). Alice Conlon, speaking of *Before Freedom, When I Just Can Remember*, states "The collection offers students a chance to use readable primary sources to research details of the everyday life of Southern slaves" (287).

That Hurmence has written so many works vividly describing black life during the Civil War, its aftermath, and the depression of the 1930s and that she has given her readership voices which ring true and reveal strength and courage speak of her immense importance in multicultural studies and in the understanding of U.S. history.

BIBLIOGRAPHY

Young Adult Fiction by Belinda Hurmence

Tough Tiffany. New York: Doubleday, 1980.
A Girl Called Boy. New York: Clarion, 1982.
Tancy. New York: Clarion, 1984.
The Nightwalker. New York: Clarion, 1988.
Dixie in the Big Pasture. New York: Clarion, 1994.

Other Works by Belinda Hurmence

My Folks Don't Want Me to Talk about Slavery. Winston-Salem, NC: John Blair, 1984.
Before Freedom, When I Just Can Remember: Twenty-seven Oral Histories of Former South Carolina Slaves. Winston-Salem, NC: John Blair, 1989.
Before Freedom: Forty-eight Oral Histories of Former North and South Carolina Slaves. Combined edition of *Before Freedom, When I Just Can Remember* and *My Folks Don't Want Me to Talk about Slavery.* New York: NAL, 1990.
We Lived in a Little Cabin in the Yard. Winston-Salem, NC: John Blair, 1994.

Selected Studies of Belinda Hurmence

Bealer, Robert C. Rev. of *My Folks Don't Want Me to Talk about Slavery*. *Science Books and Films* 21.4 (1986): 206.

"Belinda Hurmence." *Children's Literature Review*. Ed. Gerard J. Senick. Vol. 25. Detroit: Gale, 1991. 92–97.

"Belinda Hurmence." *Something about the Author*. Ed. Anne Commire. Vol. 77. Detroit: Gale. 95–100.

Bradburn, Frances. Rev. of *Tancy*. *Wilson Library Bulletin* 66.1 (1987): 60–61.

Burns, Mary M. Rev. of *Tough Tiffany*. *Horn Book* 56.2 (1980): 297.

Conlon, Alice. Rev. of *Before Freedom, When I Just Can Remember*. *School Library Journal* 35.13 (1989): 287.

Flowers, Ann A. Rev. of *A Girl Called Boy*. *Horn Book* 58.4 (1982): 404.

Freeman, Evelyn B., and Linda Levstik. "Recreating the Past: Historical Fiction in the Social Studies Curriculum." *The Elementary School Journal* 88.4 (1988): 329–37.

Wilm, Denise. Rev. of *Tough Tiffany*. *Booklist* 76 (15 February 1980): 834.

SULAMITH ISH-KISHOR
(1896–1977)

Bruce Henderson

BIOGRAPHY

Best known today for a handful of challenging and highly praised short novels on Jewish themes and retellings of Hebrew legends, Sulamith Ish-Kishor was born in 1896 in London to Ephraim and Fanny Ish-Kishor. She spent most of her childhood in London, before her family emigrated to New York City. She graduated from Hunter College, where her major fields of study were history and languages, laying the foundation for the concerns and settings of her later fiction.

She began her writing career quite early and had a number of poems published in British magazines by the time she was ten. She had an active career throughout her life, including writing for both popular and intellectual journals, such as *The New Yorker* and *Menorah Journal* and for the New York City Board of Education. Her fiction was written exclusively for a young audience, while her nonfiction (principally historical and biographical works) was written for both younger and older readers. Her 1935 biography, *Magnificent Hadrian*, included an introduction by Theodore Dreiser, with whom she struck up a professional friendship.

Though she was a working writer her entire life, she received the greatest attention and accolades for the books she wrote in the last decade of her life. She was awarded the Schwartz Juvenile Award of the Jewish Book Council in 1963 for *A Boy of Old Prague*, which was also named an

American Library Association Notable Book; she also received this award for *The Master of Miracle* in 1972. *Our Eddie*, her most celebrated novel, was a Newbery Honor Book in 1970, runner-up to William Armstrong's *Sounder*.

Sulamith Ish-Kishor died in 1977.

MAJOR WORKS AND THEMES

Two major themes may be seen as running through all of Ish-Kishor's works for young adults: the critical importance of understanding the historical past in order to make sense of present cultures and the tension between personal identity and the obligations of cultural membership. The first theme may be seen as implicit in all of her novels, a given that justifies the writer's decision not to write on contemporary issues or in contemporary settings; it was, no doubt, an outgrowth of her study of history in college and of her earlier writings on Hadrian and on the history of Israel. The latter theme, that of individual vs. collective identity, is explored explicitly in her fiction for young adults.

Most of her books are set in the distant past, whether it be Imperial Rome or sixteenth-century Prague; the most recent of settings is the turn-of-the-century London and New York City of *Our Eddie* (1969). For Ish-Kishor, one of the central aims of her fiction is the use of historical materials for contemporary young readers, and she is careful to clarify for the reader less steeped in history than herself where the lines between fact and fiction lie. In the postscript to *Drusilla* (1970), for example, the novel building most clearly on actual historical figures, she writes that "there is nothing in *Drusilla* that could not have happened. The basic facts did happen; the rest could have. . . . Some permissible liberties have been taken with date and place" (116).

In *A Boy of Old Prague* (1963), she makes a point of including enough historical material to evoke the era, yet at the same time making the fictional component clear enough. For example, she notes that the endpapers to the book are reproductions of a sixteenth-century map of the city, suggesting that the characters she has invented could very well have walked the actual streets which enclose the story. Similarly, she prefaces *The Master of Miracle* (1971) with a brief explanation of the legend upon which the novel is based.

The second theme running through Ish-Kishor's writings, perhaps the most relevant one to the reader interested in multicultural issues, is the tension between personal identity and cultural membership. In each of the four books written for young adults, Ish-Kishor presents a protagonist who must either search for literal or figurative identity and find within it a deeper understanding of his or her cultural background and traditions or one who finds a conflict between individual desires and the demands of the culture (or cultures) into which he or she has been born and raised. The struggle to reconcile personal and cultural history sometimes leads to a positive resolution, as in *A Boy of Old Prague* and *Drusilla*; in *Our Eddie* and *The Master of Miracle*, this struggle leads to tragic ends. In both of these latter works, the inability of the protagonists (Eddie Raphel and his father in the former, Gideon ben Israyel in the latter) to balance individuality with the collective wisdom and law of culture results in either death or destruction.

A Boy of Old Prague is set in feudal Prague. The character Tomas is given as repayment for a debt to Pesach ben Leib, a wealthy Jew who lives in the ghetto. While at first Tomas has the same set of stereotypes about Jews as his fellow Christians of that time, he gradually finds that Pesach and the rest of the family treat him with kindness and generosity. He is well fed, and when Pesach learns that Tomas' mother is ill, he admonishes him for his neglect of a parent and sends him home to visit her. The scene at home, where Tomas realizes how his attitudes toward Jews has changed, suggests the degree to which prejudice is built upon ignorance.

Other scenes follow the same approach to reducing prejudice: for example, one week, Pesach takes Tomas to services at the synagogue with him, not to try to convert him to Judaism (as Tomas' family suggests he should try to convert the Leibs to Christianity), but simply to help young Joseph, on his first trip to services, become less frightened, presumably because Tomas will be one more familiar face. The scene at the synagogue allows Ish-Kishor to paint a vivid picture of the religious and intellectual life of Judaism of the time, and also to show Tomas making one more step in developing an understanding of the value of different religions, to understand that his Christianity is neither superior nor inferior to Judaism or any other religion.

In the final episode, Tomas is on his way back to the ghetto from one of his weekend visits home, when he sees black smoke coming from the ghetto, and realizes that the ghetto has been set afire. When he reaches his master's home, he finds it in ruins. While Tomas' personal life ends happily, he vows "some day [to] . . . search for those whom I loved—yes, loved, Jews though they were" (90). He declares, "I shall find them, and I shall help them and work for them with my two strong hands, and among us we shall learn that the God of mercy is the same God, no matter where we find him" (90).

Our Eddie (1969), Ish-Kishor's next novel, is the most sustained work of fiction that she published. In it she tells the story of the Raphels, a poor Jewish family, living first in north London and later in the tenements of New York City. Ezekiel Raphel, the father, is a poorly paid teacher and early Zionist; he keeps the family in poverty, both economically and emotionally. In a sense, he fits the stereotype of the patriarchal Jewish holy man, but Ish-Kishor's complex characterization rescues him from any sense of flatness. Mrs. Raphel is sick with what will ultimately be diagnosed as multiple sclerosis; this illness will also plague the eldest child, Eddie, in his case fatally.

Eddie is ambitious and rebellious, wanting passionately to become a doctor, for which his father belittles him, both because it is a rejection of the sacred scholarly life Mr. Raphel envisions for his eldest son and also because he determines that Eddie does not have the intelligence for medical study. Eddie, desperate to make a life for himself, is not above petty thievery and, like many a tragic hero, seems on the road to self-destruction when the disease claims him at too young an age.

Like Anzia Yezierska's *Bread Givers*, to which *Our Eddie* bears some resemblance, this novel uses the Old and New Worlds as sites of social and cultural critique, particularly as the reader witnesses the disintegration of the family as an economic and spiritual unit and the personal disintegration of various family members (Mrs. Raphel's and Eddie's multiple sclerosis is described in detail, as is Mr. Raphel's mental breakdown). For example, the contrast between the almost Dickensian poverty in which the Raphels live (and in which Mr. Raphel willfully insists on continuing in America, even when given opportunities for economic mobility) and the relative affluence of Uncle Mark, a dentist, and his outspoken "American" wife, Aunt Sara, provides both the reader and the characters sets of different choices for constructing a new self in a new land. At the same time, Eddie's illness and Mr. Raphel's unyielding determination are reminders that the past is always present: Eddie cannot escape the inevitable legacy passed on to him genetically; in a sense, it seems that Mr. Raphel cannot (and chooses not to) forsake his ethos of economic poverty as a state of intellectual holiness. When offered an opportunity to teach the children of more affluent parents, Mr. Raphel sees it as a betrayal of his people and of his passion for the Zionist cause, and chooses to serve community and culture rather than save his family.

Such a moral choice is not an abstract one in the world of *Our Eddie*: Ish-Kishor's skills as a portraitist are such that all major characters feel multidimensional and, hence, Eddie's thievery and rebelliousness, his sister

Sybil's outspokenness, and, most important, Mr. Raphel's stubborn conviction carry much psychological and ethical weight. While most readers will agree that Mr. Raphel makes what seems like a personally unsupportable decision that leads to a tragic conclusion, it is a credit to Ish-Kishor's narrative ambitiousness that it is impossible not to be somewhat in awe of Mr. Raphel's relentless devotion to an idea—that of Zionism. The ending of the novel, as June Schlessinger has noted, is almost devoid of hope. Eddie is dead, Mr. Raphel is seemingly beyond emotional rescue; yet in the final moment, when he permits Sybil to attend the opera with Hal Kent, there is the suggestion that he is not as remote as one might think: that this gesture suggests a movement toward acceptance of the need to live in the world (1004).

Drusilla: A Novel of the Emperor Hadrian (1970) is the only one of Ish-Kishor's novels not to focus on Jewish themes and issues. Instead, Ish-Kishor returns to her earlier nonfictional work on Hadrian and weaves a brief, but affecting, story of a fictional young noblewoman, Drusilla. The plot of the novel follows Drusilla's ruminations and recollections on the day she is to plead for the life of Fuscan, the grandson of the evil Senator Servianus, accused of conspiring against the life of Emperor Hadrian. Ish-Kishor evokes the mores and manners of the period, and Drusilla is a spirited and intelligent narrator-heroine. At the end of the novel, when Hadrian offers Drusilla the option of freeing Fuscan, though also admonishing her that the choice to do so will probably result in a chain of events that will destroy the empire, she decides in favor of the government rather than the individual: it is ultimately an empty test, as she discovers after she made the "right" choice—both Fuscan and Servianus had been put to death the night before. Ish-Kishor explains Drusilla's decision, which to more modern readers might feel heartless, saying in the postscript, "We must realize that a Roman lady of that historical period would have been taught to forget personal feelings and humanitarian motives when the good of the state seemed to be endangered" (*Drusilla* 116).

In her final novel, *The Master of Miracle: A New Novel of the Golem* (1971), Ish-Kishor reclaims the legend of the Golem, the homunculus created out of earthly clay and sacred language to protect the Jews of the Prague ghetto from destruction. The narrator is Gideon ben Israyel, a foundling raised by "Mutterli," a poor but honest woman. The early part of the novel raises the question of the importance of Gideon's religious heritage in establishing his identity; some members of the community question whether he is actually Jewish, while Christians call him "Christ-killer."

Evil comes to the community in the personage of Count Batislav, who manufactures a fake kidnapping of his supposed daughter, Maria-Agnes, building on the old Blood Libel superstitions. As protection against the violence inevitably directed at them, Rabbi Loewe breathes life into the Golem. Gideon is given responsibility of watching the Golem and of removing his temporary life when it is time; he disobeys these orders and the Golem wreaks havoc. His disobedience is judged a sign of arrogance and immaturity, and he is cursed with eternal life until the "exile of the Jewish people should be ended" (in the prologue, Ish-Kishor suggests that such an ending perhaps came in 1948 with the founding of the state of Israel). Once again, a kind of hubris has put the community in jeopardy, and Gideon's punishment is a form of separation from his people, for, while he is not cast out, he is kept form joining them in the afterlife.

CRITICAL RECEPTION

Other than brief mentions in trade journals, there has been very little critical attention to Ish-Kishor's works. A few short biographical/critical entries about her and her work have been included in standard reference works, but there have been virtually no essays devoted to her writings in scholarly journals. Mentions of her work in trade journals have typically praised the richness of her use of historical materials and the elegance of her language. Zena Sutherland included *Our Eddie* in the 1966–1972 volume of *The Best in Children's Books*, saying of it, "Although there are some awkward shifts of viewpoint . . . the book has a strength and vigor that outweigh this minor flaw. The characterization is excellent, particularly that of Papa; any change in him is due to the pressure of his burdens, not to an atypical change of heart" (209). Other reviews also stress characterization and moral power as strengths of her writing. The only sustained critical essay is June H. Schlessinger's discussion of *Our Eddie* in *Beacham's Guide to Literature for Young Adults*. Schlessinger praises the novel for its realism, for its subtle use of symbolism, and for its tough unwillingness to yield to a simple narrative and thematic closure: that the family's problems are not solved as the novel ends is, for Schlessinger, one of its principal virtues (1004).

In a 1973 *Horn Book* essay calling for greater quantity and quality books for young readers on Jewish identity, Eric A. Kimmel referred to Ish-Kishor as "another Jewish writer for children worthy of considerable attention" (171). One wonders why she has not received the attention Kimmel called for. One possibility is that Ish-Kishor's novels, while relatively brief, are demanding of the young reader: they require attention to detail, an interest in history, and an appreciation of a sometimes dense style. They also do not, as a rule, have simple or comforting plots or resolutions. Also, quite pragmatically, they may have become less physically available: as of this writing, only *Our Eddie* is in print. In any case, Sulamith Ish-Kishor's body of work for young adults, while small in number, does indeed merit more critical commentary than has thus far been produced.

BIBLIOGRAPHY

Young Adult Fiction by Sulamith Ish-Kishor

A Boy of Old Prague. Illus. Ben Shahn. New York: Pantheon, 1963.
Our Eddie. New York: Pantheon, 1969.
Drusilla: A Novel of the Emperor Hadrian. Illus. Thomas Morley. New York: Pantheon, 1970.
The Master of Miracle: A New Novel of the Golem. Illus. Arnold Lobel. New York: Harper & Row, 1971.

Works for Children by Sulamith Ish-Kishor

The Bible Story. New York: United Synagogue of America, 1921.
The Heaven on the Sea and Other Stories. Illus. Penina Ish-Kishor. New York: Bloch, 1924.
The Children's Story of the Bible. New York: Educational Stationery House, 1930.
Children's History of Israel from the Creation to the Present Time. 3 vols. New York: Jordan, 1930–1933.
Little Potato and Other Stories. Illus. J. Russack. New York: Board of Education, 1937.
How the Weatherman Came. Illus. Rebecca Andrews. New York: Board of Education, 1938.
Jews to Remember. Illus. Kyra Markham. New York: Hebrew Publishing Company, 1941.
American Promise: A History of the Jews in the New World. Illus. Grace Hick. New York: Berhman, 1947.
The Palace of Eagles and Other Stories. Illus. Alice Horodisch. New York: Shoulson, 1948.
The Stranger within the Gates and Other Stories. Illus. Alice Horodisch. New York: Shoulson, 1948.
Friday Night Stories, 1, 2, and 4. 3 vols. New York: Women's League of the United Synagogue of America, 1949.
The Carpet of Solomon: A Hebrew Legend. New York: Pantheon, 1966.

Pathways through the Jewish Holidays. Ed. Benjamin Efron. New York: Klav, 1967.

Works for Adults by Sulamith Ish-Kishor

Magnificent Hadrian: A Biography. New York: Minton Balch, 1935.
Everyman's History of the Jews. New York: Fell, 1948.
Blessed Is the Daughter. With Meyer Waxman and Jacob Sloan. New York: Shengold, 1960.
How Theodor Herzl Created the Jewish National Fund. New York: Jewish National Fund, 1960.

Selected Works About Sulamith Ish-Kishor

Kimmel, Eric A. "Jewish Identity in Juvenile Fiction: A Look at Three Recommended Books." *Horn Book* 49.2 (1973): 71–79.
Roger, Mae Durham. "Sulamith Ish-Kishor." *Twentieth-Century Children's Writers.* Ed. Tracy Chevalier. 3rd ed. Chicago: St. James, 1989. 489–90.
Schlessinger, June H. "Our Eddie." *Beacham's Guide to Literature for Young Adults.* Ed. Kirk H. Beetz and Suzanne Niemeyer. Vol. 2. Washington, DC: Beacham, 1990. 101–06.
"Sulamith Ish-Kishor." *Contemporary Authors.* Ed. Frances Carol Locher. Vols. 73–76. Detroit: Gale, 1978. 309.
"Sulamith Ish-Kishor." *Something about the Author.* Ed. Anne Commire. Vol. 17. Detroit: Gale, 1979. 84.
Sutherland, Zena, ed. *The Best in Children's Books: The University of Chicago Guide to Children's Literature 1966–72.* Chicago: U Chicago P, 1973.

In addition, Sulamith Ish-Kishor's books for children and young adults were reviewed in the *Horn Book*. Refer to its indexes for the year (and subsequent year) of publication for each title.

JESSE JACKSON
(1908–1983)

Peter D. Sieruta

BIOGRAPHY

Jesse Jackson, the son of a factory worker and a domestic servant, was born in Columbus, Ohio. As the only African-Americans on the west side of town, the family enjoyed a middle-class lifestyle, but their situation changed drastically when the Scioto River flooded in 1913 and they lost their home. The Jacksons were taken in by an elderly acquaintance who lived in a lower-class, predominantly African-American community on the east side of town.

Many of Jackson's experiences in this neighborhood were recalled in his autobiographical novels *The Sickest Don't Always Die the Quickest* (1971) and *The Fourteenth Cadillac* (1972). Family life centered on the Baptist church and hard physical labor. As a child, Jackson carried newspapers, delivered laundry, and mopped floors in a factory. After the family moved to a small house near the wealthiest section of town, Jackson and his sister attended a particularly good school for several years until district lines were redrawn to prevent this integration.

Jackson's interest in reading and writing led him to Ohio State University, where he studied journalism and excelled in a number of sports, including boxing and track. During summer breaks, Jackson found jobs as a soda jerk and as a waiter at hotels and on Great Lakes steamships, and he also worked at carnivals and boys' camps. These experiences increased his awareness of the racial discrimination that African-Americans faced in the workplace.

Jackson left the university after three years to work for the *Ohio State Press*. When the newspaper ceased publication, he and a friend published their own paper for the African-American population of Columbus. Two years later he became a probation officer with the juvenile court in that city, a job that helped him refine his literary goals. Working with youthful offenders, he saw firsthand the disadvantages faced by illiterate and non-reading teenagers, and decided to write books that would appeal to this young adult audience.

In 1938, Jackson married Ann Newman Williams, a social worker, and acquired a position with the post office. Although the job bored him, it led to a series of fortuitous coincidences that ultimately established Jesse Jackson as an author. It began late one evening when he picked up a letter that had been dropped on the floor. It was addressed to an Ohio State University English professor and the return address was Bread Loaf, Vermont. Recalling that Bread Loaf hosted a major writer's conference, Jackson phoned the university professor and asked for an appointment to discuss his own writing. Professor Francis Utley reviewed Jackson's manuscripts and recommended him for the Bread Loaf Conference, where author Wallace Stegner read his stories and suggested Jackson call on Ursula Nordstrom, the legendary editor of children's books at Harper and Brothers (now HarperCollins). Nordstrom, who had been urging Richard Wright to attempt a story about African-American youth, asked Jackson if he could write a novel about the growing-up experiences of a black boy.

Published in 1945, *Call Me Charley* was considered a landmark book for its portrait of a dignified African-American boy and its realistic presentation of contemporary race relations. Shortly thereafter, Jackson, his wife, and their daughter moved to New York City, where he found work in a book-manufacturing factory, and later spent seventeen years with the National Bureau of Economic Research. During this time, he published two sequels to his first novel; wrote a book on assignment from the National Council of Churches; and authored *Tessie* (1968), his only novel to feature a female African-American protagonist.

By the late 1960s, civil rights advances, an increasing appreciation for multiculturalism, and a "new realism" in children's books rendered much of Jackson's previous writing somewhat dated and "politically incorrect," but the author took advantage of these cultural changes in writing his final two novels, which were highly acclaimed. His last publications were nonfiction—a history of African-Americans and a biography of singer Mahalia Jackson.

The author's later years were spent reaping the rewards of his pioneering work in the field of children's literature. He served as writer-in-residence at Appalachian State University in Boone, North Carolina, lectured frequently, and received numerous awards and citations.

MAJOR WORKS AND THEMES

While *Call Me Charley* was certainly a groundbreaking book in the 1940s, it is now best appreciated for its historical significance. The story of Charles Moss, the first African-American boy to live in the white community of Arlington Heights, Ohio, was one of the earliest young adult books to realistically confront issues of race relations. In the opening chapter, Charley meets a bigoted youth who calls him "Sambo" and "nigger." At his junior high school, he is placed on academic probation despite his intelligence, and is denied a role in a class play. When he and his white friend, Tom, win free passes to the community swimming pool, Charley's prize is revoked because the pool is off-limits to African-Americans.

Charley is a likable, decent character, but his acceptance of these indignities is frustrating for contemporary readers, as is the stated message that the only way African-Americans can make gains is if their white friends stand up for them. It is not surprising that many scenes in the novel are presented from the perspective of Tom, who, along with his parents, steps in to help Charley resolve critical issues.

Although they may be true to the era, the characterizations do little to dispel old-fashioned racial stereotypes. Tom and his parents have the perfect picket-fence lifestyle, complete with African-American maid, while Charley and his parents live in the garage apartment at a doctor's house where his mother is the cook and his father is a chauffeur. The characterization of Mr. Moss is particularly unfortunate because he repeatedly refers to education as "foolishness" and expresses the desire that his twelve-year-old son get a job instead of attending school.

Anchor Man (1947) and *Charley Starts from Scratch* (1958) follow the character into high school and, although less well known than their predecessor, are of interest from a multicultural perspective because they touch on such topics as job discrimination against minorities and the internecine struggles that occur among African-Americans when a group of black students enrolls in Charley's high school and resents his acceptance by the white majority.

Jackson's other literary effort from the 1950s, *Room for Randy* (1957), also tackles issues of school integration when African-American, Hispanic, and West Indian children are assigned to a formerly white school in suburban New Jersey. The novel, which was commissioned by a religious organization, is a well meaning but uninspired volume in the author's body of work.

Like the Charley series, *Tessie* (1968) features an admirable African-American protagonist confronting racial differences in an overwhelmingly white environment. Fourteen-year-old Tessie Downs lives comfortably in Harlem with her warm nuclear family and a larger community family that includes close girlfriends, schoolmates, neighbors, and a supportive librarian. However, when Tessie receives a scholarship as the first African-American student to attend the exclusive Hobbe School, she has conflicting feelings about home and school. She craves acceptance at her new school, but is unwilling to abandon her old friends and activities, so she invites her classmates from Hobbe to a Halloween dance in Harlem and asks her best friend, Floe, to accompany her to a wealthy girl's party. Throughout the novel, characters such as Floe and Tessie's mother question the girl's ability to fit in with her new crowd, but Tessie triumphs in deriving the best of both worlds. Nevertheless, some incidents seem to suggest a loss of racial pride, as when Tessie's white friends help straighten her hair using butter and a heating pad, or when—after much justification—she takes the stereotypical role of a black maid in a school play.

Issues of conformity, discrimination, and acceptance are at the core of the story, and Jackson uses several literary devices to drive home these themes, including a rather overwrought subplot about an upper classman challenged by school authorities for growing a beard. Although it is not addressed outright in the novel, there is also a subtle jab at other forms of race discrimination in the casting of the maid in the school play. The two students originally selected for the role are Asian and Jewish. By the book's conclusion, Tessie has declared that Harlem will always remain her spiritual home, but Floe—a strong voice of pride and reason throughout the novel—suggests that Tessie may find it increasingly difficult to bridge her two worlds.

In the early days of multicultural literature, ethnic characters were often idealized to an unbelievable degree. Although this was helpful in creating characters who would be accepted by a wide reading audience, it often resulted in the creation of paragons of virtue, rather than three-dimensional human beings. Thus, Tessie is depicted as an exceptionally intelligent, well-spoken teenager, so talented that she performs Shakespearean roles in local theater productions, and Charley Moss is shown to be the apotheosis of African-American youth.

The characters in Jackson's final novels, *The Sickest Don't Always Die the Quickest* (1971) and *The Fourteenth Cadillac* (1972) avoid this treatment and are instead presented as fresh, fully rounded characterizations with both positive and negative attributes. Unlike most of Jackson's previous characters, the boys occasionally curse, sometimes speak imperfect English, and in general talk, behave, and think like real children.

Set in Columbus, Ohio, during the 1920s, the novels follow best friends Stonewall and Steeplehead through a series of humorous, loosely connected incidents involving family, friendship, religion, and employment. Although the story is set in a historical era, the characters reflect the values of a more contemporary time. Racial issues are not ignored, as when Stonewall confronts discrimination during a job search, yet the tenor of the books is notably different from Jackson's previous works. Stonewall and his friends are not battling to fit into the white culture, but are rather trying to discover themselves and be accepted on their own terms.

CRITICAL RECEPTION

Because of evolving cultural attitudes, it is not surprising that critical reaction to Jackson's works has changed over the years. Initially, many critics echoed the *New York Herald Tribune Weekly Book Review* in describing *Call Me Charley* as "a contribution to understanding" (20). Early reviewers praised the Charley series for its sincerity, sensitivity, and good intentions. However, by the 1970s, the critical tide had turned. In *Written for Children,* John Rowe Townsend states that the works bear "some resemblance to the treatment of the poor in books by well-meaning Victorians. Just as the poor were expected to rely on and be grateful for the beneficence of the rich, so the black must rely on and be grateful for the beneficence of the white" (272). In "Black Perspective in Books for Children," Judith Thompson and Gloria Woodard claim the moral of *Call Me Charley* is that "the success of black endeavor is dependent upon the magnanimity of white people. In order to receive the bestowal of this magnanimity, black children must meet certain standards set by a white middle class society" (42).

The best reviews of Jackson's career were reserved for his final novels, which are considered his most accurate representations of the African-American experience, and are praised for alluding to broader implications outside the scope of the story. Reviewing *The Sickest Don't Always Die the*

Quickest for *School Library Journal*, Kay Heylman writes, that the book ends anticipating a more "cosmic scale," with "the same factors of toughness, resiliency, and faith that have kept Stonewall alive operating to help a race survive" (75).

In "Call Me Jesse Jackson," Ruby J. Lanier traces the author's career and discusses the evolving critical reception of the books, quoting Jackson's happiness that his later books could reflect an African-American perspective and writing style that was previously not acceptable to his early editors.

BIBLIOGRAPHY

Young Adult Fiction by Jesse Jackson

Call Me Charley. Illus. Doris Spiegel. New York: Harper, 1945.
Anchor Man. Illus. Doris Spiegel. New York: Harper, 1947.
Room for Randy. Illus. Frank Nicols. New York: Friendship Press, 1957.
Charley Starts from Scratch. New York: Harper, 1958.
Tessie. Illus. Harold James. New York: Harper, 1968.
The Sickest Don't Always Die the Quickest. New York: Doubleday, 1971.
The Fourteenth Cadillac. New York: Doubleday, 1972.

Other Works by Jesse Jackson

Black in America. With Elaine Landau. New York: Messner, 1973.
Make a Joyful Noise unto the Lord: The Life of Mahalia Jackson. New York: Crowell, 1974.

Selected Studies of Jesse Jackson

Heylman, Kay. Rev. of *The Sickest Don't Always Die the Quickest*. *School Library Journal* 17 (May 1971): 75.
Lanier, Ruby J. "Call Me Jesse Jackson." *Language Arts* 54:3 (1977): 331–39.
Rev. of *Call Me Charley*. *New York Herald Tribune Weekly Book Review* 11 Nov. 1945: 18, 20.
Thompson, Judith, and Gloria Woodard. "Black Perspective in Books for Children." *The Black American in Books for Children: Readings in Racism*. Ed. Donnarae MacCann and Gloria Woodard. Metuchen: Scarecrow Press, 1985.
Townsend, John Rowe. *Written for Children: An Outline of English-Language Children's Literature*. Philadelphia: Lippincott, 1974.

June Jordan
(1936–   )

Allison Wilson

BIOGRAPHY

June Jordan, the only child of black Jamaican immigrants—Granville, a postal worker, and Mildred, a nurse—was born in New York City on July 9, 1936. Her early relationship with her parents (as she would later detail in autobiographical essays and explore in confessional poetry) was ambiguous, to say the least. Their influence seems to have been instrumental in the development of her poetic voice and social awareness but destructive to the development of her sense of self. Jordan's father, who was excessively strict and physically violent, discouraged her desire to be a poet; yet, it was he who had introduced her to poetry in the first place, both the white male canon and poems that incorporated the cadences of black dialect. Her mother, who also disapproved of her poetic leanings, apparently never challenged the harsh patriarchal autocracy her husband established on the home front, even failing, for whatever reasons, to halt the physical violence; but abroad in the black community, she was the perfect social role model, a nurturing figure who was always willing to provide assistance in a medical capacity and otherwise. What is more, Jordan's ambiguous relationship with both her parents, which resulted in constant mental and physical clashes that engendered a certain amount of guilt on her part, continued long past childhood. Encounters were volatile even after she herself had become a wife and mother, even, it seems, until the ends of her parents' lives. (Her mother committed suicide in 1966; her father died in 1974.) Despite the persistent strife, though, Jordan's writings reveal that she never totally repudiated either of her parents, struggling instead to understand the complexities involved in what can only be described as a highly charged situation.

The Jordan family lived in Harlem until 1941, at which time they purchased a house in Brooklyn's Bedford-Stuyvesant area. Because Jordan spent her formative years in these two neighborhoods, both of which were significant locations in the development of the underpinnings of African-American culture, she could not have failed to internalize the rhythms of urban black life and language—or to notice the growing resentment, bubbling forth from tenements and slums, toward the historical disenfranchisement of the black race. Because her parents apparently considered a "white" education to be a superior education, however, Jordan's formal learning environment was mainstream for the most part. She attended Midwood High School, more than an hour's commute away from her home in Brooklyn, then transferred to the Northfield School for Girls in Massachusetts, a college preparatory boarding school from which she graduated in 1953.

From a positive standpoint, this "privileged" education provided the comprehensive background and sophisticated linguistic skills that would enable Jordan not only to communicate with many different audiences in many different genres but also to acquire a teaching position that would lead to a long career as a college educator. Furthermore, the instructors at Northfield encouraged her desire to write. But there was an apparent downside to this mainstream educational environment. Physically separated from other individuals of her own race (at 3,000-student Midwood, she was the only black), Jordan was greatly affected by what she saw as constant scrutiny by those for whom her skin color was her most obvious, and perhaps her only, distinguishing characteristic, a scrutiny that she would poetically dissect and deflect in her first book for young people.

Returning to New York City immediately following her graduation from high school, Jordan began her postsecondary education at Barnard College, where she met Michael Meyer, a white student attending nearby Columbia University. The couple married in 1955 and moved to Illinois, both enrolling at the University of Chicago. A year later Jordan returned to Barnard but remained only a few months. In 1958 came the birth of her only child, Christopher David Meyer, whom she would later acknowledge as the prime motivating force behind her various authorial and human successes. As her writings reveal, Jordan—given the stresses of her own childhood and adolescence—has always, on some level, identified with the plight of young people, particularly their struggle to survive in an adult world that, to her, was hostile at worst, indifferent at best. Thus, she was determined to make the most of the opportunity to be a better parent than her own mother and father had been, resolving to make her son, not her work, the center of her life. Neither seems to have suffered. All her book-length works, including the six written especially for young readers, were published after she became a mother; and her son, with whom she shares a close relationship that appears to differ markedly from the stifling familial relationships of her own youth, graduated *cum laude* from Harvard in 1981.

Jordan's relationship with her husband does not seem to have been a satisfying one, however. At the time of their marriage, interracial unions, still technically illegal in most states, were almost universally derided, even to the point of the kinds of public taunts and insults Jordan reportedly suffered. These obvious external pressures—coupled with private incompatibilities—gradually destroyed the couple's marriage, leading them finally to divorce in 1965. Though it was only then that she officially became a "single mother," Jordan had already taken full responsibility for her son some time before, always managing, one way or another, to parlay her artistic talent and intellectual strength into financial survival. She had served as assistant to the producer of *The Cool World*, a motion picture set in Harlem, from 1963–1964 and, under the name of June Meyer, had written—and continued to write until 1969—for many high profile mainstream magazines as well as for several periodicals with an African-American readership. Following her divorce, she continued to pursue a variety of occupations that served as an outlet for her artistic talents and sociopolitical concerns. In 1965 she took a job as an associate research writer in New York City's technical housing department; in 1966 she became an instructor of English and literature at City College of the City University of New York; and in 1968 she accepted a position as an English instructor and SEEK (Search for Education, Elevation and Knowledge) director at Connecticut College in New London.

Since the publication of her first book, *Who Look at Me*—which was also her first book for young people—in 1969, Jordan has taught at several other colleges, including Sarah Lawrence, Yale, and the State University of New York at Stony Brook, where she became a tenured full professor in 1982. Since 1969, she has also been the recipient of numerous honors and awards, including a Rockefeller grant for creative writing (1969–1970) and a National Endowment for the Arts fellowship (1982). In 1971 her second juvenile work, *His Own Where*, not only was nominated for a National Book

Award but also was selected by the *New York Times* as one of the outstanding young adult books of the year.

Jordan's other three fiction books for young people (*Dry Victories*, 1972; *New Life: New Room*, 1975; *Kimako's Story*, 1981) appeared over the next dozen years; and her biography for young people, *Fannie Lou Hamer*, was published in 1972. She has also edited two collections of poems, both published in 1970, that emphasize her concern for the development of the minds of young people and her belief that even the youngest human beings are capable of expressing ideas worthy of attention: *The Voice of the Children* (edited with Terri Bush), which received the Nancy Bloch Award, contains poems written by black and Puerto Rican children enrolled in a poetry workshop; and *Soulscript: Afro-American Poetry* presents poems written by young people (aged twelve to eighteen) alongside the works of established poets like Langston Hughes and Gwendolyn Brooks.

Jordan's books for adults include volumes of poems (*Some Changes*, 1971; *New Days: Poems of Exile and Return*, 1973; *Things That I Do in the Dark: Selected Poetry,* 1977; *Passion: New Poems. 1977–1980*, 1980; *Living Room: New Poems, 1980–84*, 1985; *Naming Our Destiny: New and Selected Poems*, 1989) and collections of essays (*Civil Wars*, 1981; *On Call: New Political Essays, 1981–85*, 1985). She has also written a number of plays and served as a contributing editor to several periodicals, including *American Poetry Review*.

MAJOR WORKS AND THEMES

Because Jordan's writings encompass several genres, both distinct and hybrid, and have appeared in six languages, she has been able to convey her beliefs and concerns to varied audiences all over the world, thus earning an international literary reputation. However, she is best known in her native land where she is usually thought of as a feminist poet whose works, though infused with highly personal memories and emotions, attempt to clarify—for adult audiences in the United States—the often ignored concerns of African-Americans: black alienation, black frustration, black escape, and—ultimately—black survival. As a writer of fiction for young people, she is not as well known, perhaps because the relevant works have appeared sporadically and have differed greatly in style, format, and projected audience. Nevertheless, it cannot be denied that the five of Jordan's books that are classified as juvenile fiction are infused with the same major themes that recur in her poetry and with which her stature and fame as a writer are so closely connected.

The first work of juvenile fiction—*Who Look at Me* (1969), in which the "Who" are white people—describes the intense emotions of one who is a helpless outsider in his/her own native land, even in his/her own hometown, a helpless outsider who must somehow manage to go about the daily business of survival while enduring the omnipresent stares of those who make no effort to fathom the human personality that resides beneath the black skin. The nameless narrator, speaking (in free verse) for all descendants of Africans who came to the United States in chains, is not without optimism, however, turning, finally, from the details of painful, superficial confrontation to the positive aspects of black history and culture that white society, with its selective blindness, cannot appreciate. Thus, as is emphasized by the narrator's musings as well as by the accompanying illustrations (reproductions of twenty-seven paintings, some in color, by various known and unknown artists), the black individual has survived separation and rejection by escaping into his/her own carefully nurtured sense of self.

Jordan's second book for young people carries the theme of escape a step further. In *His Own Where* (1971), an omniscient narrator, whose prose is interspersed with linguistic structures characteristic of American black English, introduces us to Buddy and Angela, inner-city teenagers. During the course of the story, the two develop a sense of self that allows them to survive the negative aspects of their environment; but they do not stop at mental evasion. They remove themselves physically from the scene, setting up housekeeping in their "own where," an abandoned building where they anticipate beginning their own family. What is more, Jordan's use of black dialect implies that this linguistic system, far from being a language of poverty and deprivation, is an important aspect of, perhaps even a contributor to, the survival of a group of Americans who have always worn shackles of one kind or another. Ironically, it was this very language that led certain school systems to ban *His Own Where* during the 1970s—on the grounds (ironic as well) that nonstandard dialect of this kind could have a negative effect on African-American children.

Dry Victories (1972), in the form of a dialogue, is also written in a prose interspersed with features of black dialect, again emphasizing Jordan's belief in the legitimacy of this linguistic code—not just from a political viewpoint. Kenny and Jerome, two young African-Americans, use this, their native dialect, to identify and dissect the events that comprised the Reconstruction era and the civil rights era, two periods in U.S. history during which their race made significant social gains. After a lengthy, detailed discussion (reinforced by numerous black-and-white photographs culled from historical and news sources) the pair conclude that much is still to be done if the triumphs of black Americans are ever to be anything other than "dry," if, in short, the members of their race are ever to find their true place in a society that is reluctant to relinquish ingrained assumptions and conclusions.

Whether in reaction to negative criticisms of the black language patterns in *His Own Where* and *Dry Victories* or because the work is aimed at a slightly younger audience, the features of black dialect are gone from Jordan's next book, with both the narrator and the characters expressing themselves in standard English. However, the theme of escape remains. When Mr. and Mrs. Robinson in *New Life: New Room* (1975)—revealed in the accompanying black-and-white drawings to be African-Americans— learn that their fourth child (the "new life") is on the way, they realize that their small apartment will be even more crowded, but, since they cannot afford a bigger home, they know that they will have to make do with the space they have. While Mrs. Robinson is at the hospital, Mr. Robinson— with solicited and unsolicited assistance from his three children (Rudy, Tyrone, and Linda) and others—finds a way to rearrange and redesign the living environment, thus creating space where none seemed to be before, much as the black race has always found a way to exist, even thrive, in any little corner of society that is available to them.

Jordan's fifth work of fiction for young people is also devoid of black dialect, though certain cultural details mentioned in the text, as well as the accompanying black-and-white drawings, reveal the ethnicity of the inner-city setting to be African-American. The title character and first-person narrator of *Kimako's Story* (1981) is a little girl, who, left to her own devices while her mother works, begins to feel isolated and stifled in her big-city apartment and goes out to explore the neighborhood. Thus, the concept of racial space is expanded from the traditional family unit to include the whole black community, an extended support structure that has always been a key factor in the survival of African-Americans.

CRITICAL RECEPTION

Jordan's fiction for children and young adults has received mixed critical reactions, not just in terms of theme and language but in terms of content as well. Where theme is concerned, the reaction has been generally positive; for most critics have applauded her attempts to articulate—for a young audience—the concerns of a race of people who have been voiceless, invisible members of society throughout most of the history of the United States. *Who Look at Me*, for example, "records with psychological deftness the evolution of the black man's racial pride," according to James A. Emanuel (52); while Diane Farrell calls the book "a strong, impassioned, splendid statement" and "if [Jordan's] intent was to startle the reader into truly seeing the faces of black America, the author succeeds powerfully"(48). Similarly, *Dry Victories* has been heralded as an effective purveyor of the historical frustration of black Americans: Rosalind K. Goddard describes the book as "an excellent, unique teaching tool" (68); and a reviewer in *The Booklist* refers to its "provocative alternate historical perspective" (449). Conversely, a few critics have noted the triteness of Jordan's themes, which were referred to in a *Kirkus* review of *Who Look at Me* as having already been presented, for the most part, by other black writers.

In relation to theme, it should also be noted that Jordan's works of juvenile fiction, though infused with the sensibilities of a single ethnic group and presented from the viewpoint of this group, generally have been considered not separatist but inclusive—thus inviting all young readers, whatever their degree of familiarity with things African-American, to identify with the struggles and triumphs of individual members of a maligned but proud group of Americans. Even Jordan's first work, in which the clash between dominant and minority cultures is the central unifying image, has not been discounted as a "feel good" book directed exclusively at African-Americans. As Susan E. O'Neal states, *Who Look at Me* "will have visual and emotional impact on readers of all ages and races as it implores them to discover others—to look at and see" (89). In a like manner, Wilkinson feels that young readers, whose identity she does not qualify in terms of race or ethnicity, "are sure to be charmed by this natural little girl [Kimako] and her inner-city world" (38). Thus, Jordan's juvenile fiction has not generally been subjected to the kinds of accusations leveled by Jennifer Farley Smith against certain children's biographies, including Jordan's *Fannie Lou Hamer*: "In their eagerness to win sympathy for . . . extraordinary black women, [Tobi Tobias, June Jordan, and Louise Meriwether] have abandoned objectivity—and at times, accuracy—altogether. Dastardly villains are white; arch-heroines are black. . . . Miss Jordan seems to be deliberately discouraging white children from reading her story" (10).

Critical reaction to the language through which Jordan presents her African-American themes has been more mixed, however, for two separate and distinct reasons. A critic for *Kirkus Reviews*, for example, has referred to "stylistic rough spots (e.g., excessive alliteration)" and "impossibly obtuse" lines in *Who Look at Me*, and Farrell has called the same book "a disjointed collection" (47). Most of the negative comments about language, though, have been directed at the nonstandard grammatical forms that recur in *His Own Where* and *Dry Victories*, with the former receiving the brunt of the criticism, not merely for the language in and of itself but, in the context of the plot, for its cultural and moral implications as well. According to Ellen Tremper, "There seems to me to be a deep contradiction between Jordan's strident nationalism whose linguistic expression is her insistence on Black English, and the absurd conclusion of her novel. . . . Whether or not black working class families agree with Jordan's evaluation of their language, they do not want their young teenage daughters and sons setting up shop and starting families of their own" (120).

His Own Where has also received most of the negative criticism related to content, critical comments ranging from the cautious ("Some may question the appropriateness of such matters for teenagers" [*Kirkus Reviews* 1021]) to the confrontational ("To propose as role models a fourteen-year-old girl and sixteen-year-old boy who are flying in the face of reality by setting up bizarre housekeeping . . . is . . . an act of social as well as literary irresponsibility" [Tremper 118]). However, Jordan's other four books have earned enthusiastic, almost universal, acceptance where content is concerned. For instance, *Who Look at Me* has been described as "a strong, impassioned, splendid statement" (Farrell 48) and "a rich and moving experience" (*Kirkus Reviews* 1021); while *New Life: New Room* has been called "a gem of a book" (Council on Interracial Books 168).

BIBLIOGRAPHY

Young Adult Fiction by June Jordan

Who Look at Me. New York: Crowell. 1969.
His Own Where. New York: Crowell, 1971.
Dry Victories. New York: Holt, 1972.
New Life: New Room. Illus. Ray Cruz. New York: Crowell, 1975.
Kimako's Story. Illus. Kay Burford. Boston: Houghton, 1981.

Other Works by June Jordan

Soulscript: Afro-American Poetry. Editor. New York: Doubleday, 1970.
The Voice of the Children. Editor, with Terri Bush. New York: Holt, 1970.
Fannie Lou Hamer. Biography. Illus. Albert Williams. New York: Crowell, 1972.

Selected Studies of June Jordan

Council on Interracial Books for Children, Inc. *Human—and Anti-Human—Values in Children's Books: A Content Rating Instrument for Educators and Concerned Parents.* Washington, DC: Racism and Sexism Resource Center for Educators, 1976. (Includes an analysis of values in *New Life: New Room.*)

Emanuel, James A. Rev. of *Who Look at Me. New York Times Book Review* 16 Nov. 1969: 52.

Fabio, Sarah Webster. Rev. of *His Own Where. New York Times Book Review* 7 Nov. 1971: 6, 34.

Farrell, Diane. Rev. of *Who Look at Me. Horn Book* 66.1 (1970): 47–48.

Goddard, Rosalind K. Rev. of *Dry Victories. School Library Journal* 19.3 (1972): 68.

————. Rev of *His Own Where. School Library Journal* 18.4 (1971): 64–65.

Harris, Janet. Rev. of *Dry Victories. New York Times Book Review* 11 Feb. 1973: 8.

Kaye, Marilyn. Rev. of *Kimako's Story. School Library Journal* 28.1 (1981): 110.

Lewis, Marjorie. Rev. of *New Life: New Room. School Library Journal* 21.9 (1975): 48.

Long, Sidney D. Rev. of *His Own Where. Horn Book* 67.6 (1971): 620.

Martin, Ruby. Rev. of *New Life: New Room. The Reading* Teacher 30 (1977): 824–26.

O'Neal, Susan E. Rev. of *Who Look at Me. School Library Journal* 16.6 (1970): 89.

Rev. of *Dry Victories. Booklist* 1 Jan. 1973: 449.

Rev. of *Dry Victories. Kirkus Reviews* 60 (1972): 809.

Rev. of *His Own Where. Kirkus Reviews* 39 (1971): 1021.

Rev. of *Kimako's Story. Kirkus Reviews* 69 (1981): 1465.

Rev. of *New Life: New Room. The Booklist* 15 June 1976: 1075.

Rev. of *Who Look at Me. The Best in Children's Books: The University of Chicago Guide to Children's Literature. 1966–1972.* Ed. Zena Sutherland. Chicago: U of Chicago P, 1973. 28.

Rev. of *Who Look at Me. Kirkus Reviews* 37 (1969): 863–64.

Rogers, Norma. Rev. of *Fannie Lou Hamer. Interracial Books for Children* 5.3 (1974): 4.

Shelton, Helen H. Rev. of *Kimako's Story. Childhood Education* 58 (1982): 258.

Smith, Jennifer Farley. "New Biographies for Children: 'What's the Author's Angle?'" *Christian Science Monitor* 7 Feb. 1973: 10. (Includes an analysis of the imbalance between historical fact and imaginative invention in *Fannie Lou Hamer.*)

Sutherland, Zena. Rev. of *Kimako's Story. Bulletin of the Center for Children's Books* 35.7 (1982): 132.

Tremper, Ellen. "Black English in Children's Literature." *The Lion and the Unicorn* 3 (1979–1980): 105–24. (Includes an analysis of this dialect as presented in *His Own Where.*)

Wilkinson, Brenda. Rev. of *Kimako's Story. New York Times Book Review* 18 April 1982, 38.

CYNTHIA KADOHATA
(1956-)

Weihua Zhang

BIOGRAPHY

Cynthia Kadohata, a young American novelist whose writing career is on the rise, is of Japanese ancestry. She was born in Chicago to her second-generation Japanese-American parents. Much of her early life was spent on the road with her family to wherever jobs would take them. From Chicago, Kadohata moved with the family to Arkansas, Georgia, Michigan, then back to Chicago and, finally, to Los Angeles when she was 15. At age eighteen, Kadohata entered Los Angeles City College. She later transferred to the University of Southern California, where she graduated from the school of journalism.

In 1977, at age twenty-one, Kadohata was badly injured while walking down a street in Los Angeles when a car jumped the curb and smashed into her, leaving her with a broken collarbone and mangled right arm. This accident made her realize the transience and the unpredictability of life. Writing has become a way for her to deal with this traumatic experience. Francie, the nineteen-year-old protagonist of her second novel, *In the Heart of the Valley of Love*, (1992), has a crushed arm resulting from a similar accident.

Coming from a minority background, Kadohata shows a strong awareness of the multicultural aspects of life in her fictional characters. There is no denying of the Japanese cultural heritage in her writing. The title of her first book is actually from an old Japanese word, *ukiyo*, meaning "the floating world." "The floating world was the gas station attendants, restaurants, and jobs we depended upon, the motel towns floating in the middle of fields and mountains," Olivia's grandmother explains in the book. Francie, on the other hand, has a mixed parentage of Chinese, Japanese, and black.

Indeed, the floating world, or the life on the road her family lived, has become a source of inspiration to Kadohata. She has twice enrolled in and later dropped out of graduate writing programs (first the University of Pittsburgh and then Columbia University). Kadohata finds the lure of the road irresistible: "I feel if I don't go out there and do wacky things, like traveling, it will make my writing dry," she told an interviewer from *Publishers Weekly*.

Several chapters in her first book have appeared as separate stories in various American magazines, including *The New Yorker*, *Grand Street*, and *The Pennsylvania Review*. Kadohata is working on her next book, which will be about the friendship between two women as they go over their lives together and separately. Having written two books in the first person, she is ready for a change: she would like to write from a different angle.

MAJOR WORKS AND THEMES

Kadohata's two novels are both published by Viking: *The Floating World* in 1989 and *In the Heart of the Valley of Love* in 1992. The former is told through the eyes of Olivia Osaka, a twelve-year-old Japanese-American girl coming of age while traveling through the Pacific Northwest with her family in the 1950s. The latter is set in the future, Los Angeles in 2052, and celebrates ordinary folks' capacity to survive. Both books have female protagonists who are either growing into young adulthood (like Olivia) or already are young adults (like Francie). Both protagonists are part of the ethnic underclass.

The Floating World centers on the Osakas, a migratory Japanese-American family on the road searching for jobs in the early 1950s. The family consists of Obasan, the maternal grandmother; Laura, the mother; Charlie Osaka (Charlie-O), the stepfather; Olivia, the twelve-year-old narrator of the book; and her three younger brothers, Ben, Walter, and Peter. Olivia and her family are living a life that is rootless, transient, full of unknown twists and turns. Coming of age in aftermath of World War II, when the horror of the mass internment of Japanese-Americans is still fresh in people's minds, when it is still hard for Japanese-Americans to find jobs, Olivia has become a reluctant witness to her parents' unhappy marriage, to Obasan's desperate hold of her Japanese past, to the hardships and humiliations her parents and other Japanese-Americans are experiencing.

Through Olivia's innocent and observant eyes, Kadohata explores the effects of racism and an alien culture on Japanese-Americans, evidenced in the lives of her family and of the many Japanese-American individuals and families in the book. After many wanderings, Olivia's family settles in Gibson, Arkansas, when she is sixteen. With the few Japanese visible among the white population, they feel the constant staring cast their way and are compelled to keep quiet in public. The family would like to move to a nearby town called Ashland, but they are discouraged by the fact that they would be the first Japanese-American family there. Racial prejudice is as subtle and telling as that.

Clearly, Gibson provides no escape for the Japanese-Americans. Here, Olivia watches with fear, shame, and protectiveness as her father loses all his money at a card game; she learns of Collie Asano, the best chicken sexer in his young and sober days, losing his wife, kids, house, and the desire for life; she feels helpless when old Mr. Tanizaki—the father of the boy she falls in love with while working in the hatchery—is fired by his fellow Japanese chicken sexers when the mechanical job has exacted a toll on him, and when his senility has become a threat to the well-being of the entire group (chicken sexers are hired and fired as a group by hatcheries); her heart bleeds over the loss of two best friends at school: one drops out, the other has left the town with her mother, leaving behind the heavily-in-debt father/husband.

But there is a sense of relief when we read about the relationship between Olivia and Obasan. Amidst the wanderings, disarrays, fears, and sufferings, Obasan, the forceful and indomitable grandmother, proves to be a much-needed spiritual guide for Olivia's growth in a hostile environment. Kadohata focuses on the ambivalent feelings that exist between Obasan and Olivia, a fact that has more to do with their being the outsiders of an alien culture trying to fit in, and, at the same time, with Obasan's effort to pass her memories to the little girl. After Obasan's death, Olivia, who has started her narrative by calling Obasan her tormentor, recalls lovingly the morning walks she used to take with the older woman—those are among her happiest memories while growing up. She also remembers how during one of the evening rides, Obasan was ready to risk her own life to protect her. To Olivia, Obasan's stories have been her possessions (like many of her valuable material ones) and figuring out the past life of Obasan has been her obsession—not for curiosity per se, but for the inspiration it brings to her own life.

In the end, Olivia is compelled to leave behind her home at Gibson and her family to search for a new life. Knowing that her parents have always wished her a happier life, she leaves for Los Angeles to attend college. Coming of age in a Japanese-American family, Olivia has witnessed and experienced firsthand what it means to grow up as part of an immigrant family; what it means to belong to America and yet to stand constantly apart; and what it means to be stable in a floating world. Her determination to grow beyond her parents' dreams, to break free from the haunting spirit of Obasan, to venture into an alien, and at times hostile, world exemplifies Kadohata's larger concern with the Japanese-Americans as a people: Will they ever claim America as their country and be acknowledged as its worthy citizens?

In the Heart of the Valley of Love, Kadohata's second book, focuses on themes and settings that are very different from her first, though the protagonist is also of mixed Asian and American background. The book takes place in 2052 Los Angeles, a futuristic world that is very much grounded in the present. Here, the author depicts a society that is plagued by government repression, police corruption, economic stagnation, moral degradation, and people's cynicism. The book provides a chilling vision of twenty-first-century Los Angeles where being arrested is a daily occurrence; where everyone is engaged in wrongdoing; where people no longer riot for change, but for destruction; where everyone carries a gun for self-protection; where pollution makes even the stars fade.

Francie, a nineteen-year-old young woman whose parents died of lung cancer several years ago, is living now with her Aunt Annie and Annie's boyfriend Rohn. Like many of the characters in the book, Rohn and Annie are engaged in illegal business dealings: they are operating a delivery business of cigarettes, food, and black-market Japanese electronics. In fact, only a few pages into the book Rohn disappears, apparently having been arrested for illegal water dealings with Max the Magician, because in this futuristic society, water and gas are rationed by the government. Rohn's whereabouts remain a mystery until the very end of the book when, during the day of the June primary, seven thousand arrests are reported, and Rohn is very likely to be released because of the overcrowded prison population.

But it is the human spirit's capacity to survive that Kadohata celebrates best in the book. In this world where people become sick and die so abruptly, where you hate to love and make any commitment to a steady relationship, Kadohata portrays a tender and inspiring love between Rohn and Annie, and Francie and Mark. Annie and Rohn are in their mid-forties, but they love like two young lovers. Their love is marked by dancing and singing at home and in motel rooms; hugging and kissing in public; sharing the risks and responsibilities of their business. After Rohn's arrest, however, Annie quickly loses her laughter and sets out to search for him. Risking arrest— one can be arrested in Los Angeles in 2052 for virtually no reason—-Annie engages in a letter-writing campaign, determined to find her boyfriend's whereabouts.

Their cheerful attitude has been a great comfort to Francie after the deaths of her parents. Less optimistic about Rohn's return, Francie stops doing deliveries for her aunt and moves out to live on her own for she can no longer bear her aunt's sadness and desperation. She decides to go to college for a change. In college, she falls in love with a young man, Mark, whose sustaining love enables her to face life with a new light. In the end of the book, Francie is able to sever herself from the past—symbolized in the burial of the rocks representing her dead parents that she has been carrying ever since their deaths—and moves in with Mark. Together they will face the unknown future, with love and trust.

CRITICAL RECEPTION

With the publication of her first book, *The Floating World*, in 1989, Kadohata has been well received by the literary circle and claimed as "a new voice on the Asian American scene—a Japanese Amy Tan" (See 48). She got very good reviews for her first book. Critics have noticed that Kadohata's writing style in *The Floating World* has the features of "Japanese colloquial poetry, *haikai*, in which images—delicate, fragmentary and fleeting—float by" (Moore 5). John Spurling lets us see how Kadohata has given her reader a different picture of what the land and home mean to an outside group: "Kadohata subtly undermines the whole North American ethos, the myth of the solid, ordinary folk at home in their land" (49). Olivia's family is not one that has its own land and home; and when they do—as they have settled down in Gibson—-they are far from feeling at home, secure, wanted, and loved. In *In the Heart of the Valley of Love*, Kadohata confirms the talent she demonstrated in her first novel. Her keen awareness of the world around her, revealed in this book, finds a strong testimony in the Rodney King riots in Los Angeles in 1992, when the chilling vision she has presented seems "more appropriate to the realm of science fiction" (See 48).

BIBLIOGRAPHY

Young Adult Fiction by Cynthia Kadohata

The Floating World. New York: Viking, 1989.
In the Heart of the Valley of Love. New York: Viking, 1992.

Selected Studies of Cynthia Kadohata

Edwards-Yearwood, Grace. "Growing Up Japanese-American." *Los Angeles Times Book Review* 16 July 1989:12.

Ehrlich, Gretel. "A Japanese Girl Wishfully Drifts across America." *Chicago Tribune—Books* 23 July 1989: 6.

Kakutani, Michiko. "Growing Up Rootless in an Immigrant Family." *New York Times* 30 June 1989: C27.

Moore, Susan. "On the Road with Charlie-O." *Washington Post Book World* 25 June 1989: 5, 7.

Ong, Caroline. "Roots Relations." *Times Literary Supplement* no. 4526 (29 Dec.–4 Jan. 1990): 1447.

Sassone, Ralph. "The Wonder Years." *Village Voice* 19 Sept. 1989: 53.

See, Lisa. "Cynthia Kadohata." *Publishers Weekly* 3 Aug. 1992: 48–49.

Spurling, John. "East, West, Which Is Best?" *The Observer* 1 Oct. 1989: 49.

Yogi, Stan. "*The Floating World* by Cynthia Kadohata." *Amerasian Journal* 16.1 (1989): 261.

JOSEPH QUINCY KRUMGOLD
(1908–1980)

Andrea O'Reilly Herrera

BIOGRAPHY

Joseph Quincy Krumgold, the first author of children's books to win the Newbery Medal two times, was born in Jersey City, New Jersey on April 10, 1908.

During his lifetime, Krumgold undertook a variety of jobs, all of which centered in one way or another on writing and filmmaking. At various points in his career he worked as a writer of adult and children's fiction, a playwright, an editor of a historical text for a local historical society, an essayist, a screenwriter, a producer, and a director. Though he is best remembered for the unusual books he wrote for adolescents—unusual in both their form and their subject matter—Krumgold actually began his career in filmmaking.

On several occasions, he admitted that his interest in movies and movie making was sparked early on by his father and brother, both of whom were involved in some aspect of the film industry. His father, Henry Krumgold, was a film exhibitor who owned and operated several movie houses in Jersey City. His older brother was an organist employed to accompany the silent films in the New York City movie palaces. Virtually weaned on "movie talk," Krumgold decided at the age of twelve that he wanted to be a filmmaker.

From all accounts, Krumgold was an exceptionally ambitious, mature, and dedicated young man. Once he had made up his mind to pursue a career in the film industry, he focused all of his energies on this goal. In his view, the years that he spent at Dickinson High School in Jersey City and New York University represent a kind of apprenticeship. Chemistry, he claimed, introduced him to film developing; in physics, he studied about the optic nerve and thereby learned about the camera lens. While attending New York University, Krumgold majored in English and history, the subjects which provided the raw material for the stories he would later turn into film scripts. In his eyes, no information was wasted upon him; everything that he learned was, in one way or another, useful.

For the next eleven years (1929–1940) he established himself in a career that would not only present him with the opportunity to work for most of the major motion picture companies in the United States but would take him from coast to coast and, in some cases, from continent to continent. Following his graduation from New York University in 1928, Joseph Krumgold relocated to California and secured employment as a publicity writer at Metro-Goldwyn Mayer. After only a short time he advanced from publicity writing to script writing and production. From Metro-Goldwyn Mayer, he went on to work as a writer and producer for Paramount, Columbia, Republic, and RKO pictures.

Roughly around the time of World War II, Joseph Krumgold stopped producing studio films and became interested in making documentaries, a career move which would take him all across the United States and to Europe and the Middle East. From 1940–1946 he served as a producer and director at Film Associates in New York; at the same time, he worked for the Office of War Information. In 1947 he moved to Israel and became associated with Palestine Films, where he served as the president in charge of production until 1951. During that time he produced fifteen films, capturing the prestigious Venice Film Festival Award for *The House in the Desert*. He later won several other prizes for both his films and his documentaries at the Edinburgh and the Prague festivals, and he was eventually nominated for an Academy Award.

In 1952 Krumgold returned to the United States with his wife, Helen Litwin, and his son, Adam, and bought a large farm in Hope, New Jersey. Shortly thereafter, he established his own film company, Joseph Krumgold Productions, which remained in business until 1960. The following year he and his wife traveled to the Southwest to gather information about sheep herders for a documentary sponsored by the United States Department of State for overseas distribution. The film received the Robert Flaherty Award honorable mention in 1954 and was remade into a movie by Universal Pictures in 1966. It was this project that inspired the editors at Thomas Y. Crowell publishing company to commission him to adapt his film into what would eventually become his most celebrated children's book, ... *And Now Miguel* (1953). Though he had already published two books (an adult novel entitled *Thanks to Murder* [1935] and a children's book *Sweeney's Adventures* [1942]), . . . *And Now Miguel* met with immediate success. The following year, Krumgold received the Newbery Medal from the American Library Association, and in 1973 the Boys' Club Junior Book Award from Boys' Club of America and the Freedom Foundation Award, for his efforts. The book was subsequently translated into at least fifteen foreign languages and reissued in 1970 by Apollo.

Though he continued to pursue his career in film, more and more Krumgold saw himself as an author of children's literature. Writing for children represented, in Krumgold's own words, "a way of going back" to "a life of choice," a time period or developmental stage in which people were open to personal growth and change. Just as his schooling had provided him with fodder for his script writing, his films provided the inspiration for his novels. Avowedly influenced by his rural surroundings, Krumgold published a second novel for adolescents, *Onion John*, in 1959. In 1960 he received a second Newbery Award, an unprecedented event in the history of children's literature. Krumgold went on to produce a third adolescent novel, *Henry 3* (1967), completing what he himself regarded as a trilogy of thematically linked stories. A year later he wrote and published his final children's story, *The Most Terrible Turk* (1969). During that same decade, he also worked as a writer, director, and producer for CBS, NBC, National Educational Television, and Westinghouse television (1960–1970).

On July 10, 1980, after a long and successful career, Krumgold succumbed to a stroke at his farm in Hope, New Jersey, dying at the age of seventy-two.

MAJOR WORKS AND THEMES

In the past reviewers of Joseph Krumgold's work have primarily focused on either the revolutionary form of his children's novels, or his sensitive handling of difficult subjects. Krumgold has almost universally been distinguished for his realistic handling of plot and character. As he himself suggested, he looked to life—"actual people and actual places"—for his source material. And thus, just as ... *And Now Miguel* was based upon the factual details of his experiences in New Mexico while filming a documentary on southwestern sheep herders, his subsequent works of adolescent fiction, *Onion John* and *Henry 3,* were based on his rural and urban surroundings respectively. (*Onion John* is set in a small town much like Krumgold's own hometown, located in northern New Jersey; and an exclusive suburb of New York City provides the setting for *Henry 3.*) All three works employ first-person narration, a literary strategy which heightens the realistic effect of Krumgold's writing. In this way he enables the reader to carefully trace, and thus identify with, the gradually developing consciousness of his adolescent protagonists, all of whom stand on the threshold of maturity.

In addition to the realistic elements in Krumgold's work, critics have also tended to comment upon the perceptive manner in which he portrays both sibling relationships and the relationships between generations, particularly in regard to fathers and sons. In the same vein, Krumgold treats with what many considered to be surprising frankness various social issues in regard to moral or religious values. For instance, Miguel of . . . *And Now Miguel* and his older brother Gabriel have a substantial discussion regarding the distinction between human desire and true religious faith and its consequent relationship to divine will. *Onion John* simultaneously treats the dual themes of respecting others who hold divergent views or desires from our own and of acknowledging what Krumgold identifies as one's "kinship" with one's own tribe. Paralleling the religious issues raised in . . . *And Now Miguel,* Krumgold also explores the relationship between mythic ritual and superstition in this second award-winning novel. *Henry 3* focuses on issues such as materialism and conformity as Henry negotiates between his schoolmates, his family, and his community. In all three cases, the main protagonists undergo an often painful process in which they eventually determine, and ultimately establish, identities independent of, though not always in conflict with, familial or communal views or attitudes. Moreover, Krumgold casts each of his adolescent protagonists in a kind of triangular relationship involving both his family and the larger community, of which he sometimes is only a peripheral member, as in the case of Henry Lovering III. In the end the reader not only witnesses each boy's psychological and emotional development, but is invited to scrutinize and evaluate the values of the family and the community at large.

Although critics have tended to praise Krumgold for his virtually unprecedented narrative form and his handling of provocative themes, what is perhaps most extraordinary about his work is that he preceded by more than a decade what would become (and still is) a multicultural trend in writing and publishing. During the 1960s the American public was made to focus its attention on issues of gender, race, and pluralism. In the wake of the Civil Rights Movement, school curricula, from the elementary level through the university, gradually began to reflect these concerns. By the late sixties and the early part of the seventies, educators and authors alike had become aware of the asymmetry between the literary representation of minorities and middle-class whites. In regard to children's literature, one need only consult the list of Newbery recipients to see that between 1922 and 1969 only two authors awarded the medal, aside from Joseph Krumgold, included minority characters in their works: Elizabeth Yates (*Amos Fortune, Free Man,* 1951) and Scott O'Dell (*Island of the Blue Dolphins,* 1961). By the mid-seventies publishing houses witnessed a proliferation of works for both children and adults that included minority protagonists or addressed minority concerns. Despite the fact that he was an "outsider" to the Mexican-American community, Joseph Krumgold numbered among the first American authors to give direct literary expression to the minority experience by featuring a twelve-year-old Chicano as the center of consciousness of his 1953 award-winning novel . . . *And Now Miguel.*

Ostensibly, . . . *And Now Miguel* depicts the life of a family of sheep herders living outside Santa Fe, New Mexico. It is a kind of rite of passage novel which chronicles the story of a young boy's desire to accompany the men in his family into the Sangre de Cristo Mountains, where they will pasture their sheep for the summer. As Krumgold himself suggested, after completing his documentary on the real Chavez family, he realized that there were many aspects of Miguel's story that could not be captured on film and, therefore, needed further exploration and attention in print.

. . . *And Now Miguel* is a remarkable novel for many reasons. In the first place, it was published well before there was any visible interest in the Chicano experience or a discernible aesthetic in Chicano literature. It was not until the early seventies, when Rudolfo Anaya published his award-winning *Bless Me, Ultima* (1972), a novel that many view as the first achieved work of Chicano consciousness, that Mexican-American writing began to be recognized as a legitimate literary genre. Though Anaya (dubbed by many as the father of Chicano literature) inspired other writers to follow in the path he had carved out, Chicano fiction did not begin to approach a state of literary maturity in terms of handling of theme and form until the seventies.

Krumgold's novel was also a maverick work of children's literature, given the time at which it was written, for it was released during a period when books for children and adolescents in general, including the textbooks educators employed in their classrooms, were primarily written by and for an essentially homogeneous audience. The foregrounding of Miguel's individual perception not only created a realistic effect, but it also gave legitimate voice to a segment of the population that had, until that time, been largely excluded from American letters. And thus, the opening sentence of the novel—"I am Miguel"—functions as a subtle political statement which tempts one to compare Krumgold's narrative strategy to that of later nonwhite writers such as Malcolm X, Maya Angelou, and Alice Walker.

In his novel, Krumgold invites the reader to explore Chicano cultural values, customs, and traditions. Although a contemporary audience might note, perhaps with some discomfort, the traditional gendered division of labor depicted in Krumgold's work, . . . And Now Miguel highlights the importance of the close-knit, extended family unit, an integral aspect of Latin culture. Throughout the novel it is clear that the members of the Chavez family base their relationships to one another on deep-rooted love, loyalty, and respect. It is also a family bound by tradition, custom, and a set of firm religious beliefs (in this case Roman Catholicism) which manifest themselves not only in the way that they shear their sheep, but in the way they pray. The emphasis on family, tradition, and religion represents a set of cultural values shared not only by the Chavez family but by the Chicano community as a whole. For us as readers, the story is not simply about the fulfillment of a child's private dream of accompanying his father and his uncle and brother into the mountains, it is also about the preservation and perpetuation of age-old traditions and values carried over from indigenous cultures and passed down through generations.

Considering the significant role that storytelling has always played in socializing and acculturating children, Krumgold's work accomplished several things. In the first place it helped explode negative stereotypes or prejudice. By emphasizing the untiring work ethic and the pride of both the men and the women in the Chavez family, Krumgold defies the stereotype, often portrayed in films, of the lazy Mexican or Chicano. Second, the novel allows the reader to identify, if vicariously, with a cultural group outside of his or her own. In . . . And Now Miguel language becomes central to this process, for by including Spanish words in the text Krumgold immediately alerts the reader to one of the fundamental differences, and perhaps barriers, for the Chicano. Years later Chicano and Chicana writers, such as Richard Rodriguez and Gloria Anzaldúa, would intermingle English with often untranslated Spanish (Spanglish) in their works in order to represent the linguistic reality of surviving in a predominantly English-speaking world.

Perhaps the greatest strength of . . . *And Now Miguel* is the idea that it is, at once, universal and culture specific. By treating universal themes of adolescence that bring the Chicano experience into focus, Krumgold not only stresses cultural differences but exposes human commonalities as well. Ultimately, his work suggests a common or shared humanity.

Onion John (1959) takes up many of the themes first introduced in . . . *And Now Miguel*. Set in the rural town of Serenity, the story revolves around a triangular relationship among the twelve-year-old protagonist, Andy Rusch, Jr., his father, and an East European hobo, Onion John. The novel opens with an episode in which Andy scrutinizes a photograph of his little league team in the local paper; unable to discern one player from another, he asks his father, "Who am I?" a question which resounds throughout the novel. In a related parallel plot, Mr. Rusch convinces the townspeople to build Onion John a modern home; his misplaced benevolence not only ends in disaster but drives the hobo out of Serenity. In his search for an identity independent of the one his father imagines for him, Andy identifies with and emulates Onion John. Though Andy at no time rejects John, the novel culminates in the boy's assertion of his desire to inherit his father's hardware store, rather than fulfill Mr. Rusch's own unfulfilled career aspirations of being an engineer at MIT or an astronaut.

Despite the fact that critics have universally tended to foreground Andy's story, the title of Krumgold's novel invites us to subordinate the boy's experiences, at least on a thematic level, in lieu of Onion John's. In other words, though Andy's maturation and his father's consequent acceptance of his son as an individual are prompted by their relationship to Onion John, the latter's experience with the people of Serenity—the epitome of a good-willed yet small-minded American town—seems to be at the heart of Krumgold's story. More specifically, the notion of cultural value and cultural difference, themes which are central to . . . *And Now Miguel*, resurface and resonate in *Onion John*. What primarily distinguishes this novel from its predecessor is the fact that we must approach these themes in a kind of refracted manner, for the Old World culture that Onion John represents—a culture replete with myth, ritual, tradition, and a sense of religious value—is represented through Andy's eyes. Unlike the other townspeople, including his father, Andy alone exhibits a willingness and openness to the difference and the richness of Onion John's culture. Once again, language plays a key role in Krumgold's work; quite literally, Andy is the only person who understands John's sometimes cryptic and garbled talk. Although the town regards John as eccentric and superstitious, an attitude embodied in the novel by Mr. Rusch, it becomes increasingly clear throughout the narrative that the somewhat ethnocentric and perhaps supremacist view that the people of Serenity represent actually prevents them from appreciating the genuine beauty and richness of John's culture. It is thus no coincidence that Andy's search for his identity cannot be completed until the town in general, and Mr. Rusch in particular, discover that they have erred in trying to modernize or civilize Onion John. In the end, the people of Serenity realize that their own set of cultural values and mores is not any better than John's; they are, quite simply, different. Like . . . *And Now Miguel*, the reader is ultimately left with the responsibility of measuring two variant, though not necessarily mutually exclusive, ways of life against one another.

Henry 3 (1967), the final novel in what is generally regarded as a trilogy, is also a first-person narrative account of a thirteen-year-old boy's maturation. Though it fails to treat the multicultural themes that appear in . . . *And Now Miguel* and *Onion John*, the main protagonist, Henry Lovering III, must also measure his own attitudes against the shallow and materialistic values maintained not only by the affluent suburban community in which he lives, but by his family as well. Like Andy Rusch, Henry ultimately has the courage to acknowledge and consequently reject the superficial, conformist attitudes and standards propagated by those who surround him. Just as . . . *And Now Miguel* opened with the simple assertion of identity, "I am Miguel," Krumgold concludes his trilogy with Henry's acceptance and affirmation, on the very first page of the novel, of selfhood: "I'm a hundred and fifty-four percent" normal.

CRITICAL RECEPTION

The multiple awards that Joseph Krumgold received for his adolescent fiction speak to the positive critical reception his writing received throughout his lifetime. The fact that both . . . *And Now Miguel* and *Onion John* remain in print more than forty years after the publication of the first novel stands in itself as testimony to significance and excellence of his work. In general, critics seem to rank . . . *And Now Miguel* as Krumgold's greatest achievement; *Onion John* follows closely in its wake. Although *Henry 3* thematically completes the trilogy, it has, since its publication, been regarded as Krumgold's weakest effort. In fact H. L. Maples of *Book World* suggested that *Henry 3* seemed like more of a "sociological treatise" than a book written for adolescents. Once again, critics almost unanimously distinguish Krumgold's writing because of its realism, its innovative literary form, its provocative subject matter, and its keen sensitivity to the difficulties and the desires of adolescents. Although all of these elements and aspects of Joseph Krumgold's work are worthy of the praise they have consistently attracted in the past, it may well be that Krumgold will be best remembered for his contribution to the growing body of multicultural literature.

Of course, in an age when the authority of an outsider to accurately and authentically depict a cultural community outside of his or her own experience is being questioned, authors such as Krumgold may be subject to a certain degree of criticism. As the ranks of primary or inside accounts of, for example, the Chicano experience expand, critics may be tempted to suggest that novels such as . . . *And Now Miguel* and *Onion John* are encoded with the author's own ideological notions and thereby create a somewhat biased or faulty picture of reality. To a certain degree Krumgold presents a somewhat idyllic portrait of the minority experience, especially in the former work. Nevertheless, one cannot lose sight of the fact that his writing was virtually unprecedented for its time in terms of its multicultural subject matter.

More recently feminist critics such as Gillian Thomas have called Krumgold to task for his treatment of women. According to the latter, females function as relational beings in Krumgold's novels; they are defined exclusively in terms of their domestic or familial roles. Indeed, in his depiction of the relationships among the various members of the Chavez household, Krumgold presents a relatively traditional, gender-biased division of labor: Miguel's mother and sisters are completely excluded from the sheep-herding activities and segregated in the kitchen and they are most frequently depicted presiding over the preparation and serving of meals. In *Onion John* women are marginalized in the plot and depicted solely in domestic roles. In *Henry 3*, as Thomas suggests, Krumgold's stereotypical portrayal of women as greedy, catty hysterics virtually reduces them to caricatures. She attributes this aspect of Krumgold's work to earlier works of literature written for boys, such as the adventure tales of R. M. Ballantyne and G. A. Henty, that "celebrate a bonding of boys and men on an exclusion of women."

Undoubtedly, Joseph Krumgold's works are informed by the ideologies that informed the historical period in which he was writing; moreover, as a white male author, he wrote from a privileged status. Although it would clearly be naive to ignore the shortcomings or the flaws in Joseph Krumgold's works, it would, indeed, be a tragedy to allow them to overshadow his accomplishments. In a word, he was a pioneer in his time who broke down barriers that still exist today.

BIBLIOGRAPHY

Young Adult Fiction by Joseph Quincy Krumgold

Sweeney's Adventures. Illus. Tibor Gergely. New York: Random House, 1942.
. . . And Now Miguel. Illus. Jean Charlot. New York: Crowell, 1953. Apollo, 1970.
Onion John. Illus. Symeon Shimin. New York: Crowell, 1959. London: Lutter-worth, 1964.
Henry 3. Illus. Alvin Smith. New York: Atheneum, 1967.
The Most Terrible Turk. Illus. Michael Hampshire. New York: Crowell, 1969.

Works for Adults by Joseph Quincy Krumgold

Thanks to Murder. New York: Vanguard; London: Gollancz, 1935.

Other Works by Joseph Quincy Krumgold

"Archetypes of the Twentieth Century." *School Library Journal* (Oct. 1968): 112–15.
Where Do We Grow from Here: An Essay on Children's Literature. New York: Atheneum, 1968.
The Oxford Furnace, 1741–1925. Editor. Local History. Belvidere, N.J.: Warren County Historical Society, 1975.

Selected Studies of Joseph Quincy Krumgold

Arbuthnot, May Hill. *Children's Reading in the Home*. Glenview, IL: Scott, Foresman, 1969.
Cameron, Eleanor. *The Green and Burning Tree: On the Writing and Enjoyment of Children's Books*. Boston: Atlantic-Little, Brown, 1969.
Donelson, Kenneth L., and Alleen Pace Nilson. *Literature for Today's Young Adults*. Glenview, IL: Scott, Foresman, 1980.
Kingman, Lee, ed. *Newbery and Caldecott Medal Books, 1956–65*. Boston: Horn Book, 1965.
Maples, H. L. Rev. of *Henry 3*. *Washington Post Book World* 2 (Nov. 1967): 8.
Meigs, Cornelia, Anne Thaxter Eaton, Elizabeth Nesbitt, and Ruth Hill Viguers, eds. *A Critical History of Children's Literature*. New York: Macmillan, 1969.
Miller, Bertha Mahony, and Elinor Whitney, eds. *Newbery Medal Books, 1922–55*. Boston: Horn Book, 1955.
Smaridge, Norah. *Authors-Illustrators for Young People*. New York: Dodd, Mead, 1973.

Sutherland, Zena, Dianne L. Monson, and May Hill Arbuthnot, eds. *Children and Books*. 6th ed. New York: Scott, Foresman, 1981.

Thomas, Gillian. "Krumgold, Joseph (Quincy)." *Twentieth-Century Children's Writers*. Ed. Tracy Chevalier. 3rd ed. Chicago: St. James, 1989. 547–48.

Ward, Martha E., and Dorothy A. Marquardt. *Authors of Books for Young People*. 2nd ed. Metuchen, NJ: Scarecrow, 1971.

Weiss, "Joseph Krumgold." Videocassette. Philadelphia: Temple UP, 1971.

EVELYN SIBLEY LAMPMAN
(1907-1980)

Denise Anton Wright

BIOGRAPHY

Evelyn Sibley Lampman was born on April 18, 1907, in Dallas, Oregon. Her parents were Joseph Sibley and Harriet Bronson Sibley. Her great-grandparents had traveled to Oregon in the nineteenth century via a covered wagon. As a child Lampman grew up hearing stories of their trip west and of Oregon's early pioneer days. She later incorporated many of these stories into her historical fiction for young people. Lampman attended Oregon State University and graduated in 1929 with a B.S. in education. On May 12, 1934, she married Herbert Sheldon Lampman, a newspaperman and the son of Ben Hur Lampman, a writer and wildlife editor. Their marriage was by all accounts a very happy one and produced two daughters, Linda and Anne. Herbert died in June of 1943 and she never remarried.

After graduating from college, Lampman worked first as a continuity writer and then as the continuity chief for KEX, a radio station in Portland, Oregon. She later fictionalized her early radio experiences in *Of Mikes and Men*, a humorous adult novel published in 1951. As the educational director for Portland's KGW radio station from 1945–1952, Lampman wrote scripts for programs which corresponded to the course work of the Portland public schools. Tapes of these programs were made available to schools throughout Oregon and were still being used in the early 1960s. Although these educational radio scripts covered a wide variety of topics, many were based upon Oregon's pioneer history. During her radio career, Lampman received two Jean Hersholt Awards for scriptwriting. In 1952, following the success of *Treasure Mountain* and her other early novels, Lampman left radio and became a full-time writer of children's and young adult books.

Lampman's juvenile books received numerous awards, among them the award from the Committee on the Art of Democratic Living for *Treasure Mountain* in 1949; the Dorothy Canfield Fisher Memorial Children's Book Award for *The City under the Back Steps* in 1962; the Western Writers of America Spur Award for *Half-Breed* in 1968 and *Cayuse Courage* in 1970; and the Children's Book Showcase Award for *The Potlatch Family* in 1977. The Oregon Historical Society Library houses many of Lampman's personal papers and speeches in addition to plays written by students in her creative writing class, research notes, foreign language editions of her published works, and drafts, rewrites, and proofs for her last novel, *Three Knocks on the Wall*.

As a way of recognizing Lampman's many contributions to children's and young adult literature, in 1982 the Children's Services Division of the Oregon Library Association created an award in her honor. The Evelyn Sibley Lampman Award is presented annually to an Oregon author, educator, or librarian who has made an outstanding contribution to either children's literature or to youth library services. Past recipients of the award include authors Walt Morey, Eloise Jarvis McGraw, Nonny Hogrogian, Ursula LeGuin, Eric Kimmel, and Rick Steber. Rebecca Cohen, director of children's services at the Newport (Oregon) Public Library and co-recipient of the 1994 Lampman Award, was particularly honored to receive this award because Lampman's *Treasure Mountain* was one of her favorite books as a child.

MAJOR WORKS AND THEMES

While Lampman was a prolific and versatile writer who was equally comfortable writing fantasy, realistic fiction, humor, and adventure, her reputation today rests largely with her sympathetic depictions of Native American life. A recurring theme in Lampman's writing is the uneasy relationship which exists between the white and Native American cultures. Nearly all of her novels are set in Oregon and many highlight aspects of that state's rich history. Lampman's historical novels often include an afterword which details her research for the work.

Lampman's fiction from the 1940s and 1950s was a mixture of fantasy, historical fiction, and adventure. Occasionally in novels such as *Treasure*

Mountain (1949) and *Navaho Sister* (1956), Lampman addressed the issue of Native Americans living in a predominantly white society. *Treasure Mountain* revolves around two children from the Chemawa Indian School who visit their aunt on the Oregon coast, search for buried treasure, and rediscover their family heritage. Oregon's Chemawa Indian School also features in *Navaho Sister* when a twelve-year-old girl experiences the conflicting values of white and Indian cultures for the first time.

Lampman's empathy for Native Americans is most clearly expressed in her later fiction. *Half-Breed* (1967), set in 1850, concerns a Crow Indian boy who encounters racial prejudice when he leaves his mother's tribe to live with his white father. *Cayuse Courage* (1970) is a fictionalized account of the small pox epidemic and resulting Whitman massacre of 1847, told from an Indian vantage point. *Once upon the Little Big Horn* (1971) is an unromanticized version of the famous battle told from a variety of viewpoints. *Rattlesnake Cave* (1974) tells the story of a sickly city boy whose life is changed by his friendship with two Indian boys. Although fiction, *White Captives* (1975) is based upon the captivity narrative of Olive Oatman, who, with her younger sister, lived among the Tonto Apaches and later the Mojave people during the 1850's. Ashamed of her alcoholic father, Plum Longor from *The Potlatch Family* (1976) longs to be like the white students in her high school. Her brother's return from the Vietnam War brings about a renewed sense of pride in their Chinook heritage. *Squaw Man's Son* (1978), set in the 1870s, tells the story of thirteen-year-old Billy who leaves his white father to live with his mother's Modoc people. There, Billy is thrust into the war between the Modocs and the United States Army.

CRITICAL RECEPTION

Throughout her long career, Lampman's novels for young people were favorably reviewed by most of the major library- and education-related periodicals. But as a white writing about the Native American experience Lampman has occasionally received mixed reviews from critics. Mary Jo Lass-Woodfin's *Books on American Indians and Eskimos* recommends eight of Lampman's novels—*Cayuse Courage, Half-Breed, Navaho Sister, Once upon the Little Big Horn, The Potlatch Family, Rattlesnake Cave, White Captives*, and *The Year of Small Shadow*—and generally praises her fair treatment of Native American issues. Hap Gilliland's *Indian Children's Books* lists seven of Lampman's novels—*Cayuse Courage, Half-Breed, Navaho Sister, Once upon the Little Big Horn, Treasure Mountain, White*

Captives, and *The Year of Small Shadow*—and among these finds only *Navaho Sister* to be objectionable in its emphasis upon white ideals.

Undoubtedly the most controversial of Lampman's novels and the one which has received the most serious critical attention is *White Captives*. Much of the criticism surrounding *White Captives* centers on what many reviewers perceive to be a negative depiction of Native Americans. Based upon Olive Oatman's 1857 captivity narrative, *White Captives* reflects Olive's lack of understanding for the Apache and Mojave people among whom she lived for several years. Opal Moore and Donnarae MacCann fault Lampman for adhering too strictly to the formula established in the Oatman narrative. As a result, they feel that *White Captives* "idealizes whites at the expense of the Indians, who are characterized as savage, unfeeling, undisciplined" (26). Nancy Lynn Carver agrees with this opinion, stating that the Indians are portrayed as "hostile, vicious, and unsympathetic" (25). In her afterword to *White Captives*, Lampman acknowledges her debt to the Oatman captivity narrative but stresses the fact that "over a hundred years later, it is possible to look at Olive's experience a little more dispassionately" and to see that "neither tribe was unnecessarily cruel" (177). Gilliland credits *White Captives* as being "a worthy attempt at telling both sides of the story" but faults Lampman for lacking "knowledge of Indian thought and culture" (154). Lass-Woodfin picks up Lampman's sentiments when she characterizes *White Captives* as a "dispassionate view of life among the Southwest Indians," but while she recommends the novel, she also warns her readers to be prepared for controversy with this title (144).

BIBLIOGRAPHY

Young Adult Fiction by Evelyn Sibley Lampman

Crazy Creek. Illus. Grace Paull. Garden City, NY: Doubleday, 1948.

Treasure Mountain. Illus. Richard Bennett. Garden City, NY: Doubleday, 1949.

The Bounces of Cynthiann'. Illus. Grace Paull. Garden City, NY: Doubleday, 1950.

Elder Brother. Illus. Richard Bennett. Garden City, NY: Doubleday, 1951.

Captain Apple's Ghost. Illus. Ninon MacKnight. Garden City, NY: Doubleday, 1952.

Tree Wagon. Illus. Robert Frankenberg. Garden City, NY: Doubleday, 1953.

Witch Doctor's Son. Illus. Richard Bennett. Garden City, NY: Doubleday, 1954.

Shy Stegosaurus of Cricket Creek. Illus. Herbert Buel. Garden City, NY: Doubleday, 1955.

Navaho Sister. Illus. Paul Lantz. Garden City, NY: Doubleday, 1956.

Rusty's Space Ship. Illus. Bernard Krigstein. Garden City, NY: Doubleday, 1957.

Rock Hounds. Illus. Arnold Spilka. Garden City, NY: Doubleday, 1958.

Special Year. Illus. Genia. Garden City, NY: Doubleday, 1959.

The City under the Back Steps. Illus. Honoré Valintcourt. Garden City, NY: Doubleday, 1960.

Princess of Fort Vancouver. Illus. Douglas Gersline. Garden City, NY: Doubleday, 1962.

Shy Stegosaurus of Indian Springs. Illus. Paul Galdone. Garden City, NY: Doubleday, 1962.

Mrs. Updaisy. Illus. Cyndy Szekeres. Garden City, NY: Doubleday, 1963.

Temple in the Sun. Illus. Lili Róthi. Garden City, NY: Doubleday, 1964.

Wheels West: The Story of Tabitha Brown. Illus. Gil Walker. Garden City, NY: Doubleday, 1965.

The Tilted Sombrero. Illus. Ray Cruz. Garden City, NY: Doubleday, 1966.

Half-Breed. Illus. Ann Grifalconi. Garden City, NY: Doubleday, 1967.

The Bandit of Mok Hill. Illus. Marvin Friedman. Garden City, NY: Doubleday, 1969.

Cayuse Courage. New York: Harcourt, 1970.

Once upon the Little Big Horn. Illus. John Gretzer. New York: Crowell, 1971.

The Year of Small Shadow. New York: Harcourt, 1971.

Go up the Road. Illus. Charles Robinson. New York: Atheneum, 1972.

Rattlesnake Cave. Illus. Pamela Johnson. New York: Atheneum, 1974.

White Captives. New York: Atheneum, 1975.

The Potlatch Family. New York: Atheneum, 1976.

Bargain Bride. New York: Atheneum, 1977.

Squaw Man's Son. New York: Atheneum, 1978.

Three Knocks on the Wall. New York: Atheneum, 1980.

Pseudonymous Works by Evelyn Sibley Lampman

————. *Timberland Adventure*. Philadelphia: Lippincott, 1950.

————. *Coyote Kid*. Philadelphia: Lippincott, 1951.

————. *Darcy's Harvest.* Philadelphia: Lippincott, 1956.

————. *Popular Girl*. Philadelphia: Lippincott, 1957.

————. *Rogue's Valley*. Philadelphia: Lippincott, 1952.

————. *The Runaway*. Philadelphia: Lippincott, 1953.

Woodfin, Jane. *Of Mikes and Men*. New York: McGraw-Hill, 1951.

Selected Studies of Evelyn Sibley Lampman

Carver, Nancy Lynn. "Stereotypes of American Indians in Adolescent Literature." *English Journal* 77.5 (1988): 25–32.

"Evelyn Sibley Lampman." *More Junior Authors*. Ed. Muriel Fuller. New York: H. W. Wilson, 1963. 131.

"Evelyn Sibley Lampman." *Something about the Author*. Ed. Anne Commire. Vol. 4. Detroit: Gale, 1973. 140–41.

Gilliland, Hap. *Indian Children's Books*. Billings, MT: Montana Council for Indian Education, 1980.

Helbig, Alethea K., and Agnes Regan Perkins. *Dictionary of American Children's Fiction, 1960–1984*. New York: Greenwood, 1986.

Lass-Woodfin, Mary Jo, ed. *Books on American Indians and Eskimos: A Selection Guide for Children and Young Adults*. Chicago: ALA, 1978.

Moore, Opal, and Donnarae MacCann. "The Ignoble Savage: Amerind Images in the Mainstream Mind." *Children's Literature Association Quarterly* 13 (1988): 26–30.

KATHRYN LASKY
(1944-)

Hilary Crew

BIOGRAPHY

Kathryn Lasky, the daughter of Marven and Hortense Lasky, was born June 24, 1944, in Indianapolis, Indiana, where she and her sister attended private school. Lasky graduated from the University of Michigan in 1966 and from Wheelock College (M.A.) in 1977. She also undertook graduate work at Harvard Divinity School. It was at Harvard that she met Christopher Knight, whom she married in 1971. They have two children, Maxwell and Meribah. The Knights live in Cambridge, Massachusetts.

Lasky's professional career has spanned that of teacher, curriculum-materials developer, and professional writer. She began writing children's books during voyages in which she and her husband crossed the Atlantic and sailed in Europe.

Many of her informational books have been produced in collaboration with her husband, a photographer and documentary filmmaker. Lasky writes for adults under the name of Kathryn Lasky Knight. These works include *Atlantic Circle* (1985), an account of the family's sailing voyages, and a series of novels about a female detective, Calista Jacobs—a children's book illustrator.

MAJOR WORKS AND THEMES

In "Creativity in a Boom Industry," Lasky writes of her concern for the creativity and diversification of children's literature in a time of mass packaging and marketing of children's books. Her body of work for young people, including fiction for young adult readers and middle graders, informational books for middle graders, and picture books for younger children, can certainly be characterized by its diversity in terms of genre, subject matter, and audience.

Lasky brings a multiculturalist perspective into the body of her work through issues that relate to ethnicity and religion. The voice of the outsider is heard in those texts of her young adult novels in which she writes about antisemitism and the treatment of Native Americans. Lasky, however, can be considered multiculturalist in broader terms as well as she deals in her texts with conflicts between different ways of knowing and between alternative value systems. Her strong commitment to intellectual freedom is evident in her fiction for young adults.

Lasky traces her Jewish heritage from both sides of her family and brings family history into several of her novels. In *Atlantic Circle* (1985) she writes of her grandfather, Joe Lasky, who worked as a machinist in a factory outside Nikolayev and escaped with his family from Russia in 1904, eventually settling in Duluth, Minnesota, where her father was born. This family history becomes the basis for *The Night Journey* (1981) in which Nanie Sashie, great-grandmother of Rachel, narrates how she and her family escaped from Nikolayev in a wagon—hidden under a consignment of chickens.

Through Sashie's voice, the subjugation of the Jews in Russia is set into the context of Rachel's family history. The fear of persecution is made immediate through Sashie's descriptions of encounters with the czar's soldiers *en route* to the border. The horror of the pogroms is represented though the character and story of survivor Wolf Levinson, marked by his experience as "a man apart"—even in the Jewish community of Nikolayev. Textual description and the stark black-and-white drawings of a burnt and blackened village through which the escaping family passes are used to convey the sense of destruction of a people—a destruction that Lasky links in the text to the Holocaust.

Jewish religion and traditions are made an integral part of the narrative through nine-year-old Sashie's plan to have the family escape during the days of Ada and dress as Purim players. The story of Mordecai and Haman is thus told as part of Sashie's story. The samovar, represented as a central symbol of the family in Russia, becomes a symbol of continuity as it serves a use in the escape itself; rediscovered by Rachel and its missing parts restored, it takes its place in the American family home before Nanie Sashie dies. The novel is thus one of inclusion rather than exclusion as Jewish tradition and family history are reclaimed and incorporated into Rachel's life.

In *Beyond the Divide* (1983), the most richly textured of Lasky's historical novels for young adults, Lasky brings a fresh perspective to bear on the history of the American West from the viewpoint of both women's history and Native Americans. Through the story of Meribah Simon, an Amish girl who has accompanied her father on the Overland Trail in 1849, Lasky brings a sense of the power of the vision of the pioneers. This vision is set against the actual frailties and cruelties of the pioneers when pitted against the hard conditions of the trail. In contrast, Lasky brings into the text, through Meribah's consciousness, the harmony and "beauty that was a part of living" of the Native Americans. Abandoned by the company and left alone when her father dies, Meribah is given shelter through the harsh winter by the remaining Yahi in the Lassen foothills of the Sierra Nevadas. In an author's note, Lasky refers to the massacre and elimination of the Yana in the Lassen foothills, including the massacre of a Yahi village in 1865.

In "The Fiction of History," Lasky writes of the "one crime" that was "assiduously avoided" in the "TV western"—the "consistent and appalling history of violence against women" (159). Lasky unveils this history through the episode in *Beyond the Divide* (1983) in which a young woman, Serena Billings, is raped. Ostracized by the company except for Meribah and her father, Serena and, later, her mother walk away from the trail to die. The writing of women into history is reinforced through Meribah's inscription of the missing initials of Serena and her mother on Independence Rock with the other names of their company.

Lasky brings a feminist perspective to the novel through the strong voice of Meribah. It is the recognition of woman to woman—"muehli"—that is first acknowledged, for example, when Meli of the Yahi offers Meribah shelter. From the beginning of the trek, Meribah mapped the trail, using her own symbols for the "shape and feel" of the land. She is represented as a young woman who has the power to map her own life as she returns to the Valley of La Fontenelle, a valley the pioneers had passed, but which Meribah knew was "home" (248).

The viewpoint of Native Americans on westward territorial expansion is heard more directly in *The Bone Wars* (1988). Set in 1874–1878, in the context of the search for dinosaur fossils in the Judith River Badlands region of Montana, Thaddeus Longsworth, a scout, meets with the young Indian "spirit traveler" Black Elk and becomes his blood brother. Although the emphasis in the text is on the "bone wars," Lasky brings in the culture and the perspective of the Native Americans during Thad's encounters with Black Elk. The competition and deceit among the fossil hunters themselves are set against the larger treachery against the Sioux, as Custer invades their sacred territory contrary to government agreements.

The violation of the Sioux's rights are made clear in the text through the unfavorable representation of Custer and government policies, the bigoted attitudes toward the Native Americans expressed by Custer's wife and others, and the descriptions by Thad of cavalry raids on the Sioux. Thad is recognized as a Sioux "warrior" for rescuing "one live child and one dead infant" as the "Bluecoats" slashed and burned the encampment. Lasky brings in the historic personages of Red Cloud, Sitting Bull, and Crazy Horse as the Sioux defend their lands against Custer and the U.S. Cavalry. The Battle of Little Bighorn is recounted in the text from the perspective of Black Elk's recollections in *Black Elk Speaks*. The emphasis, as in Lasky's other novels, is the destruction of others who live by different values and ways of living by those who may hold dominance through force, but who have no claim to moral superiority.

Lasky returns once more to her own history in *Pageant* (1986), recreating through the character of Sarah Benjamin her experience of participating as a shepherd "for four years straight" in the annual Christian pageant in a private girls school (*Atlantic Circle* 97). Set in the 1960s, the novel spans four years of life and schooling of the bright and articulate Sarah, each year beginning with yet another performance of the pageant. Her voice is representative of Lasky's intelligent young adult protagonists as she exposes the hypocrisy and prejudice of a headmistress who believes that "angels only have blonde hair and blue eyes," and the bigotry of a young man whom she dates. In this text, as in others, the "narrowness of human spirit" is denounced by the critical voice of a young person who is open to wider visions of the universe.

In *Prank* (1984), Lasky deals directly with antisemitism and the Holocaust. The focus of the novel is the desecration of a synagogue by a group of East Boston Irish boys. Narrated from the perspective of the thoughtful and observing Birdie, her brother Timmy's participation is compared to those who looked "through the peep-hole of the gas chamber" and watched "the process of death itself" (98). Effectively conveyed is the horror and disbelief of Birdie's reaction when she first learns about the gas chambers through viewing an exhibit of the Holocaust and from reading the autobiography of Rudolph Hoess. Direct quotes from Eli Weisel and Hoess add force to statements in the text that it was important to "believe it happened." The "rage" expressed by elderly Mrs. Perlowitz, a survivor of the death camps, and the first to see the swastika in the synagogue, sums up the stand taken in the text that young people must be "familiar" with the names of Auschwitz, Bergen-Belsen, and Dachau.

A feminist consciousness is heard through the voice of Birdie, who after viewing a girl's participation in a gang rape, rewrites Donne's poem in her journal as "no woman is an island, intire of itselfe. Every woman is a piece of the continent, a part of the Maine." She may not be a "radical feminist," Birdie comments, but she is a "radical human" (55). Through the representation of Birdie's battered sister and the focus on Birdie's attempt to wean her young niece from the numbing effects of watching television, Lasky brings into the text a consciousness of how the violation of individual rights and the role of passive spectator can exist daily within the microcosm of family life. Birdie, a young writer, represents the active observer who raises the consciousness of Timmy—a description that is also representative of Lasky as a writer.

Visible in Lasky's texts is her belief in the "infinite range of variation out of which life and history emerge." Questions and ideas about the mysteries of time and space, creation, divinity, and history are linked intertextually across the texts of her fiction and nonfiction works for children and adults alike. Lasky addresses multicultural issues in her texts as an integral part of recreating stories of history. Her questioning of prejudice is also visible in relation to women's history and rights and is placed in the larger context of her concern with issues of intellectual freedom, particularly in her two latest novels, *Memoirs of a Bookbat* (1994), and *Beyond the Burning Time* (1994).

In the former, the fundamentalist approach to censorship is questioned by Harper Jessup whose parents become directly involved in challenging reading materials in schools and in limiting Harper's acquisition of knowledge. In the latter novel, Lasky deals with the witchcraft trials of Salem, focusing on the anti-intellectualism and bigotry of the persecutors. An interview in *Booklist* underscores Lasky's concern with censorship.

Lasky writes to the intellectual curiosity of young people. She believes in addressing the complexity, the "mystery," and unexplainable in the universe ("Reflections" 529). Her youthful protoganists, represented as bright and intellectually aware, go "beyond the divide" in the sense that they are aware of different realities and have alternative views from those characters in the texts who have prejudicial or more limited ways of thinking about the world. Through their voices, young people are exposed to respect for cultural diversity and respect for those who have endured prejudice and persecution.

CRITICAL RECEPTION

Lasky has received numerous awards for her books for youth, including a *Parents' Choice* honor for *Monarchs* (1993); the *Washington Post*—Children's Book Guild Nonfiction Award (1986) for her contribution to children's nonfiction; the National Jewish Book Award (1982) for *The Night Journey*; and the *Boston Globe-Horn Book* Award (1981) for *The Weaver's Gift*. Her informational book, *Sugaring Time,* was cited as an ALA Newbery Honor Book in 1984. Her novels *Beyond the Divide*, *Prank*, and *Pageant* are cited as ALA best books for young adults.

The Night Journey was generally praised for Lasky's ability to "deftly" weave together the present and past through Nanie Sashie's narration to Rachel, and for its portrayal of a period of history not well documented in children's fiction. Reviews critically acclaimed *Beyond the Divide* as a "quintessential pioneer story" and for its "vivid" depiction of the pioneer's trek. One review states that Lasky "writes a vivid and stirring tale that takes the pseudo-romance out of westward migration" (Bulletin of the Center for Children's Books).

Dick Abrahamson and Natalie Babbit, respectively, refer briefly to the Native American references in the novel. Babbit writes that the most "passionate section" of the novel is Meribah's stay with the Yahi. Abrahamson mentions Meribah's "strong female" character and "will." However, unremarked in reviews by Abrahamson and Babbit is the rape of Serena Billings—a crucial part of the book—and a dark side of women's experiences of westward expansion that Lasky was particularly concerned to document. Sibel Erol's critical essay on *Beyond the Divide* refers to the novel as a "female Bildungsroman" in which Meribah's journey is described in terms of a circular journey of "female development" (8). Erol focuses on the mother/daughter aspect of the novel through "Meribah's discovery of her continuous relationship with her mother" and on the story of Serena through whom "Lasky exposes the limitations imposed on female destiny in a male plot" (7).

The feminist voice and consciousness of Birdie is not noted in reviews of *Prank*. While Michele Carlo comments that Lasky "lays a careful path to compare the observers of the death camps to those of us who watch crimes happen and don't take the responsibility to stop them," Albert V. Schwartz criticizes Lasky for "suggesting that anti-Semitism is due to troubled individuals rather than social factors." Some other reviews of *Prank* do not focus on the issue of the Holocaust. Overall, the multicultural and feminist perspectives evident in the texts of Lasky's young adult novels have, perhaps, not always received the critical attention they deserve.

BIBLIOGRAPHY

Young Adult Fiction by Kathryn Lasky

The Night Journey. New York: Warne, 1981.
Beyond the Divide. New York: Macmillan, 1983.
Prank. New York: Macmillan, 1984.
Home Free. New York: Dell, 1985.
Pageant. New York: Four Winds, 1986.
The Bone Wars. New York: Morrow, 1988.
Beyond the Burning Time. New York: Blue Sky, 1994.
Memoirs of a Bookbat. New York: Harcourt, 1994.

Works for Children by Kathryn Lasky

Agatha's Alphabet. Chicago: Rand, 1975.
I Have Four Names for My Grandfather. New York: Little, 1976.
Tugboats Never Sleep. New York: Little, 1977.
Tall Ships. New York: Scribner, 1978.
My Island Grandma. New York: Warne, 1979.
Dollmaker: The Eyelight and the Shadow. New York: Scribner, 1981.
The Weaver's Gift. New York: Warne, 1981.
Jem's Island. New York: Scribner, 1982.
Sugaring Time. New York: Macmillan, 1983.
A Baby for Max. New York: Scribner, 1984.
Puppeteer. New York: Macmillan, 1985.
Sea Swan. New York: Macmillan, 1988.
Traces of Life: The Origins of Humankind. New York: Morrow, 1988.
Dinosaur Dig. New York: Morrow, 1990.
Double Trouble Squared. New York: Harcourt, 1991.
Fourth of July Bear. New York: Morrow, 1991.
Shadows in the Water. New York: Harcourt, 1992.
Surtsey: The Newest Place on Earth. New York: Hyperion, 1992.
Think Like an Eagle: At Work with a Wildlife Photographer. New York: Little, 1992.
I Have an Aunt on Marlborough Street. New York: Macmillan, 1993.
Lunch Bunnies. New York: Little, 1993.

The Tantrum. New York: Macmillan, 1993.
A Voice in the Wind. New York: Harcourt, 1993.
Cloud Eyes. New York: Harcourt, 1994.
Days of the Dead. New York: Hyperion, 1994.
The Librarian Who Measured the Earth. New York: Little, 1994.
Monarchs. New York: Harcourt, 1994.
The Solo. New York: Macmillan, 1994.

Other Works by Kathryn Lasky

"Reflections on Nonfiction." *Horn Book* 61 (1985): 527–32.
"The Fiction of History: Or, What Did Miss Kitty Really Do?" *The New Advocate*
    3.3 (1990): 157–166.
"Creativity in a Boom Industry." *Horn Book* 67 (1991): 705–11.
Lasky, Kathryn, and Meribah Knight. *Searching for Laura Ingalls: A Reader's
    Journal*. New York: Macmillan, 1993.

Fiction for Adults by Kathryn Lasky

Atlantic Circle. New York: Norton, 1985.
Trace Elements. New York: Norton, 1986.
The Widow of Oz. New York: Norton, 1989.
Mumbo Jumbo. New York: Simon, 1991.
Dark Swan. New York: St. Martin's, 1994.
Mortal Words. New York: Simon, 1994.

Selected Studies of Kathryn Lasky

Abrahamson, Dick. "To Start the New Year off Right." Rev. of *Beyond the Divide*.
    English Journal 73.1 (1984): 87.
Babbit, Natalie. Rev. of *Beyond the Divide*. *New York Times Book Review* 21 Aug.
    1983: 26.
Carlo, Michele. Rev. of *Prank*. *Best Sellers* 44. 6 (1984): 234–35.
Erol, Sibel. *"Beyond the Divide*: Lasky's Feminist Revision of the Westward
    Journey." *Children's Literature Association Quarterly* 17.1 (1992): 5–8.
"Kathryn Lasky." *Children's Literature Review*. Ed. Gerard J. Senick. Vol. 11.
    Detroit: Gale, 1986. 112–22.
Lasky, Kathryn. "The Booklist Interview." *Booklist* 88 (1991): 246–47.
Rev. of *Beyond the Divide*. *Bulletin of the Center for Children's Books* 36 (1983):
    192.
Schwartz, Albert V. Rev. of *Prank*. *Interracial Books for Children Bulletin* 16.1
    (1985): 7–8.

JULIUS LESTER
(1939–)

Laura M. Zaidman

BIOGRAPHY

Born on January 27, 1939, in St. Louis, Julius Lester grew up in Arkansas, Kansas, and Tennessee, where his father (a Methodist minister) had churches. As an adolescent, Lester enjoyed learning, reading two or three books a day, especially westerns, detective stories, and mysteries.

One of the mysteries he unraveled as a youngster involved his multicultural heritage. Curious about his maternal grandmother's maiden name, Altschul, because of its being so unusual for an African-American, he found out that his great-grandfather, Adolph Altschul, a German Jew, had emigrated to the South in the late 1800s and married a former slave. Lester's father said that this man's descendants, store owners in their hometown of Pine Bluff, Arkansas, would never acknowledge being distantly related to African-Americans. After Lester had converted to Judaism in 1982, he discovered that all these white Jewish relatives had become Christians. This is one of the many stories he tells in his autobiographical *Lovesong: Becoming a Jew* (1988), which chronicles his long spiritual odyssey from nominal Protestantism to Catholicism and Native American faiths to Judaism. His other autobiographical work, *All Is Well* (1976), reveals the many sides of his public persona. Whether it be historical fiction, contemporary fiction, poetry, essays, or autobiography, Lester's writing reflects the strong influences of both his race and religion as well as his multifaceted interests and careers.

After receiving his B.A. from Fisk University in 1960, Lester worked as a professional musician and folk singer for Vanguard Records. This led to directing the Newport Folk Festival in Rhode Island and to producing and hosting a live television show and radio talk show in New York City in the late sixties. This radio program brought Lester unexpected national notoriety in 1968 (the year of Robert Kennedy's and Martin Luther King, Jr.'s, assassinations and the subsequent riots) when he invited an African-American history teacher from Brooklyn to read an antisemitic poem written by a student. Some critics angrily accused Lester of exacerbating the crisis by airing such inflammatory antisemitism as the following: " 'Hey, Jewboy, with that yarmulke on your head / You pale-faced Jew boy—I wish you were dead.'" The resulting controversy added to the already existing hostility from a bitter strike by predominantly Jewish teachers. According to Lester, he meant well, hoping to increase public awareness about this racially explosive anger.

Since 1971 Lester has been a professor at the University of Massachusetts at Amherst; he has also been on the faculty at the New School for Social Research (1968–1970) and Vanderbilt University (1985). He has taught African-American studies and Judaic studies, including the course Blacks and Jews: A Comparative Study of Oppression. Thus, in both his teaching and his writing he tries to encourage young people to be proud of where they come from and to know who they are.

MAJOR WORKS AND THEMES

Lester's young adult fiction portrays an intense level of social and political consciousness, reflecting American society's changing perspectives. Over the past three decades, he has woven fact and fiction to make a strong statement about the meaning of racial identity in America.

To Be a Slave, a 1969 Newbery Honor Book, is perhaps Lester's most frequently cited nonfiction work for young adults. He intersperses commentary with edited primary documents, such as narratives of slaves and Federal Writers' Project interviews of ex-slaves in the 1930s. Black-and-white illustrations by Tom Feelings effectively complement the horrific story of the slaves' capture in Africa, their journey on slave ships, sale, servitude— and for some, escape or emancipation, and freedom. Thus, the reader can better understand what it meant to be a slave: to be owned like a piece of property that could be sold at will; to be used as an object to plow fields, cook food, or nurse others' babies; and to be cruelly punished for the slightest offense. By dramatizing the strength and courage of countless unnamed heroic people into a moving, unified chronicle of human history, Lester enlivens the past for today's readers.

In the seventies Lester turned his attention to short fiction. His first collection of short historical sketches for young adults is *Long Journey Home: Stories from Black History* (1972)—six stories about common people in a variety of situations, such as a seventeen-year-old runaway slave who travels the Underground Railroad, or slaves dying in shipholds amid their own waste, or a man staying spiritually free because of the inspiration of the blues. Because Lester believes that history is made by common people whose individual lives are seldom recorded so that they may inspire others, he bases his fictionalized narratives on actual historical accounts, to which he refers briefly in the book's notes section. Shifting to contemporary America in *Two Love Stories* (1972), Lester offers two views of modern love. In "Basketball Game" fourteen-year-old Allen moves into an all-white Nashville neighborhood and has a doomed interracial romance with Rebecca, the white girl next door. "Catskill Morning" tells of two white teenagers, Emily and Mark, who enjoy a brief romance before going their separate ways.

Ten years later, Lester returned to historical fiction with *This Strange New Feeling* (1982). In the title story, a betrayed fugitive slave outwits a brutal master to escape with his beloved. In "Where the Sun Lives," Lester depicts a spirited young slave denied freedom. She is sold off to pay her freed husband's debts—a fate she chooses by rejecting her master's sexual advances. Concluding the trio of stories, "A Christmas Love Story" depicts the triumph of William and Ellen Craft, who flee slavery in Georgia to reach freedom in Philadelphia.

While Lester has written about the joys and sorrows of both African-Americans and whites, his many collections of folklore published since the 1960s represent still another dimension of his work. These illustrated tales appeal to young adult readers who delight in the oral tradition of folklore passed from generation to generation and appreciate the pictures as well. Appearing the year after *To Be A Slave* was published, another collaboration with illustrator Tom Feelings, *Black Folktales* (1969; rev. ed. 1991) contains stories about both Africa and America. Having subtexts about victory over tyranny and the weak outwitting the strong, these narratives convey social themes in lively vernacular prose. Beneath these simple tales about butterflies, snakes, and devils lies the history of slavery and Reconstruction. "Stagolee," "High John the Conqueror," and "People Who Could Fly" represent the heroic stature of those portrayed in the tales. The six folk tales in his next work of folklore for young readers, *The Knee-High Man and Other Tales* (1972), however, offer less suggestive symbolism. *John Henry* (1994), a recent Lester-Pinkney picture book collaboration, breathes new life into the famous African-American folk hero in such a way as to appeal to young adult readers interested in storytelling. But even more impressive is the Lester-Pinkney team effort of the four-volume Uncle Remus Series (1987–1994), illustrated by Jerry Pinkney. These Joel Chandler Harris stories of Brer Rabbit, Brer Fox, and others—once almost impenetrable because of the original dialect—have been made accessible through Lester's adaptation. Unlike the original versions, they present nonstereo-typical images. In his introduction to *The Last Tales of Uncle Remus* (1994), he explains that these stories have endured in the American folklore tradition because of their authentic values and vibrant language. Lester, in revising these stories for the contemporary reader, defends Uncle Remus against charges of having an "Uncle Tom" slave mentality of accommodation to whites. While he acknowledges the truth of this historical perspective, he affirms the preservation of folk culture through storytellers who seem to identify with their oppressors; moreover, Lester argues that adult readers evoke memories of Uncle Remus with a certain affection, for the distinctive narrative voice of Uncle Remus amuses with his teasing and joking, yet impresses with his dignity and love. As variants of tales of the African trickster, Anansi the Spider, Uncle Remus stories both chronicle slaves' survival and reflect universal human experiences that know no cultural boundaries or time limits. A case in point is how wily Brer Rabbit outsmarts his enemies in "Being Fashionable Ain't Always Healthy" (*More Tales of Uncle Remus*, 1988) when he takes advantage of those creatures "who ain't got the sense they ought to have been born with." To wit, Brer Rabbit obliges Brer Fox (who is so gullible that he believes that it is the fashion to take off his head when he goes to bed) by whacking off his head with an ax.

In addition to these significant contributions about mythic and historical heroes, Lester's essays reflect African-Americans' choices for heroes and their struggles in society. Ever since his days of political and civil rights activism in the sixties, the relations between African-Americans and other groups have interested Lester. He has spoken about interracial issues in public appearances and essays in national magazines and newspapers as diverse as the *New York Times Book Review, National Review,* and *New Republic.* His essay, "The Simple Truth about Blacks and Jews," in *Reform Judaism* (1989), reflects his multicultural vantage point as a prominent thinker about racial relations. Although he acknowledges that American Jews have experienced antisemitism, he refuses to equate such bigotry to the African-American legacy of centuries of slavery. Lester asserts this simple truth: Jewish Americans are among the "haves" of our society; African-Americans comprise a significant portion of the "have-nots." Consequently, Lester dismisses Jews' borrowing a "victim" identity from the Holocaust because African-Americans have been victimized by physical, economic, and social oppression on a greater scale historically. Concluding on an optimistic note, he urges new possibilities for better relations between the two groups once Jews understand that beneath the angry rhetoric is "a deep and excruciating agony which comes when it is felt that no one cares."

Five years later, Lester addressed the escalating rift between Jews and African-Americans in a *Reform Judaism* article titled "Blacks and Jews: The Politics of Resentment." Particularly interested in why many youth admire Louis Farrakhan, Jesse Jackson, and others criticized for making antisemitic statements, Lester found students' responses instructive: they refused to repudiate people such as Farrakhan because it would look like critics were telling them who they can and can not have as leaders. Rather than dismiss this attitude as childish obstinacy, Lester pleads for an understanding of hopelessness felt by many youth who recognize the chasm between themselves and the dominant society. Underlying problems in the relationship between African Americans and Jews, Lester argues, are the real issues of educational deprivation, poverty, and despair among America's largest minority.

CRITICAL RECEPTION

Lester's work has been recognized for excellence since the late 1960s, and his books have garnered numerous awards: Newbery Honor, American Library Association Notable Children's Book, *School Library Journal* Best Book of the Year, *New York Times* Outstanding Book of the Year, Lewis Carroll Shelf Award, Coretta Scott King Award Honors, National Book Award finalist, and the National Jewish Book Award finalist. His most recent publication, *John Henry*, was named a Caldecott Honor Book.

Reviewers over the years have praised Lester's vitality of language and sensitivity to human emotions. Particularly in his folklore collections, he has achieved popularity for retelling generations-old stories in a contemporary style, marked by clever humor and sharp images. In addition to revitalizing history and folk tales, Lester has the distinction of being the

first African-American to win the Newbery Honor Award, for *To Be a Slave*.
By exploring the wide range of experiences, Lester offers significant
insights into African-Americans' lives and their folklore. Though several
of his earlier works (such as *To Be a Slave* and *Black Folktales*) have been
in print for more than a generation, Lester is not without critics. For
example, Donnarae MacCann, appraising Lester's work for *Twentieth-Century Children's Writers,* faults Lester's short historical fiction for inadequate
characterization and theme; however, she recognizes the difficulty of blending social and personal experience to portray characters accurately. Some
of his short stories have been criticized for not having depth of characterization, extended treatment of theme, or tautly written style. The way
these fictional adaptations spin factual events into parables seems melodramatic to some reviewers as well.

Despite any shortcomings critics may find in his work, Lester has earned
his reputation as a noted African-American storyteller. Lester's books for
young adults reflect the need for balance and wholeness and humanity in
life. Asked why he writes for young readers, he replied, "Children's literature is the one place where you can tell a story . . . and have it received as
narrative without any literary garbage. I've done a fair amount of historically based fiction that would be derided as adult literature because it's not
'sophisticated.' I'm just telling a story about people's lives."

BIBLIOGRAPHY

Young Adult Fiction by Julius Lester

To Be a Slave. Illus. Tom Feelings. New York: Dial, 1968. London: Longman,
    1970.
Black Folktales. Illus. Tom Feelings. New York: Baron, 1969.
Young and Black in America. Ed. with Rae Pace Alexander. New York: Random,
    1971.
Long Journey Home: Stories from Black History. New York: Dial, 1972. London:
    Longman, 1973.
Two Love Stories. New York: Dial, 1972. London: Kestrel, 1974.
Who I Am. Illus. by David Gahr. New York: Dial, 1974.
This Strange New Feeling. New York: Dial, 1982. Rpt. as *A Taste of Freedom:
    Three Stories from Black History.* London: Longman, 1983.
The Tales of Uncle Remus: The Adventures of Brer Rabbit. Illus. Jerry Pinkney.
    New York: Dial; London: Bodley Head, 1987.
*More Tales of Uncle Remus: Further Adventures of Brer Rabbit, His Friends,
    Enemies, and Others.* Illus. Jerry Pinkney. New York: Dial, 1988.

Further Tales of Uncle Remus: The Misadventures of Brer Rabbit, Brer Fox, Brer Wolf, the Doodang, and Other Creatures. With Phyllis J. Fogelman. Illus. Jerry Pinkney. New York: Dial, 1990.
The Last Tales of Uncle Remus. Illus. Jerry Pinkney. New York: Dial, 1994.
Othello. New York: Scholastic, 1995.

Works for Children by Julius Lester

Our Folk Tales: High John, The Conqueror, and Other Afro-American Tales. Ed. with Mary Varela. Illus. Jennifer Lawson. Privately printed, 1967.
The Knee-High Man and Other Tales. Illus. Ralph Pinto. New York: Dial, 1972. London: Kestrel, 1974.
How Many Spots Does a Leopard Have?: and Other Tales. Illus. David Shannon. New York: Scholastic, 1989.
John Henry. Illus. Jerry Pinkney. New York: Dial, 1994.
The Man Who Knew Too Much: A Moral Tale from the Baila of Zambia. Illus. Leonard Jenkins. Boston: Houghton, 1994.

Works for Adults by Julius Lester

The 12String Guitar as Played by Leadbelly: An Instructional Manual. With Pete Seeger. New York: Oak, 1965.
The Angry Children of Malcolm X. Nashville: Southern Student Organizing Committee, 1966.
Hamer, Fanny Lou. *To Praise Our Bridges: An Autobiography.* Ed. with Mary Varela. Jackson: KIPCO, 1967.
The Mud of Vietnam: Photographs and Poems. New York: Folklore, 1967.
Look Out, Whitey! Black Power's Gon' Get Your Mama! New York: Dial, 1968. London: Allison and Busby, 1970.
Revolutionary Notes. New York: Baron, 1969.
Search for the New Land: History as Subjective Experience. New York: Dial, 1969. London: Allison and Busby, 1971.
The Seventh Son: The Thought and Writings of W. E. B. DuBois, ed. 2 vols. New York: Random, 1971.
All Is Well. Autobiography. New York: Morrow, 1976.
Do Lord Remember Me. New York: Holt, 1985. London: Dent, 1987.
Lovesong: Becoming a Jew. New York: Holt, 1988.
"The Simple Truth about Blacks and Jews." *Reform Judaism* (Summer 1989): 8–9.
Falling Pieces of the Broken Sky. New York: Arcade, 1990.
And All Our Wounds Forgiven. New York: Arcade, 1994.
"Blacks and Jews: The Politics of Resentment." *Reform Judaism* (Fall 1994): 10–11.

The Autobiography of God. New York: Arcade, 1995.

Selected Studies of Julius Lester

List, Barry. "*PW* Interviews: Julius Lester." *Publishers Weekly* 12 Feb. 1988: 67–68.

MacCann, Donnarae. "Lester, Julius." *Twentieth-Century Children's Writers.* Ed. Tracy Chevalier. 3rd ed. Chicago: St. James, 1989. 575–576.

Nelson, Harold. "Julius Lester." *Twentieth-Century Young Adult Writers.* Ed. Laura Standley Berger. Detroit: St. James, 1994. 388–90.

Zaidman, Laura M. "Julius Lester." *Authors and Artists for Young Adults.* Detroit: Gale, 1993. 115–23.

SONIA WOLFF LEVITIN
(1934-)

Karen Libman

BIOGRAPHY

Sonia Wolff Levitin was born on August 18, 1934, in Berlin, Germany, the third child of Max and Helen (née Goldstein) Wolff. Prior to the Nazi takeover in 1933 her father had prospered as a designer and producer of clothing. But, as Jews, they keenly felt the persecution of antisemitism and immigrated to the United States in 1938. The saga of the Platt family in Levitin's books *Journey to America* (1970) and *Silver Days* (1989) is based on actual incidents from her childhood: a year-long wait in Switzerland while her father worked in the United States; the poverty that greeted them as new émigrés; the family's struggle to raise their standard of living; and their eventual move to California.

Levitin attended the University of California at Berkeley and received a B.S. from the University of Pennsylvania in 1956. She also attended graduate school at San Francisco State College (University) from 1957–1960, studying with noted author Walter Van Tilburg Clark. In 1953 she married Lloyd Levitin, with whom she has two children.

Levitin's early writing was limited to press releases and articles for magazines and local newspapers. *Journey to America* began as a story for her own children, and it established Levitin's professional career as a writer for young people.

Prejudice and cross-cultural harmony were early interests. One of her first friendships in the United States was with an African-American child. This experience, along with her Jewish heritage and literary and artistic inclinations, surely combined to shape the recurring multicultural themes in her books.

Despite her prolific output of over one book per year, Levitin does not want to rest; she wants to write. Her current book projects share time with commitments to travel (she has been to Israel seven times since 1985), family, painting, teaching (part-time at the University of California, Los Angeles), and study. She resides in Beverly Hills, California.

When questioned about the impact of Judaism on her work, Levitin responded, "More and more as I mature, I try to do everything as a Jew. Not only as a Jew, but as a good and moral Jew. I want to write good books that are exciting and entertaining, but which also have something valuable to say about life." Levitin credits the Torah as a source of inspiration and guidance for her works—both secular and sacred—but notes, "Any writer writes from a value system. My values come from being a Jew and from several wonderful role models, including my mother, who taught me about courage by her own example."

MAJOR WORKS AND THEMES

Judaism and Jewish ethnic identity permeate many of Levitin's novels. *Journey to America* chronicles the experiences of the Jewish Platt family as they flee Nazi Germany and emigrate to the United States. *Silver Days* addresses the family's adjustment to life in their new country. *Annie's Promise* (1993) takes the reader into a fateful and formative summer in the life of Annie Platt, the youngest daughter. Each book in the Platt family trilogy focuses on aspects of the Jewish immigrant experience in America. The books accurately depict everyday life for the Platt children during the late 1930s and early 1940s: going to school, the war effort, trying to fit in as immigrants. The family deals with socioeconomic hardships, and the adult characters, particularly the mother, struggle with the survivors' guilt of the European Jewish émigré. Annie's summer camp experience expands the scope of the trilogy to include more universal themes concerning prejudice, difference, and friendship.

The Return (1987) also addresses issues of Jewish identity and immigration, but in a very different setting. The historic flight of the Ethiopian Jews from their repressive homeland to Eretz Israel is fictionalized through the eyes of young Desta and her family. *The Return* is rich in historical accuracy, multiethnic information, suspense, and excitement; the reader discovers much about these black Jews who courageously left their homes in the 1980s. Levitin traveled to Israel in 1985 to find out more about Operation Moses, as the emigration was called; while there she conducted dozens of interviews, and her research is reflected in the authenticity of the novel.

Levitin views the Ethiopian Jews as a symbol of the population lost in the Holocaust. In Ethiopia the impoverished Jews cried out and were saved; the Jews of Nazi Germany also cried out, but no one heeded their cries, and they perished. *The Return* illustrates the triumph of righteousness over adversity and affirms humanity's essential goodness. Levitin returned to Israel in 1987 and 1994 specifically to research the Ethiopian Jews' adjustment to their new homeland.

In *Escape from Egypt* (1994) Levitin crafts a story based on the biblical book of Exodus. The fictional account of Jesse, a young Jewish slave, and his romantic struggle with half-Syrian, half-Egyptian Jennat, is intertwined with the Jewish flight from Egypt under the guidance of Moses. Though this is not her first use of the Torah for inspiration, the use of a specific, religious incident as plot in a young adult novel is unique and reflects Levitin's current intense interest in her faith. Jesse's story is richly embellished with religious and cultural information, and the chapters are cleverly divided by translations of direct passages from the Torah. Though the book somewhat sensationalizes Jesse's feelings, it is nevertheless an exciting direction for Levitin's young adult work based on Jewish themes.

Levitin continually explores the idea of leaving one's home because of prejudice—a circumstance faced again and again by Jews throughout history. She attempts, however, to make this experience more universal by focusing on a young character's experience within the confines of a particular historical setting. She successfully conveys the Jewish experience of diaspora, while maintaining a positive and hopeful tone through the reinforcement of the concepts of home, heritage, and identity.

Faith is an integral part of these characters' lives. They frequently wrestle with what it means to be a Jew. The faith of the Jews is repeatedly tested in *Escape from Egypt*. While some are destroyed for lack of belief, Jennat eventually becomes a pious and devoted convert. *Silver Days* concludes with the Platt family celebrating the Sabbath as Mother kindles the lights and prays the traditional Baruch. *The Return* ends as the characters are praying at the holy Western Wall in Jerusalem. Though characters face adversity, they do so as Jews, with an abiding belief in God.

Levitin's work repeatedly focuses on the theme of cultural difference. In *Journey to America* Lisa stays with a Catholic family and discovers significant truths concerning difference; *Silver Days* chronicles the Platt family's desire to fit in (despite their differences) while maintaining their Jewish identity; *Annie's Promise* pushes this idea further when Annie becomes friends with Tally, an African-American girl, only to discover her parents' reaction to difference. She is horrified by their intolerance, especially in light of the ongoing Holocaust in Europe. The Ethiopian Jews in *The Return* cannot (and do not wish to) assimilate. They are shunned and punished for their differences. Difference is what drives the book's plot: the desire to escape prejudice causes Desta and her family to flee from Ethiopia.

These thematic ideas extend into her more secular works as well. In *Roanoke: A Novel of the Lost Colony* (1973) difference is exemplified by the clash of English and Native American cultures. Ultimately, it is protagonist William's ability to see beyond these differences that saves him from death. In *The Golem and the Dragon Girl* (1993) Laurel's Chinese-American and Jonathan's Jewish-American backgrounds do not prevent them from becoming friends. There is no clash of cultures in this book; their differences are explored in detail but are not the basis of prejudice or fear.

Maturation as a theme is present in all of Levitin's young adult novels, Jewish or secular. *Jason and the Money Tree* (1974) and *The Mark of Conte* (1976), both well known for their humorous styles, feature the adventures and misadventures in an adolescent's life as he confronts problematic situations. In *Smile Like a Plastic Daisy* (1984) Claudia faces sexism and must make difficult choices which alienate schoolmates, teachers, and her parents. Inky, in *A Season for Unicorns* (1986), confronts her father's infidelity, her mother's apparent indifference, and her own fears. Ken and Cassiday's decision to report the murder of a classmate, despite negative implications for them, mark their ascent into adulthood in *Incident at Loring Groves* (1988).

The maturation of the Platt girls, particularly Lisa and Annie, is plain in *Silver Days* and *Annie's Promise* and Desta's ability to continue her journey toward Israel, despite difficult obstacles, illustrates her growth as a character in *The Return*. Desta assumes the leadership role in the journey, securing her family's spot in the transport. She is even able to voice her doubts concerning her arranged marriage after her arrival in Israel. Jesse's maturation in *Escape from Egypt* is also marked by a break with tradition as he stands up for the woman he truly loves. Moses speaks to him, symbolically indicating his acceptance as a man into the tribe of Israel.

CRITICAL RECEPTION

Critics laud Levitin's ability to write sincerely about a variety of topics in multiple genres, including mystery, historical fiction, contemporary realistic fiction, and picture books. They recognize her strong sense of pacing, her dramatic and humorous styles, and her focus on characterization. The American Library Association has selected several of her books for honors, and she is also the recipient of the prestigious Edgar Allen Poe Award from Mystery Writers of America (*Incident at Loring Groves*). Though she is more often recognized as a writer of young adult fiction, her picture books have been well received, and she has collaborated with artists of such stature as Jerry Pinkney.

Her books with Jewish themes have been particularly commended. She is a two-time recipient of the National Jewish Book Award for Children (*Journey to America* and *The Return*) and has received the Association of Jewish Libraries' Sydney Taylor Award (*The Return*). Her Platt trilogy has been praised for its historical realism, honesty, and perception. *Journey to America* was called "one of the best books of the year, indeed, any year" (Graves 248). Though *Silver Days* and *Annie's Promise* were less enthusiastically received, they were nonetheless heralded by most as compelling sequels. *The Return* received much acclaim for its authenticity and historicity. Amy Kellman, in *School Library Journal*, called the adventure "totally absorbing" and lauded its emotional impact (115). Jane Anne Hannigan described it as "powerful," "haunting," and "lyrical" (578). Levitin herself believes it to be her best work, citing her son's praise as the ultimate critical reception. *Kirkus Reviews* called *Escape from Egypt* Levitin's "most ambitious novel since *The Return*" (398) and noted its emotional strength. Jayne Gardner Connor reviewed it by stating, "Strong characterizations help to give readers an understanding of the motivations and conflicts within individuals and between cultures" (152). This book's critical success exemplifies Levitin's self-appointed mission: "to be a mind bridge . . . among peoples of various colors, types and persuasions" (Collier and Nakamura 1457).

BIBLIOGRAPHY

Young Adult Fiction by Sonia Wolff Levitin

Journey to America. Illus. Charles Robinson. New York: Atheneum, 1970.
Roanoke: A Novel of the Lost Colony. Illus. John Gretzer. New York: Atheneum, 1973.
Jason and the Money Tree. Illus. Pat Grant Porter. New York: Harcourt, 1974.
The Mark of Conte. Illus. Bill Negron. New York: Atheneum, 1976.
Beyond Another Door. New York: Atheneum, 1977.
The No-Return Trail. New York: Harcourt, 1978.

A Sound to Remember. Illus. Gabriel Lisowski. New York: Harcourt, 1979.
The Year of Sweet Senior Insanity. New York: Harcourt, 1982.
A Season for Unicorns. New York: Atheneum, 1986.
Smile Like a Plastic Daisy. New York: Atheneum, 1986.
The Return. New York: Atheneum, 1987.
Incident at Loring Groves. New York: Dial, 1988.
Silver Days. New York: Atheneum, 1989.
Annie's Promise. New York: Atheneum, 1993.
The Golem and the Dragon Girl. New York: Dial, 1993.
Adam's War. Illus. Vincent Nasta. New York: Dial, 1994.
Escape from Egypt. New York: Little, 1994.
Evil Encounter. New York: Simon & Schuster, 1995.
Nine for California (tentative title). New York: Orchard, 1995.
A Piece of Home. New York: Dial, 1995.

Works for Children by Sonia Wolff Levitin

Rita the Weekend Rat. Illus. Leonard Shortall. New York: Atheneum, 1971.
Who Owns the Moon? Illus. John Larrecq. Berkeley, CA: Parnassus, 1973.
A Single Speckled Egg. Illus. John Larrecq. Berkeley, CA: 1975.
Nobody Stole the Pie. Illus. Fernando Krahn. New York: Harcourt, 1980.
All the Cats in the World. Illus. Charles Robinson. New York: Harcourt, 1982.
The Fisherman and the Bird. Illus. Francis Livingston. Boston: Houghton Mifflin, 1982.
The Man Who Kept His Heart in a Bucket. Illus. Jerry Pinkney. New York: Dial, 1991.

Other Works by Sonia Wolff Levitin

Reigning Cats and Dogs. Illus. Joan Berg Victor. New York: Atheneum, 1978.
What They Did to Miss Lily. [Writing as Sonia Wolff.] New York: Harper, 1981.

Selected Studies of Sonia Wolff Levitin

Collier, Laurie, and Joyce Nakamura, eds. *Major Authors and Illustrators for Children and Young Adults.* Vol. 4. Detroit: Gale, 1993. 1454–57. 6 vols.

Connor, Jane Gardner. Rev. of *Escape from Egypt. School Library Journal* 40.4 (1994): 152.

Graves, Elizabeth Minot. "A Selected List of Children's Books." Rev. of *Journey to America. Commonweal* 22 May 1970: 248.

Hannigan, Jane Anne. "Levitin, Sonia." *Twentieth Century Children's Writers.* Ed. Tracy Chevalier. 3rd ed. Chicago: St. James Press, 1989. 578.

Kellman, Amy. Rev. of *The Return*. *School Library Journal* 33.8 (May 1987): 115.

Klass, Sheila Solomon. "Waiting for Operation Moses." Rev. of *The Return*. *New York Times Book Review* 17 May 1987: 36.

Levitas, Gloria. Rev. of *Journey to America*. *New York Times Book Review* 24 May 1970: 26.

"Levitin, Sonia." *Contemporary Literary Criticism*. Ed. Sharon R. Gunton. Vol. 17. Detroit: Gale, 1981. 263–66.

Levitin, Sonia. "Levitin, Sonia." *Something about the Author Autobiography Series*. Ed. Adele Sarkissian. Vol. 2. Detroit: Gale, 1986. 111–26.

Levitin, Sonia. Telephone Interview. Oct. 1994.

Rev. of *Escape from Egypt*. *Kirkus Reviews* 62 (15 Mar. 1994): 398.

MYRON LEVOY
(1930–)

Suzanne D. Green

BIOGRAPHY

Young adult writer Myron Levoy was born and reared in New York City, growing up in a middle-class family in which "times were hard and toys were few" (Gallo 120). From an early age, Levoy was involved with words, books, and recitation. He recalls making constant trips to the local library with his family, and being enamored with the "smell and feel of books" (Gallo 120). He began writing at the age of eight, when he created the story of a flower growing out of a pavement crack and mused over whether the flower would survive or be crushed underfoot. "I can't remember how it ended," Levoy says, "but I know I loved writing it" (Gallo 120).

When Levoy was in junior high school, he became involved in choral speaking. His class won third place in a city contest, missing first place largely because the chorus members were intimidated by the size of the performance hall. It was through this experience that he learned that "words alone, without music, can sing" (Gallo 120). Levoy continued to write, and edited a poetry column for his high school newspaper.

Levoy studied chemical engineering at City College of New York and earned his master's degree at Purdue University. He was involved in numerous scientific projects, including an attempt to send a manned space flight to Mars, and nuclear propulsion projects for rockets and spacecraft. Although Levoy was an engineer by day, writing "remained his first love"

(Gallo 120). After his marriage to wife Beatrice, and the birth of two children, Deborah and David, Levoy retired from engineering to write full time. Levoy has written nine books for children or young adults and has also published short stories and poetry in magazines such as *Antioch Review, Massachusetts Review*, and *New York Quarterly*. He has also written several plays which have been performed Off-Broadway.

MAJOR WORKS AND THEMES

Levoy's young adult fiction is made up of a variety of different narratives, but his works are thematically similar. His novels are either survival narratives or the experiences of children of immigrant parents, and his settings generally reflect the vibrant cultural life of his native New York City. Although his young adult novels deal with adolescent coming-of-age issues, such as peer pressure, friendship, and sexuality, he generally combines these themes with a multicultural context. *Alan and Naomi* (1977) describes a young man's attempts to help a French refugee recover from the horror of seeing her father murdered by the Gestapo during World War II. Part historical fiction, part adventure, part coming-of-age story, *Alan and Naomi* has been translated into eight languages, including German, thereby widening its availability and appeal to international audiences. *A Shadow Like a Leopard* (1981) is the story of Ramon Santiago, a poverty-stricken Puerto Rican youth. His father is in Attica for assaulting a policeman during a political demonstration, while his mother has been hospitalized with a nervous breakdown. Ramon alternately attempts to be accepted by a neighborhood gang and yearns to escape this life through the writing of poetry. He strikes an alliance with Mr. Glasser, an artist who at first is a potential mugging victim, but who shows Ramon a different way of life.

Three Friends, Levoy's next adolescent novel (1984), deals with a young man's conflicting emotional reactions to two young women, one of whom ultimately attempts suicide rather than face her bisexual nature. *Pictures of Adam* (1986), a bittersweet story, describes the developing relationship between an emotionally disturbed boy who is mainstreamed into a regular classroom, and the young girl who befriends and tries to understand him. The story is told from the point of view of fourteen-year-old Lisa, an aspiring photographer, who meets Adam while photographing his house. Like most of Levoy's books, *Pictures of Adam* depends on its narrative structure to document the relationship between two unlikely characters, each of whom has something to teach the other.

Kelly 'n' Me (1992), Levoy's most recent novel, follows the same pattern. Anthony is a street performer who falls in love with Kelly. Kelly spins yarns about her destitute family, but in reality is the daughter of wealthy but troubled parents. Although she tries to convey her unhappiness to her parents, she fails and is determined to run away to San Francisco rather than continue to live with them. Anthony has his own problems, including an alcoholic mother, and in the end must choose between his mother and Kelly.

Levoy has also written four volumes of children's stories. *The Hanukkah of Great-Uncle Otto*, published in 1984, illustrates Jewish culture and tradition, while *The Witch of Fourth Street and Other Stories* (1972) is set in the lower East Side of New York, where people of differing nationalities, points of view, and religions live together. Levoy does not present the characters through a rose-colored lens, however. Natalie Babbitt in *Children's Book World* says, "These stories are about people, however, not ethnic stereotypes, and they have extraordinary freshness and charm. . . . Myron Levoy does not compromise with truth: there is pain too, and frustration—and in the final story [of *The Witch of Fourth Street*], death" (Babbitt G-17). Although Levoy presents a variety of ethnic backgrounds in his writing, he does not resort to one-dimensional, stereotypical characters. Rather, he develops an individual personality for each of his characters that incorporates their ethnicity, rather than the personality being solely based on that ethnic background.

Interestingly, Levoy does not often write of Jewish life and characters. In fact, *A Shadow Like a Leopard* focuses on Puerto Rican youth, a population with whom Levoy does not have first-hand familiarity. Indeed, this shows to some extent in the book, which uses very few Spanish words and lacks any sense of the extended family communities that many Puerto Ricans in New York have developed. In fact, it is possible to read this particular novel as not so much "multicultural" as a book that tries to inculcate white Euro-American values in its characters and readers: Ramon gives up knives and fighting at the urging of an elderly white artist, who takes Ramon to visit cultural outposts like the Metropolitan Museum and who encourages him to leave behind his Puerto Rican neighborhood and family to pursue a college degree at a predominantly white university.

In addition to novels and short stories, Levoy has written numerous stage plays. *Eli and Emily* was produced in New York City in 1969. His one-act play *The Sun Is a Red Dwarf* was performed Off-Off Broadway by the New York Theatre Ensemble, and *Sweet Tom*, a two-act play, was performed at the Playbox, another Off-Off Broadway theatre, also in 1969. *Footsteps* and *Smudge* were both produced in New York City in 1971.

CRITICAL RECEPTION

Myron Levoy has been highly acclaimed for his young adult fiction and for his children's stories. He has been favorably reviewed in the *New York Times Book Review*, whose reviewer described *Alan and Naomi* as "a fine example of honest, compassionate writing about personal responsibility. Levoy has done admirably with a subject so difficult to treat" (Meltzer 39). The *Horn Book Magazine* has favorably reviewed each of his five young adult novels, and other sources such as *Children's Book World, School Library Journal, Publisher's Weekly*, and *Booklist* have universally acknowledged the quality of his work.

When Levoy has received negative criticism of his work, it is generally for plots that have seemed to some reviewers to be overly melodramatic and perhaps too reminiscent of the problem novels of the late sixties and seventies. The *Bulletin of the Center for Children's Books* said of the recent *Kelly 'n' Me* that it was a "throwback" to the problem novels of the seventies, and certainly a number of his books contain a higher than usual percentage of socially relevant problems for the protagonists: alcoholism, confused sexuality, violence, crime, and so on.

By and large, however, Levoy has been favorably reviewed and his work has been awarded numerous prestigious prizes. *The Witch of Fourth Street and Other Stories* was named a *Book World* Honor Book; *Alan and Naomi* was designated an Honor Book by the *Boston Globe-Horn Book*, and was an American Book Award finalist. *Alan and Naomi* also won the Dutch Silver Pencil Award and the Austrian State Prize for Children's Literature in 1981, and the German State Prize for Children's Literature in 1982. The American Library Association has recognized Levoy's novels as the Best Book for Young Adults on two occasions: in 1981 for *A Shadow Like a Leopard* and in 1986 for *Pictures of Adam*.

BIBLIOGRAPHY

Young Adult Fiction by Myron Levoy

Alan and Naomi. New York: Harper, 1977. London: Bodley Head, 1979.
A Shadow Like a Leopard. New York: Harper, 1981.
Three Friends. New York: Harper, 1984.
Pictures of Adam. New York: Harper, 1986. London: Bodley Head, 1987.
Kelly 'n' Me. New York: Harper, 1992.

Works for Children by Myron Levoy

Penny Tunes and Princesses. Illus. Ezra Jack Keats. New York: Harper, 1972.
The Witch of Fourth Street and Other Stories. Illus. Gabriel Lisowski. New York: Harper, 1972.
The Hanukkah of Great-Uncle Otto. Illus. Donna Ruff. Philadelphia: Jewish Publication Society, 1984.
The Magic Hat of Mortimer Wintergreen. New York: Harper, 1988. London: Macmillan, 1989.

Works for Adults by Myron Levoy

A Necktie in Greenwich Village. New York: Vanguard, 1968.

Plays by Myron Levoy

The Penthouse Perspective. Produced Northport, NY, 1967.
Eli and Emily. Produced New York, 1969.
The Sun Is a Red Dwarf. Produced New York, 1969.
Sweet Tom. Produced New York, 1969.
Footsteps. Produced New York, 1970. New York: Breakthrough Press, 1971.
Smudge. Produced New York, 1971.

Selected Studies of Myron Levoy

Allison, Lynn. Rev. of *Kelly 'n' Me. The Book Report* (Apr. 1993): 40.
Babbitt, Natalie. Rev. of *The Witch of Fourth Street and Other Stories. Children's Book World* 7 May 1972: G-17.
Burnes, Mary M. Rev. of *Pictures of Adam. Horn Book* 62.4 (1986): 456–57.
Flanagan, Kate M. Rev. of *Three Friends. Horn Book* 60.4 (1984): 476.
Flowers, Ann A. Rev. of *A Shadow Like a Leopard. Horn Book* 57.3 (1981): 310–11.
Gallo, Donald R., comp. *Speaking for Ourselves: Autobiographical Sketches by Notable Authors of Books for Young Adults.* Urbana, IL: NCTE, 1990.
Heins, Paul. Rev. of *Alan and Naomi. Horn Book* 53.6 (1977): 664–65.
Holtze, Sally Holmes, ed. *Fifth Book of Junior Authors and Illustrators.* New York: H. W. Wilson Co, 1983.
Klein, Nancy. Rev. of *The Witch of Fourth Street. New York Times Book Review* 18 June 1972: 8.
Langford, Sondra Gordon. Rev. of *Alan and Naomi. Horn Book* 64.5 (1988): 608–609.
"Levoy, Myron." *Contemporary Authors: New Revision Series.* Ed. Susan M. Trosky. Vol. 40. Detroit: Gale, 1993.

Meltzer, Milton. Rev. of *Alan and Naomi. New York Time Book Review* 13 Nov. 1977: 39.

"Myron Levoy." *Something about the Author.* Ed. Anne Commire. Vol. 49. Detroit: Gale, 1985. 157–58.

Nilsen, Alleen Pace, and Kenneth L. Donelson. *Literature for Today's Young Adults.* Glenview, IL: Scott, Foresman & Co., 1980, 1985.

Secker, Kathleen D. Rev. of *The Magic Hat of Mortimer Wintergreen. Childhood Education* 65.4 (1988): 309.

Ward, Martha E., Dorothy A. Marquardt, Nancy Dolan, and Dawn Eaton, eds. *Authors of Books for Young People.* Metuchen, NJ: Scarecrow Press, 1990.

ROBERT LIPSYTE
(1938-)

Reinhard Isensee

BIOGRAPHY

Robert Michael Lipsyte was born on January 16, 1938, in New York. Encouraged by his parents, he spent hours reading as an adolescent and decided very early to become a writer. After finishing high school he went to Columbia University and received an undergraduate degree in English in 1957. Although he initially planned to continue his education by attending graduate school, his first summer job after graduation from Columbia turned out to be decisive for his future career. Answering a classified ad, he was employed by the *New York Times* as a copyboy for two years. Fascinated with the atmosphere and work in the sports department, Lipsyte decided to stay and to become a reporter. After receiving his M.S. in 1959 he worked as a sports reporter at the *New York Times* until 1967, followed by four years of writing sports columns. The years he covered sports for the *New York Times* made him one of the best known sports reporters in the nation. Despite his achievements in journalism, Lipsyte was frustrated by the space limitations in the papers and magazines he wrote for. He therefore began writing books while still on the staff at the paper. His first efforts as a writer resulted in a book about Dick Gregory titled *Nigger* (1964), an autobiography of Gregory's life and struggles in the sports world. With *The Contender* (1967), which followed *The Masculine Mystique* (1966)—another nonfiction piece on sports—Lipsyte published the first of his seven books for young adults.

This novel earned him immediate praise by readers and critics alike and thus strengthened his long-standing desire to introduce sports as a meaningful topic into contemporary fiction for adolescent readers. It also contributed to his reputation as an authority in the field of sports stories, both fiction and nonfiction, on a national scale.

Before he went to the *New York Post* in 1977, where he wrote a column, he visited schools to talk about his books, worked for radio programs, and taught journalism at colleges. While writing a trilogy for young adults consisting of *One Fat Summer* (1977), *Summer Rules* (1981), and *The Summerboy* (1982) Lipsyte extended his professional career to television, performing in various positions. From 1982–1986 he was employed by CBS-TV as a sports essayist for the program *Sunday Morning* and became New York City correspondent for NBC thereafter. PBS-TV New York hired him as the host of its program *The Eleventh Hour* in 1989–1990, a combination talk and interview show. In 1991 Lipsyte once again returned as a columnist to the sports department of the *New York Times,* the place where his career had begun more than thirty years ago.

His work both in the field of journalism as well as in fiction has been honored by various prestigious awards, for instance the Best Sports Stories Awards in 1964, 1965, 1967, 1971, and 1976, the Emmy Award for on-camera achievement in 1990, and the Wel-Met Children's Book Award and Child Study Children's Book Award in 1967. Moreover, his books for young adults were named outstanding books of the year by the *New York Times* and the American Library Association in 1977.

Lipsyte is married, has two children, and lives in New York.

MAJOR WORKS AND THEMES

Robert Lipsyte's background as a sports reporter and sports columnist is the major source for his remarkable work in the fields of young adult fiction, adult fiction and nonfiction, as well as journalism and screenwriting. Based on his insights into the political and cultural role of sports in American society and its impact on individuals, Lipsyte from his early days as a reporter tried to demythicize sports as represented in the media by revealing its implications for shaping (oversimplified and one-sided) values. In many ways, Lipsyte in his stories set an example for other sportswriters by covering the growing discontent of athletes, racism, sexism, distorted nationalism, and the intertwining of sports and politics. His columns about the boxer Muhammad Ali and his book *Free to Be Muhammad Ali* (1978) in particular demonstrate his strong commitment to a philosophy in which sports is no sanctuary from reality. While following Ali's boxing career from its beginnings and presenting a personal look at the individual behind the enormous success, the author does not shy away from the controversies the charismatic boxing star caused by his outspoken political views. In contrast to the negative perception Ali had for segments of the American public, Lipsyte provides insightful background material on the climate of boxing in the 1960s and on the civil unrest and growing public awareness of the role of America in the Vietnam War. In this way, he can make transparent to the reader Ali's personal motives and the values his political views are based upon, without falling back on the cynicism prevailing in other biographies. With his respectful and sensitive portrait of one of the greatest athletes in America, Lipsyte offers a convincing treatment of the problematic and complex issue of sports and the individual in contemporary society.

During the nine months he intensively worked with Dick Gregory to prepare his autobiography *Nigger* as well as during the years he closely followed Muhammad Ali's career, Lipsyte gained an extensive insight into black culture and experience. Even though he later confessed in a 1983 article in *Top of the News* that a white author might not risk creating a central black character because it might be considered arrogant, he still felt at the time of his involvement with Gregory's and Ali's stories that he could realistically relate to and write about the black experience. This attitude and his strong concern for the impact of the superstar image of sports on adolescents, especially on minority youth, caused Lipsyte to shift his writing interests more and more to the young adult novel. In his understanding, sports as a central subject matter in texts for adolescent readers was to support the process of finding one's identity rather than merely offering superficial role models and endowing sports with mystical qualities. He maintains that sports is a negative experience for most boys and almost all girls because they cannot meet the high standards set by the overwhelming images of America's media- and advertising-dominated culture. Thus, Lipsyte strongly opposes the idea that someone who does not make it in sports is a failure as a person and instead emphasizes the positive value of sports as an integral part of life where doing one's best is what matters.

In his first young adult novel, *The Contender*, the author attempts to depict sports as a special source for strengthening individual values and developing positive long-term goals and at the same time reveals the problematic nature of the myth that sports is a practical way out of the slums. Alfred Brooks, the protagonist of the novel, is a seventeen-year-old high school dropout living in Harlem. Like many of his African-American peers,

Alfred comes out of a broken home and works as a stock boy in a grocery store. His social environment seems to offer no chance for a positive change in the direction of his life. Yet, Alfred in the end succeeds in finding the inner resolve to turn his life around despite the paralyzing and dreadful conditions in the ghetto.

Lipsyte describes the metamorphosis of his main character by introducing sports as a means of acquiring the discipline necessary to survive in his environment. In this way, Alfred's search for identity is developed as the central theme of the novel. While training to be a boxer, he gradually becomes aware of the idea that it is contending rather than winning that counts in life. After his manager, Donatelli, wants him to quit boxing because he senses that Alfred lacks the killer instinct required to be a top boxer, Alfred insists on fighting one last time to find out if he really has the courage to be a contender. Although he loses the fight in the boxing ring, Lipsyte still describes him as the winner because he has discovered his own inner strength. At the end of the novel, Alfred is characterized as a confident and disciplined young man who plans to go back to school and open a recreation center for children in Harlem.

Besides the central theme of the search for self-identity, Lipsyte employs several other thematic aspects in the novel. Male adolescent friendship, to name one of the more relevant represented in the text, especially through Alfred's relationship to James, a drug addict, is depicted by including various facets of such friendship like doubt, suspicion, cynicism, despair, and responsibility. Laying special emphasis on a truthful representation of the social situation of his adolescent characters, Lipsyte arranges a setting through which the pressures and the fears, the physical conditions and psychological effects, of ghetto life are vividly evoked. His accurate reproduction of the idiom and syntax of Harlem functions as an additional element to create a corresponding atmosphere. It is here that the (white) author makes an important contribution to the process of demarginalization of subject matters in young adult fiction dealing with realities of black urban life. Even though his portrait of African-American life might appear somewhat unsophisticated and limited in the light of the present debate on multiculturalism, it is nevertheless to be appreciated as a major (and early) step in questioning the notion of a homogenous construction of American society. By choosing a black adolescent as the central character and telling the story through the eyes of this character, the author portrays forms of representations of the white world (policemen, merchants) and black world (minority group adolescents, militant African-Americans, African-American community) without forcing any social commentary on the reader.

This as well as several other features regarding theme, structure, and value orientation of the novel have resulted in an extensive and very mixed critical reception of *The Contender* during the past twenty years. Lipsyte, however, seems to have been not too much impressed by his critics and instead has relied on his readers, who were enthusiastic about the book and urged him to write a sequel. The project for such a sequel took shape when he was on an assignment at an American Indian reservation. While staying there he got particularly interested in the situation of the young people and their struggle to come to terms with an environment characterized by high levels of disease, alcoholism, and unemployment on the one hand and disillusionment and lack of value orientation on the other. The parallels he found in their lives with that of his literary character Alfred induced Lipsyte to write a book about a young American Indian who tried to escape the dead-end life at the reservation.

In *The Brave* (1991) he fictionalizes the odyssey of a seventeen-year-old half-Indian who leaves the reservation to seek a better life in New York City. The thematic focus of the novel is the clash between two different cultures as Sonny Bear, the central character, strives to make it in the white world. Inexperienced in the ways this other world works and unaware of the harsh rules of life in a big city, Sonny very soon becomes a pawn in the drug war. He can only escape the consequences of his involvement in crime by meeting Alfred Brooks, now in his forties and a police sergeant in New York. Since Alfred senses that the adolescent runaway is going through an adolescent identity crisis similar to his own before starting his boxing career, he feels responsible for him. Like his former coach Donatelli, he wants to convey to Sonny those values which changed the course of his own life when he was a teenager.

Whereas Lipsyte abstains from his favorite subject matter of sports in *The Brave* and instead lays special thematic emphasis on the search for identity itself by positioning his protagonist in a conflict of minority versus dominant culture, he employed sports as a special literary vehicle for depicting the theme of social responsibility in his earlier novel *Jock and Jill* (1982). The plot of the story focuses on Jack Ryder, a high school pitching ace. While he is portrayed as the admired star of his baseball team in the beginning, the author gradually reveals the individual behind the star. He carefully explores the problems he has to deal with in his family (a mentally retarded brother, lack of funds to pay for his college education) and in his relationship with his girlfriend Jill (who has taken therapeutic drugs for emotional problems). In this way, Lipsyte intends to present his protagonist and his problems and behavior as "typical" adolescent. Sports appears to be an important part of his protagonist's life; it is, however, not the only one nor the most relevant one. Throughout the text, the author examines sports as a source of character development of young people and questions the stereotypes related to sports stardom.

Even though Jack Ryder is aware of the fact that he has to rely on his skills as a pitcher to receive a scholarship, he still decides against sports at the end of the novel. Because of his involvement with a coalition for better housing conditions in the South Bronx initiated by a Hispanic gang leader, Jack interrupts an important game to take a public stand for this coalition and its leader. Knowing that he will probably lose his chances of winning a scholarship and that he will certainly disappoint his father, his coach, and his teammates, Jack chooses social commitment over personal success. Without doubt, Lipsyte's message here seems to be rather idealistic, but it does exactly underline his intention of deconstructing the myth of sports as a symbol of success.

With Hector, a Hispanic gang leader in the ghetto, the author introduces a minority youth who is portrayed as a strong and socially dedicated personality. In many ways, this literary character has achieved a more mature stage in life than the white characters. Yet, this very interesting question as well as the differences and similarities in the situation of Hispanic and white adolescents and their interaction in New York City are treated only marginally. Hence, the novel leaves out many of the thought-provoking issues of minority culture which seem to be essential to the conflict presented in the text.

In his young adult trilogy consisting of the novels *One Fat Summer* (1977), *Summer Rules* (1981), and *The Summerboy* (1982), Lipsyte selects a wholly different thematic focus, turning away from issues of sports as well as questions of minority youth. Set in a resort town in upstate New York, the novel is centered on the maturation process of the middle-class protagonist Bobby Marks from the age of fourteen to eighteen. The conflicts presented in the novels are designed to show three major adolescent dilemmas: lack of self-esteem and problems of body image (Bobby is the subject of public humiliation because he is overweight); problems of the first love relationship; and prejudice (Bobby, now at a summer job, is rejected by his co-workers because he is considered an affluent "summer-boy") as well as standing up for justice (Bobby leads a protest at work to improve conditions). Critics have especially praised the trilogy for the sensitive and realistic manner in which relevant questions of adolescent insecurities have been depicted. In comparison to his earlier fiction for young adults, however, Lipsyte in these novels obviously favors literary themes that relate more to the "common" issues of growing up than the "sophisticated" and controversial ones.

CRITICAL RECEPTION

The critical attention Robert Lipsyte, who generally is not regarded as a controversial author, has received is largely positive for his young adult fiction, as well as for his works for adults. His journalistic work has been praised by most critics as innovative, bold, and original. The few negative reactions to his work repeatedly categorize Lipsyte as a disenchanted writer with an intense dislike of sports because of his honest and powerful treatment of the false values, stereotypes, and idols of the sports world in modern America that he discusses in *Sports World: An American Dreamland* (1975) and *Free to Be Muhammad Ali* (1978). His seven publications for young adults have been dealt with by critics to a much greater extent. The novel *The Contender* in particular produced very mixed critical reactions.

One of the crucial arguments against the book is based upon alleged oversimplifications in depicting white and black characters. Susan O'Neal, for instance, in a review for the *School Library Journal* maintains that the literary characters are delineated one-sidedly in that the white protagonists are paragons of interest and devotion whereas the black adolescents appear to be the chief cause for Alfred's problems. In her view Lipsyte has written an outsider's book which does not increase a better understanding because it lacks a sophisticated and complex treatment of the real pressures in the ghetto. Nat Hentoff, while criticizing the plot structure as not believable and too didactic on the one hand, praises those parts of the novel which deal with boxing itself on the other hand (*New York Times Book Review*). These arguments are also utilized to some extent in the critical reviews of *Jock and Jill* and *The Brave*, although the attention of critics here is directed more toward the level of didacticism and questions of style.

On the positive side, the critical responses appreciate Lipsyte's early interest in the problems of minority youth and emphasize the complexity of the narrative and its dramatic intensity. Weaknesses concerning the somewhat imbalanced images of black and white characters, especially in *The Contender* and *The Brave*, are considered minor flaws of the novels (Simmons 117). Besides the achievements of well-rounded characterization and polished style (Sutherland) as well as "engaging urban freshness of point of view" (Klein), critics stress Lipsyte's efforts to depict adult-adolescent relations without employing the common stereotypes of adult characterization.

Considered an outstanding author of young adult fiction, Robert Lipsyte has created vivid pictures of literary characters struggling to develop self-confidence and a sense of self-worth in their search for identity. Like his protagonists, the adolescent readers of his novels are challenged to come to terms with their insecurities and fears while growing up and at the same time are encouraged to "go up the stairs" in life (as Alfred does in *The Contender*).

BIBLIOGRAPHY

Young Adult Fiction by Robert Lipsyte

The Contender. New York: Harper, 1967.
One Fat Summer. New York: Harper, 1977.
Summer Rules. New York: Harper, 1981.
Jock and Jill. New York: Harper, 1982.
The Summerboy. New York: Harper, 1982
The Brave. New York: Harper, 1991.
The Chemo Kid. New York: Harper, 1992.

Other Works by Robert Lipsyte

Nigger. With Dick Gregory. New York: Dutton, 1964.
The Masculine Mystique. New York: New American Library, 1966.
Assignment: Sports. New York: Harper, 1970. Rev. ed, 1984.
Something Going. With Steve Cady. New York: Dutton, 1973.
Liberty Two. New York: Simon & Schuster, 1974.
Sports World: An American Dreamland. New York: Quadrangle, 1975.
Free to Be Muhammad Ali. New York: Harper, 1978.

Selected Studies of Robert Lipsyte

Bachner, Saul. "Three Junior Novels on the Black Experience." *Journal of Reading* 24.8 (1981): 692–95.
Donelson, Kenneth L., and Alleen Pace Nilson. "The Old Romanticism of Wishing and Winning." *Literature for Today's Young Adults*. Ed. Kenneth L. Donelson and Alleen Pace Nilson. Glenview, Ill.: Scott, Foresman and Company, 1980. 205–27. Also in the 1989 edition. 131.
Feldman, Sari. "Up the Stairs Alone: Robert Lipsyte on Writing for Young Adults." *Top of the News* 39. 2 (1983): 198–202.

Hentoff, Nat. Rev. of *The Contender*. *New York Times Book Review* 12 Nov. 1967: 42.

Klein, Norma. "Not for Teens Only." *The Nation* 12 Mar. 1983: 312–14.

O'Neal, Susan. Rev. of *The Contender*. *School Library Journal* 14.3 (1967): 78.

"Robert Lipsyte." *Authors & Artists for Young Adults*. Vol. 7. Detroit: Gale, 1991. 139–48.

"Robert Lipstye." *Children's Literature Review*. Ed. Gerard J. Senick. Vol. 23. Detroit: Gale Research Inc., 1991. 199–210.

Simmons, John S. "Lipsyte's *Contender:* Another Look at the Junior Novel." *Elementary English* (Jan. 1972): 117.

Sutherland, Zena. Rev. of *The Summerboy*. *Bulletin of the Center for Children's Books* 36.1 (1982): 15.

STEVEN C. LO
(1949-)

David Sorrells

BIOGRAPHY

Steven C. Lo was born in 1949, grew up in Taipei, Taiwan, and attended National Taiwan University. In 1972 he began graduate studies at Texas Tech University in Lubbock, and he earned a Master's degree from Medill School of Journalism at Northwestern University. He now lives in Richardson, Texas, where his small, international business consulting firm, Asiatic International of Dallas, specializes in the Asian trade. Lo, a pioneer in trade with the People's Republic of China, claims, "I've always thought of myself as a writer, even as a boy."

Lo's background as a Chinese immigrant, his difficulties with assimilation, and his dealings with corporate, capitalist America are clearly reflected in his semi-autobiographical novel, *The Incorporation of Eric Chung*.

Lo continues to work and write in Texas.

MAJOR WORKS AND THEMES

The Incorporation of Eric Chung (1989), Lo's only published novel to date, provides glimpses of both the experiences of Eric Chung and other recent Chinese émigrés to Texas and of his later tribulations as a corporate executive in an imprudent marketing scheme, importing small electronic goods from the People's Republic of China. "I'd say September of 1972 was when all this started, September 17, 1972, to be exact. My Date of Entry," recounts Eric Chung from his lonely executive office of Coldwell Electronics International, Inc., where he and his secretary await their final dismissal from the failed importing venture.

Although Eric Chung's story is told from an adult point of view, much of the tale is in flashback and concerns his earlier difficulties in America, both with other immigrants and with the native population. Thus, his story is quite humorous to the young adult audience, who can both appreciate some of the adolescent Eric's difficulties, and can further enjoy laughing at the adult difficulties he has managed to land himself in.

Eric tells of his earlier entry into the United States and the several jobs he held prior to his position as the president of the Coldwell Enterprises division: a special advisor at Coldwell, in charge of Sino-American trade; a system programmer/analyst at Taltex; a computer operator at a small company in Lubbock. Prior to his professional employment, he was in graduate school at Texas Tech University and worked at several part-time jobs that "bordered on 'unlawful employment,'" because he did not have a work visa.

The most interesting tales Eric tells, and the ones most likely to appeal to adolescent readers, are the exploits of his circle of Asian friends, led by Victor Liu, the upper classman who not only had acclimated to Texas living but also had a car, that sure sign of being an "All-American" guy. Victor explains simple things to the new students—what a stop sign is—and not-so-simple survival strategies—how to file a penny down to the size of a dime in order to buy Cokes, and how to date American style. He also frequently takes his friends to the adult theaters to watch X-rated movies, presumably to further their accommodation to America, because "this is the way with advanced countries." The irony and the humor here will not be lost upon contemporary adolescent readers, whether they be from immigrant families or not.

Eric's job as a programmer/analyst at Taltex affords him the opportunity to meet Roger Holton, the mastermind of the international trade business for Coldwell Enterprises. Roger enlists Eric as an interpreter and cultural liaison for Chinese trade, although Eric feels unqualified for good reason: "There I was, a Chinese by birth and education, fluent only in Chinese, but knowing as much about China as any good old boy from Seminole, Texas, population 236." This points out a major difficulty of first-generation immigrants, one that is reflected in much of the literature written by them: their "homeland" feels as foreign to them as their adopted country, and they are experts neither on China nor on America. No one seems to understand them, except for other immigrants in the same predicament.

Finally Eric and Roger tackle an import agreement with a Chinese company, importing small electronic goods. The import business unfortunately eats capital prodigiously, because of the numerous production problems on the Chinese end. After pouring much good money after bad in the venture, Mr. Coldwell decides to call the import business quits. Eric Chung, the president of Coldwell Electronics International, Inc., remains sitting in his office, accompanied only by his secretary, analyzing his situation. He "telegraphs" his situation in a short message: "COLDWELL COMPANY EXECUTIVE REMOVED FROM JOB/SOON TO BE CANNED." Eric Chung is fully incorporated into the competitive and sometimes brutal world of American business—and of American life as a whole.

CRITICAL RECEPTION

Although no intensive critical work has been written on *The Incorporation of Eric Chung* to date, most book reviews are generally favorable. Reviewers have praised the book for its quiet and gentle humor. Keddy Outlaw of the Harris County Public Library, Houston, calls it "a farcical, often droll novel," while Syrul Lurie finds "Horatio Alger, An Wang, and Armand Hammer all rolled into one funny, engaging book." Amy Tan, author of *The Joy Luck Club* and *The Kitchen God's Wife* (as well as of a picture book for younger children) says, "Steven Lo provides an upside-down look at the American dream. I found myself laughing out loud about what's right, what's wrong and what's completely true about being versus becoming an American."

Lo's work shares some similarities with the work of another Chinese-American writer, Frank Chin, whose 1991 *Donald Duk* is another wry look at acculturation. Its hero, eleven-year-old Donald Duk, hates everything about being Chinese, hates being put on the spot in school to explain the China he has never visited, hates "funny" Chinese food. However, he finally learns to stop hating himself and his background when he begins to learn the truth of where he has come from.

While these two novels share certain similarities in their senses of humor, Lo's novel is a more light-hearted look at American life and capitalism: Eric fails in this endeavor, but will no doubt go on to try to succeed again, because that is the American way and he desires to succeed as an American. Chin's work is more critical of America, and of the way immigrants are taught to devalue their own culture and heritage in favor of becoming American.

Something that *The Incorporation of Eric Chung* and *Donald Duk* share is a criticism of America and its values. In earlier multicultural works of fiction, largely written by sympathetic white writers and not by Chinese (or Japanese or Polynesian, etc.), this sort of criticism does not exist. In earlier works about non-Eurocentric peoples in America, the underlying assumption was that the American way of doing things was the right way. Either overtly or covertly, there was a message that "progress" and "change" and assimilation were good things. As America has developed a generation of writers who can tell their own stories of what it is like to be living in America, but with a Chinese face, we have begun to hear more unadulterated views of America, both the good things about it and the less-than-good things, and we have also been given a view into the difficulties of assimilation. Assimilation involves losses as well as gains, which is made abundantly clear by Lo's novel and by other novels of Chinese-Americans of his generation.

Multicultural literature, at its best, should not present different cultures as simply "exotic" or "quaint" or "interesting," but as cultures that can give to America just as they take from America. And young adult multicultural literature should not only accurately reflect different cultures, but also tell stories adolescents can identify with. This is certainly true of *The Incorporation of Eric Chung*, whose wry humor young immigrants should find enjoyable. And readers who are of European background can appreciate not only the humor of the story, and the cultural information it conveys, but also the insights it offers into the difficulties all adolescents have in assimilating into the world of adulthood.

BIBLIOGRAPHY

Young Adult Fiction by Steven C. Lo

The Incorporation of Eric Chung. Chapel Hill: Algonquin-Workman, 1989.

Selected Studies of Steven C. Lo

Lurie, Syrul. Rev. of *The Incorporation of Eric Chung*. *Voice of Youth Advocates* 13.1 (1990): 31.

"New Novel Offers Chinese View of the American Work Scene." Chapel Hill: Press Kit from Algonquin Books of Chapel Hill, 1989.

Outlaw, Keddy. Rev. of *The Incorporation of Eric Chung*. *School Library Journal* 36.4 (1990): 151–52.

Rev. of *The Incorporation of Eric Chung*. *Kirkus Reviews* 57.14 (15 July 1989): 1102.

Robertson, Deb. Rev. of *The Incorporation of Eric Chung*. *Booklist* 86.2 (15 Sept. 1989): 145.

SHARON BELL MATHIS
(1937–)

Susan J. Forsling

BIOGRAPHY

Sharon Bell Mathis was born in Atlantic City, New Jersey, on February 26, 1937. Her father, John Willie Bell, had not known his parents; and Sharon was the first person he could call his own. But it was Sharon's mother, Alice Mary (née Frazier) Bell, who was her best friend until her death.

Sharon and her parents went home to her maternal grandparents' lovely Atlantic City home, provided by her Grandfather Frazier, who was a sanitation worker. This was a time when jobs for African-Americans, even those who were high school graduates like her parents, were restricted to positions as maids, dishwashers, waiters, and porters.

When Sharon's father secured a full-time job as a blacksmith's helper, the family moved on a bus, taking no furniture, to a second-floor apartment in the Bedford-Stuyvesant section of Brooklyn, New York. Her parents separated when she was five.

From the time she was tiny, Mathis liked a quiet spot of her own. The fire escape became her private refuge to read, do homework, talk with her mother in the kitchen, and just think. Her mother was a reader, and she helped her daughter discover African-American writers. Everything seemed possible to Mathis when she was on the fire escape, and she began writing little poems and short stories. Her mother was proud of her work, and her English teachers at St. Michael's Academy appreciated her writing.

The nuns let her read her stories aloud, which encouraged her to polish her work. Meanwhile, her mother worked at a multitude of jobs to keep the family together. She also suffered from a heart condition, and her condition was a constant source of worry to Mathis as she was growing up.

As graduation time approached Mrs. Bell was making plans for her daughter. Sharon was to live with her mother's best friend and her god-mother, G'Mom, and her husband, Uncle Jesse, in Baltimore and attend Morgan State College. She earned many scholarships and awards at Morgan. During her sophomore year Sharon met Leroy Franklin Mathis, and on July 11, 1957, she ran away from G'Mom's and married Leroy in front of an Arlington, Virginia, justice of the peace.

It was hard to convince her family that she would finish school, but Mathis graduated the next June *magna cum laude*. The graduation speaker was Dr. Martin Luther King, Jr. Mathis had no way of knowing that sixteen years later she would be awarded the prestigious Coretta Scott King Award for her children's biography, *Ray Charles* (1973).

Mathis' first position was as an interviewer at the Children's Hospital of the District of Columbia. Her caseload of sick children and their indigent parents was depressing, and she was happy to learn that she was pregnant with her daughter, Sherie. Three weeks later in October of 1959 Sharon accepted a position as fifth-grade teacher at Holy Redeemer School in Washington. Daughter Stacy was born four years later, and Stephanie a year after that. In September of 1965 Mathis became a special education teacher at Bertie Backus Junior High School. She took additional education courses at night, and the next year transferred to Charles Hart Junior High School where she taught remedial math.

It was at this time that Mathis began subscribing to writers' magazines. She read many books about writing. She read one genre at a time for months. Then, while the children slept, she sketched short stories and discovered that her child characters were superior to her adult ones. Before this she had never thought of writing just for children. The desire to write became overwhelming. She rented, then bought, a typewriter. The more she wrote, the more she wanted to write.

Mathis began writing for confession magazines, and after many rejections, "The Ghetto Riot Killed My Baby" was published in *Tan*, in 1969. Then, three months later, "The Fire Escape" appeared in *News Explorer*, a weekly magazine for children. Before the end of 1969 Mathis signed her first book contract for *Brooklyn Story*, a high-interest, low-vocabulary novel for teens. In February of 1970 *Sidewalk Story* took the Council on Interracial

Books for Children Award. The same year two of her poems were antholo-gized in Nikki Giovanni's *Night Comes Softly*.

From 1972 to 1985 Mathis wrote a column for *Ebony Jr!* magazine. Many of her stories, articles, and poems were published in various maga-zines in the early seventies, and she published seven books as well. She became a Fellow at the Breadloaf Writers Conference. *Teacup Full of Roses* (1972), *Cartwheels* (1977), *Listen for the Fig Tree* (1974), and *The Hundred Penny Box* (1975) were American Library Association Notable Books. *Teacup Full of Roses* was on the *New York Times* Best Book of the Year list, and *The Hundred Penny Box* was a Newbery Honor Book.

In 1975 Mathis graduated from the Catholic University of America with a master of science in library science, and in September she became a librarian at Benning Elementary School in Washington. The next year she went to Friendship Educational Center in Washington as a library media specialist.

Bad times were ahead, however. In 1978 Mathis was divorced and began to have serious writing problems. Her mother took a leave of absence from her job to see her through a difficult period of depression. In 1983 Mathis' mother and "dearest friend on earth" died of cancer of the bone. She and her brother and two sisters are devoted to honoring their mother's last wishes—to remain as close spiritually and physically as possible and take care of one another. Mathis has gone on to write *Red Dog/Blue Fly: Football Poems* (1991), dedicated to her grandson Thomas Kevin Allen II and her nephew John W. Bell III.

MAJOR WORKS AND THEMES

Mathis has said that she writes "to salute Black kids." Avis D. Matthews has written in an article about Mathis for *Book Links* that Mathis earned "a reputation for creating realistic and literate prose that authentically depicts African American children" in her early titles: *Sidewalk Story*, *Teacup Full of Roses*, and *Listen for the Fig Tree*.

In the same *Book Links* article Mathis articulates her philosophy of collection development as a library media specialist. She wants the books to give the students "ideas that strengthen them and stories that tell them it's good to be who they are, the color they are, and the race they are." Interestingly enough, Mathis provides these ideas and feelings in the books that she has written for children and young adults.

Mathis' books feature ordinary young people attempting to save lives, solve problems, and mobilize others—i.e., to be heroes in the midst of seemingly overpowering circumstances. Her characters support each other. The dialogue in her books is a mild form of black English.

Muffin Johnson from *Listen for the Fig Tree* is just sixteen and blind. The Christmas before, Muffin's father was murdered, and her devastated mother is on the way to killing herself with alcohol. Muffin wants to have a pretty dress and go to the Kwanza celebration. She wants to be away from her mother's crying and the smell of whiskey. But she does everything she can to help her mother—begging her to stay home, hiding her medications that combined with alcohol could kill her, and cleaning her mother up when she becomes ill from drinking too much. Finally Muffin realizes she has done the best she can and has to let go and allow her mother to make her own decisions.

Joe Brooks is the rock of the family in *Teacup Full of Roses*. His father is in poor health and has little impact on the family. Mrs. Brooks is so involved with her oldest son Paul, who is addicted to heroin, that she is unaware of what Joe is doing for himself and the family or of the mental brilliance and athletic talent of the youngest son Davey. Like Muffin with her mother, Joe struggles against tremendous odds to help his brother and himself. In both of these books there are shocking scenes of reality, but young readers come away with the idea that they are not helpless.

Sidewalk Story is for younger children, but again Mathis accomplishes one of her purposes in writing for children. She says that she writes so children can find solutions, so they understand that they can be courageous and face difficult situations. Nine-year-old Lilly Etta Allen is the heroine of this book. Lilly's best friend Tanya and her family are "put out" of their apartment. Workmen carry the furniture and belongings to the sidewalk and leave it. Lilly believes she can mobilize the police and newspaper and television people to help as they did in a similar case of an older woman. She eventually does marshal assistance by taking the situation into her own hands. Lilly covers the family's goods with sheets and blankets and "climbs onto the pile to hold them down" against the wind and rain. She is awakened by a reporter and cameramen.

The reality of old age and the understanding and sensitivity that a child can possess are portrayed in *The Hundred Penny Box*. Michael's great-great-aunt Dew, who raised his father, has been transported from Atlanta to live with them. She clings to an old box which contains pennies for each of her birthdays. Stories are attached to the pennies, and Michael loves the stories and Dew. The frustration and hardship of caring for an elderly person are shown through Michael's mother. But the specialness of a relationship that can develop is summarized in the last line of the book: "Michael put his head down on Aunt Dew's thin chest beneath the heavy quilt and listened to her sing her long song." Michael exhibits the same strong sense of loyalty to family or friend as Muffin, Joe, and Lilly.

Mathis continues to write in the current age of multiculturalism. Her *Red Dog/Blue Fly: Football Poems* (1991) brings her back to poetry, which was a genre of her early childhood writing. This collection gets into the mind of a young football player—the stress of learning and keeping signals straight; the independence the ball can show from what the player is trying to do with it; what it is like to be the quarterback or make a touchdown; what your parents, teammates, or coach might be thinking when you are injured; and what goes into earning a trophy. Any young football player, including those much older than the players in the book, can identify with these poems. But they also speak specifically to young African-American players. "Victory Banquet," with its menu of "curried goat and rabbit stew/fried fish chicken too/kale and mustard and collard greens," reminds them that it is good to be just who they are.

Mathis stated in *Book Links* that the world is not the same as when she last wrote fiction, and she intends to write more fiction. She says, "If you write out of a respect for the reader and an understanding of the economy—homelessness, et cetera—you will encourage the strength to stand up and go forward at all times." Thus it seems she plans to not only supply her students with "books that challenge . . . and portray them as courageous, plots that avoid hurtful stereotypes, and characters that find role models within their own racial or ethnic groups," but see that they are there to purchase by writing them herself.

CRITICAL RECEPTION

Avis D. Matthews in her article on Mathis for *Book Links* calls her "a natural storyteller, funny and charming and able to put vivid pictures of people, places, and events in your mind's eye." Her stories for the most part are page turners with the exception of *Listen For the Fig Tree* (1974), which *School Library Journal* said most readers would need lots of endurance to wade through. Muffin Johnson, Michael and his great-great aunt Dew, Joe Brooks, and Lilly Etta Allen stay with the reader because they are all clearly defined and warm, as Rochelle Cortez writes in *Black Books Bulletin* about Muffin. Christina Carr Young in *Childhood Education* said that each of Mathis' characters "is dealt with realistically and with great depth of understanding." Dale Carson writes in the *New York Times Book Review* that Mathis has a talent for characterization and the ability to describe delicate relationships. Surely this applies to Michael's relationship with Dew, Joe's with the members of his family and his girlfriend, and Muffin's with the homosexual neighbor Mr. Dale and her mother.

The Hundred Penny Box (1975) was a Newbery Honor Book with mixed reception from reviewers. Lydia Bassett in the *Interracial Books for Children Bulletin* calls it a thoughtful and sometimes touching story but also thinks the conflicts are not resolved. Annie Gottlieb writing for the *New York Times Book Review* praises it for acquainting young readers with old age and death in a way that they can compare to their own experiences, while not making the work an overt educational project. Hazel Copeland in *Black Books Bulletin* calls it "a step in the right direction toward literature that entertains and provides some positive direction for our children."

Listen for the Fig Tree was an American Library Association Notable book; but it, too, evoked mixed reactions from reviewers. *Kirkus Reviews* called it "sketchily relevant" (121) and thought too much attention was paid to the issue of patronizing black-owned stores and not enough to Muffin's reconciliation of her father's murder by blacks and her attack by a black with her growing racial pride. Jane Abramson in *School Library Journal* paints an interesting interpretation of the book as an updating of "Cinderella" with Momma as the wicked stepmother and Mr. Dale filling in for the fairy godmother. But she goes on to say that the characters are much more full blooded than stock fairy tale counterparts. She does comment, however, on "too many scenes rehashing what's already happened." That and too much repetition of how important Kwanza is to Muffin are major flaws.

Although Mathis succeeds in her desire to show black kids being black kids, she also succeeds in writing about situations that are still relevant today for any color of kid. What Eleanor Cameron writes about *Teacup Full of Roses* for the *Horn Book Magazine* could be true of all of Sharon Mathis' characters. She says that Mathis brings them alive in a situation which speaks truth in a black world, but which would speak truth just as clearly were the novels about white families. For what she talks about is the human condition.

Eloise Greenfield in the *Negro History Bulletin* says Mathis writes "love messages" to black children and tells them of their beauty, talent, and strength to survive, the "positive aspects of Black life without ignoring the fact that problems do exist." Problems exist for all children. G. Robert Carlsen wrote in the *English Journal* that *Teacup Full of Roses* was not just about black families but "every family where a parent lavishes affection on a prodigal to the detriment of the other children."

BIBLIOGRAPHY

Young Adult Fiction by Sharon Bell Mathis

Brooklyn Story. Illus. Charles Bible. New York: Hill and Wang, 1970.
Sidewalk Story. Illus. Leo Carty. New York: Viking, 1971.
Teacup Full of Roses. New York: Viking, 1971.
Listen for the Fig Tree. New York: Viking, 1974.
The Hundred Penny Box. Illus. Leo Dillon and Diane Dillon. New York: Viking, 1975.

Other Works by Sharon Bell Mathis

Ray Charles. Illus. George Ford. New York: Crowell, 1973.
Cartwheels. New York: Scholastic, 1977.
Red Dog/Blue Fly: Football Poems. Illus. Jan Spivey Gilchrist. New York: Viking, 1991.

Selected Studies of Sharon Bell Mathis

Abranson, Jane, Rev. of *Listen for the Fig Tree*. *School Library Journal* (Mar. 1974): 120.
Abranson, Jane. Rev. of *Listen for the Fig Tree*. *School Library Journal* (Mar. 1974): 120.
Bassett, Lydia. Rev. of *The Hundred Penny Box*. *Interracial Books for Children Bulletin* 6.3 (1975): 8.
Cameron, Eleanor. Rev. of *Teacup Full of Roses*. *Horn Book* 49 (Feb. 1973): 58.
Carlsen, G. Robert. Rev. of *Teacup Full of Roses*. *English Journal* (Feb. 1974): 90–91.
Carson, Dale. Rev. of *Listen for the Fig Tree*. *New York Times Book Review*, 7 April 1974: 8.
Cortez, Rochelle. Rev. of *Listen for the Fig Tree*. *Black Books Bulletin* (Spring 1974): 39–40.
De Montreville, Doris, and Elizabeth D. Crawford, eds. *Fourth Book of Junior Authors and Illustrators*. New York: Wilson, 1978. 255–56.
Gallo, Donald R., comp. and ed. *Speaking for Ourselves*. Urbana: NCTE, 1990.
Gottlieb, Annie. Rev. of *The Hundred Penny Box*. *New York Times Book Review*. 1 June 1976: 28.
Greenfield, Eloise. Rev. of *Teacup Full of Roses*. *Negro History Bulletin* (March 1973): 69.
Hanley, Karen Stang. "Guy, Rosa." *Twentieth-Century Children's Writers*. Ed. Tracy Chevalier. 3rd ed. Chicago: St. James, 1989. 647–48.

Helbig, Alethea K., and Agnes Regan Perkins. *Dictionary of American Children's Fiction, 1960–1984*. New York: Greenwood Press, 1986.

"Mathis, Sharon Bell." *Children's Literature Review*. Ed. Gerard J. Senick. Vol. 3. Detroit: Gale: 1978. 149–52.

Matthews, Avis D. "The Books of Sharon Bell Mathis." *Book Links* (Jan. 1994): 20–22.

Rev. of *Listen for the Fig Tree*. *Kirkus Reviews*. 42 (February 1974): 121.

Rollack, Barbara. *Black Authors and Illustrators of Children's Books: A Biographical Dictionary*. New York: Garland, 1992.

"Sharon Bell Mathis." *Something about the Author*. Ed. Anne Commire. Vol. 58. Detroit: Gale Research Company, 1990. 123–32.

"Sharon Bell Mathis." *Something about the Author Autobiography Series*. Ed. Adele Sarkissian. Vol. 3. Detroit: Gale, 1987. 147–74.

Young, Christine Carr. Rev. of *The Hundred Penny Box*. *Childhood Education* 52.3 (1976): 154.

FLORENCE CRANNELL MEANS
(1891–1980)

Linnea Hendrickson

BIOGRAPHY

"Whether they are red or white or yellow or black, folks are folks." This conviction, formed early in Florence Crannell Means' life, was to be reflected in more than forty books written over a span of forty years. One of her earliest memories was of the many visitors of different races and nationalities that were welcomed to the Crannell home.

Flossy Crannell was born in Baldwinsville, New York, on May 15, 1891, the second daughter of Phillip Wendell and Fannie Eleanor Grout Crannell. Phillip Crannell, a graduate of Dartmouth College and the Rochester Divinity School, was one of the strongest influences on her life. He was a scholar and a poet, and would later serve as president of Kansas City Baptist Theological Seminary for nearly twenty-five years. "I have not known another mind so deep, high, clear, and richly stocked as Father's," Means later wrote (Kunitz and Haycroft 215).

Books were important to the family. Mrs. Crannell was an avid reader who vanished into a book the moment she opened it. In the evenings Rev. Crannell often read aloud Shakespeare, the Brownings, Tennyson, or Dickens.

When Means was thirteen, her sister Effie became ill, and the family moved to Denver in hopes that the climate would improve her health. It was an unusual year that left a lasting impression on young Means. Since there were few girls to play with, she played rough with boys, riding half-broken horses, chasing lizards and "horny-toads," and racing along the prairie with her dog (Kunitz and Haycroft 215).

It was in Denver and later in nearby Boulder, that Means was to make her lifelong home. She graduated from Denver's East High School, which plays a prominent role in some of her books. After high school she studied Greek and philosophy privately with her father and also attended the Henry Read School of Art in Denver. In 1912, in the Denver house that was to be their home for many years, she married Carleton Bell Means, a young Kansas City man who had just finished law school. Carl Means also loved literature and the arts, and strongly supported his wife's writing career.

Even though her health was sometimes frail, Means wrote one or two books a year, managed her household, raised her daughter Eleanor (who grew up to be the writer Eleanor Means Hull), taught courses at the University of Denver, wrote articles and stories for periodicals such as *St. Nicholas*, *Youth's Companion*, *Child Life*, *Collier's*, and others, lectured at library and education association conferences, took an interest in church and missionary work, and traveled extensively in the United States and Mexico.

She studied the groups she wrote about, first by reading, then by talking with persons who knew about the groups, and finally by going to the groups and getting to know them. She visited Mather School in South Carolina to gather information for stories in church publications about young black children in the training school. However, on her last night on campus, the high school girls gathered around her in the dormitory, and asked her to write a book about them. The result was *Shuttered Windows* (1938), one of her most successful books. She read the book, chapter by chapter, to two senior English classes at Mather, and incorporated changes and revisions suggested by the students.

To gather information for her books about Native Americans, she visited the Navajos and Hopis in the Southwest, and perhaps twenty other tribes in other states.

Her knowledge of the Japanese dated back to her friendships early in life with two of her father's favorite students. When she began to write *The Moved-Outers* (1945), in the midst of the fear and hate generated toward the Japanese during World War II, she visited the relocation camp in Amache, Colorado, gathered information from those who had lived in the assembly centers such as the one at Santa Anita race track, and talked with young people themselves, whom she invited to her home.

Means believed that the foundation for multicultural understanding must be established in childhood, and that such understanding must be based on knowledge as well as on good intentions. She chose to write about minority groups because she wanted other children to have the same kind of knowledge and understanding that she had acquired in childhood. While adult opinions were already fixed, she felt adolescents were still open to change, especially if the characters were strong and the situations vital enough to invite self-identification.

Means wrote, "The books about minority groups have had varied motivation—more than any other the desire to introduce one group of people to another who otherwise might never know them, and so might regard them with the fear which is bred of lack of knowledge, and which in its turn breeds the hate, the prejudice which I have seen blazing out in destructive force against all Germans, against all Japanese, against all Negroes" (*Something about the Author* 155).

Means continued to write about African-Americans, Native Americans, and Hispanics, as well as other young people through the 1950s and into the 1960s. Sadly, as multiculturalism became popular in the 1960s and 1970s, Means' pioneering efforts faded from public view as newer, more radical writing took its place.

MAJOR WORKS AND THEMES

Means' first book was one in a series of six short books for younger children published by Friendship Press. These books stressed Christian ethics as a key to overcoming difficulties faced by the various ethnic groups. *Raphael and Consuelo* (1929) portrays two Mexican children who come to the United States for the sake of their education; *Children of the Great Spirit* (1932), Native Americans; *Rainbow Bridge* (1934), a Japanese family who settled in a small Colorado town; *Across the Fruited Plain* (1940), migrant workers; *Children of the Promise* (1941), Jewish children; and *Peter of the Mesa* (1944), a Hopi Indian boy who attends school at the Presbyterian Mission School at Ganado.

While writing these books for Friendship Press, Means also wrote more secular books for Houghton Mifflin. *A Candle in the Mist: A Story for Girls* (1931) and its two sequels, *Ranch and Ring: A Story of the Pioneer West* (1932) and *A Bowlful of Stars* (1934), are historical adventure stories loosely based on family history.

Themes that would be common to all of Means' work are apparent in these earliest books. Her heroines are strong-willed, independent young women who face difficult decisions, often involving a conflict between their own desires and loyalty to family members or friends.

The theme of minorities, although less central than in her later works, also emerges. While the portrayal of Native Americans contains stereotypes representative of the nineteenth-century setting of the stories and common to other children's books from the 1930s, such as Carol Ryrie Brink's *Caddie Woodlawn* and Laura Ingalls Wilder's *Little House* series, Means also describes acts of kindness and even friendships between the white characters and the Native Americans, despite fear, suspicion, and great differences on both sides.

A Bowlful of Stars (1934) raises questions about quality of life versus temporary gains, a theme that will reappear in many of Means' books. Janey must decide whether to cast her lot with her gold-mining claim in the mountains near Central City, Colorado, where beautiful canyons are being turned into noisy, ugly mines, or whether to return to ranching and farming, where wealth will not come quickly, but where there is peace and quiet and fresh air, and the landscape is nurtured rather than destroyed.

Dusky Day (1933), published between the second and third of the Janey Grant books, is the first of several of Means' school and college stories. Dusky's college roommates are an unlikely group of young women, with whom, of course, she becomes very close—a common theme in Means' school and college stories. Although ethnic minorities play a small role in this story, the themes of acceptance of individual differences, and the importance of loyalty to friends and family are strong.

The little Carmelita, the Mexican child whom the girls befriend, is typical of the delightful little children who are lovingly featured in charming cameo roles in almost every one of Means' books.

Tangled Waters (1936), Means' first book about Navajos, is one of her most powerful stories. Told from the perspective of Altolie, a fifteen-year-old Navajo girl, the story is moving and convincing. Navajo culture is portrayed sensitively, but is not idealized. The Navajo landscape, with its combination of beauty and danger, also plays an important role. Conflict between traditional Navajo culture and white culture is a major theme. Readers almost feel that Means is too hard on her protagonists. Everything that can go wrong does, and one's heart breaks for Altolie. Her last minute rescue from a loveless marriage by the faithful boy in a classic Means jalopy is gripping.

Shuttered Windows (1938), Means' first book about African-Americans, is also one of her strongest, most compelling stories. Like *Tangled Waters*, it is a story of conflict between cultures. Should Harriet, the northern-born, middle-class black, go back to her comfortable life and the well-equipped integrated schools of the North, or stay with the impoverished, superstitious, illiterate, yet warm, loving, and dignified people, such as her Granny, who live on the coastal plains and tidal islands of South Carolina?

As in *Tangled Waters*, the choice is not an easy one. The traditional way of life of the islanders is presented with sensitivity to its beauties as well as to its flaws. As in *Tangled Waters*, there is a love story, and the promise that the two young people will build a new world together—another theme common to Means' books.

Adella Mary in Old New Mexico (1939) is a historical novel depicting the journey to Taos, New Mexico, of thirteen-year-old Adella Mary Hoskins and her father, brother and sister, and their slaves, in the 1850s. Again, bits of humanity show through in the portrayals of the African-Americans, Native Americans, and Hispanics, but in many ways this seems an older book than *Tangled Waters* and *Shuttered Windows*.

Shadow over Wide Ruin (1942) is also a historical novel, and this time the Navajos are seen through the eyes of sixteen-year-old Hepzibah Emmeline Plumb, who travels from her home in Denver to the Navajo Reservation near Gallup, New Mexico. In a rather disturbing twist, the dashing, handsome Dolito turns out to be not Navajo at all, but an adopted white baby, a fact apparently known by all but Hepzibah and the reader. However, this does mean that he and Hepzibah can marry, which apparently would not have been acceptable had he been Navajo by birth.

Teresita of the Valley (1943) and *The House under the Hill* (1949) are written from the point of view of contemporary families of Hispanic descent in southern Colorado and northern New Mexico. Teresita and Elena Trujillo, the protagonists of *The House under the Hill*, are both young women from traditional rural Spanish villages in Colorado and New Mexico. Both of them face decisions regarding their education, both struggle to blend their traditional culture and new ways, both find schoolwork difficult, despite their innate intelligence, and both feel conflicts between doing what they would like to do and their loyalty to their families. Both also have attractive young men whose goals and interests influence their own.

The House under the Hill is set entirely in the tiny villages surrounding Mirador, New Mexico, but the family in *Teresita* is forced to leave its village and seek a new life in Denver. Teresita Martinez, wishing to disguise her Hispanic heritage, enrolls at her new high school under the name Teddy Jones, a decision she soon regrets. In *The House under the Hill,* likewise, a young woman who has gone to the city and now looks down on her heritage is unfavorably portrayed.

Alicia (1953) also deals with southwestern Hispanics. Whereas Teresita and Elena are unsophisticated village girls, Alicia is a well-educated, middle-class, haughty "Spanish princess," angry at the discrimination she faces because of her Hispanic heritage. She spends her junior year of college in Mexico, seeking to reinforce her pride in its grand, aristocratic culture. But, against her will she comes to appreciate the Indian aspects of Mexico, to resent the self-absorption of the rich, and to feel sympathy for the poor, with whom she decides to throw her lot.

Sumiko (Sue) Ohara in *The Moved-Outers* (1945) is, like Harriet (of *Shuttered Windows*) and Alicia, a middle-class American teenager, who is different only because of her Asian looks and her family's Japanese heritage. This book rightfully received much attention when it was first published, and it has been recently reprinted by Walker Books, making it the only one of Means' books still in print. It is remarkable that this book was written and published in the midst of World War II, when "Jap" was a dirty word and most Americans ignored the fate of loyal Japanese-Americans who were imprisoned, even when sons and fathers of some of the families were dying in battle for the United States.

The story itself reads somewhat more like a documentary than a novel, and in comparison with Uchiko Uchida's memoir, *The Invisible Thread,* it lacks immediacy; yet, it is a powerful book, amazing for its time. If there is a criticism of the character of Sue, it is that, like Harriet and Alicia, she seems almost too middle class, too American, to feel entirely real.

Although *It Takes All Kinds* (1964) received little critical attention, it is a compelling story of the family of a displaced Iowa farmer that settles into a ramshackle house next to a burning dump on the Colorado prairies. The characters and the situations are memorable, and in some ways very modern. Fifteen-year-old Florette is a mechanical genius who cannot learn to read, five-year-old Elvis has severe, undiagnosed cerebral palsy, Pop has a temper and a drinking problem, Mom is overweight and seemingly immobilized by the cruel lot that life has given her, and the beautiful, selfish Coral changes her name and pretends that she is a cousin because she is ashamed of her family.

In *Our Cup Is Broken* (1969), Means' next to last book, the orphaned Sarah, a Hopi girl adopted by missionaries, is separated from her boyfriend because of ethnic prejudice. Returning to her village on the mesa, where she no longer fits in, she is raped by a boy who, too late, learns he cannot marry her because they are of the same clan. The daughter born to her becomes blind. In the end, she marries Bennie, Hopi but also Christian, and although it is more a marriage of convenience than of love, there is hope that this family will survive.

Means also wrote plays and biographies. *Carver's George: A Biography of George Washington Carver* (1953) is a beautifully written biography for children. *Sagebrush Surgeon* (1955), the story of Clarence G. Salsbury, the "big doctor" at the Ganado Mission Hospital, and *Sunlight on the Hopi Mesas: The Story of Abigail E. Johnson* (1960) are biographies written for adults.

CRITICAL RECEPTION

Since the 1940s little has been written about Means. There has been one journal article, one conference paper, a few brief essays in reference sources, and scattered references in a few books.

Her portrayals of Native Americans, Hispanics, and African-Americans were, for the most part, highly praised by her contemporaries. E. L. Scoggin, writing of *Tangled Waters* in the *New York Times* on September 6, 1936, compared the book favorably to Oliver La Farge's *Laughing Boy* in its "richness and understanding" (10). Siri Andrews and others praised *Shuttered Windows*, the ground-breaking story of African-American high school girls in 1938.

The 1945 publication of *The Moved-Outers* received much attention, including a lengthy tribute by Howard Pease in *Horn Book*. At least one reviewer, however, while admitting that the story was moving, questioned whether anything else "could have been done for or with the Oharas" (Becker 6).

Charlemae Rollins praised *Great Day in the Morning* in 1946, and defended its use of dialect (24), and August Baker was pleased with *Reach for a Star* in 1957 (2980).

But by 1973, when Dorothy Broderick published *The Image of the Black in Children's Literature*, Means' moderate approach to the problems of America's ethnic minorities had fallen out of favor. Broderick characterizes Means as "a bleeding heart liberal," who insists on good manners and is determined to keep African-Americans in their place by insisting that they not take "an easy way out" but dedicate themselves to service to their people.

Broderick's criticism must have been bitter to Means, who had dedicated her entire life to cross-cultural understanding. If Broderick had read all of Means, she would have understood that Means allowed none of her characters, no matter what their ethnic group, to take "the easy way out." For Means, service to others always came before selfish self-interest.

Would "good manners" bring the dead Trudy, in *Great Day in the Morning*, back to life, asks Broderick (173)? She neglects the alternative— would bad manners, or perhaps a riot, have done so?

Not all latter day critics have been as harsh on Means as Broderick. Lee Kingman writes, "Her multi-layered stories of all kinds of people are not goody-goody, missionary-inspirational; they are honest, realistic, and, always, interesting and well-written."

Suzanne Rahn, in her 1987 essay in *The Lion and the Unicorn*, defends Means' role as an interpreter of one ethnic group to another, and cautions the reader not to "impose 1980's sentiments on a culture different in some ways than ours" (113). Rahn provides detailed readings of *Shuttered Windows* and *The Moved-Outers* within the contexts of their times.

Celia Catlett Anderson points out that although some critics have called Means books "too tragic" and others called them "too pat," "more often conflicts between character and situation are resolved realistically. Long before racial tolerance was a popular or even generally accepted subject for juvenile literature, Means was writing straightforward books about minority groups. Means' approach, however, is far from radical. Her minority characters are dedicated to American ideals" (*American Women*, 154).

In her detailed analysis of *Our Cup Is Broken*, Anderson points out Means' skill in analyzing "the tragic problems that are bred when a mixture of cultures has come about through conquest and patronage rather than through a free exchange among peoples" (*Cross-Culturalism*, 87).

Siri Andrews, writing in 1946, praised Means' use of "the small details of daily experience" which give the books "solidity and a convincing down-to-earth quality in spite of the idealism which inspires them." Andrews pointed out the frequent mention of food, which always sounds "luscious" even when it is simple, and the conscious use of details of the natural world, its birds, trees, flowers, and odors (26).

Andrews saw Means as "the leader in a new kind of writing for young people which will become increasingly important in a more mature postwar world" (29).Unfortunately the postwar world largely passed Means by, and her pioneering role in multicultural literature for young adults is largely forgotten.

Her heroines, whatever their ethnic background, struggle to define their identities as they learn to balance strength and independence with caring relationships with families, friends, lovers, children, old people, the handicapped, and others who need their help, just as young women do today.

Means' books may now be considered "period pieces," but their issues are with us yet. Few writers have handled them as skillfully.

BIBLIOGRAPHY

Works for Young Adults and Children by Florence Crannell Means

Rafael and Consuelo. With Harriet Louise Fullen. New York: Friendship Press, 1929.

A Candle in the Mist: *A Story for Girls*. Illus. Marguerite de Angeli. Boston: Houghton Mifflin, 1931.

Ranch and Ring: A Story of the Pioneer West. Illus. Henry Peck. Boston: Houghton Mifflin, 1932.

Dusky Day. Illus. Manning Lee. Boston: Houghton Mifflin, 1933.

A Bowlful of Stars. Illus. Henry Pitz. Boston: Houghton Mifflin, 1934.

Rainbow Bridge. Illus. Eleanor Lattimore. New York: Friendship Press, 1934.

Penny for Luck. Illus. Paul Quinn. Boston: Houghton Mifflin, 1935.

Tangled Waters. Illus. Herbert Morton Stoops. Boston: Houghton Mifflin, 1936.

The Singing Wood. Illus. Manning Lee. Boston: Houghton Mifflin, 1937.

Shuttered Windows. Illus. Armstrong Sperry. Boston: Houghton Mifflin, 1938.

Adella Mary in Old New Mexico. Illus. Herbert Morton Stoops. Boston: Houghton Mifflin, 1939.

Across the Fruited Plain. Illus. Janet Smalley. New York: Friendship House, 1940.

At the End of Nowhere. Illus. David Hendrickson. Boston: Houghton Mifflin, 1940.

Children of the Promise. Illus. Janet Smalley. New York: Friendship Press, 1941.

Whispering Girl. Illus. Oscar Howard. Boston: Houghton Mifflin, 1941.

Shadow over Wide Ruin. Illus. Lorence Bjorklund. Boston: Houghton Mifflin, 1942.

Teresita of the Valley. Illus. Nicholas Panesis. Boston: Houghton Mifflin, 1943.

Peter of the Mesa. Illus. Janet Smalley. New York: Friendship Press, 1944.

The Moved-Outers. Illus. Helen Blair. Boston: Houghton Mifflin, 1945.

Great Day in the Morning. Illus. Helen Blair. Boston: Houghton Mifflin, 1946.

Assorted Sisters. Illus. Helen Blair. Boston: Houghton Mifflin, 1947.

The House under the Hill. Illus. Helen Blair. Boston: Houghton Mifflin, 1949.

The Silver Fleece. With Carl Means. Illus. Edwin Schmidt. Philadelphia: Winston, 1950.

Hetty of the Grande Deluxe. Illus. Helen Blair. Boston: Houghton Mifflin, 1951.

Alicia. Illus. William Barss. Boston: Houghton Mifflin, 1953.

The Rains Will Come. Illus. Fred Kabotie. Boston: Houghton Mifflin, 1954.

Knock at the Door, Emmy. Illus. Paul Lantz. Boston: Houghton Mifflin, 1956.

Reach for a Star. Boston: Houghton Mifflin, 1957.

Borrowed Brother. Illus. Dorothy Bayley Morse. Boston: Houghton Mifflin, 1958.

Emmy and the Blue Door. Illus. Frank Nicholas. Boston: Houghton Mifflin, 1959.

But I Am Sara. Boston: Houghton Mifflin, 1961.

That Girl Andy. Boston: Houghton Mifflin, 1962.

Tolliver. Boston: Houghton Mifflin, 1963.

It Takes All Kinds. Boston: Houghton Mifflin, 1964.

Us Maltbys. Boston: Houghton Mifflin, 1966.

Our Cup Is Broken. Boston: Houghton Mifflin, 1969.

Smith Valley. Boston: Houghton Mifflin, 1970.

Other Works by Florence Crannell Means

Pepita's Adventure in Friendship. Play. New York: Friendship Press, 1929.

Children of the Great Spirit: A Course on the American Indian. With Frances Somers Riggs. New York: Friendship Press, 1932.

Carver's George: A Biography of George Washington Carver. Illus. Harve Stein. Boston: Houghton Mifflin, 1953.

Sagebrush Surgeon. Biography of Clarence G. Salsbury. New York: Friendship Press, 1955.

Sunlight on the Hopi Mesas: The Story of Abigail E. Johnson. Philadelphia: Judson Press, 1960.

Selected Studies of Florence Crannell Means

Anderson, Celia Catlett. "Florence Crannell Means." *American Women Writers.* Vol. 3 of *A Critical Reference Guide from Colonial Times to the Present.* Ed. Lina Mainiero. New York: Ungar, 1981. 153–55.

———. "Florence Crannell Means: Cultural Barriers and Bridges." *Cross-Culturalism in Children's Literature: Selected Papers from the 1987 International Conference of the Children's Literature Association.* Carleton University, Ottawa, Canada, 14 May 1987. Ed. Susan R. Gannon and Ruth Anne Thompson. New York: Pace U, 1988. 87–90.

Andrews, Siri. "Florence Crannell Means." *Horn Book* 22 (Jan. 1946): 15–30.

Baker, August. *Library Journal* 15 Nov. 1957.

Becker, M. L. *Weekly Book Review* 18 Mar. 1945.

Broderick, Dorothy. *The Image of the Black in Children's Fiction.* New York: Bowker, 1973.

Crosson, Wilhelmina M. "Florence Crannell Means." *Elementary English Review* 17 (Dec. 1940): 321–24, 326.

"Florence Crannell Means." *Something about the Author.* Ed. Anne Commire. Vol. 25. Detroit: Gale, 1971. 154–55.

Kingman, Lee. "Means, Florence Crannell." *Twentieth Century Children's Writers*. Ed. Tracy Chevalier. 3rd ed. Chicago: St. James, 1989. 671–73.

Kingston, Carolyn T. *The Tragic Mode in Children's Literature*. New York: Teachers College Press, 1974.

Kunitz, Stanley J., and Howard Haycroft, eds. *Junior Book of Authors*. 2nd rev. New York: H. W. Wilson, 1951.

Means, Florence. "Mosaic." *Horn Book* 16 (Jan. 1940): 35–40.

Montgomery, Elizabeth Rider. "The Book She Had to Write: *Shuttered Windows." The Story behind Modern Books*. New York: Dodd, Mead, 1949. 119–24.

Pease, Howard. "Without Evasion: Some Reflections after Reading Mrs. Means' 'The Moved-Outers.'" *Horn Book* 21 (Jan. 1945): 9–17.

Rahn, Suzanne. "Early Images of American Minorities: Rediscovering Florence Crannell Means." *The Lion and the Unicorn* 11.1 (1987): 98–115.

Rollins, Charlemae. *Bookweek* 10 Nov. 1946.

Nicholasa Mohr
(1935-)

Tara L. Rivera

BIOGRAPHY

During the 1940s, when Puerto Rico was suffering from worsening economic conditions, Nicholasa Mohr's parents, Pedro and Nicholasa (née Rivera) Golpe, migrated from Puerto Rico to the United States with hopes of giving their children a chance at the American Dream. Mohr was born in New York City's El Barrio, also known as Spanish Harlem.

Crucial events and experiences early in Mohr's life have significantly influenced her writing. In hopes that her talents would yield opportunities for her, Mohr's family always encouraged her to study and concentrate on painting and drawing. After her mother's death, the family separated, and Mohr lived with her aunt. Then it was time for Mohr, who was the best artist in her class, to select a high school. Because Mohr was an impoverished Puerto Rican female and came from a family structure that was not traditionally stable, her guidance counselor told her that she was not college material, and it would not be fair for Mohr to enter the academic track and take the place of another student who was. Thus, Mohr was placed in the vocational program. After graduation, Mohr set her goals high and enrolled at the Art Students' League in New York City. During this time, Mohr studied anatomy, Rembrandt, the postimpressionists, and muralists such as Diego Rivera, Jose Clemente Orozco, and David Siqueiros. In addition, she traveled to Europe and Mexico.

When she returned from Mexico, Mohr continued her studies at the New School for Social Research in New York City. It was there she met her husband, Irwin Mohr. They had two sons, David and Jason. At this time, her artwork expressed her personal side and depicted the environment with which she was so familiar. Her prints and paintings were filled with bold figures, faces, and various graffiti-like symbols of the city. Even though she experienced a moderate level of success as an artist and participated in exhibitions, Mohr began to explore another of her interests, to write children's books.

Wanting to present experiences of the Puerto Rican culture that were not evident in American children's literature, Mohr took her artistic talents and experiences as a Puerto Rican growing up in the city and used them to help her write books for children. Mohr's writings for children include *Nilda* (1973) a book she also illustrated; *El Bronx Remembered* (1975); *In Nueva York* (1977); *Felita* (1979); *Going Home* (1986); and *All for the Better* (1993). During the years that she has been publishing, she has written various articles, short stories, essays, and several plays.

MAJOR WORKS AND THEMES

Mohr's works focus on survival. In each work, the characters use different elements and attributes in order to survive. Mohr's first novel, *Nilda,* is a semi-autobiographical account of Mohr's life as a child in El Barrio. Set during World War II, Nilda, like Mohr, uses her artwork to help cope with her oppressive environment. The environment in *Nilda* is a tense and dark one: Nilda's family is forced to go on public assistance; Nilda's brother sees crime as the only way out; and Nilda's mother dies. However, because of her relationship with her mother, Nilda is left with means for self-empowerment. Most important is the strong drive of the Puerto Rican. Nilda is always told to do well so that she will have more alternatives later in life.

Both Nuyorican culture (the culture of Puerto Ricans living in New York) and survival are depicted again in *El Bronx Remembered.* This collection of twelve short interwoven stories, based on the experiences of Puerto Ricans who migrated to the United States from 1946 through 1956, expresses the feelings of people living in an alien environment. Although the characters live in poverty, each story is told sympathetically and with humor. The perspectives of Puerto Ricans in an urban society are illustrated through anecdotes such as those of Mrs. Suarez and her children befriending old Mr. Mendelsohn; three children who experience the death of a friend;

and a homosexual man and a pregnant girl who marry each other for widely different reasons.

Mohr continues the theme of survival in *In Nueva York.* In this darker collection of closely interconnected short stories, Mohr's characters are more clearly defined than those in *El Bronx Remembered.* The starkness of these tales helps shape the reader's view of the reality Mohr presents. The characters try to survive in a way that suits their respective personalities: from young Lali who marries older Rudi so that she can come to America; to the young boys who rob Rudi's store; to Rudi who kills one of the boys in self-defense; and finally to the mother who longs for a tombstone so that her young son's life can be remembered.

With *Felita,* Mohr returns to writing novels. Felita's family, intent on having what is best for their children, moves to a "better" neighborhood— that is, one without any Puerto Ricans. There, Felita and her family experience the fury of racism. Because her mother is light skinned and her father is dark, Felita is teased by children ignorant of the fact that the Puerto Rican peoples come in a diversity of shades. Mohr also focuses on the traditional Puerto Rican extended family. For example, Felita spends a great deal of time with her *abuelita (grandmother)* who tells Felita stories about Puerto Rico. Later, Felita must cope with her *abuelita*'s death. Although Felita returns to her old neighborhood and must survive there, she has her art, her *abuelita's* stories, and her family to help her.

Felita gets her wish to visit Puerto Rico in the companion text to *Felita, Going Home.* By having Felita, a Nuyorican, in Puerto Rico, Mohr presents a different perspective of the Puerto Rican experience. Felita experiences a conflict with her peers in Puerto Rico; they do not consider her authentically Puerto Rican because she was not raised there. In addition, since a major attribute of the Puerto Rican culture is the bilingualism of English and Spanish, Mohr explores the conflict of the Nuyorican's dependence on English. Felita struggles with some of the Hispanic traditions that her family wishes her to follow, such as boys having more freedom than girls. Although there is friction between Felita and her culture, Felita comes back to New York with a better understanding of who she is and of her Puerto Rican roots.

Mohr's most recent work is a departure from the fiction she has written previously. *All for the Better: A Story of El Barrio* is a biography of Evelina Lopez Antonetty. The message is clear in this story: one person can make a difference. That is what is seen through Antonetty's activism on behalf of the Spanish Community in New York. At age eleven, Antonetty came from Puerto Rico to New York during the depression because of the fierce economic conditions of her home. When she saw that her neighbors in El Barrio were too proud to apply for the food packages provided by the United States, Antonetty devised a plan that enabled them to survive; this event was the beginning of her career as an activist. Since this book is part of the Stories of America Series, this tale is important for the American, Puerto Rican or not.

CRITICAL RECEPTION

Mohr presents diverse images of the Puerto Rican culture. Critics have remarked upon the authenticity of her works because she reflects on many of her own experiences. Mohr's works fit within a category of Puerto Rican literature that does not provide "superficial characteristics which are supposedly Puerto Rican" (Nieto 222). "On the one hand, Mohr shows the ambiguities of history reflected in ambiguities of identity. On the other hand, she breaks free from the formulaic narratives in which Puerto Ricans are frozen in New York City" (Gregory 31). She provides "much more authentic and in-depth portrayals of relationships within the family and with the outside world" (Nieto 222). It has been said that Mohr takes the reader beyond the usual stereotypes of the inner city. Her writing reveals that there is so much more than the oppressive environment that is publicized in the media. Her awards include the Jane Addams Children's Book Award of U.S. Section of Women's International League for Peace and Freedom, the Citation of Merit at Society of Illustrators annual exhibition, and the *New York Times* Outstanding Book of the Year for *Nilda;* the American Book Award; and an honorary doctor of letters degree from the State University of New York at Albany. Her work *El Bronx Remembered* was a finalist for the National Book Award, and *Felita* was selected as a Notable Children's Book in the Field of Social Studies.

BIBLIOGRAPHY

Young Adult Fiction by Nicholasa Mohr

Nilda: A Novel. Illus. by the author. New York: Harper & Row, 1973. Houston, TX: Arte Publico Press, 1991.
El Bronx Remembered: A Novella and Stories. New York: Harper & Row 1975. Houston, TX: Arte Publico Press, 1991.
In Nueva York. New York: Dial, 1977.
Felita. New York: Dial, 1979.
Going Home. New York: Dial, 1986.

All for the Better: A Story of El Barrio. NY: Dialogue Systems, 1993.

Works for Adults by Nicholasa Mohr

Rituals of Survival: A Women's Portfolio. Houston, TX: Arte Publico Press, 1985.
"A Journey toward a Common Ground: The Struggle and Identity of Hispanics in the U.S.A." *Many Faces, Many Voices: Multicultural Literacy Experiences for Youth.* Ft. Atkinson, WI: Highsmith, 1992.

Selected Studies of Nicholasa Mohr

Forman, Jack. Rev. of *In Nueva York. School Library Journal* 23:8 (1977): 79.
Gregory, Lucille H. "The Puerto Rican Rainbow: Distortions vs. Complexities." *CLA Quarterly.* Toronto: The Association, 1992.
Haviland, Virginia. Rev. of *Felita. Horn Book* 56:1 (1980): 56.
McCracken, Ellen. "Latina Narrative and Politics of Signification: Articulation, Antagonism, and Populist Rupture." *Crítica: A Journal of Critical Essays* 2.2 (1990): 202–207.
McHargue, Georgess. Rev. of *In Nueva York. New York Times Book Review* 22 May 1977: 29.
Miller, John. "The Concept of Puerto Rico as Island Paradise in the Works of Two Puerto Rican Writers on the Mainland: Nicholasa Mohr and Edward Rivera." *Torre de Papel* 3.2 (1993): 57–64.
"Nicholasa Mohr." *Something about the Author.* Ed. Anne Commire. Vol. 8. Detroit: Gale, 1976. 138.
Nieto, Sonia. "Self-Affirmation or Self-Destruction: The Image of Puerto Ricans in Children's Literature Written in English." *Images and Identities: The Puerto Rican in Two World Contexts.* New Jersey: Transactions, Inc., 1987.
Ortiz, Miguel A. "The Politics of Poverty in Young Adult Literature." *The Lion and the Unicorn* 2:2 (1978): 6–15.
Sachs, Marilyn. Review of *Nilda. New York Times Book Review* 4 Nov. 1973: 27–28.
Sutherland, Zena. Rev. of *In Nueva York. Bulletin of the Center for Children's Books* 30:11 (July-August 1977): 178.

WALTER DEAN MYERS
(1937–   )

Simmona Simmons-Hodo

BIOGRAPHY

Presently a resident in New Jersey, Walter Dean Myers was born August 12, 1937, in Martinsburg, West Virginia. His birth parents were George Ambrose and Mary (née Green) Myers. His birth mother died when he was quite young, and he was adopted by Herbert and Florence Dean, whom he considers his "real" parents. The family relocated to Harlem when Myers was about three years old, and it was in Harlem that he grew up.

Reading came early for Myers, when he was only four, and he remembers vividly the scary stories his father told him and the gentler ones from his mother. The young Walter Dean Myers attended integrated schools and, until adolescence, his best friend was a boy of German background. He had a fairly serious speech impediment, but with the help of a sympathetic teacher overcame the problem and at the same time became an avid reader. His teen years were somewhat turbulent, and included run-ins with New York City gangs, experiences that would later be reflected in his young adult fiction.

Although Myers was a bright and talented student, and was enrolled in accelerated programs, he realized college was a financial impossibility. He has also said that in his teen years he became increasingly aware that his options were limited not only by finances, but also by race. His integrated childhood world became more segregated as he grew older: he and his best friend were separated not so much by social class as by race.

From a sense of despair and from misplaced romantic ideas of battle, Myers joined the army in 1954 and served for three years. After his discharge, still unsure of his path in life, he held a variety of jobs, and kept writing until he eventually began to be published in everything from Canadian poetry journals to *The Negro Digest*. In 1970, he became an editor for Bobbs-Merrill (where he signed Nikki Giovanni to a contract), and where he also won a contest for picture book writing for *Where Does the Day Go?*, thus launching his career as a children's writer.

Myers has said that when he was growing up "what I wanted to be was a white European. I spent much of my early writing trying to write white European" (*Children's Literature Review* 135) It was not until he discovered the work of Langston Hughes, who lived in Harlem about a half mile from Myers, that he realized it was possible to create stories based on his own neighborhood and his own people: "When I read Langston Hughes for the first time, that freed me up, and so did James Baldwin's wonderful short stories. Their work said to me you can write about Black life" (Bishop 863).

Always concerned about the lack of role models for African-American children, Myers has made an effort to write novels that are realistic about African-American life, but that also are hopeful.

Myers was the recipient in 1985 of the Coretta Scott King Award for *Motown and Didi* and in 1980 for *The Young Landlords*.

MAJOR WORKS AND THEMES

Myers' works represent and personify characters from his youth in Harlem. Although Myers began by writing picture books, he is perhaps best known as an author of young adult novels focusing on the experiences of African-American teenagers living in Harlem. Myers' protagonists confront the obstacles presented by inner-city life in addition to facing the universal problems of adolescence. An important note is that Myers addresses serious topics such as teen pregnancy, suicide, adoption, and parental neglect in an upbeat and optimistic manner.

Fast Sam, Cool Clyde, and Stuff (1975) was his first young adult novel. Episodic in structure, it follows the stories of the three title characters and five of their friends who call themselves the 11th Street Good People. It is a story of growing up African-American and urban, and while it has poignant moments concerning death and divorce, the novel is warmly humorous. Humorous writing comes easily to Myers, and even the most serious of his works have flashes of humor. *Fast Sam* also introduces some of the themes and qualities for which Myers' novels would gain critical acclaim: the language has urban, black rhythms to it; the characters are realistic; and they find a way to grow up as individuals, but also as part of larger cultural groups.

Mojo and the Russians (1977) is a hilarious account of the doings of Dean, who accidentally runs down Drusilla, a West Indian mojo, or voodoo lady, who then lays a curse on Dean, or "fixes" him. The attempts of Dean and his friends to "unfix" the curse are often quite funny, and the novel includes important information about West-Indian and African culture, as well as humor. Myers has said that the fact that Russians in the New York of his youth were the only outsiders interested in voodoo influenced the writing of this book.

The emphasis on young adults in groups, as well as the emphasis on the humorous side of adolescence, continues in *The Young Landlords* (1979), where a group of teenagers finds itself in possession of a run-down tenement building. They discover the difficulties of being landlords and the strengths of finding themselves in the course of the novel's adventures. Again, the novel was inspired by Myers' own life and by his own attempts to buy a run-down and abandoned New York City apartment building.

It Ain't All for Nothing (1978) is a more serious novel about Tippy, who faces the dilemma of whether or not to turn his ex-convict father in for committing yet another robbery. Tippy's struggle to survive his unstable family situation and the grim realities of street life make for compelling reading. The decision Tippy comes to—he must betray his father in order to save himself—is difficult but necessary. Myers does not present his reader with easy choices and decisions in his novel, nor are there any pat answers or convenient happy endings. This is one of the qualities for which Myers' novels are admired by critics and readers alike.

Hoops (1981) reflects Myers' love for all sports, and especially basketball. But unlike many young adult novels about sports, *Hoops* does not romanticize the game. The novel is filled with the problems of sports gambling and game fixing, and also provides an evocative tale of growing trust and friendship between eighteen-year-old basketball star Lonnie Jackson and his washed-up coach, Cal. Its 1984 sequel, *The Outside Shot*, presents some of the same difficulties of making it honestly in sports (Lonnie now has a basketball scholarship to a predominantly white middle western college), but also provides the reader with Lonnie's difficulties in adjusting to an alien world, as well as his difficulties in romance. Ruth Martin noted in a review that *Hoops* is "hopeful and sensitive—an example of a seventeen-year-old's decision to become an adult black person and not, as Cal says, a 'nigger'" (*Bestsellers* 440). *The Outside Shot* received even more favorable reviews.

Myers draws on his own family background in *Won't Know Till I Get There* (1982), in which an African-American juvenile delinquent is taken into foster care by a middle-class couple. He and his foster siblings get into trouble, and are sentenced to volunteer work at a senior citizens' residence, where the hero bonds with the old people and their fight for independence. Like all of Myers' books, the sharp characterization and vivid, realistic dialogue give the book its distinctive character. Also, like most of Myers' books, *Won't Know Till I Get There* concentrates on an individual coming to terms with himself or herself in the context of a group. These groups can include the family, friends, gangs, other cultural groups such as the senior citizens, but always, for Myers, the group of African-Americans is crucial. How is a teenager to find his or her place both within African-American society and within the larger, dominant white society? This is a question that has preoccupied Myers most of his life, and it pervades all of his young adult fiction.

Crystal (1987) is Myers' only attempt at writing from a female perspective, and the attempt is generally considered to be unsuccessful. This story of a black teenaged model, like Myers' other works, deglamorizes what is often thought of as a glamorous business, but his portrayal of adolescent female sexuality was generally considered to be unconvincing by critics.

Fallen Angels (1988) is a narrative monument to all persons who served in Vietnam. It is a story about Ritchie Perry, a seventeen year old who finished high school but did not participate in graduation. Since Perry cannot afford college, he chooses the army. Perry's dreams of going to college and writing like Baldwin are now delayed. This sensitive and realistic novel gives the reader insight about the war and conditions of the people of Vietnam. Sometimes using raw and graphic language, and some gruesome details, Myers delivers a compelling story.

Motown and Didi (1977) is another opportunity for Myers to portray the struggle of two teenagers, Motown and Didi, in an urban setting. Didi, a high school senior, focuses on finishing high school while Motown sees survival as a priority. The death by heroin of Tony, Didi's brother, causes Motown and Didi to make a promise that they will overcome their surroundings of poverty and crime. The novel provides romance, action, adventure, and drama.

Scorpions (1988) is a portrayal of two teenagers, Jamal and Tito, who struggle to overcome their social conditions. Even though the boys are of different ethnic heritage, they share the same concern about the drugs and violence in their Harlem neighborhood. Jamal must deal with his brother Randy's imprisonment for robbing a delicatessen and the fact that his brother wants him to take over the Scorpions, a street gang. Mack, one of Randy's peers, gives a gun to Jamal, the mere ownership of which causes emotional turmoil and forces them to think about the possible consequences of its presence.

A personal drama begins to unfold in *Somewhere in the Darkness* (1992) when Jimmy meets his father whom he has not seen since he was a baby. His father has escaped from prison, where he has been for nine years. Now critically ill, Jimmy's father, Crab, wishes to establish a relationship with his son. In his determination to reach his son's heart, Crab takes his son on a trip across country. Both Jimmy and Crab realize that Crab does not know how to be a father. With only memories of his father, who dies by the end of the novel, Jimmy returns home to his foster mother, Mama Jean. Again, Myers renders another cast of vivid and realistic characters that grab the reader's heart.

Myers' writing is not limited to young adult fiction. *Malcolm X: By Any Means Necessary* (1993) is a biographical account of the multifaceted character of Malcolm X. The text is a powerful narrative enhanced with pictures as well as copies of historical documents. It provides a chronology of significant events in Malcolm X's life, other events, and a bibliography.

CRITICAL RECEPTION

Walter Dean Myers is considered a keystone figure in contemporary African-American children's literature. He has created more than a score of books in a variety of genres: historical, contemporary realism, and fantasy fiction. One reviewer notes that Harlem, once the mecca for African-American art, literature, music, and politics, is the setting for many of Myers' books. However, Myers does not romanticize Harlem; he takes note of poverty and drug problems, and indeed they are often crucial elements of his stories.

Myers is often praised for his characterizations, for his use of natural dialogue and African-American speech patterns, for his use of timely and realistic issues, and for his attention to detail. Much of this, no doubt, is because Myers has always adhered to the dictum to "write what you know" and mined his own background in Harlem, his own love of sports, and his own troubled adolescence for material. His young adult books provide all readers, but especially African-American male readers, with hopeful protagonists who manage to succeed even in the midst of the violence, drugs, and racism that make up much of urban America today. Rudine Sims, and other critics, has praised Myers' "rendering of the style and essence of Black teenage rhetoric" (quoted in *Children's Literature Review* 137) and goes on to say that Myers' books focus on some of the positive aspects of African-American experience: "the good times, the idea that the love and the support of family, friends, and community, can prop you up. [His works] also emphasize the individual strengths and the rich resources that enable us to cope and to survive" (96).

A master of the pen, Walter Dean Myers is a successful recorder of ethnic voices, a writer who has enlarged his own life and the lives of his readers through his books. His rich-in-spirit characters from Harlem are realistic characters who rise from the printed pages to the readers' hearts.

BIBLIOGRAPHY

Young Adult Fiction by Walter Dean Myers

Fast Sam, Cool Clyde, and Stuff. New York: Viking, 1975.
Mojo and the Russians. New York: Viking, 1977.
Motown and Didi: A Love Story. New York: Viking, 1977.
It Ain't All for Nothing. New York: Viking, 1978.
The Young Landlords. New York: Viking, 1979.
Hoops: A Novel. New York: Delacorte, 1981.
Won't Know Till I Get There. New York: Viking, 1982.
The Outside Shot. New York: Delacorte, 1984.
Crystal. New York: Viking, 1987.
Fallen Angels. New York: Scholastic Inc., 1988.
Scorpions. New York: Harper, 1988.
Somewhere in the Darkness. New York: Scholastic Inc., 1992.

Young Adult Nonfiction by Walter Dean Myers

The World of Work: A Guide to Choosing a Career. New York: Bobbs-Merrill, 1975.
Now Is Your Time! The African-American Struggle for Freedom. New York: HarperCollins, 1992.
Sweet Illusions. Boston: Teachers and Writers Collective, 1992.
Malcolm X: By Any Means Necessary. New York: Scholastic Inc., 1993.

Works for Children by Walter Dean Myers

The Dancers. Illus. Anne Rockwell. New York: Parents Magazine Press, 1969.

Where Does the Day Go? Illus. Leo Carty. New York: Parents Magazine Press, 1969.

The Dragon Takes a Wife. Illus. Ann Grifalconi. Indianapolis: Bobbs-Merrill, 1972.

Fly, Jimmy, Fly! Illus. Moneta Barnett. New York: Putnam, 1974.

Social Welfare. New York: Watts, 1976.

Brainstorm. Photographs by Chuck Freeman. New York: Watts, 1977.

The Black Pearl and the Ghost or One Mystery after Another. New York: Viking, 1980.

The Golden Serpent. Illus. Alice Provensen and Martin Provensen. New York: Viking, 1980.

The Legend of Tarik. New York: Viking, 1981.

The Nicholas Factor. New York: Viking, 1983.

Tales of a Dead King. New York: Morrow, 1983.

Mr. Monkey and the Gotcha Bird. Illus. Leslie Morrill. New York: Delacorte, 1984.

Adventure in Grenada. New York: Penguin, 1985.

The Hidden Shrine. New York: Penguin, 1985.

Ambush in the Amazon. New York: Penguin, 1986.

Duel in the Desert. New York: Penguin, 1986.

Selected Studies of Walter Dean Myers

Bishop, Rudine Sims. *Presenting Walter Dean Myers*. Boston: Twayne, 1991.

————. "Walter Dean Myers." *Language Arts* 67.8 (1990): 862–66.

"Books Can Offer Avenues of Value." *NEA Today* 10.5 (1991): 9.

Hearne, Betsy. Rev. of *Malcolm X: By Any Means Necessary*. *Bulletin of the Center for Children's Books* 46 (Mar. 1993): 222.

Martin, Ruth. Rev. of *Hoops*. *Bestsellers* 41 (Feb. 1982): 440.

Nelms, Beth, Ben Nelms, and Linda Horton. "A Brief but Troubled Season: Problems in Young Adult Fiction." *English Journal* 74.1 (1985): 92–95.

Sutton, Roger. "Threads in Our Cultural Fabric." *School Library Journal* 40.6 (1994): 24–28.

"Walter Dean Myers." *Children's Literature Review*. Ed. Gerard J. Senick. Vol. 16. Detroit: Gale, 1992. 134–40.

Webb, C. Anne. Rev. of *Motown and Didi: A Love Story*. *ALAN Review* 12.2 (1985): 31.

Scott O'Dell
(1898–1989)

Meredith Eliassen

BIOGRAPHY

A descendant of Sir Walter Scott, whose fictional treatment of French and Scottish history in *Tales of a Grandfather* set the precedent for the popularity of the historical novel in nineteenth-century children's literature, Scott O'Dell was born May 23, 1898, in Los Angeles, California. The son of a railroad employee, Mennett Mason, and May Elizabeth (née Gabriel) O'Dell, he said Los Angeles was a frontier town when he was born: "It had more horses than automobiles . . . and more jack rabbits than people. The first sound that I remember was a wildcat scratching on the roof of our house" (O'Dell 1989).

As a child, O'Dell lived all over Southern California: San Pedro; Rattlesnake Island east of Los Angeles; and Julian, an old gold-mining town on the Mexican border in the heart of the Oriflamme Mountains, the ancestral home of the Diegueno Indians. Thus, many of the wonderful descriptions of landscapes in O'Dell's works come from his childhood haunts. Southern California was a focal point for his most important works. He wrote of the people and the cultures inhabiting these areas, such as Native Americans, Spaniards, and Chicanos in a land he described as "sagebrush country where descendants of the first Spanish settlers lived" (O'Dell 1989).

O'Dell had a scattered education, perhaps affecting his research methods. He graduated from Polytechnic High School in Long Beach, California. He then attended Occidental College (1919), University of Wisconsin (1920), Stanford University (1920–1921), and University of Rome (1925), but did not take a degree. Although his works are all well constructed, sometimes his lack of research (heavy reliance upon secondary sources) has given critics room to question some of the images of cultures portrayed in his writings.

Although O'Dell's first novel, *Woman of Spain*, was published in 1934, he did not start writing for children and young adults until he was in his late fifties. Then his first work for children, *Island of the Blue Dolphins* (1960), received almost instant acclaim, establishing him as a master writer of historical fiction for young adults. Although he began thinking about the story of Karana in the 1920s when he read an account of her life in an 1892 issue of *Harper's Magazine*, it took him almost forty years to resolve the concerns that were at the heart of this wonderful story (O'Dell, *Visit*).

O'Dell wrote:

Island of the Blue Dolphins began in anger, anger at the hunters who invade the mountains where I live and who slaughter everything that creeps or walks or flies. This anger was also directed at myself, at the young man of many years ago, who thoughtlessly committed the same crimes against nature. (O'Dell, "David, an Adventure")

Island of the Blue Dolphins was based upon the true story of an Indian girl who lived alone on a California island for eighteen years. O'Dell used his childhood memories of years at San Pedro and Dead Man's Island as the backdrop for descriptive narratives. Although many of his later works dealt with American, European, or Latin-American cultures, *Island of the Blue Dolphins*, pivotal to his career, illustrates his most successful use of Native American themes in young adult literature. Likewise, a character in a later novel, *Sarah Bishop* (1980), was modeled on a historic figure who touched O'Dell's world. Sarah Bishop was an actual girl who fled New York during the American Revolution, in the midst of the battle for the city, and found refuge in a cave on Long Pond in northern Westchester County. The hillside cave that she lived in was actually visible from O'Dell's residence in New York State, and children who had read the book could visit the location in the spring and summer.

Because of his avid interest in history, many of O'Dell's story ideas came from factual cultural study. His first nonfiction book was published when he was twenty-five years old. His pattern for writing books was to study the subject for two or three months and then to spend six months writing. He said that research was his favorite part of writing: "I often write of events, people, and backgrounds that I know little about, just because I want to know more."

In life, as in his writing, one could see him trying to come to terms with a rapidly changing world. Born when women did not have the vote, he discovered that women's issues and rights would play an important role in his writing. O'Dell worked as a journalist, a farmer, and he served in the United States Air Force and Army during World War II. He was a book columnist for the *Los Angeles Times* and book editor for the *Los Angeles Daily News*. He worked as a cameraman and technical director for Paramount Studios, where he worked on several Gloria Swanson films, the original *Ben Hur*, and *The Sheik* with Rudolph Valentino.

He died October 15, 1989, in Mount Kisco, New York, of prostate cancer, two weeks before his last book, *My Name Is Not Angelica,* was published. Matilda Welter, O'Dell's editor at Houghton Mifflin, said that he had been working on a novel with a Native American theme [working title: *Thunder Rolling in the Mountains*], but he had put it aside to write *My Name Is Not Angelica*, the story of an eighteenth-century slave revolt in the West Indies, as described by the daughter of a Senegalese subchief who is captured and sold to a Danish slaver. The story centers on Riasha's life choices when confronted with enslavement, cultural differences, and cultural loyalties (McDowell 1989).

In 1981 the Scott O'Dell Award for Historical Fiction was established, as an annual award for works of historical fiction set in the New World and written in English by a citizen of the United States. Although his most famous work was undoubtedly *Island of the Blue Dolphins*, he was not afraid to tackle diverse subjects and issues, such as families in crisis, slavery, religion, greed, displacement, war, runaway children, drug addiction, and others by applying these themes in different cultural settings.

MAJOR WORKS AND THEMES

Many of O'Dell's most effective themes deal with what can happen when a person is separated from normal companionship. In *Island of the Blue Dolphins* (1961) Karana befriends a dog that was once her enemy; in *Sarah Bishop* (1980) the heroine befriends a white bat which people from Sarah's community considered to be a witch's familiar; in *The Spanish Smile* (1982) Lucinda retreats into the fantasy worlds of Jane Austen and other pre-twentieth-century writers. These characters use animals or imagination to fill voids and gain strength to cope with reality.

According to O'Dell, his favorite themes were reverence for all life and forgiveness for human error (O'Dell, *Visit*). His young adult audience achieves emotional maturity through insight. The significance of *Island of the Blue Dolphins,* even more important than its Native American perspective, is an insight into the issue of a person dealing with being alone in the world—being an island.

Island of the Blue Dolphins is a straightforward portrait of a Native American girl who is a well-rounded individual, not a person doomed by any system, as in traditional views of Indians favored by white writers, but rather one who takes control of her life. The story of Karana was based upon a historical incident, "The Lost Woman of San Nicolas." It is a touching triumph of the human spirit faced with the despair that comes with tragic loss or desertion. Karana, an Indian girl, is unintentionally left behind on a Pacific Coast island when her tribe is evacuated from its island home. For eighteen years, Karana lives a female Robinson Crusoe existence. When her hopes for rescue dim, Karana makes do with her life alone and manages to survive the elements. Year after year she keeps herself alive with a commitment to survive—building shelters, finding food, and warding off wild dogs, which had killed her younger brother.

O'Dell uses deceptively simple prose to convey ideas which are complex, requiring emotional input from the reader. His skillful use of first-person narration along with historical settings, objectivity, and sensitivity in this work has given it universal and timeless appeal. O'Dell carefully maintains the first-person point of view: Karana does not pretend to know what is in the minds of others, but can only draw conclusions about others by their actions. Had O'Dell violated this first-person point of view, the reader might have lost concentration on Karana, and the story would have seemed less real and less credible. The use of first-person narration evokes the immediacy of experience. Because her thoughts are interesting to the reader, Karana is endearing. Having spent her entire life on a remote island, she is consistent and credible in her limited knowledge of the world. Karana is never demeaned by sentimentality or condescension. "Karana's story is a convincing one of survival in an adventurous setting that will appeal to adolescents and preadolescents who spurn romantic teenage stories, and to girls seeking identity and a feeling of independence" (Lass-Woodfin).

O'Dell also develops nature into a complex and real antagonist. Human relationships with and reliance upon animals are major themes in many of O'Dell's works. In *Sarah Bishop* the wilderness becomes Sarah's refuge and path to freedom, as she tries to escape the ravages of the War of Independence. *Black Star, Bright Dawn* (1988) tells the adventures of Bright

Dawn as she takes her place in the Iditarod, the challenging dog sled race that covers over a thousand miles between Anchorage and Nome, Alaska. Bright Dawn, an Eskimo girl, and Black Star, her dog—part husky and part wolf—work together to finish the race. It is more than an adventure story, it is a moral tale where Bright Dawn's character and trust for an animal reward her with knowledge and empowerment. But nowhere is this concept developed more effectively than in *Island of the Blue Dolphins*:

First of all Karana's people have always lived with nature using its bounty, conserving its offerings, and preparing for its dangers. However, when Karana is left alone, her isolation forces her to violate the taboos accepted by the tribe. Karana must make weapons to defend herself against nature, and fears that the spirits will punish her. She has to build a shelter, fight infection from an injury, fight the element of sea and earth, all of this building up to an earthquake and tidal wave. (Lukens)

O'Dell's descriptive first-person narratives often read like film shot sheets, which proved to be a highly successful technique for reaching readers in a media hungry society. Through his words, the reader sees and hears the setting and can sense its effect upon the characters and the conflict. O'Dell's style changes, yet his literary tone and rhythm remain the same. His formal and restrained language and simple sentence structure are suited to the setting, conflict, and character in *Island of the Blue Dolphins*, and he uses comparisons to nature throughout the story— whereas, in his second book, *The King's Fifth* (1966), the language is "brisk and active" (Lukens).

The underlying story of *The King's Fifth* is based on a treasure hunt. The hero of the story, Estaban de Sandoval, a Spanish cartographer, becomes part of a small band of explorers led by a daring and unscrupulous adventurer, Captain Mendoza. As they set off in search of new lands and gold, the party includes a young Indian girl, who serves as interpreter and guide, a padre, whose primary concern is saving souls, and some of Mendoza's henchmen. *The King's Fifth* is a searching tale of moral and physical exploration. The padre's hatred of the gold, and the toll on human life it was taking, is juxtaposed to the young Indian girl's unchanging nature. Gold and greed are sinister, and love for the girl's pure spirit becomes an additional issue in the young hero's choice in dealing with his moral dilemma.

Zia (1976), the continuation of *Island of the Blue Dolphins*, is the story of a young California Indian girl who is caught between two worlds—that of her mother's tribal past and the restrictive world of the Santa Barbara mission—and the drama of a young girl's struggle to reconcile the demands of two cultures. This is the sequel to *Island of the Blue Dolphins* and continues Karana's story after she leaves the Island of the Blue Dolphins. The focus of the story is Zia's determination to find her dead mother's sister, Karana. Zia and her brother, Mondo, find a boat cast upon the beach near their home at the mission at Santa Barbara (where the real Karana is buried). They repair the boat and attempt to rescue Karana from San Nicolas Island, but the journey is too treacherous: weather, distance, whalers, and shipwrecks interfere. Karana is eventually rescued by an old sea captain hunting otter and is brought to the mission. On the mainland she is isolated by language barriers. She finds life at the mission too confining, and discovers a cave on the beach and makes it into a home with her dog Ronto-Aru.

Zia and *Island of the Blue Dolphins* are two very different works. Karana is a real protagonist, whereas Zia has a self-contained strength, and her story is one of loyalty to her tribe and of betrayal by whites. Like many American teenage novels, Zia's story is a compilation of seemingly random moments, dealing with diverse lifestyles and cultures, which add up to a person's life. No one is wholly good or bad. When Karana falls ill, Zia tries to nurse her aunt and seeks help from the mission, but the padres refuse to assist unless Karana returns to the mission. Refusing to return to mission life, Karana dies, but her gifts of love and freedom have a great impact on her niece. After Karana's death, Zia leaves the mission to return to her home with the Pala Indians. "I like you but this is not my home," she tells the padre as she leaves the mission once and for all.

Sing Down the Moon (1970) deals with the issue of being uprooted from a home—in 1864 the U.S. Government forced the Navajo people of Arizona to migrate on the "Long Walk" to Bosque Redondo, New Mexico. The book tells the tragic story of the Long Walk from the viewpoint of Bright Morning, a fourteen-year-old girl. It depicts an attempt to break a centuries-old culture with the destruction of land and food supplies. With both simplicity and intensity, O'Dell depicts the grim story of how a Native American family of proud and independent people is reduced to accepting handouts. Bright Morning's story could easily have been expanded. Perhaps the strength of the story is that Bright Morning and, later, her husband possess inner strength and hope which enable them to escape the consequences of being sold into slavery and the degradation of being forced from their homes, when they begin a new life with their child. Like O'Dell's last work, *My Name Is Not Angelica* (1989), consideration for the next generation becomes a deciding aspect of the choices of the main character.

CRITICAL RECEPTION

"Deceptively simple story," "quietly told," "low-keyed, powerful writing": these phrases come up frequently when critics describe O'Dell's craftsmanship. Like all good writers, O'Dell has had his share of failures, but all of his work is consistent in establishing a moral tone and passing on messages on ecology, involving either nature or human elements, or in looking at our own cultural myths.

One cannot view Scott O'Dell's literature for young adults without taking a long look at his seminal contribution of *Island of the Blue Dolphins*. This work is important not only because it is an effective story, but because it also opened the way for children to discover important themes in Native American literature such as bravery of women, the search for self, the sacredness of nature, and the spirituality of life. O'Dell's stories cause the reader to ponder the effects that people have on one another. "Children don't relate to names of battles, dates of treaties, to statistics. Like us they relate to individuals, to emotions they can feel within themselves, to stories that arouse their curiosity" (O'Dell).

For children in California and across America, Karana was not a distant character created by a white man; she was someone real, someone who dealt with survival. What made *Island of the Blue Dolphins* more poignant was the release of the adult book, *Ishi in Two Worlds: A Biography of the Last Wild Indian in North America*, by Theodora Kroeber in 1961. These two books created a profound statement that Indians in California were being lost. In 1964, Kroeber published *Ishi: Last of His Tribe*, a nonfiction book for a young adult audience. Ishi (186?–1916) was a member of the Yana tribe, which had inhabited the western foothills of Mount Lassen in Northern California for three or four thousand years, until the California gold rush brought the first Europeans to Yana country about twelve years before his birth. After being discovered, Ishi lived long enough to leave a record of the Yana culture; the book was an attempt to look back at Ishi's life, the Yani way of life, and the world of the white man as seen through Native American eyes.

It is important to acknowledge the role of literature in shaping the lives of young adults. Books like *Ishi: Last of His Tribe* and *Island of the Blue Dolphins* emerged at a critical time. These books introduced Native American culture to readers aged ten and up between 1960 and 1965; then, by the time these children reached college age, the colleges were ripe for reform. In 1968–1969 students in universities across the country began to fight for the inclusion of Native American, African-American, La Raza, and Asian studies into the curriculum and by the early 1970s, many colleges had added ethnic studies programs.

Scott O'Dell made his reputation as a master storyteller using historical fiction to express timeless truths. *Island of the Blue Dolphins* was O'Dell's first children's book, it established his place as one of the foremost writers of historical fiction for young adults, and is considered one of the most popular children's books of all time. It is ironic that this, an author's first major work for young adults, is considered to be his best, but *The King's Fifth*, *Sing Down the Moon*, *The Hawk That Dare Not Hunt by Day*, *Sarah Bishop*, and *Black Star, Bright Dawn* are also important because they depict the possibilities for moral courage, resourcefulness, and fortitude that are present in young adults from all cultures.

In discussing multicultural literature for young adults, we often make the ethnic heritage of the author a determining element in how the literature is evaluated. Scott O'Dell was a white man who wrote about many cultures. Arguably, some of his works contain stereotypical images, but how these images come together in an entire body of work reveals much about the man and the kind of moral education that he was trying to communicate.

Feminists on Children's Media recommended *Island of the Blue Dolphins* for being a "non-sexist book about girls for young readers." Many of O'Dell's stories contain traumas, which the protagonist must overcome. The character's limitations are converted into strengths. O'Dell has a gift for assuming a feminine identity in situations that would perhaps be considered masculine in scope. Another critic pointed out that "the intricacies of daily life when one must provide for all one's needs without help are intriguing, the understated beauty of this exceptional story is awesome" (Bernstein 1983). "He has not subjected his readers to stereotypes that have been common especially in books written before the mid-1970's. Instead, his females are respected as individuals, active participants with characteristics suitable to their roles" (Thompson).

O'Dell's work using other cultures has been criticized for dependence upon stereotypes. One authority on juvenile books about Hispanic peoples and cultures said that O'Dell's views on pre-Columbian and Hispanic people and cultures were "extremely limited. It is disturbing to note that his unquestioning talents and popularity continue to promote gross misconceptions of these cultures." Specifically she cites O'Dell's trilogy: *The Captive* (1979), *The Feathered Serpent* (1981), and *The Amethyst Ring* (1983), which is based in part on a pre-Columbian legend (Schon).

O'Dell does not indicate a philosophy of life in his writing, he creates a set of circumstances which force the characters to be themselves. In an article for *Horn Book,* he admitted to using "storyteller's license" for the trilogy:

It is good for children to think that they are unique, as different from one another as are their thumb prints. But it is not good to think that their problems are unique. People before them had problems to solve—many of the same problems, or related ones by which children are now bedeviled. . . . For children, who believe that nothing much has happened before they appeared and that little of the past they do perceive has any possible bearing upon their lives, the historical novel can be an entertaining corrective, a signpost between the fixed, always relevant, and the changing present. (O'Dell 1982).

It is easy to look at only the cultural messages in literature and to forget the author's message which is placed within the cultural setting. Schon states, "The characters and plot of *The Spanish Smile* are unbelievably absurd; the references to Spanish civilization are patronizing at best; the literary and historical citations are pedantic and unnecessary; and the melodramatic setting is not what one would expect from a master story-teller."

This story, even to the youngest reader, is unmistakably fantasy—gothic literature taken to its limits—with the island castle with a mysterious crypt guarded by deadly serpents. Within this outlandish framework lies a very strong statement about our society and a warning to young adults. The sheltered heroine, Lucinda, imprisoned by her father's inability to get beyond his culture and deranged views of the world, is not allowed access to radio, television, newspapers, or even books written in the twentieth century. It takes much of the plot for Lucinda to comprehend the depth of her father's madness and to begin to assert herself. The book asks the reader to look at her own views of who she is, and where she comes from, and the book refers to a number of local incidents where people were brainwashed by real "Don Enriques." Pre-twentieth-century fiction is juxtaposed to some harsh realities of twentieth-century life, warning the reader to be aware of cultural biases that are inherent in all cultures.

As a reader experiences O'Dell's work, the most important issue is the significance of character and how young adults interact with these characters. If personal meaning is tied to values embodied in the significant people who have touched our lives—people who may include our parents, siblings, friends, and heroes—then we should be considered lucky. Many young adults in America, of all cultural and socioeconomic groups, are not so lucky; they may face broken families or communities, or they may come from cultures outside of "mainstream America." For these children, literature may offer viable solutions and role models, where significant persons need not be contemporary or historical. Scott O'Dell's Karana, Sarah Bishop, and Estaban de Sandoval may be more significant in helping young people to shape the visions and values in their lives than many of their friends and relations. Thus, the stories that we love may not always be based upon the criterion of "what really happened."

Although O'Dell wrote about many cultures, his works dealing with Native American themes were the most popular books with young adult audiences. Indeed, many adults find themselves re-reading these classics and enjoying them more, because they read them with adult perceptions and understanding. If Native American literature, religion, and culture can pass anything on to young adults, it is the concept of the circle—healing and harmony with nature. Scott O'Dell made these ideas available to a diverse group of receptive young adults. Like his Karana, O'Dell's world was limited by time and circumstances, but he, too, was able to transcend his world through literature.

BIBLIOGRAPHY

Young Adult Fiction by Scott O'Dell

Island of the Blue Dolphins. Boston: Houghton Mifflin, 1960. London: Constable, 1961.

The King's Fifth. Illus. Samuel Bryant. Boston: Houghton Mifflin, 1966. London: Constable, 1967.

The Black Pearl. Illus. Milton Johnson. Boston: Houghton Mifflin, 1967. London: Longman, 1968.

The Dark Canoe. Illus. Milton Johnson. Boston: Houghton Mifflin; London: Longman, 1968.

Journey to Jericho. Illus. Leonard Weisgard. Boston: Houghton Mifflin, 1969.

Sing Down the Moon. Boston: Houghton Mifflin, 1970. London: Hamish Hamilton, 1972.

The Treasure of Topo-el-Bampo. Illus. Lynd Ward. Boston: Houghton Mifflin, 1972.

Child of Fire. Boston: Houghton Mifflin, 1974.

The Hawk That Dare Not Hunt by Day. Boston: Houghton Mifflin, 1975.

The 290. Boston: Houghton Mifflin, 1976. London: OUP, 1977.

Zia. Illus. Ted Lewin. Boston: Houghton Mifflin, 1976. London: OUP, 1977.

Carlota. Boston: Houghton Mifflin, 1977. Rpt. as *The Daughter of Don Saturnino.* London: OUP, 1979.

Kathleen, Please Come Home. Boston: Houghton Mifflin, 1978.

The Captive. Boston: Houghton Mifflin, 1979.

Sarah Bishop. Boston: Houghton Mifflin, 1980.
The Feathered Serpent. Boston: Houghton Mifflin, 1981.
The Spanish Smile. Boston: Houghton Mifflin, 1982.
The Amethyst Ring. Boston: Houghton Mifflin, 1983.
The Castle in the Sea. Boston: Houghton Mifflin, 1983.
Alexandra. Boston: Houghton Mifflin, 1984.
The Road to Damietta. Boston: Houghton Mifflin, 1985.
Streams to the River, River to the Sea. Boston: Houghton Mifflin, 1986.
The Serpent Never Sleeps: A Novel of Jamestown and Pocahontas. Boston: Houghton Mifflin, 1987.
Black Star, Bright Dawn. Boston: Houghton Mifflin, 1988.
My Name Is Not Angelica. Boston: Houghton Mifflin, 1989.
Thunder Rolling in the Mountains. Work in progress at the time of his death.

Other Works by Scott O'Dell

"Representative Photo-Plays Analyzed by Scott O'Dell." Hollywood: Palmer Institute of Authorship, 1924.
Woman of Spain: A Story of Old California. Boston: Houghton Mifflin, 1934.
Hill of the Hawk. Indianapolis: Bobbs-Merrill, 1947.
Man Alone. With William Doyle. Indianapolis: Bobbs-Merrill, 1953.
Country of the Sun: Southern California, an Informal History and Guide. New York: Crowell, 1957.
The Sea Is Red: A Novel. New York: Holt, 1958.
The Psychology of Children's Art. With Rheda Kellogg. San Diego: Communications Research Machines, 1967.
The Cruise of the Arctic Star. Illus. Samuel Bryant. Boston: Houghton Mifflin, 1973.

Selected Studies of Scott O'Dell

Bernstein, Joanne E. *Books to Help Children Cope with Separation and Loss.* New York: Bowker, 1983.
Feminists on Children's Media. *Little Miss Muffet Fights Back: Recommended Non-Sexist Books about Girls for Young Readers.* New York: Feminists on the Media, 1971.
Lass-Woodfin, Mary Jo. *Books on American Indians and Eskimos: A Selection Guide for Children and Young Adults.* Chicago: American Library Association, 1978.
Lukens, Rebecca J. *A Critical Handbook of Children's Literature.* Glenview, IL: Scott, Foresman and Company, 1976.
McDowell, Edwin. "Scott O'Dell, a Children's Author of Historical Fiction, Dies at 91." *New York Times* 17 Oct. 1989: B8.

O'Dell, Scott. "Acceptance Speech: Hans Christian Andersen Award." *Horn Book* 48.5 (1972): 441–43.

————. "David, an Adventure with Memory and Words." *Psychology Today* 1 (Jan. 1968): 40–43.

————. "Newbery Award Acceptance." *Newbery and Caldecott Medal Books: 1956–1965.* Ed. Lee Kingman. Boston: Horn Book Inc., 1965. 99–104.

————. "The Tribulations of a Trilogy." *Horn Book* 58.2 (Apr. 1982): 137–44.

————. *A Visit with Scott O'Dell: Houghton Mifflin Author and Artist Series.* Video. Boston: Houghton Mifflin, 1983.

Schon, Isabel. "A Master Storyteller and His Distortions of Pre-Columbian and Hispanic Cultures." *Journal of Reading* 29.4 (1986): 322–25.

"Scott O'Dell, Children's Author, Dies." *Washington Post* 18 Oct. 1989: D8.

Thompson, Sally Anne M. "Scott O'Dell—Weaver of Stories." *Catholic Library World* 49.8 (1978): 340–42.

C(YRIL) EVERARD PALMER
(1930–   )

Lesli J. Favor

BIOGRAPHY

Cyril Everard Palmer was born October 15, 1930, in Kendal, Jamaica, to Cyril and Vida Palmer, farmers. He grew up in Kendal, a small subsistence farming community about 130 miles from Kingston. Much like the boys he would later create in fiction, Palmer swam and fished in rivers, cared for farm animals, traveled by donkey, and played among the lush, tropical trees and foliage of the hill country. Although his village was poor economically, Palmer's community was rich in spirit, and its people exercised a sense of humor and a spirit of fun.

Fascinated with westerns, Palmer began writing adventure stories as a young boy. While in college, he published a story in the school magazine and a number of short stories in Jamaica's *Sunday Gleaner*. He also worked for a time as a trainee journalist for the *Daily Gleaner*, covering the crime beat in Kingston. In 1955, he earned a teaching diploma from Mico Training College.

Meanwhile, Jamaica's Ministry of Education advertised for books written for Jamaican children by natives of the island, and Palmer responded. He subsequently published his first two books for young people, *The Adventures of Jimmy Maxwell* (1962) and *A Taste of Danger* (1963). These books attracted the interest of Andre Deutsch of London, who requested "realistic" books from him, and Palmer established a lasting publishing career in books for children. About his realistic children's fiction he has written, "These books are intended to revive for adults fast-disappearing or totally extinct aspects of Jamaican life and for children creating them because they have missed them." Palmer has been awarded a Certificate of Merit from the Jamaica Reading Association for his contribution to Jamaican children's literature.

Palmer moved to Canada, and in 1973, he completed a B.A. at Lakehead University in Thunder Bay, Ontario. He has continued to write novels for young adults, and since 1971, he has worked as a teacher in Red Rock, Ontario. He currently resides in Ontario.

MAJOR WORKS AND THEMES

While Palmer has written short stories, newspaper articles, and a novel for adults (*A Broken Vessel*), the majority of his work is for young people. Except for the two Houdini stories which take place in northern Canada, the books are set in Kendal, Jamaica. The lively stories of boys' adventures are rich in details of West Indian life in the small farming community, and towns and villages which characters travel to or from are actual locales in Jamaica. Palmer's fiction is rooted in reality, and while Jamaican readers are likely to relish the familiar towns, landscapes, colloquialisms, and foods, non-native readers will enjoy the carefully detailed and authentic presentations of the daily lives of West Indian islanders.

Palmer's protagonists are adventurous boys who resemble young people in any land, protecting beloved pets, running away from home to find adventure, helping manage the family farm in a pinch, and surviving natural disasters such as hurricanes and forest fires. Survival is a recurring theme in Palmer's work and serves as narrative framework in *The Cloud with the Silver Lining* (1966). Timmy and his older brother, Milton, who set their minds to managing the house and farm when their grandfather has a leg amputated, eventually earn enough money to open The Cloud, a booth selling curried goat and other savory Jamaican specialties. *Big Doc Bitteroot* (1968) is the story of a quack doctor who comes to Kendal, luring poor villagers to buy a wonder tonic and "medical" services they cannot afford. The plot culminates in a raging, tropical hurricane that causes community members to pull together to survive the crisis. In the calm after the storm, Doc begins to mend his con-artist ways. *The Sun Salutes You* (1970) is about twenty-one-year-old Mike Johnson who returns to Kendal after a five-year absence, intent on earning a living hauling sugar cane. When he discovers that a scheming Matt Southern has seized control of the haulage business and intimidates the townspeople, Mike stands up to the bully in a confrontation that culminates in a trial for arson.

In two books for younger children, Palmer provides warm tales of friendship and of the bond between boys and their pets. In *A Cow Called Boy* (1972), Josh Mahon's best friend is Boy, a pet calf that thinks it is a boy. When Boy follows Josh to school and causes upheaval by clattering into the building, Josh is forced to sell his pet. Soon, with the help of his classmates, the determined youngster uses his wits and ingenuity to win Boy back. In *Baba and Mr. Big* (1972), Jim Anderson seeks membership in a secret club by capturing a chicken-stealing hawk. He also befriends Baba, a lonely old man who helps him catch and tame the bird, which they name Mr. Big. When members of the town decide to kill Mr. Big, Jim protects his new-found pet by exposing the boys of the secret club as the true chicken stealers.

Many of Palmer's books portray nontraditional family structures of the kind with which young readers are likely to be familiar. *A Cow Called Boy* centers on a boy who lives with his widowed mother, and *The Wooing of Beppo Tate* (1972) and its sequel *Beppo Tate and Roy Penner, the Runaway Marriage Brokers* (1980) center on boys who live with foster parents. In *My Father, Sun-Sun Johnson* (1974), Rami's parents are divorced, and he lives with his father while his two siblings live with their mother. In a plot exploring interpersonal relationships and Rami's coming of age, Palmer presents a vivid portrait of familial ties that bind. This moving story has been made into a movie by the Learning Corporation of America.

In addition to his books set in lush, tropical Jamaica, Palmer has published two books set in arctic northern Canada. *A Dog Called Houdini* (1978) and its sequel, *Houdini, Come Home* (1981), are tales of a mischievous and endearing stray dog named Houdini, so named because of his persistence in eluding all attempts at his capture. By the end of the first book, he comes to live with Red O'Malley, and in the second book the boy and dog survive a forest fire together. Themes of friendship and survival enrich these books and provide a familiar point of departure from the earlier books set in Jamaica.

CRITICAL RECEPTION

Critics agree that Palmer's fiction colorfully and realistically portrays Jamaican lifestyles, speech, and community, and the amusing stories involving likable boys provide a range of reading levels suitable to skills and interests of all young people, from reluctant readers to children of diverse cultural backgrounds. The cultural and societal diversity portrayed in Palmer's body of fiction provides young readers access to a wider, welcoming, colorful world.

Palmer's spirited and fun-loving characters lead reviewers to compare them to the classic American symbols of boyhood wit and adventure, Tom Sawyer and Huckleberry Finn. In a review of *The Wooing of Beppo Tate* in "Young Readers," Gladys Williams observes that "there's definitely a Mark Twainish atmosphere about these two boys [Beppo and Roy] who learn to use their wits to balance their lack of years and general unimportance" (102). In reviewing *Beppo Tate and Roy Penner, the Runaway Marriage Brokers* for the *Times Educational Supplement*, Prabhu S. Guptara parallels the Jamaican boys with American boys, writing that Beppo and Roy "run away from home, Huckleberry fashion, in an attempt to jolt their families into appreciating them more than they do" (29).

Some critics fault Palmer for creating characters that are too purely good or bad, thereby bordering on the stereotypical. Gladys Williams comments that characters in *The Sun Salutes You* are "a bit cardboard" because of this good/bad division (41), and *Kirkus Reviews* declares that these characters are "simple caricatures" (817). In reviewing *A Cow Called Boy*, Dorothy de Wit judges the characters "flat" (2953), and in reviewing *Houdini, Come Home*, Caroline Wynburne deems the characters "flat and stereotyped" (137). Despite a lack in some books of well-rounded characters with both positive and negative traits, Palmer's characters are more often praised as colorful, entertaining, strong, and memorable.

Occasionally, reviewers remark that one of Palmer's characters is annoyingly old beyond his or her years. In "More Novels for over Tens," the *Times Literary Supplement* reports that "Beppo's head is unconvincingly old for his eleven-year-old shoulders," and in the *Library Journal*, Merrilee Anderson declares that Misty of *Big Doc Bitteroot* is "an irritating, cheeky know-it-all" who speaks "in unbelievable vocabulary." Other critics view such maturity and advanced use of language as more instructional and zestful than objectionable.

Palmer's books receive commendations for their authentic and vividly detailed portrayals of daily life in the West Indies, from the World War II era to more modern times. In *Punch*, Jane Hollowood lauds the energetic dialogue, which is "spiced with Jamaican expressions and wit" (347), and in *Bestsellers* Mrs. John G. Gray extols Palmer's prose style, which produces "an island aura—a patchwork of colloquialisms, customs, and values" (278). Finally, Marcus Crouch applauds Palmer because the author "is not ashamed to find high spirits and fun among the under-privileged of

Jamaica" (54). Overall, Palmer is an estimable writer of multicultural fiction for young people.

BIBLIOGRAPHY

Young Adult Fiction by C(yril) Everard Palmer

The Adventures of Jimmy Maxwell. Illus. Barrington Watson. Jamaica Publications Branch, Ministry of Education, 1962; 1976.
A Taste of Danger. Illus. Laszlo Acs. Jamaica Publications Branch, Ministry of Education, 1963; 1976.
The Cloud with the Silver Lining. Illus. Laszlo Acs. London: Deutsch, 1966. New York: Pantheon, 1967.
Big Doc Bitteroot. London: Deutsch, 1968. Indianapolis: Bobbs-Merrill, 1971.
The Sun Salutes You. London: Deutsch, 1970. Indianapolis: Bobbs-Merrill, 1971.
The Hummingbird People. London: Deutsch, 1971.
Baba and Mr. Big. Illus. Lorenzo Lynch. Indianapolis: Bobbs-Merrill, 1972. London: Deutsch, 1974.
A Cow Called Boy. Illus. Charles E. Gaines. Indianapolis: Bobbs-Merrill, 1972. London: Deutsch, 1973.
The Wooing of Beppo Tate and *Beppo Tate and Roy Penner, the Runaway Marriage Brokers: Two Stories*. London: Deutsch, 1980. London: Deutsch, 1972.
My Father, Sun-Sun Johnson. London: Deutsch, 1974.
A Dog Called Houdini. Illus. Maurice Wilson. London: Deutsch, 1978.
Houdini, Come Home. Illus. Gavin Rowe. London: Deutsch, 1981.

Works for Adults by C(yril) Everard Palmer

A Broken Wheel. Kingston, Jamaica: Pioneer Press, 1960.

Selected Studies of C(yril) Everard Palmer

Anderson, Merrilee. Rev. of *Big Doc Bitteroot*. *Library Journal* 96 (1971): 1508.
Bell, Robert. Rev. of *A Dog Called Houdini*. *The School Librarian* 27 (1979): 59.
"C. Everard Palmer." *Something about the Author*. Ed. Anne Commire. Vol. 14. Detroit: Gale Research, 1978. 153–55.
Crouch, Marcus. Rev. of *Beppo Tate and Roy Penner: The Runaway Marriage Brokers*. *The School Librarian* 29 (1981): 54+.
Croxson, Mary. "Palmer, C(yril) Everard." *Twentieth-Century Children's Writers*. Ed. Tracy Chevalier. 3rd ed. Chicago: St. James, 1989. 750.
de Wit, Dorothy. Rev. of *A Cow Called Boy*. *Library Journal* 97 (1972): 2953.

Edmonds, May H. Rev. of *The Cloud with the Silver Lining. Library Journal* 92 (1967): 4617.

Gray, Mrs. John G. Rev. of *The Cloud with the Silver Lining. Bestsellers* 3 (15 September 1971): 278.

Guptara, Prabhu S. "Land of Calypso." *Times Educational Supplement* 29 May 1981: 29.

Herdeck, Donald E., et al., eds. *Caribbean Writers: A Bio-Bibliographical-Critical Encyclopedia.* Washington, DC: Three Continents Press, 1979.

Hollowood, Jane. "Small Time." *Punch* (4 September 1968): 347.

Palmer, C. Everard. "Carpenter, Humphrey, and Mari Prichard." *Oxford Companion to Children's Literature.* Oxford: OUP, 1984.

"Palmer, C. Everard." *Contemporary Authors: A Bio-Bibliographical Guide to Authors and Their Works.* Ed. Ann Evory. Vols. 41–44. 1st rev. Detroit: Gale, 1979. 532.

Rev. of *The Sun Salutes You. Kirkus Reviews* 39 (1 August 1971): 817.

Rollock, Barbara, ed. *Black Authors and Illustrators of Children's Books: A Biographical Dictionary.* 2nd ed. New York: Garland, 1992.

Williams, Gladys. Rev. of *The Sun Salutes You. Books and Bookmen* 15.8 (1990): 38, 41.

Wynburne, Caroline. Rev. of *Houdini, Come Home. The School Librarian* 30 (1982): 137.

KATHERINE PATERSON
(1932–)

Joel D. Chaston

BIOGRAPHY

Katherine Paterson, one of the most widely acclaimed contemporary novelists for children and young adults, was born October 31, 1932, in Qing Jiang, China, to George Raymond and Mary Goetchius Womeldorf, Presbyterian missionaries. Growing up in China as the child of American citizens, Paterson often felt isolated and gained an empathy for outsiders in general and an interest in Asian culture, which informs many of her books. During the next few years, Paterson's family moved fifteen times and she attended schools in Virginia, North Carolina, West Virginia, and Tennessee.

Paterson eventually studied at King College in Bristol, Tennessee, where she received an A.B. in English literature. After completing her degree, Paterson taught briefly in an elementary school in Lovettsville, Virginia, and then returned to Richmond, Virginia, where she earned a master's degree from the Presbyterian School for Christian Education. From 1957–1961, she studied at the Naganuma School of Japanese Language in Kobe, Japan, and worked as an assistant to eleven pastors in the area. She completed a second master's degree from Union Theological Seminary where she met John Barstow Paterson, a Presbyterian minister. The Patersons have two sons, John Jr. and David Lord, and two adopted daughters, Elizabeth Po Lin (whose birth parents were Chinese) and Mary Katherine Nah-he-sah-pe-che-a (an Apache Kiowa).

Paterson began her career writing curriculum and other materials for her church. She began her first published novel, *The Sign of the Chrysanthemum* (1973), a historical tale about feudal Japan, in an adult-education class. Her next two novels, *Of Nightingales That Weep* (1974) and *The Master Puppeteer* (1975), also take place in Japan. Her fourth novel, the Newbery Award–winning *Bridge to Terabithia* (1977), which is set in the contemporary United States, was written in response to the death of her son David's best friend. Her other books include *The Great Gilly Hopkins* (1978), about a girl who has spent her life in foster homes; *Angels and Other Strangers* (1979), a collection of Christmas stories; *Jacob Have I Loved* (1980), a study of sibling rivalry; *Rebels of the Heavenly Kingdom* (1983), a historical novel set in China; *Come Sing, Jimmy Jo* (1985), about a boy who is part of a family of country singers; *Park's Quest* (1988), in which a boy searches for clues about his dead father; *Lyddie* (1991), a historical novel about the New England textile mills of the nineteenth century; and *Flip-Flop Girl* (1994), about two contemporary children's responses to their father's death.

Paterson has received many awards, including the National Book Award (*The Master Puppeteer*); the Children's Literature Association Phoenix Award (*Of Nightingales That Weep*); the Newbery Prize (*Bridge to Terabithia* and *Jacob Have I Loved*); the Lewis Carroll Shelf Award and Janusz Korcazk Medal (*Bridge to Terabithia*); and the Christopher Award, National Book Award, and Newbery Honor Award (*The Great Gilly Hopkins*). Paterson and her husband currently live in Barre, Vermont.

MAJOR WORKS AND THEMES

One of the major themes of Katherine Paterson's many award-winning novels is the difficult struggle that children and young adults face as they encounter new schools, towns, and cultures. Paterson, who often felt like a foreigner as she moved from place to place during her childhood, clearly empathizes with characters who feel like outsiders. Although most of the protagonists of her later novels are Caucasians, they often develop friendships with African-American, Asian, and Hispanic children who, in the end, help them overcome their feelings of isolation and begin to solve their problems.

Paterson's first two novels take place in twelfth-century Japan, the third in the eighteenth century. Together they provide important insights into the rich history and culture of Japan, including its art, music, and theater. All three of these books feature noble characters who move beyond their misperceptions and prejudices about others to form new and lasting friendships. In *The Sign of the Chrysanthemum* (1973), thirteen-year-old Muna searches for his warrior father only to come to appreciate the wisdom and abilities of the swordmaker, Fukuji. *Of Nightingales That Weep* (1974) takes place during the Gempeii wars in which two warrior clans, the Heike and the Genji, fight each other for control of the imperial family. In the novel, Takiko, the daughter of a samurai, overcomes her infatuation with the trappings of the royal family and her own notions of nobility, as well as her prejudices against the disfigured potter, Goro, whom she comes to love. *The Master Puppeteer* (1975) is set during another period of Japanese civil unrest, the famine of 1783–1787, and involves young Jiro, who, by becoming an apprentice in *bunraku* (Japanese puppetry) gains personal security, but must confront his feelings about the family he has left behind.

With *Bridge to Terabithia* (1977), Paterson has begun to focus on the United States in the twentieth century, the background for most of her other novels. While *Bridge to Terabithia* does not feature any ethnic characters, its protagonists, Jesse Aarons and Leslie Burke, despite their very different family and social backgrounds, resolve their individual differences to become best friends.

In *The Great Gilly Hopkins* (1978), Paterson more directly addresses the issue of racial prejudice. Galadrial "Gilly" Hopkins has spent her life moving from foster home to foster home and, along the way, has developed a variety of prejudices as a way to protect herself. Gilly is aghast that her newest foster mother, Maime Trotter, has befriended her blind, African-American neighbor, Mr. Randolph. Gilly is further upset when her new schoolteacher, Miss Harris, also turns out to be African-American. Ultimately, Gilly does come to appreciate both Mr. Randolph, who introduces her to the poetry of William Wordsworth, and Miss Harris, who shares her anger toward the world and leads her to the works of J. R. R. Tolkien.

Angels and Other Strangers: Family Christmas Stories (1979) is a collection of nine stories originally written to be read aloud at the yearly Christmas Eve services of Takoma Park church, where Paterson's husband was minister. Several of the stories treat prejudice and isolation. For example, in "Guests," a Japanese minister begins to create a bond with a refugee child from Korea, despite the presence of an intimidating police officer.

Like *Bridge to Terabithia*, Paterson's second Newbery Award–winning novel, *Jacob Have I Loved* (1980), does not directly deal with multicultural issues. However, its protagonist, Sarah Louise Bradshaw, leaves her home on Rass Island and travels to the mountains, overcoming her feelings of loneliness and intense sibling rivalry partly through learning to appreciate a new culture.

The Crane Wife (1981) is the first of three picture books in which Paterson again expresses her affection for Japanese culture, this time through retelling traditional folktales. *The Crane Wife, The Tongue-cut Sparrow* (1987), and *The Tale of the Mandarin Ducks* (1990) are all readable versions of these stories and can provide younger readers with insight into Japanese customs, philosophy, and language. Paterson's most recent picture book, *The King's Equal* (1992), is an original creation, a fairy tale about a mythical kingdom. It grew out of a visit to a book symposium in the former Soviet Union where Paterson met Vladmir Vagin, whose illustrations for this book have a distinctly East European flavor.

Rebels of the Heavenly Kingdom (1983), Paterson's only novel about China, the country where she was born, takes place during the revolt of the Taiping Tienkuo against the corrupt Manchu rulers. It is the story of Wang Lee and Mei Lin, who, caught up in the events of the revolt, eventually find love despite their disparate backgrounds.

In *Come Sing, Jimmy Jo* (1985), Paterson turns again to the United States. In this novel, James Johnson, an Appalachian boy, struggles with the fame and jealousies which accompany the new-found success his family has gained as country music singers. An important minor character is Eleazor Jones, an African-American boy who becomes James' salvation at his new school, serving as his voluntary bodyguard and standing up for him to their teacher, Mr. Dolman, as well as to their classmates.

Paterson's next novel, *Park's Quest* (1988), more directly explores questions of race and personal identity. Parkington Waddell Broughton the Fifth (Park) initially knows very little about his real family background. When he visits his grandfather's estate, he discovers the existence of a half-sister he never knew he had. Thanh, who is half-Vietnamese, is very hostile. The two children eventually begin to feel like they are connected to each other and their ailing grandfather. The book ends with the suggestion that the three of them are on the way to healing their psychological wounds.

Another historical novel, *Lyddie* (1991), grew out of Paterson's participation in the Women's History Project, which was part of Vermont's bicentennial celebration. Like Paterson's earliest works it is well researched, although this time the subject is the textile mills of nineteenth-century New England and the young women who worked there. The protagonist, Lydia Worthen, is, once again, an outsider. As Lyddie travels from her cabin home in rural Vermont to industrial Massachusetts, she develops a thirst for education and an obsession with money and security.

Hurt by various losses in her life, including the deaths of her parents and separation from her brother and sister, Lyddie retreats into factory life, but develops empathy for other outsiders, particularly an educated runaway slave, Ezekiel Abernathy, and a poor Irish immigrant named Brigid, both of whom she helps rescue.

The World in 1492, which Paterson co-authored with Jean Fritz, Patricia and Frederick McKissack, Margaret Mahy, and Jamake Highwater in 1992, tries to help young readers understand the complexity of various cultures which were established long before Columbus arrived in the New World. Paterson's contribution to the book is a well-researched, readable essay on Japanese life in 1492.

Like *Bridge to Terabithia*, Paterson's latest novel, *Flip-Flop Girl* (1994), deals with death and grief. In this case, Vinnie Matthews has moved to the barren town of Brownsville to live with her grandmother as a result of her father's death. Vinnie, who has no friends in her new home, is befriended by Lupe Mahoney, whose mother is Puerto Rican and father is Irish. It is only when both Vinnie and her brother, Mason, who has not spoken since their father's funeral, travel to Vinnie's house, which is situated in the middle of a pumpkin patch, that the two are able to begin the healing process.

CRITICAL RECEPTION

The author of over twenty books, including historical and realistic fiction, short stories, retellings of folktales, and literary criticism, Katherine Paterson has won nearly every award given for American children's and young adult literature. Her work has been widely praised, although there are critics who have questioned the religious themes present in many of her books, some of which they find didactic. Her historical novels set in Japan and China have been praised as detailed, convincing, and suspenseful. Writers such as Anthea Bell have, however, suggested that it "was in turning to the twentieth century that she found her own and original voice" (75).

Many critics have also praised Paterson's sensitive handling of racial prejudice in several of her books. Early reviewers of *The Great Gilly Hopkins* responded well to Gilly's relationships with Miss Harris and Mr. Randolph. An article in *Kirkus Reviews* on *Angels and Other Strangers* noted that many of its stories are about encounters between "comfortable middle-class Protestants" and those who are "poor, black, and/or outcast" and that Paterson "never falsifies the characters on either side or overplays her hand" (1211). Reaction to Paterson's treatment of the half-Vietnamese girl, Thanh, in *Park's Quest* has been more mixed. Jan Susina, in an article discussing several books about Vietnamese-Americans, finds Thanh the least convincing character of those he discusses. Thanh and Park's reconciliation, he argues, comes too quickly and is somewhat forced.

In general, Paterson's creation of sympathetic, mostly believable characters from a variety of cultures, as well as her explorations of Japanese history, are noteworthy. As a whole, her works argue that, in one way or another, everyone is an outsider and that true friendship goes beyond racial and cultural differences.

BIBLIOGRAPHY

Young Adult Fiction by Katherine Paterson

The Sign of the Chrysanthemum. Illus. Peter Landa. New York: Crowell, 1973.
Of Nightingales That Weep. Illus. Haru Wells. New York: Crowell, 1974.
The Master Puppeteer. Illus. Haru Wells. New York: Crowell, 1975.
Bridge to Terabithia. Illus. Donna Diamond. New York: Crowell, 1977. London: Gollancz, 1978.
The Great Gilly Hopkins. New York: Crowell, 1978. London: Gollancz, 1979.
Angels and Other Strangers: Family Christmas Stories. New York: Crowell, 1979. Rpt. as *Star of Night*. London: Gollancz, 1980.
Jacob Have I Loved. New York: Crowell, 1980. London: Gollancz, 1981.
Rebels of the Heavenly Kingdom. New York: Dutton; London: Gollancz, 1983.
Come Sing, Jimmy Jo. New York: Dutton, 1985. London: Gollancz, 1986.
Park's Quest. New York: Dutton, 1988. London: Gollancz, 1989.
Lyddie. New York: Dutton, 1991.
Flip-Flop Girl. New York: Lodestar Books, 1994.

Works for Children by Katherine Paterson

Yagawa, Sumiko. *The Crane Wife*. Trans. Katherine Paterson. New York: Morrow, 1981.
Ishii, Momoko. *The Tongue-cut Sparrow*. Trans. Katherine Paterson. New York: Dutton, 1987.
The Tale of the Mandarin Ducks. New York: Dutton, 1990.
The Smallest Cow in the World. New York: HarperCollins, 1991.
The King's Equal. New York: HarperCollins, 1992.
The World in 1492. With Jean Fritz, Patricia McKissack, Frederick McKissack, Margaret Mahy, and Jamake Highwater. New York: Henry Holt, 1992.
The Big Book of the Planet. Editor with Ann Durrell and Jean Craighead George. New York: Dutton, 1993.

Works for Adults by Katherine Paterson

Gates of Excellence: On Reading and Writing Books for Children. New York: Elsevier/Nelson, 1981.

Consider the Lilies: Plants of the Bible. With John Paterson. New York: Crowell, 1986.

The Spying Heart: More Thoughts on Reading and Writing Books for Children. New York: Dutton, 1989.

Selected Studies of Katherine Paterson

"Angels and Other Strangers." Kirkus Reviews 47.20 (1979): 1211.

Bell, Anthea. "A Case of Commitment." *Signal* 38 (1982): 73–81.

Chaston, Joel D. "Flute Solos and Songs That Make You Shatter: Simple Melodies in *Jacob Have I Loved* and *Come Sing, Jimmy Jo.*" *The Lion and the Unicorn* 16 (1993): 215–22.

———. "The Other Deaths in *Bridge to Terabithia.*" *Children's Literature Association Quarterly* 16 (1991–1992): 238–41.

Huse, Nancy. "Katherine Paterson's Ultimate Realism." *Children's Literature Association Quarterly* 9 (Fall 1984): 99–101.

Kimmel, Eric A. "Trials and Revelations: Katherine Paterson's Heroic Journeys." *The New Advocate* 3 (1990): 235–45.

Namovicz, Gene Inyart. "Katherine Paterson." *Horn Book* 57.4 (1981): 394–99.

Nist, Joan. "Archetypal Strands in Katherine Paterson's Novels of the Orient." Ed. Francelia Butler and Richard Rotert. *Triumphs of the Spirit in Children's Literature.* Hamden, CT: Library Professional Publications, 1986. 25–29.

Paterson, Katherine. "The Aim of the Writer Who Writes for Children." *Theory into Practice* 21.4 (1982): 325–31.

Schmidt, Gary D. *Katherine Paterson.* New York: Twayne, 1994.

Smedman, M. Sarah. "Out of the Depths to Joy: Spirit/Soul in Juvenile Novels." Ed. Francelia Butler and Richard Rotert. *Triumphs of the Spirit in Children's Literature.* Hamden, CT: Library Professional Publications, 1986. 181–97.

———. "The Quest for the Father in the Fiction of Katherine Paterson." *Literature and Hawaii's Children. Imagination: A Bridge to Magic Realms in the Humanities.* Ed. Christina Bacchilega and Steven Curry. Honolulu: Literature and Hawaii's Children, 1990. 30–39.

———. "Springs of Hope: Recovery of Primordial Time in 'Mythic' Novels for Young Readers." *Children's Literature* 16 (1988): 91–107.

Susina, Jan. "'Tell Him about Vietnam': Vietnamese-Americans in Contemporary American Children's Literature." *Children's Literature Association Quarterly* 16.2 (1991): 58–63.

GARY PAULSEN
(1939–)

Teri S. Lesesne

BIOGRAPHY

Born May 17, 1939, in Minneapolis, Minnesota, the son of a career army man, Paulsen was a typical army brat, living in various places during his youth. Because his father was overseas a great deal of the time serving as an officer on General George Patton's staff during World War II, and his mother worked in a munitions factory, Paulsen was reared mostly by his grandmother and aunts, who were to have a tremendous influence on his writing. He lived from the age of seven until he was ten with his parents in the Philippines, where his father was stationed at the time. After the family returned to the United States, they moved around continuously. Paulsen recalls never spending more than a few months in any one school. School, then, became a nightmare for him. His moving around made it nearly impossible to make friends; his grades suffered as a result. He credits a librarian with helping to turn his life around. Taking refuge in a public library led to a lifelong love of reading and books.

Paulsen attended college for a time, leaving to serve a three-year stint in the army. There, he attained the rank of sergeant and worked with missiles. Following his service in the army, he worked as an aerospace engineer. It was then that Paulsen first realized that he was destined to be a writer of more than field reports. Recognizing that he knew next to nothing about writing, he sought experiences which would provide him the education he needed to follow his dreams. He became an associate editor of a men's magazine in California, and from there went on to write screenplays, articles, and novels. It was during this early phase of his career that Paulsen first became interested in the Iditarod, a 1200-mile Alaskan dogsled race. He decided to enter the race on almost a whim and calls the seventeen days of the race a life-changing experience. It was also an experience which was to lead to several works of fiction and nonfiction.

Paulsen writes both for young adults and adult audiences. He is married to his third wife, Ruth Wright, an artist. Her work appears in a few of his more recent works. Paulsen writes because, as he puts it, it is all he can do. He has tried other things (including sculpting, teaching, farming, acting, and singing) but keeps coming back to that which he both loves and hates the most: writing. He writes because he has to. A prolific writer, Paulsen has more than forty books, two hundred magazine articles and short stories, and several plays to his credit. His works have been honored with numerous awards, including Newbery Honor Medals for *Dogsong, Hatchet,* and *The Winter Room.* Many of his books have been named to the Best Books for Young Adults list by the American Library Association Young Adult Library Services Association.

MAJOR WORKS AND THEMES

Most, if not all, of Paulsen's works feature an outdoor setting. Indeed, nature plays a pivotal role in many of his works. Water and woods are forces in his writing. Certainly, this is an environment most familiar to the author, who has run the Alaskan Iditarod race twice, who has an extensive background in hunting and fishing, and who still lives in the wilderness. The outdoors also serves as an appropriate backdrop for the coming-of-age theme inherent to many of Paulsen's stories. Whether the protagonist is a young man setting out to spend some time with his father in the Canadian wilderness, or a street smart Mexican child desperate to cross into the United States, or a young woman whose relationship with an aging Native American occurs mostly within the confines of her dreams, Paulsen presents readers with adolescent characters on the verge of adulthood. Cut off from the rest of civilization, these young men and women strive to assume their rightful places as full members of their communities. Before that can occur, however, each must undergo some test of his or her physical, mental, emotional, and/or spiritual stamina. When they rejoin their respective communities, each will be changed in some significant way.

Though not African-American or Hispanic or Native American, Paulsen frequently uses characters from these ethnic groups as protagonists in his fiction. They serve to underscore another aspect of his work: the outsider, one cut off from society who must find his or her own niche within the community. The use of non-white characters is yet another way in which Paulsen develops the coming-of-age theme; these characters are separated from society by virtue of their ethnicity in some instances. Some of the characters in Paulsen's novels must deal with ambivalent feelings about their ancestry as well. These recurring patterns, themes, and archetypal characters are apparent in much of Paulsen's work for young adult readers.

In *The Night the White Deer Died* (1978), fifteen-year-old Janet lives with her newly divorced mother in a trendy artist commune in New Mexico. There Janet meets an elderly Native American named Peter Honcho. Honcho, once a respected member of the tribe, is now an alcoholic whose only employment is posing for tourists' photographs all decked out in his regalia. At night, Peter visits Janet as the resplendent young man he once was. She is attracted to him, but each realizes that their different backgrounds make a relationship impossible. Peter prepares for his final battle as Janet again has her recurring dream about a white deer shot by a brave. Not only is this a coming-of-age story both for Janet and Peter, but Paulsen spends a great deal of time in this novel dealing with Native American spirituality. The setting in an artist commune, indeed the treatment of real art versus contrived art, is another issue which will surface in later works, most notably *The Monument* (1991). The emphasis on the spiritual quality of Native American life and religion is a theme picked up in *Dogsong* (1985).

Dogsong (1985) is the tale of fourteen-year-old Russell Susskit's crossing from childhood into adulthood. It is a story of initiation. Russell, an Eskimo, refuses to accept the ways of the modern world. Instead, he turns to the old ways of his people. With the assistance of an elder tribesman, Russell learns the songs of his history and embarks on a dogsled journey to find his own voice. During this journey he encounters many tests of his beliefs in tribal lore. The challenges he faces are at first physical. He must learn how to find food and how to seek shelter from the elements. Later, during the trip, Russell's trials are more emotional and mental in nature. He must accept the death of his mentor, Oogruk, and maintain his mental stamina through the hours of endless travel over the snowy terrain.

Though *Dogsong* is a novel of survival, it is more than that. It is the chronicle of one boy's ascension to manhood. Becoming a man for Russell means leaving behind some of the innocence of his childhood and accepting the tragedies of adulthood. It also means finding his own voice, in this case his own song which his dogs will heed and follow. During his long journey, Russell works on his song; he is working ultimately on his identity, something that will make him a unique and valued member of his community. Once again, the emphasis on spirituality is evident as Russell's trip becomes a version of the Native American vision quest. Russell shares a great deal in common, then, with the multitude of characters found in *Sentries* (1986), each of whom must find his or her place within the community.

Sentries (1986) is a collection of short fictions about various characters, almost a short story collection on a common theme. While the characters in these short pieces do not know one another, there is a common bond which they all share to some extent. Each of these men and women is facing a battle; some battles are frighteningly real while others are more metaphorical. Divided into peacetime chapters and four wartime chapters entitled "Battle Hymns," the protagonists must make choices and face their consequences. This is yet another of the recurring themes in Paulsen's works for the adolescent reader: one must learn to accept the consequences of the choices one makes. Sue must choose between the white way and her Ojibway heritage. David Garcia, a Mexican migrant worker, decides to join a group of his fellow workers. A young sheep rancher named Laura tries to prove that she is as much a part of the family business as any son could be, while Peter breaks with tradition to make his own kind of music.

Interwoven between the chapters which tell the stories of these four are the hymns which are set in Vietnam, Korea, World War II Germany, and at the precipice of World War III. Each of these hymns serves as a reminder of the tenuous nature of life and the constant threat of wartime's devastation. Paulsen's reminder of the effects of war on the innocent victims of conflict is what ties the disparate stories of *Sentries* into a unified whole. It is also evidence of another important theme in Paulsen's writings: war dehumanizes us all. To put it tritely, war is hell. The men and women who are involved in war suffer not only from the physical dangers of battle, they are left emotionally wounded as well. The scars of wartime experiences do not ever seem to heal for many of the characters in Paulsen's novels. Certainly, this is apparent for one of the main characters in *The Crossing* (1987).

Set in a Mexican border town, *The Crossing* (1987) is a dual narrative which relates the story of a young orphan who survives on the edge of society and an army sergeant whose drunken escapades serve to suppress his harsh memories of Vietnam. Manny, the young orphan, needs to cross from Mexico to the United States if he is to survive, becoming the victim of the "chicken hawks," older gangs of boys who prey on those who are more helpless than they. Manny meets up with Robert on three separate occasions. The first meeting is an auspicious one: Manny attempts to pick the pocket of the drunken soldier and perhaps use the money to purchase his safe passage across the border by bribing the officials. Robert allows Manny to go free, perhaps seeing more than a little of himself in this young boy who so desperately needs his freedom. Later, the two spend the day together, and, finally, they meet on the border itself where Robert offers himself as a sacrifice for Manny's freedom.

Manny must cross the physical and social borders which separate him from his goal; the emotional and mental borders are just as difficult to surmount. Haunted by the memories of his duties in Vietnam, Robert is too numb to act. He cannot change his life. Instead, he must obliterate the memories as best he can, with alcohol. For several characters, alcohol is a crutch used to cope with the tragedies of the past. The alcoholic characters in Paulsen's works function well on one level: they are employed, they can meet the obligations of day-to-day life. Their alcoholism seems almost apportioned to one time and place. They are not stumbling and incoherent drunks; they are people who use alcohol to forget. Even alcohol, however, cannot completely eradicate the horrors Robert suffered. Perhaps his sacrifice of self is his atonement for the atrocities of war. The emotional and mental tests which characters must undergo are pervasive in several of Paulsen's works which follow *Sentries*—such as *Hatchet* (1987), *The Island* (1988), and *Canyons* (1990).

The protagonist of *Canyons* (1990), fifteen-year-old Brennan Cole, finds a skull beneath his sleeping bag on a campout. The bullet hole in the middle of the skull compels Brennan to discover the identity of the owner and to return the skull to its rightful resting place. Brennan is certain that the skull is that of a young Native American boy, perhaps one of the Apache Nation who roamed this canyon many years ago. He is mystically connected to the young Apache warrior and vows to prevent the authorities from taking possession of the skull. Brennan is committed to helping this young brave reach a fitting burial ground.

Once again, the powerful spirituality of the Native American population is an important facet of the story. When Brennan picks up the skull, he instantly feels connected to the past. The skull brings him to a spiritual state; holding it in his hands is enough to evoke powerful emotions. As in the case of *Sentries,* Paulsen employs a dual narrative in this novel. One voice is that of Brennan, the other that of the young warrior whose death was the untimely result of the wars between his tribe and the white man, who wished to own and settle the land. This stylistic device allows readers to gain insight into the lives of both young men and to see how their journeys are parallel. Brennan struggles as he races to find an honorable grave for the skull as the young warrior once struggled to find his destiny as a brave, a goal not achieved due to the interference of "civilization."

The concept that civilized man attempts to turn nature and the course of humanity to suit his purpose despite the dire consequences of such action is another theme explored by Paulsen. Certainly, this is not a new theme. Many writers of the eighteenth and nineteenth centuries, such as Daniel Defoe, wrote about the "noble savage." Rousseau posited that when man is one with nature, he is pure; it is society that corrupts. Brennan and many other characters created by Paulsen are evidence of this corrupting influence of society. Civilized man's conceit is that he can change the course of the world; according to those who adhere more to the "noble savage" school of thought, man must give up control and become one with his world if he is to survive. This is a theme which recurs in a few of his more recent works, most notably *The Island* (1988) and *The Monument* (1991).

Rocky, the narrator of *The Monument* (1991), is an orphaned adolescent whose mixed ancestry and lame leg make her practically unadoptable until Emma and Fred come along. That her adoptive parents are alcoholics is related in a very matter of fact way by this extraordinary young woman who also notes the arrival of Mick, a rather seedy independent artist hired by the town in which Rocky lives to construct a fitting monument to those past citizens of Bolton, Kansas, who lost their lives in wars dating back to the Civil War. Through Mick, Rocky is transformed; she begins to explore her development as an artist and to understand how to view life as an artist as well.

The transformational power of art, the act of creation, is paramount to this novel. As Mick and his protégé Rocky prowl the town, they see below the surface. Occasionally, their observations are wry comments on the "paint" people apply to their lives to hide their foibles. When they reveal the inner nature of the people whose lives they observe, the reactions are mixed. Some are gratified that another person sees what lurks beneath the surface; others are appalled to find themselves laid open and, therefore, vulnerable. The monument Mick finally constructs, eighteen trees to honor the eighteen men and women who gave their lives in service to their country, returns to Paulsen's theme of being one with nature in order to be at peace with the world.

Sometimes, one is prevented from being at peace with the world due to the actions of others. That is most assuredly one of the underlying premises of *Nightjohn* (1993). Here is the story of twelve-year-old Sarny, a slave girl. Sarny, fortunately, has not yet reached menarche; when she does, she will become a "breeder." Her childhood will, in effect, end then. Her education is meager. She cannot show her natural curiosity about the world around her. A new field hand is bought by the master. Nightjohn, as he is known, fills Sarny's thirst for knowledge by teaching her the letters of the alphabet. When her new-found knowledge is discovered, the terrible events escalate. Sarny is beaten; Nightjohn's foot is mutilated. Sarny and John are not to be daunted by this brutality. Instead, under cover of darkness, they continue their lessons. Even after his escape, John returns to help Sarny learn and to pass along her knowledge to the other children.

Paulsen reiterates his belief in the importance of education in this novel. Through Sarny, he tells readers that knowledge is what sets us free. Knowledge is what matters when all else seems lost to us. Like the protagonists in his other works, Sarny does not take her new knowledge for granted but is determined to pass it along to benefit others like her. Like Manny in *The Crossing* and other characters, part of what separates Sarny from society is her ethnicity. By virtue of being born African-American, Sarny will face more obstacles and will confront more tragedy in her life. The same is true for young Rosa, one of the central characters of *Sisters/Hermanas* (1993).

The story in *Sisters/Hermanas* (1993) hearkens back to territory explored in *The Night the White Deer Died* and *Canyons*. Here is a dual narrative about two female protagonists, Rosa and Traci, both aged fourteen. These two girls are destined to meet even though their lives cannot be more different. Rosa is an illegal immigrant from Mexico whose dream of becoming a model has all but vanished in the brutal reality of survival on the streets of Houston. She can only finance her dream by selling her body. Traci is from an affluent suburban family. Her mother's dreams are for Traci to become a cheerleader as a step on the way to a beauty queen title. Traci is going along with her mother's plans at the moment, focusing constantly on how she appears to others. The story climaxes when the two girls meet in a department store where Rosa is shoplifting and Traci is trying hard to project the image her mother thinks is so important for her success.

Both girls are trapped by their circumstances despite the vast chasm which separates them. Each girl is changed by the encounter, brief though it is. For Traci, it may mean realizing that she is more like Rosa than she can comfortably admit. Rosa's experience may lead her in another direction. The ending leaves the reader to decide exactly what, if anything, will change for each of the young women. Once again, Paulsen muses about the tragedies and hardships dealt one simply due to ethnicity, something beyond one's control. Rosa is like Traci; she is bright and has hopes for the future. Unfortunately, Rosa must sell her body to make enough money to survive. It is the cruel fact of street life for her. Traci, too, realizes that she has made sacrifices for appearances' sake. Though her life has been relatively easy, Traci has avoided the truth; Rosa, despite her hard life, can admit the truth about herself. She has no illusions about what she is doing. Like Sarny and Manny, and others, then, Rosa rises above her poor beginnings and uses her dreams to vault her past the obstacles others would place in her path to the future.

In *The Car* (1994), Paulsen resurrects several of his earlier themes. Abandoned by both of his parents, fourteen-year-old Terry Anders is left to his own devices. He constructs a car from a model car kit left behind by his father, a mechanic. The Blakely Bearcat becomes Terry's ticket to freedom. He takes off on a cross-country trip, determined to find a long lost uncle. What he discovers instead is a grizzled Vietnam veteran who hitches a ride with Terry. Waylon, a forty-five-year-old "hippie," shows Terry how to see through new eyes. They visit an ancient Native American, a virtual repository of history; share a meal at a religious commune; visit the site of the Battle of Little Big Horn; and continue on their tour of America.

The trip serves as a fitting metaphor for Terry's passage from child to adult in much the same way as does Russell's journey across the wilderness in *Dogsong* or Brian's survival trek in *Hatchet*. Further, Waylon is traumatized at times by his recollections of his experiences in Vietnam. In this regard, he is reminiscent of Robert in *The Crossing* and many of the veterans of wars in *Sentries*. Once again, Paulsen incorporates a Native American as a pivotal character in the novel. As Terry and Waylon proceed on their journey, they are guided by the words passed along to them by an ancient Native American, who tells them about history from the perspective of his culture. Through these accounts Terry learns that even textbooks may not present the unvarnished truth about events of the past. Thus, Terry realizes that he must question things and not blithely accept what he reads or what he is told.

Through his various pieces of fiction and nonfiction, Paulsen continues to return to those themes which marked his early work for young adults. He extols the value of nature and natural life over civilization by setting his characters outside of the boundaries of civilized life, adrift in a boat, crossing the Canadian wilderness, sledding through an Alaskan snow storm, or trucking cross-country to learn more about life. Frequently, he uses the voices of Hispanics, African-Americans, and Native Americans to convey his messages to readers. Through these characters of color, Paulsen is able to underscore the coming-of-age theme prevalent in his writing. These characters are separated from society by virtue, in many cases, of their ethnicity; through their struggles, they win acceptance into the community which had previously ignored or rejected them. Their journey to adulthood is a perilous one in that they must fight for acceptance on two levels. They must overcome the double whammy of being adolescent and being culturally different. Though Paulsen writes from outside these cultures, his writing rings with authenticity. His works have received much praise and several awards.

CRITICAL RECEPTION

Paulsen's work for young adult readers has met with almost universal approval and considerable praise. His careful crafting and attention to detail make for vivid images, images painted with his clean prose. His sense of the importance of setting, his knowledge of place, allows readers from all areas of the United States (and indeed the world) to experience the beauty of nature. Paulsen first came to the attention of adolescents with *Hatchet,* a wonderful coming-of-age and survival story which won him his first of three Newbery Honor Medals (the other two were awarded for *The Winter Room* and *Dogsong*).

His prose has been compared with that of authors ranging from Hemingway to Farley Mowat and not found wanting. Often described as sinewy, lyric, and spare, his prose may be simple; however, his stories are not simplistic. Rather they deal with some of the crucial issues facing adolescents today. Never exploitative nor faddish, his novels present young adults wrestling with universal problems. Paulsen does not condescend to his audience as evident in the masterful prologue to *The Winter Room* entitled "Tuning." The language is pure and spare: the meanings are left for the reader to make. What Paulsen says, in essence, in this prologue holds true for all of his works. Books cannot convey sight and sound and smell and taste; the reader must bring these things to books. Paulsen compels readers to bring themselves to his works. Readers cannot remain impassive bystanders; they must bring themselves and their experiences to bear on the novels and make their own meaning.

It is difficult to pigeonhole the work of Paulsen. There is no template for his novels and pieces of nonfiction. His works resist formulas despite his prolific output. What all of his works do have in common, however, are the majestic use of language, the examination of human potential, a strong sense of humor, and the careful crafting which has won Paulsen his much deserved reputation as one of the finest writers in the field of young adult literature.

BIBLIOGRAPHY

Young Adult Fiction by Gary Paulsen

The Night the White Deer Died. Nashville: Nelson, 1978. New York: Dell, 1991.

Dancing Carl. New York: Bradbury, 1983.

Dogsong. New York: Bradbury, 1985.

Sentries. New York: Bradbury, 1986.

The Crossing. New York: Orchard Books, 1987.

Hatchet. New York: Bradbury, 1987.

The Island. New York: Orchard, 1988.

The Winter Room. New York: Orchard, 1989.

Canyons. New York: Delacorte, 1990.

The Foxman. New York: Viking, 1990.

The Voyage of the Frog. New York: Dell, 1990.

Woodsong. New York: Bradbury, 1990.

The Cookcamp. New York: Orchard, 1991.

The Monument. New York: Delacorte, 1991.

The River. New York: Doubleday, 1991.

Clabbered Dirt, Sweet Grass. New York: Harcourt Brace, 1992.

The Haymeadow. New York: Doubleday, 1992.

Harris and Me: *A Summer Remembered.* New York: Harcourt Brace, 1993.

Nightjohn. New York: Doubleday, 1993.

Sisters/Hermanas. New York: Harcourt Brace, 1993.

The Car. New York: Harcourt Brace, 1994.

Father Water, Mother Woods. New York: Delacorte, 1994.

Selected Studies of Gary Paulsen

Allen, Raymond. "Gary Paulsen: An Artist with Words." *Teaching PreK-8.* 23 (Aug./Sept. 1992): 52–54.

Barron, Donald. "Gary Paulsen: I Write Because It's All I Can Do."*ALAN Review* 20.3 (1993): 27–30.

Bartky, Cheryl. "Write What You Are." *Writer's Digest* 74. 7 (1994): 42.

Boyce, Joan. "Suggestions for Teaching a 'New' Tradebook Author." *Journal of Wisconsin State Reading Association* 35.1 (1991): 77–83.

Bushman, John, and Kay Bushman. "Gary Paulsen; the Storyteller's Legacy." *English Journal* 81.1 (1992): 85–88.

Deveraux, Elizabeth. "Gary Paulsen: Adventure and Hard Work Are Hallmarks of This Versatile Author." *Publisher's Weekly* 241.13 (1994): 70–71.

Eckwielen, Judith, and Carol Amato. "Focus On: Gary Paulsen." *School Librarian's Workshop* 12 (Mar. 1992): 14–15.

Handy, Alice. "Interview with Gary Paulsen." *Book Report* 10 (May/June 1991): 28–31.

Rahn, Suzanne. "Paulsen, Gary." *Twentieth-Century Children's Writers*. Ed. Tracy Chevalier. 3rd ed. Chicago: St. James, 1989. 763–65.

Weidt, Maryann. "The Fortunes of Poverty." *Writers Digest* 72.1 (1992): 8.

————. "Gary Paulsen: A Sentry for Peace." *Voice of Youth Advocate* 9 (1986): 129–30.

GRAHAM SALISBURY
(1944-   )

Chris Crowe

BIOGRAPHY

Graham Salisbury was born in Philadelphia, Pennsylvania, in 1944. His mother, a sixth-generation descendant of Congregational missionaries to Hawaii, was an artist, his father, a navy fighter pilot. Two months after Salisbury's birth, his mother returned with him to Honolulu. On Salisbury's first birthday, his father, a pilot assigned to the aircraft carrier *USS Essex*, was shot down and killed over Kikai Shima, Japan. Salisbury was two years old when his mother remarried—to another navy man, who died eight years later from brain cancer. When Salisbury was in sixth grade, she married a third time, to a deep sea charter boat fisherman.

Salisbury knew little of his first stepfather but was greatly influenced by his second stepfather "in a more or less regressive way. . . . [He] was a man of the sea, of the earth, of dirt and mud, of the blood and guts of hunting, of muscles and grit and beer and fishing and cigarettes hanging from scowling lips. . . . I mimicked him. I walked and talked like him. I became hard and sarcastic and demanding, and lorded over my sisters as if I were the all-time ultimate authority in their lowly lives."

Not long after his mother's third marriage, Salisbury was sent to Hawaii Preparatory Academy, a boys' boarding school in Kamuela on the Island of Hawaii, where he started and completed his secondary education. There he thrived on the discipline and structure of the preparatory school directed by

James Monroe Taylor, headmaster of the academy. Taylor instilled in Salisbury the importance of integrity, commitment, honor, character, and work. Taylor became an influential figure for Salisbury, an adult male who cared about him and his character. "That," says Salisbury, "was new to me."

After graduation from Hawaii Preparatory Academy, Salisbury spent a year at the University of Vermont and a semester at Santa Barbara City College. He did poorly at both institutions. He withdrew from school and joined a rock band that toured the Rocky Mountain states. A military draft notice called him to Los Angeles, but he was reclassified 4A, sole survivor, and exempted from military service. After some time writing music and performing with a new rock group, Millennium, he returned to college, first to Los Angeles City College and then to California State University, Northridge. While a college student, Salisbury worked as a lunch time playground supervisor at a local school. "I wanted to be an elementary school principal. . . . I loved the kids, wild and antsy. Full of life. Full of energy. Full of hope." He graduated *magna cum laude* with a B.A. in liberal studies and went to Bergamo, Italy, to study the Montessori method.

After earning Montessori certification, Salisbury left Italy for Provo, Utah, where he attended Brigham Young University briefly before working as a Montessori teacher. When the Montessori school went out of business, he worked as production manager for BYU Graphics. In 1984, he moved to Portland, Oregon, to manage five downtown office buildings, a job he still has. He and his wife, Robyn, live in Portland with their six children.

Salisbury was not drawn to writing initially. "That I have found this way of expression is truly amazing to me. Me, the one who flunked English. Twice. The one who never read as a boy." He credits Alex Haley's *Roots* with turning him on to the power and value of reading. He began reading the book during late-night feedings with his first son. The book moved him, impressed him. "From then on," he says, "I have read every day, every single day." He met Haley the year before Haley's death and told him how much *Roots* had influenced him and that he was also a writer. Haley's advice was warm and fatherly: "Remember, add to the good in the world . . . we really need it."

A fear of public speaking prompted Salisbury to enroll in a Dale Carnegie speaking course, and there he discovered that he enjoyed writing. After the course, he continued writing, teaching himself to construct effective stories, some of which were published. He later enrolled in the M.F.A. program at Vermont College of Norwich University to hone his writing skills. He graduated in 1990 with a completed manuscript of his first novel, *Blue Skin of the Sea*.

His big break in writing came following a public reading from his M.F.A. project, the draft of *Blue Skin of the Sea.* C. Michael Curtis, fiction editor for *The Atlantic Monthly,* was in the audience and asked to see the manuscript. Nothing came of that meeting, but later at a writers' conference in Oregon, Salisbury met Wendy Lamb of Bantam Doubleday Dell, to whom he told the C. Michael Curtis story. Lamb asked to see a copy of the work, and a week later, Delacorte, a Bantam Doubleday Dell subsidiary, made an offer to publish *Blue Skin of the Sea.*

Though Salisbury has had a varied and interesting life, his home, Hawaii, has remained a constant, a touchstone for him. His two novels and most of his stories are set in Hawaii with Hawaiian characters (not only native Hawaiians, but an even representation of the ethnic diversity in Hawaii) speaking and acting as Hawaiians do. His life in Hawaii, his relatively fatherless childhood, and his boarding school adolescence have made him appreciate the wonders of the islands and be sensitive to the importance of family relationships, especially the relationships between fathers and sons.

His boyhood memories of Hawaii are deep and permanent. "My first three books [his third, a memoir, is not yet published] are set in the islands, and, I suppose, the next few will also be set there. I know Hawaii. I know its people and its culture. I carry lots of wonder and history in my heart. Sometimes I listen to Hawaiian music when I write. The islands are part of my cellular make up, part of my soul. I have so much to say about this turquoise-watered place, about its diverse and generous people."

MAJOR WORKS AND THEMES

Salisbury has published a handful of polished short stories in various literary journals. His two novels, *Blue Skin of the Sea* (1992) and *Under the Blood-Red Sun* (1994) are both set in Hawaii; these novels and most of his stories reflect his Hawaiian boyhood and roots. "When I set stories in Hawaii, I set them in something I love, which deepens my writing experience, and, hopefully, my work." But his work is more than just about Hawaii, it is about boys struggling to find their place in their families, their place in the world.

A central theme in most of his work is "a boy's character building." Salisbury believes, "The world suffers far too much at the hands of boys/men who have no hearts, no conscience. If what I write can contribute anything at all toward clearing a little of the fear and hate and neglect and that damn machismo attitude out of even one boy's life, then I will have done something positive." The protagonists in his two novels often suffer at the hands of boys/men who have neither heart nor conscience. The boys are tempted at various times in their development to react in kind, but their families, their connectedness to a group of people who love them, helps them rise above rather than sink to the levels of those who persecute them.

Sonny Mendoza, the French-Portuguese protagonist in *Blue Skin of the Sea,* first learns to overcome his fear of swimming and his fear of his absent father. Through the rest of the stories that comprise this novel, he deals with the hate and fear and neglect and machismo that many young men in small Hawaiian towns lived with, and still live with. By the end of the novel, Sonny is eighteen, an enlightened adolescent who has learned by hard and often unpleasant experiences how to be a man, a human being. Sonny has learned that he has a place and a family in Kailua-Kona. That knowledge, that security, gives him the courage to leave the island in search of his own future and identity.

Under the Blood-Red Sun also deals with issues of adolescent growth and family. Tomikazu Nakaji is a first-generation American son of Japanese immigrants in Hawaii. His father is kind, wise, and loving. His grandfather is harder, more traditional and eccentric than Tomi's father, but just as loving. The young boy's nearly idyllic childhood is destroyed when Japanese planes attack Pearl Harbor. The intense anti-Japanese sentiments that follow the attack shatter Tomi's life and family. His father and grandfather are sent to mainland relocation camps, and Tomi is ignored by many, and reviled by some, of his former friends. In this isolation, he must face the harsh realities of this new world, a world stacked against him and his family.

Salisbury says, "I am fascinated by the things that shape boys into men . . . and the things that keep them from becoming men." In both books, boys face a series of crises that affect their family relationships and their places in society. These conflicts reflect both Salisbury's own childhood and his hope to portray a boy's character building in a positive way. These two boys survive and overcome their various crises through their own courage and intelligence undergirded by the support of loving family and friends. These elements are central in Salisbury's work, not because they reflect a yearning for his own fragmented childhood but because they represent what he has learned for himself about what it takes for a boy to become a man. Though his stories portray the world honestly and realistically, they are positive and upbeat without being preachy. Clearly, this reveals Salisbury's own hopeful view of life and the influence of Alex Haley's admonition to "add to the good in the world."

CRITICAL RECEPTION

Reviews of Salisbury's two novels have been universally favorable, in general citing his use of vivid, poetic language; interesting, well-developed characters; humor and emotion; and realistic portrayals of boys' dilemmas. His depictions of Hawaiian life and the issues facing Hawaiian boys in prestatehood days often receive special mention. Though both *Blue Skin of the Sea* and *Under the Blood-Red Sun* can be considered historical novels, the historical detail of the days immediately before and after the attack on Pearl Harbor in *Under the Blood-Red Sun* has been especially praised. Says one reviewer, "The author subtly reveals the dilemma of both the Americans and their Japanese counterparts—the natural suspicions of the Americans, the equally natural bewilderment of the Japanese immigrants when they suddenly become the personification of the enemy" (Bradburn 425).

The multicultural aspects of his books have been noted for both their accuracy and their universality. Salisbury's characters, representing the broad ethnic mix in Hawaii, deal with prejudice and issues unique to Hawaii, but reviews point out that many of the conflicts, or at least the attitudes behind them, are readily appreciated by mainland readers. In both books, he is praised for his presentation of life in Hawaii through the eyes of ethnic American protagonists.

Salisbury's first novel, *Blue Skin of the Sea*, was named an American Library Association Best Book for Young Adults, a *School Library Journal* Best Book of the Year, and a National Council of Teachers of English Notable Trade Book in the Language Arts. It won the 1992 Bank Street College Child Study Book Award, the Parent's Choice Award, the 1993 Oregon Book Award for Young Readers, and the 1992 Judy Lopez Book of the Year Award. In 1993, Salisbury won the PEN/Norma Klein Award. *Under the Blood-Red Sun* was named the 1994 winner of the Scott O'Dell Historical Fiction Award.

BIBLIOGRAPHY

Young Adult Fiction by Graham Salisbury

Blue Skin of the Sea. New York: Delacorte Press, 1992.
Under the Blood-Red Sun. New York: Delacorte Press, 1994.

Works for Adults by Graham Salisbury

"The Dropping Stone." *Chaminade Literary Review* (Spring 1988): 76–92.
"Jewels." *Hawaii Pacific Review* (Spring 1989): 51–60.
"You Would Cry to See Waiakea Town." *Bamboo Ridge* (Fall 1989): 112–129.
"The Old Man." *Manoa: A Journal of Pacific and International Writing* (Spring 1990): 81–91.
"Ice." *Going Where I'm Coming From: Personal Narratives of American Youth.* Ed. Anne Mazer. New York: Persea Books, 1994.

Other Works by Graham Salisbury

"Being a Boy Can Be Dangerous." *Journal of Youth Services in Libraries* 6.3 (1993): 259–64.
"Bellows Field: A Writer's Metaphor." *The Hawaii Library Association Journal* (June 1994): 15–20.
"A Leaf on the Sea." *The ALAN Review* 22.1 (1994): 11–14.

Selected Studies of Graham Salisbury

Bradburn, Frances. Rev. of *Under the Blood-Red Sun. Booklist* 15 October 1994: 425.
Corsaro, Julie. Rev. of *Blue Skin of the Sea. Booklist* 15 June 1992: 1835.
Crowe, Chris. Rev. of *Blue Skin of the Sea. The ALAN Review* 20.3 (1992): 27.
"Graham Salisbury." *Something about the Author.* Ed. Diane Telgen. Vol. 76. Detroit: Gale, 1994. 200–201.
Hearne, Betsy. Rev. of *Blue Skin of the Sea. Bulletin of the Center for Children's Books* (Sept. 1992): 22.
Lord, John R. Rev. of *Under the Blood-Red Sun. VOYA* 17.4 (1994): 216.
Meeker, Amy. "Flying Starts." *Publisher's Weekly* 13 July 1992: 22–24.
Mitchell, Sylvia. Rev. of *Blue Skin of the Sea. VOYA* 15.2 (1992): 100.
Rev. of *Blue Skin of the Sea. Kirkus Reviews* 60.12 (15 June 1992): 785.
Rev. of *Blue Skin of the Sea. Publisher's Weekly* 15 June 1992: 104.
Rev. of *Under the Blood-Red Sun. Kirkus Reviews* 20.20 (15 October 1994): 1415.
Rev. of *Under the Blood-Red Sun. Publisher's Weekly* 31 Oct. 1994: 64.
Richmond, Gale. Rev. of *Blue Skin of the Sea. School Library Journal* 38.6 (1992): 140.
Shoemaker, Joel. Rev. of *Under the Blood-Red Sun. School Library Journal* 40.10 (1994): 127.
Siteine, Alexis. Rev. of *Blue Skin of the Sea. Hawaii English Journal* (Fall 1993): 29–30.
"Word of Mouth." Rev. of *Blue Skin of the Sea. Library Journal* 117.15 (15 Sept. 1992): 120.

ANDREW SALKEY
(1928-1995)

Kwame S. N. Dawes

BIOGRAPHY

Andrew Salkey was one of the most prolific of Caribbean writers, having published more than half a dozen novels, several volumes of poetry, three travel books, ten anthologies for which he was editor, and at least ten children's books including short stories and folk tales from the Caribbean. In 1992, his prolific output and significant contribution to black literature around the world was recognized by *Black Scholar* magazine who granted Salkey its 25th Anniversary Award for Excellence in the Field of Literature. The citation read at the Commonwealth Institute in London praised Salkey for his forty years of poetry, fiction, journalism, and editing.

Salkey was born in Panama in 1928 and moved to Jamaica to live first with his grandmother and then his mother when he was two years old. His father remained in Panama where he managed to make a fairly good living renting boats and repairing them. For all of Salkey's childhood, his father was absent, and the clearest demonstration of his existence came religiously each month when money was sent to support his family in Jamaica. Salkey never met his father until he was thirty-two years old, during a furlough in Jamaica on a Guggenheim scholarship. Even a passing familiarity with Salkey's writing will reveal that this absence of a father figure greatly influenced his writing. Curiously, his children's writing sought to celebrate the presence of the father figure as the constant and reliable head of the household, while his adult novels became, among other things, involved explorations of the psychology of fatherlessness. While growing up in Jamaica, he was drawn to, and deeply influenced by, the oral tradition which was passed on to him by his grandmother and his mother. The impact of the Anancy stories shared at nighttime, complete with the inimitable improvisational style of folk telling, is clearly demonstrated in his fascination with the trickster figure in virtually all his work.

In Jamaica, he attended two prestigious boy's grammar schools: St. George's College and Munroe College. At the age of twenty-four, Salkey left Jamaica for England where he took a B.A. at the University of London. He then worked as a teacher for several years, teaching English language and literature and Latin. At the same time, he pursued his writing interests by working as a scriptwriter, editor, and broadcaster with the BBC. Salkey's voice became one of the many Caribbean voices emanating from England to the Caribbean on the BBC's broadcasts, and after the publication of his first novel, *A Quality of Violence*, in 1959, his status as a significant West Indian novelist was fairly well established.

Salkey's instinct to write for children clearly began in the early sixties and may have been prompted by a desire to provide young people in the Caribbean and children of Caribbean heritage abroad with a sense of identity and possibility. His stories modeled themselves on the adventure tales of British juvenile literature, but tried to sustain a grounding in the life and culture of Jamaican society. It is significant, for instance, that in all of his children's novels, Salkey demonstrates a fascination with food, Jamaican food. His descriptions are vivid and evocative and manage to conjure up the texture and tone of Jamaican life. Like many Caribbean writers of his generation, Salkey spent most of his life living abroad. However, he traveled extensively in the Caribbean and wrote a great deal of significant work about it. In 1971, he published his travel journal about Cuba titled *Havana Journal*, and the following year, after a 1970 visit to Guyana, he wrote *Georgetown Journal: A Caribbean Writer's Journey from London, via Port of Spain to Georgetown, Guyana, 1970*. In these as in other writings, Salkey's engagement with Marxism is demonstrated. His reaction to the Cuban revolution, for instance, is quite positive, and it seems to fit quite well with the kind of third world ethos that is apparent in much of his poetry and fiction.

In 1976 Andrew Salkey moved to Hampshire College in Amherst, Massachusetts. His time in America had an impact on the literature that he produced. In a number of his folk tales and animal lore in his children's book *Brother Anancy and Other Stories* (1994), there are numerous references to life in rural Massachusetts, American television, and childhood experiences in America. His connections to Jamaica have become more and more located in the time-honored patterns of folk tales, revealing the lasting impact that his oral education has had on his writing and his imagination. He was married and had two sons. Andrew Salkey died April 28, 1995 at the age of 67.

MAJOR WORKS AND THEMES

Salkey's writing is generally characterized by a curious thematic dichotomy between the adult works and the children's works which demonstrates how related they are to each other and how much they present, together, a rewardingly whole picture of this complex and dynamic author. Where his adult novels are distinctly pessimistic studies of violence and dysfunction in families and societies, and where they are distinguished by a propensity toward chaos and human failing, his children's novels remain rooted in a certain social and family stability. There is a tendency to celebrate the compact and stable family unit, complete with the male as head of the home and the predictability of traditional roles within the families. Indeed, Salkey's children's books thrive on the assurance of safety and acceptance such that the adventures that the characters—mostly male boys—go through are never life threatening. This is in stark and telling contrast to the characterization of the male protagonists in most of his adult novels. These men are almost always struggling with the trauma of fatherlessness and with a world that is deeply scarred by racism, political exploitation, and constant danger. Whereas the adult novels are rooted in a certain existentialist realism, the children's books are idealistic and represent an idyllic perception of the world.

But reading the two against each other, one begins to understand that Salkey is intentionally constructing works of irony that only those who read both types of work will understand. There is, for instance, an uncanny series of thematic and plot parallels between his first adult novel, *A Quality of Violence* (1959), and his juvenile novel *Drought* (1966). Both deal with droughts that cause havoc in a rural village and both follow similar plot lines when it comes to the experience of the children in the village. But while one (the adult novel) carries us to mysticism and ultimately, violent death, the other becomes a simple and seemingly innocent exploration of adolescent adventure. But the suggestion of mysticism hangs over the narrative nonetheless, in a manner that suggests that Salkey expects us to read it into the intentional idealism that he is trying to convey in the children's books. This constant effort to downplay the pitfalls of human existence continues in many of his other novels—novels that all deal with very serious issues like hurricanes, earthquakes, revolutionary espionage, and riots—but the overt optimism of these works invariably suggests the presence of danger and chaos lurking as elements of the adult world in the background.

Nonetheless, the truest value of Salkey's works for juveniles lies in the very simple, but deeply significant, act of creating imaginative narratives for and about youths who have had no such narratives with which to relate in their lives. Salkey's stories represent some of the first novels about children written in the formerly colonized Jamaica. In a sense, Salkey provides for young readers in the Caribbean, and within its own "diaspora," narratives in the form of fiction that allow them to locate themselves as part of a creative existence. In many ways, much of what we come to accept as our reality is confirmed or affirmed in the books we read. One of the dilemmas of growing up in a society that is dominated by literary images of another culture and race is that young people of marginalized communities lose a sense of the validity of their own experience and imagination—they become, literally, invisible in their own imaginative developments. Like writers Jean Dacosta, Michael Anthony, James Berry, and Victor Reid, Salkey's impressive list of children's books has provided children of the African diaspora with a crucial sense of presence in works of fiction. It is perhaps because of this "higher calling" that Salkey's writing for children is so strongly founded on intensely adhered to moral values and fairly traditional portrayals of family structure and gender roles.

But he does experiment with the very premise of the children's book in some of his later work, especially his Anancy stories, of which there are several volumes. Salkey's Anancy tales demonstrate the peculiar problem of determining how to categorize folk tales that are put in book form—are they children's stories or adult stories? does the distinction matter or mean anything at all? Salkey's Anancy tales are made up of both traditional stories from West Africa and the Caribbean, rendered afresh by this writer, or they are completely new narratives based on the Anancy character. In many of the latter, his Anancy enters the contemporary world and effectively serves as a vehicle for craftily constructed commentary on modern politics, race, and international geopolitics, to name a few. Of course, in these books which feature the Anancy character, Salkey also includes other freshly manufactured "folk" narratives which defy the concept of the folk narrative as being a static entity that is simply preserved and passed down from generation to generation. Indeed, it is the very use of the technique of creating stories and rendering them in a language that suggests the quality of myth-making and archetypal construction that distinguishes Salkey as a writer of children's stories that speak to a fascinating multicultural environment.

When one looks at his entire work, one senses then, a kind of craftiness and self-conscious trickster quality at work. The fact, however, is that the trickster is often the author himself, playing a series of ideas against each other and defying traditional ideas and structures. It is the quality of trickery, then, that allows Salkey to write such a range of materials for children. It should be understood, however, that the movement from rather standard and derivative narratives to the more complex and playful works of folk tales was a gradual one that can be tracked from book to book.

Salkey's juvenile fiction maintains certain predictable patterns in terms of narrative structure, theme, and characterization. More often than not, his main protagonist is a young male attending high school. Most of the adventures that these characters go through take place during their vacations or, as in *Riot* (1967), over weekends. Schools do not play a big part in these novels except in the fact that they provide information about the age and interests of the main characters. In many ways, these stories have an uncanny resemblance, in theme and narrative style, to the adventure stories written by such British children's authors as Enid Blyton. There are significant parallels also to the Nancy Drew and Hardy Boys series of American popular juvenile literature in that while the adventures that the characters embark on are ostensibly dangerous for the adults, the reader remains assured that the danger is not the same for the child protagonists. Stability and safety are very important elements in these works, and Salkey doggedly protects this sense of stability in a manner that suggests that he is striving to allow the children to enjoy adventure without having to contend with the encroachment of adulthood. Nonetheless, in a number of the novels, adult issues arise: death in *Drought*, gunfight and the brutal ravaging of three young divers in *Jonah Simpson* (1969), and violence and the politics of revolt and rioting in *Riot*.

But the narrative structure of his novels betrays an intense desire, on the part of the narrator, to control and dominate the nature and content of the information that is expressed in the work. Virtually all of his children's stories make use of an omniscient third-person narrator who is able to shift from the concerns and experiences of the children to those of the adults from section to section. There is little attempt to replicate the limitations of childhood experience in the character of the narrative presence. Thus, in *Riot*, Salkey is able to write passages that comment on the very adult conundrum about the validity of rioting as a political option without feeling any need to relate that to the experience of the child protagonists. They do not even overhear these conversations, and they have no impact on their own experiences. This domination of the narrative voice allows for strong moral articulations in the work, and the most striking of these is the apparent harmony that Salkey celebrates between the adult world and the children's world. There is never a suggestion of conflict or conflicting values. Rarely are adults pitted against children. All the characters, children included, accept the premise that the adults know best, and the children simply adhere to what the adults know and understand. There is perhaps only one noticeable variance from this notion in the novel *Drought,* in which the children withhold the fact that it is through their game of ritualistic activities that the well was discovered in a cave. They fear that if they disclose their game and the nature of it, the adults would censure them for toying with dangerous rituals. Beyond such isolated instances, however, it is clear that Salkey is not interested in pitting adult experience and values against those of children—which enhances the safety and security that his works seek to found themselves upon.

Salkey's first four books focus on a series of national disasters that grip small communities in Jamaica. *Hurricane* (1964), *Earthquake* (1965), *Drought* (1966), and *Riot* (1967) follow a formulaic pattern and seek to do very similar things. In each, some catastrophe presents itself to a community, and this calamity has to be dealt with. In the middle of the narratives are young boys, each with a clutch of close friends or siblings who form themselves into gangs and who basically experience the excitement of the events that are taking place around them. In many ways, these four novels have become the children's works that Salkey is best known for, and yet they represent some of the first efforts on his part to devise a way of writing for children. There are telling patterns in these four novels, however, that will guide the rest of his children's books. I should add, however, that I do not regard his Anancy books as falling into this development pattern even though I disagree with some who tend to deny their presence in the listing of children's books.

Hurricane charts the adventure of a small nuclear family as it faces a very serious hurricane in Jamaica in the early fifties. *Hurricane* is based on an actual hurricane that caused much death and havoc in Jamaica in 1950. Salkey's novel takes the reader through the process of planning for the storm, barricading, waiting out the hurricane through its various phases, and the poignant walk through the devastated city after the hurricane has passed. At the center of the novel is a young boy who experiences such a storm for the first time. There is little profound characterization in this novel and little dramatic tension between the characters—the hurricane remains at the core of the narrative and while it creates a sense of danger on the outside, there is a stability and safety inside the home because of the presence of father and mother and siblings.

Earthquake is structurally similar to *Hurricane*, complete with a prologue that sets up the narrative and the expected male youthful protagonist. However, unlike in *Hurricane* there is no real earthquake in this novel, at least not during the narrative present of the novel. At the end of the novel, and yet positioned at the center of the plot, is the grandfather's story of his experience during the painful and frightening earthquake of 1907 in Kingston, Jamaica. But the grandfather's story comes only in reaction to the questions that the main characters in the work have after experiencing a series of tremors and after a friend of theirs is overwhelmed by a landslide caused by these tremors. The central narrative surrounds a summer vacation in which three siblings meet a young Rastafarian boy who decides to enjoy their company and embark on adventures with them. The stability of a narrative structure that is provided by the hurricane in the earlier novel does not exist in this one; consequently the work is uneven and structurally weak. But the themes of security and protection are constant in this work as well, and the use of the "make-believe" games of the children prepares us for the pseudo-mysticism in *Drought*.

In *Drought* there is an actual drought, and the village has to contend with the pressures of surviving this painful natural occurrence. The landscape is bleakly drawn, and the potential for social disaster is constantly there in the adult world. In *Drought* people do die. Old Man Sands, the head of the village, dies at the height of the drought, and Elsita, a single mother, collapses in the marketplace during the drought. The reaction of the children is muted—it is almost as if Salkey tries to avoid the implications of death on the young mind. While the drought is becoming more acute, the young boys start a ritual that is intended to bring rain. It is a peculiar series of rituals that smacks of mysticism and an almost "primitive" religiosity. The boys evolve the ritual innocently, and remain innocent to the end. But they are aware that they may be seen as toying with some greater force. This hint of danger is the first time Salkey allows his juvenile characters to be in some danger that they cannot be protected from. But he understates the role of magic and mysticism in the work.

In *Drought,* moreover, we are treated to a more sophisticated narrative that shows the parallel dilemmas of leadership and strength, both in the world of the adults and in the world of the children. Seth, the central character of the novel, is faced with a series of leadership crises even as his father, Jacob Manson, is invited to lead the community upon the death of Old Man Sands. They both succeed, even if with some difficulty, in bringing about some stability and progress. The narrative reaches its climax when one of the boys, Benjamin, introduces a daring and questionable ritual in an effort to bring rain to the community. He suggests that they, on the night of the Nine Night celebrations to mourn the passing of the two dead villagers, hold a ritual sacrifice of a rooster and then talk to the dead, asking them to bring back the rain. To Double, one of the skeptics in the more superstitious among the group, sees the plan as diabolic, but the others enjoy its bizarre exoticism. They choose to carry it out. At the heart of this part of the narrative is a trickster pattern that Salkey, the author, enjoys indulging in his writing. These rituals, unbeknownst to the boys, parallel the obeah and *pocomania* rituals of rural Jamaica. That these rituals come so naturally from the boys recalls the movement toward a primordial sensibility in *Lord of the Flies*. But Salkey diffuses the potential for danger through humor. The ritual fails to make contact with the dead and the rooster escapes after pecking Benji on the hand. The rains eventually come, and the cave in which the boys have been playing produces a well. The boys virtually dig the hole themselves. They do not admit to being the ones to dig the hole, and they keep quiet about all their activities. Mystery is thus extant at the end of the novel, albeit the kind of mystery and mysticism that the narrator enjoys alone.

Jonah Simpson represents a key departure for Salkey from the disaster sequence to the more sophisticated narratives that he pursues in later works like *Joey Tyson (1974), The River That Disappeared* (1979), and *Danny Jones* (1980). Set in Port Royal, a historical town in Kingston, this novel is a mystery in the tradition of Nancy Drew, Hardy Boys, and the Famous Five. A mysterious man, a white man, is spotted by Jonah, and he keeps appearing and disappearing throughout the novel until we discover that he is probably a dangerous counterrevolutionary storing a cache of arms to attack Cuba with a small army of men. Jonah goes through a series of experiences that are mystifying and deeply complex. He is presented as a boy with a vivid and fertile imagination, but also as a child with the clairvoyant skill of predicting things in the future. Yet, this is not something he is always able to do. At times his ability is remarkable, and at other times it smacks of the simple and common phenomenon of *deja vu*. What is most telling is that Salkey never seeks to explain this ability in Jonah. It just simply is. The quest from the mysterious stranger leads to a history lesson on the peculiar and colorful background of Port Royal, Jamaica, and ultimately to a dramatic shootout between the police and insurgents on Lime

Key, a tiny island off the coast of Kingston. Jonah's preoccupation with Admiral Nelson, who once resided on Port Royal, is a fascinating example of how history can stir the imagination of a child and allow him or her to construct fascinating fictions about such historical figures. But adventure is not limited simply to the imagination in this book that also deals with diving. Indeed, people die in this work, and in a way that is brutal and painful. Three of four divers are devoured by sharks right in the presence of the entire village. The children are there to witness the mutilated bodies of the killed divers. But, as always, Salkey is determined to assure the reader that the main characters are always safe. There is never a sense of impending danger in this work, and this is largely because the adults are a constant presence in the work and are always there to bring a certain stability and safety.

Salkey rarely departs from this pattern in his works. His value as a multicultural writer must be understood in terms of his ability to locate his narrative in the life and times of Jamaican society. This ensures that the protagonists are black and have a strong sense of themselves in a distinctly unique culture—one that is quite different from the one in which these works are published. Despite this, however, there are areas in which the novels appear to reflect the indelible impact of colonial education on the author. This is so in the narrative structure and especially so in the language used by the author. Not until his later novels do we see Salkey trying to embark on the use of the dialect in a manner that is credible and natural. In his earlier works all the dialogue is in standard English or in minor variations to that pattern which do not reflect in any way the Jamaican language register. By the time we come to *Joey Tyson* and *Danny Jones* we note a shift in the language used and greater confidence and facility with the dialect. It is something that Salkey clearly had to learn, and this fact speaks volumes about the power of the colonial education on writers like himself.

The shift in landscape is most clearly revealed in his most recent collection of stories, *Brother Anancy and Other Stories*, which was published by Longman in 1994. In it, Salkey complicates the formerly simple demarcations of juvenile and adult fiction by exploring complex issues of politics and exploitation, while in the same volume, dealing with charm and wit with whimsical tales about cats and mice. There is a far greater confidence about the power of the story to convey ideas and an apparent eschewing of any inclination to speak down to a juvenile readership. In this collection, the language is rich with metaphor, imagery, and fairly sophisticated vocabulary. At the back of the book, there is a section titled "Things to Do—and Think About," which contains fairly simple questions about the stories that appear to be pitched at the elementary-aged reader. The book is, in fact, designed as a children's book, and yet it also contains some sophisticated disguised intimations about adult life in the twentieth century. However, for an introduction to Salkey's propensity toward wit and irony, and his ability to tell a story with grace and sophistication, the stories in *Brother Anancy and Other Stories* remain some of the best things to read by this writer.

The illustrations in the books go through similar patterns of transformation. The first books, illustrated by William Papas, reveal that the artist has simply darkened the faces of the characters, who have European hair and features, to create his black characters. The hair is invariably Caucasian, and where he tries to construct African features, his work becomes, at best, cartoonlike and, at worst, stereotypical caricatures of the black: thick lips in white, and dark faces that pattern the make-up worn by minstrels. For the most part, these fluid sketches in much of the early work are offensive for their lack of research. Gradually, there is an awareness of black features on Papas' part, but quite clearly there is a noticeable departure and shift when Salkey changes artists in *Jonah Simpson*. Jamaican artist Jerry Craig's sketches are often not as fluid as Papas', but there is a sounder grasp of the Jamaican landscape and the African features in his work. In his most recent collection of stories, the anonymous artist appears to have a stronger sense of the African features. The drawings are extremely naturalistic and representational, and demonstrate a sensitivity to the problems of illustration and race that crop up in the first children's novels. The difference is important, because in many of the disaster novels, the clearly positive and progressive fact of the works representing a multicultural understanding of literary experience is undermined repeatedly by the poor illustrations.

CRITICAL RECEPTION

Generally speaking, Salkey has never had the kind of critical attention that should come with the volume and quality of his work. However, most of his books have received reviews in very important journals, periodicals, and newspapers in the Caribbean, the United Kingdom, and the United States—in such publications as the *Sunday Gleaner*, the *Times Literary Supplement*, *The Listener*, and *The New Statesman*. Even less has been done with his children's stories than with his adult work. Recently, however, some significant work has been done by Peter Nazareth on the trickster motif in Salkey's fiction. Nazareth's *In the Trickster Tradition: Novels of Andrew*

Salkey, Francis Ebejer, and Ishmael Reed allows for a mechanism with which to approach Salkey's peculiar writing interests and styles. One of the more extensive studies of Salkey's children's books was done in 1968, and it clearly dismissed Salkey's work as being unimpressive. C. R. Gray's essay, "Mr. Salkey's Truth and Illusion," accuses Salkey of overt nostalgia and a failure to contend with the real issues of Jamaican life. Written before the publication of *Jonah Simpson* and subsequent novels, the criticism is understandable, even if it fails to recognize the complexity of a novel like *Drought.* Beyond that, Salkey's children's writing is still wanting of sustained critical appraisal. The commentary on his adult fiction, however, is useful for an understanding of the thematic interests of Salkey and for the very positive critical appraisal of his abilities as a storyteller and for his contribution to Caribbean writing.

There is, however, little question that his children's books remain some of the more important experiments in writing for juveniles in the Caribbean. Indeed, his anthology *Breaklight: An Anthology of Caribbean Poetry* (1971) remains one of the most influential and much used volumes in secondary schools in Jamaica. Salkey's impact on children's literature is significant.

BIBLIOGRAPHY

Young Adult Fiction by Andrew Salkey

Hurricane. Illus. William Papas. London: OUP, 1964; 1979. Harmondsworth: Puffin; New York: Penguin, 1977.

Earthquake. Illus. William Papas. London: OUP, 1965; 1979. New York: Roy, 1969.

Drought. Illus. William Papas. London: OUP, 1966.

Riot. Illus. William Papas. London: OUP, 1967; 1973.

Jonah Simpson. Illus. Gerry Craig. London: OUP, 1969. New York: Roy, 1970.

Joey Tyson. London: Bogle-L'Ouverture, 1974.

The River That Disappeared. London: Bogle-L'Ouverture, 1979.

Danny Jones. London: Bogle-L'Ouverture, 1980.

The One: The Story of How the People of Guyana Avenge the Murder of Their Pasero with Help from Brother Anancy and Sister Buxton. London: Bogle-L'Ouverture, 1985.

Brother Anancy and Other Stories. Harlow: Longman, 1994.

Adult Fiction by Andrew Salkey

A Quality of Violence. London: Hutchinson, 1959. Nendeln/Liechtenstein: Kraus, 1970. London: New Beacon, 1978.

Escape to an Autumn Pavement. London: Hutchinson, 1960. Nendeln/Liechsten-
   stein: Kraus, 1970.
The Adventures of Catullus Kelly. London: Hutchinson, 1969.
Anancy's Score. Short stories. London: Bogle-L'Ouverture, 1973.
Come Home, Malcom Heartland. London: Hutchinson, 1976.
The Late Emancipation of Jerry Stover. London: Hutchinson; Harlow: Longman,
   1982.

Poetry by Andrew Salkey

Jamaica. London: Hutchinson, 1973. London: Bogle-L'Ouverture, 1983.
In the Hills Where Her Dreams Live. Poems for Chile, 1973–1980. Havana: Casa
   de las Americas, 1979. CA: Black Scholar, 1981.
Land. CA: Black Scholar, 1979.
Away. London: Allison and Busby, 1980.

Travel Books by Andrew Salkey

Havana Journal. Harmondsworth: Penguin, 1971.
*Georgetown Journal: A Caribbean Writer's Journey from London via Port of
   Spain to Georgetown, Guyana, 1970.* London: New Beacon, 1972.

Anthologies Edited by Andrew Salkey

West Indian Stories. London: Faber, 1960; 1968.
Stories for the Caribbean. London: Paul Elek Books, 1965; 1972. New York:
   Dufour, 1968.
The Shark Hunters. London: Nelson, 1966.
Caribbean Prose: An Anthology for Secondary Schools. London: Evans, 1967.
Island Voices: Stories from the West Indies. New York: Liveright, 1970.
Breaklight: An Anthology of Caribbean Poetry. London: Hamish Hamilton, 1971.
   New York: Doubleday, 1972. New York: Anchor, 1973.
Caribbean Essays: An Anthology. London: Evans, 1973.
*Writing in Cuba since the Revolution: An Anthology of Poems, Short Stories, and
   Essays.* London: Bogle-L'Ouverture, 1977.
Caribbean Folk Tales and Legends. London: Bogle-L'Ouverture, 1980.

Selected Studies of Andrew Salkey

Allis, Jeanette. *West Indian Literature: An Index to Criticism 1930–1975.* Boston:
   Hall, 1981.
Brown, Lloyd. *West Indian Poetry.* Boston: Twayne, 1978.

Carr, Bill. "A Complex Fate: The Novels of Andrew Salkey." *The Islands in Between.* Ed. Bruce King. London: OUP, 1979. 100–108.

Gray, C. R. "Mr. Salkey's Truth and Illusion." *Jamaica Journal* 2 (June 1968): 46–54.

Griffiths, Gareth. *A Double Exile: African and West Indian Writing between Two Cultures.* London: Marion Boyars, 1978.

Herdeck, Donald E., ed. *Caribbean Writers: A Bio-Biographical-Critical Encyclopedia.* Washington, DC: Three Continents, 1979.

Huges, Michael. *A Companion to West Indian Literature.* London: Collins, 1979.

Moore, Gerald. *The Chosen Tongue.* London: Longman, 1969.

Nazareth, Peter. *The Novelist as Trickster: The Fiction of Andrew Salkey, Francis Ebejer and Ishmael Reed.* London: Bogle-L'Ouverture, 1994.

Ramchand, Kenneth. *The West Indian Novel and Its Background.* London: Faber, 1970.

DANNY SANTIAGO (DANIEL JAMES) (1911–1988)

Donnelyn Curtis

BIOGRAPHY

When Danny Santiago's novel *Famous All Over Town* was published in 1983, he was immediately and enthusiastically recognized by critics as a fresh young ethnic voice from the barrio. When it became known, a few months later, that "Danny Santiago" was the pseudonym of Daniel James, a seventy-three-year-old Yale-educated Anglo writer, the reception changed drastically as he became embroiled in a critical controversy and was accused of literary dishonesty.

This was not James' first setback as a writer. Thirty-five years earlier his screenwriting career was derailed when he was blacklisted after being called before the House Un-American Activities Committee (HUAC) to testify about his previous involvement with the Communist party. In order to keep writing, James was forced to write pseudonymously.

Daniel James grew up as an only child in a prosperous family in Kansas City, Missouri. His father had an Ivy League education, as did his grandparents, but the most famous members of the family were the outlaws Frank and Jesse James, his grandfather's cousins. Daniel's father imported and sold fine china, and in his spare time he wrote plays. He knew several of the artists and writers of the time. The family got a taste of the bohemian life during summers spent at Carmel, which served as James' "home base" for most of his life.

James graduated from Andover Academy and Yale University, where he majored in classical Greek. He became politically active in the John Reed Society during his senior year. After graduating during the depression, he held various jobs, eventually settling in California where he began writing plays. He was briefly involved in the production of plays in New York. Back in Carmel, he met Charlie Chaplin, who hired him as a screenwriter and assistant for *The Great Dictator*. In Hollywood, James joined the Communist party and continued writing plays with some success, followed by some unproductive years and disillusionment with the Communist party. Three years after quitting the party, he and his wife evoked the Fifth Amendment when questioned by the HUAC about their Communist activities. He continued writing screenplays under a pseudonym.

Dan and Lilith James became increasingly involved with the people in a small neighborhood in East Los Angeles, which, as Shamrock Street, became the setting for *Famous All Over Town* (1983). The Jameses organized theater productions and social organizations for young people in the neighborhood and became accepted into the family lives of the participants. James struggled for years to portray in fiction his experiences in the barrio community. His efforts were briefly rewarded with the acclaim he received when his novel was published. He died in Carmel at the age of seventy-seven.

MAJOR WORKS AND THEMES

Famous All Over Town is Santiago's only novel for young adults. He had some publishing success in the 1970s with short stories, some of which he reworked and included in his novel. As Daniel James, he had written *Winter Soldiers,* a somewhat doctrinaire play about the Nazi invasion of the Soviet Union; and with his wife, Lilith James, he wrote *Bloomer Girl,* which became a successful Broadway musical comedy (654 performances). After being blacklisted, he wrote two monster movie screenplays (*The Giant Behemoth* and *Gorgo*) under an assumed name (Daniel Hyatt).

Famous All Over Town portrays, in first-person episodic narrative, a year in the life of Rodolfo (Chato) Medina, a streetwise kid with a keen sense of humor and a high IQ. It is an eventful year for Chato and his family and friends, beginning with a chicken-killing coming-of-age ceremony on his fourteenth birthday and ending as he is carted off to juvenile detention after covering walls all over town with an artistic rendition of his name. During that year, Chato's family breaks up and the Southern Pacific Railroad condemns the Shamrock Street neighborhood, which it surrounds, and begins to bulldoze the houses.

Chato has near-fatal appendicitis at the same time his mother is having a baby; his sister upsets their father when she falls in love with a Mexican national; his father has troubles of his own when his pregnant girlfriend begins to make disruptive appearances. Chato glimpses his roots when the family takes a wild trip to Mexico, which is supposed to be an escape from some of their problems but only exacerbates them. He turns to his gang friends and ends up in trouble with the police more than once. In choosing to be loyal to his friends, Chato must reject the overtures of those from the "outside" who, charmed though exasperated, offer to help him transcend his environment. Chato's values do not allow him to abandon the neighborhood causes, even though they are lost causes that threaten to destroy his future, if not his life. He is a passenger when one of his friends, the driver, is killed during a joyride-turned-police-chase.

Daniel James convincingly captures the details of barrio life. Humor helps Chato deflect his pain, and the novel entertains as it delivers some subtle messages about social injustice. The episodes are short, sharp, and visual, designed to keep the attention of those who are more accustomed to electronic entertainment than to books. Chato comes across with an honest mixture of youthful naiveté and wisdom. His observations are delivered with a poignant irony that is precocious in a fourteen year old, but the structure of the novel allows some room for embellishment: at the beginning, an older Chato (twenty-eight), in the midst of an unnamed crisis, is returning to the transformed Shamrock Street where he then recalls his fourteenth year.

CRITICAL RECEPTION

James was not a prolific writer, but his writing was consistently admired and rewarded. His play *Winter Soldiers* won the Sidney Howard Memorial Award, a $1,500 prize given "to the young American playwright showing the most promise." The musical *Bloomer Girl*, based on the play he wrote with his wife, was a resounding success at the Shubert Theatre on Broadway in 1944. His story "The Somebody," which was first published in *Redbook* magazine, was included in *Best American Short Stories* of 1971.

Famous All Over Town has experienced critical ups and downs. When the first version was submitted to publishers in 1976, it was universally rejected. After it was finally published by Simon and Schuster in 1983, it garnered enthusiastic reviews and won the prestigious $5,000 Richard and

Linda Rosenthal Foundation Award for fiction from the American Academy and Institute of Arts and Letters in 1984 and the P.E.N. President's Award in 1985. According to James's obituary in the *New York Times* (21 May 1988), Simon and Schuster had wanted to submit the book for a Pulitzer Prize, but the Pulitzer rules required that a photograph of the author (which the publisher did not have) be submitted along with the book.

Initially the reviewers especially praised the author's language, his "distinctive delivery—brash but wistful, streetwise but genial, selectively broken-Englished" (*Kirkus Reviews*). Kearns, in *The Hudson Review*, was impressed by "the pleasure Santiago takes in his writing and the energy he brings to every page. . . . Fiction could not be less pretentious nor more confident in its mimetic power. . . . The language carries the book, for I suppose that without it all that would be left would be sociology. There's a good deal of sociological observation, of course, but the verve of Chato's language leaves the Social Sciences far behind" (559). It was lauded as a long-awaited Latino coming-of-age novel.

The truth of Santiago's identity became known shortly after his book won the Rosenthal Award. John Gregory Dunne was asked by the editors of the *New York Review of Books* to use it as a springboard for an essay on East Los Angeles. It so happened that Dunne and his wife, Joan Didion, had been friends of Daniel and Lilith James since renting a Hollywood house from them sixteen years earlier. Dunne, in fact, had acted as the intermediary between James and his agent, who got *Famous All Over Town* published without meeting its author. Dunne was becoming increasingly uncomfortable keeping "The Secret of Danny Santiago," as he titled his essay after persuading James to "come in from the cold" (26). The essay became a fascinating personalized account of James' literary and political life and milieu. As Jonah Raskin suggests in the *Dictionary of Literary Biography*, "His own story reflects a significant portion of twentieth-century American history" (254).

The unveiling of James unleashed "heated debates about pen names and literary hoaxes, ethnic literature and literary ethics" (Raskin 248). The issues were complex, the sides were not clearly drawn. Dunne reports that he had asked James "if he had considered the possibility of being accused of manufacturing a hoax. He shrugged and said the book itself was the only answer. If the book were good, it was good under whatever identity the author chose to use" (27), and many critics agreed, including Hispanic authors such as Thomas Sanchez and Richard Rodriguez. James flatly denied that he had any intention of deceiving his readers. He explained that his use of the Santiago persona served to loosen him up as a writer. Santiago "is like me when I'm drunk," he told *Time* (6 August 1984). In a letter to Dunne, he wrote, "He's so much freer than I am myself. He seems to know how he feels about everything, and none of the ifs ands and buts that I'm plagued with" (25).

Yet, some critics were offended, and felt that in their search for new Hispanic authors they were cheated. Felipe Ortega y Gasca suggested that "being thought of as a Latino writer was necessary to affirm the verisimilitude of the book and to promote sales of the book as a 'real slice-of-life work about Hispanic East Los Angeles' " (Haslam 248). The fact that the authenticity of the novel's narrative voice had never been doubted and that much of the praise had focused on its language brought into question the established assumption that literature about a minority group could (or should) only be written by a member of the group. James unintentionally expanded that discussion.

"We should not allow this notoriety to obscure the novel's achievement. *Famous All Over Town* remains a major work about Hispanic-American experience, even if we cannot read it exactly as we did a few months ago when we were innocent," wrote Charles Crowe in *Western American Literature* (347). The book is still in print and appears on some, but not on every, list of recommended young adult novels about the Hispanic experience. Judging from its initial critical reception, it seems likely that it would have secured a more prominent place in this canon if Santiago had really been who he was thought to be. As Hazel Rochman points out, the debate over the requirements for cultural authenticity in literature still rages. Her opinion is that "yes, authenticity matters, but there is no formula for how you acquire it. Anybody can write about anything—if they're good enough" (23). James says that he spent thirty-five years procuring his authenticity, becoming Danny Santiago, and his novel reflects that effort.

Regardless of James' success in acquiring a cultural voice he was not born with, and regardless of his intentions in perpetrating what he calls a "mild little deception" (Dunne 25), it still causes discomfort in literary circles when an author assumes a name that conveys misleading ethnic information, especially in a country that has experienced racism, cultural ignorance, and stereotyping. As Gerald Haslam points out, there are those who insist on reading novels such as *Famous All Over Town* as social documents, in which case "*who* wrote it takes on great importance" whereas "reading a novel as a work of art emphasizes the book itself and what it catalyzes in the reader" (248). "Anyone can write anything," he says, "but, given this country's discriminatory past, integrity may be as important as talent when even implicit assertions of ethnic authenticity are present"

(250). The furor over Santiago may have quieted since his death, but it will continue to rage around other writers who adopt pseudonyms denoting an ethnic identity not their own.

BIBLIOGRAPHY

Young Adult Fiction by Danny Santiago

Famous All Over Town. New York: Simon & Schuster, 1983.

Works for Adults by Danny Santiago

"The Somebody." *Redbook* (Feb. 1970): 68–69, 165, 168. Rpt. in *The Best American Short Stories*. Boston: Houghton-Mifflin, 1971; *Ethnic American Short Stories*. Ed. Katharine D. Newman. New York: Washington Square, 1975.
"Message from Home." *Playboy* 22.10 (1975): 145–46+.

Works Published as Daniel James

"Winter Soldiers." *The Best Plays of 1942–43*. Ed. Burns Mantle. New York: Dodd, Mead, 1943. 143–79.

Selected Studies of Danny Santiago

Crowe, Charles L. Rev. of *Famous All Over Town. Western American Literature* 29 (1985): 347–48.
Dunne, John Gregory. "The Secret of Danny Santiago." *New York Review of Books* 16 Aug. 1984: 17–18, 20, 22, 24–27.
Haslam, Gerald. "A Question of Authenticity, or Who Can Write What?" *Western American Literature* (Fall 1985): 246–50.
Kearns, George. "Worlds Well Lost." *The Hudson Review* 36:3 (1983): 559–60.
Raskin, Jonah. "Danny Santiago." *Dictionary of Literary Biography 122: Chicano Writers*. Ed. Francisco A. Loneli. 2nd ser. 247–254.
———. "The Man Who Would Be Danny Santiago." *San Francisco Bay Guardian* 28 Nov. 1984: 13–14+.
Rev. of *Famous All Over Town. Kirkus Reviews* 51 (1983): 126–27.
Roark, Anne C. "When Is a Pseudonym a Lie?" *San Francisco Chronicle, This World* 12 Aug. 1984: 17.
Rochman, Hazel, ed. *Against Borders: Promoting Books for a Multicultural World*. Chicago: American Library Association, 1993.

ISAAC BASHEVIS SINGER
(1904–1991)

Diana Arlene Chlebek

BIOGRAPHY

Isaac Bashevis Singer was born Icek-Hersz Zynger on July 14, 1904, in Leoncin, a Polish *shtetl* (Jewish community) near Warsaw. He was the third child and second boy of parents from devout rabbinical families. His father was a rabbi of the Chasidic Judaic tradition and was thus inclined to mysticism and a strong belief in the supernatural; his mother, Bathsheba Zylberman Zynger, was descended from the *misnagdim*, a sect of Orthodox Jews who opposed the Chasids and stressed a more rational and skeptical approach in seeking answers to problems connected with religious beliefs.

Singer received his early formal schooling in religious institutions in Radzymin, Poland. However, Singer remembers his family's rich tradition in storytelling as the best source of education in his formative years. His father would recount stories with a moral point, usually based upon the Bible, and tales of the supernatural inspired by the Cabbalah. Singer's mother would entertain him with Jewish folklore or chronicles of *shtetl* life centered in her childhood village of Bilgoray. His sister Hindele would tell stories of romantic love; his older brother Joshua, who was almost grown to manhood and had already thrust aside his father's religiosity in pursuit of secular interests, would narrate histories about foreign places and exotic cultures.

In 1908 when Singer was four years old, his family moved to Warsaw where his father set up an informal rabbinical court at 10 Krochmalna Street. The location would serve as the "spiritual address," in Singer's words, for his later evocations of Jewish life in Europe of the pre–World War II period. As a child he absorbed impressions of a crowded neighborhood teeming with colorful inhabitants who included laborers, shopkeepers, scholars, and criminal types from Warsaw's underworld—a panorama of characters who would eventually populate Singer's fictional world.

With the move to Warsaw, Singer began another phase of his education with attendance at *cheder* (Hebrew school) at the age of four. However, the books at the school, like those of his home, were all religious texts such as the Bible, prayer books, and the Talmud. To feed his imagination Singer began spending his allowance on Yiddish storybooks, penny dreadfuls whose stories sparked his own creativity and storytelling skills. Singer would combine these fantastic adventures with his family's treasure-trove of stories to entertain his classmates. Thus, his narrative art at this early age helped transform him from the school wallflower to one of the most popular boys at the *cheder*.

Secular books opened a new world of culture to Singer in his early adolescence as he began to discover classic European authors in Yiddish translation. When his brother Joshua gave him a copy of *Crime and Punishment* on his eleventh birthday, Singer found in Dostoyevsky's work a kindred intelligence that probed the conflict of faith, mysticism, and skepticism with an intensity that matched his own. The book also encouraged his taste for philosophy and spurred his lifelong interest in the literature of Russian realism.

The outbreak of World War I caused severe hardships for Singer's family, as it did for most of Warsaw's population. When food and fuel became especially scarce, the cruelty and chaos of war left a devastating impression upon the adolescent, now on the threshold of his bar mitzvah. His brother Joshua was forced to hide out in an artist's studio to avoid being drafted into the Russian army. When Singer visited his brother in this setting he was introduced to the world of the gentile and the bohemian intelligentsia. Here he saw female nudes for the first time and the casual disregard of religious laws such as that of kosher observance. Yet, the artistic, intellectual aspects of Joshua's liberated existence fascinated Singer, and the easy passage from his brother's studio to his father's study-house became an easy to-and-fro transition that he would later use as a structuring principle in his literary work.

In 1917, Singer, his mother, and his youngest brother Moishe moved to his grandparents' *shtetl* in Bilgoray, where he was to spend four critical formative years. This community was a sheltered enclave of medieval Jewish life which had preserved all of its ancient tradition and folklore. Describing Bilgoray's unique antiquity and its effect on him, Singer observed, "Time seemed to flow backwards. I lived Jewish history" (*In my Father's Court* 290).

He continued his education in Bilgoray's schools from 1917–1920 and began to read more broadly in secular literature, from the fairy tales of the Brothers Grimm and Hans Christian Andersen to the masterpieces of nineteenth-century European realism by Gogol, Chekhov, Tolstoy, and Maupassant. By the age of sixteen he was studying other languages, namely German, Polish, and modern Hebrew. His discovery of Spinoza's philosophy was a major spiritual event for him that shook the foundations of his religious belief. However, at the same time, Singer's reading of Hillel Zeitlin's *Promise of Good and Evil*, a synthesis of mystical and intellectual writing, reinforced his commitment to Judaistic tradition. During this period of his determination to pursue free inquiry, he also delved into the Cabbalah, a forbidden book for Jewish males under the age of thirty.

Growing impatient with the narrow scope of life in Bilgoray and with his own ignorance, Singer decided to continue his studies in Warsaw. He struck a compromise with his parents, who allowed him to return to the city only on the condition that he pursue rabbinical studies. Singer enrolled in Warsaw's Tachkemoni Rabbinical Seminary in 1921. He abhorred life in the institution and, having serious doubts about his commitment to religious tradition and dogma, left after his first year. He returned to Bilgoray for a short period and supported himself by teaching Hebrew. However by now, over his parents' protests, he was determined to make his living through a secular career—journalism.

In 1923 he returned to Warsaw to become a proofreader for *Literarishe Bletter*, a Yiddish literary magazine. He also supplemented his income by translating into Yiddish not only pulp novels but also classic works by literary masters such as Knut Hamsun, Thomas Mann, Erich Maria Remarque, and Stefan Zweig. As a young writer attempting to make his way in the establishment of Yiddish culture in Warsaw, Singer struggled both to find his niche in the literary world and to come to terms with his Jewish identity. He felt alienated from the mainstream Yiddish humanists and socialists whom he met in places like the Warsaw Writers' Club that he frequented. Eventually he was able to forge friendships with more conservative thinkers like Aaron Zeitlin, who encouraged his efforts at writing and also shared his interest in psychic research.

After a number of his literary submissions to Yiddish journals were rejected, one of his short stories won a prize in a contest sponsored by *Literarishe Bletter*. In 1927 his first story appeared in print, and thereafter his work was published on a regular basis, appearing under the name "Isaac Bashevis," a pseudonym he assumed after his mother Bathsheba. His first full-length work, *Satan in Goray*, was serialized in 1934 by the journal *Globus* and then published in book form in 1935.

His brother Joshua's novel *Yoshe Kalb*, published in 1932, became a great success in the Yiddish communities of Europe and the United States. The American journal, *The Jewish Daily Forward*, serialized the book and in 1933 invited the author to join its staff in New York City. Shortly after Joshua settled with his family in America, he urged Isaac to join him in 1935.

When he arrived in New York in 1935 he quickly secured a freelance position on the *Forward*. However, despite having Joshua and his family as an emotional anchor, Singer once again felt alienated, a ghost in a foreign land. In Poland, the language and literature of Yiddish was still very much alive, but in America it seemed to be a dying culture. Moreover, the chaos of American society overwhelmed him, just as it swallowed every ethnic culture that it embraced. He reacted to this discouraging situation with a form of writer's block, a literary amnesia, which lasted almost six years.

In 1937 Singer met a German émigré, Alma Haimann Wassermann, whom he married in 1940. For several years his wife's earnings as a saleswoman helped to supplement Singer's meager salary from his work on the *Forward*. *Satan in Goray* was republished in 1943 in an edition with some new short stories. When Joshua Singer died suddenly in 1944, Isaac was overwhelmed at the loss of his closest friend and mentor, but at the same time felt more freedom to write now that he was no longer working in his brother's shadow. With the publication of *Satan in Goray* in English in 1955, he began to garner a wider American audience. Singer received considerable attention from literary critics when Saul Bellow translated *Gimpel the Fool*, which was published for the *Partisan Review* in 1953.

From the 1950s on, as his Yiddish stories and novels were serialized in the *Forward*, they were reissued in book form and then published in English. With each book Singer would collaborate closely with the translator so that the final result would communicate the full flavor of the Yiddish original. In this fashion a steady succession of his novels and collections of his short stories appeared regularly over the next two decades. In 1966 the first volume of his memoirs was published; *In My Father's Court* captured the spirit of his Jewish childhood at 10 Krochmalna Street. That same year, Elizabeth Shub, his friend and editor at *Harper's,* persuaded Singer to write his first children's book. The result, *Zlateh the Goat and Other Stories* (1966), was illustrated by Maurice Sendak and won many accolades, including Newbery Honor Book status. Thereafter his children's books were published regularly, one almost every year, alongside his works for adults. Singer's reputation as an award-winning and best-selling author of books for all ages became firmly established.

In 1970 he won the second National Book Award ever granted for children's literature for *A Day of Pleasure* (1969), a re-creation of fourteen of the episodes of his Polish childhood described in the adult memoir, *In My Father's Court.* For the next several decades Singer became a frequent public lecturer and writer-in-residence at several university and college campuses. He continued his prodigious output of novels, short stories, essays, drama, and other works until his death from a stroke in Surfside, Florida, in 1991.

MAJOR WORKS AND THEMES

One of the most important reasons that Singer was drawn to writing books for the young was his conviction that children's books, unlike modern adult literature, were more likely to be rooted in what he called a "specific soil," particularly through a connection with folklore. Thus, in his first book for children, *Zlateh the Goat and Other Stories* (1966), he turns to *shtetl* life to explore a cross-section of themes also presented in his adult books. The title story, "Zlateh the Goat," is considered one of the best in the collection and is a good example of how Singer turns a Yiddish folk tale into an allegory that is significant for readers from all cultures. The frame of the narrative is a simple tale. It concerns a farm boy who sets out to sell his pet goat for slaughter when his family is hit by poverty just before Hannukah. The animal saves his young master from certain death in a freak snowstorm by sheltering him in a haystack and nursing him with her milk for three days. The details of time and place in the story have mythical overtones that are universally recognizable; the narrative's critical action, that of the life-giving process, occurs during a holy time of the year and within a womblike setting—that is, in the haystack. The special relationship between boy and animal resonates with a meaning that denotes a close, natural kinship between man and his environment.

Within the context of the Chelm and Schlemiel stories that are included in this collection, Singer recapitulates the theme of the "foolish innocent" that he examined in stories like "Gimpel the Fool." The ninny stories for children have didactic twists that transform the tales into lessons of universal application. Thus "The Snow in Chelm" relates how the citizens of Chelm strive, using their absurd illogic, to preserve one of nature's chimerical "treasures," in the form of jewel-like, freshly fallen snow. The tale illustrates the folly of man's attempts both to capture the evanescence of beauty and to exert absolute control over his environment. In the same vein, the shrewish wife in "The First Schlemiel" attempts through her careful planning to prepare her meals and her household for the proper observation of the Sabbath, as Judaic law decrees. However, like many of the protagonists in Singer's fiction, she learns that no amount of foresight or manipulation of her husband's greedy and foolish behavior can thwart the play of fate that is bound to bring disaster. Despite the humorous tone and the happy endings in these tales for the young, they illustrate the same serious lesson that Singer presents in his more sober adult tales concerning felicitous fools like Gimpel: that man's acceptance of life's deceptions and fate's cruel twists is his wisest and most noble recourse.

In 1967 Singer's *Mazel and Shlimazel* was published as a picture book for young readers. The story is based upon the traditional fairy tale motif of a battle between two spirits, one benevolent and the other malicious, who vie for the fate of a human. The Yiddish folk tale element presents the contest as a form of wager between two forces who control man's destiny, namely *Mazel* (good luck) and Shlimazel (bad luck). The story thus becomes a parable illustrating the paradoxical nature of the concept of free will. Singer consistently poses the same question throughout his works: to what extent does man have free choice if he is also at the mercy of a divine will?

The Fearsome Inn (1967), issued as a picture book, is a long tale of magic that illustrates the power of traditional religion to overcome evil in the world. Of the three male protagonists in the story, it is only the rabbinical student who is able to interpret the secret of the evil dreams used by the devil innkeepers to seduce and befuddle human victims. The student also applies his knowledge of the Cabbalah, the Judaic book of mysteries, to contain the demonic forces with what is literally white magic, namely a chalk circle drawn around the demons in order to protect himself and his companions. *The Fearsome Inn*, like many of Singer's adult books about the demonic, is a cautionary fable about the tremendous dangers and benefits that result from man's spiritual and intellectual energy. Such tales are artistic forms of cultural and psychological insight into the supernatural that Singer himself dubbed "spiritual stenography."

In 1968 with the publication of *When Shlemiel Went to Warsaw and Other Stories*, Singer presented his young readers with another gift from his Yiddish heritage. In the preface he described the collection as folk tales bequeathed to him by his mother from her mother and grandmother. He also emphasized a fundamental continuity between his stories for mature audiences and for children, affirming, "There is no basic difference between tales for adults and for young people. The same spirit, the same interest in the supernatural is in all of them." This dismissal of the age gap erases time and acts as a universalizing agent that helps the reader to cross cultural lines and brings the past world of Polish Jewry to present-day America. It establishes a framework of interpretation that combines orthodox customs and beliefs with mystical themes, but it also allows a subversion of that pattern, as this collection demonstrates. In the title story, "When Shlemiel Went to Warsaw," the protagonist has a trick played on him so that he ends up in his own town of Chelm. Choosing to accept the illogic of this situation on faith like Singer's other foolish innocent, Gimpel, he reconfigures the original Chelm into Chelm 2. Singer thus uses the folk elements of the ninny tale to demonstrate a universal lesson: man in his attempt to make sense of a confusing world or to satisfy his obsessions will convince himself that reality is a subjective construct (or vice versa).

In one of the original stories in the collection, "Menaseh's Dream," Singer deals with some of the probing questions that he had begun asking in his childhood, particularly those that dealt with man's ultimate destiny. In this story, the protagonist is an orphan who is at odds with his environment. In his dream his religious, scholarly grandfather, Tobias the Scribe, guides him through a magic palace which is filled both with his forebears and with remnants of his past, particularly the artifacts and toys associated with the Jewish holidays his family celebrated. The rooms where he observes the images from storybooks he read and visions from his dreams are also centered on figures and events from the Old Testament and from Jewish folklore. Finally, he also sees his destiny in the form of the girl he is to marry. Thus, this enchanted castle, which his grandfather calls "the place where nothing is lost," represents in man's consciousness the node of connections that teaches him about the cultural continuity between himself and his environment and about the spiritual link between life and death. Both for Menaseh and for the child within us all, the castle becomes a symbolic place of consolation, love, and hope—a crucial source of roots.

A Day of Pleasure, published the next year in 1969, also focused on the theme of origins. This memoir recreated for his younger audience the same ambiance of his childhood at 10 Krochmalna Street that he had described in his autobiography, *In My Father's Court* (1966). The focus in the juvenile version is on the activities and observations of Isaac as the protagonist of most of the episodes in the book, whereas the center of the adult memoir is the curious cast of characters and activity that passed through Rabbi Singer's religious court. Moreover, *A Day of Pleasure* becomes a document of consolation for the destroyed world of Polish Jewry through its extensive portrayals of some of the virtuous people that young Isaac observed in the ghetto: the charitable, kindly dairyman, Reb Asher, and the honest, motherly gentile washerwoman. *In My Father's Court*, on the other hand, presents a more disturbing adult world where people converge to unburden their dark secrets to the rabbi, who is often at a loss to fathom their destructive passions. However, in *A Day of Pleasure*, when young Isaac stands on the threshold of adolescence, bewildered by the transformations beginning in his body and in his intellect, Rabbi Singer is ready with consolation and with the wisdom of a religious sage. When his son reacts with confusion at his own urgent questions concerning the opposite sex and his desire to explore the secrets of the Cabbalah, a forbidden book, his father gently responds, "You are growing up, my son. That is what is happening to you."

In one of his early adult novels, *The Slave* (1962), Singer had explored the theme of cultural interface between Jews and gentiles in early Poland during its pagan period. He reworked the concept into a book for children called *Jozef and Koza, or the Sacrifice to the Vistula* (1970). In *The Slave*, which ends tragically with the death of the Jewish protagonist and his converted pagan wife, the conflict between good and evil is presented in a realistic and historical manner as a consequence of complex human passions. In *Joseph and Koza* Jewish and Slavic elements are strongly woven into the narrative; the struggle for the souls of the pagans is presented as a battle against supernatural forces represented by the witch Zla. However, an optimistic belief in the triumph of virtue and man's capacity for redemption plays a strong role in both versions of the story.

Singer's longest work for children, *Alone in the Wild Forest* (1971), is also thematically one of his most complex. The structure of the story is based on Cabbalistic magic and on Talmudic cosmology concerning the struggle of good and evil in the world and the nature of man's destiny. The protagonist must not simply overcome his evil enemy, but must also guide him in expiating his sins. Singer portrays each of the story's characters as reincarnated soul, repaying the sins of a past life through the burdens of the present in an effort to eventually unite with the Divinity. Singer saves the story from collapse into sheer abstractions by weaving into the narrative several fairy tale motifs and concrete symbols. Thus, the concept of the "wild forest," reflected in the book's title, expresses the state of a confusing world that the protagonist must confront. The image provides a continuity between Singer's works, for he uses it in other stories, most notably in "Menaseh's Dream."

With the publication of *The Fools of Chelm and Their History* (1973), Singer presents his young readers with one of the treasures of Yiddish humor. Chelm historically existed as a Polish *shtetl* near Lublin, but it was Jewish folklore that recreated it as the archetypal home of amiable fools. The book presents a Swiftian view of the follies of Chelm in a straightforward narrative with elements of slapstick that stamp the tale as simple child's play. However, Singer presents a parody of bad government and a satire of Jewish scholarly tradition in the absurd council deliberations of the Chelm "sages" that assumes a level of sophistication and knowledge of politics to be found in a more mature reader. Singer's pessimism on the fate of modern man clearly reverberates in the wry humor of the story's last sentence. After putting his country through the fruitless rigors of a phony war with a mistaken enemy, Chelm's head sage arrogantly observes, "The chances are good that someday the world will be one great Chelm" (57). The satire presents the grotesquely humorous side of the xenophobic conflicts that historically ravaged Poland and that Singer used frequently as a backdrop in his fiction.

Naftali the Storyteller and His Horse, Sus, and Other Stories (1976) is Singer's landmark collection for children. His preface dedicates the book to his defunct family as well as to his young readers who "contemplate the wonder of growing up and facing the riddle of life and love." The theme that runs throughout the collection's most significant tales concerns the crucial decision of determining one's goals in life. The title story, "Naftali the Storyteller and His Horse, Sus," is crucial in this regard, both as autobiography and as literature, tracing the growth of a writer's mind. Naftali's obsession with tales, his status as a storyteller among the boys at his *cheder*, his keen observation of human behavior and phenomena in nature are all parts of Singer's memoirs. Even as a grown man, Naftali's status is that of a childlike innocent; he roams the countryside, gathering information and impressions which he then disperses as stories to entertain others. Naftali's meeting with his kindred spirit, the bookseller Reb Zebulum, culminates in a supreme act of generosity and of destiny. With the fruits of their life's work, Naftali's artistic treasure of stories gathered and

Zebulum's monetary treasure from stories sold, the two men create and donate a monument to storytelling—a palace where tales never end, prefigured in "Menaseh's Dream" as the place where nothing is lost.

With the publication of *The Golem* in 1982, Singer explores a theme that reaches far back into the history of Judaic teaching and thought, namely, the problem of creation and the mystery of life. He uses original material from the Jewish chronicles that tell stories of conflicts between Jews and antisemitic Christians in Eastern Europe. Through his knowledge of the Talmud and of Cabbalistic mysticism, the rabbi of Prague creates the golem in order to rescue a Jew who is falsely accused of the blood-ritual murder of a Christian child. Singer's version departs from the tone of the deadly serious original chronicle in his portrayal of the golem's maturation into an outsized, exuberant adolescent; the creature rampages through the *shtetl*, insists on attending *cheder*, demands his bar mitzvah, suffers his first pangs of love for the rabbi's servant girl, and is even drafted for the country's army. It is this depiction of an alienated being who desires so intensely to become a member of the Jewish community and of the human race that renders poignant the final destruction of the golem by the rabbi.

Even as Singer's pessimism about the destiny of mankind seemed to deepen in the novels and short stories of his later career, his public lectures and interviews revealed an optimistic faith in the clarity of insight and the common-sense instincts of young people. He professed as one of his literary ambitions the publication of a history of philosophy for children, pointing out that they were "deeply concerned with so-called eternal questions." It was Singer's destiny, however, to bestow upon them an even greater gift which he himself described as "good books for children . . . the only hope, the only refuge."

CRITICAL RECEPTION

One of the fascinations that Singer's work has always held for critics is its imperviousness to definition or categorization. His early stories and novels frustrated and scandalized his colleagues in the Yiddish literary world because they saw in his writing an excess of superstition, sex, and, worst of all, immoral Jewish characters. To the Yiddish humanist, Singer's fiction seemed to be a retrograde portrayal of a lost world. However, a contemporary Jewish-American writer, Cynthia Ozick, challenged this view, pointing out that Singer was no betrayer of Jewish idealism, but rather a true moralist whose demons represent inhuman forces, such as the obsessive will that undermines mankind's best actions.

Other literary critics recognized that, despite the Old World setting and traditional moral viewpoint in his writing, Singer's fiction embodied a unique form of modernism that was also redolent of Kafka, Borges, and Nabokov. Singer's first translated works, such as *The Family Moskat* (1950), received scant reviews. But when Saul Bellow's translation of "Gimpel the Fool" appeared in 1955, it elicited admiration for Singer's mastery of the short story form. Alfred Kazin praised the artful style of "Gimpel," particularly its combination of "the abandon of modern art" with "a personal commitment to the immemorial Jewish vision of the world" (284).

Singer himself acknowledged that for him the short story was easier to plan, hence more controllable and perfect. Critics consistently praised the innovations of each of his short story collections as they were published. Singer's extraordinary range of styles and tones in his tales was perceived as the perfect vehicle to give narrative expression to the dialectic between Orthodox Judaism and modern morality. His collection *A Crown of Feathers and Other Stories* (1973) garnered him a National Book Award in 1974 and accolades such as "our greatest living storyteller."

Singer's books for the young have received less substantial criticism than his adult works. His collections of tales, such as *Zlateh the Goat and Other Stories* and *When Shlemiel Went to Warsaw and Other Stories*, were praised for their mastery of folklore elements and their poetic evocation of *shtetl* life for young audiences; both garnered award and honor status from several review sources. His longer, more complex works were criticized for structural deficiencies and arduous thematic concepts. His most ambitious work in this regard, *Alone in the Wild Forest*, was dismissed by many reviewers as humorless and confusing. Until Eric Kimmel's in-depth analysis appeared, the Cabbalistic concepts of the narrative were almost totally ignored. *A Day of Pleasure* received awards and the highest praise for its poignant visualization of the vanished Old World for the benefit of the children in the New World. Children were always Singer's most appreciative critics, and he was happy and proud of the letters he received from his young readers, including the questions and critiques about his books.

After Singer's writings were published in English, he soon acquired a worldwide audience with the majority of his works translated into at least fifteen languages. In 1978 he received the ultimate universal recognition for his value to the literary world when he was awarded the Nobel Prize for Literature. In the award, he was cited for "his impassioned narrative art which, with roots in a Polish-Jewish cultural tradition, brings universal conditions to life" (11). In his acceptance of the award, he acknowledged the hope for the world that young people represented for him, citing his ten reasons in "Why I Write for Children" (*Nobel*, 13–14). At the same time he paid tribute both to his own wonderful Jewish heritage and to all cultural heritage, stating: "In a figurative way, Yiddish is the wise and humble language of us all, the idiom of the frightened and hopeful humanity" (9).

BIBLIOGRAPHY

Young Adult Fiction in English by Isaac Bashevis Singer

Zlateh the Goat and Other Stories. Trans. Elizabeth Shub and Isaac Bashevis Singer. Illus. Maurice Sendak. New York: Harper & Row, 1966.

The Fearsome Inn. Trans. Elizabeth Shub and Isaac Bashevis Singer. Illus. Nonny Hogogrian. New York: Scribners, 1967. London: Collins, 1970.

Mazel and Schlimazel; or, The Milk of a Lioness. Trans. Elizabeth Shub and Isaac Bashevis Singer. Illus. Margot Zemach. New York: Farrar, Straus & Giroux, 1967. London: Cape, 1979.

A Day of Pleasure: Stories of a Boy Growing Up in Warsaw. Trans. Channah Kleinerman-Goldstein et al. Illus. with contemporary photographs by Roman Vishniac. New York: Farrar, Straus & Giroux, 1969. London: MacRae, 1980.

Alone in the Wild Forest. Trans. Isaac Bashevis Singer and Elizabeth Shub. Illus. Margot Zemach. New York: Farrar, Straus & Giroux, 1971.

The Fools of Chelm and Their History. Trans. Isaac Bashevis Singer and Elizabeth Shub. Illus. Uri Shulevitz. New York: Farrar, Straus & Giroux, 1973.

When Shlemiel Went to Warsaw and Other Stories. Trans. Isaac Bashevis Singer and Elizabeth Shub. Illus. Margot Zemach. New York: Farrar, Straus & Giroux, 1968. Hammondsworth, UK: Longman, Young, 1974.

Why Noah Chose the Dove. Trans. Elizabeth Shub. Illus. Eric Carle. New York: Farrar, Straus & Giroux, 1974.

Naftali the Storyteller and His Horse, Sus, and Other Stories. Trans. Joseph Singer, Isaac Bashevis Singer, et al. Illus. Margot Zemach. New York: Farrar, Straus & Giroux, 1976. Oxford: Oxford UP, 1977.

The Power of Light: Eight Stories of Hannukah. Illus. Irene Lieblich. New York: Farrar, Straus & Giroux, 1980.

The Golem. Illus. Uri Shulevitz. New York: Farrar, Straus & Giroux, 1982. London: Deutsch, 1983.

Stories for Children. New York: Farrar, Straus & Giroux, 1984.

Works for Adults by Isaac Bashevis Singer

The Family Moskat. Trans. A. H. Gross. New York: Knopf; London: 1950.

Satan in Goray. Trans. Jacob Sloan. New York: Noonday, 1955. London: Owen, 1958.

Gimpel the Fool and Other Stories. Trans. Saul Bellow et al. New York: Noonday, 1957. London: Owen, 1958. London: Secker & Warburg, 1966.

The Magician of Lublin. Trans. Elaine Gottlieb and Joseph Singer. New York: Noonday, 1960. London: Secker & Warburg, 1961.

The Spinoza of Market Street. Trans. Martha Glicklich, Cecil Hemley, et al. New York: Farrar, Straus & Cudahy, 1961. London: Secker & Warburg, 1962.

The Slave. Trans. Isaac Bashevis Singer and Cecil Hemley. New York: Farrar, Straus & Cudahy, 1962. London: Secker & Warburg, 1963.

Short Friday and Other Stories. Trans. Joseph Singer et al. New York: Farrar, Straus & Giroux, 1964. London: Secker & Warburg, 1967. Harmondsworth, UK: Longman, Young, 1970.

In My Father's Court. Trans. Channah Kleinerman-Goldstein, Elaine Gottlieb, and Joseph Singer. New York: Farrar, Straus & Giroux, 1966. London: Secker & Warburg, 1967.

Selected Short Stories of Isaac Bashevis Singer. Ed. Irving Howe. New York: Modern Library, 1966.

The Manor. Trans. Joseph Singer and Elaine Gottlieb. New York: Farrar, Straus & Giroux, 1967. London: Secker & Warburg, 1968.

The Seance and Other Stories. Trans. Roger H. Klein, Cecil Hemley, et al. New York: Farrar, Straus & Giroux, 1968. London: Cape, 1970.

The Estate. Trans. Joseph Singer, Elaine Gottlieb, and Elizabeth Shub. New York: Farrar, Straus & Giroux, 1969. London: Cape, 1970.

A Friend of Kafka and Other Stories. Trans. Isaac Bashevis Singer, Elizabeth Shub, et al. New York: Farrar, Straus & Giroux, 1970. London: Cape, 1972.

An Isaac Bashevis Singer Reader. New York: Farrar, Straus & Giroux, 1971.

The Topsy-Turvy Emperor of China. Trans. Isaac Bashevis Singer and Elizabeth Shub. Illus. William Pene du Bois. New York: Harper & Row, 1971.

Enemies, A Love Story. Trans. Aliza Shevrin and Elizabeth Shub. New York: Farrar, Straus & Giroux; London: Cape, 1972.

The Wicked City. Trans. Isaac Bashevis Singer and Elizabeth Shub. Illus. Leonard Everett Fisher. New York: Farrar, Straus & Giroux, 1972.

A Crown of Feathers and Other Stories. Trans. Isaac Bashevis Singer, Laurie Colwin, et al. New York: Farrar, Straus & Giroux, 1973. London: Cape, 1974.

The Hasidim. With Ira Moskowitz. New York: Crown, 1973.

Passions and Other Stories. Trans. Isaac Bashevis Singer et al. New York: Farrar, Straus & Giroux, 1975. London: Cape, 1976.

A Tale of Three Wishes. Illus. by Irene Lieblich. New York: Farrar, Straus & Giroux, 1975.

A Little Boy in Search of God; or Mysticism in a Personal Light. With Ira Moskowitz. Trans. Joseph Singer. Garden City, NY: Doubleday, 1976.

Shosha. Trans. Joseph Singer and Isaac Bashevis Singer. New York: Farrar, Straus & Giroux, 1978. London: Cape, 1979.

A Young Man in Search of Love. Trans. Joseph Singer. Garden City, NY: Doubleday, 1978.

Nobel Lecture. New York: Farrar, Straus & Giroux; London: Cape, 1979.

Old Love. Trans. Joseph Singer, Isaac Bashevis Singer, et al. New York: Farrar, Straus & Giroux, 1979. London: Cape, 1980.

Reaches of Heaven: A Story of Baal Shem Tov. New York: Farrar, Straus & Giroux, 1980.

Lost in America. Garden City, NY: Doubleday, 1981.

The Collected Stories. New York: Farrar, Straus & Giroux; London: Cape, 1982.

The Penitent. New York: Farrar, Straus & Giroux, 1983. London: Cape, 1984.

Yentl the Yeshiva Boy. Trans. Marion Magid and Elizabeth Pollet. New York: Farrar, Straus & Giroux, 1983.

Love and Exile: A Memoir. Garden City, NY: Doubleday, 1984. London: Cape, 1985.

Gifts. Philadelphia: Jewish Publication Society, 1985.

The Image and Other Stories. New York: Farrar, Straus & Giroux, 1985. London: Cape, 1986.

The Death of Methuselah and Other Stories. New York: Farrar, Straus & Giroux, 1987. London: Cape, 1988.

The King of the Fields. New York: Farrar, Straus & Giroux, 1987. London: Cape, 1988.

Scum. New York: Farrar, Straus & Giroux; London: Cape, 1991.

Selected Studies of Isaac Bashevis Singer

Alexander, Edward. *Isaac Bashevis Singer*. Boston: Twayne, 1980.

Buchen, Irving H. *Isaac Bashevis Singer and the Eternal Past*. New York: New York UP, 1968.

Farrell Lee, Grace. *From Exile to Redemption: The Fiction of Isaac Bashevis Singer*. Carbondale: Southern Illinois UP, 1987.

Kazin, Alfred. "The Saint as Schlemiel." *Contemporaries*. Boston: Little, Brown, 1962. 283–88.

Kimmel, Eric. "I. B. Singer's *Alone in the Wild Forest*: A Kabbalistic Parable." *Children's Literature in Education* 18 (Fall 1975): 147–48.

Kresh, Paul. *Isaac Bashevis Singer: The Magician of West 86 St*. New York: Dial, 1979.

Malin, Irving, ed. *Critical Views of Isaac Bashevis Singer*. New York: New York UP, 1969.

Miller, David Neal, ed. *Recovering the Canon: Essays on Isaac Bashevis Singer*. Leiden: E. J. Brill, 1986.

Rosenblatt, Paul, and Gene Koppel. *Isaac Bashevis Singer on Literature and Life*. Tucson: U of Arizona P, 1971.

GARY SOTO
(1952–)

Ronald Edwards

BIOGRAPHY

Gary Soto was born in Fresno, California, on April 12, 1952, and grew up in the barrio amidst the agriculturally rich San Joaquin Valley. A third-generation Chicano raised in the predominantly Hispanic, poor, west side of the city, Soto experienced many of the disadvantages associated with poverty and his ethnic heritage. Having gained firsthand knowledge during his youth working as a migrant laborer, he sought to bring these early childhood experiences to light through his poetry, and later his prose.

Mostly autobiographical in nature, Soto's literature is replete with the plight of the poor and economically disadvantaged. Many of his poems focus on his own relatives who themselves labored long hours in the fields of the San Joaquin Valley picking fruit and cotton, as well as toiling in the packing houses of the Sun Maid Raisin Company and other industries.

As with many Mexican-Americans, Soto's parents and grandparents also worked in these same packing houses and fields in the Central Valley. Both his parents were American born, but it was their Mexican heritage which greatly influenced Soto's growth and development. These cultural traditions instilled during his childhood and the recollections of growing up in the barrio with his mother, stepfather, and grandparents served as a foundation for most of Soto's literary contributions for years to come.

At the age of five, Soto and his family moved to a Mexican-American community on the outskirts of the city of Fresno. Unfortunately, tragedy struck Soto almost immediately with the accidental death of his father who was only twenty-seven. Suddenly, his mother became responsible for raising three children primarily by herself, although with some assistance from Soto's grandparents.

Educated in the local schools, Soto admits to not being a good student in elementary and secondary school. He was more concerned with sports and games than with studying. After graduating from high school in 1970, but lacking any literary aspirations, Soto enrolled at Fresno City College, intent upon pursuing a major in geography. This initial inclination soon dissipated in favor of studying literature.

This transformation in Soto's life and his desire to pursue a literary career occurred around the age of twenty while he was still attending City College in Fresno. Like so many artists, Soto became interested in writing after he discovered how much the art form personally affected him. Reading some of the "Beat" poets such as Ferlinghetti, Corso, and Ginsberg, as well as Pablo Neruda and Theodore Roethke, Soto became hooked. His infatuation with poetry was so intense that he proceeded to write his own poetry and eventually took classes at California State University-Fresno.

After graduating *magna cum laude* from the university in 1974 with a degree in English, he got married the following year to Carolyn Sadako Oda, the daughter of Japanese-American farmers. Soto then went on to obtain his master's degree in creative writing from the University of California-Irvine in 1976, and became writer-in-residence at San Diego State University shortly thereafter. Since then he has gone on to hold associate professorships in both Chicano studies and English at the University of California at Berkeley.

Considered by many to be the best Chicano poet of his generation and an accomplished writer of young adult fiction, Gary Soto has garnered numerous prestigious awards for his literary efforts. In 1975 he won the first in a long series of awards, the Academy of American Poets Prize and *The Nation* Award. Since then the list of accolades have included the following: United States Award of the International Poetry Forum, 1977; Bess Hokin Prize for poetry, 1978; Guggenheim Fellowship, 1980; National Endowment for the Arts Fellowship, 1981 and 1990; Levinson Art Award for poetry, 1984; American Book Award, Before Columbus Foundation, 1985; Best Book for Young Adults designation, American Library Association, 1990; and *Parenting Magazine*'s Reading Magic Award, 1990.

Currently, Soto resides in Berkeley, California, with his wife and daughter Mariko. Among his hobbies are reading, traveling, and karate.

MAJOR WORKS AND THEMES

Poetry and young adult fiction have undergone a gradual, but distinct, transformation in the last twenty-five years. Instead of the concern with formal rhyme, specific poetic forms, and traditional literary devices, a focus on less-structured qualities and multicultural themes has emerged. Soto reflects these changes in his poetry and prose and represents this new wave of artists who have moved away from using regular rhythm and meter to a more narrative structure and style. And although he writes poetry more often than fiction, his poetry is often so narrative that it reads *like* fiction.

The narratives which Soto presents depict the way he interprets the world he has experienced. By using this poetic device, Soto is able to accurately tell the stories he feels are important and in the process show the connection that exists among the main characters in his literature.

Through his autobiographical writing, he is able to exhibit a harsh realism about life, as well as examine the social inequalities that exist for those growing up Chicano in the barrio. His concern for precise language and use of metaphors describing urban violence and the despair of the migrant laborer in the rural areas of the California agricultural fields reinforce his desire to create a sense of place in his literature.

These unique artistic characteristics are clearly revealed in *The Elements of San Joaquin* (1977), Soto's highly acclaimed first volume of poetry. Without resorting to rhyme and the use of conventional meter, Soto vividly captures the essence of life for the migrant laborer and the way in which all of these individuals seek a better existence beyond life's daily drudgery and routine. On the one hand, there is the social oppression and economic immobility of urban life and the physical hardships of rural life. In this setting, migrant laborers are spiritually demoralized by the futility of their position in the overall socioeconomic marketplace. On the other hand, Soto reveals his own personal optimism in his longing for a better way of life for Mexican-Americans and people in general.

Soto's concerns for the economic condition of the Mexican-American have prompted some people to compare his work with that of Philip Levine, one of Soto's instructors at the California State University-Fresno. In fact, in *Speaking of Poets*, Soto credits Levine with not only inspiring in him the ability to read poetry correctly, but also with instilling the desire and ability to eventually manufacture his own style of poetry (Copeland 94).

In most of Soto's poetry and prose there is a common affinity for the extended family and the security that is discovered or rekindled by this affiliation. According to Juan Bruce-Novoa, the family acts as the stabilizer afloat in a sea of conflict and chaos (213). Likewise, it is here that Soto has so often recreated his own childhood experiences in the poetry and prose he sculpts for his audience.

This emphasis on the family unit is very evident in the volume *Black Hair* (1985). Soto focuses in these poems on his own family and friends by distinctly portraying his adolescent experiences and the moments he spends with his young daughter. Although not critically well received when first published, *Black Hair* is considered significant in that it surpasses mere reflections of his own life and travels into previously unexplored territory. With the advent of *Black Hair*, Soto departs from the common themes of despair and social chaos into a world focused more on love. He is able to transcend cultural boundaries and articulate themes common to other ethnic groups. That same year, 1985, also saw publication of Soto's first prose work, *Living up the Street*. Thus, there emerged not only a change in writing style concerning his poetry, but also a serious exploration into the field of prose.

Living up the Street reveals yet another major theme in Soto's repertoire. Although he writes from his own particular worldview, Soto also believes that there are specific values and feelings that are universal. These beliefs transcend ethnic barriers and affect everyone similarly. While relating the recollections of his childhood, adolescence, and adulthood, Soto makes every effort not to proselytize his readers. Instead, he stresses that cultural diversity does not always bring about harmony, but may, instead, result in more confusion and conflict. This situation manifests itself in a dual consciousness, whereby the socializing forces of the mass media are so pervasive that they completely dominate the Chicanos' own cultural expression (Erben and Erben 43). This theme is often repeated in Soto's works where he sees the influence that fashion, television, and other forms of popular culture have in the lives of his family and on Chicano identity itself.

Most of Soto's literature since the beginning of the 1980s has centered on nostalgic recollection of his youth and is geared primarily for young adults. This scenario surfaces in his highly touted and award-winning *Baseball in April and Other Stories* (1990). Having received both the American Library Association's Best Book for Young Adults designation and the Beatty Award, this collection of eleven short stories carries on Soto's interest in describing everyday life and growing up poor and Mexican-American in California's Central Valley. The themes of youth and age, love and friendship, success and failure reveal in convincing detail the experiences of contemporary young adults in our multicultural society. As Soto has accomplished so often before, he is able to effectively make his characters come to life, as well as the families who care for them. His ability to portray adolescents and the cultural dynamics they experience in our diverse society is unique among today's writers. The vast majority of his literature focuses on a Hispanic neighborhood similar to the one he grew up in, but Soto is able to transcend this locale and make his themes and characters universally applicable.

Although he still writes on social issues and the need to examine the urban condition, Soto's later undertakings have dealt more with a positive approach to life as opposed to one concerned with despair and the ordeal of growing up in the barrio. Soto has made a conscious effort to make his literature readable to a diverse audience by rejecting obvious political content (Tatum 158). His recent artistic endeavors clearly reflect this literary shift. This change in Soto's writing is clearly displayed in *Fire in My Hands* (1991). Soto realigns himself by eliminating events that are more indigenous to the barrio. Instead, he focuses more on situations which are ordinary to children across the spectrum. Social criticism gives way to an examination of childhood activities, sans the psychological impediments.

Likewise, in *Neighborhood Odes* (1992), Soto celebrates life in the neighborhood. Joy, love, and childhood reminiscences are abundant. Charles Tatum has talked about the pain and misery of Soto's earlier literature (158), but this attitude has waned as reflected in *Neighborhood Odes*. The collection also reveals a more universal approach in its examination of adolescents and their experiences.

Finally, Soto comes full circle in *Local News* (1993). Ordinary events in life are given new meaning through the author's precise narrative. In the end, Soto's maturity as a writer, given over twenty years to develop, culminates. In his attempt to transcend cultural boundaries, Soto has mollified the demands he places on his readers. Only traces of the social criticism evident in his earlier works remain. Because of this modification in writing style, he is more effective in eradicating the racial barriers that might have existed if this change had not occurred. Consequently, the audience Soto now attracts is more diverse.

CRITICAL RECEPTION

Most critics agree that Gary Soto is the most recognizable Chicano writer of this generation. Whether this opinion is the direct result of objective critical analysis or due to the fact that, overall, there is a paucity of Chicano young adult writers to critique, remains unanswered. Regardless of the reasons for Soto's critical reception, he has inspired an abundance of criticism during his career, reflecting a number of common denominators.

A self-professed imagist, Soto is adept at using images to depict the human condition. As he so often does, Soto resorts to the image of the street to metaphorically unify his poetry. By implementing these cultural markers, Soto is able to include a Chicano perspective regarding issues which are, in fact, universal in nature. Julian Olivares clearly points out Soto's ability to organize the elements in his poetry to allow the reader to see a broader vision (46). Because of his meticulous use of the language, Soto's message is delivered unobtrusively.

In "Ambiguity in the Poetry of Gary Soto," Patricia de la Fuente reinforces these attributes by referring to Soto as having achieved an "exceptionally high level of linguistic sophistication" (35). This can only be interpreted in a positive way and certainly one denoting an advanced level of creative development.

Heiner Bus maintains that Soto uses his poetry to emphasize the need for coherence in one's life. In effect, "to create islands of stability" (196). Bus also believes that it is this continuity which is so vital for the autobiographer in his work (192). In essence, Soto is able to rectify the discontinuity of life through the continuity of his poetry (Olivares 43).

A sense of confusion and disorder is prevalent in Soto's literature. Although this is not an uncommon thread in other pieces of poetry and prose, Soto employs the family to focus on this chaos. The family acts as an instrument in connecting the past to the present. This legacy of familial relationships that Bruce-Novoa discusses does not always promote a positive environment, but instead may be laden with distrust (214).

By refraining from telling people what to think, in favor of letting individuals judge for themselves, Soto has effectively served his audience. His unmistakable philosophical resonance has proven to be a key ingredient in his success as a writer. He remains detached from the characters he portrays, as well as the tone of the literature he writes. Soto allows his readers to interpret and reflect on the images he conveys in a very unobtrusive fashion (Varela-Ibarra 383).

In a similar manner, Soto succeeds in not politicizing with undue rhetoric. His style of writing does not indoctrinate, but serves as a conduit for disseminating ideas to a diverse clientele. Tatum understands Soto as being determined to generalize the Chicano cultural experience, thus making it more applicable and relevant to his readers (158).

Soto has not been reticent concerning his desire to inspire other Chicanos to write about their culture and experiences. He has been successful in instilling this passion and assisting young Chicanos to believe that they possess an identity worth sharing with the rest of the United States. In this respect, Soto reveals yet another of his attributes, his desire to promote his craft.

BIBLIOGRAPHY

Young Adult Fiction by Gary Soto

Living up the Street: Narrative Recollections. Portland, OR: Strawberry Hill Press, 1985.
Baseball in April and Other Stories. New York: Harcourt Brace, 1990.
Taking Sides. New York: Harcourt Brace, 1992.

Fiction for Children by Gary Soto

Cat's Meow. Portland, OR: Strawberry Hill, 1987.
The Shirt. Illus. Eric Velasqauez. New York: Delacorte, 1992.
Pool Party. Illus. Robert Casilla. New York: Delacorte, 1993.
Crazy Weekend. New York: Scholastic, 1994.

Poetry for Children and Young Adults by Gary Soto

A Fire in My Hands. Illus. James M. Cordillo. New York: Scholastic, 1991.
Neighborhood Odes. Illus. David Diaz. New York: Harcourt Brace, 1992.

Works for Adults by Gary Soto

The Elements of San Joaquin. Pittsburgh, PA: University of Pittsburgh Press, 1977.
The Tale of Sunlight. Pittsburgh, PA: University of Pittsburgh Press, 1978.
Father Is a Pillow Tied to a Broom. Pittsburgh, PA: Slow Loris Press, 1980.
Where Sparrows Work Hard. Pittsburgh, PA: University of Pittsburgh Press, 1981.
Black Hair. Pittsburgh, PA: University of Pittsburgh Press, 1985.
Small Faces. Houston, TX: Arte Publico, 1986.
A Summer Life. Hanover, NH: University Press of New England, 1990.
Who Will Know Us? San Francisco: Chronicle Books, 1990.
Home Course in Religion. San Francisco: Chronicle Books, 1991.
Pacific Crossing. San Diego: Harcourt Brace Jovanovich, 1992.

Local News. San Diego: Harcourt Brace Jovanovich, 1993.

Selected Studies of Gary Soto

Bruce-Novoa, Juan. *Chicano Poetry: A Response to Chaos.* Austin, TX: U of Texas P, 1982.

Bus, Heiner. "Sophisticated Spontaneity: The Art of Life in Gary Soto's *Living Up the Street.*" *The Americas Review* 16:3–4 (Fall-Winter 1988): 188–97.

Copeland, Jeffrey S. *Speaking of Poets: Interviews with Poets Who Write for Children and Young Adults.* Urbana, IL: National Council of Teachers of English, 1993.

de la Fuente, Patricia. "Ambiguity in the Poetry of Gary Soto." *Revista Chicano-Riquena* 11.2 (Summer 1983): 34–39.

———. "Mutability and Stasis: Images of Time in Gary Soto's *Black Hair.*" *The Americas Review* 17:1 (1989): 100–107.

Erben, Rudolf, and Ute Erben. "Popular Culture, Mass Media, and Chicano Identity in Gary Soto's *Living Up the Street* and *Small Faces.*" MELUS 17:3 (1991–1992): 43–52.

Magill, Frank N., ed. *Masterpieces of Latino Literature.* New York: HarperCollins, 1994.

Olivares, Julian. "The Streets of Gary Soto." *Latin American Literary Review* 18:35 (Jan.–June 1990): 32–49.

Shelton, Pamela L. "Gary Soto." *Authors and Artists for Young Adults.* Ed. Kevin S. Hile. Vol. 10. Detroit: Gale Research, 1993.

Tatum, Charles M. *Chicano Literature.* Boston: Twayne Publishers, 1982.

Trejo, Ernesto. "An Interview with Gary Soto." *Revista Chicano-Riquena* 11.2 (Summer 1983): 25–33.

Varela-Ibarra, Jose. "Gary Soto." *Chicano Literature: A Reference Guide.* Ed. Julio A. Martinez and Francisco A. Lomeli. Westport, CT: Greenwood Press, 1985.

ARMSTRONG SPERRY
(1897–1976)

Caroline C. Hunt

BIOGRAPHY

A native of New England, from a family that included sea captains, merchants, and whalers, Armstrong Sperry fulfilled his family's tradition of sea travel and yet departed from that tradition in his fascination with other cultures, particularly the Polynesian. Sperry was born November 7, 1897, in New Haven, Connecticut, the son of Sereno Cark Sperry and Nettie (née Alling) Sperry. He was fortunate in having a great-grandfather who told the youngster stories about the South Seas—including an account of his own experiences on Bora Bora, where he had once spent some time following a shipwreck. A favorite book, Frederick O'Brien's *White Shadows in the South Seas*, later reinforced what the young Sperry had learned from Captain Armstrong. Though he had drawn pictures from earliest boyhood, Sperry's formal artistic training began at the Yale Art School. As soon as the United States entered World War I, however, young Sperry enlisted in the navy; after the war, he attended the Art Students League in New York for three years, followed by a year studying in Paris at the Académie Colarossis. Returning to the United States, Sperry worked in New York at an advertising agency, but gave it up to join an expedition to the South Seas with the Bishop Museum of Honolulu—serving, despite his lack of formal training, as assistant ethnologist.

After two years in the South Pacific islands, Sperry once again returned to New York, this time working as an illustrator from 1924–1932, when he began writing books for children. During this period he married Margaret Mitchell (1930), and they had two children, Susan and John Armstrong. For over twenty years he continued to illustrate other writers' juvenile titles, particularly those about exploration and about American history, while building his own reputation as a children's writer. Sperry's most memorable titles concern the sea, particularly the South Pacific, but he also wrote about Eskimos, the rain forest, and the pioneer settlers of the American West, among other topics.

For most of his working life, Sperry divided his time between New Hampshire, where he and his family lived, and Vermont, where they had a small farm. From time to time he felt his great-grandfather's spirit urging him to travel, and he would pack up and go to sea or travel in Europe, returning with material for a new book. Sperry continued illustrating, though less and less frequently, until 1956, and writing his own books until the later 1960s; he died April 28, 1976.

MAJOR WORKS AND THEMES

Sperry's works may most logically be categorized by their settings. Those that take place in the United States include *Wagons Westward: The Old Trail to Santa Fe* (1936); *Black Falcon* (1949); *River of the West* (1952); *Thunder Country* (1952); and the nonfiction titles *John Paul Jones, Fighting Sailor* (1953) and *Great River, Wide Land: The Rio Grande through History* (1967). These reflect, logically enough given Sperry's background, a kind of unquestioning patriotism that now seems somewhat simplistic. Seafaring tales like *All Sail Set* (1935); *Storm Canvas* (1944); *Hull-Down for Action* (1945); *Danger to Windward* (1947); and *South of Cape Horn* (1958) reflect his own enthusiasm for nautical adventure. Sperry's multicultural works are set in numerous locales, from the frozen north (*One Day with Tuktu, an Eskimo Boy* [1933], *All about the Arctic and Antarctic* [1957]) to the tropics (*One Day with Jambi in Sumatra* [1934], *All about the Jungle* [1959]). However, it is in the Pacific, especially the South Seas, that Sperry sets the largest number of his important books, including his Newbery Medal winner *Call It Courage* (1940).

Starting with the cleanly written but didactic "One Day with" books, Sperry attempted to expose young readers to the lives of ordinary people, particularly children, in other cultures. Recent commentators have pointed at the somewhat condescending nature of these early efforts, but during the

America-first era in which they appeared, Sperry's books made a distinctly progressive statement. Notable, too, is the fact that he explored what are now called third world cultures, whereas most earlier internationalists (such as Lucy Fitch Perkins and Hendrik Van Loon) had concentrated on European civilization.

Tuktu, Manu, and Jambi never come alive as characters, though their clothing, diet, and daily activities are described in great detail. Indeed, much of what Sperry was attempting in the three "One Day with" books would have been better suited to nonfiction. His next effort, though not itself multicultural in theme, solved this dilemma. With *All Sail Set*, a story about the era of the great clipper ships, he was able to embed his factual material into a compelling narrative; the book was issued in a Cadmus edition and as a Junior Literary Guild selection in addition to its 1935 publication by Winston. Several of Sperry's other books from the period 1935–1945 also appeared in multiple editions. From the success of *All Sail Set*, Sperry learned the importance of plot, and thereafter he carefully separated material which could successfully be fictionalized from material which required a more straightforward expository format. At the end of his career, Sperry turned more and more to nonfiction.

Despite a lifetime of writing about other cultures, Sperry's reputation rests almost entirely on a single book, *Call It Courage*. What distinguishes *Call It Courage* from all of Sperry's other works is the primacy of story. At one level, this is a simple survival story in which a teenage boy, Mafatu, is swept onto a volcanic island and overcomes threats from a shark, a wild boar, cannibals, and—most significantly—the sea itself, on which he and his people depend. This primal tale is framed by scenes on Hikueru, the coral island on which Mafatu lives. Thus the story is cast in the familiar form of a circular journey in which the protagonist leaves home, becomes an adult, and returns.

At the beginning, Mafatu is an outcast because he fears the sea; as a small child, he was swept out to sea by a storm in which his mother, saving him by risking her own life, died. Throughout the journey part of the story, which occupies most of the book, Mafatu is accompanied by the traditional helping animals of folklore—in this case a dog, Uri, and an injured bird, Kivi. Upon his return to Hikueru, Mafatu can take his place in society as a man. The book ends with the same paragraph with which it began (minus the qualifying last line), emphasizing the circular nature of the story. In his Newbery acceptance speech, Sperry said he "had been afraid that perhaps . . . the concept of a spiritual courage might be too adult for children," noting with relief that "the reception of this book has reaffirmed a belief I have long held: that children have imagination enough to grasp any idea, and respond to it, if it is put to them honestly and without a patronizing pat on the head." Sperry's admiration of the Polynesian culture comes through almost as clearly as the story itself.

CRITICAL RECEPTION

At the time of their publication, most of Sperry's early books were very favorably reviewed. The fact that he was already a successful illustrator of children's books worked to his advantage, as for some years he continued to illustrate other writers' stories as well as his own. Thus, among his early recognitions were a Newbery Honor Book designation in 1936 for his own *All Sail Set*, and a second Newbery Honor Book designation the following year for *Codfish Market*, a story by Agnes D. Hewes for which Sperry provided the illustrations. (Although the designation was for Hewes' story and not specifically for Sperry's pictures, the sizable circulation afforded to Honor Books gave Sperry added public, and critical, exposure for the second consecutive year.) Of particular interest to modern readers are two multicultural stories which Sperry illustrated during this transitional period. *Shuttered Windows*, by Florence Crannell Means, depicted with great sensitivity a young African-American girl in South Carolina, and the dignified illustrations did the book justice. William Stone's *Teri Taro from Bora Bora* gave Sperry another chance to share with young readers the scenery of his favorite island; this book appeared in the same year as the author's own *Call It Courage*, also set in Polynesia.

The author's critical fame peaked with *Call It Courage*, which received the Newbery Medal for 1941. This timeless story was immediately recognized as a classic survival tale, a coming-of-age narrative in a unique and beautifully rendered setting. Of all Sperry's fiction, *Call It Courage* is the only title which is still consistently found in reference books, recommended lists, and library collections. After the war, Sperry garnered two further awards: the *New York Herald Tribune* Children's Spring Book Festival Award in 1944 for *Storm Canvas*, and the Boys' Clubs of America Junior Book Award in 1949 for *The Rain Forest*.

With the advent of multiculturalism, beginning in the late 1960s, Sperry's work has been reevaluated. While recognizing his laudable intention in introducing far-flung cultures to young readers in the United States, critics have become uncomfortable with the attitude tacitly conveyed in some of the books. Such terms as "savages," the word Sperry often used for native populations, now cause problems that Sperry could not have imagined. *The*

Rain Forest, for instance, contains childlike natives with "bushy" hair and amusing antics which are apt to embarrass the modern reader. Similarly, his patriotic tales of early World War II (and, indeed, much of his historical fiction as well) now seem almost jingoistic in their approach, and much of the nonfiction appears simplistic by more recent standards. To the classic *Call It Courage,* however, these considerations do not apply; it remains as compelling a tale as it was over fifty years ago.

BIBLIOGRAPHY

Young Adult Fiction by Armstrong Sperry

All Sail Set: A Romance of the "Flying Cloud." Philadelphia: Winston, 1935. London: Lane, 1946.

Wagons Westward: The Old Trail to Santa Fe. Philadelphia: Winston, 1936. London: Lane, 1948.

Lost Lagoon: A Pacific Adventure. New York: Doubleday, 1939. London: Lane, 1943.

Call It Courage. New York: Macmillan, 1940. Rpt. as *The Boy Who Was Afraid.* London: Lane, 1946. Rpt. as *The Boy Who Was Afraid.* Illus. William Stobbs. London: Bodley Head, 1963.

No Brighter Glory. New York: Macmillan, 1943. London: Hutchinson, 1944.

Storm Canvas. Philadelphia: Winston, 1944.

Hull-Down for Action. New York: Doubleday, 1945. London: Lane, 1948.

Danger to Windward. Philadelphia: Winston, 1947.

Black Falcon: A Story of Piracy and Old New Orleans. Philadelphia: Winston, 1949.

The Voyages of Christopher Columbus. New York: Random House, 1950.

River of the West: The Story of the Boston Men. Illus. Henry C. Pitz. Philadelphia: Winston, 1952.

Thunder Country. New York: Macmillan, 1952. London: Lane, 1953.

Captain James Cook. Evanston, IL: Row, Peterson, 1953.

John Paul Jones, Fighting Sailor. New York: Random House, 1953.

Captain Cook Explores the South Seas. New York: Random House, 1955. *All About Captain Cook.* Rev. ed. London: W. H. Allen, 1960.

Pacific Islands Speaking. New York: Macmillan, 1955.

Frozen Fire. New York: Doubleday, 1956. London: Lane, 1957.

All about the Arctic and Antarctic. New York: Random House, 1957.

South of Cape Horn: A Saga of Nat Palmer and Early Antarctic Exploration. Philadelphia: Winston, 1958.

All about the Jungle. New York: Random House, 1959. London: W. H. Allen, 1960.

The Amazon, River Sea of Brazil. Rivers of the World Series. Champaign, IL: Garrard Press, 1961. London: Muller, 1962.

Great River, Wide Land: The Rio Grande through History. New York: Macmillan, 1967. London: Collier Macmillan, 1967.

Works for Children by Armstrong Sperry

One Day with Manu. Philadelphia: Winston, 1933.

One Day with Tuktu, an Eskimo Boy. Philadelphia: Winston, 1933.

One Day with Jambi in Sumatra. Philadelphia: Winston, 1934.

Little Eagle, A Navajo Boy. Philadelphia: Winston, 1938.

Bamboo, the Grass Tree. New York: Macmillan, 1942. London: Lane, 1946.

Coconut, the Wonder Tree. New York: Macmillan, 1942. London: Lane, 1946.

The Rain Forest. New York: Macmillan, 1947. London: Lane, 1950.

Works Edited by Armstrong Sperry

Story Parade: A Collection of Modern Stories for Boys and Girls. Philadelphia: Winston, 1938–1942. 5 vols.

Selected Studies of Armstrong Sperry

Aside from early book reviews, nearly all the secondary material on Sperry consists of short entries in standard reference works. Most of these are listed in Muriel Brown's *Newbery and Caldecott Medalists and Honor Book Winners: Bibliographies and Resource Material*, 2nd ed. (Neal Schuman, 1992). The best recent (extended) treatment of *Call It Courage* is in *Beacham's Guide to Young Adult Literature*, cited below, with selective bibliography. Some useful articles, as well as recent additions not included in other sources, are listed below.

Johns, Jolinda. *The Boy Who Was Afraid.* Suva, Fiji: Institute of Education, 1985.

McGrath, Joan. "Sperry, Armstrong." *Twentieth Century Children's Writers.* Ed. Tracy Chevalier. 3rd ed. Chicago: St. James, 1989. 912–13.

Miller, Bertha Mahoney, and Elinor W. Field, ed. *Newbery Medal Books:1922–1955.* Boston: Horn Book, 1955.

Mosley, Mattie. "Call It Courage." *Beacham's Guide to Young Adult Literature.* Ed. Suzanne Niemeyer. Vol. 4. Washington, DC: Beacham, 1991.1605–10.

Troy, Anne. *Call It Courage: Study Guide.* Palatine, IL: Troy and Green, 1987.

Wilkin, Binnie T. *Survival Themes in Fiction for Children and Young People.* Metuchen, NJ: Scarecrow, 1978.

MILDRED D. TAYLOR
(1943-)

Anita Moss

BIOGRAPHY

Mildred D. Taylor was born in Jackson, Mississippi, in 1943. According to one of Taylor's Dial editors, Phyllis J. Fogelman, Taylor's father was involved in a disturbing racial incident when his daughter Mildred was only three weeks old. The incident convinced him that Mississippi was too dangerous a place for African-Americans to rear young children in. He left the same day for Toledo, Ohio. When Taylor was three months old, her father sent for his wife and daughters.

Taylor thus grew up in Toledo, but the family remained deeply rooted in Mississippi earth. The Taylors often returned to the family farm for visits, and throughout her childhood Taylor listened to the stories—some warmly humorous, some terrifying—that all suggested the enormous strength of the Taylors and Davises to survive amid the worst kind of racial prejudice and injustice.

Taylor received her education in the Toledo schools, which were integrated at the time. However, Taylor was often the only African-American in her college preparatory classes. She performed best in her English classes and had decided by high school that she would eventually become a writer. Fogelman notes that her senior class prophecy read: "The well-known journalist Mildred Taylor is displaying her Nobel Prize winning novel" (411).

In addition to her desire to write, Taylor had decided by age sixteen that she wanted to join the Peace Corps. During her years at the University of Toledo, she learned as much as possible about the Peace Corps and Ethiopia. After graduating from college, Taylor did indeed join the Peace Corps. She served several years in Ethiopia, where she taught English and history and where she grew to love African landscape, music, song, and story.

When Taylor returned to the United States, she recruited for the Peace Corps and taught in one of its training programs. She then entered the School of Journalism at the University of Colorado. After completing her master's degree, she worked in the Black Education program until she decided to concentrate full-time upon her writing. She then moved to Los Angeles, took an undemanding eight-to-five job, and spent her evenings writing. Taylor found that this life did not provide enough emotional and social support to sustain her. As she later explained to Fogelman, "Writing alone made me too weak emotionally; I needed an outside social force, something in which I could also be creative but which would be people-oriented in a different way. It was then that I decided to return to school and to receive a degree in international training" (433).

Before departing from California, Taylor had submitted a manuscript of *Song of the Trees* to the Council on Interracial Books for Children; the manuscript won first prize in the African-American category for 1973. The council sent *Song of the Trees* to several publishers, and Taylor decided to accept the offer from Dial Books. She has maintained her publishing relationship with Dial and has continued to develop as a writer. Phyllis Fogelman has described the exceptional rapport and friendship which developed between herself, Taylor, and another Dial editor, Regina Hayes.

In her Newbery Award acceptance speech, Taylor describes her vivid childhood memories of the house, land, and family in Mississippi. In early childhood the trips from Ohio to Mississippi seemed like "a marvelous adventure, a twenty-hour picnic that took us into another time, another world; down dusty red roads and across creaky wooden bridges into the rich farm country of Mississippi, where I was born" (401).

Later Taylor and her sister became aware that the family took their own food because restaurants would not serve her family in the segregated South. The Taylors drove straight through on these trips because motels refused them service. These early experiences with racism, discrimination, and the threat of violence would later be reflected in her fiction.

Through all of these ordeals, Taylor says that her father imparted to her strength of character, self-respect, and a strong identity, as well as his gifts as a master storyteller. She notes that her Logan characters are drawn from various members of her own family. If readers of her books find them autobiographical, Taylor observes, "it is because I have tried to distill the essence of Black life, so familiar to most Black families, to make the Logans an embodiment of that spiritual heritage" ("Newbery Award" 403). Drawing still upon her own cultural heritage, Taylor continues to write about the Logans. She plans further books about the Logans, as well as other writing projects. She makes her home in Colorado, where she devotes herself full-time to her writing.

MAJOR WORKS AND THEMES

In the emotionally concentrated *Song of the Trees* (1975) the reader meets Cassie Logan, the nine-year-old narrator; her courageous father, David; Cassie's strong, nurturing grandmother, Caroline (called "Big Ma" by the children); as well as Cassie's older brother, Stacey, and her younger brothers, Christopher John and Clayton. In *Song of the Trees* Taylor stresses the Logans' closeness to their land, especially Cassie's imaginative and emotional engagement with the trees in the Logan forest—"shaggy-bark hickories and sharp-needled pines. . . . blue-gray beeches and sturdy black walnuts" (16). Playing among these magnificent ancient trees, Cassie rejoices as she imagines that the trees sing to her. Her affinity with the forest may remind readers that African-American literature has frequently portrayed the forest as a friend, the beneficent place where runaway slaves took shelter in their quests for freedom.

The central action in the narrative occurs when Cassie suddenly realizes that she can no longer hear the trees singing and that many of them have been marked with a large and ominous *X*. A white man, Mr. Andersen, and his crew plan to buy the trees at a fraction of their cost, after threatening the life of David Logan. Later, however, David confronts Mr. Andersen. Holding the plunger to ignite the dynamite that he and his son Stacey have planted all over the forest, David demands that Andersen and his crew leave at once. When the white man suggests that David is bluffing, David reveals a significant key to his strength of character: "One thing you can't seem to understand, Andersen, is that a black man's always gotta be ready to die. And it don't make me any difference if I die today or tomorrow. Just as long as I die right" (43). When Andersen suggests that David will not always have the plunger, he answers resolutely, "That may be. But it won't matter none. Cause I'll always have my self-respect" (46).

Song of the Trees establishes Cassie as the central consciousness in the novels, underscores the close identity between the Logans and their land, exposes the racial terrorism which held the entire South in its grip at the time, and stresses the strength, courage, and loyalty of the Logans to one another, to their land, and to their community. In the three full-length novels to follow, Taylor explores these themes at length through dramatic events while developing her characters, their intense conflicts, and the social and historical background in much greater depth.

In some respects Taylor's fiction reminds readers of many other works of southern agrarian fiction that idealize the yeoman farmer and his family as they labor in cooperation and love upon the land. Southern writers from William Faulkner to such contemporary authors as Reynolds Price, Lee Smith, and many others have centered their fictional families on land which may appear as both a blessing and a curse. Children's writers, too, have made use of what Phyllis Bixler Koppes has described as a tradition deriving from the "georgic version of pastoral myth" in which the ideal community includes a family at work in a green place such as farm, garden, pasture, or forest (203–204). Taylor blends these agrarian traditions with the strategies of social realism; that is, within her narratives of family history and land ownership, Taylor also reveals dark social, racial, and economic realities. She does not flinch from depicting horrific details of racial terror, such as the burning of members of the Berry family at the hands of the Wallace brothers, violent white men who own a local store.

Despite important similarities to mainstream American literary traditions, Taylor's fiction asserts profound and distinct differences from such fiction. As J. D. Stahl explains, "In American children's literature, the predominantly white perspective on race relations in the South, extending from *Uncle Tom's Cabin* to *Sounder,* can be complemented and in part counterbalanced by a work such as Mildred Taylor's *Roll of Thunder, Hear My Cry!*" (16). Rudine Sims describes Taylor's work as "culturally conscious fiction" because it represents "the social and cultural traditions with growing up Black in the United States" (49). Sims explains her terms: "The label 'culturally conscious' suggests that elements in the text, not just the pictures, make it clear that the book consciously seeks to depict a fictional Afro-American life experience. At minimum this means that the major characters are Afro-Americans, that the story is told from their perspective, the setting is an Afro-American community or home, and the text includes some means of identifying the characters as Black—physical descriptions, language, cultural traditions, and so forth" (490). As Mary T. Harper has observed, Taylor's fiction employs all of these strategies, "to identify itself as representative of African American life" (75).

Throughout her Logan novels Taylor weaves strands of Logan family history as well as larger events of African-American history. One of the significant ways that Taylor establishes her fiction as culturally conscious is through her characters' storytelling. As Taylor's father had instilled a sense of pride and strength in his children through his stories, so Caroline ("Big Ma") Logan inspires Cassie by revealing specific details of Logan family history. As the two sit by the pond, hidden in the forest as if to escape from the perils of their racist society, Caroline tells Cassie how her husband had been born into slavery in Georgia, had learned the skill of carpentry and had traveled to Mississippi after the Civil War, where he worked as a carpenter to buy the first two hundred acres of land from a northern carpetbagger.

Taylor features Caroline telling Cassie this family history in her own voice, suggesting that Caroline is the articulate and inspired keeper of family and cultural history. Caroline embeds her own family's history within centrally important historical events—slavery, the Civil War, Reconstruction, World War I, the Great Depression—events which changed patterns of life for all families, black and white. Caroline's narrative is a strong story of cultural identity. Caroline, Taylor's own father, and countless other storytellers took care to pass on the stories which would one day find expression in distinctive works of African-American literature.

A consistent motif throughout Taylor's fiction is that African-Americans must resist the racial injustice of their society in any way possible. When the Wallaces burn members of the Berry family, Mary Logan takes her children to visit the barely living charred body of Mr. Berry because she wants them to understand why they must not go to the Wallace store. She explains that not only have the Wallaces committed the atrocity, but that the racist criminal justice system of the time will do absolutely nothing about it. The Logan children watch as their brave mother organizes a boycott against the Wallace store, a venture made possible by Mr. Jamison, the white lawyer, who backs the credit of anyone who wishes to shop in Vicksburg.

Without resorting to preaching or excessive exposition, Taylor dramatizes throughout her fiction the ways in which African-Americans were systematically degraded, exploited, humiliated, and sometimes tortured and murdered in their segregated society. The most painful encounter Cassie Logan experiences in *Roll of Thunder, Hear My Cry!* (1976) occurs when her family takes her to Strawberry for the first time. Until this incident, Cassie had been fairly insulated from the pain of racism. She does not understand the harsh realities outside her immediate family and community. First, she wonders why Big Ma parks her wagon so far behind the wagons of the white farmers. When she goes to the dry goods store, she does not understand why Mr. Barnett interrupts his service to her and her brother to wait upon a young white girl. Finally she does not understand why Lillian Jean Simms insists that Cassie address her as "Miz Lillian Jean" or why the white girl's father, Charlie Simms, knocks her off the sidewalk when she does not. When Cassie's Uncle Hammer hears of the incident, he drives off to seek revenge from Charlie Simms for treating Cassie so badly. Only Mr. Morrison, who jumps in the car at the last minute, talks him out of it. Mary Logan must explain to her spirited daughter that Mr. Morrison has probably saved Hammer's life. Black men in the community, Mary sadly comments, have been murdered for much less. Cassie learns that since she is an African-American, white people will never regard her as equal to even the worst white people. Taylor presents this experience with exceptional narrative skill and dramatic power. The reader senses at a profound level that Cassie Logan will never be the same again—never quite as sure and confident—as she was before her ill-fated journey to Strawberry.

While many of the white characters who populate Taylor's fiction are violent, bad people, Taylor does not demonize all white characters nor idealize all African-Americans. She presents the white lawyer, Wade Jamison, as fair, open-minded, and racially moderate. When Mr. Jamison agrees to back the credit of the families participating in the boycott against the Wallace store, he remarks to the Logans that many white people disapprove of the crimes against African-Americans in the community, but he adds that there are just not enough whites who feel as he does to make the needed changes. David Logan also mentions that Mr. Harrison, another powerful landowner, is a just and decent man.

Taylor presents the problems of forming and maintaining friendships between the races with exceptional emotional power. Jeremy Simms desperately desires the friendship of the Logan children, especially Stacey. When the young white boy carves a windpipe and presents it to Stacey for Christmas, David Logan explains to Stacey that the friendship will ultimately be impossible because eventually the white boy will grow up and consider himself a man while still viewing Stacey as a boy. Mr. Logan adds that because friendships between the races in Mississippi can never be based on equality, they are essentially impossible.

In *Let the Circle Be Unbroken* (1981) David and Hammer Logan drive this point home even more vehemently when they discover that Cassie has a photograph of Jeremy. Hammer explodes in anger and views it in the light of the history of white male abuse and exploitation of black women: " 'A white man think he can have his way with colored women, can have them for the taking'" (175). When Cassie complains to her father that her Uncle Hammer just does not understand about Jeremy, her father angrily replies, "'He understood all right. Jeremy's a white boy. You got no business with his picture'" (178). Mr. Logan adds that his own grandfather had been a white slave owner who had raped his grandmother and expresses his own deep rage: "White men been using colored women for centuries—they still doing it—and believe me, it's a mighty hurting thing. . . . mighty hurting, and I feel just like your Uncle Hammer do 'bout it" (179).

Taylor's interest in Jeremy Simms is sufficient for her to allow him to narrate her short, intense book *The Mississippi Bridge* (1990). In this narrative Charlie Simms and other white men abuse Josias Williams when they learn that he has come to the Wallace store to catch a bus in order to secure a lumbering job off the Natchez Trace. Charlie Simms immediately resents the black man's job opportunity when so many white men are out of work. Ultimately Josias cannot even get on the bus because there are too many white passengers. Jeremy states how much he dislikes his father's violent behavior toward black people and that he knows full well his father's actions were deeply wrong. When the bus crashes off the bridge, Josias and Jeremy participate in sad equality as they recover the drowned white bodies from the submerged bus.

Even long-term interracial friendships were subject to the betrayals of community pressure, the central subject of Taylor's short book, *The Friendship* (1987). Mr. Tom Bee, an elderly African-American, has been the life-long friend of John Wallace, owner of the Wallace store. Tom visits the Wallace store and because he has saved the life of John more than once, he addresses "John" by his first name. Cassie, the narrator, describes the racist customs of address: "We both knew this name business was a touchy thing. I didn't really understand why, but it was. White folks took it seriously. Mighty seriously. They took it seriously to call every grown black person straight out by their first name without placing a 'mister' or 'missus' or a 'miss' anywhere" (28).

When Tom continues to address John by his first name, Charlie Simms and Kaleb and Dewberry Wallace taunt him for allowing an old Negro to "disrespect" him. In the horrifying climactic scene, John shoots Tom's right leg open with a shot gun blast. Dragging himself along the road with his torn and bleeding leg, Tom shouts, "Ya was John t' me when I saved your sorry life and you give me your word you was always gonna be John t' me as long as I lived. So's ya might's well go 'head and kill me cause that's what ya gon' be, John. . . . Till the judgment day" (53).

Taylor dramatizes with cold, stark power the extent to which John Wallace has allowed his racist culture to trivialize what was probably the most profound emotional relationship of his life—that of father and son. In denying the man who had not only saved his life but had also acted as the only real father he had ever known, John passed on a legacy of violence and false values to his own sons. Lillian Smith's words are instructive: "They who so gravely taught me to split my body from my mind and both from my soul, taught me also to split my conscience from my acts and Christianity from Southern Tradition" (27). Smith's explanation shows why a host of violent white racists who populate the pages of Taylor's fiction emerge as distorted, monstrous, and not fully human. While some critics might be tempted to say that Taylor has presented unfair racial stereotypes of white characters, a study of southern history reveals how tragically many white southerners made monsters of themselves. Taylor fully articulates the African-American experience of southern life, and she has also perceptively presented the tragic ways in which white southerners denied their own true human feelings. Such white southerners clearly hated and feared African-Americans, but not nearly so much as they hated and feared themselves.

Taylor reveals, too, that just as white southerners, such as Wade Jamison and Jeremy Simms, could behave with justice and friendship to their black neighbors, so also African-Americans were capable of envy, violence, and betrayal of one another and of their community. In *Roll of Thunder, Hear My Cry!* T. J. Avery displays his lack of character from the beginning of the novel. He admits placing the blame for his own misdeeds on his younger brother, Claude. He allows Stacey to assume the blame and take the punishment for his cheating on an examination, and ultimately he betrays Mary Logan to the white school board which fires her for teaching black history accurately. Ultimately, then, T. J. isolates himself completely from his own community, a condition vividly demonstrated when he brings R. W. and Melvin Simms to the revival meeting at Great Faith Church. He brags to Stacey that he has new white friends and does not need Stacey any more. As noted earlier in this essay, T. J.'s relationship with R. W. and Melvin ultimately costs him his life. Throughout *Roll of Thunder, Hear My Cry!* Taylor demonstrates T. J.'s laziness, sneakiness, dishonesty, as well as his poisonous envy of the Logans. T. J. never commands Cassie's respect, nor the reader's. Yet at the end Cassie, who has disliked T. J. the most, finds herself grieving and crying for T. J. and the land.

If friendship between the races was complicated and difficult in the American South at this time, romantic relationships were even more forbidden—not only by custom but by state law as well. Taylor introduces the delicate subject of interracial marriage in *Let the Circle Be Unbroken.* Mary Logan's nephew, Bud Rankin, visits the Logans unexpectedly from New York and after a day or two admits that he has married a white woman, that he and his wife have a fifteen-year-old daughter, Suzella, who feels shame for her father and for her own status as a person of mixed blood. Bud wants Suzella to stay with the Logans for a while in order that she may come to appreciate, understand, and accept her African-American heritage.

Hammer Logan reacts to the news that Bud has married a white woman by bluntly remarking that he is a fool. Clearly all of the Logans deeply disapprove of Bud's action and at some level regard it as an act of betrayal. Bud's daughter, Suzella, turns out to be so light skinned that she can pass for white, and frequently does so. When young white Stuart Walker mistakes her for a white girl, she does not correct the impression, an act which Cassie and her brothers rightly interpret as a rejection of her kinship to them. Eventually Suzella's deception results in a truly ugly incident when Stuart and his friends force her father to strip in the presence of Suzella and the Logan children. Taylor makes it painfully clear that Suzella will never live comfortably in either community.

While Taylor effectively exposes the injustice of racism in the lives of her African-American characters, she also celebrates positive aspects of the Logans' lives. As noted earlier in this essay, storytelling is one of the most important ways of knowing the Logans' experience. As Caroline Logan appears to be the keeper of the family's oral history, so Mary Logan, trained as a teacher and obviously a woman of considerable scholarly and academic skill, introduces her children to reading, writing, and thinking. In *Roll of Thunder, Hear My Cry!* the children all receive books for Christmas even though there is little money for other necessities. Mary carefully sets aside a time and a place for her children to read and to study. She supervises their studies, questions them, and challenges them to think. The Logans' literacy is one important way that they hold on to their land. When Harlan Granger genially offers to pay the taxes on their land, for example, David fortunately knows the tax laws. He realizes that if Harlan paid the taxes on the land, he could eventually take the land away from them.

Although Mary has lost her teaching position at Great Faith School, she finds other ways to teach. She not only instructs Miss Lee Annie Lees in the intricacies of the state constitution; she also holds a tutoring session on Saturday mornings for children in the community. Taylor indicates that Cassie is in training not only to carry forward the traditions of storytelling but also to follow Mary's example by mastering the skills of reading, writing, and reasoning. When someone in the community needs a letter written, Cassie is often called upon to write it. Taylor makes it clear that the Logans' literacy is one important way they avoid being victims of their racist society.

In sum, Taylor celebrates and affirms the values, strength, and vitality of African-American culture even as she exposes and indicts the most painful social realities. All of Taylor's books resonate with the great love and loyalty the Logan family shares with one another and for their four hundred acres of rich Mississippi farm land. As a body of work, Taylor's fiction represents a significant contribution to American literature.

CRITICAL RECEPTION

One strong indication of the positive critical acclaim Taylor's fiction has enjoyed is the large number of prestigious awards she has won for her writing. As noted earlier, *Song of the Trees* won the Council on Interracial Books for Children competition. The *New York Times* listed it as an outstanding book of 1975, and in 1976 it was named a Children's Book Showcase book. *Roll of Thunder, Hear My Cry!* has generally been regarded as a significant masterpiece of twentieth-century American fiction. An American Library Association Notable Book in 1976, winner of the New-bery Medal for 1977, and a *Boston Globe/Horn Book* Award Honor Book, the novel was also a finalist for the American Book Award. A *School Librarian* reviewer declared that Mildred Taylor "had done for Depression era black southerners what Laura Ingalls Wilder did for the pioneers" (367). The novel has also received prominent international critical attention as well. Translated into several languages, the novel received in 1985 the Buxtehuder Bulle, a prestigious German award for excellence in children's literature.

Let the Circle Be Unbroken was a 1982 American Book Award nominee and a Coretta Scott King Award winner. The American Library Association listed it among the American Library Association's Best Books for Young Adults in 1981. *The Friendship* won the *Boston Globe/Horn Book* Award and the Coretta Scott King Award in 1988. Also in 1988, the Children's Book Council honored Mildred D. Taylor "for a body of work that has examined significant social issues and presented them in outstanding books for young readers." *The Gold Cadillac* won the Christopher Award, and *The Road to Memphis* won the Coretta Scott King Award in 1991.

Critics and reviewers have praised Taylor's powers of description, her skill in representing African-American speech, her ability to write convincing dialogue, and her ability to weave social and historical information into the dramatic and emotional contexts of her narratives.

Some reviewers of Taylor's fiction note that the most significant narrative problem in her fiction is her use of a child narrator. Cassie, a nine-year-old girl in the first two books, must sometimes report and analyze difficult and baffling adult realities. Her ability to do so seems often beyond that of a nine-year-old. David Rees notes that the novel's only weakness is that "Taylor seems uncertain about how much she can involve the children . . . in areas that are the preserve of the adults: the result is that she is obliged, too often, to make them eavesdrop at keyholes or through floorboards on their parents' discussions of what atrocities have recently occurred, and what actions should be taken in reprisal" (109).

Let the Circle Be Unbroken has also received highly positive critical reception. Virtually all reviews praise the novel for its honest exploration of racial injustice and for presenting social issues in dramatically convincing narrative scenes. *The Road to Memphis*, though it won a prestigious award, has not faired so well. Some reviewers complained that while the novel contains compelling scenes, the characters sometimes make speeches to one another. A *Horn Book* reviewer complained that "much of the dialogue seems repetitious, and minor pieces of business overlong" and suggests that only the reader's familiarity with the Logan family brings the characters to life (610).

Taylor's short novels have also received positive critical assessment. A *Horn Book* reviewer writes of *The Gold Cadillac* that Taylor makes her point skillfully by contrasting the comfortable, carefree life the sisters have always known surrounded by their large, extended family up North and later in Mississippi with the hostile no man's land between" (606). Both *The Friendship* and *The Mississippi Bridge* received praise for their emotional concentration, their eloquent understatement of moral and social dilemmas, their characterizations, and their plot development.

As a body, then, Taylor's books have consistently been praised as outstanding works of American children's literature. Adam Hochschild sums up her achievement admirably:

A masterful storyteller, Taylor is one of those rare writers whose ability to create full, vividly memorable characters is matched by a sense of class and history. You are drawn very deeply into Cassie Logan's growth from childhood to adolescence, from innocence into a knowledge of human good and evil. Yet the knowledge is one that must encompass the social world as well. . . . Among children's literature, these are the only books I know that have, in the way they show deeply realized characters against a social background of equal richness, a quality one can almost call Tolstyan. (58)

While reviewers have virtually all praised Taylor's achievements, her fiction has seldom received the sustained critical attention it deserves. A notable exception is Mary T. Harper's essay, "Merger and Metamorphosis in the Fiction of Mildred D. Taylor," a perceptive article which places Taylor's fiction in the context of African-American literary and cultural traditions. According to Harper,

Like Alex Haley, Taylor creates her own "faction." As she blends the stories heard in her childhood with her own knowledge of history, she creates a fiction that is functional—one that enables young readers to experience a world sometimes alien to them but, at the same time, one that allows them to establish a kinship with characters in their own age group who must confront the challenges of growing up in a less than ideal world. . . . Mildred Taylor weaves stories that are contemporary revelations of the spirit and will of those enduring characters John and Brer Rabbit. (77–79).

BIBLIOGRAPHY

Young Adult Fiction by Mildred D. Taylor

Song of the Trees. Illus. Jerry Pinkney. New York: Dial, 1975.
Roll of Thunder, Hear My Cry! New York: Dial, 1976. New York: Puffin, 1991.
Let the Circle Be Unbroken. New York: Dial, 1981. New York: Puffin, 1991.
The Friendship. New York: Dial, 1987.
The Gold Cadillac. New York: Dial, 1987.
The Mississippi Bridge. New York: Dial, 1990.
The Road to Memphis. New York: Dial, 1990. New York: Puffin, 1992.

Other Works by Mildred D. Taylor

"Newbery Award Acceptance." *Horn Book* 53.4 (1977): 401–409.
"Sidelights." *Something about the Author.* Ed. Anne Commire. Vol. 15. Detroit: Gale, 1979. 277.
"The Color of Skin." *The Marble in the Water: Essays on Contemporary Writers for Children and Young Adults.* Ed. David Rees. Boston: Horn Book, 1980. 104–13.
"Acceptance of the *Boston Globe/Horn Book* Award for *The Friendship.*" *Horn Book* 65.2 (1989): 179–82.

Selected Studies of Mildred D. Taylor

"Canon Formation: A History and Psychological Perspective." In Glenn Sadler, ed. *Teaching Children's Literature: Issues, Pedagogy, Resources.* New York: MLA, 1992.

Fogelman, Phyllis J. "Mildred D. Taylor." *Horn Book* 53.4 (1977): 410–14.

Harper, Mary T. "Merger and Metamorphosis in the Fiction of Mildred D. Taylor." *Children's Literature Association Quarterly* 13 (1988): 75–85.

Hochschild, Adam. "Bedtime Stories." *Mother Jones* 7 (Dec. 1982): 56–58.

Koppes, Phyllis Bixler. "The Child in Pastoral Myth: A Study in Rousseau and Wordsworth, Children's Literature, and Literary Fantasy." Diss. U of Kansas, 1977.

Moss, Anita. *Literature Guide to Roll of Thunder, Hear My Cry! by Mildred D. Taylor.* Cambridge, MA: Book Wise, 1990.

Rees, David. "The Color of Skin: Mildred Taylor." *In the Marble, in the Water.* Boston: Horn Book, 1980. 104–13.

Rev. of *Roll of Thunder, Hear My Cry! SLJ* 23 (March 1977): 367.

Sims, Rudine. *Shadow and Substance: Afro-American Experience in Contemporary Children's Fiction.* Urbana, IL: NCTE, 1982.

Smith, Lillian. *Killers of the Dream.* Rev. ed. New York: Norton, 1949; 1961.

Vasilakis, Nancy. Rev. of *The Gold Cadillac. Horn Book* 63.5 (1987): 606.

———. Rev. of *The Road to Memphis. Horn Book* 66.5 (1990): 609–10.

Wright, David A. "Mildred D. Taylor." *Dictionary of Literary Biography.* Ed. Glenn E. Estes. Vol. 52. Detroit: Gale, 1986.

THEODORE TAYLOR
(1921-)

Dona J. Helmer

BIOGRAPHY

Theodore Taylor, the son of Edward Riley and Elnora Alma Langhans Taylor, was born June 23, 1921, in Statesville, North Carolina. He was married in 1946 to Gweneth Goodwin whom he divorced in 1977, and in 1981, he married Flora Gray Schoenleber. He is the father of three children: Mark, Wendy, and Michael. Taylor is a former newspaperman, scriptwriter, and publicist who has also written under the pen name of T. T. Lang.

According to his article in *Something about the Author Autobiography,* his parents were two totally different types of people. His father was a rugged man and his mother was a deeply religious woman. During the depression, his father was often absent from home because he was looking for work. As a young boy, Taylor worked picking up trash, selling junk, and delivering newspapers until he got his first "real" job as a cub reporter for the *Portsmouth Star* in 1934, at age thirteen. He eventually worked his way up to sports editor. After graduation from the Fort Union Military Academy in Virginia, he convinced the managing editor of the *Washington Daily News* to hire him as copy boy. He referred to that experience as "my college, my seamy side university, my graduate school. I've often regretted I didn't attend college. City rooms were the substitutes, newsmen were the teachers" (Taylor 307).

In 1942 he entered the Merchant Marine Academy at Kings Point, New York, and joined the naval reserve. Although Taylor did not participate in any of the big naval battles of World War II, he fell in love with naval history and was later to write highly praised, accurate, historical naval novels. His first book, entitled *The Magnificent Mitscher,* was written during his tour of duty with the naval reserve during the Korean War. He would later use the experiences from another tour of duty in the Caribbean providing relief to hurricane victims as the background for *The Cay* (1969).

After the service, Taylor worked as a press agent for a Hollywood film company and later became a scriptwriter. He now writes full-time for adults as well as young adults. He said in an interview with Norma Bagnall:

I'm proud to write for young people, but when I sit down to write I do not consciously think, "Now, you're writing for young people." I let the story go the way that story should go; the worst thing a writer can do is write down to children. I am just not conscious of whether I am writing for young people or adults. But I will probably do other books with characters like Ben O'Neal, Jose, Phillip, and Teetoncey. They are the kind of peer models children can like and respect; all of them are self-reliant; all are self-sufficient. They find their own way without constant reference to adults. I like that kind of kid; I think kids like that kind too, and if it helps them aim toward self-reliance, then I've done a good job. (91)

MAJOR WORKS AND THEMES

Taylor's novels often include multicultural characters based upon composites of people he has known. Sometimes, they are primary characters. Sometimes, they are secondary or tertiary characters who serve only to add to the sense of setting and place and are not fully developed characters. The works which have important multicultural characters are *The Cay* (1969), *Timothy of the Cay* (1993), *The Children's War* (1971), *The Maldonado Miracle* (1973), and *Maria: A Christmas Story* (1993).

Taylor usually writes about growing up, surviving a challenge, learning self-reliance and self-respect, and often about the clash of cultures. His accurate settings are often the product of his travels or military experiences.

The Cay is a Robinsonnade about Phillip, a young white Dutch boy, and Timothy, an old black West Indian sailor, who are marooned on an island together. When the ship they are sailing on sinks, Phillip is placed in a life raft but he is struck by a piece of wood and blinded. Despite his rather racist upbringing Phillip is forced to rely on Timothy. Timothy teaches the boy about survival, about living, about friendship and respect. At the time of its publication, death was often a subject that was ignored in juvenile literature, but here Timothy's death is an integral part of the story. Taylor skillfully interweaves the themes of maturing, innocence versus wisdom, and white versus black in this adventure tale.

Over twenty years later, Taylor returned to these characters. He used a new format which he called a "prequel/sequel" to tell the story. *Timothy of the Cay* alternates between the first-person accounts of Phillip's rescue and third-person accounts of Timothy's life. In this prequel/sequel, the reader learns about the events leading up to the time when the characters are stranded on the Caribbean island and about Phillip's eventual return to the island after he regains his sight.

The Children's War is the story of twelve-year-old Dory Scofield who lives in the Alaskan village of Sedluk, which is invaded by the Japanese during World War II. Although the island and the characters are fictional, the events in the story and the relationship between Dory and Bakutan, the Eskimo, have a ring of authenticity. Dory learns to respect the environment and life.

The Maldonado Miracle is the tale of twelve-year-old Jose Maldonado, an illegal alien who plans to join his father in California. Along the way he encounters greedy men—both Anglo and Mexican—is injured while fleeing from some men, and hides in a church. When the blood from his wound drips down on a statue of Christ, the local parishioners think it is a miracle. The parish priest is skeptical, and Jose tells him the truth. The priest is instrumental in helping Jose tell his father that he does not wish to go to the United States—he wants to go home to Mexico and study art. Once again, Taylor's young protagonist must develop self-reliance and learn to negotiate with the adult world.

Maria: A Christmas Story is the story of a young woman who goes to a predominantly Anglo school. When her rich white classmates talk about how their families are going to participate in the town's Christmas parade, Maria becomes angry when she learns that no Hispanic family has ever participated in this event. She decides to try. Her family becomes involved, and eventually the whole Hispanic community joins in to win the prize.

CRITICAL RECEPTION

Taylor has received mixed reviews for his work. Many critics initially praised *The Cay*, perhaps Taylor's best-known work, because of its fast-paced plot and vivid characterizations. The book, which was dedicated to Martin Luther King, Jr., received the Jane Addams Children's book award in 1970 and the Lewis Carroll Shelf Award. However, in the 1970s the book was attacked as racist because of its stereotypical portrayal of Timothy. Critics, particularly the Council on Interracial Books for Children, objected to the West Indian dialect that Taylor used for Timothy. The Jane Addams committee requested that Taylor return the award, which he did in 1975.

Taylor told Jim Roginski that although he got the idea for the book in 1956, he did not begin writing it until 1968. The story is based upon a true incident, "a very thin true incident, but nonetheless the kid got on the life raft and drifted away. . . . I used a friend of mine from St. Croix as the model for the black guy." The character of the Dutch boy was also based on someone Taylor had known, a boy he had known in North Carolina who was "passionate" about hating black people, even at the young age of eight. "It seemed the right combination to use him as the little Dutch kid and to put him on that raft with a person whom he immediately hated, and let the story work out from there" (Roginski 211).

Polly Goodwin's review for *Book World* in the *Washington Post* stated that the weeks the boy and man spend shipwrecked "make unforgettable reading." Goodwin also found that Timothy, in his role as teacher to Phillip and in his role as martyr/hero, was "a wonderful human being, whose heart and courage matched his big frame." Still, the image of a black man sacrificing himself for a white boy and for the education and edification of potentially racist readers is problematic.

C. Dorsey wrote that "Taylor has skillfully developed the perennially popular castaway plot into a good adventure story," but also notes that the story has deeper significance once Phillip realizes that "racial consciousness is merely a product of sight: to him Timothy feels 'neither white nor black.' . . . The idea that all humanity would benefit from this special form of color blindness permeates the whole book. . . . The result is a story with a high ethical purpose but no sermon" (26).

M. R. Singer gave the book a starred review although she found that the "minor flaws . . . are dwarfed by the fully realized setting, the artful, unobtrusive use of dialect, the impact of Timothy." She also found that the book's "essential value lies in the representation of a hauntingly deep love, the piognancy of which is rarely achieved in children's literature" (Singer 2505). She also cited it as one of the Best Books of the Year in the December 1969 *School Library Journal.*

Zena Sutherland wrote that the prejudiced Phillip finally realizes that Timothy's every action is based upon loving kindness, and that the story of Phillip's growing perception and maturity "is very well written, the bleak setting a foil for the dramatic situation. The two characters and their relationship are developed with skill; pace and suspense are artfully maintained" (183).

Albert Schwartz provides one of the most negative commentaries on the novel, noting that *The Cay* is an initiation story of an upper-middle-class white boy into his adult role as a participant in a colonial, sexist, and racist society. He states that Taylor never criticizes the way of life on Curagao, in which blacks are "owned" by outside white powers, and that he never questions that the black man is the servent of the white boy throughout the novel. He finds it "incredible" that in a contemporary children's book a writer would be so "racially insensitive" as to make the adult Timothy the servant of the white boy Phillip, "a servant who risks his life for the boy and, in the end, sacrifices his life so the white boy may live" (7).

Theodore Taylor answered this by saying that "in my own mind, I did not set out to write a 'racist' novel . . . the goal was to the contrary. Directed primarily toward the white child (thinking that the black child did not need to be told much about prejudice), I hoped to achive a subtle plea for better race relations and more understanding." Taylor went on to say, "I have been faulted for the derogatory use of dialect by Timothy, even though most West Indian sailors of 1942 spoke dialect. To me, calypso is the single most pleasing, if not musical dialect on earth; a black treasure, I would think. It may jar some white ears, and some black ears, but I would use it again without hesitation" (Taylor 284–86).

The prequel/sequel to *The Cay*, *Timothy of the Cay*, garnered some of the same criticisms as the first book, although it also struck some reviewers as being less offensive than the earlier book. Susan Knorr stated that the book is "faithful in tone, dialect, and characterization to the earlier title," but that it does not develop the theme of racial prejudice, focusing rather on Phillip's "appreciation of his friend and guardian angel, and on the adventures and touching yarns of the West Indian man's life at sea." She also felt that the book is important because it "adds depth to Timothy's character" (132).

In a starred review in *Publisher's Weekly,* Diane Roback said that the novel does explore social and racial imbalances, and also "draws a graceful parallel" between Timothy's youthful struggle to achieve the dream of capturing his own boat and Phillip's courage in choosing to undergo risky eye surgery that might improve his vision. She does note that at times Taylor seems apologetic about Timothy's illiteracy and his belief in spirit magic, called jumbi, "which seems unnecessary, given the character's obvious dignity and deep-rooted wisdom." Ultimately Roback sees the novel as "somewhat more thoughtful" than its predecessor, and also "boldly drawn" and "commanding." (98).

Stephanie Zvirin sees the novel as a "complicated entwining of two personal narratives" and thinks that Timothy's is the more compelling story. "There's a strong sense of place in its telling. . . . Taylor is true to the characters he created for the original book. . . . But unlike the first book, this one is underscored with an indictment of prejudice" (153).

Reviews of *The Children's War* praised the work for some of the same qualities as *The Cay*, primarily the vivid and dramatic writing. "The events, characters and location are fictional. But Theodore Taylor. . . has taken the imaginary event and turned it into a dramatic and compelling story. His descriptions of the country and people are so vivid that the reader is convinced the story is true" (*Publisher's Weekly* 50).

The review in the *New York Times Book Review* compared the novel to *The Cay*, noting that the strongest relationship in the book is that between the boy and an elderly and taciturn Eskimo hunter he idolizes. "Like the bond between Phillip and an old West Indian, Timothy, in *The Cay*, . . . this friendship is achieved between two cultures and two age levels" (8).

Not all reviewers were as enthusiastic. M. Dorsey found it an "average historical fiction" whose "routine characterization and slow unfolding of Dory's life on the sparsely populated island will cause reader interest to lag long before the action starts" (Dorsey 4193).

The Maldonado Miracle also received mixed reviews. "Although the plot is trite the story reads well, and the characterization of Jose has special appeal" (*Booklist* 911). Ruth Robinson felt that by the end of the story, Jose is sure his father will accept his new maturity and his decision to go to Mexico City to become an artist, which for Jose would be the miracle of Maldonado. "Taylor realistically depicts the plight of migrant workers whose dreams of a better life compel them to resort to illegal means of entering the U. S. and make them prey to the greedy and unscrupulous of both races" (Robinson 2657). Once again Taylor's work suggests some of the difficulties of being an outsider trying to write of a culture not one's own.

Norma Bagnall asked Taylor if he felt there was any racial prejudice in *The Maldonado Miracle*, and Taylor replied that there was some, because he was trying to deal with both themes of survival and themes of national pride. He wanted to send Jose back to Mexico in order to make him proud of his own country and his own heritage. "Sometimes we do think too highly of our own way of life (89).

Maria: A Christmas Story also tackles questions of racism. Ruth Semrau found that "Taylor's brief tale is more about perceived barriers of economics and race than about Christmas," noting that Maria joins the parade not because she is full of holiday spirit, but because she no longer can stand by silently and listen to the bragging of others. Her father agrees out of similar annoyance. "After the difficulties and subsequent coming together of the community, winning the trophy in the parade pales. . . . Useful, perhaps, in multicultural studies" (104).

Chris Sherman, on the other hand, felt that "Taylor's portrayal of the Gonzagas—their ethnic pride, their sense of responsibility to their people, and the frustrations they experience—is vividly accomplished" and that the story would leave readers both satisfied and gently reminded of the true meaning of Christmas" (148).

Taylor's fiction is generally well written, and sometimes well received, but it does raise questions about the ways in which writers of the dominant society can perceive—and misperceive—peoples of other cultures. He is sincere in his efforts to portray people of color in a positive way, but still at times becomes condescending and perhaps even stereotypical in his treatment of minorities.

BIBLIOGRAPHY

Young Adult Fiction by Theodore Taylor

The Cay. New York: Doubleday, 1969.
The Children's War. New York: Doubleday, 1971.
The Maldonado Miracle. New York: Doubleday, 1973.
Teetoncey. New York: Doubleday, 1974.
Teetoncey and Ben O'Neal. New York: Doubleday, 1975.
The Odyssey of Ben O'Neal. New York: Doubleday, 1977.
The Trouble with Tuck. New York: Doubleday, 1981.
Sweet Friday Island. New York: Scholastic, Inc., 1984.
The Hostage. New York: Delacorte, 1987.
Walking Up a Rainbow; Being the True Version of the Long and Hazardous Journey of Susan D. Carlisle, Mrs. Myrtle Dessery, Drover Bert Pettit, and Cowboy Clay Cramer and Others. New York: Delacorte, 1987.
Sniper. New York: Harcourt, 1989.
Tuck Triumphant. New York: Doubleday, 1991.
The Weirdo. San Diego: Harcourt, 1992.
Maria: A Christmas Story. New York: Avon, 1993.
Timothy of the Cay. San Diego: Harcourt Brace, 1993.

Selected Studies of Theodore Taylor

Bagnall, Norma. "Profile: Theodore Taylor: His Models of Self-Reliance." *Language Arts* 57.1 (1980): 86–91.

"Best Books of the Year." *School Library Journal* 94.22 (1969): 4583.

Dorsey, C. "*The Cay.*" *New York Times Book Review* 29 June 1969: 26.

Dorsey, M. "*The Children's War.*" *Library Journal* 96.22 (1971): 4193.

Goodwin, Polly. "*The Cay.*" *Washington Post Book World* 4 May 1969: 36.

Knorr, Susan. "*Timothy of the Cay:* A Prequel-Sequel." *School Library Journal* 30.10 (1993): 132.

Rev. of *The Children's War*. *New York Times Book Review* 9 Jan. 1972: 8.

Rev. of *The Children's War*. *Publisher's Weekly* 18 Oct. 1971: 50.

Rev. of *The Maldonado Miracle*. *Booklist* 69.18 (1971): 911.

Roback, Diane. "*Timothy of the Cay.*" *Publisher's Weekly* 6 Sept. 1993: 98.

Robinson, Ruth. "*The Maldonado Miracle.*" *Library Journal* 98.1 (1973): 2657.

Roginski, Jim. *Behind the Covers: Interviews with Authors and Illustrators of Books for Children and Young Adults*. Vol. 2. Englewood: Libraries Unlimited, 1989. 210–23.

Schwartz, Albert. "*The Cay*: Racism Still Rewarded." *Interracial Books for Children Bulletin* 3.4 (1971): 7–8.

Semrau, Ruth. "*Maria: A Christmas Story.*" *School Library Journal* 39.1 (1993): 104.

Sherman, Chris. "*Maria: A Christmas Story.*" *Booklist* 89.2 (1992): 148.

Singer, M. R. "*The Cay.*" *Library Journal* 94.12 (1969): 2505.

Sutherland, Zena. "*The Cay.*" *Bulletin of the Center for Children's Books* 22.11 (1969): 183.

———. "*The Maldonado Miracle.*" *Bulletin of the Center for Children's Books* 26.11 (1992): 178.

Taylor, Theodore. *Something about the Author Autobiography Series*. Vol. 4. Detroit: Gale, 1987. 303–20.

Zvirin, Stephanie. "*Timothy of the Cay: A Prequel-Sequel.*" *Booklist* 90.2 (1993): 153.

Yoshiko Uchida
(1921–1992)

Cathryn M. Mercier

BIOGRAPHY

Yoshiko Uchida draws widely upon her personal and family experiences in all her fiction. She was born in Alameda, California, and was the second daughter of Iku (née Umegaki) and Dwight Takashi Uchida, Japanese immigrants to the United States. Uchida claims the stories of her parents' lives were integral to her own growth and identity as a Japanese-American. She outlines their history in the young adult/adult autobiography *Desert Exile: The Uprooting of a Japanese American Family* (1982) and touches upon it in her memoir for children titled *The Invisible Thread* (1991). Elements of their courtship and marriage appear in *Picture Bride* (1987). Uchida's individual and collective relationship with her parents serves as a model for the parent-child dynamics in her thirty-six books.

Her father spent three years teaching Japanese in Hawaii before arriving in San Francisco, California, in 1906. Dwight Takashi Uchida's aspirations to study medicine at Yale were never realized; a move to Seattle to be with his mother and an opening at a general merchandise store launched Takashi on his future as a store manager. He returned to San Francisco to operate a branch of Mitsui and Company in 1917 and later that year married Iku Umegaki.

Yoshiko Uchida portrays her mother as an unusual Japanese woman and influential role model. The daughter of a samurai who then became involved in regional politics, Iku Umegaki was the oldest of five children; her father died when she was twelve. Overcoming family hardship and some cultural resistance to a young woman pursuing a higher education, she attended Doshisha University in Kyoto. At this well-known Christian institution, Iku met Louise DeForest and Ellen Emerson Cary, two teachers of English literature who would change the course of her life. She studied with these professors, worked for them, and became a close friend. In fact, they, with the president of Doshisha University, served as the go-betweens in her arranged marriage to Takashi Uchida.

The separate lives of these two individuals played a key role in Uchida's life. Not only does she respect her parents, but she also pays tribute to their strength and their courage as first-generation Issei in the United States. Through them she begins to explore her own split identity as an American who is also Japanese. She remarks on their bravery in leaving their homeland, especially that of her mother who left behind her entire family. Stamina and dual national loyalties became particularly difficult issues during World War II when the Uchida family was uprooted from their comfortable, hard-working home in Berkeley, California, and moved into makeshift internment camps.

Uchida comments upon her early life as a time rich in Japanese tradition. However, it proves to be that cultural binding which challenges the young girl in school. She resisted Japanese language school and was puzzled at her mother's annual celebration of the Dolls' Festival. She recounts moments when Japanese customs embarrassed her. In yearning to be free from asking such questions as "do you cut Japanese hair?" upon her first professional haircut, Uchida describes humiliation and bafflement at the Japanese segregation which accompanied her childhood and adolescence. Even before the wide-scale internment of Japanese-Americans, Uchida felt apart from, felt "other-than," white Americans.

It is the internment of the Uchida family and the other 120,000 Japanese-Americans which marks this woman, finding extensive expression and exploration in her writing. Her father first was removed from the family and sent as a prisoner to a camp in Montana. With less than ten days' notice, she, her sister Keiko, and her mother were required to pack all their belongings and vacate their suburban home and lifestyle. Bewilderment, anger, and finally endurance accompanied them first to the Tanforan Assembly Center and then across country to the Central Utah Relocation Center in Topaz.

Uchida depicts this dark chapter in America's history in all its racism and human cost; however, she also demonstrates a remarkable ability to celebrate the Japanese-Americans who suffered and those who survived this experience. She completed her final semester of work at the University of California at Berkeley while interned and graduated *cum laude*. As a teacher at both internment camps, she participated in community building activities in response to the fragmentation of life in the camps. When offered the opportunity to secure sponsorship and placement outside the confines of Topaz, both Yoshiko and Keiko left. Uchida's difficulty in leaving her own parents behind in such deplorable conditions became tolerable only because they yearned for her to complete her education, and she believed she would be able to work for their release.

Upon leaving Topaz, Uchida's life followed a celebrated path: she graduated with an M.Ed. from Smith College in 1944, taught at a Friends' school, then served as secretary to the Institute of Pacific Relations from 1946–1947 and to the United Student Christian Council in New York from 1947–1952. Even though she began writing at the age of ten, her first book was not published until 1951. Yoshiko Uchida received a two-year Ford Foundation Fellowship in 1952 which enabled her to visit Japan for the first time. While discovering new aspects of herself in her parents' native land, she researched Japanese folk arts, documented the lives of a well-known potter and a poet, and collected the folk tales which she would retell and publish later. She completed a series of articles about Japanese folk arts and crafts for the *Nippon News* (1953–1954) and later became a regular columnist for *Craft Horizons* (1955–1964). She wrote regularly for children and young adults from 1951 through 1987, with two newly illustrated folk tale picture books published posthumously in 1993 and 1994; she published a single novel for adults in 1987 and four works of nonfiction between 1953 and 1982. For *The Happiest Ending* (1985), she received the Bay Area Book Reviewers Award for Children's Literature. In 1981 the University of Oregon honored her life and work with its prestigious award. Her manuscripts and papers are housed at the Kerlan Collection at the University of Minnesota, the University of Oregon Library, and the Bancroft Library at the University of California at Berkeley. Uchida died in her childhood—and adulthood—hometown of Berkeley, California, in 1992.

Yoshiko Uchida believed that "a sharing of ideas will someday bring about the kind of peaceful world we all hope for" (*Magic Listening Cap*, vii). Clearly, her experiences of harsh institutionalized and governmentally perpetuated racism fuel this drive. All her writing speaks to the humanitarian necessity of personal cultural identity and the possibility of a heterogeneous, complementary human community.

MAJOR WORKS AND THEMES

Yoshiko Uchida best states the unifying theme of her work: "I hope to give young Asians a sense of their own history, but at the same time, I want to dispel the stereotypic image held by many non-Asians about the Japanese-Americans and write about them as real people. I also want to convey the sense of hope and strength of spirit of the first generation Japanese-Americans. Beyond that, I want to celebrate our common humanity" (*The Dancing Kettle* 174). Uchida accomplishes these goals in four distinct genres of writing for children and young adults: folk tales, including the picture book retellings as well as volumes of collected tales; stories for the young reader; historical novels; and autobiography.

Uchida's best-known volumes of Japanese folk tales fall within the earlier part of her career. The collection *The Dancing Kettle and Other Japanese Folk Tales* first saw publication in 1949 with Harcourt Brace and was reissued with a new cover, but with Richard Jones' original illustrations, in paperback in 1986 by the Creative Arts Book Company in Berkeley. These fourteen tales establish Uchida as a skilled reteller. She does not translate the stories directly from their Japanese source; rather, she adapts them to meet a contemporary and largely Americanized, if not American, audience. In this volume, too, Uchida provides a glossary and a pronunciation guide. This tactic enables her to use original Japanese words throughout the stories, resulting in a natural flow and ease of language. In addition, these appendixes also encourage unfamiliar readers to discover items, foods, places, or characters specific to Japanese culture; the pronunciation guide especially educates them in a new way of speaking and of sounding. *The Magic Listening Cap: More Folk Tales from Japan* (1955) also contains Uchida's original, simple illustrations to fourteen tales. *The Sea of Gold and Other Tales from Japan* (1965) adds twelve more tales. It echoes the other two volumes in their vivacity and freshness. Uchida's voice in all three captures the humor and color of Japanese folk characters. Uchida briefly establishes a Japanese setting in these three volumes as she describes rice fields, flower gardens, high mountains, and the ever-present sea. These three collections stand not only as authentic in their voice and research, but also as authoritative in their unique contribution of Japanese folklore to children's literature. Perhaps their importance is just now being understood as Japanese and non-Japanese artists return to these sources to select individual tales for picture book-length versions. Margot Zemach illustrated *The Two Foolish Cats* in 1987; Keiko Narahashi chose *The Magic Purse* for a 1993 book; and Martin Springett painted scenes for *The Wise Old Woman*, a 1994 publication.

Though not a folk tale in origin, *Rokubei and the Thousand Rice Bowls* (1962) takes its pattern and characters from folklore. Rokubei works in the rice fields all day but enjoys making pottery rice bowls in his free time. Soon the hundreds of rice bowls overwhelm his studio and threaten to push his wife and two children out of their home. Just as the family is about to revolt, a wealthy lord buys all of the bowls and appoints Rokubei as chief potter. Uchida's direct, simple telling of the story makes its ending, Rokubei's return to his beloved country home, not only predictable but also deeply satisfying.

By far, the largest and most inclusive group of Uchida's fiction falls under the category of books for young readers. The earliest of these publications was illustrated for and addressed to an audience of children ages five to eight. They contain straightforward stories told with wit and humor; they focus on a single event in a young protagonist's life. Though the setting may be Japan or the United States, though it may be ancient times or the modern day, Uchida instills the book with a profound sense of community and the underlying, sustaining potential of family. Like Rokubei, these characters discover the wonder and tranquillity of home.

Takao and Grandfather's Sword (1958) features one of Uchida's few male protagonists. At ten years old, Takao yearns to help his father make the twenty-five tea sets just ordered by a prominent shopkeeper. It is unfortunate that Takao seems to create havoc wherever he goes, no matter how good his intentions. When his best efforts result in ruination of the kiln, Takao sells his treasured legacy, his grandfather's sword. Uchida's appreciation for the potter as artisan infuses this book and underscores Takao's respect for his talented father. A forgiving family and a village wise man help Takao restore his own pride as he helps his father rebuild from disaster.

Uchida combines the Christian celebration of Christmas with the Japanese winter in *The Forever Christmas Tree* (1963). In Sugi Village in Japan, bored Takashi and his school-aged sister Kaya venture into the backyard of the annoying Mr. Toda to decorate the only appropriate tree for Christmas. The children's daring eventually brings them the friendship of the old man. As she did with Takao, Uchida keeps the world of these two children limited to their immediate family at first, then she slowly expands that world to include an elderly man from the village. The children grow beyond their original expectations as they cross intergenerational boundaries with their respect and friendship.

Seven-year-old Sumi in *Sumi's Prize* (1964), *Sumi's Special Happening* (1966), and *Sumi and the Goat and the Tokyo Express* (1969) has one best friend in all of Sugi Village: its oldest resident, Mr. Gonzaburo Oda. In the first book, Sumi's father helps her to design and construct the most beautiful butterfly kite for entry in a contest. In this story, Sumi crosses an unspoken gender boundary to become the only girl entered in the contest. Rather than chastising her, the community welcomes her and recognizes the uniqueness of her contributions. This departure from gender-defined expectations of female characters appears in many of Uchida's books. As she discovers cultural differences in the treatment of gender, Uchida devises female characters who push the confines imposed by a Japanese perspective; however, she does not reconfigure completely the Japanese girl into a liberated American female. Thus, Uchida boldly exposes Japanese attitudes without merely replacing them with an American counterpart. She creates a tension between the two cultures which resides within the emerging personality of the female protagonists.

In the second book, Sumi's relationship with Mr. Oda develops. She yearns to give him an exciting, meaningful ninety-ninth birthday present. With the help of her schoolteacher-mayor, she takes him on a ride in the village's first fire engine. The third book once again starts at Sumi's school. However, Sugi Village undergoes change when the Tokyo Express extends its line along the edge of town. As Uchida introduces subtly the implications of this event, she holds true to the child's perspective and shows the school children's curiosity in the train and its passengers on the day Mr. Oda's red-hatted goat stops the train in its tracks. Uchida enlarges the tight circle of Sumi's family to include the larger community, and, through the symbolic train, to places beyond the familiar village.

Two of Uchida's picture books fall toward the end of her career, though they continue the themes she invokes in earlier books for young readers. In *The Birthday Visitor* (1975), Emi Watanabe wants to protect her seventh-birthday celebration from the intrusion of yet one more in her parents' long line of visitors from Japan. Emi's birthday turns out to be a fine party not just because her special friends the retired Wadas come, not just because five-year-old Benji stays, but especially because the visiting Reverend Okura appreciates a seven year old's perspective. Once again, Uchida combines children, adults, young, and old in joyful ways. Similarly, *The Rooster Who Understood Japanese* (1976) shows the reassuring results when a young child helps an older friend. Mrs. Kitamura's neighbor called the police to cease the disturbing daily cock-a-doodle-dooing of her rooster. Miyo devises a plan and finds the perfect home in the country for this beloved pet. The young characters operate within a safe, loving environment which instills self-esteem and makes success possible.

Large, bold print and small page decorations point to the older intended readership for *Makoto: The Smallest Boy* (1970). In the third grade, Makoto already feels a failure because others excel in ways he cannot. Uchida extends the special relationship between old and young explored in the Sumi books as Mr. Imai directs Makoto to discover his hidden, distinctive talent as an artist. Family and friends remain the central empowering components for the young artist.

Children ages seven to eleven can learn much about the city of Tokyo in *In-Between Miya* (1967) and *Hisako's Mysteries* (1969). Twelve years old and the middle child, Miya feels caught "in-between" and trapped by her plain house, family, and friends. She quickly accepts an invitation to do chores and household duties for her sick aunt and struggling uncle living in Tokyo. Miya expects more fun than work; she discovers she just may be too young to cope with the demands of running the house. Miya returns to her family with appreciation of them and their quiet, simple lifestyle. It is Hisako's curiosity about a mysterious birthday and about life outside her grandparents' house, her home since her parents' deaths, that prompts her to accept an invitation to visit her cousins and a friend in Tokyo. Hisako learns that her father is alive; yet, like Miya, she also finds that she may be too young to accept the full implications of some secrets. With these two books, Uchida's characters begin to venture outside their immediate families and towns into an extended family and into a larger sphere of activity and expectation.

Throughout these books, Uchida depicts a childhood of comfort and safety. Like Sumi, Takao, Miya, and Makoto, these children grow up within firmly identified, traditional families. Elders within the family and the community are respected and even befriended. It is this world that shifts dangerously when Uchida crosses the ocean to set her stories in America. That effect began in *Samurai of Gold Hill* (1972), and escalates in the Topaz books. This change also defines a change in Uchida's audience. As she tackles material of increased emotional complexity, she turns to an older audience and more intricate storytelling in slightly longer novels. The characters in these books are older, ranging in ages from eleven to fourteen, and they assume significant responsibilities within the household as they grow in independence and reliability.

The Promised Year (1959) signals Uchida's interest in stories of immigration. For middle readers, she describes Keiko's journey across the ocean to live in California with her Aunt Emi and Uncle Henry. Keiko decides she can endure her visit with this difficult uncle because of its limit to a single year. Uchida uses that time frame to demonstrate the tremendous growth that can occur. In that short time, eleven-year-old Keiko helps to run the household during her aunt's hospitalization, and she risks Uncle Henry's displeasure when she warns him about an oncoming smog that threatens his carnation business. Keiko goes well beyond her desire to be accepted as she assumes the role and the trust of an older child.

Samurai of Gold Hill (1972) also moves from Japan to America. Living in a historically distant Japan of 1869, Koichi yearns to be his father's companion and apprentice. When his father joins with other men in town to pool their funds to emigrate to America, Koichi wonders what will happen to his dream of continuing the family tradition of samurai. Their life in California becomes less peaceful than imagined as the Japanese fall under racist attack and Koichi devotes his best, most noble samurai efforts to ensuring peace and goodwill in the Wakamatsu colony on Gold Hill. Koichi moves from his self-centered wishes into full participation as a reliable community member.

Somehow, *Journey to Topaz* (1971) and *Journey Home* (1978) never betray Uchida's domineering belief in hope as they shape fiction around a bleak episode in America's history. Despite the shameful treatment of the Japanese-Americans during World War II, Uchida's two novels demonstrate a pervasive trust of and loyalty to the American government. The novels hold tenaciously to an eleven-year-old child's perspective as they describe the prisoners' existence: Uchida speaks of inadequately met basic needs of shelter, clothing, and food. She traces the four Sakane family members' evacuation from their beloved, cultivated Berkeley home to the Tanforan Race Track Assembly Center and then to the windy, dusty, incomplete relocation center in the Sevier Desert at Topaz. Father eventually joins them from his location in Montana while older brother Ken answers the army's call to join a special Nisei, second-generation Japanese-American unit. Uchida describes the concentration camp in all its dispiritedness and gloom. Yet, both novels simultaneously depict resilient characters whose constant tie to family and willingness to reach out to others allow them to persist and even to flourish.

Twelve-year-old Yuki makes a lifelong friend in Emi; the neighbors on the other side of the Sakane's barracks share despair and happiness; a community builds itself up, complete with schools, dances, funerals, and weddings. The move home proves nearly as devastating as the journey to Topaz. Once again, the family surrounds itself with good friends, with others in need, and they organize a solid foundation from which to build a future. Uchida does not shy away from showing the historically accurate hate crimes and resistance to the released Japanese; however, she uses the opportunities to bind together further the tight community. Most importantly, Uchida contrasts those who continue to hate with those who start to see individuals beyond appearance. When Ken returns, injured and broken, from his army service, only the Olssens can free him from his emotional pain—they understand because their only son died fighting against Japan. Uchida resists overplaying these moments. She inserts them into the fabric of the fiction, presents them with understated subtlety, and invites the reader to determine their magnitude.

The Topaz books certainly offer the generational "link to the past" and provide young readers "with the cultural memory they lack" (*Desert Exile* 146). Noting Uchida's desire to convey to "Japanese-American young people an understanding of their own history and pride in their identity" (Hoyle 990), her final trilogy of novels makes a fitting conclusion to her fictional work. In these books, Uchida continues to portray the closely knit Japanese family, to examine how it nurtures its young, and to envision a future of promise and hope. Uchida departs from her characteristic third-person narrator to develop the first-person voice of eleven-year-old Rinko in *A Jar of Dreams* (1981), *The Best Bad Thing* (1983), and *The Happiest Ending* (1985). Rinko's adventures in just over a year immerse the reader in Japanese traditions. Rinko's favorite foods and festivals are given full description here. Additionally, Rinko feels the pull between her Japanese heritage and her American culture. She discovers no easy answers, but learns to look at and to listen to individuals. Here, Uchida truly realizes her goal to expose a common humanity. For example, Rinko resists the idea of the arranged marriage of an acquaintance and tries to make a match for romantic love. Only when she sees the intended bride and groom as complex people, truly capable of independent choice, can she forgo the American romantic ideal for the better advised Japanese tradition. Throughout these three books, Rinko emerges as a typical, and an exceptional, Uchida character. She defeats stereotypes, both those she holds and those others cast her in, to materialize as an individual thinker and confident young woman with a firm sense of her own identity. That identity combines the dual cultures which shape her personality in original, exciting ways.

Uchida's narrative skills and her interest in personal life stories combine in a very early book, *The Full Circle* (1957). Umeko Kagawa, a teenager growing up in Japan, feels burdened by the celebrity of her father, a world renowned Christian leader. His popularity disturbs her quiet time, often makes him unavailable, and sometimes challenges her with insurmountable expectations. In this fictionalized story of the daughter of Dr. Toyohiko Kagawa, Uchida enters fully the reality of an adolescent girl. Readers quickly sympathize with Umeko's difficulty in part because they also recognize the fun and the joy characterizing her life. Umeko's mother and her friends help her to see past her own, at times, selfish need to recognize the contributions made by her father, and to see what individual attributes she shares.

In her two autobiographies, *The Invisible Thread* (1991) for children, and *Desert Exile: The Uprooting of a Japanese American Family* (1982) for young adults and adults, Uchida continues to explore a momentous, defining experience of being Japanese-American: the 1941 forced internment. Both books detail the full range of Uchida's life experience. *The Invisible Thread* follows Uchida's childhood and includes the internment episode: it focuses on her life within a stable, strong family. In contrast, *Desert Exile* turns explicitly on recounting the tragedy of the Japanese-American internment. A search for truth, a prevailing desire for understanding an incomprehensible historical reality, and the triumph of resilience, fortitude, and hope distinguish the books. Readers will find many biographical facts which Uchida re-forms into story elements or into aspects of a character in her fiction. Young readers, especially, delight in this overlapping of fact and fiction as they discover the person who also is the author.

Picture Bride (1987) fits neatly into none of these genres. While published as an adult novel, *Picture Bride* could be read by a young adult audience, too. Though requiring greater reading skill than Umeko's story, adolescents, particularly adolescent females, will take immediately to the urgency felt by the twenty-one-year-old Japanese woman Hana. The match making of Hana with Taro Takeda and her need to relocate to the United States will pique their romantic curiosity. Even more so will the irresistible attraction Hana feels to Taro's best friend. Hana's and Taro's marriage sustains; they fall in love slowly as they develop a life together. Adolescent readers will see in the Takedas' daughter Mary, who wants to forget her Japanese roots and become a fully integrated, fully accepted American, their own struggle for personal identity. And, like the Topaz books for younger readers and the autobiography *Desert Exile*, this novel recounts the Japanese-American internment experience; however, here Uchida adopts the more controlled, patient, yet equally confused perspective of two mature first-generation Japanese-Americans.

CRITICAL RECEPTION

Yoshiko Uchida has won citations from prestigious professional organizations such as the National Council of Teachers of English, the American Library Association, the California Association of Teachers of English, the Japanese-American Citizens League, the International Reading Association, the National Council for Social Studies, and the Children's Book Council.

Uchida's work continues to receive critical applause. Her work consistently garners favorable reviews in journals such as *School Library Journal, The Horn Book, Kirkus Reviews, The Bulletin for the Center of Children's Books, Booklist*, and the *New York Times Book Review*. Her work is praised for its age-appropriateness: Uchida speaks to her different audiences in ways which respect their emotional and intellectual maturity even as she asks them to grow beyond themselves as a result of reading. Crafted stories and well-developed characters who lead complex lives and whose decisions are often difficult continue to earn the admiration of reviewers, educators, and children alike. Uchida's willingness to explore the rich theme of cultural identity makes her a daring author, and one of the first authors to break the boundaries of stereotype. She manages to describe the ceremonies, traditions, and customs of each culture without diminishing the other. Reviewers generally applaud the central place of the family in Uchida's work; some comment upon the distinct sense of morality and living a morally responsible, humanitarian life which define the core of Uchida's work.

While no definitive critical, or biocritical, study of Uchida's work has been published, she does earn substantial attention in both *Major Twentieth Century Writers* and *Twentieth Century Children's Writers*. These essays remark upon Uchida's accomplishments as storyteller, be it in retelling Japanese folk tales or in writing original fiction. They note her ability to establish character through description and through a masterful use of dialogue. They compliment Uchida's success in depicting Japanese and American settings. Karen Nelson Hoyle honors Uchida's writing from a multicultural perspective when she states that the "author has worked diligently in describing an ethnic group and interpreting cultural patterns as a step toward the 'creating of one world'" (991).

BIBLIOGRAPHY

Young Adult Fiction by Yoshiko Uchida

The Promised Year. Illus. William Hutchinson. New York: Harcourt, 1959.
Journey to Topaz. Illus. Donald Carrick. New York: Scribner, 1971.

Samurai of Gold Hill. Illus. Arti Forberg. New York: Scribner, 1972.
Journey Home. Illus. Charles Robinson. New York: Atheneum, 1978.

Works for Children by Yoshiko Uchida

The Dancing Kettle and Other Japanese Folk Tales. Illus. Richard Jones. New York: Harcourt, 1949. Berkeley: Creative Arts Book Company, 1986.
New Friends for Susan. Illus. Henry Sugimato. New York: Scribner, 1951.
The Magic Listening Cap: More Folk Tales from Japan. New York: Harcourt, 1955.
The Full Circle. Illus. by author. New York: Friendship Press, 1957.
Takao and Grandfather's Sword. Illus. William Hutchinson. New York: Harcourt, 1958.
Mik and the Prowler. Illus. William Hutchinson. New York: Harcourt, 1960.
Rokubei and the Thousand Rice Bowls. Illus. Kazue Mizumura. New York: Scribner, 1962.
The Forever Christmas Tree. Illus. Kazue Mizumura. New York: Scribner, 1963.
Sumi's Prize. Illus. Kazue Mizumura. New York: Scribner, 1964.
The Sea of Gold and Other Tales from Japan. New York: Scribner, 1965.
Sumi's Special Happening. Illus. Kazue Mizumura. New York: Scribner, 1966.
In-Between Miya. Illus. Susan Bennett. New York: Scribner, 1967.
Hisako's Mysteries. Illus. Susan Bennett. New York: Scribner, 1969.
Sumi and the Goat and the Tokyo Express. Illus. Kazue Mizumura. NY: Scribner, 1969.
Makoto, the Smallest Boy. Illus. Arkihito Shirakawa. New York: Crowell, 1970.
The Birthday Visitor. Illus. Charles Robinson. New York: Scribner, 1975.
The Rooster Who Understood Japanese. Illus. Charles Robinson. New York: Scribner, 1976.
A Jar of Dreams. Atheneum, 1981.
Tabi: Journey through Time: Stories of the Japanese in America. El Cerrito, CA: Sycamore Congregational Church Board of Education, 1981.
The Best Bad Thing. New York: Atheneum, 1983.
The Happiest Ending. New York: Atheneum, 1985.
The Terrible Leak. New York: Creative Education, 1989.
The Invisible Thread. New York: Messner, 1991.
Bird Song. Privately printed, 1992.
The Bracelet. Illus. Joanna Yardley. New York: Macmillan, 1993.
The Magic Purse. Illus. Keiko Norahashi. New York: Macmillan, 1993.
The Wise Old Woman. Illus. Martin Springett. New York: Macmillan, 1994.

Other Works by Yoshiko Uchida

We Do Not Work Alone: The Thoughts of Kanjiro Kawai. Kyoto: Folk Art Society, 1953.

The History of Sycamore Church. Privately printed, 1974.

Margaret de Patta. Exhibition Catalog. Oakland, CA: Oakland Museum, 1976.

Desert Exile: The Uprooting of a Japanese American Family. Seattle: U of Washington P, 1982.

Picture Bride. Flagstaff, AZ: Northland Press, 1987.

Selected Studies of Yoshiko Uchida

Chang, C. E .S. "Profile: Yoshiko Uchida." *Language Arts* 61.5 (1984): 189–93.

Dreyer, S. S. *The Bookfinder: A Guide to Children's Literature about the Needs and Problems of Youth Ages Two through Fifteen*. Circle Pines, MN: American Guidance Service, 1981.

Hoyle, Karen Nelson. "Uchida, Yoshiko." *Twentieth-Century Children's Writers*. Ed. Tracy Chevalier. 3rd ed. Chicago: St. James, 1989. 989–91.

Mercier, Cathryn M. "Yoshiko Uchida." *American Women Writers from Colonial Times to the Present*. Ed. Carol Hurd Green and Mary Grimley Mason. New York: Continuum, 1994. 455–57.

"Uchida, Yoshiko." *Contemporary Authors, First Revision*. Ed. Clare D. Kinsman. Vols. 13–16. Detroit: Gale, 1975. 814.

"Yoshiko Uchida." *Something about the Author*. Ed. Anne Commire. Vol. 53. Detroit: Gale, 1989. 147–57.

Paul R. Yee
(1956-)

Jim Cope

BIOGRAPHY

Paul Yee was born October 1, 1956, in Saskatchewan, Canada, to Chinese immigrant parents who were owner/operators of a small café. His parents died when he was a young child, and he and his younger brother moved to Vancouver, British Columbia, to live with their Aunt Lillian. He grew up in his aunt's home in Strathcona, the Chinese section of Vancouver, where he attended elementary and high school.

While both schools' student bodies were almost entirely Chinese, Yee was uninterested in his Chinese roots. The closest he came was a fondness for the Chinese "sword-fighting" movies from Hong Kong and his Aunt Lillian's stories based on the rich folk tradition of Chinese-Canadians. It was not until he entered the University of British Columbia that Yee became interested in his Chinese heritage. While in college as a history student, he began studying the history of Chinese-Canadians. This study was soon combined with volunteer work in Chinatown, a visit to China, and his beginning to speak Chinese again.

Despite this deep interest in his Chinese heritage, Yee always considered himself a Canadian. As a child he often felt uncomfortable being "between" cultures. This personal experience of trying to live in two cultures comes through very clearly in Yee's writing. His current position as archivist for Toronto, Ontario, allows him to combine his love of history with his love of writing. His research into the history of Chinese-Canadians and their contributions to Canada, combined with his personal experiences, provide inspiration for his writings for children and young adults.

MAJOR WORKS AND THEMES

As stated above, Paul Yee's writing draws very clearly from his experiences growing up "between" cultures as well as from his professional work as an archivist. The impact of personal experiences comes through most clearly in his first work, *Teach Me to Fly, Skyfighter! and Other Stories* (1983). This collection of short stories for upper elementary students focuses on the lives of three Chinese-Canadian children and one white Canadian child growing up in the Strathcona section of Vancouver. While the Chinese students are concerned with the normal pursuits of children everywhere, they are also deeply concerned with finding their place in both cultures. Their parents and grandparents insist that they study and obey Chinese customs that seem terribly alien to them. At the same time, they are struggling to find a home in a Canadian culture that they know and love even though it does not always welcome them. Yee skillfully blends the children's struggles to find their cultural identities into stories that are universal.

In the title story, Sharon Fong is a young girl who strongly resists all attempts to teach her about her Chinese heritage. Her inability to speak Chinese is the center of her resistance to learn about a culture she wants nothing to do with. This resistance is melted away when an elderly friend of her grandfather gives her a kite that allows her to beat her rival, Samson, in a kite-flying contest. In the process of helping her with the kite, the old man teaches her an appreciation of her Chinese heritage through stories of his youth, building and flying kites in China.

In another of the stories, "Never Be Afraid," John Chin decides to take kung fu lessons after he is roughed up by some older boys. The martial arts training brings him closer to his Chinese heritage, but at the same time moves him away from his place in the Canadian culture of his classmates. The time he spends taking kung fu lessons causes him to miss hockey practice and gets him into trouble with his friends on the hockey team. Yee uses the pull of everyday childhood interests to subtly demonstrate the awkward place children often find themselves in as fully accepted members of no culture. This struggle for cultural identity is further illustrated in the stories as the children constantly compare and make distinctions between classmates who were born in Canada and those who are newly arrived from

China. These distinctions are carried further when they then compare themselves to their white Canadian classmates, causing the children to feel trapped between both cultures.

This comparison comes through most effectively in "Who Set the Fire" where Samson has to find out who set the fire at the playground so that he can save his white teammate from being falsely blamed. During his investigation, Samson discovers that his white classmates have lives very similar to those of his Chinese friends. Yee writes of these cultural conflicts as integral parts of the characters' lives and not as didactic lessons grafted onto typical stories of childhood.

Yee's second work, *The Curses of Third Uncle* (1986), relies both on his experiences as a historian and his personal experiences centered on the stories told him by his Aunt Lillian. The heroine of this adolescent novel is fourteen-year-old Lillian Ho. Lillian's father is a fundraiser for Dr. Sun Yat-sen and his revolutionary cause. When her father disappears for five months, the family sewing business goes broke and her mother grows ill, placing her unborn baby in danger. These problems are compounded by her Third Uncle's greedy desire to sell everything they own and send Lillian, her mother, and her sisters back to China.

Desperate to save her family, Lillian sets off in search of her father. Her search leads her to a remote mining village and the even more remote home of an ancient Chinese healer. At the healer's cabin, Lillian finds out about her father's job as fundraiser and learns about a form of spiritual healing, "chay gung." Back at home, she finds Third Uncle has betrayed her father by stealing his notebook that contains all of his financial contributors. Lillian uses her new knowledge of chay gung to save her mother, and with the help of Dr. Sun, she tricks her uncle into giving back her father's book. The end of the story finds the family saved financially by a collection taken in honor of her father at a rally for Dr. Sun.

The novel's core is based on an actual visit to Vancouver by Dr. Sun to raise funds for his revolution to free China from Manchurian rule. Yee uses this historical fact as the basis for his plot, but fleshes it out with ideas taken from his aunt's stories and his own experiences growing up in Strathcona. Lillian's struggle to appreciate Chinese culture while finding a place for herself in the Canada of the time reflects Yee's own childhood ambivalence about his cultural identity. Yee's childhood love for Chinese sword-fighting movies even makes an appearance in the form of a young Chinese woman Lillian meets on her search.

Yee's third major work, *Saltwater City: An Illustrated History of the Chinese in Vancouver* (1988), grew entirely out of his work as a historian, but reflects much of what appears in his earlier fiction. The book developed out of the Chinese Cultural Center's "Saltwater City" exhibition in honor of Vancouver's centennial in 1986. Using old newspaper articles, legal documents, official census data, and two hundred black-and-white photographs, the book traces the contributions of Chinese-Canadians to Vancouver's growth from their first arrival in number before the city was even founded through the centennial celebration. The book clearly describes the economic, social, and racial struggles the immigrants endured in building new lives. Many of these struggles were due to white prejudice and the ensuing legal and illegal tactics used in an attempt to halt the immigrants' economic and social achievements.

The book also does an excellent job of weaving the voices of individual Chinese-Canadians into the larger history of the city and its Chinese heritage. The voices of adolescents in the 1920s and 1930s bemoaning the fact that they are made to go to Chinese schools in addition to public schools or one young woman's laments about trying to live as a normal teenager while attempting to adhere to Chinese customs demonstrate how Yee's historical research finds its way into his fictional characters. In both he is concerned with the story of his people and the difficulty they, and others, face when they are forced to live between cultures.

In his award-winning *Tales from Gold Mountain: Stories of the Chinese in the New World* (1989), Paul Yee uses a spare but muscular style for eight "folk tales" based on the real labors of Chinese-Canadians in building Canada. From the son who finds and lays to rest his father's ghost in an unfinished railroad tunnel in "Spirits of the Railway" to Lee Jim's revenge on the cannery owner who replaces him with the "Iron Chink," Yee combines the style of the traditional Chinese folk tales he heard from his Aunt Lillian with his research into the history of Chinese-Canadian contributions to building Canada to create new stories for Chinese Canadians. In "Sons and Daughters," he tells the story of Merchant May's obsession with passing on his name. When twin daughters are born to him and his wife, Merchant May gives away the girls and buys twin boys from a poor peasant family. Years later his "sons" marry beautiful twin sisters that turn out to be May's real daughters. Before his "sons" and their wives are allowed to give him grandchildren, the gods force him to have his "sons" change their names and thus crush his dream. This story illustrates how Old World customs cause problems when used in the New World.

Two other stories tell of misfortunes brought about by prejudice. In "Gambler's Eyes," a man pretends to be blind to hide his green eyes that are a result of his mixed heritage. By pretending to be blind, he develops his hearing to the point that he never loses at gambling. This constant success is no small comfort for never being accepted in either culture. Prejudice brings a sad end in "Forbidden Fruit" when a father prevents his daughter from marrying the man she loves because he believes her loved one is beneath them in social status. His prejudice keeps the lovers apart and causes his daughter to pine away. In the end he understands what his narrow-mindedness has wrought.

Yee's stories are made even more compelling by the powerful illustrations of Simon Ng. Ng's strikingly magical illustrations combine with Yee's spare and muscular style to create a work that is hauntingly beautiful. These "New World" folk tales bridge the gulf between the two worlds to create stories that would be familiar in both.

Roses Sing on New Snow: A Delicious Tale (1991) is Paul Yee's newest work and builds on the stories from *Tales from Gold Mountain* to create another New World folk tale. Maylin loves to cook but is forced to slave away in the kitchen of her father's restaurant while her brothers get all of the credit. She finally receives recognition for her cooking when the visiting governor of South China raves over her new creation, "Roses Sing on New Snow." But Maylin's big moment is stolen when her cruel father tells the governor that Maylin's oafish brothers are the true cooks. When the governor demands to see how the dish is prepared, the brothers are unable to produce it. The truth comes out, and he asks Maylin to show him how to make it, but she replies that it would be impossible for him to prepare the dish back in China because it is truly a "dish of the New World." The illustrations by Harvey Chan do much to support this feminist story of the New World. They clearly show Maylin's strength in the face of her father and the governor and the greed and cowardice of her father and brothers.

Maylin's insight that the dish is truly one of the New World sums up the experience of reading Yee's works. His weaving together of history, personal experiences, and Chinese folk tales into stories that depict the lives of Chinese-Canadians creates characters and voices that are universal but that clearly belong to the world of Chinese Canada.

CRITICAL RECEPTION

In her review for *Books in Canada,* Mary Ainslie Smith describes *The Curses of Third Uncle* as "an ambitious book" that deals with important aspects of the immigrant experience of Chinese-Canadians. While she finds problems with the novel's "flow" and the use of coincidence to drive the plot, she describes the work as "a worthwhile addition to the general collection." The novel was voted Honorable Mention, 1986 Canada Council Children's Literature Prize.

In her review in *The Journal of the West*, Judy Yung praises *Saltwater City* for its ability to tell the history of Chinese-Canadians in Vancouver in a short, yet powerful format: "*Saltwater City* has that rare quality of being an informative, enlightening, and attractive book." She remarks on Yee's use of "quality" photographs and the "effective" use of sidebars to tell the more personal stories of the immigrant experience. Yung's praise of the book's visual qualities is in contrast to a review of the book from *Publisher's Weekly*. The review in this journal praised the historical depth and accuracy of the book, but criticized the black-and-white photography because "many have a grainy or washed-out quality." *Saltwater City* received the 1989 Vancouver Book Prize.

The highest acclaim for Yee's works comes for *Tales from Gold Mountain*. Betsy Hearne describes the work as "dramatic blends of realism and legend" while praising Yee for his lack of stylistic "pretensions" and for his "piercing portrayals." In a review for *The Horn Book*, Hanna B. Zeiger is struck by Yee's "richly evocative language." *Tales from Gold Mountain* was awarded the 1990 Imperial Order of the Daughters of the Empire National Children's Book Award, the 1990 British Columbia Book Prize, and the Sheila Egoff Award for Children's Literature.

Booklist found *Roses Sing on New Snow* to be told with "grace and economy" and commended the book for its "substance and visual appeal" (Hutt). This was echoed by Elizabeth S. Watson's review in *The Horn Book* that described the book as "delicately told and illustrated." Maggie De Vries criticizes the ending of the book as "flat" while commending the way the text and illustrations complement one another.

BIBLIOGRAPHY

Young Adult Fiction by Paul R. Yee

Teach Me to Fly, Skyfighter! and Other Stories. Illus. Sky Lee. Toronto: James Lorimer & Company, 1983.

The Curses of Third Uncle. Toronto: James Lorimer & Company, 1986.

Tales from Gold Mountain: Stories of the Chinese in the New World. Illus. Simon Ng. Toronto: Groundwood, 1989. New York: Macmillan, 1990.

Roses Sing on New Snow: A Delicious Tale. Illus. Harvey Chan. Toronto: Groundwood, 1991. New York: Macmillan, 1992.

Works for Adults by Paul R. Yee

Saltwater City: An Illustrated History of the Chinese in Vancouver. Vancouver: Douglas and McIntryre, 1988. Seattle: U of Washington P, 1989.

Selected Studies of Paul R. Yee

Burke, Kathleen. Rev. of *Roses Sing on New Snow: A Delicious Tale. Smithsonian* (Nov. 1992): 196.

Carver, Peter. Rev. of *Tales from Gold Mountain: Stories of the Chinese in the New World. Quill & Quire* (Dec. 1989): 23.

Chang, Margaret A. Rev. of *Tales from Gold Mountain: Stories of the Chinese in the New World. School Library Journal* 36.5 (1990): 121.

De Vries, Maggie. Rev. of *Roses Sing on New Snow: A Delicious Tale. Canadian Literature* 137 (Summer 1993): 95.

Hearne, Betsy. Rev. of *Tales from Gold Mountain: Stories of the Chinese in the New World. Bulletin of the Center for Children's Books* (Mar. 1990): 178.

Hutt, Karen. Rev. of *Roses Sing on New Snow: A Delicious Tale. Booklist* 1 Mar. 1992: 1288.

Lottridge, Celia. Rev. of *Roses Sing on New Snow: A Delicious Tale. Quill & Quire* (Aug. 1991): 19.

Marton, Diane S. Rev. of *Roses Sing on New Snow: A Delicious Tale. School Library Journal* 38.5 (1992): 95.

Meet the Author: Paul Yee. Videocassette. Color. Produced by School Services of Canada. Clearvue/EAV, 1992. 15 min.

Rev. of *Saltwater City. Publisher's Weekly* 236 (21 July 1989): 49.

Smith, Mary Ainslie. Rev. of *The Curses of Third Uncle. Books in Canada* (Dec. 1986): 18.

Stattaford, Genevieve. Rev. of *Saltwater City. Saturday Night* (Nov. 1988): 69.

Watson, Elizabeth S. Rev. of *Roses Sing on New Snow: A Delicious Tale. Horn Book* 68.2 (1992): 196.

Wieland, Gernot. Rev. of *Tales from Gold Mountain: Stories of the Chinese in the New World. Canadian Literature* 130 (Autumn 1991): 142.

Wilms, Denise. Rev. of *Tales from Gold Mountain: Stories of the Chinese in the New World. Booklist* 15 Mar. 1990: 1464.

Woodcock, George. Rev. of *Saltwater City. Saturday Night* (November. 1988): 69.

Yung, Judy. Rev. of *Saltwater City. Journal of the West* (Apr. 1993): 109.

Zeiger, Hanna B. Rev. of *Tales from Gold Mountain: Stories of the Chinese in the New World. Horn Book* 66.4 (1990): 459.

LAURENCE MICHAEL YEP
(1948–   )

Kay E. Vandergrift

BIOGRAPHY

Born on June 14, 1948, Laurence Yep is a third-generation Chinese-American who spent his childhood in San Francisco where his family owned and operated a corner grocery store and lived in the apartment upstairs. He attributes his diligence as a writer to his Jesuit education and the discipline he learned working in that family store. The neighborhood was predominantly African-American, but Yep commuted to Chinatown to attend grammar school where he was a very successful student in the English curriculum but an utter failure in the Chinese curriculum because of his inability to speak the language. Since students spoke Cantonese to conceal things from the nuns, Yep was also left out, not privy to the jokes and "insider" information of his classmates. It was not until he attended high school that he participated in the largely white American culture which he says he approached "as something of a stranger." His father, mother, and brother, ten years his senior, were all athletes, which added to Yep's feelings of being inadequate and an outsider even where he was most at home, feelings he has used to advantage in his writing. In his autobiography, *The Lost Garden* (1991), Yep describes his father making kites, particularly butterfly kites, later used in *Dragonwings* (1975). His father was also a basketball coach and an ardent gardener, priding himself on what he could grow in the small concrete space in back of the store. Yep, like many of the characters in his stories, has always tried to live up to the expectations of a very accomplished father.

Yep was an avid reader and a good student, who discovered his local library and eventually the main branch of the San Francisco Public Library, where he searched out aliens in the adult science fiction collection. He has said that, as a child, stories about boys with bicycles who live where no one locks their doors "seemed like fantasy to me. Ironically, what seemed 'truer' to me were science fiction and fantasy because in those books children were taken to other lands and other worlds where they had to learn strange customs and languages—and that was something I did every time I got on and off the bus." In high school, he was particularly successful in science but soon realized that he preferred making stories to making explosives. While at Marquette University, as a journalism major, he became friends with fellow writer and his future wife Joanne Ryder, who later encouraged him to write for young people. Unhappy at Marquette, despite his grandmother's caring food parcels that provided a strong link to home, he transferred to the University of California, Santa Cruz and received his B.A. there in 1970. Later he went to the State University of New York at Buffalo where he delighted in working with Leslie Fiedler. He completed his doctoral dissertation on William Faulkner in 1975.

MAJOR WORKS AND THEMES

Yep has written for young people of all ages and in an extraordinary range of genres. His novels for young adults include science fiction, fantasy, historical fiction, mystery, and contemporary realism. He has also written short stories, plays, and folk tales for this audience, as well as texts for picture books based on Chinese legends or folk tales that would be of interest to older youngsters studying the culture. In one of his most recent picture books, *The City of Dragons* (1995), a boy with the saddest face in the world is driven from his village because he makes others sad. Giants misinterpret the boy's looks and take him to the dragons where he uses his strangeness to advantage to help them cry real pearls.

Yep began his writing career at age eighteen while a student at Marquette University when his first published story appeared in a science fiction magazine which paid him a penny a word. This story, "The Selchey Kids," was later anthologized in *The World's Best Science Fiction of 1969*. As Yep wrote in his autobiography, "in looking back at those early stories, I was writing either about alienated heroes or aliens—even trying to tell the alien's viewpoint in the first person. All those years I had been trying to solve puzzles when the biggest puzzle had been myself." Yep's first young adult novel, *Sweetwater* (1973), was also science fiction. This is a complex story of life on the planet Harmony where three cultures lead completely separate lives until Tyree Priest, the young protagonist, crosses racial and social barriers to form a musical bond with old Amadeus. Thus, Yep continued to use the conventions of science fiction to explore the theme of those alienated because of race or culture. In the Star Trek novel *Shadow Lord* (1985), Spock and Sulu come to the aid of young Prince Vikram of the alien planet Angira in a romp through Kik-Kik attacks and sword-wielding enemies. As in *Sweetwater*, Yep creates an interesting juxtaposition of modernization versus alien culture.

Yep has also explored both his Chinese heritage and the role of the outsider through fantasy in his series based on Chinese dragon myths. In *Dragon of the Lost Sea* (1982), Shimmer, the exiled dragon princess, and the boy Thorn search for the evil Civet who has stolen the sea home of the dragons. His skillful blending of the real and fantasy worlds with history and mythology in lively adventure stories continued in *Dragon Steel* (1985), *Dragon Cauldron* (1991), and *Dragon War* (1992). Discussing these books in *The ALAN Review*, Yep wrote "the dragons have taught me that there is more than one way to reach the truth and more than one way to portray it. There is more than one way to discover a heritage and more than one way to explore it. Fantasy may be the longer path, but its rewards are far more satisfying" ("A Garden of Dragons").

The work of Jon Lee who collected stories in Oakland's Chinatown for the original WPA Writing Project of the 1930s was the basis for Yep's retelling of many of these tales of the Chinese agriculture and railroad workers in *The Rainbow People* (1989) and *Tongues of Jade* (1991). These collections use mythology and tradition to give voice to cultural links forged through story. Yep moved into the larger Asian-American community with his editing of twenty-five stories and poems representative of these cultures in *American Dragons* (1993). With *Tree of Dreams* (1995) Yep reaches even further to render beautiful dream stories drawn from cultures throughout the world. As he says in the preface, "Dreaming is a bond that unites us—beyond language and custom, beyond geography and time itself."

In *Dragonwings* (1975) Yep dealt with the alienation of Chinese-Americans in this country directly and realistically. In the process of researching the history of Chinese-Americans in California, he discovered the story of Fung Joe Guey who built and flew his own plane about the time of the Wright Brothers. Using this event as a pivotal incident, he built a story focusing on the aviator's young son, Moon Shadow, who came from China to join his father at a Chinese laundry in San Francisco. This book is authentic historical fiction with vivid pictures of the Chinese bachelor community of San Francisco's Chinatown at the turn of the century. It portrays believable multi-dimensional characters, both Chinese-American and white; a strong father-son relationship; and powerful symbols from Chinese myth and legend as well as the airplane as symbols of one man's dreams and the power of the imagination for all humanity. Yep adapted this novel into a play performed at the Berkeley Repertory Theater and at Lincoln Center in New York.

Dragon's Gate (1993), published almost twenty years later, shares its beginnings with *Dragonwings* and even has a character, Bright Star, in common. Here Yep tells the story of the Chinese immigrants who labored under brutal conditions to build the transcontinental railroad just after the Civil War. Fourteen-year-old Otter led a somewhat pampered life in China until he accidentally killed one of the barbarian Manchus and had to flee China and join his adoptive father and the legendary Uncle Foxfire in "the land of the Golden Mountain." On his arrival, he is forced into what amounts to slave labor and learns that America's other nickname, "the Land of the Demons," may be more apt. This challenging novel is both an exciting adventure story of a young man's coming-of-age and an informative picture of immigrant life in the last century.

Child of the Owl (1977) is the first of three realistic novels based on Yep's own family life. Set in San Francisco's Chinatown of the 1960s, this is the story of twelve-year-old Casey who confronts the Chinese part of herself for the first time when she goes to live with her grandmother Paw-Paw. Again a legend, in this case that of the owl created by Yep, provides thematic unity as the young protagonist comes to appreciate her Chinese-American roots. The intergenerational elements are also compelling as Casey recognizes her beloved father for the compulsive gambler he is, learns about her mother who died when she was young, and comes to love and appreciate Paw-Paw, who is one of the most interesting grandmothers in fiction for young people. Like other Yep characters, Casey develops her own sense of identity by accepting her Chinese heritage into her American consciousness. In *Thief of Hearts* (1995), a sequel to *Child of the Owl*, Stacey, daughter of Casey, considers herself all American until her school forces her into a relationship with a new girl named Hong Ch'un. Now, just as her mother had before her, Stacey must reconcile her Chinese heritage with her American way of life.

Craig Chin of *Sea Glass* (1979) has greater difficulty in establishing his identity than previous Yep protagonists because he is rejected by both

Chinese-American and white American society. In this semi-autobiographical story, Craig moves from Chinatown to a small town of white Americans. He is pushed by his father to pursue sports, for which he has no aptitude and little interest, as a way of fitting in. The conflict of cultures and that between father and son are played out against an array of complex and finely drawn minor characters. Craig's voice in this first-person narration will ring true to young people trying to find their place as outsiders in an alien world, even if the "aliens" they contend with are only adults.

The Star Fisher (1991) is a fictionalized account of Yep's grandmother's family, the first Chinese family to move to Clarksburg, West Virginia, in the 1920s. They move into an old schoolhouse and open a Chinese laundry, but many of their neighbors are hostile to anything "foreign." With the help of their landlady and Mama's apple pie, the Lee family gains acceptance and gradually becomes a part of this American town without losing touch with their Chinese past. The star fisher of the title, a bird that belongs in both heaven and earth without ever being completely at home in either, is symbolically akin to the teenage protagonist, Joan Lee.

Yep's young adult fiction deals with marginalized teenagers seeking their own authentic, if dual, identities, often facing racial discrimination as they move from one culture to another. Young protagonists most often tell their stories in the first person, balancing adolescent angst, alienation, and intergenerational conflicts with an offbeat sense of humor. The roots of Chinese-American culture are embedded in both time and place and in the oral traditions of the people. Yep incorporates myths, legends, and folk tales from ancient China into contemporary Chinese-American life, most often in San Francisco. He also gives readers a sense of the history that drove Chinese-Americans to this country and the ways that history shaped their lives here. Above all, Yep creates strong and memorable characters, many of whom are based on members of his own family. Minor characters are as believable as major ones, with those from all cultures exhibiting both positive and negative traits. Unlike many contemporary teen characters, Yep's protagonists accept the help of adult mentors such as Uncle Quail in *Sea Glass* and Amadeus in *Sweetwater*. Of special interest are his strong older female characters who often play pivotal roles in helping young people build bridges between their two cultures. The Chinese grandmother, Paw-Paw, from *Child of the Owl* and white Americans Miss Witlaw from *Dragonwings* and Miss Lucy from *The Star Fisher* serve in this role.

One of Yep's great strengths is his ability to build connections among conflicting elements of human life. His courageous young characters create their own independence without severing ties either with cultural history or with the generations they rebel against. They face racism and bigotry, often matter-of-factly, but also find caring and inclusion among those of different races and cultures. Yep's voice is as true and as powerful in his female characters as in the males. He even bridges the gap between children's and young adult literature.

CRITICAL RECEPTION

Yep's multicultural stories have been honored with many awards. *Dragonwings* was a Newbery Honor Book, A Notable Children's Book, and won numerous other awards shortly after its publication. In 1995, twenty years later, it won the Phoenix Award of the Children's Literature Association. The *New York Times Book Review* stated that "as an exquisitely written poem of praise to the Chinese American people, it is a triumph." *Publisher's Weekly*'s commentary on *Dragonwings* indicated that "it would be impossible for a reader of any age to retain even a trace of the stereotyped Chinese image after reading this thrilling book."

Eighteen years later, Yep won another Newbery Honor for *Dragon's Gate*. The committee chair described this book as "carefully researched and well written. . . . Told with humanity and compassion, *Dragon's Gate* is a tribute to the survival and courage of these immigrants." This book was also a Notable Book and won the John and Patricia Beatty Award of the California Library Association.

Child of the Owl was a winner of the *Boston Globe-Horn Book* Fiction Award and the Jane Addams Children's Book Award, as well as being included on both the Notable Children's and Best Children's Book lists of 1977. *Kirkus Reviews* called this novel "a beautifully transmuted Chinatown legend, and an odds-on popular favorite as well."

In discussing *Dragonwings*, *Child of the Owl*, and *The Star Fisher*, Mingshui Cai wrote, "By combining old myth with contemporary life, the three novels achieve a rich, colorful texture that appeals to the imagination. They take children into the fantasies of the faraway and long ago, yet also bring them back with new insight into the problems of the present world. In Yep's historical and contemporary realistic fiction, we find an element of fantasy, while in his fantasies, there is close relevance to problems in the real world."

Yep has commented that when he was a boy there were no books for children about Chinese-Americans. He has certainly been a leader in filling that void for today's young people and has received critical acclaim for those stories. His Asian-American heritage has perhaps given him special insight into the young adult sense of being a "stranger in an 'alien' culture" that is the essence of the coming-of-age experience and the search for personal identity. Critics have praised Yep for his complex, multidimensional characters, his first-person narratives, the use of figurative language and elements of traditional literature within realistic stories, and especially for the authenticity of historical details. The only major criticism of his multicultural stories has been that they are often slow paced, but that pace may provide time for readers to consider the many layers of meaning in Yep's work.

BIBLIOGRAPHY

Young Adult Fiction by Laurence Michael Yep

Sweetwater. New York: Harper, 1973.
Dragonwings. New York: Harper, 1975.
Child of the Owl. New York: Harper, 1977.
Sea Glass. New York: Harper, 1979.
Dragon of the Lost Sea. New York: Harper, 1982.
Kind Hearts and Gentle Monsters. New York: Harper, 1982.
The Mark Twain Murders. New York: Four Winds, 1982.
Liar, Liar. New York: Morrow, 1983.
The Serpent's Children. New York: Harper, 1984.
The Tom Sawyer Fires. New York: Morrow, 1984.
Dragon Steel. New York: Harper, 1985.
Mountain Light. New York: Harper, 1985.
Shadow Lord: A Star Trek Novel No. 22. New York: Pocket, 1985.
The Rainbow People. New York: Harper, 1989.
Dragon Cauldron. New York: Harper, 1991.
The Star Fisher. New York: Morrow, 1991.
Tongues of Jade. New York: Harper, 1991.
Dragon War. New York: Harper, 1992.
Dragon's Gate. New York: Harper, 1993.
Later, Gater. New York: Hyperion, 1995.
Thief of Hearts. New York: Harper, 1995.
Tree of Dreams: Ten Tales from the Garden of Night. Illus. Isadore Seltzer.
    Mahwah: Bridgewater, 1995.

Works for Children by Laurence Michael Yep

The Curse of the Squirrel. Illus. Dirk Zimmer. New York: Random House, 1987.

When the Bomb Dropped: The Story of Hiroshima. Illus. Robert Andrew Parker. New York: Random House, 1990.

The Butterfly Boy. Illus. Jeanne M. Lee. New York: Farrar, 1993.

The Man Who Tricked a Ghost. Illus. Isadore Seltzer. Mahwah: Bridgewater, 1993.

The Shell Woman & the King: A Chinese Folktale. Illus. Yang Ming-Yi. New York: Dial, 1993.

The Boy Who Swallowed Snakes. Illus. Jean Tseng and Mou-Sien Tseng. New York: Scholastic, 1994.

The Ghost Fox. Illus. Jean Tseng and Mou-Sien Tseng. New York: Scholastic, 1994.

The Junior Thunder Lord. Illus. Robert Van Nutt. Mahwah: Bridgewater, 1994.

Tiger Woman. Illus. Robert Roth. Mahwah: Bridgewater, 1994.

The City of Dragons. Illus. Jean Tseng and Mou-Sien Tseng. New York: Scholastic, 1995.

Hiroshima. New York: Scholastic, 1995.

Works for Adults by Laurence Michael Yep

Seademons. New York: Harper, 1977.

Monster Makers, Inc. New York: Arbor House, 1986.

The Lost Garden. Autobiography. Englewood Cliffs: Messner, 1991.

Plays by Laurence Michael Yep

Pay the Chinaman. Between Worlds: Contemporary Asian-American Plays. Ed. Misha Berson. New York: Theatre Communications Group, 1990. 176–196.

Dragonwings. New York: Dramatist Play Service, 1993.

Works Edited by Laurence Michael Yep

American Dragons: Twenty-Five Asian American Voices. New York: Harper, 1993.

Other Works by Laurence Michael Yep

"Writing Dragonwings." *Reading Teacher* 30.4 (1977): 359–63.

"Fantasy and Reality." *Horn Book* 54.3 (1978): 136.

"The Green Cord." *Horn Book* 65.1 (1989): 318–22.

"A Cord to the Past." *CMLEA* 15 (Fall 1991): 8–10.

"A Garden of Dragons." *The ALAN Review* 19.3 (1992): 6–8.

Selected Studies of Laurence Michael Yep

Burnston, Patrick. "In the Studio with Laurence Yep." *Publishers Weekly* 16 May 1994: 25–26.

Cai, Mingshui. "A Balanced View of Acculturation: Comments on Laurence Yep's Three Novels." *Children's Literature in Education* 23 (June 1992): 107–18.

Dinchak, Maria. "Recommended: Laurence Yep." *English Journal* 71 (1982): 81–82.

"Laurence Michael Yep." *Children's Literature Review*. Ed. Gerald J. Senick. Vol. 17. Detroit: Gale, 1989. 201–209.

"Laurence Michael Yep." *Major Authors and Illustrators for Children and Young Adults*. Ed. Laurie Collier and Joyce Nakamura. Vol. 6. Detroit: Gale, 1993. 2522–25.

"Laurence Yep." *Authors & Artists for Young Adults*. Ed. Agnes Garrett and Helga P. McCue. Detroit: Gale, 1990. 245–52.

"Laurence Yep." *Contemporary Literary Criticism*. Ed. Daniel G. Marowski. Vol. 35. Detroit: Gale, 1985. 468–74.

"Laurence Yep." *Speaking for Ourselves: Autobiographical Sketches by Notable Authors of Books for Young Adults*. Comp. and ed. Donald R. Gallo. Urbana, IL: NCTE, 1990. 222–24.

Molsen, Francis J. "Laurence Yep." *Twentieth-Century Children's Writers*. Ed. Tracy Chevalier. 3rd ed. Chicago: St. James, 1989. 1074–75.

Morgan, Karen Ferris. "Laurence Yep." *Twentieth-Century Young Adult Writers*. Ed. Laura Standley. Detroit: St. James, 1994. 723–25.

Pelimas, R. H. Rev. of *Dragonwings*. *New York Times Book Review*, 16 November 1975: 30.

Rev. of *Child of the Owl*. *Kirkus Reviews* 45 (1 Feb. 1977): 99.

Rev. of *Dragonwings*. *Publishers Weekly* 207 (16 June 1975): 82.

Stines, Joe. "Laurence Yep." *Dictionary of Literary Biography*. Ed. Glenn Estes. Vol. 52. Detroit: Gale, 1986. 392–98.

Wigutoff, Sharon. "Junior Fiction: A Feminist Critique." *The Lion and the Unicorn* 5 (1981): 4–18.

"World Building." *Innocence & Experience: Essays and Conversations on Children's Literature*. Ed. Barbara Harrison. New York: Lothrop, 1987. 182–84.

SELECTED BIBLIOGRAPHY: WORKS RELATED TO MULTICULTURAL LITERATURE

GENERAL WORKS

Alexander, Jayne. "Multicultural Literature: Overcoming the Hurdles to Successful Study." *The Clearing House* 67 (1994): 266–68.

Allen, Adela Artoka. *Library Services for Hispanic Children: A Guide for Public and School Libraries.* Phoenix: Oryx Press, 1987.

Bacon, Betty, ed. *How Much Truth Do We Tell the Children? The Politics of Children's Literature.* Minneapolis: Marxist Education Press, 1988.

Blair, Linda. "Developing Student Voices with Multicultural Literature." *English Journal* 80.8 (1991): 24–28.

Bortolussi, Marisa. "Culture and Identity in Canadian Children's Literature." *Canadian Literature* Supp. 1 (1987): 138–45.

Bushman, John H., and Kay Parks. "Diversity in Young Adult Literature: Ethnic, Cultural, and National." *English Journal* 82.6 (1993): 80–82.

Camarata, Corinne. "Making Connections: Introducing Multicultural Books." *School Library Journal* 37.9 (1991): 190–91.

Carlson, Ruth Kearney. *Emerging Humanity: Multi-Ethnic Literature for Children and Adults.* Dubuque, IA: William C. Brown, 1972.

Carter, George E., James R. Parker, and Sara Bentley, eds. *Minority Literature and the Urban Experience: Selected Proceedings of the Fourth Annual Conference on Minority Studies.* LaCrosse, WI: Lacrosse Institute for Minority Studies, University of Wisconsin, 1978.

Dyson, Anne Haas, and Celia Genishi, eds. *The Need for Story: Cultural Diversity in Classroom and Community.* Urbana, IL: NCTE, 1994.

Foster, Frances Smith. "What Matters the Color of the Tiger's Stripes? The Significance of Bibliographies by Ethnic Identification." *Children's Literature Association Quarterly* 13.1 (1988): 80–83.

Gannon, Susan R., and Ruth Anne Thompson, eds. *Cross-Culturalism in Children's Literature: Selected Papers from the Children's Literature Association, Carleton University, Ottawa, Canada, May 14–17, 1987.* New York: Pace U, 1988.

Gibson, Lois Rauch. "Children's Literature as Social History." *Teaching Children's Literature: Issues, Pedagogy, Resources.* Ed. Glenn Edward Sadler. New York: MLA, 1992. 175–77.

Hansen-Krening, Nancy. "Authors of Color: A Multicultural Perspective." *Journal of Reading* 36.2 (1992): 124–29.

Harris, Violet J. "'Have You Heard about an African Cinderella Story?' The Hunt for Multicultural Literature." *Inspiring Literacy: Literature for Children and Young Adults.* Ed. Sam Sebosta and Ken Donelson. New Brunswick, NJ: Transaction, 1993. 27–40.

Hunt, Peter. "Cross-Culturalism and Inter-Generation Communication in Children's Literature." *Cross-Culturalism in Children's Literature: Selected Papers from the Children's Literature Association, Carleton University, Ottawa, Canada, May 14–17, 1987.* Ed. Susan R. Gannon and Ruth Anne Thompson. New York: Pace U, 1988.

Khorana, Meena. "The Ethnic Family and Identity Formation in Adolescents." *The Child and the Family: Selected Papers from the 1988 International Conference of the Children's Literature Association, College of Charleston, Charleston, South Carolina, May 19–22, 1988.* Ed. Susan R. Gannon and Ruth Anne Thompson. New York: Pace U, 1989.

Kissen, Rita M. "Multicultural Education: The Opening of the American Mind." *English Education* 21.4 (1989): 211–18.

Kruse, Ginny Moore. "'No Single Season': Multicultural Literature for Children." *Wilson Library Bulletin* 66.6 (1992): 30–33.

Lewis, Valerie. "With Many Voices: Talking about Multicultural Children's Literature." *Instructor* 103.6 (1994): 38–41.

Lindgren, Merri V., ed. *The Multicolored Mirror: Cultural Substance in Literature for Children and Young Adults.* Ft. Atkinson, WI: Highsmith Press, 1991.

Madigan, Dan. "The Politics of Multicultural Literature for Children and Adolescents: Combining Perspectives and Conversations." *Language Arts* 70.3 (1993): 168–76.

Manna, Anthony L., and Carolyn S. Brodie, eds. *Many Faces, Many Voices: Multicultural Literary Experiences for Youth.* Ft. Atkinson, WI: Highsmith, 1992.

Martinez, Julio, and Francisco Loreli, eds. *Chicano Literature: A Reference Guide.* Westport, CT: Greenwood, 1985.

Marzollo, Jean. "Multicultural Books for Every Classroom." *Instructor* 100 (Feb. 1991): 41–43.

Miller-Lachman, Lyn. "The Audience for Multicultural Literature." *Journal of Youth Services in Libraries* 6 (Winter 1993): 163–65.

————. *Our Family, Our Friends, Our World: An Annotated Guide to Significant Multicultural Books for Children and Teenagers.* New Providence, NJ: Reed Reference Publishing, 1992.

Minderman, Lynn. "Literature and Multicultural Education." *Instructor* 99 (Mar. 1990): 22–23.

Moebius, William. "Cultural Entitlement in the New Age." *The Lion and the Unicorn* 16.1 (1992): 57–65.

Moore, Opal, and Donnarae MacCann. "On 'Reading' Institutions." *Children's Literature Association Quarterly* 13.4 (1988): 198–200.

Norton, Donna E. "Teaching Multicultural Literature in the Reading Curriculum." *The Reading Teacher* 44.1 (Sept. 1990): 28–40.

Pugh, Sharon L., and Jesus Garcia. "Multicultural Trade Books for Adolescents: A Definition and Sampler." *Social Education* 56.5 (1992): 303–307.

Rasinksi, Timothy V., and Nancy D. Padak. "Multicultural Learning through Children's Literature." *Language Arts* 67.6 (1990): 576–80.

Reissman, Rose. "Leaving Out to Pull In: Using Reader Response to Teach Multicultural Literature." *English Journal* 83.2 (1994): 20–23.

Richard, Kerri J., and Gisela Ernst. "'Understanding the Other, Understanding Myself': Using Multicultural Novels in the Classroom." *Clearing House* 67.2 (1993): 88–90.

Roney, R. Craig. "Multiethnicity in Children's Fiction." *Social Education* 50.6 (1986): 464–66, 468, 470.

Rudman, Masha Kabakow. *Children's Literature: An Issues Approach.* 2nd ed. New York: Longman, 1984.

Sasges, Judy. "Connections—Young Adult Publishers, Young Adult Librarians, Young Adult Readers: Linking Multicultural Needs." *Journal of Youth Services Librarians* 6 (Winter 1993): 166–68.

Scarpaci, Jean. "Multi-Ethnic Literature for Children." *MELUS* 3.3 (1976): 2–3.

Shields, Charles J. "Multicultural Literature: Does a Book's Locale, Customs, and Characters Take Priority over Good Literature?" *Curriculum Review* 33.1 (1994): 8–12.

Smagorinsky, Peter. "Towards a Civic Education in a Multicultural Society: Ethical Problems in Teaching Literature." *English Education* 24.4 (Dec. 1992): 212–28.

Stinton, Judith, ed. *Racism and Sexism in Children's Books.* London: Writers and Readers Publishing Cooperative, 1979.

Stotsky, Sandra. "Academic Guidelines for Selecting Multiethnic and Multicultural Literature." *English Journal* 83.2 (1994): 27–34.

Stover, Lois. "Exploring and Celebrating Cultural Diversity and Similarity through Young Adult Novels." *ALAN Review* 18.3 (1991): 12–15.

Sue, Stanley, and Nathaniel N. Wagner, eds. *Asian Americans: Psychological Perspectives.* Palo Alto, CA: Science and Behavior Books, 1973.

Yeh, Phoebe. "Multicultural Publishing: The Best and the Worst of Times." *Journal of Youth Services in Libraries* 6 (Winter 1993): 157–60.

Yokota, Junko. "Issues in Selecting Multicultural Children's Literature." *Language Arts* 70.3 (1993): 156–67.

LITERATURE ABOUT AFRICAN-AMERICANS

Anderson, Celia. "Florence Crannell Means: Cultural Barriers and Bridges." *Cross-Culturalism in Children's Literature: Selected Papers from the Children's Literature Association, Carleton University, Ottawa, Canada, May 14–17, 1987.* Ed. Susan R. Gannon and Ruth Anne Thompson. New York: Pace U, 1988. 87–90.

Bishop, Rudine Sims. "Strong Black Girls: A Ten Year Old Responds to Fiction About Afro-Americans." *Journal of Research and Development in Education* 16.3 (Spring 1983): 21–28.

Broderick, Dorothy. *The Image of the Black in Children's Fiction.* New York: Bowker, 1973.

Capan, Mary Ann, and Cynthia Suarez. "Biracial/Biethnic Characters in Young Adult and Children's Books." *Multicultural Review* 2.2 (1993): 32–37.

D'Costa, Jean. "Expression and Communication: Literary Challenges to the Caribbean Polydialectal Writers." *Journal of Commonwealth Literature* 19.1 (1984): 123–41.

Deane, Paul. "Black Characters in Children's Fiction Series since 1968." *Journal of Negro Education* 58.2 (Spring 1989): 153–62.

Dowd, Frances S. "Evaluating Children's Books Portraying Native American and African Cultures." *Children's Literature in Education* 68.4 (Summer 1992): 219–24.

Foster, Frances Smith. "Literature for Children by Afro-American Writers: 1976–1986." *Children's Literature Association Quarterly* 13.1 (1988): 83–87.

Graham, Joyce L., and Susan Murphy. "Growing Up Black: Fiction about Black Adolescents' Experiences." *Journal of Reading* 36 (April 1993): 590–92.

Hamilton, Virginia. "On Being a Black Writer in America." *The Lion and the Unicorn* 10.1 (1986): 15–17.

Harris, Violet J. "From Little Black Sambo to Popa and Fifina: Arna Bontemps and the Creation of African-American Children's Literature." *The Lion and the Unicorn* 14.1 (1990): 108–27.

———. "Race Consciousness, Refinement, Radicalism, Socialization in *The Brownies' Book*." *Children's Literature Association Quarterly* 14.3 (1989): 192–96.

————. "Research in Review: Multicultural Curriculum, African-American Children's Literature." *Young Children* 46 (Jan. 1991): 37–44.

Haskins, Jim. "The Triumph of the Spirit in Nonfiction for Black Children." *Triumphs of the Spirit in Children's Literature.* Ed. Francelia Butler and Richard Robert. Hamden, CT: Library Professionals Publications, 1986. 88–96.

Hoyle, Karen Nelson. "Resources for Study of Black Children's Literature at the University of Minnesota." *Children's Literature Association Quarterly* 13.1 (1988): 87–88.

Huse, Nancy. "*Sounder* and Its Readers: Learning to Observe." *Children's Literature Association Quarterly* 12.2 (1987): 66–69.

Johnson, Dianne. "The Chronicling of an African-American Life and Consciousness: Lucille Clifton's Everett Anderson Series." *Children's Literature Association Quarterly* 14.3 (1989): 174–78.

————. "Perspectives on Writing and the African Diaspora: Examples from the Children's Literature of Lucille Clifton and Rosa Guy." *Work and Play in Children's Literature: Selected Papers from the 1990 International Conference of the Children's Literature Association.* Ed. Susan R. Gannon and Ruth Anne Thompson. New York: Pace U, 1990.

Kiah, Rosalie Black, and Elaine Page Wilty. "The Portrayal of the Black Mother in Fiction for Children and Adolescents." *Adolescents, Literature and Work with Youth.* Ed. J. Pamela Weiner and Ruth M. Stein. New York: Haworth, 1985. 81–91.

Kruse, Ginny Moore, and Kathleen T. Horning. *Multicultural Literature for Children and Young Adults: A Selected Listing of Books 1980–1990 by and about People of Color.* 3rd ed. Madison, WI: Wisconsin Department of Public Instruction, 1991.

Lester, Julius. "The Storyteller's Voice: Reflections on the Rewriting of Uncle Remus." *The Voice of the Narrator in Children's Literature: Insights from Writers and Critics.* Ed. Charlotte F. Otten and Gary D. Schmidt. New York: Greenwood, 1989. 69–73.

MacCann, Donnarae. "Effie Lee Newsome: African American Poet of the 1920's." *Children's Literature Association Quarterly* 13.1 (1988): 60–65.

————. "Racism in Prize-Winning Biographical Words." *The Black American in Books for Children: Readings in Racism.* 2nd ed. Ed. Donnarae MacCann and Gloria Woodard. Metuchen, NJ: Scarecrow, 1985. 169–79.

MacCann, Donnarae, and Gloria Woodard, eds. *The Black American in Books for Children: Readings in Racism.* 2nd ed. Metuchen, NJ: Scarecrow, 1985.

————. *Cultural Conformity in Books for Children: Further Readings in Racism.* Metuchen, NJ: Scarecrow, 1977.

Madsen, Jane. "Historical Images of the Black Child in Children's Literature and Their Contemporary Reflections." *Minority Voices: An Interdisciplinary Journal of Literature and the Arts* 4.2 (1980): 1–36.

McCloskey, Audrey T. "Tell the Good News: A View of the Works of Lucille Clifton." *Black Women Writers 1950–1980: A Critical Evaluation.* Ed. Mari Evans. Garden City, NY: Anchor Doubleday, 1984.

Mikkelsen, Nina. "But Is It a Children's Book? A Second Look at Virginia Hamilton's *The Magical Adventures of Pretty Pearl.*" *Children's Literature Association Quarterly* 11.3 (1986): 134–42.

———. "Censorship and the Black Child: Can the Real Story Ever Be Told?" *The Child and the Story: An Exploration of Narrative Form. Proceedings of Ninth Annual Conference of the Children's Literature Association, Univ. of Florida, Mar. 1992.* Ed. Priscilla Ord. Boston: Children's Literature Association, 1983. 117–27.

Mitchell, Arlene Harris. "Black Adolescent Novels in the Curriculum." *English Journal* 77.5 (1988): 95–97.

Moss, Anita. "Frontiers of Gender in Children's Literature: Virginia Hamilton's *Arilla Sundown.*" *Children's Literature Association Quarterly* 8.4 (1983): 25–27.

———. "Mythical Narrative: Virginia Hamilton's *The Magical Adventures of Pretty Pearl.*" *The Lion and the Unicorn* 9.1 (1985): 50–57.

Nodelman, Perry. "The Limits of Structures: A Shorter Version of a Comparison between Toni Morrison's *Song of Solomon* and Virginia Hamilton's *M. C. Higgins the Great.*" *Children's Literature Association Quarterly* 7.3 (1982): 45–48.

Quinlivan, Mary E. "Race Relations in the Antebellum Children's Literature of Jacob Abbot." *Journal of Popular Culture* 16.1 (1982): 27–36.

Russell, David L. "Virginia Hamilton's Symbolic Presentation of the Afro-American Sensibility." *Cross-Culturalism in Children's Literature: Selected Papers from the Children's Literature Association, Carleton University, Ottawa, Canada, May 14–17, 1987.* Ed. Susan R. Gannon and Ruth Anne Thompson. New York: Pace U, 1988. 71–74.

Sims, Rudine. *Shadow and Substance: Afro-American Experience in Contemporary Children's Fiction.* 2nd ed. Chicago: NCTE/MLA, 1982.

Taxel, Joel. "The Black Experience in Children's Fiction: Controversies Surrounding Award Winning Books." *Curriculum Inquiry* 16.3 (Fall 1986): 245–81.

Tremper, Ellen. "Black English in Children's Literature." *The Lion and the Unicorn* 3.2 (1980): 105–24.

Williams, Helen E. *Books by African-American Authors and Illustrators for Children and Young Adults.* Chicago: ALA, 1991.

LITERATURE ABOUT HISPANIC-AMERICANS

Arenas, Bibi. "José Martí: Escritor para niños?" *José Martí ante la crítica actual: En el centenario del Ismaelillo.* Ed. Elio Alba-Buffill, Alberto Gutiérrez de la Solana, and Esther Sánchez-Grey Alba. Miami, FL: Circulo de Cultura Panamerica, 1983. 115–23.

Baker, Houston A., ed. *Three American Literatures: Essays in Chicano, Native American and Asian-American Literature.* New York: MLA, 1982.

Duff, Ogle B. "Expanding the Secondary Literary Curriculum: Annotated Bibliographies of Amer-Indian, Asian-American, and Hispanic American Literature." *English Education* 22.4 (1990): 220–40.

Freundlich, Joyce. "Images of the Puerto Rican in Young Adult Books: Fact or Fancy." *Journal for the National Association of Bilingual Education* 5.2 (1980–1981): 69–80.

Jackson, Shirley. "The Special Gift of Literature." *Monographic Review/Revista Monográfica* 1.1 (1985): 83–89.

Lucas, Fábio. "Ideologia e Literatura Infantil." *Colóquia* 84 (Mar. 1985): 20–27.

Michel, Fiume Gomez de. "La literatura en la formación de los niños." *Punto* 71.6 (1985): 27–29.

Moore, Opal, and Donnarae MacCann. "Paternalism and Assimilation in Books about Hispanics." *Children's Literature Association Quarterly* 12.2–3 (1987): 99–102, 110, 154–57.

Nieto, Sonia. "Puerto Ricans in Children's Literature and History Texts: A Ten-Year Update." *Interracial Books for Children Bulletin* 14.1–2 (1983).

———. "Self-Affirmation or Self-Destruction: The Image of Puerto Ricans in Children's Literature Written in English." *Images and Identities: The Puerto Rican in Two World Contexts.* Ed. Asela Rodriguez-Seda de Laguna. New Brunswick, NJ: Transaction, 1987. 211–26.

Ortego, Philip D., and Jose A. Carrasco. "Chicanos and American Literature." *Young Adult Literature: Background and Criticism.* Ed. Millicent Lenz and Ramona M. Mahood. Chicago: ALA, 1980. 279–84.

Schon, Isabel. *A Hispanic Heritage: A Guide to Juvenile Books about Hispanic People and Culture.* 3rd ed. Metuchen, NJ: Scarecrow, 1991.

———. "A Master Storyteller and His Distortions of Pre-Columbian and Hispanic Cultures." *Journal of Reading* 29.4 (1986): 322–25.

———. "Noteworthy Books about Hispanic People and Cultures for Adolescents." *Journal of Reading* 36.10 (1992): 158–60.

———. "Noteworthy Books in Spanish for Adolescents." *Hispania* 76.1 (March 1993): 152–55.

———. "Recent and Notable and Dumb Books for Young Readers from Spanish-Speaking Countries." *Hispania* 66.1 (1983): 87–91.

———. "Recent Good and Bad Books About Hispanics." *Journal of Reading* 34.9 (1990): 76–78.

———. "Recent Hispanic Children's Literature: A Selected Annotated Bibliography." *Monographic Review/Revista Monagráphica* 1.1 (1985): 97–110.

———. "Recent Noteworthy Books about Hispanic People and Cultures for Students in the Middle Grades." *Journal of Reading* 36.9 (1993): 431–32.

LITERATURE ABOUT NATIVE AMERICANS

Baker, Houston A., ed. *Three American Literatures: Essays in Chicano, Native American and Asian American Literature.* New York: MLA, 1982.

Caldwell-Wood, N. "Native American Images in Children's Books." *School Library Journal* 38 (May 1992): 47–48.

Carver, Nancy Lyn. "Stereotypes of American Indians in Adolescent Literature." *English Journal* 77.5 (1988): 25–32.

Charles, Jim. "Celebrating the Diversity of American Indian Literature." *ALAN Review* 18.3 (1991): 4–8.

Coulon, Janet. "American Indians in Children's Books." *Fiction International* 20 (Fall 1991): 167–81.

Dowd, Frances S. "Evaluating Children's Books Portraying Native American and African Cultures." *Children's Literature in Education* 68.4 (Summer 1992): 219–24.

Duff, Ogle B. "Expanding the Secondary Literary Curriculum: Annotated Bibliographies of Amer-Indian, Asian-American, and Hispanic American Literature." *English Education* 22.4 (Dec. 1990): 220–40.

Falkenhagen, Maria, and Inga K. Kelly. "The Native American in Juvenile Fiction: Teacher Perception of Stereotypes." *Journal of American Indian Education* 13.2 (1974): 9–13.

Gellert, James H. "Circling the Square: The Role of Native Writers in Creating Native Literature for Children." *Cross-Culturalism in Children's Literature: Selected Papers from the Children's Literature Association, Carleton University, Ottawa, Canada, May 14–17, 1987.* Ed. Susan R. Gannon and Ruth Anne Thompson. New York: Pace U, 1988.

Goding, Deborah. "Images of Native American Girls for Young Readers." *Feminist Collections* 14.4 (1993): 8–11.

Helbig, Alethea. "Teaching American Literature from Its Real Beginnings: Native American Stories." *Young Adult Literature: Background and Criticism.* Ed. Millicent Lenz and Ramona M. Mahoud. Chicago: ALA, 1980. 259–66.

Lewis, Magda. "'Are Indians Nicer Now?' What Children Learn from Books about Native Americans." *How Much Truth Do We Tell the Children? The Politics of Children's Literature.* Ed. Betty Bacon. Minneapolis: Marxist Education Press, 1988: 135–56.

Lickteig, Mary. "*Julie of the Wolves* and *Dogsong*: The Cultural Conflict between the Inuits and the Dominant American Culture." *Cross-Culturalism in Children's Literature: Selected Papers from the Children's Literature Association, Carleton University, Ottawa, Canada, May 14–17, 1987*. Ed. Susan R. Gannon and Ruth Anne Thompson. New York: Pace U, 1988.

Madsen, Jane M., and Rebecca Robbins. "Native American Visual and Verbal Images in the Caldecott and Newbery Award Books." *Minority Voices: An Interdisciplinary Journal of Literature and the Arts* 5.1–2 (1983): 17–40.

Maher, Susan Naramond. "Encountering Others: The Meeting of Cultures in Scott O'Dell's *Island of the Blue Dolphins* and *Sing Down the Moon*." *Children's Literature in Education* 23 (Dec. 1992): 215–27.

Markstrom-Adams, Carol. "Coming-of-Age among Contemporary American Indians as Portrayed in Adolescent Fiction." *Adolescence* 25 (Spring 1990): 225–37.

Moore, Opal, and Donnarae MacCann. "The Ignoble Savage: Amerind Images in the Mainstream Mind." *Children's Literature Association Quarterly* 13.1 (1988): 26–30.

Mura, David. "Strangers in the Village." *Multi-Cultural Literacy*. Ed. Ricke Simonson and Scott Walter. St. Paul: Graywolf, 1988. 135–53.

Slapin, Beverly, and Doris Seales. *Books without Bias: Through Indian Eyes*. Berkeley, CA: Oyate Press, 1988.

Stensland, Anna Lee. *Literature by and about the American Indian: An Annotated Bibliography for Junior and Senior High School Students*. Urbana, IL: NCTE, 1979.

Stott, Jon C. "Form, Content, Cultural Values in Three Inuit (Eskimo) Survival Stories." *American Indian Quarterly* 10.3 (1986): 213–26.

———. "Native American Narratives and the Children's Literature Curriculum." *Teaching Children's Literature: Issues, Pedagogy, Resources*. Ed. Glenn Edward Sadler. New York: MLA, 1992.

Williamson, Norman. "The 'Indian Tales': Are They Fish or Fowl?" *Children's Literature Association Quarterly* 12.2 (1987): 70–73.

LITERATURE ABOUT ASIAN-AMERICANS

Bacchilega, Cristina. "Adapting the Fairy Tale for Hawaii's Children." *The Lion and the Unicorn* 12.2 (1988): 121–34.

Baker, Houston A., ed. *Three American Literatures: Essays in Chicano, Native American and Asian American Literature*. New York: MLA, 1982.

Canham, Stephen. "'Da Kine': Writing for Children in Hawaii—and Elsewhere." *Children's Literature Association Quarterly* 9.4 (1984): 174–76.

————. "Images of Hawaii for Children: Cultural Deprivileging and Reprivileging." *The Image of the Child.* Ed. Sylvia Patterson Iskander. Battle Creek, MI: Children's Literature Association, 1991. 89–99.

————. "Mythic Consciousness and Hawaiian Children's Literature." *Triumphs of the Spirit in Children's Literature.* Ed. Francelia Butler and Richard Rotert. Hamden, CT: Library Professionals Publications, 1986. 127–36.

Chi, Marilyn Mei-Ying. "Asserting Asian-American Children's Self and Cultural Identity through Asian-American Children's Literature." *Social Studies Review* 32.2 (1993): 50–55.

Cooper, Nancy M. "Multiethnic Literature in America: Korean Literature for American Students." *English Journal* 69.4 (1980): 100–103.

Duff, Ogle B. "Expanding the Secondary Literary Curriculum: Annotated Bibliographies of Amer-Indian, Asian-American, and Hispanic American Literature." *English Education* 22.4 (Dec. 1990): 220–40.

Egoff, Sheila. "Inside and Out: A Canadian's View of Traits and Trends in Contemporary Children's Literature." *A Track to Unknown Water.* Ed. Stella Lees. Metuchen, NJ: Scarecrow, 1987. 337–55.

Egoff, Sheila A., ed. *One Ocean Touching: Perspectives from the First Pacific Rim Conference on Literature.* Metuchen, NJ: Scarecrow, 1979.

Inokuma, Yoko. "The Present Situation of Stories about Minority Groups in Japan." *A Track to Unknown Water.* Ed. Stella Lees. Metuchen, NJ: Scarecrow, 1987. 69–84.

Johannessen, Larry R. "Young-Adult Literature and the Vietnam War." *The English Journal* 82.5 (1993): 43–49.

Kai, Kei-ye Hsu, and Helen Pablubinkas. "Introduction from Asian-American Authors." *Young Adult Literature: Background and Criticism.* Ed. Millicent Lenz and Ramona M. Mahoud. Chicago: ALA, 1980. 279–84.

Lo, Suzanne, and Ginny Lee. "Asian Images in Children's Books: What Stories Do We Tell Our Children?" *Emergency Librarian* 20.5 (1993): 14–18.

Louie, Ai-Ling. "Growing Up Asian-American: A Look at Some Recent Young Adult Novels."*Journal of Youth Services in Libraries* 6.2 (Winter 1993): 115–27.

Mahy, Margaret. "On Building Houses That Face towards the Sun: Proceedings of the Second Pacific Rim Conference on Children's Literature." *A Track to Unknown Water.* Ed. Stella Lees. Metuchen, New Jersey: Scarecrow, 1987. 104–18.

Matsuyama, Utako K. "Asian and Asian-American Literature for Adolescents." *Journal of Reading* 35 (Mar. 1992): 508–10.

Matsuyama, Utako, and Kristi Jensen. "Asian and Asian-American Literature for Adolescents." *Journal of Reading* 33 (Jan. 1990): 317–20.

McVitty, Walter. "Children on the Rim: Proceedings of the Second Pacific Rim Conference on Children's Literature." *A Track to Unknown Water.* Ed. Stella Lees. Metuchen, NJ: Scarecrow, 1987. 3–12.

Natov, Roni. "Living in Two Cultures: Bette Bao Lord's Stories of Chinese-American Experience." *The Lion and the Unicorn* 11.1 (1987): 38–46.

Palomino, Harue. "Japanese Americans in Books or in Reality? Three Writers for Young Adults Who Tell a Different Story." *How Much Do We Tell the Children? The Politics of Children's Literature.* Ed. Betty Bacon. Minneapolis: Marxist Educational Press, 1988. 125–34.

Saxby, Maurice. "Minority of One: Proceedings of the Second Pacific Rim Conference on Children's Literature." *A Track to Unknown Water.* Ed. Stella Lees. Metuchen, NJ: Scarecrow, 1987. 356–66.

Susina, Jan. "'Tell Him about Vietnam': Vietnamese-Americans in Contemporary Children's Literature." *Children's Literature Association Quarterly* 16.2 (1991): 58–63.

LITERATURE ABOUT JEWS

Allison, Alida. "Guess Who's Coming to Dinner? The Golem as Family Member in Jewish Children's Literature." *The Lion and the Unicorn* 14.2 (1990): 92–97.

Farnham, James F. "Holocaust Literature for Children: The Presentation of Evil." *University of Hartford Studies in Literature* 18.2–3 (1986): 55–62.

Freeman, Deborah J. "Isaac Bashevis Singer on Writing for Children." *Children's Literature* 6 (1977): 9–16.

Guzlowski, John Z. "Telling through Untelling: The Genesis of Isaac Singer's *A Day of Pleasure.*" *Studies in American Jewish Literature* 10.2 (1991): 197–209.

Jurich, Marilyn. "Once Upon a Shtetl: Schlimazels, Schlemiels, Schnorrers, Shadchens and Sages: Yiddish Humor in Children's Books." *The Lion and the Unicorn* 1.1 (1977): 9–25.

Mendelsohn, Leonard M. "The Survival of the Spirit in Holocaust Literature for and about Children." *Triumphs of the Spirit in Children's Literature.* Ed. Francelia Butler and Richard Rotert. Hamden, CT: Library Professional Publications, 1986.

Mersand, Joseph. "The Literary Impact of Jewish Culture." *English Journal* 64 (Feb. 1975): 39–46.

Mirel, Barbara. "Lost Worlds of Traditions: *Shtetl* Stories for Suburban Children." *Children's Literature Association Quarterly* 9.1 (1984): 6–9.

Natov, Roni, and Geraldine DeLuca. "The Darkest Side: Writing for Children about the Holocaust: An Interview with Aranka Siegal." *The Lion and the Unicorn* 12.2 (1988): 76–96.

Nilsen, Alleen Pace. "We Should Laugh So Long?" *School Library Journal* 33.3 (1986): 30–34.

Patterson, Sylvia W. "Isaac Singer: Writer for Children." *Proceedings of the Eighth Annual Conference of the Children's Literature Association, Uni-*

versity of Minnesota, March 1981. Ed. Priscilla Ord. New Rochelle: Department of English, Ithaca College, 1982. 69–76.

Patz, Naomi M., and Philip Miller. "Jewish Religious Children's Literature in America: An Analytical Survey." *Phaedrus* 7.1 (1980): 19–29.

Riggio, Thomas P. "The Symbols of Faith: Isaac Bashevis Singer's Children's Books." *Recovering the Canon: Essays on Isaac Bashevis Singer*. Ed. David Neal Miller. Leiden: Brill, 1986. 133–44.

Sherman, Ursula F. "Why Would a Child Want to Read about That? The Holocaust Period in Children's Literature." *How Much Truth Do We Tell the Children? The Politics of Children's Literature.* Ed. Betty Bacon. Minneapolis: Marxist Educational Press, 1988.

Stadtler, Bea. "Six Decades of Books for Jewish Children." *Jewish Education* 60 (Summer 1993): 26–28.

———. "What's New in Jewish Juvenile Literature?" *Jewish Education* 52 (Winter 1984): 43–45.

Tannenbaum, Abraham J. "Jewish Texts, Education and Identity: Inseparable." *Jewish Education* 57 (Summer–Winter 1989): 7–12.

INDEX

About the Editor and Contributors

MIRIAM BAT-AMI is Associate Professor of Children's Literature at Western Michigan University, and has written articles on multicultural and historical fiction for *Children's Literature in Education* and *Language Arts Journal of Michigan*. She has also acted as primary consultant for the multicultural adolescent textbook *Tapestry*. Bat-Ami is a children's writer herself. Her works include *Sea, Salt and Air* and *When the Frost Is Gone*.

ANN M. CAMERON teaches children's and young adult literature, American literature, and writing at Indiana University, Kokomo. She has written articles on a number of authors for young adults, including Robert Westall, Margaret Mahy, and Bruce Brooks, as well as articles on the poetry of Whitman and Taylor.

JOEL D. CHASTON is Associate Professor of English at Southwest Missouri State University where he teaches children's and young adult literature. He is the co-author of *Theme Exploration: A Voyage of Discovery* and is currently completing *Lois Lowry*. He his published extensively on contemporary children's writers, including Katherine Paterson.

DIANA ARLENE CHLEBEK is Associate Professor in the Library at the University of Akron, Akron, Ohio. She has expertise in bibliography, language, and literature, and has previously published on Eastern European literature and on children's literature of both the nineteenth and the twentieth centuries.

JIM COPE is an Assistant Professor of English at Longwood College in Farmville, Virginia. He is a former high school English teacher who has also taught at the University of Georgia and the University of Central Florida.

HILARY CREW is a children's librarian at Westfield Memorial Library in Westfield, New Jersey, and is a Ph.D. candidate in the School of Communication, Information and Library Studies at Rutgers University.

CHRIS CROWE is Associate Professor of English at Brigham Young University in Provo, Utah, where he teaches adolescent literature, secondary English teaching methods, and creative writing.

DONNELYN CURTIS is a reference librarian at New Mexico State University who specializes in information technology. She is the editor of the *New Mexico Library Association Newsletter* and the compiler/maintainer of Children's Literature: Electronic Resources, an area of the New Mexico State University Library Gopher.

JULIE A. DAVIES is a visual artist and independent historian. She is currently affiliated as a teaching associate with the Canadian Studies Program and the Women's Studies Program at SUNY Plattsburgh.

KWAME S. N. DAWES is an Assistant Professor of English and the Chair of the Division of Arts and Letters at the University of South Carolina at Sumter. He has published articles on theater, race, Commonwealth and postcolonial literature and theory in several journals, including *Journal of West Indian Literature, Arts Review,* and *Ariel*. His volumes of poetry include *Progeny of Air* (1994), *Prophets* (1995), and *Resisting the Anomie* (1995).

RONALD EDWARDS is an Assistant Professor of Libraries & Learning Resources and Head of the Curriculum Resource Center at Bowling Green State University in Bowling Green, Ohio. He is currently Chair of the Curriculum Materials Center Interest Group of the Academic Library Association of Ohio and a Member of the American Library Association's Curriculum Materials Committee. Edwards has published on multicultural issues for *MultiCultural Review*.

MEREDITH ELIASSEN lives in the San Francisco Bay area and works at San Francisco State University's J. Paul Leonard Library with the Marguerite Archer Collection of Historic Children's Books. In 1991, she wrote A *Guide for Emmy Award-Winning Programs 1974–1986* for the Northern California Chapter of the National Academy of Television Arts and Sciences.

KAREN FAULS-TRAYNOR is a graduate student in the School of Information Studies, Library Science Program at Syracuse University. She has a long-standing interest in children's literature, especially in multicultural children's literature. She has previously published in *School Library Journal*.

LESLI J. FAVOR teaches literature and writing at the University of North Texas, and her research interests include nineteenth- and twentieth-century narrative fiction.

SUSAN J. FORSLING has been a library media specialist in Alaska and Iowa and a public librarian. She served as a reviewer for *Every Teacher's Science Booklist* and is a frequent reviewer for the State of Iowa Department of Education's *DE Reviews*.

SUZANNE D. GREEN is a doctoral candidate at the University of North Texas in Denton, Texas. She has interests in children's literature and in ethnic literatures.

DONA J. HELMER is an Associate Professor at Montana State University at Billings, where she is the Education Librarian and the Director of the Curriculum Resource Center. She has taught courses in children's and young adult literature and has served on both Caldecott and Newbery Award Committees. Helmer has also lived in a Yupik Eskimo village in Alaska and on a remote naval air station in the Aleutian chain.

BRUCE HENDERSON earned undergraduate and graduate degrees from the Department of Performance Studies at Northwestern University. He is at present Associate Professor of Speech Communication at Ithaca College. Publications include *Performance: Texts and Contexts* (co-authored with Carol Simpson Stern). He is an Associate Editor for *Text and Performance Quarterly*. Current research interests include storytelling and folklore; camp aesthetics; contemporary literature and cultural performance; children's literature; twentieth-century American and British poetry and fiction.

LINNEA HENDRICKSON is the author of *Children's Literature: A Guide to the Criticism* (1987). She teaches children's literature at the University of New Mexico, and has been a Vista Volunteer, a New York City caseworker, a teacher at a small college on the Navajo Reservation in Arizona, and an academic reference librarian.

KAREN HERC has published on adolescent fiction for Simmons College's *Essays and Studies*.

ANDREA O'REILLY HERRERA is Assistant Professor in the Department of English at SUNY Fredonia, where she teaches Victorian and Edwardian literature and multicultural literature with a special focus on Latina/o writers. She is also certified to teach secondary school. She has published essays on Marguerite Duras and Sandra Cisneros.

CAROLINE C. HUNT teaches at the College of Charleston in Charleston, South Carolina. She has contributed to numerous reference works and has written on Sperry and his historical context in recent articles in *The Lion and the Unicorn* and *Journal of Children's Literature*.

SHERRIE A. INNESS is an Assistant Professor of English at Miami University, Ohio. Her research interests include lesbian fiction, girls' serial novels, women's basketball, nineteenth-century women missionaries, and female domestic servants. She has published articles in *American Literary Realism, Edith Wharton Review, Journal of Popular Culture, NWSA Journal, Studies in Short Fiction, Women's Studies*, as well as in three anthologies.

REINHARD ISENSEE is currently an Assistant Professor at the Institute for English and American Studies, Humboldt University, Berlin (Federal Republic of Germany). His more recent publications include articles on Robert Cormier and Todd Strasser for *Beacham's Guide to Literature for Young Adults* and several articles on young adult fiction for German academic journals.

LINDA C. JOLIVET is a media specialist librarian in California. She has special interests in African-American and other minority literatures, as well as in literature and media for children.

MITCHELL KACHUN is a Ph.D. candidate in American history at Cornell University, currently finishing a dissertation on historical memory among African-Americans in the postemancipation period. He holds masters' degrees from Cornell University and Illinois State University.

M. DAPHNE KUTZER is Associate Professor of English at SUNY Plattsburgh. She has published extensively in the field of children's literature, including essays in *College English* and *Children's Literature Association Quarterly*. She has been a Plenary Session speaker at the International Children's Literature Association conference, and is currently working on a critical study of Beatrix Potter.

TERI S. LESESNE is an Assistant Professor in the Department of Library Science at Sam Houston State University, where she teaches graduate and undergraduate courses in literature for children and young adults. She writes the "Books for Adolescents" column in the *Journal of Reading* and is an active member of the Assembly on Literature for Adolescents of the National Council of Teachers of English.

KAREN LIBMAN currently teaches Literature for Children at SUNY Cortland and freelances as a professional storyteller.

JOHN P. MADISON has published articles on reading, language arts, mathematics, and children's literature. He is currently writing a book on using multicultural children's books in elementary classrooms. He is a Program Professor in the Graduate Teacher Education Program at Nova Southeastern University.

CATHRYN M. MERCIER is an Assistant Professor and the Associate Director at the Center for the Study of Children's Literature at Simmons College in Boston, Massachusetts. A regular reviewer for *The Five Owls*, she contributes to a range of children's an young adult literature review journals and reference sources. She co-authored *Presenting Zibby O'Neal* (1991) and currently is working on *Presenting Avi*. She chaired the 1993 *Boston Globe-Horn Book* Award Committee and served on the 1994 Caldecott Committee.

THOMAS J. MORRISSEY is Professor of English and Director of College Writing at SUNY Plattsburgh. His critical articles and reviews have been published in such journals as *Science Fiction Studies*, *Eire-Ireland*, *Centenniel Review*, and *Children's Literature*. His poetry has appeared in *Green Fuse* and *Blue Line*.

ANITA MOSS is Professor of English at the University of North Carolina at Charlotte, where she teaches courses in children's and young adult literature. She is the Editor of *Children's Literature in Education* and the author of numerous articles and reviews.

JANICE E. PATTEN is currently a Lecturer at San Jose State University, San Jose, California. She has given many papers at conferences in the United States and in England and Scotland on romanticism, the theater, and children's literature, and is working on a text for teaching literature in the young adult classroom.

JEANNE WHITEHOUSE PETERSON lives in Albuquerque, New Mexico, where she serves as Co-director of the Rio Grande Writing Project and Adjunct Professor of children's and adolescent literature with the Department of Curriculum and Instruction in Multicultural Teacher Education at the University of New Mexico. She writes books for young people, including *I Have a Sister—My Sister Is Deaf* and *My Mama Sings*. She is also the Author-in-Residence of the Zuni Young Author Conference, and served in Malaysia in the Peace Corps. She met Ann Nolan Clark in 1981.

TARA L. RIVERA is currently a graduate student at Purdue University with concentrations in Children's Literature, Multicultural Literature, and Adolescent Literature.

KAREN SANDS is a freelance writer whose previous biographical works include several twentieth-century mathematicians. She is currently completing graduate work in Children's Literature at Hollins College and is writing her thesis on L. Frank Baum's *The Wonderful Wizard of Oz*. She wishes to thank Wendy Keen of Hollins College for her help in locating some of the material about Cliff Faulknor.

PETER D. SIERUTA, who works at the Wayne State University Libraries in Detroit, is a freelance writer and critic. He is the author of a young adult book, *Heartbeats and Other Stories*, reviews for *Horn Book* publications, and has contributed over one hundred essays to a forthcoming Houghton Mifflin reference book on children's authors.

SIMMONA SIMMONS-HODO is Head of Reference, Kuhn Library and Gallery, University of Maryland, and has been a contributor to *Notable Black American Women* and *The Bulletin of Bibliography*.

DAVID SORRELLS has presented papers at numerous professional conferences, including the Modern Language Association Conference and the South Central Modern Language Association Conference. His publications include critical articles on *The Scarlet Letter*, Irish playwrights, Texas authors, and technical writing pedagogy. A publishing poet, he did his doctoral work at the University of North Texas, and currently teaches at Lamar University in Beaumont, Texas.

SHIRLEY A. TASTAD has co-authored several articles for *BookLinks*, focusing on American history. Currently she is Assistant Professor of Library Media Education at Georgia State University in Atlanta, Georgia.

KAY E. VANDERGRIFT is an Associate Professor, School of Communication, Information and Library Studies, Rutgers University, teaching children's and young adult literature. She has authored several books, including *Child and Story*, *Children's Literature: Theory, Research and Teaching*, and *Power Teaching: A Primary Role of the School Library Media Specialist*, and has edited several others. She has contributed over thirty chapters to books as well as articles to a number of academic journals. Her current research is a combination of feminist and reader-response criticism in the meaning-making of young people. Two edited books, *Ways of Knowing: Literature and The Intellectual Life of Children* and *Mosaics of Meaning: Enhancing the Intellectual Life of Young Adults through Story*, will be published in 1995.

ALLISON WILSON, a Professor of English at predominantly black Jackson State University, received her doctorate from Columbia University, where she specialized in the teaching of writing. Her short stories, poems, and articles have appeared in numerous popular, literary, and scholarly periodicals and anthologies.

DENISE ANTON WRIGHT is a librarian and storyteller who lives in Bloomington, Illinois. She is currently a Reference Librarian at Illinois State University in Normal. She is also the author of *One-Person Puppet Plays* (1990).

LAURA M. ZAIDMAN, Professor of English, teaches children's literature at the University of South Carolina at Sumter. She edited *British Children's Writers, 1880–1914* (*Dictionary of Literary Biography* 141) and a section of the *Children's Literature Association Quarterly* (Winter 1991–1992). Articles on multicultural literature have appeared in the *Dictionary of Literary Biography, Twentieth-Century Young Adult Writers, Authors* and *Artists for Young Adults*, and *The ALAN Review*.

WEIHUA ZHANG, a native of the People's Republic of China, is a DA candidate at SUNY Albany and has published critical essays on Ann Petry and Nikki Giovanni.

ISBN 0-313-29331-7

9 780313 293313

90000>

HARDCOVER BAR CODE